DEBUNKING
WOMEN'S
HISTORY

DEBUNKING WOMEN'S HISTORY

*Myths & Legends About
101 Infamous Women Exploded*

ED RAYNER & RON STAPLEY

AMBERLEY

First published 2010

Amberley Publishing plc
Cirencester Road, Chalford,
Stroud, Gloucestershire, GL6 8PE

www.amberleybooks.com

ISBN 978-1-84868-217-7

Typeset in 10pt on 12pt Adobe Caslon Pro.
Typesetting and Origination by Amberley Publishing.
Printed in the UK.

CONTENTS

PREFACE

This book deals with the role in history of over a hundred women of different sorts, chosen from the entire female species. The authors hope that our women readers will not resent the fact that both of us are men; both of us in fact appreciate that women have played a vital part in human history – and that furthermore they make up about fifty per cent of our readership.

Nor do we wish to tangle with the ranks of professional feminists who make a career out of 'women's studies'. Both the authors date from a generation when such specialisms scarcely existed, and when we thought that men's history and women's history amounted to much the same thing – i.e. part of *human* history. Neither of us is aware of the existence of any conspiracy against the female gender, nor would we wish to take part in it if we knew of it. Perhaps we may be accused of playing an unwitting part in such a conspiracy, but we would like to say that we both hope that such a charge is unfounded.

Some women, of course, like Helen of Troy, have myths woven about their very existence, but in many cases the 'myth' arises from some misunderstanding, or some misapprehension, about their true historical significance. These misunderstandings we have endeavoured to put right. It is not the women we have 'debunked'; it is the male stereotype of them that we have tried to correct.

This is why we have written this book – to contribute to the re-evaluation of the role of women in the late twentieth century after years of their being written down, or ignored, or obliterated, and so to restore them to a position of proper importance. We have not concentrated on female pioneers struggling towards female emancipation, though their role, of course, is very important; nor have we concentrated on women in positions of power, like queens or mistresses, many of whom have been written about already. We have tried to produce a cross-section of all kinds of women in all kinds of situation, and to produce a fair and balanced statement of their role and importance.

A glance at the Table of Contents will reveal how we have chosen and arranged these women.

Ed Rayner and Ron Stapley

HELEN OF TROY:
GODDESS, PRINCESS, WHORE

Helen of Troy, semi-mythological beauty and heroine of Greek history, was said to be the daughter of Zeus and Leda, and sister to Clytemnestra and the twins Castor and Pollux. She was the most alluring and beautiful of women, and captivated the hearts of all men. As a result she was the cause of the Trojan War, when she was abducted by Paris and carried off into captivity by him and his followers to the city whose name she traditionally bears. Later she was supposedly granted immortality by the god Apollo. The roots of this story are nourished by four sources: ancient polytheistic religious beliefs, classical poetry, ancient Greek folklore, and history of a more archaeological and written sort; but this last is not the strongest element in the story. There is no doubt that Troy was destroyed in war, but whether the cause of that war was trade conflict and imperial expansion, or whether it was brought about merely by the abduction is not immediately obvious.

What is the nature of the Helen myth? In Sparta, her home city, tradition has it that Helen was worshipped as a goddess and as a heroine; in Greece generally, she was regarded as a spirit of the earth, air and sky; while in Egypt she is looked upon as the decorous and seemly wife. At sea, in the Aegean, where she widely travelled, she was said to have brought the frightening illumination of St Elmo's Fire to storm-tossed sailors, and they were as much terrified by her presence as they were grateful to her for her ministrations. Regarded by many as the daughter, sister and incarnation of Aphrodite, she continues even today to be revered by masses of followers.

It is generally agreed that Helen was the daughter of Leda, wife of Tyndareus, King of Sparta, one of the great cities of the Peloponnese. The story of her birth, however, is much less certain. One day, it is said, as Leda bathed on the banks of the River Eurotas, Zeus himself caught sight of the beautiful young queen, and was enraptured. Determined to possess her, Zeus transformed himself into a giant swan and ravished her. Sometime later, Leda produced a curious clutch of eggs, which she left to hatch in the foothills of Mount Taygetus, where they were found by a shepherd and taken back to the Spartan palace. Here Helen was born, with a number of siblings who were either her brothers, like the twins Castor and Pollux, or her half-sister, Clytemnestra. Helen was more beautiful even than her own mother, and became the matrilineal heiress to the kingdom, and later queen of it. When Helen was little more than a child she was snatched by Theseus, King of Athens, said to be elderly though not too old to fight in battle, and afterwards was raped by him. This brought about an invasion of Athens in a war of revenge by Castor and Pollux, and much later was sometimes advanced as the excuse for a series of wars in the early sixth century between Attica (the territory of Athens) and Laconia (the territory of Sparta). Helen later went on to marry Menelaus, warrior king of Sparta, while still in her teens, in a splendid and elaborate ceremony involving feasting, dancing and various competitions in which suitors demonstrated their fitness for her, and then ruled an empire which was totalitarian in government, belligerent and secretive,[1] its warrior-citizens employing slaves for the more tedious of their daily obligations, while they themselves lived and trained as professional soldiers as they continued to celebrate their devotion to Helen. During her lifetime she spent much time on a strict training regime for Spartan girls, trained not only in typically feminine things like music and poetry, but also in riding, racing, athletics and wrestling, where all of the practitioners were naked. While young, adolescent girls cropped their hair short, with a bushy forelock and a pony-tail, but when they were of marriageable age they let it grow, and mature women usually had a full head of luxuriant locks. Girls, of course, still made use of the *pyxis* – the cosmetic compact – but this was something they did in private to enhance their natural beauty. Of course, in Mycenaean Greece at this time there was great opulence as well, with treasure, material possessions and a slave-based economy, but wealth was somewhat less valued in a society such as Sparta.

In the early and happier period of her marriage to Menelaus, Helen produced a daughter for him, Hermione. At this point Paris appears, or rather re-appears, in her life. They had met already, and it was said made love, and he may even have been one of the competitors at the time of her wedding ceremony. He had been banished from Troy[2] by his father, King Priam, because of a prophecy that he would bring ruin upon Troy, and so was living as a simple herdsman. Now Zeus nominated Paris as judge in a beauty contest between Hera (Zeus' wife), Athena (his daughter) and Aphrodite (goddess of sexual love). All made him promises: the first, an empire; the second, invincible prowess in war; and the third, possession of the most beautiful woman in the world – so Aphrodite got the golden apple, and Paris secured the promise of Helen. But he incurred also the lasting enmity of powerful goddesses.

The story goes that the beautiful Paris sailed to mainland Greece from Troy, on the Aegean coast just south of the Dardanelles, a dependency of the province of Wilusa, a puppet state of the Hittite Empire; and, together with his hoard of gifts, was given a royal welcome in Menelaus' palace. King Menelaus was on the point of departure for Crete, to partake in his grandfather's funerary rites, and in his absence Paris violated the marriage bed and slept with Helen, either with her consent, or, worse still, without it. Claiming he was her legitimate spouse (on account of having competed for her at her marriage feast) he carried her off back to his native Troy. This was a large, rich city, several miles from the sea, and famed for its breeding and training of horses; Helen would have been a 'secondary wife' in a society that permitted polygamous marriages (Priam himself was famous for having fathered fifty sons). Menelaus, returning to Sparta after his melancholy journey, at first attempted diplomacy as a way of recovering his wife; when this failed, he resorted to war. A massive Greek fleet,[3] held up for a time at Aulis awaiting favourable winds, reached Troy, and, when their demands for Helen's return were rejected,[4] besieged it. The siege is supposed to have lasted ten years in the earlier part of the twelfth century BC, though this, too, was probably poetic exaggeration, since such a siege would have destroyed the besiegers as effectively as the besieged. Helen is said to have stood on the city's ramparts and picked out the Greek leaders – Agamemnon, Odysseus, Ajax, Achilles – to identify them to their enemies. The story told by Homer in the *Iliad* (though only covering a few days of the conflict) is gruesome in its minutiae of death and suffering. In the end, the Greeks seemed to have relinquished Helen, and made as if to withdraw, leaving behind them only a great wooden horse as an ironic parting gift. The Trojans debated whether to take it into the city or pitch it over the nearby cliffs to destroy it; they made the wrong choice, and at night the warriors it concealed within its flanks crept out and opened the gates to admit Greek forces into Troy. Havoc and massacre followed: Priam and his followers were brutally slain, women raped and sold with their children into slavery. Paris is never heard of again, though there were those who claimed he had been killed by an arrow.

With the end of the war, Helen was taken back to Sparta by Menelaus to resume her reign. He had contemplated cutting her throat, but the very sight of her deterred him, and he forgave her. But they were caught up in a furious storm, and blown off course as far as Egypt.[5] The royal couple gathered up stories and treasures to take back to Sparta, where they lived for some years afterwards. Orestes, murderer of his mother Clytemnestra, under a sentence of death which Menelaus refused to revoke, with his accomplice Pylades, hatched a plot to avenge himself on the King by killing his beloved Helen. This done, the corpse of Helen vanished. Apollo appeared, explaining that he had snatched Helen up to safety and immortality as a star, always brilliantly shining, and like herself just out of reach.

With the end of Helen came the end also of the Mycenaean civilisation: it imploded not exactly overnight, but in a short space of time afterwards. The end of the Bronze Age in the late thirteenth century BC was the time of an outbreak of intensified seismic activity, with a series of massive earthquakes, of upwards of 6.5 or 7 on the Richter scale, which devastated the land and destroyed many of the often splendid buildings the Mycenaeans had erected on it. Built out of a mixture of mud brick and stone, these buildings, however grand and impressive they may have seemed, lacked the sophistication of later buildings and collapsed into ruins more easily. The Mycenaean, Hittite and Egyptian civilisations were intimately linked, and all were undermined and collapsed. It is surprising how little remained when this period of destruction passed. But with the end of a brief Dark Age that followed, the way was cleared for Archaic Greece, and after it the age of Classical Greece.

Helen, however, never passed away. She remained at the heart of classical Greek theatre in the later centuries BC, where successive plays such as Euripides' *The Trojan Women* warned of the dangers of beautiful charismatic women; her cult remained central to early Greek religious beliefs. Her vital statistics provided the dimensions for the breast-shaped cups employed in the temples of the islands of the Greek archipelago throughout the period of Greek cultural dominance. Her influence may be seen in the teachings of Simon Magus in the first century AD, with his ideals of free love and his leanings towards drug abuse and sexual excess. She survives in a wide mix of historical writings, from those of Dictys and Dares in the second century AD, self-styled historians of Helen's times, to the *Troye Book* of John Lydgate in the early fifteenth century. More modern archaeological work has uncovered evidence of Helen-worship in Palestine in pre-Mohammedan times. Her statue remained in the Hippodrome of Constantinople as late as 1204, before it was destroyed in the fighting of the Fourth Crusade. From the eleventh century onwards the Franks and the Normans perpetuated myth-histories by claiming descent from the rulers of Troy. Even in the reign of Henry IV, the King buttressed his claim to the fealty of the Scottish king by thus extending the genealogy of his family. Earlier, Eleanor of Aquitaine, wife of Henry II, a woman struggling for dominance in a man's world, had developed a striking rapport with Helen, and even incorporated Benoît's epic *Roman de Troie* in her Bible as part of the Book of Exodus. But perhaps the most telling tribute to Helen is found at the end of the sixteenth century in Kit Marlow's *Tragical History of Dr. Faustus*, where he says of her:

> Was this the face that launched a thousand ships,
> And burnt the topless towers of Ilium?
> Sweet Helen, make me immortal with a kiss,
> Her lips suck forth my soul; see where it flies –
> Come, Helen, give me my soul again!

PART 1

ARTISTS

BEATRICE AND DANTE ALIGHIERI:
A STORY OF UNREQUITED LOVE

The story of the poet and dramatist Dante degli Alighieri and his loved one, Beatrice Portinari, is one of the most famous and poignant in the history of courtly love. In an age when tender sentiment was much less in evidence than coarse brutality, chivalrous devotion was perhaps always something of a myth; nevertheless, even today, the story still retains its elegance, its beauty and its charm. He was an Italian Florentine poet born in 1265, and author of The Divine Comedy, *often considered the finest literary statement of love and redemption produced in Europe in the medieval period, and the basis of the modern Italian language. She was the passion of his heart, adored from the very first time he met her as a boy until her death at the early age of twenty-four in 1290. Even after her demise, the memory of Beatrice haunted his life and continued to inspire his writings until he died himself in 1321.*

In 1274 Dante first met Beatrice when he was nearly nine at a gathering at her father's *palazzo* in Florence. She was a few months younger than him, but he was allured by her at the first sight. She was dressed in soft crimson, with a beautiful girdle about her slim waist, and appeared to him as an angelic being with divine as well as noble qualities. She captivated him completely. He took to frequenting places where he could catch a glimpse of her, but there is no evidence that she returned his passion, or even noticed him. It was not until nine years afterwards that she actually spoke to him. One afternoon in 1283 he saw her dressed in white, walking down a street in Florence, accompanied by two older women. Beatrice turned and greeted him. The occasion filled him with such joy that he returned to his lodging to relish the memory. He fell asleep, and had a dream that in his hands became the subject of the first sonnet in his work *The New Life* (1292), the story of his searing passion told with unquenchable pathos in one of the world's greatest love poems.

In thirteenth-century Florence, arranged marriages were the norm, especially among the upper classes to which both Dante and Beatrice belonged. In 1287 she was married to her intended bridegroom, Simone de' Bardi, but neither this, nor the poet's own marriage to Gemma Donati, the daughter of a powerful neighbouring Guelf family, interfered with his pure and platonic devotion to Beatrice, which intensified with her early death only three years later. Dante and Gemma produced seven children, six sons and one daughter, whom he called Beatrice and who became a nun at Ravenna. After a military and diplomatic career in which he was sent in an embassy to Pope Boniface VII and quarrelled with his own state, he was banished from Florence in 1309, and sentenced to death in his absence. He led a wandering life in a number of Italian cities, including Verona and Lunigiana near Urbino, eventually settling in Ravenna in 1318. He completed The New Life in 1294, when he was twenty-nine years old, but he continued to feel that mere love poems could not do justice to the honour or beauty of his beloved Beatrice, and so embarked on composing *The Divine Comedy*, which he completed only three years before his death.[1] This work is his spiritual testament, narrating his journey from Hell through Purgatory to Paradise. At first he is guided by the poet Virgil up to the Heights of Mount Purgatory; after that point only Beatrice could guide him to Paradise. *The Divine Comedy*, which Dante began in Latin, successfully established Italian as a literary language.

The Divine Comedy remains even today the chief exemplar of religious and amorous verse, the forerunner of the religious writings of Milton and the romantic school of eighteenth- and nineteenth-century poets. To the modern reader it seems abstract and unworldly to the point of being anaemic, but to the reader of the time it was a delicate story of unfulfilled passion. And Beatrice's role in it, though quaint and unfashionable, and certainly passive by modern standards, remains the yardstick by which romantic composition is measured.

APHRA BEHN:
ONE OF THE VERY FIRST ENGLISH WOMEN TO WRITE FOR A LIVING

Women who earned money from writing were a great rarity in the seventeenth century. Women who wrote plays and novels were an even greater rarity. Aphra Behn was unique in that she had a temporary career as a government agent before taking up writing. Her works enjoyed great vogue in her day, but went out of fashion on account of their explicit sexuality. Her work was too amorous for the affected prudery of the Victorians, but has now enjoyed a revival.

Aphra's early life can be pieced together only very sketchily. She was born on 10 July 1640 to Bartholomew Johnson, a barber by trade, and Elizabeth Denham. It is likely that she was born near Canterbury and grew up with the children of the rich Culpeper family, with whom her mother was employed as a nurse. Little is known of her upbringing and education, but she seems to have been brought up as a Catholic and her writings are sufficiently imbued with classical references to suggest a good scholastic background. But she had not learned the classical languages, and was later, through one of the characters in her plays, to bemoan her inability to read Homer and Virgil in their vernacular. In 1663, possibly through her connection with the Culpepers, she visited an

English sugar estate on the Surinam river,[1] close to the shores of the Caribbean. Her experiences on the trip were to give her material for *Orinooko*, the most famous of her novels. Soon after her return to England in 1664, Aphra is said to have married Johan Behn, a merchant of mysterious Dutch or German origin who disappeared from Aphra's life so quickly that it is often asserted that he was a fiction of Aphra's inventive mind, devised in order to give herself the protection of a widow's status.

Aphra was a committed Tory at the time, early in Charles II's reign, when political parties were beginning to form. Her choice may have been in part due to her Catholic upbringing and partly because Thomas Culpeper had introduced her to the exciting Restoration court of Charles II. Soon after the Second Anglo-Dutch War of 1665 had broken out, Aphra went to the Netherlands as a secret agent, codenamed *Astrea*. There she took on a man of high rank and influence as a lover, and pumped him for information that would benefit her English paymasters. Except that they did not pay. Charles neither paid her for her information nor for her expenses; she even had to borrow money to get back from Holland to England. She spent a year politely pestering Charles for money, but in the end she was consigned to a debtor's prison, having received little or nothing for her efforts. In 1669 she was released from prison after some unknown person paid her debts.

Having given up espionage as dangerous and unprofitable, Aphra had to find other ways of making a living. She was not keen to be a courtesan, especially as it was believed that she was bisexual, and her marriage, if it ever existed, seemed to have fizzled out, so she turned to writing. Her connections at court gave her an advantage, and by writing under the name *Astrea* she could, when she chose, keep her identity and even her gender secret. She began in 1670, and over a period of nineteen years wrote seventeen plays, four novels (some call them novelettes because of their relative brevity), some short stories and a collection of *Poems on Several Occasions (1684)*. Although some of her work was published posthumously, her writings gave her enough income to support the contention that she was the first English woman to earn her living by writing.

But although her plays were popular in her day they, like her poetry, were dismissed by subsequent ages as smutty. Aphra, drawing upon her experiences as a spy, was able to explore the relationship between sex and power and she attacked the contemporary conventions relating to race, class and gender. She tended to portray women as the dominant sex, and in her poem *The Golden Age* men are depicted as impotent. *The Golden Age* in some ways mirrors Ovid's depiction of the Golden Age in his *Metamorphoses*. But hers is not just a harking back to the age of innocence; it is the creation of a pastoral paradise in which free love and uninhibited sexuality are liberated from social and sexual morality. Her hedonism shines through much of her work. The transitory nature of human existence – 'Faith, sir, We are here today and gone tomorrow' – leads her to assert that 'Variety is the soul of pleasure', that 'Love ceases to be a pleasure when it ceases to be a secret', and 'Come Away; Poverty's Catching'. In 1681 she dedicated the second part of her most famous play *The Rover* to the Catholic Duke of York, recently returned from his second exile.[2] Whether she deserved her subsequent reputation for undermining conventional morality can be seen by her giving one of the characters the typical declamation that 'One hour of white down is worth an age of living dully on.'

Not surprisingly she had a very caustic view of marriage, regarding it as a social convention for the entrapment and enslavement of women, claiming that marriage would bring 'a cradle full of noise and mischief, with a pack of repentance at my back' *(The Rover)*. There would be no place for marriage in her pastoral paradise where women were the superior sex, yet she could not resist a tilt at contemporary bluestockings, and in *Sir Patient Fancy* the character of Lady Knowall is based on her assessment of Mary Astell.

So there is much division among critics about the quality of her work. But there is no doubt about its timing. Britain had no other female playwright until at least twenty years after her death on 16 April 1689, no female novelist for at least another fifty years, and no female poet of note for many years to come. She was buried in Westminster Abbey, not in Poets' Corner, but near to an actress, and her tomb carries the epigraph:

> Here lies a Proof that Wit can never be
> Defence enough against Mortality.

And no one could dispute that.

JANE AUSTEN AND HER WORLD

Jane Austen was born in Steventon, Hampshire, in 1775, the sixth of eight children of a country rector. Before her death in Winchester in 1817 she spent the first twenty-five years of her life in Steventon, and the last eight in nearby Chawton; her middle years were spent in fashionable Bath, where she saw at first-hand the social behaviour of the upper classes and the intimate workings of the marriage market. She herself never married, though she had a number of suitors, and wrote wittily and perceptively on the subjects of courtship and marriage in her novels. Her main subject was the closely observed and often ironically drawn morals and customs of country life, as in perhaps her best known works Sense and Sensibility *(1811),* Pride and Prejudice *(1813),* Emma *(1816) and* Persuasion *(1818, though published only posthumously). Her personal letters, though carefully censored by her sister Cassandra after her death, give us perhaps the most revealing written sources on her life. Sir Walter Scott praised her for the 'delicate observation and fine judgment' in her work, but she herself was more modest in her comments. She had begun to write mainly for her own amusement and that of her family, and had graduated to burlesquing popular fiction by ridiculing the current taste for Gothic novels in her* Northanger Abbey *(not published until 1818), but ended in a more documentary style by providing her own, and subsequent, generations with a finely drawn and accurate pen portrait of the lives and attitudes of gentlefolk in the early nineteenth century.*

Jane Austen's writings came at the end of a rather fallow period in English literature when names such as Richardson and Fielding were well in the past, but when there were few new writers coming forward to replace them. It was a time when there was little creativity: the plotlines of stories were stolen and regurgitated, society scandals were thinly disguised and dished up as fiction, old books were reissued with new titles, and old magazine stories were tacked together to form new books. There were a few writers whose names are today barely remembered, like Fanny Burney and Maria Edgeworth, and some prose compositions by Lord Byron, but generally there were few real literary names in the field. Classicism fell before the advance of Sentimentalism and Gothicism.[1] The *Monthly Review*, in 1790, lamented that 'novels in general have arrived at mediocrity ... we are indeed so sickened with this worn-out species of composition that we have lost all relish for it'. Only Sir Walter Scott was the shining exception. His annual earnings did not fall far short of £10,000 by 1818: *Waverley* sold 9,500 copies between 1814 and 1817, *Rob Roy* 10,000 in three weeks in 1817. Jane Austen's performance was much more modest: *Sense and Sensibility* sold about 1,000 copies in the two years after 1811 and made her about £140; *Pride and Prejudice* sold about 1,500 copies and made her about £110. Others, like *Emma*, were more modest still; her income from this book in 1815 amounted only to £39. In her letters she frequently bewailed her own commercial failure, and regretted that the critics did not acknowledge her achievements as fully as she would have liked. Contemporary critical comments were for the most part cool, criticising her for her omissions rather than praising her achievements.[2] It could be said, therefore, that she did not exactly wow her contemporaries, but came to be appreciated fully only after her death.

Scott was perhaps unique in the generosity of his comments on her work. He heralded the arrival of a new kind of novel whose art consisted of 'copying from nature as it really exists in the common walks of life, and presenting to the reader, instead of splendid scenes of an imaginary world, a correct and striking representation of that which is daily taking place around them'. He believed she was capable of depicting scenes of such 'spirit and originality' and so 'finished up to nature' that she achieved 'something of the merits of the Flemish school of painting'. This was high praise indeed, but praise with which modern opinion seems inclined to agree much more readily than with the other, lesser, contemporary evaluations. The circumstances of their respective deaths were also strikingly dissimilar: while Scott in 1832 was mourned nationally with 'almost every paper announcing the event in Scotland, and many in England, with the signs of mourning usual on the demise of a king', Jane Austen passed almost unnoticed, and her gravestone in Winchester Cathedral did not even mention that she was a writer.

And what can be learned of this social scene that she so faithfully described at the end of the eighteenth century? In her work there is little evidence of the impact of French Revolutionary ideas, or of the years of conflict with the Napoleonic Empire, but there is a great deal of minute description of social life in England at that time. Together the landed gentry and the peerage numbered about 25,000 families, their yearly incomes varying from those of the great landowners (about 400 families) at £10,000, down to the families with from £1,000 to £5,000 a year (about 5,000 families), with the majority receiving less. The landed families in Jane Austen's novels probably were about the £2,000 mark. A few of her characters had made their money through trade, though this was rather frowned on, some (in the navy) by the capture of prizes, and with professional people such as lawyers and clerics being also well represented. But the basic source of income in the books was from land, and took the form of rents. Landed estates were usually *entailed*, the object being to preserve the estate from generation to generation by preventing estates from broken up between the children or sold off. Entailment preserved the family estate and secured its income to one individual, but the process created a problem[3] for the younger sons and daughters who were debarred from their share of the income. The widow was provided for by a *jointure*, usually in the form of an annuity whose value would have been fixed in her marriage settlement. The position of younger sons was often straitened by entail, and was reinforced also by the convention among landed families whereby they voluntarily precluded themselves (within certain modest limits) from earning money independently.[4]

The landed gentry did not, however, exclude themselves from the professions. Entry here usually entailed a considerable financial outlay, and even then could not be relied on to generate an adequate income. Normally only four occupations were included on the list – the army, the navy, the church and the bar. In the Army, the purchase of a commission from an existing holder cost several thousand pounds, according to rank, and occasioned little opportunity for an income during service, but generated income to the retiring holder only when it was sold on. The position was much the same in the Navy, except there was more opportunity here for loot from captured vessels. Lawyers, if they were merely solicitors, were not treated much better than family servants; but if they were barristers could make a good living if they were talented and lucky, and stood a fair chance of making a good marriage.[5] In the Church, many livings were in the gift of the landowner, but if he gave the appointment to one of his own younger sons he deprived himself of the possibility of selling it to someone else; in any case, many stipends were often not much more than about £200 and would not afford a younger son much of a life.[6] In the cases of all these professions the establishment of younger sons required a considerable financial outlay from the family, and when this had been done there was still often little hope that the son in question would have enough money to improve his standing. The best way for them to do this was by an advantageous marriage.

The same applied even more markedly to women. A young woman's dowry (or 'portion' as it was usually called) was not so much intended to provide her with an income as to enable her to make a suitable marriage. The amount of the portions was a family matter,[7] and was often laid down in the marriage settlement of the girl's parents. There was, of course, no intention of a young gentlewoman *earning* anything, and almost no chance that any of them would do anything so vulgar as *take a job*. The custom of dowries arose from the circumstances of the time and reinforced the custom of entail and of the partial bar on gainful employment as the only way in which families could increase their financial resources. The system in the long run benefited the landed class as a whole because it supplied the necessary circulating capital for people whose incomes were normally static.

All these – widows, younger sons and, above all, daughters – placed burdens on entailed estates, many of which were saved from decline only by the very device they hated most – the augmentation of their fortunes by the inclusion of monies made from manufacture and trade. So marriage created much more than a relationship between a man and a woman; it was a *business proposition*. It gave rise to the doctrine of the 'equal alliance'. As in any bargain, it often occurred that one side would try to get the better of the other, and the losing family would consider that such an alliance was not an 'equal' one.[8] Such an unequal marriage would cause resentment and adverse social comment from landed neighbours, and perhaps ruin the marital relations of the young couple.

There were thus two sides to family alliances in Jane Austen's days. In her writings her characters were as much concerned with the notion of the 'equal alliance' in marriage as with marriage as the outcome of a romantic encounter between two individuals. Some of her characters are concerned with romance, some with settlements.[9] Sometimes the conflict between the two becomes pivotal, as with Mr. Darcy in *Price and Prejudice*, who knows he is marrying beneath him, but eventually allows his romantic attachment to Elizabeth Bennet to overcome his better judgement. He says: 'In vain have I struggled. It will not do. My feelings will not be repressed.' One wonders whether the violent objections of Lady Catherine de Bourgh will not resurface after the book is finished: she is certainly not in any doubt but that Elizabeth is a cunning little schemer worming her way into the family.

In practice the two aspects of the undertaking were combined. The enamoured couple took the initiative in meeting, falling in love and making outline plans; then parents were consulted and consent obtained, for it was they who financed the marriage settlement. If consent was refused the couple might elope, or else might prolong the engagement in the hope that agreement might finally be given.[10] But in the last analysis the two components of marriage – equal alliance and mutual affection – were fitted together by the landed gentry in the early nineteenth century as best they could to ensure their financial security and the continuing stability of their social system. These were problems which did not trouble the working classes at all, or even the manufacturers and shopkeepers, to anything like the same extent.

ELIZABETH BARRETT BROWNING: THE POET'S POET

Elizabeth Barrett Browning was one of the most prominent and influential poets of the nineteenth century. Her compositions were popular both in Britain and the United States, published either by her during her lifetime, or by her husband, Robert Browning, after her

early death in 1861. She was also read and studied by other literary figures, and exercised
a discernable influence on many of her contemporaries like Emily Dickinson, Dante and
Christina Rossetti, Edgar Allan Poe and Algernon Charles Swinburne. She also branched
out into critical prose writings, and eventually came, through her enormous reading and her
equally enormous correspondence, to devote herself to what she called the 'life of the mind', i.e.
to formulate a whole philosophy of life and art. Her illness and early death, accelerated by the
use of palliative opiates, extinguished a spiritual influence that might ultimately have put her
among the leading artistic figures of her age.

Elizabeth Barrett Moulton-Barrett was born in 1806 in rural County Durham, daughter of Edward Barrett Moulton-Barrett and Mary (*née* Graham-Clark). She was the eldest of a family of twelve. The family were part Creole, having lived in Jamaica for generations, where they owned sugar plantations worked by coloured slaves (Elizabeth's father chose to live in Britain while his fortune steadily accumulated in the West Indies). The Graham-Clark family were almost as well-off as the Barretts. Elizabeth was baptised in 1809 at Kelloe Parish Church, the family moving later that year to Hope End, an estate in the Malvern Hills in Herefordshire. Elizabeth was educated at home by a tutor, and received a good education at his hands, reading Milton and Shakespeare by the age of ten, and soon developing into a studious, precocious child. The family attended services at a nearby dissenting chapel. By the time she was fourteen, her father paid for the publication of a long Homeric poem she had written called *The Battle of Marathon*, and by the age of twenty she had learned Greek, Latin, some Italian and Hebrew, and had read the whole of the Old Testament in the original language. It was at this age that Elizabeth began her battle with a lifelong illness which the doctors could not diagnose; she began taking morphine to ease the pain and eventually became addicted to the drug.

After this, and in spite of it, her artistic life developed very rapidly. From 1822 onward she absorbed a good deal of Greek literature, studying such authors as Homer, Pindar and Aristophanes. In 1824 she published her *Stanzas on the Death of Lord Byron*, and in 1826 her *Essay on Mind and Other Poems*, which also showed the influence of the Greek and Latin classics on her. She also published *The Rose and the Zephyr* in 1825, her first excursion into scholarly thought. After her mother's death in 1828, and the abolition of slavery in 1833, the family's finances took something of a knock, and the family had to sell up Hope End, moving three times in almost as many years, first to Sidmouth in Devon, then to Gloucester Place in London and finally to Wimpole Street. Here she began contributing to a variety of literary magazines such as the *Literary Gazette*. At Wimpole Street, too, a place she had first got to know as a child, she made the acquaintance of many of the other leading literary figures of the age such as William Wordsworth, Samuel Taylor Coleridge, Alfred, later Lord, Tennyson and Thomas Carlyle. She became a friend of Mary Russell Mitford, who helped to further her literary ambitions at the time of her publication of *The Seraphim and Other Poems* in 1838. In this year, at her physician's request, she moved to Torquay for the sake of her health, but the death of her brother Edward from drowning in a boating accident set back her recovery and she returned in 1840 almost an invalid and a recluse. She blamed herself for her brother's death, since she had been so keen for him to be in Torquay with her, and from this time she graduated from morphine to crude opium, which weakened her for the rest of her life. Nonetheless, she continued to write furiously: in 1842 she wrote *The Cry of the Children*, a poem condemning child labour and helpful in the formulation of legislation against it in the mines and factories, and two other volumes of poems, *A Drama of Exile, A Vision of Poets*, and *Lady Geraldine's Courtship*, as well as critical prose pieces contributed to a publication called *A New Spirit of the Age*.

It was her 1844 poems that first brought her to the attention of Robert Browning through the intermediary of Richard Henry Horne, the editor of *A New Spirit of the Age*. Browning wrote to her to tell her how much he loved her work, and the two came together in a secret engagement and then marriage with the primeval force of an earthquake.[1] She was six years older than him, but was swept off her feet by his passion. The pair were married very privately at St Marylebone Parish Church in 1846, and Robert imitated his hero Shelley by spiriting his love off immediately afterwards to Italy, living first in Pisa and then, in 1847, in Florence, where their son Robert Wiedermann Barrett Browning (1848–1912) was born.[2] The Brownings were well-respected in Italy, and popular among the English colony living in Florence. Elizabeth's health also benefited from the climate, and she grew stronger and began to recover. At her husband's bidding she published a second edition of her poems, including her love poems, and this enhanced her reputation and the high critical regard in which she was held. On the death of Wordsworth in 1850 she was even regarded as a serious contender for the post of poet laureate (though the post was eventually accepted by Tennyson). By 1860 she was often regarded as the favourite Victorian poetess.

The end, when it came, was swift. With the death of an old friend, G. B. Hunter, and of her father in 1860, she took ill once more, and had to move from Florence to their summer home in Siena. Here she wrote and published a collection of poems on the wars in Italy called *Before the Congress*, and finally one called *A Musical Instrument*, which together with *Last Poem* was the last she ever composed. She finally returned to Rome, and died in June 1861. The nature of her illness is still disputed, but medical specialists have speculated that it was probably due to some condition of the lungs such as pulmonary tuberculosis, aggravated by the large number of opiates she consumed. She was buried in an ornate tomb in the English cemetery in Florence.

In the years after her death, her reputation steadily declined until she was rediscovered by the feminist movement in the later twentieth century. Some contemporaries found her religiosity off-putting: she had studied Milton's *Paradise Lost* and Dante's *Inferno* in some detail, linking them with her poetry – she said 'Christ's religion is essentially poetry: poetry glorified' – and she was perhaps too fond of theological debate. In 1899 Lilian Whiting depicted her life as 'the Gospel of applied Christianity'; to her 'art for art's sake' is less important than what she calls 'the intuitive gift of spiritual divination'. Others, such as Edgar Allan Poe and Emily Dickinson, in the 1840s, ignored this and concentrated on her poetic capabilities, saying 'her poetic inspiration is of the highest; her sense of art is pure in itself'. By 1931, in her play *The Barretts of Wimpole Street*, even Besier concluded rather more modestly that 'literary criticism of Browning's works suffers from the popularity of the poet rather than her poems'.

When she was rediscovered by the feminist movement of the mid-twentieth century, her work was made subject to some re-evaluation. Some feminists[3] suggested that the importance of her voice was partly stifled by the fact that she was writing in an age dominated by masculine superiority, and that even her husband, in spite of his obviously genuine attachment to her, believed that there was 'an inferiority of the intellect in women'. This evaluation, it may be thought, is on the whole only slightly less insulting than the neglect into which her work since 1860 has sunk.

HELEN BRADLEY AND POPULAR ART

As well as being a painter of considerable charm and style, Helen Bradley was also a child-like and observant commentator on the life of industrial Lancashire in the early twentieth century. Her pictures take as their subject the streets and the mill towns of early twentieth-century Lancashire, but they often stray into more picturesque rural areas of that county, or stroll observantly along the sands at Blackpool.

'Child-like', however, does not mean 'childish'. Though expressed in a style that, like the style of her contemporary J. S. Lowry, was naïve, her paintings reflected a personal and more intensely felt time before the First World War. It was an era when children were seen, not heard, but nonetheless never missed anything and were quite capable of describing it in detail afterwards, whenever the mood took them. There is an impish sense of humour behind the little men and women in her work; indeed, the acute observer may often detect the child herself somewhere in the picture. On the back of most of the paintings she often provided neatly written notes, sometimes quite lengthy, describing the scene, and supplying them with other clues. An observant critic[1] said of her that she interwove actual characters and episodes from her own childhood with flights of pure fancy, 'producing a unique blend of reality and fiction' that was 'the hallmark of the true artist'.

It is true that her paintings never attained the acclaim that awaited the canvases of Lowry, but they teemed with as much incident as his, and in some respects were more action-packed and colourful, and even more intimate. The seaside pierrot show with bright-faced children absorbed in the magic of the performance; the hay being brought in from a tiny field surrounded by working-class streets and mill buildings; the washing being put through the dolly-tub and the mangle in the yard while dresses, stockings and old-fashioned underwear are being hung out on the line to dry; two tiny dogs tussling together over a child's discarded hair-ribbon under the kitchen table – all these depict life as she saw it in early twentieth-century Lancashire. Sunday school seems to have its place in the events of the artist's life: one picture shows the Whit Walk of boys and girls behind the bands at Piccadilly, Manchester. Another shows poor children at a street party ascending Jacob's ladder, broken into two, and dancing on the clouds like a pink feather bed. Yet another depicts a boy called Jonah with a stick, poking at the enormous black head of a whale emerging from the lake in the local park. Sedate walks in Sunday best in the woods in all weathers; summer picnics by the lake; street scenes with someone with a bucket and shovel collecting horse manure after the tradesman's cart had passed; the local railway station – all these appear on Bradley's canvases. She was too shy at first to sign her pictures; instead she painted a small fly in the corner.[2] Many of her characters reappear in other pictures to continue the story. There was Miss Carter (who wore pink); Aunt Mary; Grandmother Shaw; the Murgatroyds, a rough lot who lived in the next street; The Reverend Albert Green, the new curate; and Mr Taylor the bank manager – and they keep reappearing to continue with the story like a children's comic. A picture of pre-war industrial Edwardian England as seen through the eyes of a child comes completely to life in the streets of Lees, the northern fringe of Oldham, with its back-to-back housing, its chimneys and its cotton mills, its teeming streets with shawls and clogs, a few trams and trains but chiefly still horse-drawn carts and drays. The flush water closet is still a novelty. Many of the people who appear here were plainly only just above the subsistence level, but the tone of these pictures is not depressing, but full of uncomplicated youthful fun.

Helen Bradley was born Nellie Layfield in November 1900 in Lees, Lancashire. She came from a musical family and was called Nellie in honour of Dame Nellie Melba, the soprano her father much admired. However, she hated the name and adopted for herself the name of Helen. Even after she was married, she continued to use the name 'Helen Layfield' to sign her pictures. She was the eldest of the four children born of the marriage between Jane Shaw and Frederick Layfield, both lower-middle-class tradespeople in a working-class environment. The Shaws were connected with tailoring, the Layfields with hosiery. Their home was a large double-fronted stone house in High Street, Lees, and was also the premises of David Shaw & Son, Tailors, Helen's maternal grandfather, whose products were displayed for sale inside the bow front window. Helen grew up surrounded by the members of her numerous family, especially the female ones, while grandfathers and uncles were away at work. Little details of her childhood recur constantly in her paintings, such as the lace-edged tablecloth which she remembered from her visits to see her numerous aunts, just as she remembered the gossip she overheard sitting silently in the corner as a little girl. Family life for the Layfield children centred on music, and Sundays were devoted to music rather than to religion, which Helen's father rather despised. He had founded the Oldham Orchestral Society, some of whose members visited the Laycocks on Sundays to take part in string quartets, with Frederick on the violin. Hence all the children learned to play music – the other three violin or cello, and Helen herself the piano, so that she could be the accompanist.

Grandfather Shaw had a younger brother who was a painter, some of whose pictures were hung at the Royal Academy at least once, and this seems to have inspired Helen to be a painter rather than a musician. As a child she painted Christmas cards, and a number of small pictures, on scraps of hardboard about six inches by three, of various local scenes.

She had relatively little regular schooling, though, after the family moved to Clarksfield, closer to Oldham, she put in about two years' regular attendance at the Council School there. Her headmaster encouraged her to apply for a scholarship at Oldham Art School, where she intended to study jewellery design, but her father thought this was a waste of time, and diverted her to City and Guilds evening classes, while during the day she worked for his business, tramping the streets with a small attaché case of samples and an order book. Later she was allowed to use the pony and trap. Her slight, girlish figure (she was only a little over five feet tall) was well known throughout the district. She worked through the war, only once being caught in a Zeppelin raid during the hours of the blackout. At art school she met Tom Bradley, who was later badly gassed, wounded and left for dead on the Western Front. She married him in 1922. By this time he had diverted from Fine Art – he hoped at one time to go to the Slade School in London – to become a designer in the textile trade. Helen's domestic commitments to her new home, and her obligations to her own two children, born in 1927 and 1931, took her once again away from her beloved art, but she enjoyed herself in creating home furnishings and learning to make shoes.

It was not until the end of the Second World War that she resumed her interest in painting. The family had meanwhile moved south to Stanmore in Middlesex on account of her husband's work as a designer and his involvement with the John Lewis Partnership. Helen was able to take up painting again as a hobby. She visited the London art galleries and looked at their pictures avidly. Dutch, Mughal and Chinese artists all made their mark on her, and she had great fun experimenting with their artistic methods. After 1952, when her husband retired from textile design, they moved house again, first to Cheshire and finally, in 1964, to Cartmel on the edge of the Lake District.

At first she wanted only to show her grandchildren what life was like in Edwardian England, but later painting became for her almost an obsession. She threw herself wholeheartedly into fulfilling her long-cherished ambitions to be an artist. She experimented with both watercolours and oils, soaking the paper in the bath overnight for the former before drying it off the following day when she started work, and using for the latter household implements of all sorts – old knives, fish-slices and even ordinary nails for removing and applying paint. This she did thickly, hardly ever using brushes. Some of the detail in her pictures is minute and delicate; her watercolour landscapes are fluid and watery, and often quite Chinese in atmosphere. With her husband she joined the Saddleworth Art Group, though through a self-imposed limitation she largely confined herself to providing tea and cakes for the society's members, many of whom had little idea that privately she was an artist. Suddenly her imagination was fired. The main focus of her attention remained the scenes of her childhood, and the depiction of a host of figures now long dead but still vivid in her memory. Her daughter Betty, recalling her newfound flood of enthusiasm, said of her: 'Once she got to her figures there was no stopping her. She had found something that was herself. In the past she had never been so determined; she always gave in to her husband and her children – it was always what *they* wanted.'

In 1965, though well into what were commonly regarded as retirement years, she put on her first one-woman exhibition of her work, exhibiting under her maiden name of Helen Layfield. A local admirer of her paintings, Lord Rhodes of Saddleworth, was so struck when he saw her pictures that he gave her the name of a London gallery, the Mercury Gallery in Cork Street, who offered her an exhibition in 1966, and at this and later exhibitions she found to her delight that the public could not get enough of her work. By the end of the 1960s, private commissions for her paintings were coming in thick and fast, not only from British clients but from abroad as well. As a dumpy, motherly, unassuming figure, happy in her domestic kitchen, she was delighted with her success and tried not to be surprised. She began to make a good deal of money, though she remained consistent in her refusal to commercialise her work by allowing her designs to be used on tea-towels and jigsaw puzzles. At about this time, the publisher Jonathan Cape suggested that her pictures would make an excellent children's book, and got her to agree to publish in 1971 a very successful selection, *Miss Carter Wore Pink: Scenes from an Edwardian Childhood*. She also went on to what she considered the pinnacle of artistic achievement – an exhibition at the Royal Academy in 1973, and also at about the same time in Los Angeles in the United States. By the mid-1970s, Helen had become famous, setting up Miss Carter Publications, first in Manchester and later in Bolton, where it still operates today. In 1979 she received an MBE in the Queen's Honours List, but never travelled to London to receive it since she suffered a heart attack in the weeks before the investiture and died in July of 1979.

A close examination of her work reveals how much she owed to the work of earlier artists, though how relatively little to J. S. Lowry, whom she met only once.[3] Her figures are drawn with loving attention to detail, pleasing lines and a colour that is at the same time dainty and accurate; they were never much like Lowry's matchstick men. She took her inspiration from a wide variety of sources, many of them dating back to her visits to London Galleries in the 1950s and 1960s. Many of those who inspired her she saw when she was living at Stanmore. It was during one of her visits to the National Gallery that she became fascinated by the winter landscapes of the Dutch painter Hendrick Avercamp (1585–1634). She was so much influenced by his work that at least one of her early works is entitled 'After Avercamp'. She derived inspiration, too, from the early Mughal painters, whose works served as a visual diary of court life in India in the seventeenth century. These paintings were teeming with tiny but vividly coloured figures whose neat dress and wide eyes can be seen as she imitated them in her work. She admired also the work of the seventeenth-century watercolourist Tao-chi (1630–1707), on whose elegant and fluid painting style for trees, gardens, landscapes and figures she modelled her own. She never ceased to learn from a wide range of quite esoteric sources, and absorbed as much of their style and painting techniques as she could. Close examination of her work shows that they were much more the source of her inspiration than the paintings of Lowry.

COCO CHANEL:
THE EMPRESS OF STYLE

Coco Chanel liked to say 'Fashion passes; style remains'. During a long, hardworking and wonderfully successful lifetime, she made an international name for herself, and at the same time a name for Paris as the home of haute couture *during the twentieth century. Her pioneering spirit was directed towards the production of menswear-inspired fashions conceived in pursuit of an elegant but expensive simplicity, and executed in fine materials. She was so highly esteemed in the realm of* haute couture *that, when it appeared, hers was the first name on* Time *Magazine's list of the 'most important people of the twentieth century'. Karl Lagerfeld took over from her shortly after her death in 1971 as chief designer of Chanel's fashion house, and continued to work for the firm until well into the twenty-first century, but by then her name was firmly established as perhaps Europe's leading fashion guru.*

Gabrielle Bonheur ('Coco') Chanel was born in Saumur, Maine et Loire, France, the daughter of a small travelling salesman Albert Chanel and his partner Jeanne Devolle in the summer of 1883. Her parents got married in the year of her birth. She was the second of three sisters, two of them born before her parents' marriage, and the third, and also her three brothers, in the interval before the early death of her mother in 1895. In the later, successful, period of her life she felt herself forced to rewrite and embroider her own biography, conjuring up an unhappy childhood in which her mother died very young (not too far from the truth), her father abandoned her and emigrated to America in search of work, and she was sent to live with two cold-hearted spinster aunts – much of which, of course, was untrue. Also she pretended, as was not uncommon at the time, to be much younger than she really was, claiming to have been born in 1893.

In fact, she was born ten years earlier in the poorhouse, to which her father had committed her mother because of his inability to maintain her. When her birth was reported at the local *mairie* by two employees of the hospice, both of whom were illiterate, the mayor enrolled the birth in his register, but not knowing how to spell 'Chanel' spelt it with an 's', and so recorded it as 'Chasnel'. Brought up in great poverty, Coco did not have an easy life, a situation further worsened by her mother's death from tuberculosis in 1895, after a protracted illness, when the little girl was only twelve. Her father was still looking for a steady job, and so, while he was looking for work, committed her to the care of the orphanage of the monastery of Aubazine, where she was brought up and given instruction as a seamstress. As a result of this training she was able, when she left the orphanage at the age of eighteen, to take up work for a local tailor. An attractive, though rather skinny, young woman, she was taken up by a local playboy, Étienne Balsan, who gave her a taste of the good life by lavishing dresses and jewellery on her, and taking her to live with him at his apartment in Paris. After some experience as a cabaret singer (where she acquired the nickname of 'Coco' on the strength of her singing of the vaudeville number 'Ko Ko Ri Ko'), she began designing ladies' hats, and, when she broke with Balsan, opened her first shop in central Paris in 1910, where she also sold a range of fashionable raincoats and jackets.

Coco went on to make the acquaintance of Arthur ('Boy') Capel, a wealthy English industrialist and a former friend of Balsan. She fell in love for a second time, this time with Capel.[1] With his help she was able in 1913 to introduce a new line in women's sportswear at the new shop she established in Deauville. She acquired the Countess de Gounaut-Biron (daughter of a US diplomat) as her first aristocratic client, and went on from there to establish further shops, for example in the fashionable spa town on Biarritz, where, during the First World War, her simple clothes and hats became extremely fashionable and popular.

Chanel furthered her own image of the twentieth-century liberated woman, embodying independence, personality, confidence and style. As her distinguishing mark in the French fashion world, she took cheap jersey fabric, previously only used in underwear, and manufactured this in the form of short knee-length skirts. These were matched with boxy jackets with big, piled pockets and no waistline, traditionally made from woven wool. By the end of the 1920s her new chemise set the fashion trend with its 'little boy' look. Her clothes were in sharp contrast with the uncomfortable, stiff corseted garments of the Edwardian period, and gave the 'flapper' of the 1920s a great sense of athleticism and freedom. Chanel herself wore mannish clothes, usually combined with chunky costume jewellery. In 1925 she introduced her signature 'cardigan jacket', followed in 1926 by a 'little black dress', so popular that it entered the fashion vocabulary in the form of its initials – the 'LBD' – because of its versatility for being worn either during the day or in the evening. It was strapless, backless and, because it required only a minimum of underwear, more than a little risqué; but it soon became the fashion rage, and has remained so ever since.

Her most famous fragrance, Chanel No. 5, was introduced in 1922, and even today remains popular.[2] It was created by Chanel's associate Ernest Beaux, who described it (misleadingly) as a 'woman's perfume with the scent of woman'. It was the very profitable product of her own perfume company, managed by Pierre Wertheimer, who after 1924 was her business partner, and possibly also her lover. The Wertheimers fought for the control of the business, and continue to run it today.

During World War Two, Chanel served for some time as a nurse. She also took up residence in the Ritz Hotel, Paris, which she made her home during the Nazi occupation. At this time, she had an affair with Hans Gunther von Dincklage, a German officer with intelligence connections,[3] who arranged for her to remain at the Ritz during the war, in addition to having her own apartment above her shop in the Rue Cambon. Her behaviour excited criticism and brought her some loss of popularity, as did her building of a new home on the Riviera in unoccupied France. In 1945 she went into temporary voluntary exile in Switzerland, but eventually returned to Paris in 1954 and re-entered the fashion world. She never quite recovered her popularity with the Parisians, but her collections in the postwar years came to be much applauded, not only by the French but internationally as well. Her casual, natural clothing once again caught the eye of fashion-conscious ladies, as well as being within the reach of their purses. She introduced pea-jackets and bell-bottomed trousers for women, both of which proved to be sensationally successful. Though she claimed to have retired, she was still working even in her old age.

She could also be a tyrant. She herself was slim and boyish, and she had no time for fleshier females.[4] She squabbled with Gloria Swanson as early as 1931 at the fitting of her new dress when she disregarded her instructions to 'lose five pounds' but instead came back for her second fitting even plumper than before. She also strongly disapproved of miniskirts, such as those worn by Jackie Kennedy, who had 'horrible taste' in clothes, and frequently declared her hatred for 'tight girdles' and 'sagging bottoms'. Even when she was old, she carried on the struggle for liberating women from their servitude to uncomfortable underwear. The octogenarian Chanel finally had to deal with not only bad temper but terrible bouts of sleepwalking. She was several times found naked in her bedroom, holding a pair of scissors and having reduced her pyjamas to a 'heap of scraps'.

Still treating her servants with the same cutting disregard as she had practised throughout her life, she died in January 1971, in her private suite at the Ritz, eighty-seven years old, and was buried in Lausanne, Switzerland in a tomb bearing the carved heads of lions representing her birth sign, Leo.

Chanel's career had something of the fairytale about it. Though born in circumstances of gruelling poverty, she managed, by a combination of good fortune and hard application, to rise to the top of the tree of *haute couture*. She achieved international fame and adulation, great wealth, which she managed with a petit-bourgeois devotion to detail, and, though she never produced a family, enjoyed a varied succession of lovers throughout her life. She, and the garments she designed, remain even today widely admired and respected, and her example stands as a beacon to those wishing to follow in her footsteps.

ENID BLYTON: STORY-TELLER

Enid Blyton achieved great popularity in the twentieth century as one of the most prolific contemporary writers of fiction for children. Her work, chiefly themed into a number of popular series such as the Famous Five, *the* Secret Seven, *and the* Noddy *books (concerning the adventures of an impish little cartoon character and his friends) ran into thousands of titles; she also wrote more serious Bible stories, retelling Old and New Testament stories and introducing them to children, and edited an Enid Blyton magazine, as well as writing for a number of other children's papers. The wordage of her books ran to such vast dimensions as to encourage the idea that the author, who wrote sometimes as much as 10,000 words per day (a feat that outshone the achievements even of Anthony Trollope), employed a team of ghost-writers to maintain her output. She had a great respect for her juvenile readership, and always claimed to know what they wanted – fantasy alternating with cosiness – but she was herself the deliberate victim of the same sort of juvenile day-dreaming that appears in her books. Extending from her fiction into her own private existence, this fantasising finally obliterated the true reality of her life and experience.*

Enid Blyton was born in August 1897 in East Dulwich, London, the eldest child of Thomas Blyton and his wife Theresa Mary. As a girl, Enid adored her father, a cutlery salesman, who took her and her younger brothers Hanley and Carey for long walks in the woods, where he taught them the names of the trees and flowers they encountered. The family later moved to the nearby suburb of Beckenham. Here, from 1907 to 1915, Enid was educated at St Christopher's School. She was a bright pupil both in academic subjects and at sports, and finished by becoming Head Girl. A talented pianist, she nevertheless decided to give up music and undertook teacher training at Ipswich High School, later teaching for five years in a variety of local schools. In her spare time she took up writing, and succeeded eventually – after the usual difficulties of a new author finding a publisher – in getting her first book, *Childhood Whispers*, a collection of children's verse, published in 1922. The editor of the book department of George Newnes, the firm that took up her first two books for publication, was Major Hugh Alexander Pollock, whom she met when she visited the firm; he married her in 1924. The couple moved to rural Buckinghamshire, and finally to a house whose name – Green Gables – was chosen for her in a competition among her readers and where her children, both girls were born in 1931 and 1935. There, provided with a new typewriter, she embarked in a serious fashion on fulfilling her literary ambitions.

From the beginning there were problems in her relationship with her husband. She dwelt a good deal on her early experiences, which she invested with an aura of fantasy. She believed her father to have been an admirable figure let down by his wife, though in fact he was something of a womaniser, and she was more sinned against than sinning. Enid cut her mother and her brothers out of her life, and seemed to believe in her own story that her mother had died shortly after the separation – though in fact she lived on until 1950. She did not see her brothers for over thirty years, and was even reluctant to go to her mother's funeral. In spite of – or perhaps because of – her vivid imagination, she somehow contrived to remain undeveloped and childish in her attitudes. Physically, too, she found out from her doctor in her twenties that she had the uterus of an undeveloped twelve-year-old; and, even after she had produced children, remained conspicuously lacking in affection for them, writing furiously and resigning their upbringing to a succession of nannies. Her husband Hugh was stung as much by her self-delusion as by her coldness, saying with some bitterness that she thought only in terms of 'bunnies and picnics and talking bloody golliwogs', and saying that children loved her only 'because they didn't really know what she was like'. She had little awareness of the world about her at the outbreak of the Second World War, writing a steady stream of books, up to about twenty a year, and totalling over 750 altogether, while the world about her and her own marriage steadily foundered on her own neglect and indifference.

In 1941, quite by chance, she met and fell in love with Kenneth Waters, a London surgeon, and in 1943 the two married at City of Westminster Registry Office, after both had secured a divorce from their existing spouses. It is perhaps typical of Enid's selfishness that she attempted beforehand to escape from the social blame involved in her divorce by trying to persuade Hugh to provide her with the grounds for it. When she remarried, Enid made out to the youngsters that her new husband was the girls' father as well as her new husband, and changed their names to Waters. Typically, but astonishingly in the light of her attachment to her own father, she ignored their feelings for their biological father. Throughout her life she continued to demonstrate her lack of consideration for her children, but nonetheless she herself remained devotedly attached to her second husband, as he was to her. She cast herself in the role of a doctor's devoted wife, and so fulfilled her own as well as her husband's expectations. Kenneth suffered from a hearing disability and wore a hearing aid – indeed, he said hers was the only voice he could ever understand. When eventually, at the age of forty-eight, she became pregnant in 1945, she miscarried after a fall while collecting fruit from the trees in her garden, and so never succeeded in giving him the son they both wanted. It is a bizarre footnote to her obsession with her world of fairyland that she promptly reinvented this lost son as the fictional Noddy, and created for him a popular range of infantile adventures.

Enid's husband died in 1967. This event brought her life and career into violent collision with reality, and succeeded in disturbing her emotional balance. Thereafter she became increasingly affected by forgetfulness, and this state eventually developed into full-blown dementia. She could not even remember the names of her two brothers. Shortly before her death she was moved into a nursing home in Hampstead, where she died in November 1968. She was cremated at the Golders Green Crematorium, where her ashes remain.

Opinions of the importance of her work remain today much divided. Many literary critics believed she had an accurate intuitive understanding of children's minds, and this was why she was so successful in her writings. Her books were vastly popular in many of the countries of the world, including Australia, New Zealand, the countries of the former Yugoslavia, India, Sri Lanka, Malaysia, Singapore and Japan, and were translated into nearly ninety languages. They reflected the fantasies of younger children. Children in them were free to play and to develop without adult interference; grown-ups were often portrayed as authoritarian figures without sympathy for children's thoughts, or else as adversaries engaged and finally defeated by children. In her books, children are of three types: ordinary children in extraordinary circumstances, having adventures and solving crimes, often proving themselves superior to the rather stolid policemen in the tale; boarding-school stories where pupils emerge from the day-to-day routine of school to have exciting and unusual adventures; and magical stories, where children escape into a world of make-believe where they have adventures with fairies, elves and goblins. Certainly children hung on her every word, spellbound by her writings. She won numerous literary prizes for her output, as in the case of the 2008 Costa Awards, when she was posthumously voted the best-loved children's author, ahead of Roald Dahl and J. K. Rowling. Indeed, she always contended that she was not interested in the views of any critic over the age of twelve.

On the other hand there were many who held a different view of her work. At times, her books in the 1950s and 1980s were banned from the shelves of children's libraries in New Zealand, Australia as well as in Britain, and sometimes their contents were censored by a number of her publishers. Most were said to be quite outdated, reflecting the thinking of earlier times – unreflectingly patriotic, xenophobic, authoritarian, her language imbued with racist overtones, her households always staffed by respectful and submissive servants, and organised on typically bourgeois lines. She developed a stereotyped portrayal of 'decent' (i.e. middle-class) folk contrasting with the 'rough' (i.e. the coarser) working people, these being usually responsible for any law-breaking that went on in her pages; and this gave a facile but misleading picture of society, though it doubtless illustrated Blyton's own view on the world. Many of the features of her stories seemed be lacking in political correctness. Her easy use of the term 'nigger' to refer to black people, though still quite common in her time, came to be resented as racist, and even her publishers were of a mind from time to time to replace her 'golliwogs'[1] with 'teddy-bears'. Sexism was another accusation made against her. Even the children of the Famous Five were all aware of the distinctions that ought properly to be drawn between the roles of men and women in society – one of them says to another: 'You may look like a boy and behave like a boy, but you are a girl all the same, and, like it or not, girls have got to be taken care of.'

The BBC was among Blyton's severest critics. Many there took the prissy, but quite sincere, view that her books were shallow and childish, her style very flat and uninspired, and her stories boring. They were not impressed by her reputation, or her sales figures and royalties, but took the strict Reithian line that she was to be kept off the air for the good of broadcasting. She protested, she remonstrated, but the answer remained the same – she was to be barred from the BBC in the interests of literary and artistic standards. She eventually succeeded in making a brief appearance on *Woman's Hour*, but for the whole of her career she was never really welcome at Broadcasting House. Nonetheless, demand for her books even today remains strong, and many parents turn instinctively to her place on the booksellers' shelves when they think of buying something suitable for their children, and hundreds of her books are sold each year all over the world by the publisher handling her intellectual estate, Chorion of London.

PART 2

ENTERTAINERS AND STARS

GRETA GARBO:
WAS SHE THE BRIGHTEST STAR
IN THE FIRMAMENT?

A Swedish film star of historic pre-eminence, Great Garbo was oddly rather less remarkable for how she performed in her films than for the deliberate air of mystery with which she cloaked her existence, and the tantalising lack of communication with the outside world that eventually became her individual trademark. In the end she became totally reclusive; what had been a curious quirk of her nature became an obsession. Even today, the books are full of her professional accomplishments as an actress, and bulging with lists of the films in which she appeared before 1949, the last year she chose to appear on celluloid; but precious little else is known of her opinions, her character, her relationships or of anything more individual than the characters of the persons she chose to portray in her work.

She was born Greta Lovisa Gustafsson in Stockholm in 1905, the youngest of three children of Karl Alfred and Anna Lovisa Gustafsson, her elder brother seven years older and her sister three years older than herself. When she was fourteen, her father, with whom she was very close, died, and she had to leave school to go to work. Her first job was as a soap-lather girl in a barber's shop, then as a sales assistant in PUB, a department store in Stockholm, where finally, after winning a bathing beauty competition, she became a photographic model for the store at the age of sixteen. She appeared in her first moving picture when she appeared in two short advertisements filmed by the store. She had no ambitions in the direction of acting until these publicity films were seen by the comedy director Eric Petschler, and he recommended that she go into the theatre, which put the idea of acting into her head.

From 1922 to 1924, Greta studied at the Royal Dramatic Theatre in Stockholm, where she met and worked under the film director Mauritz Stiller. It was he who invented the surname 'Garbo' for her, and cast her in her first major role as Gosta Berling, opposite the Swedish star Lars Hanson. The pair of them were brought to Metro-Goldwyn-Mayer by Louis B. Mayer, who was much impressed by Garbo's acting, sensitive expression and screen presence. Her career was made from then on, with Stiller insisting that MGM give her a proper contract in Hollywood. She went on to do film work for MGM and for Paramount Pictures. When her sister Alva died of cancer in 1926 at a very early age, Greta felt her loss deeply. At the same time, she experienced homesickness at being so far from her homeland in Sweden. When she was denied permission to return home to attend the funeral she felt resentful towards MGM for the studio's heartlessness.

Garbo's film career in a way parallels the history of the whole film industry. She grew up with it, and added a glamorous dimension to its sometimes rather seedy history. She began in the silent era, when films were adorned with captions to provide the dialogue; she went on to films whose soundtrack was strictly limited to music and sound effects; she was a star in an age that was at first exclusively and later chiefly black-and-white, and turned to colour only about the time of the Second World War. Garbo proved to be an actress of remarkable talent and legendary beauty, as her roles in a number of silent films from 1926 to 1929 revealed. She featured in *Flesh and the Devil* (1927), and Love (1927), both with the popular leading man John Gilbert, of whom it was said, after their steamy performances together, that he managed to persuade her to marry him, only to be left standing at the altar when she failed to show up for the wedding. She went on to star in *The Mysterious Lady* and *A Woman of Affairs*, both in 1928, and *The Kiss* (1929), the last film to be made without a soundtrack for the dialogue – it used it for the music and the sound effects only. Her voice was first heard on screen in Eugene O'Neill's *Anna Christie* in 1930, widely publicised under the headline 'Garbo talks!' Other films followed in a great rush. She appeared in *Romance* (1930), *Mata Hari* (1931), *Grand Hotel* (1932), *Queen Christina* (1933), *Anna Karenina* (1935), *Camille* (1936) and *Ninotchka* (1939)[1] receiving high praise from fellow actors and actresses, and being three times nominated for the Best Actress award at the Academy Awards. There was a fallow period during the Second World War, apart from another attempt (an unsuccessful one) at comedy with *The Two-Faced Woman* (1941), which was a success at the box office, but was generally panned by the critics. This seems to have been the occasion when Garbo decided to retire from the screen, for, though Walter Wanger tried to tempt her back in 1949 with *La Duchesse de Langeais*, she never appeared before the cameras again. She did, however, receive some sort of recognition when she was awarded an honorary Academy Award in 1955 for her 'unforgettable screen performances', an award that she agreed to accept, but only by proxy, when the award was accepted on her behalf by another actress, Nancy Kelly.

Garbo had always been taciturn in her dealings with the press, giving out little information and maintaining a strict regard for her own privacy. This tendency to withdraw from social contacts grew more pronounced as she grew older: she granted no interviews, signed no autographs, attended no premieres and answered no fan mail. She became something of a mystery to others, including her fellow actors. It was suggested, rather unkindly and probably also without much truth, that she was reclusive because she was ashamed of her origins, for although she was proud to count herself Swedish, she was alleged to have been ashamed of her father's occupation (a humble one – indeed at one time he was said in a Sunday newspaper article to have been a latrine-cleaner). She was well known for her reluctance to mingle and the saying for which she gained a reputation: 'I want to be alone',[2] a motto she translated into action at every opportunity. But in reality she knew how to be loyal and faithful to her friends. When she broke with John Gilbert in 1927 and unexpectedly refused to marry him, the two remained friends – indeed she insisted on providing him with a role in *Queen Christina* in 1933, despite the fact that his film career had collapsed by this time and the MGM head of studios,

Louis B. Mayer, was reluctant to give him a part. A biography of Greta Garbo published in 1995 makes the point that privately she had a number of close and warm relationships – for example with the actor George Brent, the orchestral conductor Leopold Stokowski, the nutritionist Gayelord Hauser and her manager George Schlee, the husband of the designer Valentina Schlee.[3]

But Garbo nevertheless remained a very isolated figure after she retired from filming. She never disappeared from the public eye, and resolutely refused to re-enter public life. She became a naturalised US subject in 1951, and in 1953 bought a seven-room apartment on East 52nd Street in New York, where she lived for the rest of her life. She was well known for walking anonymously through the streets of New York dressed in casual clothes and wearing big sunglasses, which she imagined kept her from being recognised by the paparazzi and the public at large, but in fact she was nearly always recognised, though not accosted. She lived frugally because of her sensible upbringing and her Swedish carefulness; she invested her considerable wealth wisely. She bought up land and property in Beverley Hills in California – the home of many wealthy film stars – which eventually became very valuable, and she never indulged in anything like conspicuous consumption. Unlike the character later played by Gloria Swanson, she never attempted a comeback, but is today remembered for her momentous performances of yesterday.

She died in New York Hospital in April 1990, aged eighty-four, as the result of pneumonia following renal failure, and was cremated. After her death her ashes were interred under a simple headstone in Skogskyrkogården Cemetery in Stockholm.

JOYCE GRENFELL: THE PERENNIAL AMATEUR

Even when she was at her most professional, Joyce Grenfell never lost the air she cultivated of being a gifted amateur. She had a sharp ear and a discerning eye for mimicry, and possessed the modest but endearing capacity to present herself as ordinary, when in fact she was extremely gifted. She was upper-class in every way. Like her extraordinary mother, Nora Langhorne, and her very forthright aunt, Nancy Astor, the first woman MP, she could spontaneously produce the telling phrase that made her famous if not universally popular.[1] A gifted comedienne, Joyce performed on the radio and appeared on television and on film as a performer and personality, and was one of the few whom the Royal Mail immortalised as 'Heroes of Comedy' with her face on a postage stamp in 1998.

Joyce Grenfell was born in London in February 1910 as Joyce Irene Phipps, daughter of an unsuccessful architect Paul Phipps[2] and her madcap American mother Nora

Langhorne. Nora was a delight to Joyce and to other children, whom she loved to play with, being herself a child at heart, but was fickle, flippant and lived very extravagantly. She was eccentric to the point of lunacy, falling in love with every attractive man she met, and, when she eventually ran away with one, never even grasping that bigamy was a crime. From her Joyce inherited her untiring ability to improvise and to entertain, from her father her discipline and determination, and from her Virginian grandfather her energy and her ambition. From her childhood she was surrounded by the aristocratic, the rich and the privileged – even to name them would be invidious, since they were so numerous that not even the most brash of social climbers could have invented the list. Perhaps the most influential, among entertainment people like Mrs Patrick Campbell, Noel Coward and Ivor Novello, was the accomplished American monologist Ruth Draper, who remained for many years Joyce's lodestar. Though Joyce was upper-class, she was at first not at all rich. She said: 'There's no denying my privileged background. I had holidays, fee-paying schools and marvellous hand-me-down clothes from generous cousins.' She was brought up not by her mother, who was generally much too busy entertaining, but by a nanny she adored. She eventually attended Francis Holland School in Central London, but did not like it, and spent much of her time mimicking her teachers. She loved literature, good books and beautiful music, but learned this love from her family and not from her schooling. In her teens, she was converted to the Church of Christ, Scientist, by her aunt Lady Mary Astor, and she remained a Christian Scientist[3] to the end of her days.

In the middle 1920s she gained admission to RADA (one of its Directors, George Bernard Shaw, was a friend of the family), where she made the acquaintance of Celia Johnson. Although she learned to act, Joyce was more interested in 'being an actress' and did not persist in her studies. In 1927 she met Reggie Grenfell, and two years later married him. In the interval, like many young upper-class girls of the period, she was presented at court, though with her big feet and large legs she was rather ungainly for a successful debutante. The couple were given a house on the Cliveden estate by Nancy Astor. While at a luncheon party at Cliveden, she met the editor of the *Observer*, and, telling him how interested she was in listening to radio, was given the job of writing the first wireless critic column that the paper produced. Among her other 'good works' she helped with a welfare clinic, worked briefly in nursery schools, and did her stint for the Women's Institute – all of which were used later as sources of her acutely-observed and entertaining monologues.

In 1939 she made her theatre debut. Having amused the radio producer Stephen Potter with the impersonation of a toothy woman she had met at the WI giving a little talk on how to make a 'useful little *boutonnière* from empty beech-nut husk clusters', she was persuaded to take part in a show, *The Little Revue*, which appeared at the *Little Theatre* off the Strand in 1939. The show ran until the outbreak of war, and Joyce took home nearly £11 a week (including her share of the profits). The critic James Agate of the *Sunday Times* thought she was the funniest thing he had ever seen.

During the war, Joyce was 'called up'. She did not want to work in munitions, and was thrilled when she was given a chance to become a singer with ENSA.[4] She performed in camps and military hospitals, and in 1944 set off for a tour of the Middle East in which she visited Egypt (where she had a touch of the high life as she was the niece of the British High Commissioner in Cairo, Mile Lampson, Lord Killearn), and afterwards Iraq and India. Fifteen months and fourteen countries later, she felt justified in entering on her passport the job description 'Writer-Entertainer'.

From 1946 to 1954 she was heard, and later seen, on TV in *We Beg to Differ* – a light-hearted discussion programme – alongside such figures as the cantankerous Gilbert Harding and the equally opinionated radio doctor Charles Hill (it was one of BBC's darkest secrets that Joyce's fee was more than twice that paid to her male counterparts), and then in other stage revues such as *Penny Plain,* then *Tuppence Coloured,* and finally *Joyce Grenfell Requests the Pleasure,* which ran from June 1954 to January 1955. But this type of entertainment had long felt dated and it faded away altogether in the 1950s. Instead, playing alongside such stalwarts as Alistair Sim and Margaret Rutherford, she appeared in a series of films set in the imaginary scenario of a girl's school, St Trinians, beginning with *The Happiest Days of Your Life,* and continuing with *The Belles of St Trinians, Blue Murder at St Trinians* and *The Pure Hell of St Trinians,* in all of which she played the lanky gym mistress Miss Gossage – 'Call me Sausage'. Though producing her material was hard work and took hours before the mirror, refining and perfecting it until she found it acceptable, Joyce had the gift of making it look very easy. Others used to ask her to write for them, but her answer was always the same – 'You must do it for yourselves.'

But there was a serious side to her work. In 1961 and 1962 she spent almost two years as a member of the Pilkington Commission into the standards and the future of radio and television. Invited by Reginald Bevins, the Postmaster General, to join the Commission, she was pleasantly surprised, but she was well-chosen for the work, which she did assiduously and with great success. Alongside her, the only other woman on the eleven-strong panel was the Scottish broadcaster and social worker Elizabeth Whiteley, with whom she worked very well. She also struck up a friendship with the university lecturer Richard Hoggart, author of *The Uses of Literacy,* and made famous by the Penguin trial of *Lady Chatterley's Lover,* and with him she worked to achieve higher standards and more professionalism in broadcasting. The Report of the Commission inveighed against advertising and roundly declared that 'triviality is worse for the soul than wickedness'. It was an epoch-making document when it appeared in 1962, and, though it bore the imprimatur of the Postmaster General, the government took no notice of it whatsoever. But she herself, now taken more seriously, went on to be invited on to quality TV programmes like *Any Questions,* where she appeared alongside heavyweights like Enoch Powell, Bernard Levin and Malcolm Muggeridge.

In 1966 Joyce embarked on one of her favourite TV programmes, *Face the Music,* hosted by the pianist Joseph Cooper, with a regular panel of 'gifted amateurs' such as Bernard Levin, David Attenborough, Richard Baker and Robin Ray. The programme featured the popular 'hidden melody' idea, when Cooper improvised a well-known tune in the style of another composer, such as 'John Peel in the style of Mozart'. As well as being very entertaining, Joyce also proved herself extremely perceptive, as on the occasion when she recognised one note – the D-flat above middle C – as the start of Debussy's *Girl with the Flaxen Hair*.

With age, Joyce grew more and more like her own stereotype. Always conservative in her outlook (though she felt that politics was not the 'sort of thing for a woman'), she wasted little sympathy on the political manoeuvrings of the late 1960s or on Miners' Strike of 1974. She also 'mothered' those she came into contact with: she tried to stop Richard Hoggart smoking; she kept an eye open on *Face the Music* to see whether Richard Baker had a glass too many of the BBC 'hospitality', and she even tried to smarten Patrick Campbell up – until she discovered that he preferred the rumpled look.

As she gradually gave up acting as a career in the 1970s, she did more and more unpaid work, for charitable garden parties, for the House of St Barnabas, a women's hostel in Soho, and, after 1974, as a member of the Churchill Memorial Trust, deciding who should receive travel scholarships. But her health was in decline. She felt tired, and her left eye ached and was swollen. She visited her Christian Science practitioner and confessed to 'discomfort' in her eye. Her husband sent her – and like a dutiful wife, she went – to see his doctor, who sent her to see the ophthalmologist at St Thomas'; he gave her pills and drops to reduce the inflammation in the eye. Joyce reconciled her behaviour with her principles by acknowledging that Mary Baker Eddy had said if the pain was really bad it was permissible to use medication to ease it, but she went no further than this by way of conventional treatment, and members of her family did not press for it. She remained constant to her faith until the end. One of her favourite quotations was from Marcus Aurelius: 'Man is made for kindness, and whenever he does an act of kindness and helps forward the common good, he fulfils the law of his being and comes by his own.'[5] This view seemed to uphold her in her difficulties. Early in 1974 she went blind in her left eye, and had a 'cosmetic contact lens' fitted which was so good that people did not realise her sight was less than normal.

Of course, the end product of her convictions was that the extent of her illness went unrecognised and untreated. Consequently it got worse. She finished the book she was writing, *In Pleasant Places*, early in 1979, and continued to live in retirement until October, when she finally went into hospital. She was treated quite quickly and discharged, but she was still obviously unwell, and the pain got worse. Tests on the removed tissue showed that she had cancer of the eye, and that the pains in her neck were due to the fact that it was rapidly spreading into her spine. She continued, active and undeterred, but finally died in November 1979, aged sixty-nine. She had requested no service, but the Thanksgiving for her life put on in Westminster Abbey in February 1980 was at least as much a sell-out as any of her stage shows.

Joyce Grenfell was a remarkable woman. Her songs and monologues were taken up by Maureen Lipman, who performed them nearly twenty years after her death, and she would have been pleased when she appeared in a question on *University Challenge* in 2000. There can be no doubting the memorable and very individual mark she made on British comedy in the second half of the twentieth century.

THE LIFE AND DEATH OF MARILYN MONROE

There were two Marilyn Monroes. One was a simple, innocent, pretty youngster; the other was a moody Hollywood star, a sultry sex queen who was enslaved to drugs. The two did not even look very much alike. This is the story of how the second ruined and finally ended the life of the first.

Marilyn Monroe was born in the charity ward of Los Angeles County Hospital in 1926 under the name of Norma Jeane Mortenson. Her mother Gladys, previously the wife of Jasper Baker, in 1924 remarried Martin Mortenson, though the marriage did not last long and he was thought by some not to have been Norma's real father at all, and the real father to have been Charles Gifford, an employee of RKO Pictures, where Gladys worked as a film-cutter. While still a child, Norma was placed with foster parents in Hawthorne, California, whence her mother recovered guardianship of the child and moved her into her own house. However, her mother lost her mind and was removed to an asylum, and in 1935 Norma became a ward of state and was sent to the first of a succession of Orphans' Homes. When she was barely sixteen, in 1942, Norma married James Dougherty, a seaman in the Merchant Marine, and went to work in an aircraft factory during the Second World War. Her simple prettiness was recognised by an army photographer as marketable, and she was signed on by Blue Book Modelling Agency in 1944. For two years she was one of the agency's most successful models before she was discovered by a film talent scout, and offered a standard six-month contract by 20th Century Fox at a salary of $125 a week. She ditched her rather shabby name and adopted the name Marilyn (after the actress Marilyn Miller) and Monroe (after her maternal grandmother). When, after a couple of films, Fox did not renew her contract, she moved in 1948 to Columbia Pictures, but later returned to Fox when her contract was not renewed again. Fox vice-president Darryl Zanuck, however, remained unconvinced of her talent, and only offered her a few bit parts until *Don't Bother To Knock* in 1952, which, though it was only a B-movie, brought her to the forefront of public attention. In the course of the next year, *Gentlemen Prefer Blondes*[1] and *How To Marry a Millionaire* established her 'dumb blonde' screen persona, as well as her needle-sharp comedic timing. She did, however, land herself in some trouble by agreeing to the publication of earlier nude photos, taken by photographer Tom Kelly, in *Playboy* magazine.

After completing work on *The Seven Year Itch* in 1955, and tiring of the stereotypic roles that Zanuck insisted on offering her, Marilyn broke her contract with Fox and fled east to study acting at the Actors' Studio in New York. With the growing success of *The Seven Year Itch*, however, she was tempted back to Hollywood with an improved contract, and Zanuck finally admitted her star quality. She formed her own production company to release *The Prince and the Showgirl* in 1958 opposite Laurence Olivier, who also directed the film. But she was already getting something of a reputation in the studios for lateness and for being temperamental, in spite of the raft of film awards[2] that she won for her work.

After this there was no looking back.[3] In 1959 she scored her greatest hit with Tony Curtis and Jack Lemmon in Billy Wilder's comedy *Some Like It Hot*, when her performance earned her a Golden Globe award as the best actress in a musical or comedy. After this came *Let's Make Love*, with Yves Montand and *The Misfits*, Clark Gable's last film, during which he died of a heart attack in the Nevada desert. Returning to Hollywood, she planned to embark on her last great project, *Something's Got to Give*. A little of the film was shot, but only in fragments, and sometimes over and over again. So legendary had she become for her lateness, temperament and abuse of drugs[4] that the film was never completed, and later roles in other films were patched in by Shirley MacLaine and Kim Novak. Her last significant appearance was in May 1962 when she sang *Happy Birthday, Mr. President* for a televised birthday party for John F. Kennedy.

She was found dead by her housekeeper at her home in Brentwood, Los Angeles, in August 1962. Her death, which came like a bombshell to Hollywood and the world, created puzzlement, scepticism and finally a full-blown conspiracy theory to explain the events of the night of 4/5 August 1962, which came to be presented as a simple accident, or, at most, the suicide of a deeply-troubled woman. So many different accounts have been given of these events that it seems impossible to arrive at the truth, but the overwhelming probability is that they involved representatives of the highest authorities in the USA.

Marilyn Monroe's acquaintance with J. F. Kennedy began at a luxurious Christmas party in December 1961, not long after his election as US President. Thereafter they met on frequent occasions, and became intimate; he even provided her with a telephone number that connected directly with his desk at the White House. Marilyn was not aware – any more than the rest of America was aware – of the persistent and incorrigible tendencies of JFK towards womanising: this was, after all, scarcely compatible with the whole Camelot legend. She, building castles in the air like any love-stricken schoolgirl, imagined he might divorce Jacqueline ('that frosty statue' as she called Mrs Kennedy) and marry her.[5] He, always on the hunt for a tasty bit of skirt, aimed to fulfil his wish to bed the most brilliant film star in the firmament. The sexual encounters of the two were frequent but always distressingly brief; Marilyn generously put down his mediocre performance in bed to the state of his injured back – it was always 'in-and-out', as she put it. The elderly patriarch of the Kennedy family, Joseph Kennedy, at first ignored the relationship, but he always cherished a deep regard for the family's public reputation, and, in his desire to keep the Kennedy name squeaky clean, eventually ruled against it. JFK then tried to wriggle out of the relationship, using his younger brother, Robert Kennedy, the US Attorney General, to act as go-between and shelter him from

Marilyn's attentions, and then, when this failed, brutally broke off the affair without any explanation. Marilyn simply found that his telephone number no longer worked, and all she got was the cool voice of a secretary at the White House who refused to put her through to speak to him.

It was Bobby Kennedy who sent a helicopter to pick up Marilyn at the studios to whisk her off to the east coast to attend JFK's birthday party in May 1962. The management of Fox, tired of her uncooperative behaviour on the set, refused to let her go. Bobby asked, he wheedled, he shouted, he swore, he threatened, but all to no avail; in the end she just walked out without leave, reassured that the powerful Kennedy clan would sort out the details. She wore a fabulous $12,000 gown at the party and performed a brilliantly successful turn, but it did not rekindle the President's ardour. As good as their word, Fox sacked Marilyn. Only the intervention of her co-star, Dean Martin, turned the tables and succeeded where the Kennedys had failed. At the actor's behest, she was actually rehired by the studios at a salary of $1 million a year, and promised to get back to work without any more delays.

By this time it was Robert Kennedy who had replaced JFK as lover and companion. His style of love-making was almost as peremptory as his brother's, but there was also an intellectual dimension to the new relationship. While Marilyn's education was sketchy, she had a sharp natural intelligence, and the pair discussed Kennedy's work as Attorney General; she was interested enough to keep a series of spiral notebooks on the subject, and questioned him on a number of things, including US dealings with Cuba.[6] They talked a good deal over the telephone, and it was not uncommon for his pale blue helicopter to be seen landing in and around Hollywood for their more personal encounters.

Then in July 1962 there was a new bombshell. Marilyn suddenly found that the telephone number Bobby had given her no longer worked. When she rang the switchboard at the US Justice Department she was told that the Attorney General was in conference and could not be disturbed. That was the end of a beautiful friendship. She was furious at the Kennedys' duplicity. She demanded that someone – anyone – explain the shabby way in which she had been treated by both of them. But explanation there was none.

In late July 1962, Marilyn checked into hospital under a false name, some said for treatment and advice in her drugs problem, others to abort a baby (although which Kennedy was the father no one could be certain). She was getting more and more outspoken in her criticisms of both the President and the Attorney General, and both were getting more and more alarmed that she might blow the gaff on their conduct.

Her end was as mysterious as it was sudden. On the Saturday evening of 4 August 1962, Marilyn was at home battling as usual with sleeplessness and taking pills to avoid it. Bobby was helicoptered in to have a last meeting and light supper with her, but no record remains of what transpired at that meeting, though it seems likely that both he and she secretly tape-recorded what was said. He left before eleven o'clock, and sometime during the night Marilyn died of a drugs overdose. It was not yet 5.00 a.m. when the Los Angeles police were summoned to her house following a phone call from her housekeeper. The policeman parked outside, having found everything quiet. When he secured entry, he found that Marilyn had been dead probably for some time, and there had been a string of visitors already at the house. Her filing cabinet had been rifled, and three drawers of studio material had been scattered about and much of it burnt in the fireplace. Her tape-recording equipment had been tampered with and various tapes removed. Her phone records had been wiped and her spiral notebooks stolen. When the police entered the bedroom they found Marilyn stretched out naked on the bed[7] with some evidence that she had been dead for some time. The body was removed and taken for police examination, but the results of the autopsy were suppressed[8] and the tissue samples that had been taken from her liver and kidneys were immediately afterwards destroyed. So massive was the overdose that unless she had been given a fatal injection in the rectum or the armpit she must have taken some hundreds of pills to accumulate such a lethal quantity, and she would have passed out before she had been able to finish swallowing them. The secrecy surrounding the case was watertight, and the investigation bore all the hallmarks of a CIA and/or an FBI operation. The final verdict of 'possible suicide' was a fairly obvious attempt to shut down the enquiry, and later efforts to reopen it were all frustrated.

It seems overwhelming likely that Marilyn Monroe, whatever her intentions, was murdered, if not by Robert Kennedy then by federal agents acting on Kennedy's instructions, in order to silence her and to frustrate any attempt to publicise her recent involvement with members of the Kennedy family. This was her personal contribution to the Camelot legend.

GRACIE FIELDS:
WAS SHE A STAR OR A DISAPPOINTMENT?

Gracie Fields was born Grace Stansfield in Rochdale, Lancashire and later awarded the DBE and known as Dame Gracie Fields. She was early in her life a performer on the stage, and later on the screen, in singing and comedic roles. She was hailed as one of the brightest stars of music hall and cinema, but later, through no fault of her own, suffered before her death in 1979 an eclipse from which she never recovered.

Grace Stansfield was born over her grandmother's fish-and-chip shop in Rochdale in 1898 of solid working-class stock. Her father, Fred, worked for a local firm engaged in maintaining motor coaches, and her mother, Jenny, in the local cotton mills. The two of them fulfilled the traditional husband-wife relationship: he was quiet and caring; she, with her strong and positive character, the dominant element in the marriage. Both

Grace's sisters, Edith and Betty, and her brother Tommy, went on to appear on the stage, but Gracie herself was by far the most successful, first appearing as a child performer at the age of five, and undertaking her professional debut at the Rochdale Hippodrome in 1910. At the theatre, she met comedian Archie Pitt. He was at first was her manager, then the two began working together and were married in 1923. The pair appeared chiefly in a series of revues, and with the latest of which, *Mr. Tower of London*, she came to the West End in 1922. But the marriage was not a successful one: though they owned a house in London, her husband took a mistress and Gracie soon took to performing by herself on stage, and eventually appeared at the Alhambra Theatre in 1925, where she was booked by Sir Oswald Stoll. She signed with Basil Dean as her manager, though she detested him and he did not much care for her. She made the first of ten Royal Variety performances in 1928, soon building up a great reputation through self-deprecating jokes, comic songs and humorous monologues for her simple style, her 'no-airs-and-graces' northern accent and her tremendous rapport with her working-class audiences. The 1930s saw her as one of the most successful comic performers in the country during the Depression era.

Gracie Fields was famous for her songs. Some were confections of simple and unashamed sentimentality, like 'When I Grow Too Old to Dream'; others were marching songs like 'Sing as We Go' and 'Wish Me Luck as You Wave Me Goodbye', or plainly comic ditties in the old Marie Lloyd tradition, such as 'The Biggest Aspidistra in the World', 'If I'd Known You Were Coming I'd've Baked a Cake' or 'Walter, Walter, Lead Me to the Altar'. Her biggest hit was 'Sally', and this provided the title of her first film, *Sally in Our Alley* (1931), a great financial success if a rather indifferent film. She went on to make a number of other, chiefly comic, films both in Britain and the USA, though, with her warm and immediate human touch, she always preferred the stage to the screen. In many ways her film persona resembled her real one: she was impulsive, generous, optimistic, and with a strong sense of personal duty to what she saw as her calling, however adverse the situation in which she found herself might be.

The later 1930s saw her popularity come to a peak. She was honoured by a number of charitable bodies such the Order of St John for the support she gave them; she received the Freedom of the Borough of Rochdale and she became a CBE for her services to entertainment. For the first time she went to Capri, originally on holiday, but so loved the island that she bought herself a villa and increasingly spent long periods there. In Britain in 1939 she was taken ill with cervical cancer, but she rallied to her treatment and eventually went into remission, yet she was still convalescing when war broke out in 1939. She threw herself wholeheartedly into the war effort, not sparing her health, and was soon, like Vera Lynn (the "forces' sweetheart", whom she genuinely admired) giving concerts all over the country for the troops. She gave a series of concerts both at home and in France, and later in the war in the Far East as far as Australia and New Guinea to help entertain the troops.

Following her divorce from Pitt in 1939 she had met and married Monty Banks, then a film director living in America but originally a Keystone Cop, a friend of Stanley Laurel and a number of other Hollywood figures. Banks, however, though widely travelled and pretty international by temperament, was – and remained – an Italian national (his real name was Mario Bianci), and it was this that led to her great personal problem, especially after Italy entered the war on Germany's side in 1940. They were no longer able to spend time in their beloved property in Capri, where she had spent a small part of her convalescence. Now, as an enemy national, Banks, though quite non-political, was liable to internment under Regulation 18b, and this created difficulties for Gracie. She was encouraged to leave the country for a tour of Canada, partly to encourage that Dominion's war effort, and partly to raise funds to support Britain's efforts, all of which she did with considerable success. But of course similar arrangements existed in Canada for the treatment of enemy aliens, and Banks was threatened here too with internment. Eventually a compromise was reached, permitting him to return to his home in the United States, while she continued with her organised tour of concerts, a separation that she felt most deeply.

Her personal situation was further darkened by the lack of understanding at home in Britain for her problems. The attitude towards her on the part of her previously adoring public changed: she was widely supposed to have deserted her country in a cowardly fashion, and even to have taken a fortune with her out of the country in cash and jewellery. Such suggestions astonished her and cut her to the quick; in fact she was loyally patriotic and selfless, and to be thought of as a scheming careerist and a profiteer was more than she could bear. What she regarded as the ingratitude of her public came near to breaking her heart. Nonetheless, she put a brave face on her predicament and determined to continue with what she saw as her war work.

When the war ended, Gracie returned from long periods of foreign touring and resumed her domestic career on a more limited footing. Monty Banks died in 1950; then in her mid-50s, she married a third husband, Boris Alperovici, two years later. Most of her time was spent at her beloved villa in Capri, which she had bought with Banks at the end of the 1930s. By the postwar era, much of the magic had disappeared from her reputation, and her public image, however frivolously lost, never recovered.

She took part in the Festival of Britain celebrations in 1951; she played a role in the US TV production of Agatha Christie's thriller *A Murder is Announced* in 1956; she opened the Gracie Fields Theatre in her home town of Rochdale in 1978, and in that year appeared for the final time in a Royal Command performance in London at the age of eighty; and in 1979, shortly before her death, she became Dame Commander of the British Empire.[1]

Her life falls into two distinct halves: the first popular and successful part, for which today she is chiefly remembered, and the second much less dramatic part when she lost the sparkle of success as she lost her youth, so that her death, at the age of eighty-one, passed almost unnoticed. Her career proved ephemeral: she did not expect, and often felt she did not deserve, such spectacular fame in the 1930s; and she did not deserve the dismal decline of her fortunes in the years after 1945.

MARGOT FONTEYN:
DANCING WITH NUREYEV

There are not many ballet dancers who capture the public imagination as completely as did Margot Fonteyn. There are fewer still who are famed to the degree that their names are inextricably coupled with the name of another, as Fonteyn's name was coupled with Rudolf Nureyev – one of the few classical double acts of the ballet world. To most observers of the world of dance, Margot and Rudi were ballet royalty, the undisputed stars of the Royal Ballet in the 1960s and 1970s. Until Darcy Bussell broke the mould in the 1980s, Margot was to most people the model of the perfect woman and the perfect dancer – 5 ft 4 in, with dark almond-shaped eyes, raven hair, a porcelain skin and a face as open and radiant as a schoolgirl's. Her passionate relationship onstage with Nureyev was breathtaking and palpably sincere – or was it? Ballet, after all, was the world of art, and the world of art is the world of make-believe. The truth of her personal relationship with Rudi remains to this day no more than a matter of conjecture. In the words of the popular press: 'Did she, or didn't she?'

Margot Fonteyn was born Margaret Hookham in May 1919 in Reigate, Surrey, to an English father and an Irish mother, Hilda, of Brazilian extraction, who exercised a powerful influence over her life almost to the end. Early on, Margaret changed her mother's name Fontes into the more theatrical Fonteyn, and adapted her first name into Margot, thus providing herself with a name that was more enduring than she could ever have imagined.

She joined the Royal Ballet while she was still a teenager, and was trained by some of the greatest ballet teachers of the day, like Olga Preobrajenska and Mathilde Kschessinska. By 1939 she was the company's *prima ballerina*, and the star of many of the ballets of Sir Frederick Ashton, Director of the Royal Ballet, such as *Daphnis and Chloe* and *Ondine*. Another dominant figure was Dame Ninette de Valois, who built up a tradition of ballet in Britain and created for it a structure that proved to be the model handed down through generations.[1] At the heart of this structure was de Valois, or 'Madam' as she was always known.[2] She ruled over the company with a rod of iron, claiming to know what was best for the ballet as a whole and individually for each dancer in the troupe; ballet was never a democracy. With its strict organisation, the Royal Ballet toured the USA in 1949 and Fonteyn became a worldwide celebrity. To see her in action was the realisation of the dream of many visitors to Covent Garden. Performances were a picture. Nylon and Lycra were capturing the market in dancewear, transforming the visual world of ballet, with its pale pink costumes and white foaming tutus, putting paid, once and for all, to wrinkly knees.

In her early career in the 1940s and 1950s, her reputation was still building. She had a very successful dance partnership in the 1940s with Robert Helpmann, and the pair toured together throughout the UK. In the 1950s she danced with Michael Soames, reviving the success the two had had when they danced Constant Lambert's *Horoscope* in 1938. But her greatest partnership came in 1962, at a time Madam was really expecting her to retire from the ballet altogether, when she danced for the first time with Rudolf Nureyev.

In 1961 Nureyev had defected from the Soviet Union at Le Bourget airport in Paris, seeking greater freedom in the West. He was half-boy, half-satyr, promiscuously bisexual, a spoilt, self-centred creature with no other idea than to gratify his primal urges. But he was an unrestrained and quite brilliant performer.[3] He and Fonteyn appeared first onstage in a performance of *Giselle*, and it brought the house down. During three curtain calls, Nureyev dropped to his knees and extravagantly kissed Fonteyn's hand, cementing a relationship between them that lasted until her final retirement in 1979. They went on to appear together many times. Fred Ashton choreographed *Marguerite and Armand* for them; they performed Kenneth Macmillan's *Romeo and Juliet* for the first time; they danced together in a film version of *Swan Lake* as well as appearing in *Les Sylphides* and *Le Corsaire*. Despite their differences in temperament and character, and a difference of nineteen years in age, they were deeply attached and absolutely loyal to each other and close, lifelong friends. They remained friends even after she retired, forty-five years after making her debut with Sadler's Wells ballet in the corps de ballet as a snowflake in the *Nutcracker*. They spoke frequently by telephone after her retirement to Panama; when she was treated for cancer Nureyev paid many of her medical bills and visited her often; he remained loyal to her[4] even when his own health began to decline – until in fact he died of AIDS in 1993. Both were consummate professionals: he quixotic, swift, athletic; she tender, lyrical, graceful.

For a star so expressive of her simulated feelings onstage, Fonteyn was curiously uncommunicative about her real life. In the 1940s, her name was linked with that of the composer Constant Lambert, but, though it is said his ballet *Horoscope*, in which she appeared, was written to commemorate some features of the affair, their association did not lead to marriage. The man she chose to marry, and to whom she was loyal throughout his extraordinary career, was Dr Roberto Arias (known to her and his other associates as Tito), a Panamanian diplomat, ambassador to the UK, and something of a playboy. He was involved from time to time in the shadier features of Latin American politics: he drew a considerable income from gunrunning, from the seedier sort of brothels, and was known to be occasionally a little too close to revolutionary movements than was comfortable. The couple quarrelled, the marriage was a shaky one, yet throughout Fonteyn remained loyal to him. He was aware of, but professed indifference to, his wife's association with Nureyev, and himself was rather lax in the observance of his own marriage vows with a whole string of women. In 1959 he was involved in an attempted coup against the Panamanian President, Ernesto de la Guardia. Tito was arrested and detained and Fonteyn was deported back to England. In 1964, he was shot and crippled by a rival Panamanian politician, Alberto Jimenes, and remained a quadriplegic until his death in 1989.[5]

Margot was a deeply passionate woman, but she usually reserved her displays of emotion for the stage. It is quite possible that she gave herself to Nureyev and became his sexual partner – he certainly bragged to his friends that she had – but she never entirely relaxed her self-control and always kept at least part of herself private. Rudi was not only much more extrovert and impulsive than she was; he was also nineteen years younger and never lost his air of being no more than a spoilt boy. Dancing together, she might forget this momentarily, but she could always be reminded of it, as she was when a young acquaintance of Rudi approached them in a London restaurant and referred to her slyly as 'Mamma!' She was always conscious of how much she had given up for her art, as on the occasion when she turned furiously on her mother and sobbed that she had changed her name, her voice, her nose and even the chance of having children ('God knows there were no babies to get in the way of my dancing!') The main obstacle that stood in her path, however, was her loyalty to her husband Roberto. The role in life that remained the dearest to her throughout her career – even more than *prima ballerina* – was that of loyal wife; never was she more aware of it than when he was a helpless cripple totally dependent on her for love and support. It was costly to her artistically, financially and in every way, but she did it willingly; she danced into her sixties – until her feet literally bled – to pay her husband's medical bills. And, in spite of Nureyev, she ended her days on a cattle ranch in Panama, devoted to Roberto's children from an earlier marriage.

In her lifetime, other honours were piled upon her, but none so highly valued as that bestowed in her old age in 1979 when she was dubbed by the Royal Ballet *prima ballerina assoluta*. She was already a DBE, a title bestowed on her in 1967; she became Chancellor of the University of Durham from 1981 to 1990, the main room in the student union building being named after her. She died from cancer in 1991. The last time she had danced with Nureyev was in September 1988, when she was sixty-eight and he was fifty. They performed together the pas de trois from Baroque. It was again a triumph in spite of the difference in their ages, and bore out her dictum: 'Genius is another word for magic, and the whole point of magic is that is inexplicable.'

PART 3

BATTLEAXES

LAURA ORMISTON CHANT: NIT-PICKER OR MORAL REFORMER?

Mrs Chant was the Mrs Grundy of Victorian England, the self-appointed guardian of public morality against the sinister and insidious growth of corruption and wickedness in social life. Though today her name is almost forgotten, she aroused strong feelings at the time either in favour of her campaign for the preservation of moral decency, or else against it by furious opponents of her strait-laced, joyless and narrow-minded puritanism. But this, of course, was a caricature of her work, which in fact ranged over a wide variety of social, political, religious and moral issues generally thought at the time to be important.

Laura Ormiston Chant was born Laura Dibdin in Chepstow, South Wales, on the border of Monmouthshire and Gloucestershire, in 1845. Brought up in the Congregationalist Church, she imbibed its evangelist teachings, and became when she grew up one of the leading members of the local church community. In 1876, at the age of thirty, she married a local doctor, and in due course produced a son and three daughters. Her husband died in 1913. Educated at home, she went on to take courses offered by the Association of Arts and became an Associate of Arts at the Apothecaries' Hall. Afterwards she did some school-teaching, and also some hospital nursing, including a spell at the London Hospital. For a time, in the voluntary sector, she was assistant manager of a lunatic asylum.

Instances of her sermons delivered to Congragationalist meetings, and of her speeches to other more overtly political conferences that she attended in the course of her life, are still extant. They are generally full of moral and religious uplift rather than doctrinal teachings. She takes the line that 'religion is bound to conquer in the end', and that 'we will not accept sin, sorrow and failure as eternal, longer than our love can let them be'. She says she does her best towards the 'redeeming of the world out of darkness into light, out of sin and misery into righteousness'. It was this faintly dogmatic moral tone when applied to matters that they thought of quite minor significance that irritated her opponents as much as it gratified those who agreed with her message.

During all this time, her extra-curricular commitments were increasing. As a doctor's wife, with money and a certain amount of leisure behind her, involvement in topical causes was expected of her, and her performance here did not disappoint. In 1881, she was one of the founder-members of the Society for Promoting the Return of Women as Poor Law Guardians, and shortly after became a member of the Vigilance Association for the Defence of Personal Rights. She was interested, too, in the question of the female suffrage, and in 1888 represented the question as a delegate to the first International Council of Women in Washington. She was also elected to the executive committee of the Women's Liberal Federation, and in 1893 also attended the World Congress of Representative Women in Chicago. Throughout this time, like many women of her class and outlook, she supported the Repeal of the Contagious Diseases Act, maintaining they constituted an affront to the dignity of women.[1] She was also an outspoken supporter of the Anti-Opium League, campaigning at the time for restrictions on the ready availability of opium and other dangerous drugs over chemists' counters.

But perhaps her most controversial role was over what she regarded as issues of 'public decency'. Here she was a vigorous social purist. She was much exercised over the question of 'proper dress', especially for women. She objected to the wearing of anything daring, unusual or revealing – corsages that were cut too low or too daringly, or skirts that were too short, or slashed to reveal the petticoats underneath. During the 1880s she came to edit a periodical, called the Vigilance Record, for a body known as the Women's Vigilance Association. This publication had a considerable subscription, both on the part of its supporters, and also those roused to exasperation by its very existence. Those who craved to know the correct etiquette for a lady to choose and wear her gloves turned to its columns for advice, the others to heap derision on its 'fatuous edicts'.

But, undoubtedly, her pinnacle of fame, or her nadir of unpopularity (depending on whether or not you approved of her well-intentioned meddling), came over the question of the late Victorian music halls. Many of these, at the rear, were provided with 'promenades', resembling lounges, often with tables and chairs, where people could meet in the theatre intervals, or even in the course of the performance, and take a drink or engage in conversation. Some, like the promenade of the Empire Theatre, were large and luxurious, and were often used as places of assignation between the sexes. Here it was possible for young 'ladies', often of the professional kind, to empty the pocket-books of raffish young gentlemen by having them buy sweet fizzy wine, masquerading as champagne, or getting them to provide overpriced boxes of chocolates (often sold back by their recipients to the barmen after purchase) before they moved on to more private premises to conduct the main agenda of their assignation. This was prostitution of the most polished and discreet kind. Critics of this system were scandalised: they saw no real difference between these over-dressed young women touting for custom in these comfortable promenades and their less fortunate sisters standing bedraggled on the street corners outside waiting for a profitable 'pick-up'.

It was Mrs Chant who took it upon herself to denounce this disgraceful practice. She visited the Empire, and noted grimly that onstage the acts were in questionable taste, the young women were flashily and vulgarly dressed, and performing in lewd and suggestive style, while the visiting clientele were not much better, their voices loud, their language coarse and their dress bordering on the indecent. She opined that there was 'too much pulling and jostling' between them and the men, too much drinking and (when she could find the vocabulary to describe it) too much sexual titillation by the prostitutes of their clientele. She protested to the theatre manager, Mr George Edwardes, asking him to restrain their improper conduct, and, when her protests were ignored, took it upon herself to oppose the renewing of the theatre's performing licence before the London County Council (LCC) Watch Committee.

At the Committee hearing, she easily outshone the rather startled barrister representing the Empire. It was her view that the theatre promenade was the 'habitual resort of prostitutes in pursuit of their traffic'; she then produced, in succession, a battery of witnesses who testified that it was a 'place of procurement', a place whose dancing was 'calculated to incite impure thought and passion', where 'the moral character of the women there could be inferred from their dress', where 'accosting' was commonplace – an establishment, in short, that was 'the worst place in Europe'. Middle-class hypocrisy was seen here at its most prejudiced. In spite of a stout defence based on common sense put up by the applicants' lawyer, renewal was refused on the grounds that the place was used 'for purposes such as the Council could not properly recognise by its licence'.

Immediately, a furious counter-attack was launched by the supporters of the music halls against the intolerable female busybodies who deprived them of their entertainment. The *Morning Post* and the *Daily Telegraph* produced columns of letters (sometimes six or seven columns daily) generating a fine lather of indignation against what one correspondent called 'prudes on the prowl' – a resounding phrase which soon became the title of a popular song. One of these letters, signed, tongue-in-cheek, by 'Puritan', complained bitterly about 'disgusting dress' and said he had counted no fewer than twelve so-called 'ladies' at the Empire where 'not one was wearing gloves'.

Mrs Chant nevertheless had what could only be called a field day. She wrote and spoke repeatedly on the subject, producing more of her pamphlets in which she made mincemeat of her critics.[2] She was constantly being interviewed by the press. To the *Pall Mall Gazette* she revealed that she was not hostile to the music halls 'as such'; that she was 'passionately fond' of dancing; that her French friends, though accustomed to performances at the Moulin Rouge, nevertheless walked out of the Empire with the comment: 'C'est trop fort!' Her assertion that she knew theatre girls who regularly made £20 or £30 a week from prostitution evoked the thoughtful reply from George Bernard Shaw that 'the problem for Mrs Chant is to make it better worth an attractive girl's while to be a respectable worker rather than a prostitute'. Even *Punch* joined in the attacks on her, producing a full-page cartoon showing 'Mrs Prowlina Pry' surveying the Empire theatre, placarded with '3,000 Employees Will Be Thrown Out Of Work'.

Meantime, demonstrations by the public, and even one by a trade union, the Amalgamated Society of Railway Servants, continued to draw attention to the situation, and Mr George Edwardes continued to pursue his opponents through the courts. All this was in vain; in 1894, the LCC confirmed its earlier decision and the Empire was compelled to close for alterations to its notorious promenade. Members of the LCC were compelled to submit to being booed in the streets. The manager of Toole's Theatre offered his premises for benefit performances for former Empire employees, and they were put on half pay during the dispute.

However, alterations took only a few days, and the theatre returned to business after November with a modified licence involving a slight reduction of the promenade area and the erection of canvas screens to separate the auditorium from the bar area. A young Sandhurst cadet called W. S. Churchill,[1] and other young gentlemen in his company, soon found that these screens were as flimsy as they looked, and made short work of them by attacking them with their walking sticks one Saturday night, crying 'Long live Edwardes!' while they simultaneously wrecked his theatre. Edwardes magnanimously forgave their youthful high spirits and in 1895 resumed his activities with an unconditional licence. Shortly afterwards, the Palace and Alhambra theatres followed the Empire's lead and established promenades of their own. All Mrs Chant's effort on behalf of public decency had been in vain. Thus the scandal of music hall promenades became one of the main features of Edwardian England. It was only in 1916 that Alfred Butt announced his intention to do voluntarily what the LCC had failed to force him to do; he was closing his promenade in response to a change of public feeling in the dark days of the First World War. He was followed by Sir Oswald Stoll, who had recently bought control of the Alhambra. These actions did not, as pessimists had thought, put an end to the classic music hall – that decline was accelerated only by the coming of talking pictures at the end of the 1920s.

By then, Mrs Chant herself was dead, her campaigns for public decency largely forgotten. She died in 1923. She never saw the Charleston, or the flappers of the later 1920s in their short and skimpy dresses, gloveless, boyish and flat-chested (a few wearing brassieres instead of the restricting bust-binders), jigging recklessly in public with their long tortoiseshell holders for their cigarettes: the sight would surely have killed her.

MARY WHITEHOUSE:
SCOURGE OF THE BROADMINDED

Mary Whitehouse was not a typical product of the swinging 1960s. On the contrary, she was the butt of all broadminded comics, she was the scourge of the BBC, and she was depicted in the national press as an antediluvian relic of a bygone age. Her objections to portrayal in the media of obscenity, blasphemy, sodomy, incest and the like were out of touch with the spirit of the age, and out of touch with the new breath of moral liberation that was transforming and captivating the nation. Did she actually achieve anything?

Mary Whitehouse was born Constance Mary Hutcheson on 13 June 1910 in Nuneaton, Warwickshire. When the family moved to Chester, Mary won a scholarship to the City and County School and, after completing her schooling, joined St John's School as an apprentice teacher. She then moved on to the Cheshire County Teacher Training College in Crewe where she trained as an art teacher. Her religious upbringing influenced her decision to join the Student Christian Movement which required deep religious commitment and motivation. After qualification in 1932 she taught art in Staffordshire for eight years, and while there joined the Oxford Group, which was later known as Moral Re-armament. Originally a fundamentalist Protestant organisation, Moral Re-armament sought to re-establish and consolidate the four moral absolutes of honesty, purity, love and unselfishness. With these it hoped to change the world.

It was at MRA sessions that Mary met Ernest Raymond Whitehouse. They married in 1940, and after having five sons (two of whom died in infancy) Mary resumed teaching at Madely Modern School in Shropshire where she became Senior Mistress. There was a profound culture shock between her teaching experience in the 1930s when children had a strong ethical background, and resuming teaching in the 1960s when to her they seemed to have no ethical background at all. She had taken on responsibility for sex education, and the response of her pupils to issues of morality appalled her. For this she blamed the media and in particular the BBC, whose moral standards seemed to her to have declined rapidly. In its early days under Lord Reith, newsreaders dressed formally and bad language was not allowed.[1] Indeed, in 1935 a reporter was sacked for saying 'bloody' on air, but he *was* also drunk. By the 1960s the BBC had changed. Profanities were sprinkled liberally in kitchen sink drama in order to create realism, and even the sex act was occasionally simulated for the same reason. But Mary was convinced that titillation rather than realism was, if not the BBC's aim, at least its result, and set out on a crusade to restore the BBC to its former glory. The Director-General of the BBC in 1963 was Sir Hugh Green. And upon him she turned her full artillery.

Her letters to Sir Hugh went largely unanswered – he regarded her as an interfering busybody – so Mary appealed to the wider public. In April 1964 the 'Clean Up TV Campaign' attracted 2,000 people to its meeting in Birmingham, and in 1965 half a million people signed a 'Clean Up TV' petition which was sent to the Queen. In the same year the National Viewers' and Listeners' Association was established, which demanded higher standards of taste from both the BBC and ITV. Mary inundated Downing Street with her strictures on innumerable television programmes, some of which were relatively innocent. Downing Street's response was to lose the letters in civil servants' files to avoid having to answer them, a common enough tactic. Nevertheless, when Green left the BBC in 1969 it was widely, although erroneously, believed that Mary had significantly hastened his departure. Even so, despite Mary's campaign and Green's departure, television continued to become more daring and risqué.

The advent of Mrs Thatcher to power in 1979 seemed to provide Mary with a sympathetic ear in high places. Indeed, in 1980, she was awarded the CBE for public services. But the Conservative government's championship of market forces made it reluctant to introduce broadcasting restrictions that might reduce the number of BBC viewers or ITV's advertisers. In the late 1970s, Mary was increasingly turning to the courts for support. Here she had little success. She managed to secure a libel conviction against the editor of *Gay News* in 1977, but most of the other cases failed. The most notorious was in 1982 when she started a private prosecution against a National Theatre production for its portrayal of anal sex on stage. Since her only witness was sitting in the back row of the stalls, his description of what he alleged to have seen from that distance was torn to shreds by the defence, and the prosecution collapsed.

Despite these failures, Mary could claim to have influenced various pieces of legislation of the 1970s and 1980s which aimed to protect children from exposure to obscenities, placed some control on sex shops, and imposed restrictions on the contents of videos. It is unlikely that the Broadcasting Standards Council, set up in 1990, would have seen the light of day had it not been for her prolonged campaigning.

But to the sexually liberated, Mary was an easy target. Her blue rinse and spectacles became the standard make-up for those comediennes (or men in drag) who wanted to poke fun of her. Caricatures of her appeared under the names of Mrs Blackhouse, Desiree Carthorse and Mary Lighthouse. TV producers feared praise from Mary would give them too squeaky clean an image to such an extent that the Goodies introduced a touch of risqué into their second series to avoid her accolade. Songwriters made her a figure of fun, and satire programmes had a recurring field day. Most of the hostility provoked no response from Mary, but she did react with a complaint when provoked in 1980 by Tim Brooke-Taylor's appearance on a BBC stage in underpants sporting a large carrot motif.

Mary retired as president of the National Viewers' and Listeners' Association in 1994. The Association, now called Mediawatch-uk, still has over 30,000 members, although at its most active it had 150,000. Mary's ability to campaign was undermined both by advancing age and by a spinal injury she sustained in 1997. Increasingly infirm and fragile, she died in a Colchester nursing home on 23 November 2001, aged ninety-one. Many of her former enemies paid tribute to her. Michael Grade, whose time at the BBC was made more difficult by her persistent demands for higher standards of decency, praised her courage and sincerity, but thought she was 'out of touch entirely with the real world'. One comedian commented: 'She'll be sadly missed, but not by me.' A more generous opinion was that, although she was treated by the BBC as a figure of fun and of little consequence, her campaign had forced both the BBC and ITV to pay significant attention to standards of decency in broadcasting. Mary, however, would not have considered that she had achieved much. Things have got even worse, or public taste has become far more tolerant, than they were when she was at her most active. Sexual intercourse is now commonplace in many serious dramas, and even innocuous cookery programmes are littered with expletives. But how much worse would it have been without her?

PART 4

SCIENTISTS

MARGARET ANN BULKLEY
AKA DR JAMES BARRY

The extraordinary story, first told in the Manchester Guardian *shortly after Margaret Ann Bulkley's death, related to the imposture of this person as a military doctor and surgeon for the whole of her mature lifetime until her death at the end of her military service in 1865. Whether this imposture sprang from some kind of transgender proclivity, or whether, as seems likely, because she was aware of the greater possibilities of freedom and success as a man rather than as a woman, was never clear; but the affair created a sensation in Victorian England, and would have been widely disbelieved if it had not been so thoroughly and officially documented in army records at the time.*

Margaret Ann Bulkley was born the daughter of Jeremiah and Mary-Ann Bulkley in the early 1790s, probably in 1792. She was of Irish extraction. Her mother was the sister of the famous Irish painter (and Professor of Painting at the Royal Academy in London) James Barry. Acting with the collusion of her uncle and other male relatives, she enrolled as a medical student in the University of Edinburgh in 1809 and travelled with her mother by sea to Edinburgh in the November of that year to begin her studies. Her uncle, James Barry, commented in a letter at the end of the year that it was 'useful for Mrs Bulkley to have had a gentleman on board ship, and in a strange country', which seems to suggest that it was at this time that the fictive change of gender was made. It was under her uncle's name that she studied during the next four years.

James Barry qualified as a medical doctor in 1812, and served for a few months in London at the United Hospitals of Guy's and St. Thomas'. In 1813 she passed the examinations of the Royal College of Surgeons, and was commissioned in the Army as a hospital assistant, in time for the Battle of Waterloo in June 1815. She served in India and South Africa around 1817, where she soon became Medical Inspector for the Colony. It was while she was here that in the course of her duties she performed a successful Caesarean section and delivered to the mother the first baby in African history born in this fashion. Later she was posted successively to Mauritius, Trinidad and Tobago and St Helena (she visited the island while Napoleon was in captivity there,[1] and incurred an official reprimand for quitting the island without formal permission). Later Dr Barry served in Jamaica, Canada, Malta, Corfu and, during the Crimean War, in the Crimea. She finally retired from military service in 1864, the year before her death.

During this time Dr Barry was several times promoted. In Canada she became Inspector-General, HM Army Hospitals, and in the West Indies, after a brief demotion to Staff Surgeon, Principal Medical Officer. In Corfu she became Deputy Inspector-General of Hospitals, and then in 1857 returned to Canada as Inspector-General of Hospitals once again.

This chequered career casts some light on Dr Barry's rather volatile character. She was always devoted to the welfare and management of the troops under her charge, and, though she was reputed to have crossed swords with Florence Nightingale when the two met during the Crimean War, she showed herself entirely devoted to sanitation, proper medical care and better, fresher food for the patients under her care. She showed admirable professional surgical skill – in the days before general anaesthesia, she was accurate, decisive and rapid in the performance of her duties – and had a good bedside manner, unlike Nightingale, who was obsessed with administration and throughout her career remained somewhat frosty towards the patients in her care. Dr Barry did her best to alleviate any unnecessary suffering on the part of her patients and took great pains over their proper nourishment. She was hostile towards any attempt to treat 'gentlemen' patients better than the more common sort, and always took pains to see that these patients, even though indigent, were properly treated, and their feelings, and the feelings of their families, considered. Her later work in Canada with civilian prisoners and even with lepers became legendary.

Nevertheless, Dr Barry could be peremptory, opinionated and quarrelsome in her manner. She was several times reprimanded for insubordination, and this helps to explain why her career was marred by occasional demotions. Even in 1864, she was disinclined to take retirement, and had finally to be forced into it by her superiors. She remained prickly and quarrelsome in her relations with others, disliking any adverse comment on her medical or surgical accomplishments, and objecting particularly strongly to any adverse comments about her slight appearance or the light timbre of her voice. She is said to have fought a duel – and to have challenged more opponents still – over matters springing from such personal observations. Those who met Dr Barry, however, were generally deeply impressed by her level of competence and expertise, and spoke highly of her work.

Dr Barry never married, and died of dysentery in July 1865, alone and unbefriended. It was only when her housekeeper, Sophia Bishop, undressed the body to wash it in preparation for the funeral, that she discovered that her master was a woman.[2] The Army authorities were shocked, and sealed all records for a hundred years.

Dr Barry's extraordinary career somewhat dents the record claimed by Elizabeth Garrett Anderson to be the first woman medical practitioner. On account of the sex barrier to women which prevented them from qualifying in medicine, Mrs Anderson obtained her licence to practise only in 1865, the year of Dr Barry's death at the age of over seventy, and then she got it merely from the Society of Apothecaries; and she did not establish her first somewhat tentative clinic, the London Dispensary for Woman and Children, until the following year, 1866.

ELIZABETH GARRETT ANDERSON

Employment opportunities for Victorian women depended very much on class. Most lower-class women would find paid employment an absolute necessity if they were to avoid abject poverty; for such women there was work in factories or in the fields or for the more fortunate there was always the lure of domestic service. Middle-class women could work in the retail trade or even in business, or if well educated perhaps as a teacher or governess. But such avenues were denied to gentlewomen. Class snobbery prevented them from engaging in commercial activities and male chauvinism and legal obstacles denied them access to the professions. A few might become authors while writing under a pseudonym, but the armed forces, the church, the law, politics and medicine were male preserves and were mainly recruited from the universities to which female access was banned. The first major professional bastion to give way to female pressure was medicine, and this was very largely due to the determination, single-mindedness and obstinacy of Elizabeth Garrett Anderson.

Elizabeth was not born with an upper-class silver spoon in her mouth. Perhaps if she had been, a career in medicine would have been out of the question. When Elizabeth was still in her infancy her father, Newsom Garrett, had moved his family from London to Aldeburgh in Suffolk in order more effectively to pursue his business interests. And he pursued them so successfully that he soon became the most important businessman in Aldeburgh. He made occasional bad investments which put the fear of God into him, but in no way inconvenienced his family, which was always very well provided for, and he was able and willing to finance private education for both Elizabeth, her four brothers and five sisters. At first they had a governess whom they heartily disliked, but then, in 1849 when Elizabeth was thirteen, she and her sister Louie were sent to London to join the Academy for the Daughters of Gentlemen. This was owned and run by two maiden aunts of Robert Browning, the poet. The girls never met Browning but the Academy seemed to have succeeded in its main task of turning young girls into young ladies. For Elizabeth it had the added, and subsequently very useful, bonus of making her fluent in French, which the Misses Browning insisted on using as a lingua franca throughout the school.

Elizabeth left the Academy when she was sixteen and returned home to enjoy the life of an affluent gentlewoman, to which the family's rapidly growing wealth entitled her. Most of her family expected her to marry. It is said that when they were children, Elizabeth and her sister Millicent (subsequently Millicent Garrett Fawcett the suffragist leader) had decided to force their way into the professions, Elizabeth as a doctor and Millicent as a politician. But there was a twelve-year difference in their ages and such a childhood commitment seems unlikely. Elizabeth did, however, meet Emily Davies, who was to achieve fame as a feminist and who was to have a considerable influence over Elizabeth's life and ambitions. In March 1859 Elizabeth and Emily attended three lectures on 'Medicine as a Profession for Ladies' given by a visitor from the USA, Elizabeth Blackwell. Miss Blackwell had read medicine at a small college in New York State, and had been allowed to qualify in 1849. She was now both a successful medical practitioner and a world-famous publicist. Her lectures reinforced Elizabeth in her determination to pursue medicine as a career, and her developing friendship with Emily Davies gave her vital support and encouragement.

Elizabeth had no science, nor any natural affinity for medical work, and when she announced her intention to her family her father could not contain his disgust nor her mother her tears. She was immediately subjected to all the usual arguments: medicine was only suitable for men; it would expose women to horrific sights and smells which would appal any lady; in those days before antiseptics surgeons measured their experience and ability by the amount of blood and pus on their operating jackets. Moreover, it would mean learning about and examining male anatomy; and, even more importantly, whatever would the neighbours think? Florence Nightingale was as yet only on the threshold of making nursing a respectable career for women, and Elizabeth's argument that nurses were involved in the care of patients both male and female drew the response that nurses were usually of the vulgar sort and were quite suited to situations that would be unseemly and revolting to a lady of breeding. But Elizabeth persevered.

Her father was appalled at first, but, seeing his daughter's steely determination, he agreed to take her to London to sound out the practicalities of medical training for her. They were rebuffed at every quarter. Eminent surgeons and doctors refused to take Elizabeth seriously; they suggested she should take up nursing or find herself a husband. It may be that, at first, Newsom was humouring his daughter, thinking that she would give up her ambition in view of the obstacles to be overcome, but the high-handed way Elizabeth was treated rankled with him. He told Elizabeth that he would support her financially, and in any other way he could.

It was through a friend of Emily Davies that Elizabeth was allowed to join the Middlesex Hospital in August 1860, ostensibly as a nurse but in reality to receive clinical tuition from senior medical staff sympathetic to her career aim. Other nurses, recognising that they had a lady among them, offered to prepare her meals and help with washing and ironing; these offers Elizabeth declined. During the next few months, she familiarised herself with ward procedures and attended medical lectures alongside the medical students. She was even allowed into the dissecting room provided there were staff present. At first most of the male students tolerated her presence, but when she began to do well in class tests they realised that her interest in a medical career was not ephemeral, but was serious and committed. In June 1861 some of the students she had outshone got up a petition against her.

We the undersigned students consider that the mixture of sexes in the same class is likely to lead to results of an unpleasant character.

The lecturers are likely to feel some restraint through the presence of females in giving that explicit and forcible enunciation of some facts which is necessary.

The presence of young females in the operating theatres is an outrage on our natural instinct and feelings and calculated to destroy those sentiments of respect and admiration with which the sex is regarded by all right-minded men. Such feelings are a mark of civilisation and refinement.

So the hospital administration panicked, the students won, and Elizabeth was asked to leave the Middlesex. She had no immediate option but to return to Aldeburgh.

If Elizabeth was to pursue her medical studies, there seemed no alternative but to obtain private tuition, yet it seemed foolish to do so unless she could obtain a recognised qualification. In 1858 Parliament had passed an Act to regularise the medical profession. Until then charlatans and quacks had plied their trade with little restriction, and could set up a practice without any formal medical training. The Act required all new doctors to become members of the College of Surgeons, the College of Physicians or the College of Apothecaries, all of which required applicants to pass appropriate examinations. The first two restricted membership to men, but the Apothecaries had no such explicit restriction and reluctantly promised to examine Elizabeth when she had completed the required courses. She found eminent surgeons willing to take her on as a private pupil, particularly in the Scottish universities of St Andrews and Edinburgh, and also sympathetic medical staff who had worked with her at the Middlesex Hospital. In 1864 she worked for a time in the London Hospital, again in the guise of a nurse, where she gained valuable experience, particularly in midwifery. A year later she had completed her courses and was ready to submit herself to examination, but to her consternation the Apothecaries refused to allow her take the examination. They had broken their promise of four years earlier and her father was incensed; he threatened legal action and the College of Apothecaries gave way. Elizabeth took the examination and passed comfortably. Fortunately there was no order of merit to arouse further male jealousy. Even so, the Society of Apothecaries hastily altered its constitution to prevent other women following in her footsteps. But Elizabeth was now able to be enrolled on the British Medical Register and to set up her own consulting rooms in 20 Upper Berkeley Street, London, a house that her father had leased for her.

Her new practice soon had plenty of patients, especially women attracted by the novelty, and by the absence of the embarrassment usually associated with examination by a male doctor. Despite her heavy workload Elizabeth found time in 1866 to support Emily Davies in gathering signatures for John Stuart Mill's petition to Parliament in support of female suffrage. Parliament rejected the petition but Elizabeth had demonstrated early her commitment to the cause of women's rights. Soon after, she lost her sister Louie to appendicitis, a grievous blow because the sisters had been very close. All the while Elizabeth had been conscious of the limited nature of her medical qualification. If she was to compete with male doctors for clients she needed to secure an MD. This would require entrance to university and no British university would accept her. But the University of Paris had recently opened its medical degrees to women and Elizabeth determined to take her MD there.

Elizabeth now committed herself to a programme of rigorous home study in which her school French was very useful, but even so she had to relearn vast numbers of technical medical terms in the French language. She had already, in 1866, established the St Mary's dispensary for sick women and children to which she gave much of her time during the next twenty years, so that fitting in her studies with her work was a considerable burden. In June 1870 she went to Paris to take her MD and lodged with the family of a sympathetic professor at the Sorbonne. She gained her MD with distinction, but at first the British Medical Register refused to include it in her list of qualifications. The year proved to be a busy one for her. At the end of November she was elected to the London School Board, which had just been set up to administer the new Education Act. She wrote pamphlets on contagious diseases; she developed her ambition to turn her dispensary into the New Hospital for Women; since 1869 she had run not only her own practice and studied for her MD, but had also become honorary physician to the children's hospital near London docks. It was here that she met one of the governors of the hospital, James Anderson, whom she married in the following year. He was a wealthy shipping agent and his support, as she pursued her full-time career, became a vital part of her armoury.

During the next five years she had three children, one of whom died in infancy. She had a nanny for the children, a cook and enough household servants to relieve her of all the chores usually associated in Victorian times with the role of a wife. Money was never a problem. She charged 6*d* for a consultation at her dispensary, which covered her expenses and helped to limit the enormous number of would-be patients. She presided for a time over the Kensington Ladies' Discussion Society, which met four times a year. The huge demand for her time caused her to take on two female colleagues who had only been able to qualify abroad and thus were denied registration in Britain. The BMA rather grudgingly admitted her to membership in 1873, but hastily voted against admitting any more women, a policy it retained rigidly for the next nineteen years. In 1874 she helped found the London School of Medicine for Women. This was exclusively for women, both patients and staff, and the lack of registered colleagues placed heavy responsibility on Elizabeth. But, in 1876, one of her earliest male sympathisers, Russell Gurney, now an MP, managed to persuade Parliament to pass legislation allowing universities to admit women to medical degrees. Dublin was the first to do so but London soon followed in 1877. Elizabeth's colleagues were now able to qualify and the pressure on her was somewhat relieved.

Elizabeth was regarded by feminists as committed to their cause, but her support for the Contagious Diseases Acts dismayed them and brought her into collision with Josephine Butler. The Acts were attempts to deal with the evil of prostitution: women who were prostitutes or alleged prostitutes could be forced to be subjected to intimate and embarrassing internal examination by male doctors. There were no indignities provided for the prostitutes' male clients. Elizabeth took the view that such legislation was necessary to deal with the rapidly growing problem of venereal disease; feminists led by Josephine Butler took an opposite view and fought vigorously against the legislation, attacking its inhumanity and its sexism. Despite strenuous medical opposition the feminists managed, after a long fight, to get the Acts suspended in 1883 and repealed in 1886. But Elizabeth was still a moderate feminist at heart and her views are summed up by her words to the Privy Council in 1876: 'We are not asking for special privileges, only for the removal of special disabilities.'

The next few years were frenetic. Elizabeth lectured in her medical school, of which she became dean in 1883. She continued to practise in her clinic and was heavily involved in planning and raising funds for new buildings for the medical school. She became a member of the Central Committee of the National Society for Women's Suffrage in 1889; she was much in demand as a public speaker; she was elected president of the East Anglian branch of the BMA in 1896. Her close friendship with Emily Davies led her to accept appointment to the committee of Emily's college at Cambridge (Girton), which necessitated occasional trips out of London. The appointment of qualified female staff to her hospital should have eased her burden, but the rapidly escalating number of patients severely taxed the hospital's resources and added to Elizabeth's burdens both administrative and medical. She found the pressure so great that she gave up her school board work, but tried to fit in time for her children, taking them for carriage rides, visiting places of interest in London and arranging parties for them.

Women who took up medicine were still very few in number, regarded curiously by other women and suspiciously by men. There was still a battle to be won. In 1893 Elizabeth's contribution to the founding of the John Hopkins Medical School was conditional upon it being open to women. Yet by the 1890s, most universities other than Oxford and Cambridge were admitting women to medical degrees, and in 1898 she at last received a royal accolade when the Prince and Princess of Wales formally opened the new buildings of the London School of Medicine. But by now Elizabeth was in her sixties and tiring. She had already given up most of her practical work, and in 1903 she resigned her position as dean. By 1906 she and James had retired permanently to Aldeburgh, where he was elected mayor. He died in the following year and Elizabeth was invited by Aldeburgh council to succeed him, thus becoming Britain's first woman mayor.

So her activities switched from medical to political. She attended and spoke at women's suffrage meetings in which she played quite an active role until 1912. But by then she was seventy-six and lacked the youth and energy needed for the fight. Moreover, she was concerned about the militancy and increasing violence of the suffragette campaign, and after 1912 her suffragette activity ended. Her last years were clouded by loss of memory and increasing dementia. When war broke out in 1914 she neither understood whom Britain was fighting nor why it was fighting, yet the Women's Hospital Corps – which she saw departing from Victoria Station in 1914, laden with medical supplies and staffed by women doctors – would not have existed but for her. Her death in 1917 passed almost unnoticed amid the carnage of war.

Elizabeth Garrett Anderson was a pioneer, but a pioneer who had come at exactly the right time. Had she been born a hundred years earlier, her aim to become a trained and qualified physician would have been universally laughed to scorn, and there was no avenue by which it might have been achieved. But by the mid-nineteenth century the USA had allowed its first female to qualify in medicine, the University of Paris opened its medical degrees to women, and Britain had laid down by statute the route to qualification – a route which did not specifically bar women. Elizabeth did not fight her battle alone. She was sustained by the support of such influential women as Elizabeth Blackwell and Emily Davies, and a number of men rallied to her cause, notably the doctors and surgeons who taught her, the MP Russell Gurney and her husband John Anderson. Above all, she had the unwavering support of her father Newsom and his money. She was not opening the door to the professions to *all* women as there was no way for women without money, education, friends or influence to follow in her footsteps, but she was an example to those of similar background to herself, and one by one over the next century the professions exclusive to men were compelled to accept the entry of women; the disabilities Elizabeth had so strongly argued against had been, if not swept away, at least undermined.

MARIE CURIE: MATHEMATICIAN AND PHYSICIST

Marie Curie was remarkable in three ways: as a woman, for her romantic and ultimately tragic association with her husband, the distinguished French doctor and scientist, Pierre Curie, by whom she raised two almost equally famous daughters, Irene, a nuclear physicist, and Eve, a musician and writer, who also worked during the Second World War in the USA on behalf of the French Resistance; as a Polish patriot, for her devoted service to her homeland and her support of Polish independence; and, most importantly, for her work in the fields of physics, magnetism and radioactivity, and for her isolation of two new elements, radium and polonium (which she named after her native Poland).

Maria Sklodowska was born in 1867 in Warsaw, formerly the capital of the Kingdom of Poland, and at that time in the Russian-occupied portion of Poland, a country then denied an independent existence but partitioned between the three major eastern European powers: Prussia, Austria-Hungary and Russia. She was the youngest of five children, and, after the premature death of her mother from tuberculosis while she was still only a child, was brought up in dismal poverty by her father, a mathematics graduate of the University of St Petersburg who was denied work by the Russian authorities for political reasons. The whole family experienced petty political discrimination at the hands of the occupying power. Maria was a clever girl who showed a retentive memory and a formidable capacity for concentration, and performed brilliantly in her studies at high school. However, she was denied entry to university because of sweeping Russian reprisals after the Polish rising of 1863, and was compelled to work for eight years as a governess to a wealthy landed family some distance from her home while she scraped together the money to send her sister Bronislawa to Paris to study. She followed her there in 1891, where, after two years of eking out a miserable life in a garret, she graduated as top student in physics in her undergraduate class at the Sorbonne in 1893, and the following year took a first in her master's degree in mathematics. This success entitled her to an Alexandrovitch Scholarship from Poland, and on the strength of this she went on to apply for admission to Krakow University. She was, however, denied a place, partly for political reasons, but chiefly because she was female. She met and fell in love with Pierre Curie in 1894, and the two were married the following year. Her husband, born in 1869, was the son of a doctor and was already established as an expert on the properties of magnetic materials.

Together, Pierre and Marie Curie worked on magnetism and radioactivity (a term she coined in 1898). By 1897, Marie had settled down to her work on her doctoral thesis on uranium rays. No woman as yet had completed a PhD at any European university, and her career there was therefore something of a novelty. As a female researcher she was rather grudgingly allocated the use of a wooden shed for her experiments; she was banned from the main laboratories for fear that the presence of a female scientist might unduly overexcite the sensibilities of the other, male, researchers.

Her first great discovery in early 1898 was that pitchblende (the ore from which uranium is extracted) was more radioactive than the uranium it contained; from which she deduced that it must contain another, even more radioactive, substance. This discovery was so dramatic that it induced Pierre Curie to abandon his own research to join with Marie in her efforts. In effect, there were two such substances, both discovered by the young couple: one was 'polonium', and the other 'radium', because of the radioactivity it produced. It took until 1902 to produce one-tenth of a gram of radium, a sufficient quantity for it to be analysed chemically and allocated its place in the periodic table. Marie was awarded her DSc a year later – the same year that she and her husband were awarded their first Nobel Prize for Physics (jointly with Antoine Henri Becquerel,[1] her supervisor in the University of Paris, who was given most of the credit for her work). Marie and Pierre went on to discover the amazing amount of energy that radium produced – enough from every gram of radium to heat 1⅓ grams of water from freezing point to boiling, without significant change in the radium itself. This apparent violation of the law of the conservation of energy created a bigger stir than the original discovery of the new element itself, and brought fame to the couple, enabling them to move home and embark upon a more comfortable standard of life.

In April 1906, however, Pierre Curie, leaving his publisher's office in Paris, was killed when he slipped crossing the road and had his head crushed under the wheels of a passing horse-drawn wagon. Prior to the accident he had been suffering from dizzy spells, and modern opinion inclines to the view that his ailment was probably due to the onset of radiation sickness brought about by his long exposure to atomic radiation.

Distraught at her husband's death, Marie nevertheless agreed to continue her husband's teaching work at the Sorbonne, where she was eventually promoted to Professor. In 1911 the Royal Swedish Academy of Sciences awarded her a second Nobel Prize, this time in chemistry, but essentially for the same work for which she had won her first in 1903.

During the First World War, Marie pushed for the establishment of mobile radiography units for the treatment of wounded soldiers, known as 'petites Curies', whose treatment tubes were powered by the colourless, radioactive gas given off by radium, and eventually identified as radon. After the war she twice visited the United States to raise funds for further research into radium, and the second of these, in 1929, enabled her to complete the equipment of the Warsaw Radium Institute, established in 1925 in the newly independent state of Poland. Marie lived until July 1934, when she died of leukaemia at a clinic in the Haute-Savoie, a victim of the same radiation sickness that had earlier helped to kill her husband. Unaware of the danger involved, she had long been in the habit of carrying about test tubes containing radioactive isotopes in her overall pocket, and had stored them in the drawer of her desk, admiring the pretty blue-green light they emitted in the dark. Even now, her laboratory notebooks are still so highly radioactive that they are kept in a lead-lined safe, and only removed occasionally and with the appropriate precautions.

The scientific impact of Marie Curie's career has been tremendous, overturning established ideas in both chemistry and physics. Her investigations into the properties of radium, whose behaviour seemed to undermine the laws of the conservation of energy, led to a wholesale reconsideration of the basic laws of physics, while, at the experimental level, her extraction of pure metallic radium (in 1910, as distinct from the radium chloride she had isolated in 1902) provided other scientists such as Ernest Rutherford with the material with which he could further investigate the structure of the atom. Furthermore, she gave her name to the Curie (symbol Ci, the unit of radioactivity), and to the element curium, atomic number 96, which was also named in her and her husband's honour. Radioactive materials were also named after her, such as curite and sklodowskite. Numerous seats of learning such as Pierre and Marie Curie University (Paris) and of cancer hospitals came to be named after her like the Curie Institute of Oncology in Warsaw – even a station on the Paris Metro (the Pierre and Marie Curie station). Her image appeared on a Soviet stamp in 1987, on the Polish 20,000 zloty note in the 1980s, and on the last French 500F note issued just before the franc was replaced by the Euro.

But Marie Curie was not only a scientist. Because during her lifetime she experienced difficulties as a Polish woman, she was involved in the current movements of her age, sociologically and politically. As a woman she blazed a trail for others: she was the first to attain the rank of experimental scientist, PhD and university professor, while throughout her life she suffered from discrimination on account of her gender, as well as because of her nationality. She made no attempt to disguise her strong feminist and nationalist feelings, but seems to have invited controversy by constantly reaffirming them. Not only did she chafe at the discrimination she encountered from her own and her adoptive country, but in spite of the mounting Prussian and Russian feeling against her, remained a stout patriot devoted to the idea of a free Poland. At the outbreak of war in 1914, she even surrendered her two Nobel gold medals in order that the gold they contained could be used to help the war effort. She saw herself, and was seen by others, as a free, emancipated and independent woman. According to her biographer, Wojciech Wierzewski, Albert Einstein said of her that she was the only woman he knew who remained uncorrupted by the fame she had won.

PART 5

MISTRESSES AND FAVOURITES

ROXELANA:
SIXTEENTH-CENTURY
SULTANA OF TURKEY

Roxelana was the slave, concubine, eventual wife and Sultana, or Queen, of Sultan Suleiman
of the Ottoman Empire, when Turkey was at the peak of its power in the middle years of the
sixteenth century. By 1530, Sultan Suleiman I (known to his people as 'the Magnificent') had
extended his power deep into Europe. His writ ran from his capital in Constantinople, on the
Sea of Marmora, into the Black Sea, much of whose coasts he controlled, and across the Balkans
as far as the gates of Vienna, while at the same time he controlled the whole Mediterranean
rim of North Africa as far as Gibraltar, and lands throughout the Near and Middle East as far
as the Persian Gulf. Roxelana rose in power and importance until she became virtual co-ruler
of the Turkish Empire until her death in 1558; when she died she left the way clear for her
son, Selim, to inherit the Empire after his father's death in 1566; and she left, too, the legacy
of female influence over Turkey for a century or more, when the government of the Ottoman
Empire was known as 'the sultanate of the women'.

Roxelana[1] was born in the early years of the sixteenth century, far away from the
centre of power in the Ottoman Empire, a Ukrainian peasant girl and the daughter of
an Orthodox priest in the town of Rohatyn, south-east of Lvov, a major city of Galicia,
at that time part of the Kingdom of Poland. She was beautiful, with pale creamy skin
and long red hair, bewitching enough to attract the attention of the Tartar raiders who
streamed at that time into the Ukraine from the Crimea. They kidnapped her and took
her as a slave, probably first to the Crimean city of Kaffa, a centre of the slave trade, and
afterwards to Constantinople, where she was selected for the Sultan's harem and bought
by Ibrahim Pasha, Grand Vizier to the new Sultan Suleiman I.

Suleiman was regarded not only as one of the greatest of Ottoman sultans, but also
one as one of the most civilised, enlightened and humane. His troops were disciplined
and orderly, his towns and cities ordered and quiet. His subject populations were
loyal and accepted his rule without complaint, partly because he was so powerful that
complaint was useless, but chiefly because if subjects behaved themselves and paid
their taxes promptly their Turkish masters left them alone. Taxes were heavy, but fair.
The surrender of one child in ten to the state for army service[2] was the most severe;
but since no attempt was made by the Turks to impose Islam on the subject peoples,
and the non-Turkish people were left largely to their own devices, the peasants and the
townsfolk were generally no worse off in the Ottoman Empire than they would have
been elsewhere; indeed, justice was administered with remarkable fairness.

There were, however, features of Turkish rule that were more unusual. The sultan took numerous wives (a feature permitted by the Islamic faith but not always imitated, since many ordinary Turks simply could not afford the expense it entailed), kept in his harem as concubines and guarded by a body of eunuchs specially employed for the purpose. The sultan's harem was a glittering, pampered and often conspiratorial world, under the eunuchs who guarded and protected slaves and concubines.[3] When Ibrahim Pasha bought Roxelana he was well aware of the new sultan's preference for fair-skinned women; he also knew that she had the gift of amusing men by her verbal wit as well as her feminine charms (hence the nickname 'the laughing one'). When he saw her, Suleiman fell in love with her immediately. Among those in the harem when Roxelana arrived there was his chief favourite, Gulbehar, who had a privileged status because she was the mother of Suleiman's eldest son, Mustafa. Cunningly, Roxelana set about marginalising Gulbehar so as to make herself indispensable to the sultan and to become the first woman in the harem. In 1524, the year after her arrival, she gave birth to her first son, Selim,[4] and afterwards went on to bear him four other children. She persuaded Suleiman to marry off many of the other young girls surrounding him, because she was afraid of the rise of other rivals, and the sultan, besotted by her, agreed to her terms, and finally, in 1534, even consented to marry her. This was unprecedented; some contemporaries thought he had been somehow bewitched. After her marriage, Roxelana set about the more unfamiliar task of extending her influence beyond the gilded, claustrophobic world of the harem into the world of Turkish politics.

In his infatuation with his lover, Suleiman began to consult with Roxelana on affairs of state. The two were always together; even when they were apart they wrote each other love poems. But they were frequently separate. Her principal problem was the distance separating the Old Palace, which housed the harem, and the New Palace, which was the centre of Ottoman government. She reckoned that the closer she was to the centre of government, the more influence she would have over the sultan. For some time, Roxelana could make no progress in this direction, but fate came to her aid. In 1535 fire broke out among the flimsy wooden buildings on the waterfront of the Bosphorus, and in the conflagration that followed the Old Palace was completely destroyed. She asked her husband to give her accommodation in the New Palace, and he agreed. She gave orders for a new door to be built between her apartments and those of Suleiman, and, with the new peephole that she persuaded the sultan to install through a shuttered window over his council chamber, she was able to observe and listen to the dealings that went on in the divan, or council of ministers. Her triumph was complete, and her influence now virtually unchallenged.

Roxelana seemed to have had considerable force in the world of foreign affairs and international politics. A few of her letters to the Polish king, Sigismund II Augustus, have survived, and she seems to have brought about some improvement in Turkish-Polish relations. She also tried to control the operation of Tartar slave-dealers in the Ukraine. Roxelana had a lively interest, too, in matters of domestic concern. She engaged in the construction of a number of major buildings from Mecca to Jerusalem. Among her foundations in Constantinople were a mosque, two Koranic schools, a public fountain and a women's hospital near the slave market. She also commissioned a bath to serve the community of worshippers in the nearby Hagia Sophia. Some of her fine embroidery has also survived, in gifts given to the Shah of Persia in 1547 and to the aforementioned King of Poland in 1549.

After 1540 two obstacles alone remained between her and supreme power and the succession of her son: the Grand Vizier, Ibrahim Pasha, whose devoted friendship was one of the more pleasing aspects of Suleiman's reign, and Mustafa, the sultan's eldest son, whose reputation with the Janissaries was legendary, and who was little short of a hero to the Turkish people. This leads on to the second undesirable feature of Turkish government at this time – the prevalence of court intrigue, and the time-honoured custom of dispatching political opponents secretly by assassination by means of strangulation. Roxelana was particularly ruthless in this respect.

She first of all embarked on a vicious campaign of gossip and innuendo against Ibrahim Pasha's reputation. Ibrahim was of fairly humble Albanian origin, and his steady and trusting relationship with the high-born sultan had been found by the common people to be especially inspiring, and seemed to belie the traditional jealousy of the sultans for their powerful ministers. But Roxelana worked on her husband, and eventually persuaded him that Ibrahim was working to a secret and ambitious agenda of his own, and should be removed. The legend has it that Suleiman and Roxelana were sleeping in the next room when the murder took place; she covered her husband with kisses so that he should not hear the sounds of the struggle as Ibrahim was throttled. This was in 1536. The incoming replacement was Rustem Pasha, her daughter's husband and her own close friend. With his appointment, Roxelana became effectively co-Grand Vizier.

Together, Roxelana and Rustem set about the task of undermining Mustafa, the sultan's son and her own popular rival. It took seven years of intrigue and suggestion to convince Suleiman that Mustafa was inciting disaffection and rebellion against his own father, a task complicated by his reputation as a military hero who was handsome, clever, popular and able. Mustafa could not believe that his own stepmother should be engaged in such a wicked and spiteful cause, and, refusing to heed warnings of her intentions, made no effort to escape. Ultimately, Mustafa's gifts and his popularity worked against him; they led Suleiman to believe the young man was working against him for his own ends, and the sultan ordered his assassination. As was usual, this murder led almost inevitably to others. Selim had a brother who might also prove a threat to his ascendancy; he was removed from the succession and his five sons were all strangled. In this fashion the way was cleared for Selim to succeed to his father's throne on the latter's death in 1566 – although he soon proved himself to be drunken and second-rate as a ruler, and his sultanate lasted for only eight years.

By then, the author of all these wicked deeds was herself dead. She died in 1558, as she was approaching her sixtieth birthday. In her lifetime she set the precedent whereby the favourites and mistresses of sultans could intrigue for the royal succession, and in so doing, dictate the course of foreign and domestic policy in the Ottoman Empire. This was the beginning of the 'sultanate of the women', which lasted until the middle of the eighteenth century. Turkey remained for long a mighty state and a threat to the security of the western world, but the beginnings of the decline may be seen in the reign of Selim II.

NELL GWYNN:
ACTRESS AND ROYAL MISTRESS

Eleanor ('Nell') Gwynn was one of the earliest actresses to achieve national stardom, and was a long-time mistress of King Charles II. She was first spotted by Charles Sackville, Lord Buckhurst, in 1667, when she was playing a rumbustious part in a comedy known as All Mistaken, or the Mad Couple, *when she rolled about on the stage, feet towards the audience and showed her drawers. On the strength of these exciting undergarments she became his mistress for the next couple of years. She later made the King's acquaintance at another play,* She Would if She Could, *and became his lover and his playmate for much of the rest of his reign.*

Nell's youth, passed in obscurity and impoverishment, remained hidden from her public, although she was not ashamed of it and was always willing to talk about it. Her mother was Eleanor (or perhaps Helena) Gywnn, more frequently referred to simply as 'Madame' Gwynn, and she lived in the parish of St Martin-in-the-Fields, in inner London. Her husband was probably a captain in the Cavalier Army during the Civil War, and it seems likely from his name that he was of Welsh origin. Madame Gwynn kept a bawdy house (i.e. a brothel – hence perhaps her name 'Madame') and was a prodigious drinker of cheap brandy. Nell herself was born in 1650 in Pipewell Lane near Covent Garden (renamed in the nineteenth century as Gwynne Street on her account), and spent much of her youth selling vegetables or hawking herring. She grew up in Coalyard Alley, a poor slum off Drury Lane. She may have sometimes worked as a child prostitute for her mother in her bawdy house. Around 1662, though still only twelve, she seems to have struck up a relationship with a man called Duncan, and it was he who secured her first job on the stage at one of the theatres being built at this time in Drury Lane.

Charles II, newly restored to the English throne after a decade of strait-laced Puritan rule under the Commonwealth and then under Cromwell, set about restoring not only royal government, but also some of the fun that had recently gone out of English life. One of his early acts was to license the formation of two new acting companies, and in 1663 the King's Company, headed by Thomas Killigrew, opened a new playhouse in Bridges Street, later rebuilt and renamed as the Theatre Royal in Drury Lane. Here Mary Meggs, a former prostitute, was hired to sell the small sweet 'china' oranges that her 'orange girls' used to sell at sixpence a time to audiences to suck (and sometimes, if they felt like it, to throw at actors they did not like). Mistress Meggs hired Nell and her older sister Rose for this work. Here Nell's opportunities immediately expanded.

She began to meet a much superior type of person to those she already knew (indeed, the King himself sometimes came to see the play), and as the girls sometimes served as messengers between members of the audience and the actors backstage, picked up handsome tips and even did a bit of discreet pimping for the more gallant of the young men. If Nell was not a prostitute already, there can be little doubt that in this environment she rapidly became one.

The Restoration theatres were the first to employ women for the female roles. They had earlier, as in Shakespeare's days, been played by boys or young men, whose smooth faces and unbroken voices were actually preferred by audiences. Nell seemed cut out for such a job. She was already a theatre employee, had good looks, a strong clear voice and a ready wit, and promised well, but as yet she had no acting experience and was totally illiterate, which made the learning of lines very difficult. However, she got her first trial in Dryden's heroic drama *The Indian Emperor* in March 1665, where she played Cydaria, Montezuma's daughter and Cortez's love interest. She was not really up to the role, and expressed her disappointment at her own performance.[1] It was in comedy roles that she found her *métier*. Later that year, in May ('runs' of plays were often distressingly short in Restoration times – seats were dear and the section of the public to which plays appealed was extremely limited, so that you might get fifty plays in the course of a single season) she made her first successful appearance in *All Mistaken, or the Mad Couple*, in which, with Charles Hart, an established comedian, she played the female role in the 'gay[2] couple' so often featuring in comedies at that time. The play was typical of many of the comedies of the time: a pair of antagonistic, witty lovers, he trying to avoid the entrapment of marriage, and she pretending to do the same to keep him at arm's length, rather like Shakespeare's Beatrice and Benedick in his *Much Ado About Nothing*. It was in this comedy role that Nell Gwynn first came to the notice of the upper classes. She featured also in what were called 'breeches roles', where plots made some excuse for female actors to appear in men's costumes, so as to show off their figures better in close-fitting male attire. Lord Buckhurst fell for her heavily, inveigled her away from the theatre, set her up in his own house and provided her with spending money of £100 per year. They took a country holiday together in the summer of 1667 in Epsom. Their affair, however, did not last long, and by the autumn they parted.

Before the end of the year, George Villiers, Duke of Buckingham, became the unofficial organiser of Nell's social life. Buckingham, one of the King's principal advisers, was looking for an eligible female who might be promoted to the rank of the King's mistress, in place of Barbara Palmer, his current lover, who, in spite of being Buckingham's cousin, was thought to have outlived her usefulness. His plan at first backfired, chiefly on account of Nell's demanding £500 a year for taking the King on, but after a brief dalliance with her rival, Moll Davis,[3] Charles turned back to Nell and their affair started to roll in the spring of 1668. Legend has it that the King, his brother the Duke of York (the future James II) and Buckingham's brother, went to the theatre together to see George Etherege's *She Would if She Could*, and afterwards went off to supper; the three gentlemen having discovered none of them had brought any money, poor Nell found herself obliged to pay the bill. Whether this story is true or not, Nell did not find herself so completely out of pocket thereafter. Having already enjoyed the patronage of Charles Hart, the actor, and Charles Sackville, Lord Buckhurst, she dubbed the King 'Charles III', which seems both witty and accurate.

Nell did not, however, give up her acting career. Indeed she found her new notoriety as the King's wanton gave her even greater popularity than she had enjoyed previously. She played at least three major roles in the course of 1668 and the first half of 1669, with even more élan and popularity than usual, and it was only as her commitment to the King built up that she began to wind down her acting career. Though Charles continued his habit of taking multiple mistresses, and continued to do so in spite of what seems his genuine affection for Nell, and in spite of the rather prim resistance of his legal wife, Queen Catherine of Braganza,[4] Nell found herself increasingly in competition with others much better born than she was, like Louise de Kérouaille, who came over originally as lady-in-waiting to Queen Catherine, but who proved a powerful rival.[5] In May 1670, she gave birth to the King's son, Charles Beauclerk (later Duke of St Albans) – the King's seventh son by five different mistresses. When she fancied the King's ardour was cooling, Nell did return to the theatre briefly once again, appearing in Cryden's *Conquest of Grenada* in 1671, but this seems to have been her last play after a stage career that had lasted seven years. By this time she had moved into a town house in fashionable Pall Mall, whose lease had been transferred to her by Charles. She complained that she had *given*, not *leased*, her favours to the King, and expected to be treated likewise; and in fact was granted the freehold in 1676.[6] It was in this solidly built brick house that Nell in 1671 gave birth to her second son, James Beauclerk, who was sent to school in Paris at the age of six, and died there suddenly in 1681.

The King later gave her also Burford House (on the edge of Home Park, Windsor), and another summer residence in King's Cross Road, London, where she continued to receive the King towards the end of his reign. It was said that it was she who persuaded Charles to set up Royal Chelsea Hospital in 1682 for old soldiers who had been wounded in war or grown sick. When Charles II died in 1685 at the early age of fifty-four, James II, Duke of York, succeeding him, granting Nell a handsome pension of £1,500 a year.[7] He did not, however, succeed in persuading her to become a Catholic.

Nell Gwynn, never losing the common touch, continued to live in considerable luxury until 1687, when she suffered a stroke which left her paralysed down one side. A second stroke shortly afterwards immobilised her altogether, and she died in November 1687, at the age of thirty-seven, little more than two years after her royal master and patron. She was buried at St Martin-in-the-Fields.

ABIGAIL MASHAM:
ROYAL FAVOURITE

Anne, Queen of England from 1702 to 1714, was always in need of a royal confidante; without one she was emotionally insecure and politically ineffective. From the age of eleven she was guided and advised by Sarah Jennings (Sarah Churchill[1] after her marriage to John Churchill) and she retained Anne's confidence after she became queen until Sarah was replaced by Abigail Hill (Abigail Masham after her marriage to Samuel Masham). The transfer of royal favour from Sarah to Abigail generated much unpleasantness and had important political consequences.

Abigail's date of birth is uncertain but was probably 1670. She was the elder daughter of Francis Hill, a merchant trading with the Near East, and his wife, Elizabeth Jennings. Abigail was first cousin to her future rival Sarah and second cousin to Robert Harley, the Tory Earl of Oxford. Abigail's childhood was fairly uneventful, but in the late 1680s her father's unfortunate financial mismanagement led to bankruptcy, and the family was virtually destitute. It must have been demeaning for Abigail to look for employment, but she joined the household of Sir George Rivers whose family was connected to the Harleys. She was in effect little more than a domestic servant, a post unworthy of her family connections. When Sarah Jennings realised that her cousin's family was in such financial straits she stepped in to help them, and she asked Princess Anne to find Abigail a place as a bedchamber woman whenever a vacancy should arise. She is not listed in Anne's household until 1700, but, on Anne's accession in 1702, Abigail's post was confirmed with a very generous salary for such a menial post of £500 a year.

Abigail's duties consisted of dressing her mistress, waiting at table, emptying slops and sleeping on her bedroom floor. This gave plenty of opportunity for intimacies between Abigail and Anne, and as early as 1703 their relationship was one of affection rather than formality. Anne was already suffering from poor health, and she was one of eighteenth-century Bath's very earliest visitors to seek the waters. Abigail jibbed at the Bath lodging which had been assigned to her, and Anne is recorded as having run after her, begging her to go back to the bed she had spurned, and addressing her frequently as 'Dear Hill'. Robert Harley now began to realise that he might be able to make political use of his kinship with Abigail. The Tories and Whigs had joined forces in order to fight the War of the Spanish Succession against France under the leadership of Sydney Godolphin, a man of undoubted Whig credentials, and Sarah's husband, the newly created Duke of Marlborough, who, although a Tory at heart, favoured a government of mixed parties for the successful prosecution of the war. The Tories were glad enough to wage war if there was a Tory general in charge of it, while the Whigs were glad enough to have a Tory general as long as there was a war. But by 1706 the Tories were growing increasingly restless at the cost of the war and were alarmed at Godolphin's promotion only of Whigs to vacant ministerial posts. Abigail and Harley began to argue the Queen out of her support for the Whigs, which in any case had only been reluctantly given, and Abigail kept Harley closely informed of the Queen's political confidences by meeting him at evening concerts at which the Queen was also present.

Until 1707 Sarah believed herself to be fully in the Queen's confidence and had no idea how close Abigail had come to supplanting her. It was Abigail's wedding to Samuel Masham that alerted her. It was generally agreed that Abigail was not a particularly attractive woman, but an unmarried status was something of a handicap to an ambitious woman. A number of men had shown interest in her when it became clear that she might be politically useful, but Samuel Masham seems to have been genuinely attracted to her. He was groom of the bedchamber to Anne's husband Prince George. They married in the spring of 1707; the Queen was present and she gave them a very generous £2,000 dowry. But the wedding took place without Sarah's knowledge, and it was this failure to inform her that alerted Sarah to the danger posed by Abigail. Sarah did not help her cause by ranting at the Queen, emphasising that Abigail owed her rise to Sarah's generosity towards her family ('I raised her from a broom') and worst of all that the relationship between the Queen and Abigail was an improper one.

Harley resigned from the cabinet in 1708 but continued to meet the Queen behind the Whig ministers' backs. Abigail arranged these assignations. The Marlboroughs were now thoroughly alarmed. The Duke tried to secure a parliamentary address to the Queen to have Abigail removed from court, but the Tories opposed this tactic and it failed. The Whigs were still in power in 1709, but the war was universally regarded as expensive and unpopular, and Anne finally felt bold enough to dismiss the Whig ministers in 1710. A Tory triumph at the general election inevitably followed.[2] Abigail was now supreme, and she had the satisfaction of seeing her rival ignominiously dismissed from court and deprived of almost all her offices. The crucial post of Keeper of the Privy Purse was given to Abigail, a position that had once been held by Sarah and which showed how deeply the Queen trusted its holder. Anne would have liked to confer a degree of nobility upon Abigail but was concerned in case she would 'lose a useful servant about her person, for it would give offence to have a peeress lie on the floor and do several other inferior offices'. But Anne's need to strengthen the Tories in the House of Lords led her to create twelve Tory peers in December 1711, of whom Samuel Masham was one. Anne persuaded Abigail to 'do as she used to do' and remain as a bedchamber woman.

Now that the Tories were in power, Harley, newly elevated to the Earldom of Oxford, had less need of his cousin's influence with the Queen, but he thought it worth continuing to cultivate nevertheless. Abigail had six children from 1708 onwards and frequent pregnancies meant long absences from court. But Abigail maintained her hold over Anne who would not agree to any policy of the new government without Abigail's approval. Oxford's preoccupation with government led Abigail to respond to the overtures of Oxford's Tory rival Henry St John, Viscount Bolingbroke, especially as he was prepared to further the career of her brother. Bolingbroke was a more committed Tory than Oxford, and it seems likely that they discussed the possibility, though not necessarily the desirability, of a Jacobite restoration. Anne disliked her Hanoverian relatives, and whether Abigail and Bolingbroke would try to persuade her to overturn the Act of Settlement[3] remains a matter of conjecture since Anne died on 1 August 1714 after a very short final illness. But in Anne's final weeks Oxford had been dismissed from office, Bolingbroke was now supreme, and his Jacobite sympathies were an open secret.

Anne's death took everyone by surprise but the pro-Hanoverians were ready; the Jacobites were not. George I succeeded without any serious challenge, and appointed a Whig Ministry. Abigail who, unlike Sarah, had genuine affection for the Queen, not only greatly mourned her loss, but also found her own political influence had completely ebbed away. The Hanoverians had no use for her, and anyway rightly suspected that her influence had been exercised against their interests. Abigail retired into private life and political obscurity. In 1723 after the death of her father-in-law she moved into his property at Otes in Essex where she died on 6 December 1734 after a protracted illness.

Even after the Glorious Revolution of 1688, the English monarchy was still very powerful. It could still veto parliamentary legislation; it could appoint and change ministers; it could determine foreign policy; it could call a general election. Most of these powers, in Anne's reign, came under the control, not of the leading male politicians, but of her two closest women friends. Sarah was always the controller; Abigail began as the trusted listener. But as Abigail became more politically powerful she, too, began to mould Anne's policies in the way that Anne had found so irksome with Sarah. Sarah and Abigail were unique; not until the twentieth century did an English woman politician ever enjoy such power.

SARAH CHURCHILL: ROYAL ADVISER

Sarah Churchill was the wife of John Churchill, Duke of Marlborough, one of England's most successful soldiers. But she did not shelter under the umbrella of his success; she was successful in her own right. She became a close friend of Princess Anne, later Queen Anne, and was able to exert considerable influence in the politics of her reign, even to the extent of determining the rise and fall of ministers. She had a formidable reputation among her contemporaries, who often had reason to fear her temper, but among her darker qualities there were a number of redeeming features.

On 5 June 1660 Frances Jennings gave birth to another daughter. Frances (*née* Thornhurst) was the wife of Richard Jenyns (Jennings), an impoverished member of Hertfordshire's landed gentry. They named their new daughter Sarah, and while Richard was endeavouring to recover some of his lost lands, Sarah was given the usual upbringing of a female, short on learning but rich in social graces. Richard's business efforts brought him into contact with James, Duke of York, and he secured for Frances the post of maid of honour to the Duke's first wife, Anne Hyde. When Richard died, Frances remarried and the family spent some time in France, but James did not forget them and in 1677 appointed Sarah as maid of honour to his second wife, Mary of Modena. Through this appointment Sarah became very close to Anne, and since Anne was in great need of a confidante whom she could trust and lean on, Sarah filled the bill admirably.

But neither Sarah nor Anne forgot the primary purpose of seventeenth-century females: the propagation of the species. Sarah was seventeen, well-proportioned, with fair hair and blue eyes, but not a great beauty. Nevertheless, John Churchill had seen her at court, was smitten, and proceeded to pursue her. It was not her money he was after because she didn't have any, and nor did he since the Churchill estates were heavily entailed. Thus, not surprisingly, the courtship was so strongly disapproved of by both families that the couple married in secret. It is significant that Anne was kept informed of it, but Sarah, who was never very good at family relationships, quarrelled with both her mother and her elder sister, and the breach was not easy to repair. Soon after the marriage, the Popish Plot[1] resulted in James' temporary exile from England and he was accompanied to the Netherlands by John and Sarah. It is said that through Sarah's experiences at James' court she took a dislike to the ritual and ceremonial of the Catholic Church, and she became an advocate to Anne of Church of England Protestantism.

James was grateful for Churchill's loyalty and secured a peerage for him, and when Anne married Prince George of Denmark[2] in 1683, requiring a separate household, Sarah was appointed one of her ladies of the bedchamber. Sarah and John enjoyed a surprisingly good marriage. John soon learned how to ride or control her temper tantrums, and Sarah gave birth over the years to five daughters and two sons. Their accommodation problem eased in 1684 when they were able to buy the Jennings' family seat at Holywell. But raising a family did not weaken her hold on Anne. James became king on Charles II's death in 1685, and while he did not question John's loyalty he was suspicious that Sarah's firm Protestantism would have too much of a resonance in Anne. He should have paid more attention to Churchill, who changed sides in 1688 and at the very last minute sided with William of Orange. Angrily he attempted to arrest Sarah, but not only did she challenge the validity of the arrest warrant, but she even managed to spirit Anne away from Whitehall and out of her father's reach.

Churchill's late change of sides meant that he had earlier opposed Parliament's offer of the throne to William, and William was always a little suspicious of him. Queen Mary, William's wife, resented the excessive influence Sarah had over her younger sister. It was no coincidence that it was in 1691 that Anne and Sarah adopted the names of Mrs Morley and Mrs Freeman in their secret correspondence, so that little damage would occur if the letters fell into the wrong hands. Like many other politicians, Churchill had taken out political insurance by maintaining his links with the Jacobite court, and Sarah had been corresponding with her Jacobite sister, Frances. In the political panic which ensued in 1692 over the alleged Jacobite threat, Churchill was briefly imprisoned. But Queen Mary died in 1694 and William found it expedient to try to improve relations with his sister-in-law; after all, it was Anne and her children who would succeed him. Sarah persuaded Anne that it was in her interest to mollify William, and her influence was such that when it was deemed appropriate for Anne's son the Duke of Gloucester to have a separate establishment it was Sarah who suggested most of the appointments to it. But the young duke died in 1700, and Anne had no other surviving children. Sarah gave Anne sound advice not to obstruct the Act of Settlement whereby the Dowager Electress Sophia of Hanover was to be her successor, and in the War of the Spanish Succession, which England entered in 1702, Anne had no qualms about appointing Churchill Captain-General of the English forces. In 1689 Sarah had been made Countess of Marlborough, and in 1702 her husband became the Duke of Marlborough at Anne's insistence. Sarah had shown some hesitation about this elevation as she feared that she and John lacked the finance necessary to sustain a dukedom. After Marlborough's great victory at Blenheim in 1704, Parliament granted the Marlboroughs the Woodstock estate with the finance to build a country house worthy of such distinguished owners. Preoccupation with this could occasionally distract Sarah when she should have been keeping a careful eye on Anne, especially as she managed to antagonise not only the architect Vanbrugh but also most of the skilled craftsmen engaged in its construction.

Sarah became closely involved in the politics of war. Marlborough had never been a committed Whig, but had thrown in his lot with the Whigs who wanted to continue vigorous prosecution of the war with its opportunities for enhancing his military career. To do this he must control the government through Sarah's hold over Anne, and must abandon his ideal of a government of all parties. At first Marlborough was partnered in government by Sydney Godolphin, a man of impeccable Whig connections. While Marlborough was abroad it was Sarah's job to keep him informed, to keep Anne under control, and to keep the Tories, such as Harley and St John, out of office. Sarah's power was so great that those who had business with the Queen had to see Sarah first. In 1706 Sarah insisted on the appointment of her son-in-law, the Whig Earl of Sunderland as Secretary of State. Anne unwillingly complied, after a particularly nasty show of temper by Sarah, despite the fact that Anne did not like Sunderland's politics and thought him arrogant.

From the first, Anne's relationship with Sarah had been that of a young girl with a wiser and older companion. But Anne was no longer the wide-eyed girl of eight which she had been when the relationship started. She was now a mature woman, not as worldly-wise as Sarah was, but with a mind of her own and an obstinacy to rival Sarah's. What she yearned for was a loving friend and counsellor, what she got was a self-opinionated and controlling mentor. Anne was beginning to find Sarah tiresome and restrictive. In 1700 Sarah had introduced her penniless cousin Abigail Hill into Anne's court as a bedchamber woman, a post which was confirmed when Anne became queen in 1702.[3] Sleeping on the floor of the Queen's bedroom gave Abigail plenty of opportunities to have intimate conversations with her, especially as Sarah was so often absent from court. By the spring of 1707 Sarah realised that Abigail had replaced her in the Queen's affections. She quarrelled bitterly with Anne over her familiarity with Tory politicians, her reluctance to continue the war, and over Sarah's frequent absences from court for successive childbirths and to be with her husband John. She was incensed when she learned that Abigail had married Samuel Masham with the Queen's knowledge and consent, but without reference to her. And it was Abigail, not Sarah, who consoled the Queen when she was prostrate with grief over the death of George of Denmark. Perhaps Sarah could not understand why anyone should be so upset over the death of such an insignificant prince.

In 1710 Anne and Sarah had their final meeting. Soon afterwards the Tories triumphed in the general election which followed Anne's dismissal of the Whig ministers and her replacement of them with Harley and St John and their friends. Marlborough continued an expensive and desultory war in the Netherlands, and begged his wife not to alienate Anne further. But in 1711 Anne asked Sarah to give up most of the multiplicity of offices she held; Sarah was so furious that she vented her spite on the rooms in St James's palace that she was asked to vacate. She stripped them of all their curtains and fittings, and even tried to dismantle the chimney breast. At first the Marlboroughs retired to Holywell, but after a few months they set off on a European tour. It was a triumphant success. They were everywhere greeted as the saviours of Europe from Louis XIV. They were feted by princes and treated like conquerors. But Sarah was homesick, and their return to England coincided with the death of Queen Anne on 1 August 1714. The Marlboroughs were keen supporters of George I and the Hanoverian succession, but the new Whig government, although grateful for their support, was anxious that they should not enjoy the same influence they had possessed in the time of the late Queen. Sarah contented herself with the construction at Blenheim and in securing suitable marriages for her descendants. In 1717 Lady Henrietta Godolphin, her granddaughter, married Thomas Pelham-Holles, Duke of Newcastle, a rising politician destined for high office.[4] Two years later, Blenheim was finally near completion and the Marlboroughs were able to move in. In 1720 Sarah invested in the South Sea Company and made a killing before the collapse came, although some of those she had advised to invest lost heavily in the bursting of the bubble. The Duke had suffered a stroke in 1716, but another in 1722 killed him. Theirs was an admirable marriage; they had genuine affection for each other and remained loyal to each other for forty-five years; Sarah's grief at his passing was deep-felt and sincere.

Sarah was now an enormously wealthy widow, and she had to fend off aristocratic suitors, some of whom hoping to recoup their finances at her expense. She continued her habit of quarrelling with her relations and descendants – with her son-in-law Sunderland, and with her daughter Henrietta on account of her liaison with the playwright William Congreve. She disliked Sir Robert Walpole as she thought his policy of peace at any price damaged the country's prestige, but even worse helped to keep interest rates low, thus depressing the interest she received from government bonds. Opposition politicians thought her sufficiently influential to be worth seeking out, and Princess Caroline (later queen of George II) made overtures to her. But Caroline and Sarah were too much alike, and Caroline found Sarah haughty and condescending. Even so, Sarah toyed with the idea of marrying one of her granddaughters to Caroline's son, Prince Frederick, but Walpole stepped in to prevent it, thus intensifying Sarah's dislike of him. As Walpole's power declined in the 1730s, Sarah used some of her huge financial resources to fund the opposition to him, even with the odd Jacobite. The government showed its resentment of these activities by temporarily ceasing to borrow from the Marlborough trust in 1737, but the threat of war in 1738 helped the government to reverse its decision. Even when she was in her eighties, politicians like Henry Pelham thought it worth their while to cultivate the cantankerous old lady, whose acerbity was not helped by increasingly debilitating attacks of gout. Sarah died at Marlborough House[5] on 18 October 1744. She was buried at Blenheim Palace, and her husband was brought back from Westminster Abbey to be reinterred with her. She left an enormous fortune, with many generous bequests to servants and friends, including one of £10,000 to the promising young politician William Pitt.

Sarah's achievements easily outweigh her failures. Without her urgings and encouragement her husband would probably never have progressed so far in his military career. She gave him the strength and commitment that were needed to complement his military genius. She gave Princess Anne wise guidance on steering through the many political pitfalls on her way to the throne, even if later she failed to pay Anne the deference that was due to a monarch. She certainly had unfortunate relations with most of her family, but she did try to make sure that they were financially secure, and that, as far as possible, they made good marriages. Her political power was great, and, fortunately for England, was usually exercised in England's best interests. Maybe she was too keen on war, but her support for the Act of Settlement and the Hanoverian succession helped to consolidate political stability and the acceptance of the Hanoverian dynasty by many who were wavering, and she refused to flirt seriously with Jacobitism. Many great male politicians have left lesser political legacies.

MADAME DE MAINTENON AND THE COLLÈGE DE ST CYR

Mme de Maintenon has long enjoyed the reputation of wielding considerable power as the mistress of the Sun King of France, Louis XIV. After 1670 he came to be very much influenced by her in matters to do with politics, economics, and especially religion; and after the death of the Queen, Maria Theresa of Spain, he was privately married to her in a morganatic marriage by the Archbishop of Paris. This strengthened her influence over him so that afterwards many matters to do with the government of France were discussed with her, and her influence felt especially in matters to do with the faith. She was an ardent Catholic, despite having been brought up a Huguenot,[1] and the influence of her faith may be seen in a number of crucial decisions taken by Louis in the later part of his reign e.g. the revocation of the Edict of Nantes, by which Huguenots had enjoyed freedom to worship since the reign of Henri IV.[2] Undeniably she was devout, but she was also shrewd. She may have made some mistakes, for example the choice of one unsuccessful general (Villeroi) over another (Catinat) in Louis' later campaigns, but the major errors in French diplomacy were made by Louis XIV himself and not by his mistress.

What is less well known is her interest in educational matters, largely on account of her own early experiences. She had been born Françoise d'Aubigné in 1635 in prison at Niort, where her father, Constant, had been imprisoned as a Huguenot. On his release in 1639, he fled to Martinique, where he gambled away all his money, forcing Françoise's mother to entrust her daughter to her sister-in-law, Mme de Villette, who brought her up in her own faith as a Huguenot. Released by royal order to her godmother, Mme de Neuillant, she was brought back to Catholicism, and eventually returned to live with her mother in very reduced circumstances with no more than a small pension of 200 livres a year. She was befriended by the writer Paul Scarron, who, though he was deformed and an invalid, married her in 1651 (thereafter her detractors at court always referred to her contemptuously as 'Madame Scarron'). When Scarron died in 1660, the Queen increased her pension to 2,000 livres, but her son, Louis XIV, when he assumed full power from his mother in 1661, refused to continue with it in 1666, and she contemplated leaving for Portugal as a lady attendant to the Queen of Portugal; but before she did, she made the acquaintance of the King's mistress, Mme de Montespan, who, thinking that Scarron was unlikely to prove a rival with her prim ways and her black gown and crucifixes,[3] appointed her as one of her staff at her mansion at Vaugirard. Later the King brought his illegitimate children to court, and through Mme de Montespan met Mme Scarron, later elevating her estate at Maintenon to a marquisate and entitling her Mme de Maintenon. By the middle 1670s the King was constantly in her company, and de Montespan found herself out of favour.[4]

These experiences brought her to feel sorry for the children of minor provincial nobility, her own social class, girls who were often ill-educated and destined to go into convents if they did not finish up as servants of someone better off. Mme de Maintenon began to take an interest in such girls, and with the support of Mme de Brinon, an Ursuline nun whose convent had been closed by lack of funds, she set up one of her own in 1685 at Reuil. She prevailed on the King to move it to St Cyr on the edge of the park at Versailles, where a new building was put up by the military under the direction of Mansart on the detailed instructions of Mme de Maintenon. She ordered an open square of a building rather like a barracks, plainly built without elegance or grandeur. There was room for 250 girls between six and nineteen, taught by thirty-six lady professors, called *Les Dames*, and assisted by twenty-four lay sisters. The pupils were to be brought up to live in the world, and were to be provided with a good general education. They were to be taught to speak and to write good French; they should learn embroidery and poetry, which they should learn by heart and be able to recite. The 'constitution' of St Cyr was approved by Père la Chaise and by Maintenon's confessor, its grammar corrected by Racine and Boileau, and the final document submitted to the Pope for his acceptance. An apartment was set aside for her at the Academy, and she often came to visit and to help.[5]

The girls were to be chosen by the monarch himself – four degrees of nobility on the father's side were required, and the girls were never to forget their noble origins. The King took a lively interest in the school uniform. He wanted the girls to look like nuns, but with plenty of white muslin and ribbons. Brown woollen material was chosen for their gowns, with an apron over it edged with the colour of the form to which the wearer belonged; their capes were to be fur-lined in winter and made out of striped cotton in summer. Hair had to be neat, and the girls were enjoined to take a pride in their appearance since 'beauty is a gift from God'. Their teachers wore a simple gold cross.[6] When the school was opened in 1686 the King visited, inspected it, talked to the girls, attended mass and thanked Mme de Maintenon for her splendid efforts. She herself was now there three or four times a week, often arriving early in the morning, helping the girls and staying to help in the preparation of their meals.

Drama was one of the things that Mme de Maintenon encouraged for the girls, but she found the little plays written for then by Mme de Brinon rather silly, and asked Racine whether he could find time to write something suitable for them, a request that at first he found rather beneath him. By the time he got to writing *Esther*, a biblical play that really amounted to Versailles in Old Testament garb, Mme de Brinon had quarrelled with her old friend and had been given her marching orders.[7] But the King was delighted with the play, and invited all and sundry to see the production (though what his ministers and the members of the Paris *Parlement* thought of it no one stopped to ask). He insisted that Mme de Maintenon allow them to rehearse Racine's *Athalie* as well, which he had also written for them later.

This seems to have been enough to make Mme de Maintenon change her approach to her school. Instead of seeing it as a finishing school for future ladies, she now transformed it into a freezing penitentiary, with no literature lessons, no new books and a severely restricted cuisine. She completed her little intellectual revolution by appointing the strait-laced Bishop of Chartres as Director. He brought with him six priests as confessors, and interviewed the twenty-four teachers in private, telling them that they were at liberty to leave if they wished, but that if they stayed on they must take perpetual vows instead of simple ones. They had to give up their contacts with the outside world and perform nightly vigils; there was no warmth in winter and when the food ran short they had to give what there was to the girls.

Then the school found itself embroiled in doctrinal controversy. The puritanism of the place was acceptable to figures such as Bossuet and Fénelon, but Mme de Maintenon made the mistake of allowing a Mme de Maisonfort to take up a post, a giddy and brilliantly intellectual woman who found difficulty in adapting herself to the strict regime of the convent. Shortly afterwards, her cousin and in some ways her exact opposite, a Mme Guyon, introduced her own persuasion of Quietism to St Cyr.[8] There was a long and acrimonious tussle between the Jesuits and the Quietists (the Jansenists chuckling at the plight to which the Jesuits had reduced the faith) in the course of which the King roundly denounced any form of religious enthusiasm, packed off Fénelon to the vacant see of Cambrai, and referred the whole question of Quietism to the Pope, who condemned it in 1698. In the meantime, the Bishop of Chartres twice subjected St Cyr to an episcopal visitation, in the course of which he found literary material he deplored and had removed from the college.

The episode tested the patience both of Louis XIV and of Mme de Maintenon. The King did not go near her and she took to her bed. When he learned she was really ill he visited her and with some feeling told her 'this affair is killing you, Madame'. The two were finally reconciled, but things were never the same again. In her last years St Cyr was her refuge, and *Les Dames* her adoring slaves. She outlived Louis XIV, and the Regent Orleans continued her pension of 48,000 livres. When she died in 1719, she was buried in the choir there, and the whole college became her memorial.

THE MARQUISE DE POMPADOUR AND THE DECLINE OF THE FRENCH MONARCHY UNDER THE ANCIEN RÉGIME

Jeanne-Antoinette d'Étioles, Marquise de Pompadour, is famous as the mistress of the French eighteenth-century king, Louis XV. She was actually more than a mistress, of whom Louis XV had a great many, but his 'official mistress' ('maitresse déclarée'), and recognised as such even by the Queen. Her influence was so important that she came to be regarded not only as the royal mistress, but also as 'Mistress of France' with an enormous authority at the French court, treated with reverence and circumspection by French courtiers and aristocrats.

To Pompadour came to be attributed not only a good deal of the excess and extravagance at Versailles, but, more seriously, many of the errors in domestic policy and external affairs that weakened and humiliated the country in the eyes of its subjects and its neighbours. Beliefs such as these are not entirely without foundation, but in a number of ways were an exaggerated version of the true state of affairs in the eighteenth century – the period often referred to as the *ancien régime*. In three respects the received view of the Marquise ought to be modified: that, considering the limitations of her background, she was as often right as she was wrong in her views; that, though she never attained the status of 'prime minister' to the King, as she occasionally claimed, her advice was no worse, and often quite markedly better, than that of the King's official advisers;

and, finally, that the faults and weaknesses of the French political system were endemic and institutional rather than political, and that the King himself must be held finally responsible for his failure to remedy, or even give serious attention to, the public issues it was his duty to resolve.

The focus of all this popular denunciation was born Jeanne-Antoinette Poisson in Paris in December 1721, only six years after the five-year-old Louis had succeeded his great-grandfather, the 'Sun King' Louis XIV, to the French throne.[1] If the Regent, Philippe, Duke of Orleans, had had his way, the young prince would have moved back into Paris and, through his commitment to his people and to business, would have rebuilt the popularity the Regent thought was essential to the future health of the dynasty; but the youthful Louis did not appreciate the Regent's instinctive populism, and when Orleans died in 1723, worn out by his excesses, the King grew increasingly indifferent to his people's needs and wishes, and centred his life on the court at Versailles.

Jeanne-Antoinette's family were middle-of-the-road *bourgeois*, who lived in modest but comfortable circumstances in Paris in the Rue de Cléry. Her mother came from the very respectable la Motte family living at Les Invalides; one of her aunts was a nun, another was married to a fruiterer who supplied the royal household. Her father, François Poisson, was a procurement agent working for the French Army, a rather stolid man, and worked in close conjunction with the four Pâris brothers, all of whom were affluent and worked in the world of finance, banking and army supplies. François was often away from home for protracted periods, and in his absence his wife, a lively and attractive woman, consorted with a succession of rich men (one of whom was even suspected of being Jeanne-Antoinette's father). One of the Pâris brothers, Pâris de Montmartel, an affluent banker and financier, stood as godfather to the infant girl. Another associate of her mother was Charles Lenormand de Tournehem, a tax-farmer and a director of the immensely rich East India Company.[2] Jeanne-Antoinette had a brother, Abel-François, born in 1725; for him she later worked ceaselessly, while she was at court, to secure preferment.[3] In 1726 François, her father, was involved in an embezzlement scandal when another of the Pâris brothers spent some time in the Bastille before he could clear his name; he remained abroad in Germany for ten years as the result of this scandal, leaving his wife in Paris to fend for herself as best she could. She had her little daughter, already strikingly pretty, educated at the Ursuline convent at Poissy, some miles out of Paris, under the eye of two aunts who were nuns there. She stayed there for three years; afterwards, under the protection of '*oncle*' Tournehem, she took singing lessons, lessons in acting and declamation, and learned embroidery, how to play the harpsichord, and how to ride a horse and to drive her own carriage. Finally at nineteen, she was married off in 1741 to Tournehem's nephew, whom he had made his sole heir by a will of 1740, the rather shy and timid Charles-Guillaume Lenormand. He now took the name of 'd'Étioles' after his uncle's estate. The family now thought that Jeanne-Antoinette d'Étioles was ready to launch herself into French court society.

Meantime, Louis XV had fallen thoughtlessly into the routine of hunting and socialising at Versailles. He was a rather listless, dull young man, surrounded by fawning courtiers struggling to entertain him, and vainly seeking diversion from the endlessly boring routine of court ceremonial. As time went by, hunting stags and seducing pretty young women became his chief entertainment. He got through daily business as quickly as he could, content to leave the routine of government to his former tutor, the Cardinal de Fleury, a man of advanced years who nevertheless managed to keep the various departments of government ticking over. Louis hardly ever visited Paris. In 1730 he married a Polish princess, Maria Leczinskaya, who, studiously avoiding comment on his conduct, did her duty by him by producing in due course five children. Even before he met Madame d'Étioles in 1745, Louis had had at least three mistresses already; now he found himself dazzled by the beauty and attracted by the coy cunning of the woman who was to dominate much of his life.

The two met for the first time – officially – in February 1745, when the King gave a spectacular masked party at Versailles to celebrate the marriage of his first son, the Dauphin Louis, to the Infanta Maria Theresa of Spain. He was barely sixteen; she was little more than a child. The King was keen on gardening, and had dressed the dauphin as a gardener, his bride as a flower-seller; he himself, in a group of others, was disguised in papier-mâché branches as a yew tree. By the end of the evening, by the delighted and sustained attention the King bestowed on his young companion, it was obvious they were an item.

Thereafter, Louis was besotted by his vivacious partner. She became virtual queen of the warren of little rooms (*les petits cabinets*) above his own in his wing of Versailles, where, two or three times a week, she presided over select gatherings of ten or a dozen favoured courtiers who squabbled for an invitation to her *petits soupers*. She put on elaborate and costly performances at her little theatre there, in which she always played the leading role, and afterwards the audience danced and gambled at her card-table. She adored the intimacy of such gatherings, at which it was easier to shine, and her royal partner, too, found a chance to escape from the crushing routine of the formal court, and sometimes made his guests coffee instead. Even before she was presented at court, Louis hunted out an appropriate title to give her, and settled finally on the tiny marquisate of Pompadour, an estate in Limousin, whose name she immediately fell for.[4] As Marquise, she was able to indulge her craving for jewellery and other expensive little trinkets, and in particular for pretty new homes, like that at Crécy, near Dreux, or Bellevue, not far from Meudon, which she built, equipped and then tired of and abandoned. The citizenry of Paris felt bitter at the King's thoughtlessness and neglect, but more particularly resentful of the Marquise's ascendancy and the extravagance to which it seemed inevitably to lead. They felt the pinch of rising taxes, while she spent money like water. Members of the court, too, jealous at her ascendancy, added to her discomfort by criticising her bitterly, though not to her face, and regretting their declining influence over the King, while seeing only too clearly that he preferred her to them, brightened visibly when she approached, and obeyed even her slightest whim. Soon, the only way to gain the King's attention was to approach him through her, and this intensified their resentment.

She came first to feel the true extent of her power in the later stages of the War of Austrian Succession, which was fought from 1740 to 1748. Before his death in 1740, the Emperor Charles VI Habsburg had secured the agreement of Europe to the provisions of what was called the Pragmatic Sanction, whereby his daughter Maria Theresa was accepted as heiress to all the Habsburg dominions. He hoped, too, that her husband, Francis Stephen of Lorraine would be elected as Holy Roman Emperor. In fact, both Frederick II of Prussia and Louis XV had reason to be uneasy at this succession: the first had his eye on the province of Silesia, which he invaded and overran at the beginning of the war; the second resented the growth of Austrian influence that would result from Francis' election, and put up a Bavarian Wittelsbach instead. He was duly elected as Emperor Charles VI. The war in Germany did not go well. Successive French commanders were overshadowed by the superior performance on the battlefield of Frederick II.[5] Fortunately, Marshal Saxe, one of the marquise's *protégés*, did better against the Dutch; he captured Brussels in 1746 and overran most of the Netherlands. But she was right over French failures in the war in Germany, and desired to end the struggle. Unfortunately, the treaty of Aix-la-Chapelle in October 1748, concluding the war, proved to be no triumph for French diplomacy, and scarcely worth the treasure that had been spent on the fighting. The French were forced to withdraw from the Austrian Netherlands, the 'barrier fortresses' were granted to the Dutch to help protect them, and though Louisburg was guaranteed to France at the mouth of the St Lawrence, there could be little doubt that the English had not given up in their drive to take over French overseas colonies.

In the 1750s, the story was much the same. While Louis was dithering over a radical proposal to abandon his relationship with fickle Frederick of Prussia and ally himself with Austria, it was the Prussian king himself who broke off his alliance with France and began to negotiate with Britain, whose armies had already taken the offensive in America and India against the French settlements there. Louis XV rather tamely fell into line with his new imperial ally, but in the Seven Years' War that followed did not do well. Though the French army overran Hanover, the French commander, the Duc de Richelieu – whose bungling was just as bad as it had been during his campaigns in Germany in the 1740s – managed to let Cumberland and most of his troops escape beyond the Elbe, while Prussia was successively defeated by the co-operation of the Austrians, the Russians and even the Swedes. Frederick actually saw his capital, Berlin, occupied by the Austrians. In fact, Britain proved to be of little real help to its Prussian allies, concentrating on Canada, the Mississippi valley, French islands in the West Indies and on India in its efforts to mop up the French colonies. Britain even sent a fleet and 8,000 troops to support a threatened rising by French Protestants near the Île de Rhé. France was goaded to retaliate. They toyed with the idea of an invasion of England, imagining that this would redress the military balance, but not only did the English move swiftly against the French invasion transports in Quiberon bay in Brittany, they also went on to smash the main French fleet under Conflans, inflicting losses of ten ships-of-the-line and over 2,000 men. The Marquise looked on with increasing frustration at her country's successive humiliations. It was not until 1763 that peace was made in Paris. France retained Martinique and Guadeloupe in the West Indies, but gave up Canada, the Ohio Valley and Louisiana, India and Senegal; restored Minorca to the British; demolished the fortifications at Dunkirk; evacuated Hanover, Hesse and

Brunswick; and restored the Rhineland possessions of the King of Prussia. Louis was bitterly disappointed in the treaty, and commented: 'The peace we have just made is neither good nor glorious.'

Domestic affairs were almost as bad. Louis was engaged in a long-running struggle with the Paris *Parlement* over royal proposals to remedy the country's financial predicament by imposing a new tax, the *vingtième*,[6] from which he suggested there should be fewer exemptions; but the *Parlement*, claiming much the same kind of constitutional control over taxation as was exercised by Parliament in Britain, stubbornly resisted, and had to be forced into it by successive *lits de justice*.[7] *Parlement's* stubbornness kept the King and the court in penury, and increasingly forced Louis to anticipate taxes by farming out their collection to financiers who paid a lump sum down and then recouped by collecting the taxes themselves through their own agents. The Marquise, who recognised a grasping bourgeois when she saw one, would have none of their claim to be defending the rights of the people; she saw them, quite correctly, as defending their own privileges and those of the nobility whose ranks they aspired to join. She likewise harboured deep suspicions of the French Church. Though she herself, as her physical attractions declined, from time to time sought to reconcile herself with her religious advisers by various strategies such as renouncing the eating of meat (not just during Lent), she objected to many of the Church's privileges and pretensions, and suspected, not without reason, that some religious leaders were in cahoots with the *parlements*. While no Jansenist herself, she was suspicious of the insistence placed by the Archbishop of Paris and the clergy he instructed on religious conformism in insisting that the dying should procure a *billet de confession*[8] before last rites could be given. She likewise sniffed at Church claims to be exempt from taxation, since the *dons gratuits*[9] it contributed to the Exchequer were handsome but in effect just another example of the network of financial immunities from which the upper classes benefited at the time. Finally she was suspicious of popular disaffection among the masses at the time. To Parisian surliness (which she was careful enough to escape simply by avoiding the city itself) she could turn the other cheek, but she knew from her provincial contacts that the country often simmered with disaffection on account of over-taxation and administrative mismanagement by the government, and she struggled to find a way to remedy the problem. Worse still, she strongly suspected that people such as the Prince de Conti, the haughty cousin of the King who was so far above her in the Versailles ranking that he need not disguise his contempt for her, allowed and even fomented resistance to the King's wishes; she suspected him of encouraging, for motives of his own, parliamentary resistance, church pretensions and popular opposition all at the same time. There may have been a grain of justification for her suspicions, but she failed to see that if her suspicions were true the fault lay with the King, since if he were a better and a stronger man he would have dealt with Conti as imperiously as Louis XIV had dealt during his reign with Conti's grandfather.

The fact was that the reason for France's misfortunes at the time was that the country was burdened with a plethora of mediocrities and incompetents, none of whom made much contribution towards halting the country's decline. Cardinal de Fleury was about the best of them, but he died in 1743 at the age of ninety and his successors were a sorry lot. One of the worst was the Duc de Richelieu, who represented the most reprehensible type of the *noblesse*. A brilliant man of fashion, he was thoughtless, frivolous and vicious. Quite apart from his foolish support of the fashionable philosophic movement and his want of sympathy for the classes below him, he lacked also any sense of responsibility or patriotic feelings, and was generally incapable of either personal bravery or military skill, in spite of his high military calling. There was also the Comte de Maurepas, witty, laconic and faintly sinister, who occupied a string of Council appointments; Machault d'Arnouville, who was Finance Minister, Minister for the Navy and Keeper of the Seals in turn; the two d'Argenson brothers, the Marquis and the Comte, who also occupied positions of central importance, the elderly Maréchal de Noailles, who was War Minister and the Marquis de Puysieulx, who succeeded one of the d'Argensons at the Foreign Office. There were also others who were little more than cyphers, like Antoine Rouillé, Jean Moreau de Séchelles and Henri Bertin at the Finance Ministry, none of whom had the talent to contribute much to the country. The best two seemed to be the Abbé Bernis, the short, rosy-cheeked and portly Ambassador to Madrid and later Minister of Foreign Affairs, and Étienne-François de Stainville, later Duc de Choiseul, upon whom the King relied the most heavily as a minister and a diplomatist – and they were both closely linked in sympathy with the Marquise and depended on her patronage. As *Dame du Palais* (Lady-in-Waiting to the Queen) after 1756, her position was highly prestigious, while her sway over Louis was such that it was said of her: 'The Mistress is Prime Minister, and becomes more and more despotic, such as no mistress has never been before in France.'

For Louis seemed to be bored with politics, and spent as little time on it as he could. His normal life at court was weighed down with ceremonial from the first waking moments of his *petite levée* and the *grande levée*, to his final *coucher*, when he allowed his current favourite to carry the royal candlestick. He did not escape this entirely, even when he took up his endless pilgrimages from castle to castle in search of novelty, from Versailles to Fontainebleau, to Choisy, Compiègne, Trianon, Marly and La Muette, and to others for whose upkeep the *Bâtiments* was responsible. He also spent long hours in the field in the forests around Paris, hunting for stags. His evening conversation was taken up with the number of those he had killed during the hunt. As well as the Queen and Pompadour, he also had a whole string of other mistresses at court, fully accepted by Pompadour so long as they did not challenge her supremacy. She actually encouraged his nymphomania by supplying him with 'young birds' who were little more than schoolgirls[10] brought specially from Paris in shuttered sedan chairs for him to deflower at his various residences in and around Versailles. First he groomed them, then he undressed them, then he impregnated them, one after the other. Today, he would have been regarded as a paedophile.

In the meantime, in spite of his title of *Louis le Bien-Aimé* (hardly ever used derisively, even by turbulent Parisians), the King's conduct in office constituted the most damning indictment imaginable of despotic government. What was needed was some sort of constitutional framework, which would have kept a hold on policy. For, to the King, public policy always took second or third place. He took advice as indiscriminately as a chicken pecks up grain, some of it good, some bad. Much of this advice he pursued for a while, and then abandoned, when it began to bore him. He lacked tenacity, and abandoned a policy as soon as difficulties presented themselves. A little persistence would have enabled him to remedy many of France's problems, whether administrative, financial or diplomatic, but he never spent enough time at the job. Generally, the advice he got from Madame Pompadour was more good than bad, because her instincts were sound, even if she did constantly underrate the importance of France's overseas commitments and grow impatient at what she saw as financial restrictions on her spending. But she was not prime minister, and finally, as her health declined,[11] had no wish to be. So the ship of state, with no firm hand on the tiller, drifted from problem to problem until finally, under Louis' grandson and successor, it ran on to the rocks of the Revolution.

JEANNE BÉCU, COMTESSE DU BARRY: DID SHE DESERVE THE HATRED OF THE REVOLUTIONARIES?

The Comtesse du Barry has received a very bad press from most historians. They see her as selfish and greedy, the archetype of the extravagant aristocracy of the ancien régime, *and they have little sympathy for the hysterical woman who went to her death on the guillotine in a state of abject terror. Yet she did have some redeeming features: loyalty, and, surprisingly enough, courage.*

Marie-Jeanette Bécu was born at Vaucouleurs, Lorraine, in April 1743. Her paternity was in some doubt, but her father was reputed to be Jean Baptiste Gourmand de Vaubernier, a local friar. Her mother, Anne Bécu, was renowned for her beauty, and also made a living from her sewing and possibly her cooking. Marie-Jeanette's education at the convent of St Aure was paid for by her mother's long-term lover. At the age of fifteen she moved to Paris, and, adopting the name of Jeanne Rançon, she worked first as a hairdresser, briefly as a lady's companion and later as a milliner's assistant. During this time she had an affair with her first employer, and may have had a daughter by him. Afterwards she became a close friend of the owner of the milliner's shop's daughter who was later to become a famous painter, Adelaide Labille-Guiard. Jeanne's reputation as a great beauty brought her to the notice of Jean du Barry, a noted procurer and pimp who made her his mistress in 1763. Through him she gained access to the upper echelons of Parisian society, and this enabled her to choose men of wealth as her lovers.

Jeanne had not only remarkable good looks; she also had considerable charm, was easygoing and good-natured and had compassion for others less fortunate. It was not surprising that she took Paris by storm and became a favourite of the aristocracy. One of her frequent clients was the Maréchal de Richelieu; but Jean du Barry aimed high and wanted to use Jeanne as a means of gaining influence with the King, Louis XV. She had first met him in 1768 on a visit to Versailles. He was captivated, but she could not become the official royal mistress unless she was a member of the aristocracy. Du Barry therefore arranged a marriage between Jeanne and his brother, Comte Guillaume du Barry, using a false birth certificate which credited her with noble descent and lopped three years off her age. So she was able to be presented at court in April 1769, wearing a gown of the utmost beauty and extravagance, and such was her charm that even the King's three daughters were impressed.

Jeanne did not slip into her new role as official mistress without making enemies. She had no malice towards anyone, but the Duc de Choiseul's sister had tried for several years to take Mme de Pompadour's place as the King's mistress, but to no avail. Now she saw this bastard and upstart newcomer occupying the role that she herself had coveted. The Duc de Choiseul had been the pro-Austrian foreign minister who had pushed the marriage of the dauphin and Marie Antoinette, daughter of the Empress Maria Theresa. Shortly after the marriage in 1770, Choiseul was dismissed from the office. Marie Antoinette believed that Choiseul's dismissal was due to Jeanette's influence. Here she was mistaken, but she never wavered in her hatred of the King's new mistress and what she considered to be her blowsy vulgarity. Certainly Jeanne dipped heavily into France's meagre revenues, bought expensive clothes, and covered herself in diamonds, so that in 1774 the court jewellers were making for her a diamond necklace of the utmost extravagance, and of a style that was so heavily ornamented that Marie Antoinette considered it vulgar.[1]

Early in her role as mistress, Jeanne had demonstrated that she would use her influence for the good of others. She begged, on bended knee, for the lives of two murdering aristocrats to be spared. Louis was so amazed that she was not asking for anything for herself that he granted the rather undeserving murderers their reprieve. Jeanne found the King more pliant than Marie Antoinette, who continued her hostility to Jeanne unabated. Her refusal to speak to Jeanne at court was so persistent and so noticeable that after nearly three years, Jeanne, out of character, lost patience and complained angrily to the King. But his intervention brought no real improvement. Choiseul's and Marie Antoinette's hostility pushed Jeanne into becoming a supporter of the King's new triumvirate of ministers, D'Aiguillon, Maupeou and Terray. So those who opposed the ministers included scandalous attacks on Jeanne in their broadsheets and pamphlets. Unbelievably, Jeanne's circle was, according to these, a 'festering cesspit of promiscuity, adultery, incest and buggery'. These allegations, of course, were far from the truth. Fortunately her critics were unaware of the more damaging fact that Jeanne knew of the King's *secret du roi* by which he conducted his own foreign policy through his own secret agents and unknown to his ministers, who might themselves be pursuing a very different path. Jeanne knew state secrets, and knew how to keep them secret; but she herself made no major impact on policy, apart from her inability to get on with Choiseul.

The reforms of the new ministers, especially Maupeou's tax innovations, might have prevented, or at least slowed down, France's drift towards revolution. But unfortunately

Louis' death in 1774 brought to the throne a new king, Louis XVI, whose wife was Jeanne's enemy. It also brought into office a minister, Maurepas, whose sole concern was for a quiet life. Jeanne had been accused by her enemies of introducing smallpox through a girl Jeanne had provided for the King. He, when he knew death was imminent, ordered Jeanne to remove herself from court in order that he should be free to receive absolution. At first she entered a convent, but in 1776 she moved to her main residence at the Chateau de Louveciennes.

Hated by the new queen, Jeanne did her best to keep out of harm's way. She had few friends, and she kept the entertaining of them down to a minimum. But she did take lovers, the most important of whom was the Duc de Brissac. She also undertook a great deal of charity work. On one occasion she ordered her servants at the chateau to provide a fully pregnant poor woman with soup, wine and linen. She preferred not to discuss her time at court in order not to give needless offence to those who were still there. But as the Revolution approached she shared with Marie Antoinette the dubious distinction of being the most hated woman of the *ancien régime*. In 1792, Jeanne made several trips to England partly to recover some stolen jewellery, but probably also to assist French *émigrés* who had fled to England. Although the Terror had not yet started, the situation in France was dangerous enough for her English friends to plead with her to stay in England for her own safety. Her jewels would have enabled her to lead a comfortable existence in England, and her friends even went so far as to unharness the horses from her carriage. But Jeanne was determined to get back to France and to Louveciennes, where the Duc de Brissac was hiding. Her loyalty to Brissac was to cost her her life.

The Reign of Terror, which had begun in the late spring of 1793, intensified in the autumn. It was only a matter of time before her enemies would seek her out, especially after Brissac was seized and murdered and his bleeding head brought to Jeanne as a warning of what was to come. It was said that she was denounced by her servant, a black boy by the name of Zamore, but her arrest was certain once the Terror gathered pace. Jeanne offered her inquisitors to reveal the whereabouts of her jewellery (most of which, in fact, was in England). But to no avail. In December 1793, Jeanne was condemned by the Revolutionary Court, and, soon after, on 8 December, was bundled into a tumbril to be taken to the guillotine. Jeanne did not show the stiff upper lip of many of the aristocratic ladies who suffered at the block. Her courage failed her, she collapsed several times in the tumbril, and, on reaching the guillotine, screamed in terror. She begged for mercy from the hostile *tricoteuses*,[2] who had no power to grant it anyway. She asked her executioner for a moment more (*'encore un moment'*), which, if conceded, would only have prolonged her suffering. He, however, preferred to dispatch this troublesome woman as quickly as possible. After her death, her jewels were sold at Christie's in London for £8,791 4*s* 9*d*, a sum worth about a million pounds in today's equivalent. Oddly, although Britain and France were now at war, the proceeds were sent to the Revolutionary Tribunal, since Jeanne had no legal heirs to inherit them.

The Comtesse du Barry had shown human frailty at her terrible end, and the revolutionaries for their part, in very poor taste, made much fun of it. Their hatred for her cannot be fully justified. She was personally extravagant at a time when France needed economy, her circle may have encouraged promiscuity but not the blacker peccadilloes, and she had no real influence over affairs of state. She was plainly not the she-wolf that her enemies depicted. Without her they would have found some other target, and the French Revolution would have continued on its course.

PEGGY EATON AND PRESIDENT JACKSON

Margaret (Peggy) O'Neale, originally a Washington innkeeper's daughter, was remarried to Major John Eaton, Secretary of State for War in the Jackson Administration, who was one of the leading politicians of the United States in the 1820s, and she was not so much a mistress as a publicly-recognised hussy. Her unsavoury reputation, and the social slights it provoked, became the starting point of an embarrassing political crisis, and exercised a lasting effect on the later careers of two of her new husband's most ambitious colleagues.

Though only sixteen years old at the time, Peggy O'Neale had already acquired something of a reputation as the attractive, free-and-easy daughter of one of Washington's leading publicans. In 1816, after a whirlwind courtship, she married John B. Timberlake, young, blond and tall, and the not very efficient purser aboard the US frigate *Constitution*. He got himself into trouble with the Navy on account of discrepancies in his accounts, but was assisted by his father-in-law, who lent or gave him money. One of those who stayed at his inn was John Henry Eaton, one of the senators from Tennessee, and he, too, was generous with financial aid. But all this was in vain, for the young officer died aboard ship in 1828. The ship's log gave the cause of death as 'pulmonary disease', but the rumour ran that it was his wife's misconduct with the 'lodger' that had sent him to an early grave.

Senator Eaton, as well as being a close friend of Andrew Jackson, was a member of the influential 'Nashville Junto', who had been planning since 1823 to secure Jackson's election as President. In 1828 they succeeded, and his riotous reception at the White House was something that made polite Washington society run for hiding.[1] Although opponents attacked him as a swaggering frontiersman, an ambitious and ruthless army commander and an illiterate lout, Jackson was a simple man, a loyal supporter of his friends, an unforgiving opponent of his enemies and a chivalrous defender of his wife Rachel and of his other women acquaintances.[2] The new President carried out a purge of the political system, giving hundreds of public appointments to his supporters,[3] and appointed a new cabinet in which John Eaton became the new Secretary of War. Mrs Rachel Jackson ignored the malicious rumours surrounding Peggy, and received her graciously when they met. For appearances' sake, and in order to stifle the boarding-house gossip that was aimed at ruining Eaton, Jackson probably encouraged his old friend to marry her, and he probably also discussed the matter with his wife, but Mrs

Jackson died just before her husband's inauguration (killed, he believed, by the vicious rumours circulated by opponents concerning her allegedly bigamous marriage with him years before) and he was left a grieving widower, believing Peggy Eaton another victim of the same sort of gossip that had ruined his wife.

Feelings over Peggy Eaton were deeply divided from the beginning. Mrs Floride Calhoun, wife of the Vice-President, was a proud Carolinan to whom her flamboyant husband deferred in matters of social etiquette, and she took the lead in snubbing the unfortunate Peggy. The wives of other cabinet members followed suit, determined to give the hussy no countenance. In the White House itself, Emily Donelson, who kept house for her widowed uncle, was cool with her. Only Martin Van Buren, Jackson's Secretary of State (a widower himself) and Charles Vaughan, the British Ambassador (a bachelor) paid Peggy any attention – which was not difficult, since she had considerable wit and beauty. But the invitations to the dinners they laid on in her honour were declined by the other ladies, and at balls she was systematically 'cut' until she began to give up hope of social recognition. The embattled President mulishly dug in his heels. He called a cabinet meeting on the subject, where he pronounced her 'as chaste as a virgin', but the rebellion of the strait-laced ladies continued. Even Mrs Donelson would not call on her, and when Jackson gave her the choice of either doing so or quitting the White House, she quit the White House. The quarrel was not only undermining the stability of the administration, it was making Jackson look a fool.

The breach crystallised the political differences within Jackson's cabinet. Martin Van Buren, the New York political 'Boss', was a suave businessman, an effective operator and one of the first creators of a political machine – the so-called 'Albany Regency' which ran New York State while Van Buren was absent in Washington. Though he enjoyed only limited backing in the federal capital, he was a great survivor, and eventually succeeded Jackson to the presidency in 1836. His opponent, John C. Calhoun from South Carolina, Jackson's Vice-President, on the other hand had much more substantial backing, and was the recognised spokesman of southern interests, a Jeffersonian Democrat and was soon the leader of the southern states' claims to secession from the Union.[4] Jackson thought that such a threat to the union would imperil the whole future of the United States, and stoutly resisted it. Relations between Jackson and Calhoun were further weakened when Calhoun's critics revealed to the President that, far from being his devoted follower at the time of the 1812 war, as he liked to pretend, when Jackson had invaded Florida, Calhoun had actually opposed Jackson's actions. The crunch came in 1829, when Jackson, acting on behalf of the small farmer, declined to support the renewal of the Charter of the Bank of the United States, and embarked on a campaign to undermine and destroy the Bank.[5] But Calhoun kept silent over the issue and refused to give Jackson the support he demanded, a final affront that Jackson was slow to forgive. All this was the real meat of the differences between the two, though apparently the battle was fought over a triviality of social protocol – whether Peggy Eaton was a suitable lady to admit to Washington society.

This particular problem did not get any better. Peggy's critics continued to undermine her social pretensions; Jackson persisted in his belief that attacks on her were intended as slights on his own person. Invitations to dinners, though accepted by his colleagues, were universally declined by their wives, they said, insultingly, on grounds of 'circumstances unnecessary to detail'. The newspapers had caught wind of the scandal, and published cruel cartoons of 'Bellona, the goddess of War' – a thinly disguised reference to Mrs Secretary Eaton – then they backed up their attacks by scathing articles on the Secretary's own fitness for the office he occupied. There was another – utterly trivial – occasion when Mrs Eaton accidentally collided on the dance floor at a state reception with the wife of Maj.-Gen. Alexander Macomb, and had to be restrained from resorting to fisticuffs. Even foreigners found themselves involved. At a ball given by Baron Krudener, the Russian Ambassador, the innocent placing – strictly by rank – of Mrs Eaton next to Madame Huygens, wife of the Dutch Ambassador, at the supper table led to protests and ill-feeling. Jackson took all this very seriously, and began to think there was a petty social conspiracy operating against himself and his whole government.

The whole scandal concerning the social boycott of Mrs Eaton had the effect of moving the President towards attitudes more radical than would have been reached in the normal course of events. Jackson discussed the issue in his 'Kitchen Cabinet',[6] and gradually the influence of Calhoun ebbed away. A plot engineered by Van Buren achieved the resignation of Eaton, together with a handful of others, and this paved the way for Jackson's reorganised cabinet in 1831, in which Van Buren was supreme, and the troublesome Calhoun was shunted sideways into an ambassadorial role as the US minister at the court of St James. Eaton, now out of office, blustered and vainly threatened his former colleagues with violence if they persisted in refusing his challenges to a duel; while his wife was eventually abandoned by Jackson (at Van Buren's insistence) with his conviction that in 'his past anxiety on her account he had at least overrated her own susceptibilities'. With Calhoun now far away in London, there was nothing to stand in the way of the vice-presidential ambitions of Van Buren, in which role he was seen after 1833 as a champion of popular democracy, and a Jackson man, against the entrenched opposition of the older vested interests. In due course he became the presidential candidate for the Democrats at the 1836 election.

LILY LANGTREE

Lillie Langtry won fame both as a renowned actress and as an even more renowned mistress. Whether she deserved her reputation for either is debatable, but there is no denying that in her youth she was a great beauty; it was her beauty that propelled her into her notoriety and fortune.

Emilie Charlotte Le Breton was born in St Saviour's parish church rectory, Jersey, on 13 October 1853. She was the daughter of the Anglican Dean of Jersey, William Corbet

Le Breton, and his wife Emilie Davis. It was convenient for the family to nickname her Lillie, partly to avoid confusion with her mother, and partly on account of her considerable natural beauty which she had inherited from her mother. Lillie was the sixth of her parents' seven children, and their only daughter. She enjoyed a happy childhood, and, as the only girl among so many boys, a rather boisterous one. Although her father sent the boys to the local Victoria College, Lillie, as was fitting for a girl, was educated at home. But it was no second-rate education. She shared her brothers' tutors, learning Latin, Greek, French and Mathematics, supplemented with art and music, an education that would have been envied by most contemporary girls of similar background.

In her teens Lillie found herself deputising for her mother at official functions because of her mother's intermittent ill-health, and this enabled her to gain valuable experience in public speaking and social graces. When she was just fourteen she attracted the attention of one of the sons of the Archbishop of Canterbury, who hastily retreated when he realised how young this beautiful and mature-looking girl was. Her first attempt to enter London society, at the age of sixteen and chaperoned by her mother, was not a success. Lillie felt gauche and out of her depth. For the next few years Lillie confined herself to broadening her knowledge of literature and busying herself in the social activities of the parish.

In 1873, when Lillie was twenty, she attended the wedding of her brother William. Here she met Edward Langtry, the recently widowed husband of William's bride's sister-in-law. Whether she found him or his luxury yacht more attractive it is difficult to judge, but within a few weeks of meeting Edward she married him. Finding Jersey's social whirl too restrictive, the couple moved to London, but at first they were not welcomed in high society and Edward missed his yachting. In 1877 Lillie arrived late for her younger brother's funeral in Jersey, but wore a simple black dress as mourning attire when she returned to London. Her disappointing social life might have continued had it not been for a chance meeting with an acquaintance from Jersey who secured her an invitation to a social gathering at Lady Sebright's residence. Lillie felt very out of place in her simple black dress and tried to retreat from the gathering by lurking in a corner. She was noticed there by John Millais who heard that Lillie was from Jersey where he himself had spent much of his early life. He had been for many years a painter with a formidable national reputation. He asked Lillie to sit for him, and later that evening another artist, Frank Miles, drew several sketches of her. His sketches were soon put on sale in London, photographers clamoured to take her picture, and she gained instant fame as a ravishing beauty. Society, which had previously ignored her, welcomed her with open arms. Invitations to social gatherings and events poured in. When the Millais painting was ready to display in the Royal Academy it had to be roped off from crowds desperate to see it. He entitled the portrait 'A Jersey Lily' and thus gave Lillie the nickname she was to retain for the rest of her life, even though the lily she is shown holding in the painting is actually from Guernsey.

There were no society functions, apart from royal ones, from which Lillie was now excluded. Shortly after her triumphant entry into society she was invited to a dinner party given by Sir Allen Young and there she met Edward (Bertie), Prince of Wales.

He sat next to her, and despite her initial awkwardness he was greatly impressed by her. They began to ride together in Hyde Park, and people soon came to the conclusion that Lillie had become his mistress. For poor Princess Alexandra, Bertie's long-suffering wife, the Prince's philanderings were nothing new, and, like Lillie's husband, Alexandra resignedly accepted it; she even became Lillie's friend and showed her kindness when the rest of society might have rushed to judgement. Bertie lavished money on a new hideaway for them both at Bournemouth, and Lillie was introduced to his mother, Queen Victoria. The Queen's reception of her was anything but fulsome, but after the introduction no doors were barred to her and she became a regular guest at Buckingham Palace receptions. It was now that she became acquainted with Oscar Wilde, the famous playwright and socialite.

Such was Bertie's reputation that it seemed unlikely that the affair would last long, even though he was at first besotted. It continued through the rest of 1877 and throughout 1878, but in June 1879 Sarah Bernhardt arrived in London.[1] Fickle Bertie soon transferred his affection to the newcomer, but Lillie had already begun an affair with the Earl of Shrewsbury and Edward Langtry was threatening divorce, citing Bertie as co-respondent. The threat came to nothing, but Bertie and Lillie were no longer inseparable companions, even though Bertie always retained some affection for her. The end of the royal connection brought financial problems for the Langtrys. Lillie had abandoned the little black dress and had begun to indulge in a sumptuous wardrobe to show off her beauty, and an extravagant lifestyle to accompany her new social status. This the Langtrys could ill afford, and only the arrival of the bailiffs in October 1880 and the removal of much of Lillie's furniture staved off official bankruptcy.

The year 1880 added to Lillie's discomfort when her father's behaviour led to his losing his post as Dean of Jersey and being demoted to a vicarage in London. Lillie's response was to develop an affair with Bertie's cousin, the young Prince Louis of Battenberg and to get herself pregnant by another lover, Arthur Clarence Jones. Prince Louis was sent to sea by his horrified parents, while Lillie went to Paris with Arthur and there gave birth to a baby girl, Jeanne Marie. For many years it was widely believed that the child was Prince Louis', even by the Battenberg family.[2] But there seems little doubt now that she was Arthur's.

Lillie did not let childbirth interrupt her busy life for long. She forsook Paris, left Jeanne Marie with her mother in Bournemouth and headed back to London, virtually penniless. Oscar Wilde suggested she try acting, and in December 1881 she took to the stage in Goldsmith's *She Stoops to Conquer*. At first she was very nervous and got mixed reviews, but she soon gained in confidence and skill, and attracted adoring audiences. To mitigate the social stigma attached to acting she became a friend of the Prime Minister, William Ewart Gladstone, who was always prepared to forgive women in the less respectable professions. Within a few months she was in a position to embark on an acting tour of the USA, and was a huge success with American audiences, even if critics panned some of her performances. Box office receipts broke records; so did her salary. Despite her lack of experience she took on Shakespearean roles; she was greatly in demand and toured the USA in five successive years.

She soon was introduced to the American millionaire, Freddie Gebhard, and she became his mistress in 1882, a liaison that was to last nine years. He bought her a house in New York and a personal railway carriage costing $1 million. She bought herself a Californian vineyard and took up horse racing, purchasing several horses. Through this interest she met George Alexander Baird, a Scottish amateur jockey and boxer. He, too, was a millionaire, but he also had a vicious temper. The black eye he gave Lillie was so vicious that she was hospitalised for ten days, and he only won her back by giving her a 200-foot yacht. Needless to say, the American press delighted in giving its own name of *Black Eye* to the new yacht.

Baird died in 1893, and Lillie's acting career continued to prosper. In 1897 she became an American citizen and divorced Edward, who died following an accident a few months later.[3] She was now free to remarry and in 1899 she became the wife of Hugo Gerald de Bathe, an important racehorse owner and heir to a baronetcy. There was a large age difference: he was the younger by nineteen years, and after buying a property in Jersey in which to embark on married life the youthful Hugo insisted on enlisting in the British army to fight in the Boer War. Lillie decided to resume her acting career in London and after this, although they remained married for the rest of Lillie's life, they met only for social occasions. Lillie's constant companion in her final years was her butler's widow, Mathilde Peat, and she very rarely saw her own daughter. Lillie had alienated her by concealing from Jeanne Marie the truth about her parentage, and Jeanne Marie was allowed to believe that Lillie was her aunt, not her mother. When she found out the truth she felt badly let down and humiliated, and broke off all connection with Lillie.

Lillie's renewed success in the new century enabled her to play a vital part in the early days of commercial advertising, and she could be seen on posters giving her approval to soaps, perfumes and other products, a form of early celebrity endorsement. But she gave up acting in 1906, made her debut in vaudeville and appeared in one of the very early films. She became an inveterate gambler, frequently visiting Monte Carlo, and had the distinction in 1907 of being the first woman to break the bank there. On the death of her father-in-law in that year she became Lady de Bathe. Soon afterwards she took up her main residence in Monte Carlo while her husband lived at Nice, no great distance away. Such was her wealth that she was able to subsidise her husband, even though he had considerable means of his own.

As the years went by her beauty was transformed into maturity, and maturity gave way to signs of old age. In 1929, when she was seventy-five, she developed bronchitis, and this led to pleurisy. She lay ill for weeks, and then caught influenza. It was too much for her weakened body and she died on 12 February 1929. She was returned to Jersey for burial in accordance with her wishes, and her husband neither attended the funeral, nor sent flowers.

It is difficult to say whether Lillie was a great actress. She was certainly a popular one. She received the adulation that today is reserved for superstars, and was probably the first actress who could not go out of doors without being mobbed. Her accomplishments as a mistress are even more difficult to judge, but she certainly was an experienced one, and probably one of the very few to have flouted social convention so successfully and with such impunity.

EVA BRAUN:
THE FÜHRER'S DARLING

Eva Braun (1912–1945) was the long-time companion and later, briefly, wife of Adolf Hitler, Führer of Nazi Germany at the time of the Second World War. Part of his household at the Berghof near Berchtesgaden, she lived a sheltered and privileged life, a private person almost unknown to the general public until well into 1944, always keeping well out of politics and exercising no discernable influence on the leader's character or decisions. As the Third Reich crumbled towards the end of the war, she swore her undying loyalty to Hitler and went to be by his side in the Führerbunker under the ruined Reich Chancellery in Berlin. Here she died with him at the end of April 1945 at the age of only thirty-three.

Eva Anna Paula Braun was born in Munich in February 1912, second daughter of schoolteacher Friedrich Braun and his wife Franziska (Fanny) Braun, both coming from respectable middle-class Catholic families. Her elder sister Ilse was born in 1909; her younger sister Marguerite (or Gretl) in 1915. The three girls went to the local lycée, and then Eva went on to business school in a nearby convent, after which she worked briefly as a medical receptionist before becoming become a lab assistant and a photographer's model for Heinrich Hoffmann, official photographer for the Nazi Party, whose headquarters at that time were in Munich. It was here in 1929 that she first met Hitler, twenty-three years her senior. He was introduced to her under his security name 'Herr Wolff' (a childhood nickname he liked to use when he felt important enough to claim anonymity); she later described him as 'a gentleman of a certain age with a funny moustache, a light-coloured English overcoat and carrying a big felt hat'.

At first the two saw little of each other. At first Hitler appears to have been attached to the daughter of his half-sister Angela, a young woman called Geri Raubal, but she committed suicide – it was rumoured because she was jealous of Eva, though this seems unlikely, since Eva had hardly heard of her. Another early attachment of Hitler, the actress Renate Müller, also died in mysterious circumstances, and suicide was mentioned here as well. Gradually, however, Eva and Hitler became better acquainted, even though her family was much against her liaison with an older man – and one dabbling in dubious fringe politics. But Hitler seems to have had a curious effect on the women he knew, for on two occasions, in 1932 and 1935, Eva, too, attempted to kill herself, on the first occasion by shooting herself in the chest with her father's revolver, and on the second by an overdose of sleeping tablets. Steadily the pair grew more intimate. It is difficult to see exactly what Eva saw in Hitler to attract her: his treatment of her was never very close, at best a sort of distant paternalism where he might pat her hand and exchange pleasantries with her. He gave her small gifts, and as a gesture of his supposed fondness for her, he arranged for the royalties from his widely published photographs at the Hoffmann studios to be paid to her. This helped towards her purchase of a house in Munich, and eventually was enough to cover the provision for her of a Mercedes, a chauffeur and a maid. Her younger sister Gretl moved in with her to counter any scandalous gossip that might result from the relationship.

Hitler's attitude towards women always seems to have been psychologically flawed. He grew more vain as he got older, but took care to keep at arms' length from any particular woman in case intimacy somehow impaired his popularity with German women in general – an attitude which caused some of the more sniggering of observers to impugn his underlying manhood. Perhaps in some emotional or perhaps physical way he was incapable of showing affection, perhaps even of feeling it, so that throughout his life he always veered away from personal intimacy. He remained sharply focused only on political matters. Nevertheless, observers noted that when Eva was present, Hitler was always more relaxed than on other occasions. By 1936 Eva was an integral part of Hitler's household. She was at Berchtesgaden whenever he visited, and her parents, though still entertaining doubts, were invited to dinner there a number of times. In 1938, Hitler nominated Eva in his will for a substantial income on his death; he also from time to time gave her tokens of his regard by giving her jewellery. It was always a one-sided relationship; she clearly was much more devoted to him than he was to her. His attitudes towards her were conventional: he was never less than gallant, as he felt a man ought to be towards a woman, but nevertheless he treated her as an inferior – as he felt women should be treated.

Eva remained, however, curiously unpolitical in surroundings that were always intensely devoted to politics. She never joined the Nazi party, and there is no reason to suppose she ever wanted to. She never took part in political discussions, and Hitler habitually banished her from the room whenever political matters were under discussion.[1] Her only known intervention in politics came in 1943, when Hitler, as part of a drive towards a 'total war economy' threatened to impose a ban on the manufacture and use of women's cosmetics (which he disapproved of in any case); Eva is said to have approached him in 'high indignation' to register her protest – and in fact he relented and substituted a cessation of production for an outright public ban. Otherwise she led a sheltered and privileged existence away from the hurly-burly of government. She spent much of her time reading cheap novelettes, watching romantic films, exercising, and swimming. She was also fond of nude sunbathing, and in spite of Hitler's disapproval liked to be photographed doing it. She had a lifelong interest in photography and had her own dark room, where she processed the snaps she took herself. Besides this, she liked to keep herself smart and so concerned herself a good deal with her hair, her dresses and her personal appearance. She was always tastefully dressed, well made-up, and wore valuable jewellery – but she was not allowed to change her hair style. Once when she tinted it differently and piled it up on top of her head, she was ordered to change it back immediately by a horrified Hitler (he had at least noticed). Eva was fond of her two Scottie terriers, Negus and Stasi, which she took for regular walks (she also was careful to keep them well out of reach of Hitler's German shepherd, Blondi). To the outside observer hers seemed a pampered but pretty useless existence. She was never a sex toy: Hitler treated her as something halfway between a daughter and a domestic. When Hitler was too busy to pay her attention, as he often was, she 'would often be in tears', but he did not seem to notice.

In June 1944, Eva's younger sister Gretl married Hermann Fegelein, Himmler's liaison officer on Hitler's staff.[2] It was only from this time that he began to allow Eva to be present at official functions. This was the first time that many Germans got to see her or to know anything about her. After he survived the bomb plot of July 1944 Eva wrote him a loving letter, saying: 'From our first meeting I swore to follow you anywhere, even unto death, I live only for your love.'

Early in April 1945, Eva motored from Munich to Berlin to be at her husband's side. By this time the Russians were in the eastern suburbs of the German capital, and the writing was on the wall for all Germans to see. Hitler divided his time between making grandiose plans for a counter-attack to fend off the enemy with troops that existed only in his imagination, and futile recriminations with his staff for their real and imagined shortcomings. The few professional soldiers about him, fearing his explosive temper, dared to say nothing, though in private they were disgusted with his petulant behaviour. He ordered Eva to leave and to save herself; she made it quite clear that she was not going to go, and that she intended to share his fate. She was one of the few who remained loyal to him to the end. 'Better that ten thousand others should die than he be lost to Germany,' she said. Finally, on 29 April Hitler and Eva were married (though Hitler was not a well man and it is extremely doubtful whether the marriage was ever consummated). The next afternoon she committed suicide by biting on a cyanide capsule, minutes before Hitler took his own life. On his orders both bodies were taken up into the open air, doused in petrol and burned in the garden of the Reich Chancellery, where the charred bodies were discovered by the advancing Soviet armies in the following days, together with the corpses of the members of the Goebbels family.

The remainder of Eva's family survived the war. Her mother, Franziska, who still lived in Bavaria, died at the age of ninety-six at her farmhouse in 1976.

CLARA PETACCI:
HER LIFE AND DEATH
AS MUSSOLINI'S MISTRESS

Like Eva Braun, Clara Petacci fell under the spell of one of the Great Dictators on the European stage at the time of the Second World War. Like Eva Braun, too, she shared the dictator's life, and chose also to share his death. As a wayward daughter of the Church, she chose a brief career of parasitic pre-eminence during thirteen years of her lifetime, followed by a dismal death at the hands of communist partisans. As a result, she earned while alive the contempt of the Italian nation, and afterwards in her death its quite unmerited vengeance.

Twenty years younger than Mussolini, Clara (or its diminutive 'Claretta') Petacci was born of a well-heeled Roman family in February 1912. Her father was a physician – at one time personal physician to the Pope. She had a younger sister, Miriam (1923–1991), who became an actress and a film-star, and a brother, Marcello, an egoist and a self-proclaimed follower of Mussolini, who was captured along with her near Lake Como, and shot at Dongo in 1944 while trying to escape.

Clara first met Mussolini on the road to Ostia in 1932, some years after he had become *Duce* and Fascist dictator of Italy. She was in a car as he was driven past; she turned and waved to him, shouting '*Duce! Duce!*' She was a very pretty girl, with green eyes, long straight legs, a full bosom (which Mussolini liked), a husky voice and curly hair. She took great pride in her personal appearance, and yet her clothes were always a bit fussy. She was generous, hysterical, vain, obsessively sentimental and fundamentally stupid. Mussolini, as well as a good Catholic wife Rachele, had had a string of mistresses already, including one Ida Dalser, a strange neurotic woman by whom he had had a mentally retarded son called, like himself, Benito, and who never ceased to pester him for recognition and support; and Magda Corabœuf, a rather loud actress whose stage name was Fontanges, who reacted violently when she was rejected, tried to poison herself and then made up for her failure by shooting the French Ambassador to Rome and nearly killing him. Clara, however, seemed to be more successful and durable than the others. Even Rachele seemed to imagine she might supplant her as a permanent fixture in the household. She knew how to resort to real and imaginary ailments as a method of bringing his attention back to her when he strayed. Once, when she contracted peritonitis after a miscarriage she did nearly die, and Mussolini impressed even her parents by the regularity of his visits; he even insisted on being present in the theatre while they operated on her. Usually she went to visit him at the Palazzo Venezia, his official residence in Rome, entering by a side door and going straight up to a flat on the upper floor where he often nipped up between interviews for a spot of fornication. Like many other womanisers he was never too busy to spare a moment for the ladies, but, unlike them, he never allowed himself to be dominated by them.

Mussolini brought Italy into the Second World War with great éclat in the summer of 1940. But although his own performance as leader left little to be desired, that of Fascist troops in Greece and North Africa was little better than it had been in his earlier campaigns against the ill-armed Abyssinians, and soon his troops were falling back on all fronts. By the autumn of 1942 his reputation was dwindling. He seemed to be physically shrinking. His cheeks were sunken, his eyes hollow, his neck suddenly scrawny – he was rapidly losing the embonpoint that had earlier distinguished him. His daily cold bath before breakfast, his sudden breaks for riding, swimming, or violent games of tennis, were things of the past – the only exercise he now took was a gentle scything of the long grass in the grounds of his villa. He still kept the light in his study burning until late into the night, but this was only to generate an impression of industry to those passing his curtained window. To one of his ministers, Giuseppe Bottai, he confessed to being unable to face his adoring public any more, admitting that he spent a 'solitary life at the Palazzo Venezia wrestling with my problems and deciding them all by myself'. It might have been better, Bottai later remarked, if he had been by himself, but most of the time in fact he was wrestling with Clara Petacci.

But in fact, as Clara could have told him, the progress of their relationship was also severely under challenge. By early 1943 his visits to her became fewer and more perfunctory; for hours she lay alone on a divan bed in the sitting room of the upstairs flat waiting for him, designing new clothes, painting, playing sentimental songs on the gramophone and reading love stories. But when he arrived he was often depressed, irritable, and sometimes angry; many times he did not come at all. He talked constantly about betrayal. Clara felt sure he had found another mistress and was doing the betraying himself. She even took to writing him plaintive letters. Her brother's mistress, Zita Ritossa, suggested the remedy might be to make herself less available instead of being always to hand when he wanted her. Clara replied pathetically: 'But if I did that, he wouldn't bother about me at all!' Indeed, he did try to shut her out. One day, an embarrassed policeman at the Palazzo Venezia told her he had orders not to let her in. She swept past him and sought out Mussolini to confront him. He looked at her icily, and said: 'I consider the cycle closed.' But he relented and took her back almost immediately: 'The war is going badly,' he explained, 'and the people might criticise me for my weakness.' All the same, he still snapped at her frequently, he taunted her, he quarrelled with her, he criticised her family, her brother's disreputable financial speculations, her calculating, hook-nosed mother's idle boasting and promises of patronage. Once he struck Clara so hard during a quarrel that she hit her head on the wall and had to be revived with an injection.

But it was true that their relationship was leading to a major scandal. Count Ciano, the Foreign Minister and Mussolini's son-in-law, agreed with a senior policeman, Angelo Carica, who asserted that his affair with Petacci 'was doing the Duce much more harm than losing fifteen battles'. Their family, he said, 'meddles in everything, grants political protection, threatens from above and intrigues from below'. Clara, perhaps unjustifiably, got much of the blame for this. In fact it was her brother, Marcello, who was chiefly to blame.[1] But in the end it was Mussolini himself who suffered. Senior figures in the Fascist Party warned Ciano of the rising tide of dissatisfaction with Mussolini's leadership and threats to replace him with another party figure; the only trouble was that no one dare face him and tell him so. He was always told how well the war was going: armament production figures were inflated, slight military gains turned into major achievements, reverses either minimised or suppressed altogether. The Duce was so pathetically pleased to hear good tidings that they were fabricated just to keep on the right side of him. But all the time the murmurings continued.

When the Allies invaded Sicily in June 1943 and Rome was subjected to it first serious air raids, he made an appeal to Hitler at a specially convened summit meeting at Klessheim near Munich on 19 July to allow him to make a separate peace with the invading Allies. But Hitler did not even pretend to listen to him. In Rome the group of Fascists who were critical of his leadership gave him a further body-blow by summoning a meeting of the Fascist Grand Council, which, after a seven-hour meeting, carried a resolution of no confidence in him, a verdict which Mussolini quietly accepted. The following morning, 25 July, the King informed Mussolini that he accepted the decision of the Grand Council and had appointed Marshal Badoglio in his place as Head of Government. As Mussolini left the royal villa he was placed under arrest. He was removed to an inaccessible ski resort high in the Appenines with strict orders as to his detention, but in early September, in a brilliant commando operation, Col. Skorzeny and a handful of soldiers landed a small plane there and rescued him, so that he was now effectively the prisoner of the Germans rather than of his own countrymen. Under their direction he set up the short-lived Salò Republic in Northern Italy.[2] From here he issued the Verona Manifesto, promising genuinely democratic reforms in the Fascist system, and blaming the conspiracy against him for all Italy's troubles. But it was a whitewash. In his purge of the administration he allowed the indictment of five senior Fascists[3] for their alleged misdeeds, and on their conviction stood by and let them be shot. But by this time even he recognised that he was no more than the cat's paw of the occupying Germans. With the rapid Allied advance northwards, even this hollow bubble of power was pricked: the Salò Republic collapsed, and Mussolini was once again on the run.

Mussolini's only consolation was that now at last Clara had been restored to him, even though the motives of the German officials who arranged this were less disinterested than he thought.[4] His own family had failed to give him the support he needed: his wife Rachele found not only his fall from political grace unendurable, but still burned with jealousy over his affair with Clara; his children gave him little or no support (apart from Vittorio, and he proved quite unsuitable for the political role Mussolini assigned him); only his more distant family were in touch with him, and then only because they wanted small gifts and favours from him. By April 1945 he was virtually on the run, a shadow of his former self (he had lost over twenty kilograms and was by now quite gaunt). But his courage did not fail him. He rejected the suggestions that he flee,[5] and determined to make a last stand in the Valtellina; he might be finished, but Fascism, he believed, would live on. So he headed for Milan en route for the mountains and the lakes. On 23 April he learned that Mantua had fallen to the advancing Americans, and that Brescia was threatened. He phoned his family and advised them to make good their own escape; he gave the same advice to Clara, but she refused to leave his side, but stayed with him. Two days later he and his small party left Milan without knowing exactly where they were going, he in the uniform of the Fascist Militia and with a machine-gun across his knee in an open Alpha-Romeo, Clara in another Alpha-Romeo just behind, in a procession of about thirty cars and lorries.

The party arrived in Como by about ten o'clock that evening. By now Milan was in the hands of the partisans; the Americans were only a few miles away, and the Germans had evacuated. He did not stay long. The next morning he was off again heading northwards towards Menaggio; from here he moved off the lakeside road and headed for the little village of Grandola, only fourteen kilometres from the Swiss frontier (where many in the Italian party imagined he was headed). Then he was moved by his escort twice again, finishing in Count Bellini's villa at Blevio. Clara, left behind in the headlong flight, finished in Dongo, locked up in the Town Hall, in the hands of the Count. From here he allowed her to go to rejoin Mussolini. Finally the couple, the partisans by now hot on their heels, took refuge in a farmhouse well off the road, where the farmer's wife turned her two sons out of their double bed and let Mussolini and Clara sleep in it. It was in the early hours of the following morning, 28 April, that they were roused by partisans, told to get dressed,[6] bundled into a car, taken back down to the village and there confronted by the partisans and their weapons. A few words, possibly of condemnation, were mumbled. Then a machine-gun jammed; a pistol was drawn, Clara screaming all the while that they should not do it, and this jammed as well; finally another machine-gun was produced, and this fired. Clara died first, shot in the head; Mussolini followed, the first shot wounding him, the second finishing him off. The bodies were loaded on to a removal van and carried off back to Milan.

On the morning of 29 April, the van stopped at a half-built petrol station at the Piazzale Loreto, Milan, and the four bodies were strung up by their legs to the girders of the roof of the forecourt. Mussolini's face was badly disfigured by the crowd's kicks at his head; Clara's skirt fell back, revealing her nakedness underneath. The crowd jeered as a woman in the crowd took pity on her, pulled her skirt into position and tucked it between her tightly-bound legs. The bodies were left for some days before they were cut down and taken away for final burial.

Clara's last wish had been granted: she had died, as she had lived, alongside her lover and sharing his final fate. His wife Rachele and her children survived into the postwar world, to see the communists fail in their efforts to seize power in Italy; his lover Clara, with his other lovers, passed into oblivion.

PART 6

WIVES

ANNE HATHAWAY: WIFE OF WILLIAM SHAKESPEARE

It is sometimes imagined that there could be no happier fate than to be married to the greatest playwright and poet the English language has ever produced. But such a judgement is hasty, as a number of writers, such as Hubert Osborne, Edward Bond and others in their plays and James Joyce in Ulysses, *have already pointed out. Anne Hathaway, Shakespeare's wife, is sometimes depicted as a shrew, sometimes as a martyr; the truth is that she was simply a very unhappy woman.*

Anne Hathaway was born in 1556 and grew up in the little village of Shottery, near Stratford-upon-Avon, the daughter of a yeoman farmer called Richard Hathaway. The house she lived in still exists today, and is the goal of many modern tourists to the area: a substantial thatched building with a stout timber framework and a solid earthen floor. When her father died in 1581 he left his daughter a tolerable sum, £6 13s 4d, to be paid as a dowry on the day of her marriage. Anne married Will Shakespeare the following year. He was eight years younger than she was; the fact that she was already pregnant has led some students to conclude that this was a shotgun wedding forced on the couple by indignant relatives.

This is not the case. A difference in their ages is not a reason to suppose anything was amiss in the relationship between two affianced persons in the mid-sixteenth century. At the time it was in fact not unusual for orphaned girls to have to stay at home to take care of the remaining members of the family when the father died, so that girls were often married in their late twenties, quite often to somewhat younger eligible men. Besides, it was not then (any more than now) unusual for brides to be pregnant at the time they wed. There may have been some family pressure for the two to marry, for fear the girl should be shamed by producing a baby out of wedlock, but the mere fact that Will had got her pregnant is not alone evidence of any long-term commitment on his part towards marriage. The suggestion that about the same time he had been involved with another girl is probably untrue, and may have arisen solely from a clerical error, since, at about the same time, a document from the Worcester Episcopal Register shows an application from a 'Wm Shaxpere' to marry one 'Anna Whately' of 'Temple Grafton'; but the recording clerk seems to have misheard or misspelt the name, because on the following day a surety was signed for £40 guaranteeing the wedding of 'William Shakespere and Anne Hathwey'. The respective families may well have known one another, and expected the couple to marry, but nothing survives to suggest unwillingness on the bridegroom's part.

The children who followed from the match were born soon after: Susanna was born in 1583, and the twins Hamnet and Judith in 1585. Again there is no real indication of any rift between the couple, and no evidence or correspondence to support it; indeed, three children in less than three years tends towards the opposite conclusion. But, towards the end of the 1580s, Will left Stratford to seek his fortune in London, after a brief spell which he spent as an actor working with small companies resident with a number of local recusant families. However, evidence of strong Catholic sympathies is difficult to detect in his work, when he eventually began writing in London around 1588. His sketchy education – his 'little Latin and less Greek', probably acquired at Stratford Grammar School – did not seem to tell significantly against him, and quite a number of his acquaintances in London had minor aristocratic connections (a few, such as Henry Wriothesley, Earl of Southampton, were quite eminent). He spent much of his London acting career after 1594 with the Lord Chamberlain's company, which became at James I's accession in 1603 the King's Company, and he also acquired interests in two other theatres, the Globe in 1599 and Blackfriars in 1609. But he was certainly very busy. He did not have much time or money for the long and difficult journey back from the capital to Stratford, and this caused some distress and unhappiness to his wife Anne; but when he retired from the theatre in 1613 he came back to live in the house he had bought for himself in 1597 as a token of his worldly success, New Place, a substantial residence close to the centre of the town (subsequently demolished, though its garden still exists). Here he embarked on the considerable task of revising and editing his dramatic work for later publication, before dying in 1616.

Anne, struggling with a young family and left alone in a small provincial town, experienced the consequences of isolation and poverty in her everyday life, and was obliged to endure the intolerance and the spiteful gossip of small-minded neighbours. She was not, however, completely poverty-stricken; indeed there are indications that she was financially solvent, if not completely secure in her income. She did have a house to live in, and her daughter Susanna, when she grew up, secured for herself a financially sound husband. But such security – if she regarded it as such – was little consolation for being alone, lacking the guidance and the practical help of a husband in the house. She could not turn to him to salt a ham, or knock a nail in; he would probably not have been much good at it if she had. By the time Will retired and came home he was forty-nine, a comparatively old man for his years, and she, at fifty-seven, was already in need of help and support from her children. There had been many years in which she had needed his help, but he was absent; even when he was there his head was always full of his stage business and professional matters relating to the theatre, and the help he could find time for was necessarily limited in time and deficient in skill.

But there is nothing in surviving letters or other documents to suggest that their relations during his retirement were strained. The children by now had grown up and moved away, and were looking forward to their own lives. Though not an old man, Will died on his birthday[1] in 1616, still only in his early fifties.

Much has been made out of the fact that Shakespeare in his will left Anne only his 'second-best bed'. It seems likely, however, that this does not betoken any lack of warmth in their married relationship. The UK National Archives, in which the original will is lodged, have stated that 'beds and other pieces of household furniture were often the sole bequest to a wife', since customarily the children would be bequeathed the best pieces and the widow only the second-best. Certainly, in Tudor times, the 'best bed' was habitually reserved for guests, so that the second-best bed would have been the marital bed, and the one he gave her. It may well have been, too, that a condition of the marriage of Susanna, Shakespeare's eldest child, when she married her comfortably-off husband, was that she should inherit the bulk of her father's estate.[2] Since Anne was meant to live with her married daughter for the rest of her life, this did not signify a marked degree of meanness on the part of Will towards his wife.

History has been a little unkind towards Anne. James Joyce in *Ulysses* sees her as adulterous in her conduct, and speculates that the 'second-best bed' was a punishment for her adultery. She also appears in Hubert Osborne's *Shakespeare Play* (1911) and its sequel *The Good Men Do* (1917), where she is shown as spiteful and shrewish. The US dramatist and actress Yvonne Hudson takes the opposite, and probably the more truthful position. In her *Mrs Shakespeare, Will's First and Last Love* (1989), she sees Will as continuing fundamentally loyal to his wife in spite of long periods of separation; she even uses his sonnets as supporting evidence for her view, and allows her to have a country wife's respect for her educated husband's work and career far off in the capital. Germaine Greer's more historical approach to the subject, *Shakespeare's Wife* (2007), gives a measured and documented treatment of her life, re-evaluating some of the legends that have accumulated about their marriage and their subsequent lives.

In her later years, Anne may well have been feeble and dependent on the affection and support of her two daughters. At the age of sixty-seven, she died, as she had lived throughout her life, in Stratford in 1623. There is no extant documentary evidence that relates to her views or her beliefs; she led a subdued and almost a mute life, and there is no reason to suppose that the unsympathetic opinions that were held by her critics of her actions and attitudes were true or accurate ones.

ELIZABETH PEPYS: DUTIFUL WIFE OR UNGRATEFUL REBEL?

Samuel Pepys, the great seventeenth-century diarist, was renowned in his day both for his work as a civil servant and for his proclivity as a philanderer. There is no doubt that he married for love, but he tended also to love other women. Elizabeth, his wife, took Pepys as a husband, not so much out of love, but out of the need to make a successful marriage as the only worthwhile career for a woman of the age. But she felt, certainly early on, that she had married beneath her, and showed her discontent by leaving him. Later, as Pepys' career progressed, their marriage became less turbulent, but never smooth, while Pepys tried to do the juggling act of continuing to please his wife and continuing to please himself.

Elizabeth was born on 23 October 1640, possibly in Bideford, Devon, although her husband Samuel was later to record her birth as having taken place in Somerset. Her father, Alexandre le Marchant de St Michel, was of the minor French nobility, with which France was overgenerously endowed at this time. His noble ancestry provided him with lands and money, which he lost by converting from Catholicism to Protestantism, and by fighting as an adventurer during the Thirty Years' War. Her mother, Dorothea, was the daughter of a baronet and the widow of a gentleman of Cork in Ireland. Cromwell's invasion of Ireland led to the escape of the St Michel family to mainland Europe, and by 1652 Dorothea had abandoned her husband and was living alone in Paris with her children. Presumably finding life with limited resources difficult, Dorothea placed her children into the safe keeping of Catholic friends who promptly consigned Elizabeth to an Ursuline convent. This was not to the liking of Elizabeth's father who brought the family back to London. But Elizabeth never entirely lost her Catholic faith which the Ursuline convent had instilled, although she found it necessary after her marriage to at least pay lip service to the Church of England.

How she first met Samuel Pepys is not known. But she was a very attractive girl of fourteen, and Pepys was smitten. It would have been better for him to use marriage as a stepping-stone to further promotion. Or at least he should have chosen a girl who could give him entry to the upper echelons of society, and who would provide a handsome dowry. Yet Pepys decided that such considerations were unnecessary and that he could maintain a decent household on his meagre clerk's salary of £50 a year. For Elizabeth, Pepys' ardent wooing would not in itself have won him her hand, but despite her father's noble ancestry her relative poverty meant that she brought with her no dowry, and her prospects of finding a husband with both influence and money were remote. Pepys' was the best offer she was likely to get, and he was a presentable young man, so she was not unattracted to him. Church marriages had been banned by the Commonwealth in 1653 and the young couple were married before a magistrate on 1 December 1655. But they had already made their vows at a religious ceremony on 10 October, and that is the date on which they later celebrated their wedding anniversaries. Both families disapproved of the marriage, the Pepyses thinking it would not advance his career, and the St Michels because she was marrying beneath her. After the wedding Pepys took his bride to the one-roomed attic lodging that he had in the house of his employer. It was more squalid than she had expected.

Elizabeth was not afraid of work. She cooked, cleaned, washed and sewed for her husband. But while he was absorbed in his career, she was lonely. He had not yet been able to prise open the door into society for her. Moreover marital relations were hampered by her genital cysts which came with the puberty that coincided with her marriage. She tended to believe that Pepys had given her the pox; he rather wondered whether he might have done. When Pepys failed to listen to Elizabeth's complaints, she left him when they had only been married a few months, probably to take refuge with her parents. It was some months before she returned to her husband, but she really did not have much choice. Yet she did not return as a submissive and cowed wife; she had a strong will of her own, they rowed frequently, and if he struck her in anger she was quite capable of striking back. He complained of her flightiness, her carelessness with money, and her fondness for fine clothes; she complained of his wandering eye, his meanness and his spending more money on fine clothes for himself than for her.

In the summer of 1660, Pepys was given the post of clerk of the Acts with the Navy Board on a salary of £350 a year. With it went a substantial house in Seething Lane. Elizabeth was quick to profit from their good fortune. Now Elizabeth could have more time to indulge in her taste for theatre, parties and high spending. She liked a public spectacle and it was more likely curiosity rather than ghoulishness that saw her attending the grisly execution of some of the regicides[1] in October 1660. Her ambition to have a proper household establishment was partially satisfied by raising their number of servants from one to four. But Elizabeth had little idea how to manage servants. Jane had been almost one of the family, while the new servants tended to be undisciplined, and since they were usually chosen by Samuel they were pretty rather than hardworking. Samuel and Elizabeth quarrelled about her inability to control them. He appointed them, she dismissed them. Just before Christmas 1664, Samuel blacked Elizabeth's eye following a bitter row, and the couple remained estranged well into the New Year. Almost at the height of the plague in 1665, Elizabeth took her mother-in-law around London, shopping and visiting places of interest. But at last, when London was virtually empty of anyone of consequence by early July, Samuel moved his wife and household to a friend's house in Woolwich. Elizabeth stayed there for the rest of the summer, occasionally visited by her busy husband, but when the plague subsided in the autumn Elizabeth was anxious to return home to Seething Lane, and in fact moved back there to make the house ready before she could persuade her husband to return in January 1666. It was not fear of the plague, but fear of losing his bachelor-like freedom which made him so tardy in returning home.

Pepys had used his enforced separation from Elizabeth to embark on several brief amorous adventures. Elizabeth retaliated by using her undoubted charm to captivate male admirers. She was worshipped by Will Hewer who entered the Pepys' household in 1660 as Samuel's clerk and personal servant; Lord Sandwich, Pepys' superior at the Navy Board, had asked Elizabeth to become his mistress in 1662, an invitation which flattered her, but which she politely declined. Later she was to flirt with Henry Sheeres, a naval engineer. And there had been other admirers.

On 2 September 1666 the Great Fire of London began. At first the Pepyses were unconcerned and Samuel took Elizabeth on a boat trip on the river Thames to join other sightseers. They were turned back by sparks and smoke. By 5 September, when much of the city had been destroyed, the fire was approaching Seething Lane. There was some frantic last minute packing. Valuables, including furnishings curtains and pictures, were taken into store, and Elizabeth and the servants were sent to Woolwich, where Elizabeth had stayed at the height of the plague. But the worst of the fire was now over. The ferocious wind, so responsible for driving the fire into the city, had abated, and Seething Lane was untouched. The servants returned to Seething Lane to use the opportunity to carry out a thorough house cleaning; Elizabeth, as befitted a lady both of birth and now of substance, returned when all was completed.

One great disappointment to both Samuel and Elizabeth was their failure to have children. Elizabeth tended to blame Samuel for this, because of his numerous liaisons, about which she was aware but did not have any specific knowledge. Samuel rather tended to think that perhaps she was right. But this did not cause him to pause in his philandering. In 1667 the couple took in a young and pretty girl of seventeen as a servant and companion for Elizabeth. Almost from the outset Deborah Willet was subjected to Samuel's advances, at first subtle and low-key, eventually more adventurous and explicit. Then one evening in the autumn of 1668 Elizabeth came unexpectedly upon Samuel in the act of intimately groping Deborah. Elizabeth's rage knew no bounds. She threatened to hurt Samuel physically by brandishing red-hot fire-tongs at him, and materially by announcing that she was a Catholic. If it were generally known that Pepys had a Catholic wife his career, at a time when Catholics were believed to have been involved in spreading the plague, causing the fire and inviting the Dutch[2] up the Thames, would have been irreparably damaged. Elizabeth's bitter recriminations were loud and long, and continued well into the late autumn. What made matters much worse was that Pepys still continued to seek out Deborah, long after she had been ignominiously dismissed from the Pepys household by Elizabeth. When Elizabeth discovered this she threatened to leave Samuel if he gave her a few hundred pounds, and she threatened to slit Deborah's nose.

Even when the Deborah affair died down Samuel still persisted in clandestine affairs, but things were sufficiently repaired between himself and Elizabeth for Samuel to agree at last to take his wife to France. She had wanted to visit France, partly for the shopping and the culture, but also to visit places from her childhood and possibly look up some of her relatives. She certainly went shopping when she eventually got to Paris, after a detour to Holland to visit the naval shipyards. This had little interest for her, and she was even more put out when Samuel cut short the holiday in order to get back to his Admiralty office. But immediately on their return in October 1669 Elizabeth was taken ill and retired at once to bed. She was subjected to the usual ministrations by doctors – for fevers this invariably consisted of bloodletting to reduce the fever, but with the disadvantage of greatly weakening the patient. Samuel thought it politically expedient not to summon a Catholic priest to give her absolution in her final hours, even though he knew her Catholic sympathies. Elizabeth died on 10 November 1669, and was buried in St Olave's church. Samuel was greatly affected by his wife's death, and was genuinely upset by it; he had loved her at first, and remained very fond of her until her death. She was only twenty-nine.

Elizabeth was not a typical seventeenth-century wife, nor the ideal one, meek, submissive and fecund. Pepys' account of her in his diary is probably close to the truth. Elizabeth was shrewish, had a vicious temper, and was ambitious and careless with money. But she had a fighting spirit, and she had plenty of provocation for her tantrums and her long sulks. She was well-read, loved books and was bilingual in English and French – the Ursuline convent had done its work well, and it had given her a basic Catholic faith which never left her. She was generous and generally kind to her servants, and, unable to have children herself, she did on at least one occasion act as midwife to one of her friends. There is no indication that she had any political influence, although she moved on the edge of great events and among the great and powerful. But had she lived, her faith would have dragged Samuel even deeper into the political maelstrom of 1678–81.[3]

MARY ANNE DISRAELI: PRIME MINISTER'S WIFE AND SUPPORT

Mary Anne Wyndham-Lewis in 1839 married Benjamin Disraeli, a Christian Jew who was twice Prime Minister of Britain, in the 1860s and 1870s. She was his loyal and loving wife until her death in 1872. She was twelve years older than he was, and some people thought he was looking for a mother figure because of his uneasy relations with his own mother Maria. Though he appeared in some ways to take her for granted, Disraeli was deeply attached to Mary Anne and seems to have loved her at least as much as he said he did – and not only because of her money, as some of the less charitable of his acquaintances alleged. He certainly dealt very brusquely with anyone who dared slight her in his presence. His relationship with his wife seemed much more intimate – even volatile – than those between Mrs Gladstone and her husband, his great parliamentary rival, who always preserved a certain distance and formality in their marital relations; and few who knew him suspected there was any lack of warmth of his attachment to his own Mary Anne.

She was born Mary Anne Evans in 1792, daughter of Lt John Evans, RN, and his wife Eleanor, who came from a respectable middle-class farming family in Gloucestershire. Mary Anne's father died when she was only two, and in 1810 her mother remarried, this time to a Thomas Yate, and the pair lived at Clifton near Bristol. Neither of Eleanor's husbands was truly a man of means, so it was pleasant for Mary to meet Wyndham Lewis at a ball in Bristol, to find that he fell in love with her, and afterwards to marry him in 1815. Living in grander circles in South Wales, and, later, when her husband entered Parliament, entertaining lavishly in London, she met the Duke of Wellington and other leading figures. The couple eventually moved to Grosvenor Gate, where she continued to provide balls and dinners for London society. It was here that Disraeli first met her, at a soirée given at Bulwer's in 1832. To begin with, he rather frightened her with his ready rapier wit, his foppish appearance, his brocade waistcoat and his kiss-curl plastered to his forehead. He was quite the opposite of her. He was shrewd, witty, incisive, ambitious, and always with an eye to the main chance. She was a chatterbox (what contemporaries called 'a rattle'), impulsive, warm-hearted, kind, affectionate, often ignorant and even slightly 'common'. She, after the death of her husband in 1834, was something of a social butterfly, still quite attractive to men and bringing out their instincts to protect her. It was only after Disraeli became Member of Parliament for Maidstone in 1838 that they saw much of each other when he began to address letters to her that one of his biographers suggests were full of 'a sort of mock devotion'. Perhaps his bantering tone was due to the fact that at first he did not take her seriously. Indeed, she was prone to social gaffes and blunders; they often got her into hot water.[1] She was not totally uneducated, nor stupid, but she still was capable of silly mistakes.[2]

Precisely when he first thought of marrying her is obscure. Perhaps it had to do with money. Disraeli was perpetually embarrassed by lack of funds, and even in the early days of their acquaintance had touched her for a loan of several hundred pounds. Now he was in trouble in Maidstone, where he was accused of promising bribes in 1837 and then refusing to pay. The matter nearly went to the courts, but Mary Anne saved him from the embarrassment by lending him more money. Perhaps she had been warned about his predatory instincts, because the pair rowed furiously over the matter, and only a grovelling letter prevented a rupture. Mary Anne did not break with him when she received it, but forgave him completely, and went on to marry him at St George's, Hanover Square, in August 1839.

At first, perhaps, he did not know that she had only a life interest in her former husband's fortune (it was a substantial one all the same, the capital yielding about £5,000 a year); when he found out he persisted nevertheless. The financial restrictions this life interest imposed on her use of the capital would have made a great difference to a mere fortune-hunter in the days before the Married Women's Property Act. If her money had been hers absolutely he could have come into ownership of it on his marriage, and would have been able to pay off all his debts.[3] As it was, he could not sequester her funds, and thus had only a marginal interest in her wealth.

He soon found that money was not everything. By 1840 he had reached the age when home, affection, security were all-important and when feminine sympathy, admiration, and even idolatry were essential to his self-esteem. It is true that they never had children, but the devotion he showed for her was genuine enough. To say they lived happily ever after would be an exaggeration, but it was as true as it is of any marriage. Disraeli, who had shown himself already to be something of a flirt in his younger days, when he had set his cap at Lady Blessington, Mrs Gore, Mrs Norton, Mrs Bulwer, and later Lady Chesterfield and others (as well as dismissing Mrs Wyndham Lewis as 'that insufferable woman'), settled down with her with a respect and a devotion that even Gladstone would have admired. As for Mary Anne, he recognised that she was shrewder than her silly manner and her non sequiturs seemed to suggest, and that she gave him the love, devotion and worship he needed and protected him from the domestic trivia he detested. He was too embarrassed to let her know how deeply he was in debt, and she was understandably annoyed at the successive revelations that took place, but all the same she let him use her income and he benefited from it in the improvement of his credit. In the end, it is reckoned, she let him have not less than £13,000.

Both he and she came to desire a suitable country house for their out-of-town residence: he because it was fitting for a major leader in the protectionist wing of the Tory party after Peel's allegedly injudicious repeal of the Corn Laws in 1846, and she simply because she fancied the move. So they came to purchase Hughenden Manor, about a mile north of High Wycombe in Buckinghamshire. It was a three-storied eighteenth-century building, the garden and lawns sloping down to the south, and flanked by woods, falling steeply to the east towards the little church that lay in the grounds. It cost him £35,000, and a protracted delay over the valuation of the timber that the woods contained. Neither of them could find such a sum, and Disraeli had to borrow £25,000 from Lord George Bentinck and Lord Titchfield, both party associates, to complete the deal. They did not move in until the winter of 1848.

But neither he nor she ever regretted it. She loved to run it as their marital home, playing the part of the country lady, and he loved to come down from London to recharge his batteries there at the weekend, strolling gently round the grounds and in his woods,[4] and browsing among the books in his library. Autumn sessions were rare in those days, and the pair loved the long run-up to Christmas in the comfort of their own home. Mary Anne was not much interested in politics, though she took a pride in reading his many books and pamphlets 'to see if his name is in any of them', and she was proud of the honorary degree bequeathed on him by Oxford. His tenure at Hughenden, however, was not popular among the locals. His predecessor had taken a lively interest in their affairs and had under-rented his land to them: Disraeli was much sharper, distant, exacting and not very concerned. He did, however, become a close friend of Mrs Brydges Willyams, an elderly lady of Jewish extraction to whom he wrote lengthy and revealing letters, and from whom on her death in 1863 he inherited a fortune, so that their joint income rose to £9,000 per annum, of which at least half was his own.

At the time of Disraeli's defeat by the Liberals in 1868 after the 1867 Parliamentary Reform Act, he took the unusual step of asking Queen Victoria to bestow a peerage on Mary Anne, though not for himself, as he wished to stay leader of his party in the House of Commons. Victoria consulted with General Grey, who also found the request embarrassing, but Disraeli insisted and the Queen complied, making Mary Anne a peeress in her own right as Viscountess Beaconsfield of Beaconsfield in the County of Buckingham. Disraeli himself did not become Earl of Beaconsfield until 1876, when he decided, after a Commons career of nearly forty years, to continue to lead the Conservatives from the House of Lords.[5]

By the start of the 1870s, now in her eighties, Mary Anne's health was in decline. Periodic illness pursued her for the following two years. She got to know from her doctor that she was suffering from cancer of the stomach; she had not told her husband, who knew anyway but had refrained from discussing it with her. She insisted on accompanying him to Manchester for his speech at the Free Trade Hall in April 1872, but the experience took a good deal out of her and she never properly recovered. After a brief stay at Hughenden for Whitsun, she returned to Grosvenor Gate, but at a reception for the Duchess of Cambridge, collapsed again in July and never appeared in society again. She rallied at the end of September, and Disraeli was able to take her down to Hughenden, where generous neighbours bombarded her with appetising concoctions from their chefs. She tried vainly to receive visitors such as Rosebery and Harcourt, but it was too much for her in her weakened state. She died in December 1872. She was buried, eventually with him, in a vault in the small church at Hughenden that stood on his land, and gave its name to the manor.

Disraeli had been unimpressed with Mary Anne when he first met her, but came to appreciate that she was shrewder than her silly manner made her appear. He came to depend on her heavily for his domestic comforts at Hughenden, and she turned out to be a great help to him, not least with the editing of a series of successful political novels,[6] a portion of which he wrote there during his vacations. She was twelve years older than he was, but their romance continued until the day she died. He used to joke that he married her for her money, but that he would do it all over again, for love.

THE LIFE AND DEATH OF JANE CARLYLE

Jane Baillie Welsh was born in Haddington, East Lothian, in 1801, a 'wee Scots farm girl' who was strictly brought up and tutored by the revivalist minister Edward Irving. She had a powerful sense of her own identity and individual worth and considerable literary talent. It was her tutor who first introduced her to her future husband, Thomas Carlyle, whom she married in 1826. They lived on her estate at Craigenputtock, Dumfriesshire, from 1828 to 1834, and then moved to London where they lived in Chelsea. The marriage was a stormy one, marred by her husband's ill-temper and his ill-use of her, and her own (and his) chronic illness and hypochondria. All this was related in some detail by James Anthony Froude, a cleric and a renegade from the Oxford Movement who, though one of the most careless and inaccurate of historians, became eventually Professor of Modern History at Oxford. He described how Jane, in spite of her natural literary talents, refused to become a writer, but how she is nevertheless remembered for her vividly written letters and diaries which were published after her death and which reveal her to have been one of the greatest letter-writers in the English language.

When Thomas and Jane moved to London in 1834, they took possession of one of those tall, narrow houses which today accommodate professional families from Islington to Camberwell. No. 5, Cheyne Row, had two rooms on each floor, a small addition at the back that accommodated a larder, a closet and a dressing room, and eventually a loft extension that provided a soundproof study for the great writer. There was an outside lavatory and no bathroom.

Jane's mother warned her of her husband's ill-temper even before their marriage. Jane put it down to his enforced poverty and his chronic dyspepsia, but whatever the reason for it nothing could be done to alleviate his condition, and it continued throughout his life. Jane soon learned not to complain about her own aches and pains; they never received any sympathy, anyway, and her hurt pride prevented her ever mentioning them again. He got on with his books; she stuck to the task of being his housekeeper rather than his wife. The couple had no children; there were even those who doubted whether the marriage had ever been consummated. Her great talent was for frugal housekeeping and for spinning out their limited funds; this she combined with patience in dealing with her monstrous husband, whose tantrums would have tried the patience of a saint. It seems significant that after her death, though he lived on for a further fifteen years, he never wrote anything of note.

As time passed, Jane became steadily more and more shrewish. There was nothing too small to complain about – food, clothing, decorating, pets and above all servants. It seems quite likely that she was unable to find intellectual or imaginative fulfilment in the marriage, and that her relentless bottling-up of her creativity help to produce her dyspepsia. Only in her letters did she find an outlet, where her caustic wit, her self-mockery and her sarcasm towards others gives us a glimpse the woman she might have been.

Their home was the meeting place for many of the eminent individuals of the period, including Charles Dickens, Giuseppe Mazzini, Edward Irving, John Stuart Mill and a host of others. They thought well of her in an indulgent way as his muse and confidante, and at the centre of his salon. But they had no real idea. Thomas was often barely civil to her. Nor was she ever content or truly well. Her sympathisers called her complaint neurasthenia, her critics hypochondria. Always hovering on the uncomfortable margin between illness and health, she was ever keen to learn of the medical advances that were being made daily, and of trying out new remedies if she could, whether in the comfortable alcoholic form of laudanum or (the often deadly remedy) mercury. She tried champagne, she tried morphia, she tried 'blue pills' (whatever they were), she tried castor oil; she even contemplated submitting herself to 'electrical treatment'. She endeavoured to rig up various gadgets and mechanical devices in her bedroom, operating them from the bed, but succeeded in nothing more than irritating her husband further. Indeed, nothing she did brought about permanent improvement. When one of her friends, a Mr Venturi, died suddenly in 1866, his doctors diagnosed his complaint as 'quite imaginary' and 'the result of an unsatisfactory life'. But a post-mortem revealed it was due to heart disease. Jane found this very significant, and questioned the competence of doctors. She also worried about the health of her husband, at that time lecturing in Edinburgh; also about Landseer's illness; and about a female suicide in Scotland due to the 'intolerable pain of neuralgia'; she even worried that her husband might catch a cold when he returned to London and got the housemaid to sleep in his bed so as to air it.

In mid-summer 1866, while Thomas was still in Edinburgh, Jane went for a drive in her brougham round Hyde Park. Just before four o'clock she got down from her carriage to let her little dog have a run, and at the Serpentine bridge she and the dog got back in and she continued the drive towards the Bayswater side of the park. She stopped again at Victoria Gate, and the dog was put out to run alongside the carriage, but another passing carriage frightened it and she got out again to pick the dog up, and then remounted. Her coachman, Silvester, asked if she was all right, but she did not appear to hear. He could see her hands motionless folded in her lap in the carriage. He took the carriage twice round the Serpentine drive, but then became concerned at the lack of further instructions, so he stopped at the gatekeeper's lodge and asked a lady to look in the carriage, and then on her instructions drove her to nearby St George's Hospital. But Mrs Carlyle was already dead.

Thomas Carlyle returned to London distraught, remorseful over his treatment of his wife. He managed, through the intervention of influential friends, to avoid the normally obligatory coroner's inquest and post-mortem, but the pain of his bereavement hit him hard. Although he had never moved in court circles, Queen Victoria herself, also recently bereaved from Albert, sent her condolences. Jane was buried in the churchyard of her birthplace in Scotland. Carlyle told Froude that when he died he wished to be buried by his wife's side, but not even this came about, since, as if in recognition of their profound incompatibility, he was buried miles away in the churchyard at Ecclefechan in Dumfries. Froude did something to compensate for Carlyle's protracted neglect: book succeeded book,[1] reminiscences of Carlyle, the editing of Mrs Carlyle's prolific stock of letters, and, when he became Professor of Modern History at Oxford, further books on a wide variety of subjects from Catherine of Aragon to Disraeli. But Froude nevertheless remains the major chronicler of the often moving story of the unhappy match between Thomas and Jane Carlyle.

LADY EMILY TENNYSON: WIFE AND SECRETARY OF A POET LAUREATE

Emily Tennyson was chiefly famous for being Alfred Lord Tennyson's wife, and the mother of his two sons, but she was more than this. She was also his friend, his confidante, his secretary and, perhaps most important, his lover. Though herself never very strong physically, she was the main driving force in the family, and it was her moral courage and her unquenchable spirit that held the family together.

Emily Sarah Sellwood was born in July 1813 in Horncastle, Lincolnshire, to Michael and Sarah Sellwood, and was the eldest of three daughters. Her mother died while she was still only small. She had problems all her life with a weak spine and was regarded as a semi-invalid who easily became tired. She had quite a happy childhood, though marred by a series of family deaths, and was looked upon by all who knew her as a bright and happy child. While still a teenager, Emily met the man she was to marry. She was walking in the woods with Arthur Hallam, a close friend of Alfred Tennyson's when they came across Tennyson, and she fell in love with him at first sight. In 1836, Emily's sister Louisa married Tennyson's elder brother, Charles, and Emily was maid of honour at the wedding. It was there that Alfred confessed he had fallen in love with her when he saw her tears of joy at her sister's wedding. They became engaged to each other shortly afterwards. He said he would 'break stones on the road' to have his Emily; she for her part found him 'kingly' and could 'scarcely consider anything more glorious in human form'. Their engagement, however, was not without incident. Louisa was not happy with Charles, who renewed his old opium addiction, and the Sellwood family were not willing to allow Alfred to continue his engagement[1]; the result was that their proposed marriage did not immediately go ahead. Alfred had money worries, and his lack of strong religious conviction also troubled Emily. He offered her her freedom, but her love for him continued, until in 1849 his financial position improved, and he published the poem *In Memoriam* which first made him famous. He had lost his best friend, Arthur Hallam, with whom he had developed strong ties, and now turned to women for consolation. Finally Emily and Alfred married at Shiplake in 1850, he at the age of forty, she thirty-six.

Their life thereafter was lived in a harmony that was almost unnatural. The couple lived in a pleasant country house at Farringford, Freshwater (Isle of Wight). She presented him with a son at Easter 1851, but he was stillborn; she became pregnant again very soon and produced another son whom they called Hallam after Tennyson's great friend. In 1854 they had a third son, this time called Lionel. Emily was overjoyed to be a mother and doted on her sons. She kept them in skirts with their hair long, and could not bring herself to think of sending them away to school. The only cloud in their sky was the news of the Crimean War. The little boys played at soldiers, falling down and saying, 'This is how the Russian soldiers fall down when they are killed', but it made Emily unhappy and distracted Alfred from his work.[2] Then there appeared a slim green volume, *Maud, and Other Poems* (1855), and just before that he was appointed Poet Laureate. His reputation stood so high that a trip to Farringford for his many visitors was almost like a pilgrimage to Mecca. American tourists flocked in; Prince Albert came to visit him even before he had got his books on the shelves. Life by the end of the 1850s became quite giddy: Edward Lear came and charmed them by singing for three hours; Charles Kingsley burnt the guy for them on Guy Fawkes Day; Dr Jowett, then Professor of Greek at Oxford, played Blind Man's Buff at Christmas. The eminent lady photographer Julia Cameron came and was so enchanted that she bought two cottages at Freshwater Bay, knocked them together and moved in, naming the place Dimbola after her husband's tea estates in Ceylon. For several years she kept their lives busy and exciting with showers of gifts and the loan of a grand piano.

In 1862 there began another momentous friendship with a distinguished neighbour. Queen Victoria had suffered the loss of her beloved Albert, and was so moved by reading *In Memoriam* that she summoned the Tennysons to Osborne, entertained them and afterwards sent them a signed photograph of herself and three of her children. Their friendship did not end until Tennyson's death thirty years later. Then, in 1864, Garibaldi, the Italian nationalist leader, enjoying his perennial popularity in England, paid a visit to Farringford, and he and Alfred recited Italian poetry to one another, and even discussed Italian politics.[3]

During the whole of this time, Emily worked as hard as her health would allow her not only at domestic chores, but also as his adviser and secretary, handling the whole of his correspondence. She wrote letters to his friends; she responded to well-wishers; she answered the letters of aspiring poets who sought the advice of the Poet Laureate. She kept a detailed journal of their life together on the Isle of Wight. Through it all there shines her devotion to her husband, and his high regard for her.

In 1869 the Tennysons moved to Aldworth. The new house stood on the summit of a hill near Haslemere, with a view across the Sussex Downs to the Channel. Designed by Alfred's friend James Knowles, the house had everything for Emily, from the text across the façade, *Gloria Deo in Excelsis*, to the delightful hot-water bathroom where the poet had three baths a day. For most of the rest of her life, however, Emily was only of moral succour to her husband; she was no longer fit for much active work. It is almost impossible to diagnose her illness, but the fact that her hair was still auburn, her complexion perfect and that she lived to the age of eighty-three suggest that she did not suffer from any mortal disease. Perhaps, like a number of others of her class and generation, her weakness was mainly due to 'nerves', or to her oversensitive mind. Whatever the cause, she was now almost completely confined to her sofa and her chair. Her son Hallam came down from Oxford and took up the secretarial work she had been accustomed to do. In 1883, Queen Victoria conferred a barony on Tennyson; Emily became a baroness and was called Lady Emily Tennyson at her own request. In 1886 her second son Lionel, who had an office career in India, died of a fever on his way home by ship, at the age of thirty-two, leaving a young widow and three children. The whole family were devastated by the news.

She accepted her ill-health with fortitude, continuing to perform her secondary role with devotion. She knew her sphere and accepted it, and in her perfect, unselfish acceptance of her duties and her limitations lay her genius as a wife. Her intellectual and artistic tastes were developed alongside her husband's; she put up with her own ill-health to safeguard the health of her loved one.[3]

In 1892, after a short illness, Alfred died. He was buried, his Shakespeare beside him, in Westminster Abbey. He was eighty-three; she was seventy-nine. She wrote to her sister: 'It is a wonderful thought that he is known and loved throughout the world, and a blessed one that his influence can only be for good.' She devoted the remainder of her days with her son Hallam to compiling materials for a biography on Alfred. Her health was no better, and she died in August 1896 at the age of eighty-three. Her last words were supposed to have been: 'I have tried to be a good wife.' She was buried at All Saints' Church on the Isle of Wight.

ALICE LIDDELL: THE LITTLE GIRL THROUGH THE LOOKING-GLASS

Alice Liddell, known for most of her life by her married name, Alice Hargreaves, was the little girl who inspired Charles Dodgson's children's classic Alice's Adventures in Wonderland *(1863)[1], a story that, with its equally famous sequel,* Alice Through the Looking-glass, *(1871), has delighted countless children from that day to this. The relations between Alice, a little girl of ten, and Charles Lutwidge Dodgson, a middle-aged mathematics don from Oxford, who wrote children's stories under the pen name of Lewis Carroll, has been the subject of much innuendo and speculation; her life, on the other hand, was that of an exemplary wife and mother who died at the age of eighty-two in 1934.*

Alice Pleasance Liddell was the fourth child of Henry Liddell, Dean of Christ Church, Oxford and his wife Lorina Hanna Liddell (*née* Reeve). She was born in 1852, and had three elder brothers (of whom one died at the age of three in 1853) and an elder sister Lorina (known as Ina). She also had a younger sister called Edith, born two years after her. In 1856 the family moved, when her father left a post as Dean of Westminster School to go to his new appointment in Oxford. The family became acquainted with Dodgson, who taught mathematics at the same college. He soon became a close friend of theirs. Dodgson also had a lively interest in photography, and it was while he was photographing the cathedral that he first met the Liddells. Among his other photographic subjects were portraits of little girls, including Alice herself on several occasions. Dodgson also enjoyed the company of children, and spent a good deal of time rowing and having picnics with them during the long summer afternoons.

Alice grew up mainly in the company of her two sisters, Ina, who was three years older than she was, and Edith who was two years younger. The family regularly spent their holidays at their holiday home, Penmorfa, near Llandudno, and when she was a young woman she went on a grand tour of Europe with her sisters, where the youngest of them, Edith, became involved with Prince Leopold, the youngest son of Queen Victoria. Nothing came of the acquaintance, however, since Edith died shortly afterwards. Alice herself married Reginald Hargreaves in 1880 at the age of twenty-eight in Westminster Abbey. She later gave birth to three sons, Alan Knyveton, Leopold Reginald, both of whom were killed in action during the First World War, and Caryl Liddell Hargreaves (whose name 'Caryl' she always stoutly denied was in any way connected with Dodgson's pen name). She also had a daughter, Rose Liddell Hargreaves. Her husband inherited a considerable fortune, and Alice became in her mature years a noted society hostess.

On her husband's death, Alice found the costs of continuing to maintain their family home too great, and found it necessary to sell her manuscript copy of *Alice's Adventures Under Ground*. Sotheby's auction fetched the amazing price of £15,400. The book was bought by an American, Eldridge Johnson.[2] In her later years, Alice lived in the New Forest, where she died at the age of eighty-two in 1934. She is buried in the churchyard of St Michael and All Angels, Lyndhurst.

The connection between Alice and her older admirer Charles Dodgson is still a matter of speculation. It was in 1862, when she was only ten, that Dodgson and his colleague the Revd Robinson Duckworth took her and her sisters Edith and Ina, then aged eight and thirteen respectively, for a picnic outing on the river from Folly Bridge, Oxford, to Godstow, with Duckworth doing the rowing while Dodgson entertained the girls with fairy tales he made up on the spur of the moment. The story he told dealt with the fantastic adventures of a girl named Alice, after she fell down a rabbit-hole. It introduced a whole cast of fantastic characters such as Tweedledum and Tweedledee, the White Rabbit, the Cheshire Cat and the March Hare, and a whole crowd of characters who turned out, like the King and Queen, to be taken from a pack of cards. The girls loved it, and Alice made Dodgson promise to write it down for her, which he eventually did, presenting the bound manuscript copy to her in November 1864. Dodgson later saw that the book might become a commercial venture, and published it in 1865, and its sequel *Alice Through the Looking-glass* in 1871, in both cases with line illustrations by John Tenniel.

The truth behind the supposedly platonic relationship between a grown man and a girl of ten has been the subject of a good deal of supposition, with hints and inferences taking the place of actual evidence of any baser motives. The facts are that Dodgson did not meet the Liddell family until 1855, and that it was her elder brother Harry that he first befriended. The older man took the boy on boating trips on the Thames and afternoon picnics. Later, when Harry went to school, Alice and her sister joined the party, and he told them impromptu stories to amuse them. He also spent time taking their photographs, a number of which still survive. There was never any suggestion that his conduct towards them was in any way improper.

However, there occurred a sudden and inexplicable break in the relationship between Dodgson and the Liddell family, as recorded in his diaries in June 1863, as well as the loss or accidental destruction of Dodgson's diaries from April 1858 to May 1862. The Liddells never referred to it, and hence it was a matter of pure conjecture what might have occurred to cause the rift, though it was suggested that Dodgson's relationship with Alice may have been at the root of it. However, in 1996, a document was published (known as *The Cut Pages in the Diary*) which indicated the existence of a note allegedly written by Violet Dodgson, Charles' niece, saying that the break was caused by concern in the Liddell family that Charles was pursuing the Liddell family governess and was using the children to further this pursuit.[3] The truth about this allegation, and about who made it, was never decided,[4] and the matter is still being disputed between the descendants of the two families. However, the fact remains that Dodgson avoided the Liddell household for some months after the incident, and that even when visiting recommenced, relations between the two groups were never so warm again – though the differences may have been more due to college politics than to Dodgson's misconduct.

There has even been some disagreement about whether the figure portrayed by Dodgson in his *Alice* can be identified with Alice Liddell at all. Dodgson himself claimed that she was not, but that she was an entirely imaginary child. Certainly his own sketches of her, for Tenniel's benefit, look nothing like her; one writer has even suggested that the younger Edith was the model (though there is no explanation offered, if such a suggestion is true, why he did decided to call her Alice). On the contrary, there is some textual evidence suggesting otherwise. In *Through the Looking-glass*, he sets Alice's 'half-birthday' as 4 November, which, considering that Alice was born on 4 May, is exactly right; and, secondly, at the end of that story, there is printed an acrostic poem referring to the scenario of the book, the first letter of each line of which spells out the name 'Alice Pleasance Liddell'. The motives of Dodgson in so strenuously denying that he had Alice in mind when he wrote either book seem mysterious in themselves unless the author himself felt he had something to hide.

Later works by a variety of authors have not clarified the situation, but instead have added further fanciful speculations to the mix. The 1985 movie *Dreamchild* promotes the popular assumption that Dodgson was romantically attracted to Alice, though producing no evidence for such an assertion. If Dodgson in fact entertained any such paedophilic yearnings for Alice Liddell, he kept very quiet about it, and never translated his cravings into reality.

MAGDA GOEBBELS: FIRST LADY OF THE THIRD REICH

After a very varied earlier career, Magdalena ('Magda') Quant married Josef Goebbels in 1931, and as the wife of a leading and highly visible Nazi official became 'first lady of the Third Reich' until her death in the Führerbunker at the beginning of May 1945. Her short and troubled life was at first cushioned by luxury but later cut off in bizarre circumstances at the climactic point of twentieth-century German history. It provides a parable of the dangers of uncritical submission to a regime that was the ruin not only of a political ideology but a whole nation in the mid-twentieth century.

Johanna Maria Magdalena ('Magda') Reitschel was born in 1901 in Berlin, daughter of Oskar Reitschel and Auguste Behrend (shortly afterwards married, but divorced in 1904). While Magda was still little, her mother sent her to join Oskar in Cologne, and he enrolled her in an Ursuline convent school in Vilvoorde. In 1908 Auguste married

Richard Friedländer,[1] a wealthy industrial manufacturer and a Jew, and the pair moved with Magda to Brussels. Auguste did not, however, adopt her husband's faith, but remained Catholic. Expelled as German nationals after the invasion in 1914, they moved back to Berlin and Magda was sent first to the Kolmorgen Lycée and in 1919 to the very reputable Holzhausen Ladies' College near Goslar.

Magda was still a schoolgirl when she was swept off her feet by Günther Quant, a man old enough to be her father, and a rich and successful German industrialist. He was, furthermore, a large shareholder both in BMW and Daimler-Benz. He asked her to accept the Protestant faith in place of her previous nominal Catholicism, and, having no strong religious convictions, she agreed; then he went on to marry her in 1921. She was still not yet twenty-one years old. In 1921 she presented him with a son, Harald, and set about bringing him up. Her husband, however, was far too busy to spend more than a little time with his young new wife, and as a result she was left rather to her own devices. She fell for his seventeen-year-old son (her stepson) Helmut, but was saved from scandal when he died from appendicitis in 1927. Later that year, she went to the USA on a business trip to Philadelphia in the company of her husband. Günther still, however, was obsessed with business matters, and paid little attention to her, with the result that their marital relationship steadily went downhill, until finally he divorced her with a generous financial settlement in 1929.

The start of the 1930s saw Magda young, single, attractive, rich, and at something of a loose end. Her life so far, though endowed with many worldly benefits, had been somewhat aimless, not based on any sound spiritual values; so it is hardly surprising that she fell victim to the rather superficial attractions of the Nazi ideology when she became acquainted with it. Attending a party rally in the depth of the economic depression in 1930, she was moved, partly by the persuasiveness of successive speakers' arguments, and not least by the strong sense of unity and conviction among the eager crowd attending. In particular she was impressed by the performance of one of the speakers, Josef Goebbels, at that time the Nazi *Gauleiter* of Berlin. She joined the party in September 1930, and, after doing some volunteer local work, moved to party headquarters where she became secretary to Hans Meinshausen, Goebbels' deputy. Later she was invited to take charge of Goebbels' private archives. Hitler, when he met her as he did in 1931, found her an impressive woman and was impressed as much by her Prussian upper-class background and her refined comportment as by her commitment to the cause; and though he seems to have wished himself to remain single, it is sometimes said he thought it a good idea that by marriage she should give the appropriate social cachet to the regime and even fulfil the role of 'first lady' to the Nazi movement. He was always close to Magda: after an abortive attempt to poison him in Berlin at the Kaiserhof Hotel in January 1933, he asked her to take personal care of the preparation of his food; he was also a firm ally and a political collaborator of Goebbels, the two of them planning and organising often quite late into the night, so that Goebbels was as close to Hitler as anyone was. Although, with his club foot and his rather unprepossessing appearance, Goebbels did not appear to be very impressive material, he was devotedly attached to Hitler's cause and used his considerable talents to promote the advance of the party in every way he could.[2] Goebbels married Magda in December 1931, with Hitler as witness.

Though Magda was clearly attracted to Goebbels as he was to her, their relationship was never a passionate one. For his part, Goebbels had a number of affairs, not least with the Czech actress Lida Baarova. Magda, too, was reputed to have had an affair with Goebbels' deputy, Karl Hanke. But the marriage was certainly fruitful. In the course of the 1930s, she presented him with six children – five girls and a boy. In order of their births they were:

> Helga Susanne
> Hildegard ('Hilde') Traudel
> Helmut Christian (the only boy)
> Holdine ('Holde') Kathrin
> Hedwig ('Hedda') Johanna
> Heidrun ('Heide') Elisabeth

Both parents seemed accustomed to the limelight of their social status in Germany and both had high-profile jobs – the one as a Nazi minister of state and the other as his devoted wife. Like all the Nazi leaders, Goebbels did well out of his ministerial appointment: his salary was a high one and there were plenty of fringe benefits coming to him either officially or else through the graft rampant in the system.

From the outbreak of the Second World War in 1939 the pair threw themselves enthusiastically into the cause. Magda helped her husband promote his propaganda work by public appearances and speaking appointments; she carried out her other official functions conscientiously by receiving the wives of foreign heads of state or diplomats, she helped to encourage and support the troops, and she did her bit to comfort war widows. She sought to create for herself the status of a patriotic worker by training as a Red Cross nurse; she also took a job with the electronics company Telefunken. She even cultivated the common touch by insisting on going about by bus and not in an official car. Her first son, Harald Quant, now in his early twenties, became a Luftwaffe pilot and fought in the war.[3]

At the same time, during the war, especially when campaigns were not going well in Africa and later in Russia, Magda provided later researchers with evidence of her occasional disenchantment with Nazi ideas if not with Nazi leaders.[4] Privately she began to express doubts about whether Germany was going to win the great victory everybody had been led to expect; the inconsistency between her own husband's rosy reassurances and the military realities of 1942 and 1943 seemed too glaring. She is said to have turned off a radio address by Hitler in December 1942 with the impatient exclamation: 'God! What a load of rubbish!' Her qualms increased as German forces were inexorably driven back upon Berlin in 1943 and 1944 and Allied air raids on the capital increased in frequency and intensity. Her health began to deteriorate in this latter year: she was suffering from a recurrent condition in her cheek known as trigeminal neuralgia which necessitated hospital treatment and gave her acute and chronic pain. At the same time she was concerned about the future fate of her children, most of whom were still only very young.

By the spring of 1945 the Soviet armies were at the gates of Berlin, and the whole Goebbels family retreated to the Führerbunker, a deep bolthole that had been constructed beneath the ruined Reich Chancellery. Conditions here were crowded and unpleasant: not only were the group of thirty or so leading Nazi figures cramped close together, vexed by a defective air-conditioning system, and continually threatened by the bombardment of enemy artillery, but this was scarcely the place for Minister Goebbels and his wife, and for their six young children. The only bathroom that had a bath was that of Hitler himself; he did not mind their using it, but for the children and for Magda herself the arrangements were scarcely satisfactory. Soviet troops had meanwhile entered Berlin, occupied the Reichstag building and run up the Soviet flag on it, and were fighting their way through the streets, looting and pillaging as they went. Hitler was urged to flee, but refused; he did not believe he could get away, and he dreaded to be captured, especially by the Russians – if he was to die, he would rather do it himself. So, after several days of fruitless raging against his fate, and the drafting of his last 'Testament', Hitler decided on suicide[5]; he and his new bride Eva Braun killed themselves on the afternoon of 30 April 1945, and the Goebbels family did the same the following day.

When Soviet troops entered the bunker a day later they found the bodies. There is still some doubt as to the actual course of events that produced the deaths of the entire Goebbels family. One version states that the children were given sugary drinks laced with cyanide by an SS doctor in the bunker; another tells the more likely story that Frau Goebbels killed her children herself. Only one, twelve-year-old Helga was awake, and struggled before she died. All of them were found in their night clothes. There is a similar discrepancy over the fate of the adults: Goebbels and his wife took poison and went up out of the bunker, and either he shot her and then himself, or else they ordered an SS trooper to carry out their execution by gunfire. Their bodies were doused in petrol and then an attempt was made to cremate them, but conditions of wind and weather and constant enemy gunfire were such that this proved impossible, although both bodies were badly damaged by fire. All the bodies were interred by Soviet troops, though subsequently in 1970 they were recovered and cremated and the ashes scattered in the River Elbe.

RUTH BELL GRAHAM: WOMAN EVANGELIST

As the wife of perhaps the most famous evangelist in modern American history, Ruth Bell Graham inevitably played the subordinate part of a close adherent of her husband, William Franklin Graham, known as 'Billy', and as a support for his work on the road and in the pulpit.

She accepted this supporting role without complaint, saying in her Journal, *when she married him 'he will be increasingly burdened for lost souls and increasingly active in the Lord's work', adding 'I will slip into the background. In short I will be a lost life – lost in Bill's.' All the same, she was a considerable student of, and college teacher in, the Scriptures, a counsellor of troubled students in prison and elsewhere, and an author of fourteen books, including a book of poetry and a personal memoir. She also supervised the creation of a retreat, the Billy Graham Training Centre on a 1,500-acre site near the family home at Montreat in North Carolina.*

Ruth McCue Bell was born in 1920 in Qingjiang, in the Jiangsu Province of eastern China, where her parents were Presbyterian missionaries and her father ran a hospital. As Christian expatriates they found themselves caught up in the middle of a civil war between the Chinese Nationalists and the Communists, facing grave danger from either left-wing bandits or right-wing warlords. From there, she went on to school in Pyongyang in North Korea, and at seventeen enrolled at Wheaton College near Chicago. It was here she met Billy Graham, already an ordained minister and a charismatic and successful preacher. After their marriage she gave up her personal plans to become a Christian missionary in Tibet, and devoted herself to being his helper and support.

She did, however, persuade him to move their family home to Montreat in North Carolina, near her parents, and it was here that she brought up their five children, with comparatively little help from her husband. She concentrated on researching the cities he visited on his preaching tours, so that he could bring a touch of local colour into his sermons by showing a familiarity he did not really possess with the places where he spoke. But she clearly retained a mind of her own, and was not averse to revealing its working to him. She was always strongly against any involvement in US politics, and, when he met Lyndon Johnson at the Democratic Convention of 1964, discouraged him from discussing who Johnson's running mate should be for Vice-President. Likewise she firmly quashed any suggestion that her husband should run for President himself – she even threatened to leave him if he did.

She always continued with her own religious work, too. She taught religious studies to prison inmates and to ordinary high school students, and she wrote and published poetry inspired by her religious work. In addition she wrote over a dozen other books, including her memoir *Footsteps of a Pilgrim*. At her home in North Carolina, she brought up her children almost single-handedly, her husband being always absorbed in his work. Teaching Bible studies in North Carolina Women's Prison and in a local college with a difficult reputation, she found herself concentrating on disturbed students. She explained her actions by saying: 'Just because they are unattractive or warped in their thinking doesn't mean the Lord doesn't love them.' One of the young women she helped was Patsy Daniels, later famous as the best-selling writer Patricia Cornwell. She later said that it was the success of the biography of Ruth Graham she wrote in 1983 that provided the spur to her writing career. It was the beginning of an unlikely friendship between the crime writer and the minister's wife lasting for many years, and was believed by some to imply that their relationship was a lesbian one. The biography was the cause of some tension between the two women, but nevertheless it was reissued in 1997 as *Ruth, a Portrait*.

Ruth supervised the building of a retreat in North Carolina, the Billy Graham Training Centre, known as 'the Cove', on a 1,500-acre site near her home. This matter became a reason for controversy when her son Franklin built a Billy Graham Memorial Library in Charlotte, commemorating his father's rural roots and featuring a talking cow, to which his mother objected. Ruth called it 'a circus' and issued a statement rejecting it and expressing her wish to be buried at the Cove, saying 'under no circumstances am I to be buried at Charlotte'. In 2007, however, when she died at the age of eighty-seven, Ruth Graham deferred to her husband for the final time when she agreed to be buried at the Library.

PART 7

HEROINES

LADY GODIVA: EXHIBITIONIST OR SAINT?

Very little is known about Lady Godiva's origins. That she was a real person and not just a name in a legend is beyond dispute, but whether she rode naked on a horse through the streets of Coventry seems highly unlikely, and lacks any contemporary record.

The name Godiva is a later adaptation of the common Saxon name of Godgifu. Her parentage is unknown but from the dowry lands she was known to hold in 1066 it is likely that she came from a wealthy noble family in north-west Mercia, the great earldom that straddled middle England. By 1010 she was married to Leofric, earl of Mercia, suggesting firstly that Leofric had married her to consolidate his hold on that part of Mercia, and also that she was probably born near the beginning of the last decade of the tenth century since eligible noble maidens were usually married off while they were still in their teens. Leofric was a great religious benefactor, and Godgifu's name appears in a number of charters and sources relating to these. Some of the land grants must therefore have come from the lands Godgifu had brought with her to her marriage.

The city of Coventry was founded jointly by Leofric and Godgifu, and she is said to have given 'her whole store of gold and silver' to provide Coventry with appropriate church service vessels. She was generous to a considerable number of religious foundations, but she did retain some lands promised to the church; these Leofric had intended for the church and were to be handed over on his death, but Godgifu was determined to keep them and tried to compensate with gifts of rich vestments and expensive ornaments. Perhaps she was not quite as devoted to God as legend would have us believe. Godgifu's son, Aelfgar, died around 1062, and since her lands passed directly to Godgifu's grandsons, Edwin and Morcar, without reference to Aelfgar, there is a presumption that Godgifu survived her husband and son. Whether she survived the Norman Conquest is uncertain, but she certainly is recorded in Domesday Book as having held lands before it. Later sources suggest she died in 1067, and since there is no record that her lands were taken from her she could have been the only Anglo-Saxon noblewoman to have been a major landholder after 1066, if only briefly. There is some dispute as to where she was buried, but it was probably with Leofric at Coventry.

The earliest reports of her, apart from her landholdings and pious gifts, began to appear in the mid-twelfth century, and were already the stuff of legend rather than history. It was said that she was renowned for her beauty as well as her religious devotion. Not until the turn of the century was the story of her naked ride through Coventry first told by Roger of Wendover, who died in 1236. He says that she was promised by her husband Leofric that he would reduce Coventry's taxes if she would ride naked through the town, and that she did so, using her long golden hair to cover her nudity, and flanked for protection by two men-at-arms. Through the centuries the legend gathered corroborative detail, until by the seventeenth century it was celebrated in verse, and proclaiming that citizens were ordered to remain indoors during the ride, so that her nakedness should not be a public spectacle. By the eighteenth century there was another added embellishment in the person of 'Peeping Tom' who watched through a keyhole and was struck blind. If there was any truth at all associated with the legend it may be that a noble lady did undertake such a ride, clad only in a shift, as part of a religious festival, but there is no corroboration for this.

So the legend gathered pace over the centuries, but the real Lady Godiva, Godgifu, has only a shadowy historical basis. That she was a great Anglo-Saxon lady is beyond dispute, as is the fact that she was well-endowed with lands. It seems, too, that she was not a mere cipher to her husband Leofric, and that she appeared in a number of his charters and grants of land; her piety is also documented. Beyond that everything is either mere conjecture or the mythology of later centuries.

JOAN OF ARC:
HOW IS SHE TO BE EXPLAINED?

There is general agreement among historians that Joan of Arc was a historical figure of such importance that her greatness bordered on the supernatural. People with strong religious convictions have generally regarded her beliefs and her actions as the result of a series of miracles sent to save her country at a time of its great testing in war; others not sharing this view have put her influence down to witchcraft or to some other similarly malign force. Some have said that she was no more than a complaisant puppet operated by a powerful and ambitious French Church; others that she was simply delusional. The would-be scientific experts have put her extraordinary behaviour down to attacks of some psychiatric illness, and have put forward schizophrenia or auto-suggestion as their diagnosis of her condition. But about the critical importance of her contribution to fifteenth-century French history there has been little dispute.

Jeanne d'Arc was a peasant's daughter born in eastern France at Domrémy in 1412. After a blameless childhood, her grief at the woes afflicting France became linked with what she said were visions of the Archangel Michael, St Margaret and St Catherine, all of whom urged her to rescue her country. She secured from the local Dauphinois captain an escort to accompany her to Chinon in 1429 to see the Dauphin Charles, where she impressed upon him that he was the son of King Charles VI and the true heir to the throne of France. She won over to her viewpoint an ecclesiastical commission set up to examine her, and soon brought new energy and fire into the faltering counsels of Charles. Dressed as a knight, Joan led a large relieving force through English lines to recapture Orleans, and, winning another victory at Patay, secured Charles' crowning in Rheims. She now wished to return home, but she was too valuable an asset to be relinquished. She reconquered much of Champagne from the English Duke of Bedford, whom she drove back into Paris, and then turned on the forces of his ally Philip of Burgundy around Compiègne in 1430, where the hesitations of Charles VII allowed her to be captured by the Burgundians and imprisoned at Rouen.

Here she was tried by an ecclesiastical court composed of French adherents of England and Burgundy and presided over by Cauchon, driven from his see at Beauvais. The court was determined to entrap her and for several months sought to outwit her. Joan, an unlettered peasant girl, replied to their provocative and insidious questions with plain answers of simple sincerity, until eventually she was ensnared into an admission of guilt, and, before she could withdraw it, was convicted of heresy at the age of nineteen, and in May 1431 was burned alive in the marketplace of Rouen with a final cry of '*Jhésu*'. Her remains were thrown into the Seine to prevent them becoming relics. The Pope pronounced her innocent of any offence twenty-four years later. In 1909 she was beatified and in 1920 canonised as a saint of the church.

Joan's sturdy good sense, her rationality and the uniform consistency of the workings of her mind tend to cast doubt on any suggestion of insanity as being at the root of her troubles.[1] Her own description of her condition is relevant here. She said that from the age of twelve she started to have unusual mixed sensations of *light* and *sound*, coming to her *from her right*, together with *touch* and *smell*. She says she saw crowned heads, heard voices speaking, was able sometimes to touch these visions, and smelt an agreeable odour. These sensations were generally accompanied by a bright light. She was not sure why, but she believed that her supernatural visitors were St Michael, St Margaret and St Catherine, her favourite saints. At first she saw her divine visitors occasionally, then weekly, and by the time of her trial she said she saw them twice or three times a day. She became ill from time to time, and twice during her trial in 1431 for periods of up to one week, when she suffered from a mild fever and bouts of vomiting (which her warders put down to her having eaten fish that had gone bad).

This evidence has been studied according to modern clinical methods, and has been related to studies of the functions of different areas of the brain. The results point to disturbances in its temporo-sphenoidal lobe. Injuries or diseases situated in this area create sensations of noise and lights which do not come from the external sensory organs, but are nevertheless interpreted by the brain as if they did, thus creating the impression of 'seeing faces' or 'hearing voices'. It seems, on account of Joan's age and other evidence,[2] less likely that the condition was due to a brain tumour, and more likely that it came from a tuberculoma, that is, an abscess or series of abscesses in the brain of a cheese-like composition caused by the ingestion of milk from cattle inflicted with bovine tuberculosis. It must be remembered that many people suffered from minor ailments owing to this cause in the fifteenth century, and fashionable people even wore high collars or ruffs to conceal tubercular glands in the neck. Joan almost certainly grew up in an area where herds of cattle grazed alongside the Meuse, and the odds are that she could have easily contracted some mild form of tubercular infection.

This diagnosis fits well with other features we know of her condition as a teenager. The records show that she suffered from amenorrhoea, a condition in which the menstrual flow was small or irregular.[3] Her jailers also said she had trouble with her kidneys, another recognised complication of tuberculosis. Finally, her executioner observed at her execution that her entrails would not burn, which would not be surprising if there were calcified lymph glands situated in the abdomen and intestines. All this points to the accuracy of a diagnosis of bovine tuberculosis as the underlying cause of the lesion in Joan's brain. It seems likely that if she had not been burned, Joan would have eventually succumbed to her tubercular condition and died unobserved in some dank medieval prison.

None of this medical analysis belies Joan's historical greatness, nor does it deny the importance of her achievements for France. In any case, according to Dunois, the French commander at Orleans, Joan's voices said little more to her than *'Fille de dieu, va, va, va! Je serai à ton aide!'* ('Keep going, daughter of God! I shall be there to help!') It was as the result of her staunch vitality and her formidable will-power that she defeated her enemies at Orleans and Patay, and crowned a King of France. These achievements cannot be belittled by offering a medical explanation for them.

GRACE DARLING:
ANGEL OF MERCY

Grace Darling of Bamburgh was never meant to be a heroine, though this is how she turned out. Through the support of her father, William Darling, lighthouse keeper, this simple girl, raised in poverty and in rural isolation, became a legend in her own lifetime and is now an eternal part of English folklore, endowed miraculously with bright, streaming hair, mythic beauty and indestructible selfless courage. It is true that her father kept a diary, but this tells us nothing of his daughter; the only real authority is a small book written by Grace's sister Thomasin, later published by one Daniel Atkinson of Harrogate in 1880 under the title of Grace Darling: Her True Story.

Grace was born seventh in a family of nine in 1815, and before her eleventh birthday moved from her humble home at the light on Brownsman Island to the newly built lighthouse tower on Longstone Rock further out to sea off the north-east coast of England, but inshore from the Farne Islands, whose reefs and rocks at that time were a serious danger to shipping. The family was virtually self-sufficient, and Grace continued to grow the crops and tend the animals they left behind at the Brownsman when they moved. In 1838, when she was twenty-two and when the rest of the family had grown up and left, leaving the two girls to look after their mother and father, the lighthouse family achieved a sudden fame when the four of them found themselves involved in the tragic wreck of the *Forfarshire*. This was a small vessel, owned by the Hull & Dundee Steam-packet Company, which weighed only 450 tons, and was carrying a mixed cargo of cloth and hardware and had sixty-three persons aboard. It ran into difficulties as she passed the Farnes when the wind suddenly backed north and increased to gale force, and the starboard boiler sprang a leak. The master, John Humble, attempted to head for the Inner Sound, which would have given him shelter from the weather, but the storm was too fierce to permit him to do this and he was driven aground on that part of the reef known as Big Harcar Rock (then known as Harker's Rock). The crew tried to lower a boat, but it was caught up in the fierce tide and swept away with the mate and eight of the crew; almost immediately afterwards, at about four in the morning, the ship broke in two near the paddle-boxes and the after end was swept away with the captain, his wife and forty-one other people still aboard it. They were never seen again. Twelve survivors were left clinging to the rocks or crouching in what remained of the vessel. Darling launched his small cobble boat[1] when he espied men clinging to the rocks at about 7.00 a.m. the following morning and in two perilous trips in his little rowing boat he and his daughter rescued eight men and one woman from the sea. The woman was still clutching the dead bodies of her two drowned children. For the second trip, Grace was replaced at the oars by two of the rescued crewmen. The North Sunderland lifeboat was also launched, but arrived too late for the rescue, and recovered only three dead bodies, which it carried to the Longstone Rock, where all of them remained marooned for several days.

Darling promptly reported all this to Trinity House in a dispatch more distinguished by its precise detail than by the stylistic elegance of its English. The odd thing is that nowhere in it does he make any mention of the role played in the rescue by his daughter Grace. Her role was completely overshadowed by the scandal that arose as a result of the wreck. There were shortly afterwards two inquests held as the result of the loss of the *Forfarshire*: at the first, evidence was given by a crew member, Daniel Donovan, that the wreck was due to a combination of the appalling condition of the ship's boilers and the criminal incompetence of its master (opinions he had freely offered earlier during his stay on the Longstone to anyone who would listen), as a result of which a fine of £100 was imposed on the ship's owners; at the second, shortly afterwards, on the drowned body of one William Doughty, fireman aboard the *Forfarshire*, the court disputed Donovan's evidence of negligence and found that the man had perished simply as the result of the vessel 'being wrecked in consequence of tempestuous weather'. The newspapers seized on this discrepancy, and inflammatory articles were produced to fuel the flames.

It was during the siege of the Longstone by crowds of reporters struggling to find a new angle on the story that the Grace legend was conceived. A letter written to the

Duke of Northumberland drawing his attention to the 'gallant rescue' aspect of the story produced an immediate effect – one that would not have disgraced even today's enthusiastic journalists. Grace's fame spread like a forest fire. She was awarded three silver medals by the Humane Societies of Glasgow, Leith and Edinburgh, and a fourth from Royal National Institute for the Preservation of Life from Shipwreck (later the Royal National Lifeboat Institution). The Duke himself, not to be outdone, got her a gold medal from the Royal Humane Society (of which he was president); and along with the medals came the gifts of money – twenty pounds here, thirty pounds there, and finally, from Queen Victoria herself, a gift of £50. No less a person than William Wordsworth praised her heroism in verse. Bibles galore, and other works of devotion, showered down on the Longstone. A covey of artists descended on her, all eager to paint Grace, not so much for posterity as for the profit they could make out of selling prints to the public.[2] Grace was worked off her feet. As well as looking after her parents, keeping the lighthouse spick and span and doing a little modest sewing as a spectacle to impress the crowds of visitors that descended upon her, she had to sign hundreds of cards sent out to well-wishers, provide autographs for those demanding them, and had to keep popping off to Bamburgh Castle to receive addresses and awards, and give interviews to all and sundry. History does not record how the poor girl managed to cope with all this attention, but she must have thought that the whole world had gone mad.

Of course, like most newspaper campaigns, it did not last long. Before the end of 1838 a lot of more doubtful characters had started to jump on the bandwagon. She was offered £50 (plus expenses) to appear for a five-week run at the Adelphi Theatre, London; she was contacted by one William Batty, proprietor of the Equestrian Circus in Edinburgh, who offered her the £20 he had raised in a benefit performance for her. The same twittering ladies who had crowded round her to congratulate her on her gallantry now began to question her motives and suggest less than charitable motives for her behaviour.

Finally the Duke of Northumberland himself had to intervene to save her embarrassment. But she still found herself overwhelmed by the obligations that her newfound fame imposed upon her; each gift had its price in the form of some commitment or other. Invited to Newcastle in 1839 by the Mayor and his Corporation, she dithered between accepting and giving further ammunition to her critics, and refusing and giving mortal offence to the Mayor. She eventually found an escape formula that saved faces all round. Her new life continued into 1840. Eventually the Duke took pity on her and decided to wind up the funds she had generated. They were not enormous. They amounted to £1,061; of this amount her father got £175, the North Sunderland boatmen got £161 and Grace herself got the remaining £725, but it was so securely tied up by the trustees that she never got to spend a penny of it. In the spring of 1842 she took the first holiday she had ever had in her life; but by midsummer she had developed a troublesome cough, and the Duke suggested more airy lodgings for her in Alnwick and actually sent the Duchess' own physician to attend on her. But by now she had taken all she could manage of his well-meaning condescension, and she returned to Bamburgh, where she died in October at the age of only twenty-seven in the same little cottage where she had been born.

The heroine was dead, but the legend lived on. There was a whole industry generating memorabilia, from doorstops and boot scrapers to commemorative plaques and figurines, and postcards, portraits, linen and tableware. Even the clothes she wore were shredded for the souvenir hunters. Grace Darling was an early manifestation of the terrifying power of sustained press publicity, a phenomenon that is still very much with us nearly two centuries later.

MARY SEACOLE:
THE BLACK NIGHTINGALE?

Much less well-known to British readers than her contemporary, Florence Nightingale, Mary Jane Seacole was one of the heroines of the Crimean War, chiefly, like Miss Nightingale, on account of the work she did in nursing during the course of the struggle. Her career contrasts markedly with that of her contemporary: she was concerned with the day-to-day treatment of the dying and the wounded more or less at the battle-front; unlike Nightingale she had little or no official backing or recognition for her work, but travelled to the Crimea at her own expense to set up what she called the 'British Hotel' – a tin shack – for Allied servicemen there; she provided food, lodging and domestic comforts to those out of the front and so disengaged from the action, as well as care for frontline soldiers suffering from wounds and from sickness; she even ventured into the front line herself to provide emergency treatment, whereas the nearest that Nightingale normally came to the battlefield was Scutari, twelve hundred miles away in the military hospital on the Asian side of the Bosphorus. Though famous in her homeland of the West Indies, it is perhaps a little surprising that the colourful details of Seacole's nursing career remained so long comparatively unfamiliar to Europeans.

Mary Jane Grant was born in Kingston, Jamaica in 1805, the creole[1] daughter of a Scottish father, an army officer serving in the colony, and a Jamaican mother, a free black who ran a boarding house in the capital. Throughout her life she remained always alert and articulate, and possessed a ready awareness of the social, political and national problems with which she, a black woman, was surrounded. She claimed to have inherited her energy and ambition from her parents: from her father her perception in recognising her problems and her vigour and determination in dealing with them; from her mother her domestic skills and her sound knowledge of medical matters, both European and native, and including what was later to prove invaluable to her, traditional Jamaican medicine, which enabled her to apply herbal remedies to diarrhoea, dysentery and even cholera. Boiled thistle seeds were used as a remedy for diarrhoea, water lily roots to quench thirst, lemongrass to quieten fever, and fig tree sap to 'cleanse the stomach'.

Her marriage to Edwin Horatio Seacole (a godson of Admiral Lord Nelson[2]) ended in 1844 when he died suddenly after eight years of marriage; and the loss of her husband, together with the loss of her mother shortly afterwards, left her free to travel more widely than before. She increased her knowledge of nursing when a cholera attack swept Jamaica at the end of the 1840s, and when she also picked up invaluable hints about its treatment, using the herbal remedies with which she was familiar. In the early 1850s she went to join her brother on the Isthmus of Panama, or New Grenada as it was called. Here she encountered the scarcely-veiled hostility between the native Panamanians and the Americans passing through – she was there when the US General Ulysses S. Grant made his way with US troops to do military service in Panama or in California. She also became acquainted with many prospectors en route for the Californian goldfields. In Panama she continued her social and medical work and helped to deal with a massive outbreak of cholera there in the early 1850s. She became a victim herself, but managed to recover. In 1854, she was rejected by the official organisations responsible for sending nursing orderlies to the Crimea; yet, undeterred, she undertook the 2,000-mile journey there anyway, using her own funds, and soon established herself in the peninsula as a useful but independent appendage to the nursing team there.

The War Office and other departments had already rejected her application to serve in the war, and Florence Nightingale herself refused to make her part of her team of nearly fifty nurses. This was not so much on grounds of racial prejudice, as Seacole – having witnessed other black volunteers rebuffed as she was herself – thought, but because she was concerned that 'her' nurses should not mix socially with the 'Seacole establishment', whom she believed, whatever their nursing qualifications, to be rowdy and drunken in their behaviour.[3] Mary regarded such an accusation as monstrous. She herself firmly believed that Miss Nightingale, if not actually racist in her attitudes, was looking either for ladies, who would be in charge, or for skivvies, who would do the hard work. Mary thought she was no 'lady', in Miss Nightingale's narrow bourgeois sense, nor a 'skivvy', considering her proven skill and her long record of successful nursing. But Nightingale's rejection upset her nonetheless. Two other factors also explain the ill-feeling between the two: one, that Mary Seacole in the early 1840s was alleged to have had an illegitimate child,[4] which Nightingale thought would set her nurses the wrong kind of example, and two, that Mary Seacole had sought, and had successfully achieved, the protection of Nightingale's great adversary Dr John Hall, Inspector-General of Hospitals in the Crimea, who approved of her conduct and helped her in the provision of bandages, needles, thread and various sorts of medicaments.

For eighteen months, Mary Seacole worked hard at her self-imposed war service, securing the commendations of the British press (*The Times* reporter in the Crimea, William Howard ('Billy') Russell, gave favourable publicity to her work) and of Alexis Soyer, the French chef, who admired her industry and the ingenuity of her cooking for servicemen at her 'British Hotel' at Spring Hill, three miles along the road from Balaclava. Miss Nightingale was not appeased, though she did later admit, rather grudgingly, that she had 'done some good' in the Crimea.[5] On 5 September 1855, Mary Seacole was the first woman to enter the blazing town of Sebastopol after the siege. She exhausted not only herself, but also her always rather slender financial resources. She got no financial aid from either the British or the French governments, and at the end of the war found it impossible to dispose of her remaining supplies and equipment, and so was forced into bankruptcy.

When she returned to England Mary fell on hard times.[6] Public affection for her for a while remained unabated. She was awarded several medals for her bravery, including the British Crimea Medal and the French *Légion d'Honneur*. She also enjoyed a rapturous reception at a benefit in her honour at the Royal Surrey Gardens in July 1857, where she was received with members of her family by many of the military establishment, but the affair was mishandled and little was forthcoming in the way of funds. The publication of her autobiography, *The Wonderful Adventures of Mary Seacole in Many Lands*, in the same month, describing her achievements with great gusto, kept her name in the public eye. As well as providing an inspiring example of Mary's candour and her spirit of independence, the book was also instrumental in reinforcing the influence of anti-slavery activity, especially in the strong defence she gave of English 'independence' against the continuation of slavery in the United States. The book speedily went into a second edition; however, it achieved only moderate long-term commercial success. It was not until the late twentieth century that the book really made its mark.

Mary Seacole eventually became known as 'the black Nightingale', commemorating her singular contribution to nursing. Whereas Miss Nightingale was a formidable administrator, Seacole far outstripped her in practical nursing experience, her work including diagnosis, minor surgery, preparing and administering medicines, and carrying out her 'first and last' post-mortem examination on a Panamanian baby to learn more about the effects of cholera. 'Mother (or Aunty) Seacole', as she came to be known, was later briefly employed by Alexandra, Princess of Wales and wife of the future Edward VII, on account of her fame as a nursing pioneer.[7] However, she was not fully recognised until 2004, when a poll voted her the 'greatest black Briton in history'. Mary Seacole later made her home in London after 1857, where she died in 1881. She was buried in the Roman Catholic Cemetery at Kensal Green.[8]

EDITH CAVELL: SAINT OR SUBVERSIVE?

The story of Edith Cavell, the British nurse trapped by the Great War in Belgium who used her position there to smuggle out about 200 captured Allied troops to neutral Holland in contravention of German security regulations, provides for English audiences one of the great

*stories of selflessness and heroism in the First World War. For the Germans, the symbolism is
quite different. Britain made a propaganda use of her execution from the beginning, regarding
her as the 'victim of Germany's most barbarous crime' and representing her as a brave and
patriotic girl (she was actually a mature woman of nearly fifty at the time of the supposed
offences) who devoted her life to nursing and died saving others; the Germans on the other
hand regarded her not as a heroine, not even as a foreign agent, but simply as a troublesome
nuisance. They acknowledged the fact of her execution but did nothing to use the incident either
for publicity or for propaganda, merely admitting that it happened, and pointing out that
France had also executed a number of people – including two German nurses who had aided in
the escape of prisoners-of-war taken by the French – and furthermore that they had a perfect
right to do so.*

Edith Louisa Cavell (the name is pronounced with the stress on the first syllable, Cávell, to rhyme with 'travel') was born in 1865 at Swardeston in Norfolk, where her father served as a priest for forty-five years. She trained as a nurse at the Royal London Hospital, and in 1907 was appointed Matron at the Berkandael Institute in Brussels. Shortly after, she became the first director of a new nursing school, the *École d'Infirmière Dimplonier*, set up by Antoine Depage. When the First World War broke out with the German invasion of Belgium in August 1914, the hospital was taken over by the Red Cross, but Edith continued to work there even during the German occupation.

In the first months of the war she helped in the delivery of large numbers of captured British soldiers from prison camps, whence they absconded to neutral Holland, and from here they were transported back to England. She found herself arrested by German military police in August 1915 on a charge of sheltering escaped British soldiers contrary to military regulations, and was held in prison for ten weeks (the last two in solitary confinement) while the authorities prepared their case against her. Then she was court-martialled, rather than being tried in a civilian court. The matter was brought to the attention of the British government by diplomatic officials, but the Foreign Office, while expressing its regret, took the line that in wartime there was nothing they could do. Nurse Cavell admitted her guilt, saying that she had acted solely from humanitarian motives. The United States (which at this time was not yet at war) protested that the trial, and similar events such as the wartime burning of Louvain and the sinking of the *Lusitania,* were compromising the friendship felt by the USA for Germany; but the authorities on the spot pushed on with the prosecution for fear that the government in Berlin should relent in its intention, and hastily found her guilty. Edith Cavell was executed by firing squad in the early hours of 12 October.[1]

Nurse Cavell immediately became a martyr in the eyes of the British people, and acquired the reputation of a national heroine that has endured to this day. In the period immediately after her death, and continuing into much later years, and even today, she was presented as a mature, patriotic and brave woman who devoted her life to nursing and to helping and saving others. Her story was told in countless newspaper articles, pamphlets and books; and a film was made on the subject in 1939.[2] She became an iconic figure for the recruitment drive in Britain, being used to imply that men had to enlist in the armed forces immediately in order to stop the murder of innocent British females, and was used also in the USA to encourage favourable attitudes towards the Allies in the period before America joined the war. Because of her sex, her noble calling as a nurse, and because of her heroic approach towards her own execution, she was held up to universal admiration as a figure to be revered and imitated; her execution was portrayed as an act of barbarism and moral depravity by the Germans, and on a par with their (equally fictitious) raping of Belgian nuns during their advance. British propaganda ignored any feature of her case that did not fit the one they were spreading, such as the suggestion that in the course of her interrogation she gave out information that incriminated others – indeed, in 1915, the Foreign Office specifically denied that anything she had said was used in the prosecution of others of her comrades. In fact, she knew perfectly well that what she was doing was against German military regulations, but all the same allowed her sympathy for fleeing prisoners to override her natural lawfulness.

At the end of the war, Nurse Cavell's body was exhumed and brought back to Britain. Her coffin, covered by the Union Jack and pulled by six horses, led a procession from Victoria Station to Westminster Abbey through crowded streets to a funeral service attended by George V and Queen Mary in May 1919. The cortège then afterwards travelled to Liverpool Street Station and her coffin was conveyed to Norwich where it was taken to Norwich Cathedral, where after a further service it was finally taken to Life's Green at the east end of the cathedral. Here a memorial had been erected to her memory, and the body was finally reburied near it. A service is held at the memorial every year to celebrate her life. Her name also survives in the names given to streets, squares, and buildings all over the world, and to hospitals, clinics and schools, and survives in scholarships and funds connected with nursing.

EVA DUARTE DE PERÓN: HEROINE OF THE PEOPLE

Maria Eva Duarte de Perón (1919–52) is still regarded as somewhere between a saint and a heroine by masses of Argentinian people. She was the second wife of President Juan Domingo Perón (1895–1974) and was created by him First Lady of Argentina from 1946 until her early death in 1952. She is often called simply Eva Perón, or by the affectionate diminutive Evita ('Little Eva') by the people who adored her.

Maria Eva Duarte was born of unmarried parents in Junin, close to Buenos Aires, in 1919.[1] Her father, Juan Duarte Ibarguran, was an aristocrat from nearby Chivilcoy. He never married her mother, because he was married already, and had run away with her as his mistress. In 1920, when she was only one, he left Juana and other children, and returned to his legal wife, leaving his little family in a severe state of poverty. Juana took in sewing to support her children, and moved into a one-room apartment in Junin. All that her father left the family was his surname Duarte. Young Eva was bright and very pretty, but almost completely uneducated. She took part enthusiastically in school plays and concerts, and had the dream of becoming a famous actress. In the meantime, with her elder brother's financial help, the family had moved to a bigger place where her mother set up a boarding house. In 1935, at the age of fifteen, Eva ran away to Buenos Aires to pursue her dream of movie stardom. Her mother, who seems to have had some idea of the young girl's intentions, arranged for her to live with the Bustamontes, who were friends of the family. Eva struggled to find employment, and in 1936 appeared with a theatre company, worked as a photographic model, and was cast in bit parts in a few B-grade movies. As the result of her modest success in films and on the stage, she was able to rent a respectable apartment in Buenos Aires, and in 1943 helped to set up the Argentine Radio Syndicate (ARA). It was in the January of the following year that, on the occasion of an 'artistic festival' to raise funds after a serious earthquake in San Juan, she first met Juan Perón.[2] It was not long after this that Eva and Perón began to live together. At the time, entertainment and politics were regarded as totally different spheres, and there was some surprise and not a little gossip when Perón introduced Eva to his political associates, even allowing her to sit in on political meetings. Up to this point Eva had had no knowledge of, or interest in, Argentinian politics, but she soon developed a feel for it.

The difference in their ages (he was forty-eight and she was only twenty-four in 1944) gave a populist and a celebrity feel to his career, and his next move, to organise radio and stage performers into a trade union met with considerable popular support, especially when she was elected president of it. Shortly afterwards, Eva embarked on a series of daily broadcasts entitled 'Towards a Better Future' in the ordinary language of an everyday woman which brought her to popular attention as a rising political star. By early 1945 a group of senior army officers, known from their programme as GOU (*Gobierno, Orden, Unidad* – Government, Order, Unity) earned a considerable following, and, fearing they might prove too powerful with the backing of the *decamisados*,[3] the new President, Eldemiro Farrell, in October 1945 ordered Peron's arrest and imprisonment. A massive demonstration of over a quarter of a million formed in front of Casa Rosada, the Argentinian government house, and on 17 October his release was secured.[4]

All this persuaded Juan Perón to enter the contest for the Argentinian presidency in 1946. He campaigned strongly, and Eva used her broadcasting skills to publicise his message every week, highlighting her own humble beginnings to show her solidarity with the underprivileged. She also travelled the campaign trail with him, so that the masses got to know her as 'Evita'. After Juan's election to the presidency, Eva embarked on a goodwill tour of Europe – the so-called 'Rainbow Tour' – when she visited not only Franco and the Pope, but many other European countries as well. She was well-received by De Gaulle in France, and visited Versailles, but was less warmly received in Switzerland, and snubbed by Britain, where she called off her visit when she learned that the royal family would not meet her. Perón's critics back home suggested the real reason for the tour was not to enhance Argentinian standing in Europe, but rather to put money on deposit in numbered Swiss bank accounts. Certainly Eva returned from Europe with fashionable Paris hair styles and *haute couture* in place of the rather flashy film-star costume she had worn previously.

On her return to Argentina, Eva concerned herself with charitable undertakings, and, rejected by the ladies of the so-called Society of Beneficence (*Sociedad de Beneficence*) on account of her less than distinguished origins, established her own Eva Perón Foundation to raise money for the impoverished, in the absence of adequate social service provision in the country. It was not, as its enemies suggested, merely a machine for funnelling money into private Swiss bank accounts, but one for collecting voluntary contributions from charitable societies and even from private businesses and trade unions (later with a government-funded levy from casinos and horse-racing tracks) to supply the needs of those in want – gifts in the form of footwear, sewing machines, kitchen equipment and other practical things. The Foundation also provided scholarships and built homes and hospitals,[5] employed 14,000 workers and controlled funds of over 3 billion pesos (about $200 million at the prevailing rate of exchange). She spent a great deal of time dealing with the sick and the diseased, and in a short time had acquired a saintly reputation, being idolised and almost worshipped by humble people.

Gradually her interests widened to include more specifically political programmes. She supported women's suffrage in her broadcasts, but at first lacked the clout to achieve very much. It took over two years to get a bill passed through Parliament decreeing equality of political rights, but in 1947 this was eventually accomplished. One of the major consequences of the reform was the foundation, immediately afterwards, of the Female Perónist Party, which soon boasted a membership of over half a million women. With female support, Juan Perón was able to secure a 63 per cent majority in the 1951 presidential election.

In 1951, Eva aimed at achieving nomination for the vice-presidency, a spectacular rise to political importance which surprised even Perón himself, and seemed to threaten his opponents with the possibility of her achieving supreme power as President if he were to die. There was a massive political rally in August in the Avenida Nueve de Julio, near the Casa Rosada in Buenos Aires, where the enormous crowds were addressed both by Perón and Eva on a vast scaffolding backed by enormous portraits of the pair. She begged to be given more time to decide whether she wanted the nomination, promising to broadcast her decision within a few days. When she did so, she turned the nomination down. The reasons for her reluctance became clear only later. Partly it was due to pressure from powerful political colleagues, from the military and even from the Argentinian upper classes, who feared her political ambitions and preferred she be kept out of power – a view shared to some extent even by her husband; but chiefly it was due to Eva's rapidly declining health by reason of rapidly advancing cervical cancer. As early as 1950, though she was barely thirty, there had been advance warnings of illness of the gravest sort; she had suffered fainting fits even before the time of the 1951 rally, and had undergone an appendectomy; but she continued to suffer from vaginal bleeding, and after her 'Renouncement' (as her abandonment of her vice-presidential candidacy was rather grandly known) submitted to a radical hysterectomy as a way of treating it. She rallied briefly, but continued a very sick woman.

Eva was well enough to take part in the celebrations of Perón's re-election as President in June 1952, but only as the result of physical support to keep her upright, and the administration of repeated and severe doses of pain medication to mitigate her suffering. She underwent chemotherapy (a fairly novel treatment at that time), but rapidly wasted away, and weighed less than ninety pounds at the time of her death on 26 July 1952. She was given a state funeral; hundreds of thousands of admirers, chiefly women, flocked to her funeral and Buenos Aires florists found their shelves bare, as mountains of flowers were piled up outside the official presidential residence. Her body, from the beginning sadly decomposing, was hastily embalmed[6] and held for burial, and a monument planned, even bigger than the US Statue of Liberty, in which her corpse was to be enshrined.

Her massive monument, however, was never completed. In 1955, Juan Perón was overthrown in a military coup, and a military junta took control in Argentina, ruling until 1971. Perónism was legally banned, and it became an offence to possess a picture either of him or of Eva, or even to mention their names. The new military dictatorship removed Eva's body, and its whereabouts remained a mystery for sixteen years. Eventually the body was found. It had been buried in a crypt in Milan, was now reburied at Perón's house in Spain, and finally restored to its homeland. In 1973 Juan Perón had come out of exile, returned to Argentina and now became President for the third time. Perón died in office in 1974, and his third wife, Isabel Perón, succeeded him as President – the first female president in the western hemisphere. She put the two bodies briefly on display together, then they were buried separately, Eva's body in La Recoleta cemetery in Buenos Aires, in an elaborate thief-proof crypt.

Eva Perón became a legend in Argentina, loved and respected by masses of people in much the same way as Che Guevara. Though it is not a public holiday, the anniversary of her death is marked by Argentines every year; her image has appeared on Argentine coins, and a denomination of currency called 'Evitas' was named in her memory. Ciudad Evita (Evita City) is located just outside Buenos Aires, and remains a thriving suburb today. Her supporters continue to regard her as a shining example of passion and sincerity, rejecting any suggestion that either she or her husband were fascists. After the Malvinas War, in 2002, a museum was opened in one of the very buildings that had housed the Eva Perón Foundation, to commemorate her, and called in her honour 'Museo Evita'. Though rejected by many foreigners as a heroine,[7] her story, the subject of a world-famous musical play by Tim Rice and Andrew Lloyd-Webber, called *Evita*, remains for many people, Argentinians included, the legend of the oldest of theatre clichés, the rags-to-riches story, and she remains a very powerful popular cultural icon.

PHYLLIS THOM:
JAPANESE PRISONER OF WAR

Phyllis Thom found herself caught up in the Japanese invasion of Malaya in 1941 while working as a young nursing sister in the colonial Nursing Service in the General Hospital at Alor Star in Kedah in the Malay Peninsula. The story of her captivity was the basis of a programme called Tenko[1] *broadcast by BBC TV from 1981 to 1985, and running to three series. The story also appeared in a book by Lavinia Warner and John Sandilands called* Women Beyond the Wire, *published in 1982, and in the feature film* Paradise Road *in 1997.*

Phyllis Mary Erskine Briggs was born in Bexhill-on-Sea, East Sussex, in June 1908, to an English couple who met while working in the Caucasus. She spent her early youth in Paris, where her father was chaplain of Christ Church in Neuilly-sur-Seine, and of the English Hospital in central Paris. She was orphaned in her early teens, and care of her was taken over by her aunt and uncle in northern England. She moved on to take up nursing in Manchester, and later at King's College, London. Her passion for travel took her to Malaya, where she was caught up in the Japanese invasion in December 1941 while working as a sister in Kedah. She was evacuated first to Singapore, where she worked in a hospital taking in air-raid victims; then she was placed aboard the cargo ship *Mata Hari*, which, overloaded with women and children, was taken prize by the Japanese navy, and they were unceremoniously dumped ashore on the coast of Sumatra, and left without food or water for twenty-four hours before being marched to their first prison camp.

In spite of Japan's having signed the Geneva Convention in 1929 regarding the humane treatment of prisoners of war and non-combatant civilians, and quite contrary to their previous good record in respect of their behaviour during the Russo-Japanese War of 1905, the Japanese earned for themselves worldwide condemnation for their brutal treatment of prisoners from 1941 to 1945. Their brutality was sometimes explained away by the suggestion that customarily to the Japanese soldier, death was preferable to capture, so that maltreatment in captivity was to be expected, if not welcomed; but the real reason for this cruelty was the rise of Japanese fatalism regarding their future destiny in Asia and the world, which combined with the new spirit of militarism in senior military circles, and the emergence of a discipline based on physical violence in the training for the armed forces, together with the Japanese Special Police for the Protection of the State, the Kempei Tei, and the suicide cult among Japanese airmen training for service against the more powerful US Pacific fleet.

Together with hundreds of other women, and a great many young children, Phyllis Briggs was held prisoner in one camp or another for the next three and a half years, and obliged to endure constant hunger, pointless cruelty, hardship and indignity in ramshackle camps scarcely fit for animals. On the jetty, the very first day she landed, she took off her watch and the scraps of jewellery she had with her, tied them in her handkerchief and hid them in her hair. They were to prove invaluable later as currency with which to buy food and medicines.

Her first camp, for forty women, was improvised by her captors from a camp originally designed for a mere twenty Chinese coolie labourers in the tin mines at Muntok in Sumatra. Their sleeping accommodation was a sloping concrete slab, and their lavatory an open drain. After three months most of the women and children were moved away, but Phyllis and five others with some experience remained behind as nurses to care for the 500 male soldiers and civilians who were drafted in to replace them, working in the mines. Later the women were moved to a group of former Dutch bungalows in what was named the Women's Internment Camp, Palembang, and this became their prison for the next twenty months. It was in this camp that Phyllis became seriously ill, passing blood to an alarming extent, but, with the aid of a few medicines bought or scrounged from a Roman Catholic Caritas Foundation in the vicinity, she was steadily nursed back to health by a friend, Alice Rossie, so that she managed to recover. She and the other nurses with her devoted themselves to a daily round of the male prisoners in the camp, and to bringing serious cases to the notice of the few doctors working among them.

In September 1943 the women, and a few children remaining, were given twenty-four hours' notice of their captors' intention to move them. Their hopes ran high that perhaps they were to be shipped to Java, where it was thought conditions were better and where food was more plentiful. Instead, they found themselves being marched only about a mile to a former men's camp that had recently been evacuated. After the tolerable privacy of the bungalows they found themselves in a much inferior place, ramshackle and infested with rats. Here, in April 1944, their already scanty food rations were reduced further, and the women were forced to resort to growing their own vegetables outside the prison compound.

In August 1944, Prelambang was bombed by Allied aircraft, a development which lifted the spirits of the prisoners more than it frightened them, and the next week, a batch of cards from the outside world reached them, kept back, it appeared, for several weeks from delivery by the prison guards. In October the women were moved back to Banka, and landed on the same jetty as had brought them to Sumatra in 1941. There, contrary to all their expectations, they found a spanking new camp with a proper kitchen purpose-built to receive them.

Finally, in April 1945, they were moved again, to a rubber plantation in south-western Sumatra. It was here that, on 26 August 1945, twelve days after the end of the war, the camp commander announced to them that Japan had surrendered.[2] Phyllis Briggs, weighing less than six stones, was flown on a stretcher to join family members in New Zealand and to embark on a period of slow recuperation.

She returned to nursing in Malaya in June 1946, and in the following year was married to Robbie Clifton Thom, who became head of the Malayan Police Special Branch, and subsequently a security officer in British Guiana before its independence. After her husband died in 1967, she retired to Bournemouth, where she became a volunteer for Barnardo's. She died at the age of 100 in 2008.

ANNE FRANK:
MARTYR TO NAZI RACE POLICIES

Anne Frank was the symbol of the Nazi tyranny inflicted on Germany and much of the rest of Europe at the time of the Second World War, seeing and feeling the effect of Nazi policies on the everyday lives of ordinary people. She kept a diary in which she recorded the everyday occurrences that made up her and her family's life during the Nazi era. It is not that she was more important, or that her experiences were more significant than those of many thousands of others, or that they produced more pain, but that they tell a truthful story of the consequences for ordinary people of a tyrannical regime inflicted on a nation and a continent, and its dire historical consequences for the whole world.

Annalies ('Anne') Marie Frank was born the second daughter to Otto and Edith Frank, a Jewish family living in Frankfurt am Main in Weimar Germany in June 1929, shortly before the end of the Weimar Republic. The family was not well off; Otto was a small businessman employing about half a dozen workers in his factory, Edith a hausfrau looking after her two daughters. When the Nazis came to power in 1933 they felt the impact on their lives of a party that tolerated and even encouraged the expression of popular anti-Jewish feelings – slogans painted in whitewash on the windows of shops, insults and even blows exchanged on the streets, attacks on synagogues – and as a result decided to leave the country, along with about 300,000 others. The family moved to Amsterdam in the Netherlands, where Otto established a company, Opetka, to produce the fruit extract pectin for domestic and various industrial uses. In 1938 he went on to set up another company, Pectacon, for wholesale dealings in herbs, pickling salts and spices used in the manufacture of sausages.[1] He took premises on the Prinsengracht, an old street facing one of Amsterdam's many canals, where he took on about half a dozen Dutch employees. Edith found conditions here more tolerable, and the two girls were enrolled in local schools where they both did well.

In the spring of 1940, the German armies invaded France and the Low Countries and the family fell once again under Nazi control. It did not take long for Nazi policies of anti-semitism to begin to bite. There were a number of restrictions on Jews' lives, soon followed by mandatory registration and segregation. Anne and her sister Margot found themselves excluded from school and compelled to go to exclusively Jewish schools; their mother Edith was shunned and insulted as she shopped; none of the family was allowed to go to the cinema (though Anne had in mind to become a film actress later in life). Otto found that the Nazi laws against Jews being employers of Gentiles and Jewish ownership of businesses were now also to apply in German-occupied territories, and would mean he would lose the ownership of his companies. As a result, in the course of 1941, he transferred the ownership of his shares in Pentacon to Johannes Kleiman, and his directorship to another Gentile, Jan Gies; he did the same with his interests in Opetka, though he still retained a small income from his businesses on which to support his family. The crunch came in July 1942 when Margot received a call-up notice from the Central Office for Jewish Emigration (Zentralstelle für jüdische Auswanderung) directing her to report to a work camp, a move almost certainly involving her deportation back to Germany. The family took the decision to disappear and go into hiding.

The place they chose for their refuge was the rear portion of their premises in the Prinsengracht, known in Dutch as the Achterhuis, the 'rear premises', referred to in Anne's diary as the 'secret annexe'. This was a three-storey space entered from a landing above the Opetka offices, a space comprising two small rooms, with a bathroom and toilet, and, on the floor above, a larger living room with another smaller room alongside, and from this room a ladder leading upwards to the attic, used for sleeping. To prevent detection, the door to the Achterhuis was hidden behind a bookcase. Only six people knew of their concealment,[2] and it was these who brought them foodstuffs and other supplies, as well as news of the outside world. Later, the numbers of the refugees increased when the Franks were joined by the van Pels family, Hermann, Auguste and their sixteen-year-old son Peter, and later still by Fritz Pfeffer, a dentist who was a friend of the family. This meant a certain amount of overcrowding of their sparse accommodation, and provoked frequent friction between the eight of them.

These were the dramatis personae whose lives, friendships and quarrels were recorded in Anne's diary. For her thirteenth birthday in June 1942, just before the family went into hiding, Anne's father bought her a cloth-bound autograph book with a lock on it, which Anne decided she would use as a diary, and she began to record in it almost immediately her thoughts, her beliefs and her impressions. She wrote a lot, and when it was full she supplemented it with sheaves of loose pages, nearly all of which survived her ordeal. In her diary she detailed the squabbles that occurred over the fair division of their limited supplies of food; her anxious anticipation of the daily visits from the 'helpers', especially the young typist Bep with whom she formed a close bond; her first girlish affair with Peter van Pels and her first kiss, though later they drifted apart as her ardour for him cooled; her differences with her mother, whom at first she found sarcastic and overbearing, though she later came to respect and love her; and her differences with her elder sister Margot, whose placid manner pleased her parents but irritated Anne, though later they too grew closer and finished by being inseparable chums. She wrote assiduously each day, her style maturing from its original, childish form into something surprisingly adult and mature. Her childhood ambition to be a film star gave way to the wish to become one day a journalist or an author. Her last entry in her diary was for 1 August 1942.

Three days later, their hiding place was stormed by the German Security Police (Grüne Politzei) on a tip-off from an informant whose identity the inmates never discovered, and the whole group were taken to the Gestapo Headquarters and held overnight for questioning.[3] On 5 August, they were transferred to the local House of Detention (Huis van Bewaring) and afterwards transferred to Westerbork, nominally a transit camp, though through it by this time over 100,000 Jews had passed on their way to deportation. From here, at the beginning of September, the group was sent to Auschwitz in Poland.[4] On arrival, after a gruelling journey lasting three days, the men were separated from the women, and any children under fifteen were immediately sent to the gas chambers. Anne, who escaped execution by a matter of weeks (she had had her fifteenth birthday the previous June) was stripped, her head shaved and her arm tattooed with her prisoner number, then set to work in a thin uniform hauling rocks and cutting turf which was then bundled into rolls and sent away, and then she was crammed into overcrowded barracks at night with neither heat nor light. Food was scarce, working hours extremely long. Surviving witnesses described her as a tower of strength to the others; she even managed to arrange extra bread rations for her mother and sister, both of whom had become ill and were confined to barracks. Disease among the prisoners was rampant: Anne herself was affected by scabies, which broke out in patches all over her skin. Margot was removed temporarily and Edith permanently to the infirmary, also dark and unheated, where eventually Margot recovered enough to be released. Edith remained seriously ill. She stopped eating altogether, but contrived to pass her food to her daughters through a hole she had made at the base of the infirmary wall.

At the end of October, about 800 of the women were relocated to Bergen-Belsen in Lower Saxony, the number including Anne, Margot and Auguste van Pels.[5] At first the prisoners were under canvas in spite of the inclement weather, and the death toll rose. Anne thought that both her parents were dead and grew deeply depressed, but work went on for her even in her emaciated condition, and witnesses testified how ragged, thin and sick she looked. Margot again fell ill and was confined to her bunk, and Anne got the additional job of looking after her. In March 1945, after a harsh winter, a typhus epidemic broke out at the camp, killing eventually 17,000 prisoners. By this time the condition of the inmates was desperate: they were dressed only in rags, they were hungry, they were exhausted, and nearly all of them suffering from some illness or other. Margot fell from her bunk in her weakened state and the shock of the fall killed her. A few days later, Anne herself died of exhaustion and starvation. She was not yet sixteen years old. Not long after, British troops liberated Belsen on 15 April 1945, and the scenes of horror they found there are too well-known to warrant description here.[6]

Otto Frank, in spite of his slight frame and weakened condition, was the only one of the family group to survive imprisonment in the camps. Others of the more extended family also survived, as they had fled Germany in the 1930s but had gone further afield, to Britain, Switzerland and the USA. After the war, the diary came into his hands, and, having revised it, he determined on publishing it as a family record and as a record of the war as it had affected her. After a number of references to it in the Dutch press by those to whom Otto had shown the diary, it was published in the Netherlands in 1947, and then in Britain and the USA in 1952. At first it got rather a mixed reception, but by the mid-1950s it was firmly established as a valuable war record, and in 1955 a play based on the story was produced on Broadway (where it was awarded a Pulitzer Prize for drama), followed by the movie *The Diary of Anne Frank* in 1959.

The diary, of course, also attracted the critics. There were those who asserted that it had been heavily edited, or even totally fabricated, by Otto Frank as a money-making stunt (in fact, from the very beginning, subject to the provision that the first 80,000 Swiss francs each year were set aside for the family's benefit, much of the revenue raised went to Jewish charitable causes connected with the war). He went on to win a chain of legal cases challenging the authenticity of the diary, and was awarded substantial damages by the courts from a number of detractors. But mainly the praise exceeded the blame: the diary was extolled for its content and qualities by a wide section of eminent people like Eleanor Roosevelt, Hillary Clinton, Nelson Mandela and Václav Havel, and was translated into more than thirty languages for world reading. When Otto Frank died in 1980, he willed it to the Dutch Institute for War Documentation as a major historical document.[7]

The Prinsengracht premises were saved from demolition in 1957, and the Achterhuis opened as a museum in 1960, receiving by the end of the century nearly a million visitors. Even the horse chestnut tree referred to in the diary by Anne Frank – she said she could see it from the window – was preserved from felling, and treated for the fungal disease that had been affecting it. If Anne had been alive to know it, she would have been greatly gratified by the renown that history heaped upon her; being dead, however, her name was firmly inscribed in the record of war martyrs.

SOPHIE SCHOLL:
GERMAN RESISTANCE LEADER

It is a commonly held opinion in Britain that the mass of the German people, bitterly disillusioned at the treatment of Germany after the First World War, were solidly behind Hitler as Führer and Nazi policies in general during the Third Reich, and that consequently they must share the blame for German policies in the war and, at home, in respect of the suppression of public liberties and the extermination of the Jewish minority in their society. Perhaps many Germans did; but there were also opposition elements to Hitler's rule that suggest not only that some did not agree with his views and actions, but that they were actually prepared to run the risk of saying so in public. Sophie Scholl was one of these.

Sophia Magdalena Scholl was born in 1921 not far from Stuttgart in central Germany, in the Town Hall of Forchtenberg on the Kocher, where her father was mayor. She was fourth in a large family of six children. The whole family was Lutheran. She had a happy childhood at junior school, but her family moved to Ludwigsburg in 1930 and two years later to Ulm, where her father had a business consultancy. In 1932 Sophie started secondary school, and, after the Nazis came to power in 1933, like the great majority of schoolgirls at the time, she joined the League of German Girls (*Bund Deutscher Mädel*), the female Nazi youth movement equivalent to the Girl Guides. Her initial enthusiasm soon gave way to dissatisfaction: she was aware of the relentless stream of political propaganda to which they were subjected, and shared the critical outlook towards the Nazi regime of her father, her friends and a number of her teachers. The arrest of her brother Hans and a number of her friends in 1937 because of their attitudes made a strong impression on her; this, together with her interest in pictorial art from about this time and her interest in philosophy and theology and her fundamental Lutheran belief in the value and importance of the individual, all led to an increasing dissatisfaction with Nazism.

In 1940, in the early stages of the war, she left secondary school and became a kindergarten teacher in Ulm, hoping that service there would be accepted as a qualification for university entry instead of the normal National Labour Service (*Reichsarbeitsdienst*). This, however, was not the case, and in 1942 she was obliged to embark on a six-month spell of auxiliary war service as a nursery teacher in Blumberg. She disliked the regimentation of military service, and the restrictions it imposed on her freedom to think for herself. On the termination of this service, in May 1942, she was in fact admitted to the University of Munich to study biology and philosophy. Her brother Hans, who was already there studying medicine, introduced her to his circle of friends, and together they developed their interest in art, music, literature and philosophy, as well as sharing their love of hiking, swimming and skiing. On the whole, this was a happy time, though marred by the demands of the regime on the individual, as when Sophie was forced to spend her summer vacation doing war work at a metallurgical plant in Ulm. This was the time, too, that her father was arrested and detained on account of critical observations to a fellow employee about Hitler.

Her boyfriend at the time was Fritz Hartnagel,[1] with whom she conducted a lively correspondence before he was drafted to the Eastern Front in May 1942. Before he left, he gave a copy of Cardinal Newman's *Sermons*, the reading of which was important in focusing her mind on questions of religious faith, and strengthened her determination to oppose the Nazi regime as it operated in Germany. Although by persuasion she remained Lutheran, she paid heed to the pronouncements at that time of Cardinal Clemens von Galen, Roman Catholic bishop of Münster, who in his sermons was irrepressible as a critic of the regime. Hartnagel informed her in his letters from the Russian Front of the execution of Soviet prisoners[2] and of the mass rounding up and murder of Jews, and she found all this deeply repugnant. The upshot of this deep disquiet was the formation of a society called 'The White Rose', urging Germans to think critically about the actions of their authorities during the war, and to offer passive resistance to the most heinous of its decisions.

The original members of the White Rose were only half a dozen or so, chiefly students, the three most important of whom were friends and associates of Sophie: Hans her brother, and two of his friends Willi Graf and Christopher Probst. Between them they produced six anti-Nazi political resistance pamphlets, indicating ways in which the regime might be peacefully resisted. No one spoke of blowing up bridges or sabotaging railways; the idea was to point to Christian moral principles and enhance the awareness on the part of ordinary people of the atrocities that were being carried out in their name. These pamphlets were duplicated by their authors and distributed clandestinely among the students and other citizens of Munich. It was while the sixth of these was being distributed at the University of Munich that almost the entire membership of the White Rose was arrested by the police.

The accused faced charges of high treason before the People's Court in Munich in February 1943. Sophie Scholl, though afraid, never flinched in her indictment of Nazi wrongdoing. She declared: 'Somebody, after all, had to make a start. What we wrote and said is also believed in by many others. They dare not express themselves as we did.' But her defence fell on deaf ears. Their trial lasted less than a day, and at the end of it all the accused were condemned to death for high treason, and on the second day, before 5.00 p.m., all the convicted students were beheaded by guillotine in the Stadelheim Prison, Munich, by the public executioner. Sophie's final comment was: 'Such a fine, sunny day and I have to go; but what does my death matter if through us thousands of people are awakened and stirred to action?' Unfortunately, the deaths of these protesters did not even ripple the calm of German public opinion generally; the grip of Nazi propaganda control over the media was so secure that most people never even heard of their sacrifice. Though a copy of the sixth leaflet was smuggled out of Germany and thousands of copies scattered over Germany by the RAF in the following weeks, the outcome of the trial created few repercussions in Germany as a whole, and the episode subsided into oblivion.[2]

In 2009, Dr Frank McDonough, the first person since the war to examine Gestapo interrogation records and court files, published his definitive account of her career and trial in *Sophie Scholl: the Woman Who Defied Hitler*, though there have been a number of German accounts of the short-lived blossoming of the White Rose in stage and screen productions relating to the movement.

DIANA:
THE 'PEOPLE'S PRINCESS'

Diana Spencer, a representative of one of the oldest aristocratic families in Britain, who, after her marriage to Charles, the heir to the throne, became Princess of Wales, developed into one of the great personality icons – if not the greatest – of the later twentieth century. How and why did this come about? In order to answer such a question, it is necessary to examine the reality of both the 'personality' and the 'icon' of the statement.

Diana was born the third of three girls in July 1961 on one of the family's estates in Norfolk, near Sandringham. The only boy in the family was deformed and had not long survived his birth in 1960, leaving her father John with a grim determination to produce a male heir, which he eventually did in 1964, when Charles Spencer was born. Diana, his elder sister, was an angelically pretty but rather stubborn little girl, with a chequered childhood; even at the age of six her school report commented that she was 'the most scheming child' her teacher had ever met. Her grandfather, Earl Jack, at Althorp House in Northamptonshire was a mean old codger who was always short of money. He refused to follow the trend of opening the house to visitors, and instead hand-washed the family china, dusted the books in the library and produced his own covers for the furniture, needle-pointing them by hand, while refusing to sell a single one of the treasures he had hanging on the walls. He kept Diana's father short of cash, too; hence the money Johnny got from his wife Frances, originally the daughter of Lady Fermoy,[1] proved a life saver, though she still got treated like a brood-mare. As a teenager, Diana, never a great scholar, read a good many of the 723 romantic novels churned out by Barbara Cartland, and provided unwitting evidence of their brain-rotting qualities by swearing she would only ever marry 'for love'. Eventually her mother did just that: she left Viscount Johnny for the wallpaper heir Peter Shand-Kydd, and there was an acrimonious divorce, giving him custody of the children and making them even more unhappy. Diana stood by the open door for weeks, waiting for her mother to come back. Eventually, her father, by now even more monosyllabic than usual, remarried without even telling the children. Diana's new stepmother was Raine, Countess of Dartmouth, the daughter of that very same authoress Barbara Cartland. Diana did not like either of them (though Raine had modern ideas and soon opened Althorp and managed to make it into a profitable concern). In 1975 Jack died and Johnny became the 8th Earl Spencer. Diana became Lady Diana Spencer.

By the time she was seventeen, Diana had been to a variety of schools: an English school, where she failed all her O-levels (twice) and a girls' finishing school in

Switzerland, leaving her with low-grade academic objectives but good skills in flower arranging. Then she persuaded her parents to allow her to move to London, where an apartment was purchased for her and for her three flatmates in the Earls Court area. She became one of the 'Sloane Rangers', with their affected accents, socially very active but intellectually rather limited, or 'nice-but-dim' as they preferred to put it. Diana tried her hand at a number of things, such as dabbling in a cookery course, nannying well-to-do children, and teaching dance also to small children, but nothing too demanding and certainly nothing that interfered with her extended holidays. She even worked as a cleaner and a cocktail waitress. Already she was showing what became increasingly obvious later, that, in spite of her awareness of her intellectual inferiority, she was good at meeting people, particularly hospital or mental patients, joking or dancing with them and having extended conversations during her frequent visits. Such visits became an important part of her early life. She met Prince Charles once, in a ploughed field at Althorp, and immediately fell in love with him in a big way.[2]

The more she got to know of the royal family, the less pleased she was with the humourless, starchy atmosphere with which they surrounded themselves: Margaret was the most icy of the younger generation, and among the older representatives she found Philip rude, fierce and aggressive, and the Queen, whom she would have dearly liked to love, aloof and much absorbed by her high sense of duty to her 'red boxes'. Buckingham Palace she found full of little cliques from the posses of servants upward, with all the great figures living in their own little empires.[3] The whole period of her engagement proved a severe trial, though never once did she question the wisdom of marrying the Prince of Wales. But the British public worshipped her, and, whereas members of the family hated and feared the newspapers, Diana quite enjoyed the constant attentions of hordes of newspapermen, enjoyed playing pranks on them and enjoyed girlish jokes with them. She seems to have thought that when her position was established she could bring a breath of fresh air into the royal family's stifling lives. She even quite enjoyed her grand wedding at St Pauls in July 1981, and the interest of the public and her national reputation had never stood so high.

The reality of her married life turned out to be quite different. Twenty-year-old Diana was a little girl at heart, but Charles had been born middle-aged, and neither was prepared to make any allowances for the other. The Queen was distressed at her ignorance and sullenness; Philip thought she was 'pushy' and hogged some of the adoration that should have been bestowed on the Queen; Charles was angered at her bulimia and her refusal to enjoy his relaxations in the field; she constantly felt her nose rubbed in her own intellectual inferiority and was increasingly obsessed by what she thought was his lingering regard for Camilla Parker-Bowles, the old flame she thought he would give up after their marriage.[4] Diana brightened when she left Buckingham Palace for private apartments in Kensington Palace. She could now escape some of the suffocating formality of court. Meantime, the press continued their relentless pursuit of Diana; the public, too, as during their tour of Wales, when ecstatic crowds clustered round the Princess, giving her gifts, and Charles was heard to grumble, 'I'm just the chap who carries the Princess' flowers.' When eventually Diana became pregnant public interest in and concern for her knew no bounds.

The birth of Prince William in June 1982 did something to re-establish concord between Charles and Diana. The Prince shared the birth with her in St Mary's Hospital, and his comments, then and afterwards, seemed to indicate a brighter future for the marriage.[5] But the improvement was only temporary.

Diana's insistence on attending the funeral of Princess Grace of Monaco (a figure in some ways rather like herself) in September 1982, and the royal family's total failure to recognise it or comment on it, and the state visit of Charles and Diana to Australia in March 1983, with Diana's easy populist success and Charles' more ponderous performance, all added to the widespread impression that relations between the married pair were rocky. On their return to Kensington Palace the image began to crystallise of Diana as a moody fantasist and Charles as a sad, eccentric figure racked by self-doubt and appalled by the megastardom of his wife. The marriage steadied a little with the birth of a second son to Diana in September 1984, but Charles, when he saw the baby, cried out in dismay to his wife, 'But he's got red hair!' – the Spencer trademark, since many of the family were auburn – and however much Diana tried to recapture his affections she had little success. The truth is that, with she being the easygoing Sloane and he the bookish eccentric, the pair had precious little in common.

In public the couple tried to preserve some sense of harmony, but privately whenever they were speaking at all they were usually quarrelling, even throwing things at each other. Diana spent much of her time in tears, and Charles in demanding peevishly, 'What are you crying about now?' Diana's conduct grew progressively more unpredictable and her bulimia worse. No one could deny Diana's spontaneity; the only trouble is that she acted first and then thought about the consequences later. The result of this unreliability was that she landed herself in some deep holes, and often contrived to hurt many who thought themselves her friends. For example, she at first welcomed the appearance in Buckingham Palace of Sarah Ferguson, whom she thought of as an ally and a confidant; she saw her meeting the same responses and making the same mistakes as she had made herself when she was new to the scene – hence she felt very sorry for her. But Fergie, whose marriage to Prince Andrew finally ended in divorce, was astonished to learn later that several times she had let her down, and had tactlessly breached what should have been sacred confidences. Where she never went wrong was in her unerring instinct for playing to the gallery; her judgement of what was good for her brightly burnished public image was faultless, and much better than anything the Windsors could achieve. For example in November 1985, in Washington, she dazzled the President[6] and Mrs Reagan and an assembly of over 400 people in a spectacular dance with John Travolta (after which, he said, he 'just turned back into a pumpkin'); in December 1985, at an evening at Covent Garden, she slipped from the royal box and went up on stage with Wayne Sleep to perform a sparkling dance routine to the music of Uptown Girl.

She remained obsessively concerned over the role of Camilla in Charles' life but refused to pay him back in his own coin by taking a lover. Yet in the end she did have a number of friends with whom relations were extremely close. One of them was one of her own bodyguards (or 'Personal Protection Officer' – her PPO), Sgt Barry Mannakee, who was moved on when the affair came to light; another was James Hewitt, a staff captain in the Life Guards, who got himself posted to Germany after a torrid affair, and left her life. Others were Philip Dunne, David Waterhouse, Rory Scott and James Gilbey (an upmarket car salesman related to the Gilbey gin family). Because of their easy charm and beauty, they got themselves referred to in Savile Row tailors' language as '42 longs'.

As if this were not enough, Diana also began to unburden herself, in confidence, to psychiatrists, and later even agreed to collaborate with Andrew Morton in the writing of her side of the whole affair, in the columns of the *Sunday Times*, a work later published as a book *Diana: Her True Story*. Far from clearing the air, which she seems to have wanted to do, this could not help but illuminate the full horrors of the experience and deepen the resentment with which the royal family regarded her.[7] She deepened the offence further by denying at first that she had anything to do with it, which gave her an air of duplicity as well as of treachery. All this resulted in January 1993 in a 'trial separation' between the couple, a suggestion by the Queen herself, and Diana's moving out of Highgrove, the Prince's Gloucestershire home, and back into Kensington Palace.

Operating from an office in St James Palace, the Princess now set about the task of selling the Diana franchise like a being possessed. Part of her effort was due to the recognition that this 'touchy-feely' philanthropic endeavour was a project close to her heart and something which redeemed her otherwise useless existence, but there was also the sure knowledge that such activity drew the unremitting attention of the newspapers to her and sustained their interest in her. With 'big-tent' names like Angelina Jolie, Bob Geldof and Madonna, and no longer constrained by the polite reticence of the royals, she went off jetting round the world, visiting India, Egypt, Zimbabwe,[8] Nepal, America North and South, doing work of great sympathy and generating marvellous pictures and headlines. Buckingham Palace persisted in its arthritic efforts to promote a reconciliation; Charles (much against their instincts) went on TV in his Dimbleby interview in June 1994 and squirmed uncomfortably as his interviewer extracted confessions of disloyalty and infidelity from him.

Diana now became obsessed with the idea of making public her side of the story, which she did in a Panorama broadcast for the BBC in November 1995, when she allowed herself to be exclusively interviewed by Martin Bashir. This interview, breathtaking in its simplicity and its intimacy, exploded in the public's face like a Bonfire Night firework, created immense sympathy for Diana's plight, and at the same time put an abrupt end to any slim hope of her reconciliation with the royal family. The frankness and openness of the interview even created the feeling in the court that the Princess was totally unhinged. The Queen concluded that divorce was the only answer, and eventually one went ahead, Diana taking care not to be so easy a pushover as Fergie had recently been when she divorced Andrew. Diana eventually got her divorce in August 1996, giving up her title of 'Her Royal Highness', being known instead as 'Diana, Princess of Wales', but having a settlement of £17 million to compensate her. Since she was mother to the first and second in line to the throne she remained a member of the royal family and kept her apartments at Kensington Palace.

After the divorce, Diana continued her useful charity work, particularly for the Red Cross and in her campaign for ridding the world of landmines. At the same time she pursued her interests in philanthropy, music, fashion and travel, and indulged her eccentric tastes by consorting with New Age healers and spiritualists, and personalities like Gianni Versace, Elton John and Michael Barrymore, with whom she made occasional visits to nightclubs. She never forgot, however, that she was the mother to a future king, and while her sons were at school she assuaged her loneliness with visits to the gym and the cinema, or easily prepared meals-for-one at home. She put behind her the little affaires she had indulged in with men like the international rugby player Will Carling, and set her sights on more solid achievements, dealing with the mutilations inflicted by landmines in places like Angola and Bosnia. She was even partially responsible for the Ottawa Treaty banning anti-personnel landmines, though this was not actually signed until after her death.

She had a brief affair with Hasnat Khan, a dedicated heart surgeon and a serious man with too much respect to play games with her. She even contemplated converting to Islam to make herself acceptable to him, but to him such an idea was ludicrous and he kept her at arms' length. It eventually got through to Diana that such a match was out of the question, and she allowed the affair to fade away.

Her last male partner was Dodi Fayed, the son of the ambitious Mohammed Al Fayed, millionaire and proprietor of the great retail empire, Harrods. She was never serious about him[9]; he was no more than a distraction and an amusement for her, but his intentions may have been more in earnest. The pair visited Paris together in August 1997, where she, Dodi Fayed, and Henri Paul, the driver of the Mercedes-Benz S280 Sedan and allegedly drunk at the wheel, were killed and her bodyguard seriously injured in a high-speed car crash late at night in the Pont d'Alma road tunnel on the Paris Périphérique.[10] Diana's funeral in September 1997, with its solemn procession from Westminster Abbey by hearse to Althorp in Northamptonshire was watched on TV by an estimated 2.5 billion people worldwide. Charles, her brother and now 9th Earl, gave his eulogy to his sister lying before him, a remarkable cry of defiance to the prissy conventions of royalty from a pedigree line much more ancient than that of the Hanoverians, and was as effective in the stony silence it produced in the Abbey as in the roar of applause it generated among the crowds standing outside.

The phenomenon of national mourning created by this event, and the mountains of flowers that were heaped by thousands of people outside Kensington Palace, saw a paroxysm of national grief that the nation had never experienced before. Members of the press beat their breasts in remorse and published headlines like 'Forgive us, Princess' – indeed, if they had dared to show their faces they would have been summarily lynched by the mob. The inexplicable spirit that persuades people to leave little bunches of flowers at the scene of an accident involving persons they have never known was the same as the spirit which moved citizens nationwide to mourn the passing of a person they had only ever met in the columns of the newspaper; the strange unearthly howl, like a jungle animal caught in a trap, that went up when her coffin left the gates of Kensington Palace, signified, too, a nation that was beside itself with an unprecedented and mysterious grief. This crowd turned nasty, like a mutinous football crush, when they saw that Buckingham Palace flew no flag, either at full-mast or at half-mast, to symbolise Diana's passing (though every other building in London flew one). The Queen had to hasten back from Balmoral, and publicly acknowledge the Princess' importance to her family in order to shore up the dyke protecting the Windsors from a simmering republicanism. Tony Blair, the new Prime Minister – a man in many ways on the same wavelength as Diana – had the gift of realising at once the importance of 'helping the Queen to get through this', and the theatrical savvy to come up with the phrase 'the People's Princess' to sum up the nation's feelings. Others more coolly wondered why the public celebration of grief, of total strangers embracing each other and weeping, had become so much a public pastime; and why such people needed a princess, when they themselves saw the whole episode in exasperation as 'celebrity culture meets the democratisation of monarchy'.

More than ten years after her death, the question still remains: was she a visiting angel, inspiring the world with her brilliant, fragile beauty and her selfless humanitarian missions, or was she a manipulative, unpredictable neurotic who acted first and thought afterwards, and came within an inch of bringing down the monarchy? Perhaps, in reality, she was both.

PART 8

TROLLOPS

SKITTLES:
THE VICTORIAN COURTESAN

Skittles was the last great courtesan, her name synonymous with scandal. By profession she was a prostitute; the Victorians, broad-mindedly raffish as many of them were, would have called her a 'whore', while the effete twentieth century would have applied to her the much paler and more euphemistic term 'call-girl'. Whatever the name by which she went, she led a colourful and glamorous life in London and Paris which lasted through the whole of the Second Empire in France and for most of the later Victorian and Edwardian periods in England. She was in France at first the protégée of the elderly Achille Fould, finance minister of Emperor Napoleon III, while in England she counted among her many acquaintances the Marquis of Hartington and numerous other members of the Cavendish family, and Edward VII himself (whom she referred to rather disrespectfully as 'Tum-tum'). She was honest and directly spoken, remaining fresh-faced and curiously unsophisticated in a florid and overdressed age. Parisians loved, and even cultivated, her English accent, Englishmen loved her northern dialect with its hint of Liverpudlian, a local touch she was proud to maintain. She remained for most of her life a celebrated, and sometimes notorious, figure in both countries.

She was born Catherine Walters in 1839 in the backstreets of Toxteth, Liverpool, close to the docks. Her father, Edward Walters, a retired sailor, was by trade a 'tide-waiter', i.e. he was one of the many casual labourers who waited for ships to come up the Mersey on the high tide and then helped to unload them; in more modern times he would have been called a stevedore. He and his numerous family later moved to the Wirral when Catherine was only eleven and with the help of a small pension from his seafaring work set himself up as an alehouse keeper. The sailors she met with there were rough and hard-swearing, with money in their pockets from their last voyage and willing to spend it on anything female that crossed their paths. Catherine knew very early about the effects of drunkenness and coarse and violent language, and as a slum child knew all about shared bedrooms, shared beds and communal lavatories; her father beat her regularly and her stepmother (her real mother had died and been buried in Toxteth) was cowed and bullied just as she was herself. But she remained independent and self-reliant, and in spite of the dirt and poverty with which she was surrounded retained her intelligence and her pert elfin charm. By the time she was a teenager she left home and went to live with her grandmother back in Toxteth, where she got herself a job in the Black Jack Tavern close to the docks, working in the skittle alley and earning herself the nickname that was to accompany her for the rest of her life. Her vivacity, allure and quickness in repartee made her name locally, and she was soon working successfully as a prostitute much sought after by the inn's clientele. The age of consent for females at that time was thirteen, but Catherine had probably lost her virginity while she was still a child. The family moved again, this time to the Cheshire Hunt area near Tarporley, where she learned to ride. She already had acquired the rudiments of riding, either because she had access to livery stables, or else because as a child she had been fond of going to the circus. Now she became a very accomplished horsewoman and was allowed to ride with the county folk. When she was twenty, however, she decided to seek her fortune in London, perhaps as the companion of a young man of means who had persuaded her to run away with him.

In London Catherine soon became a *habituée* of the fashionable West End. She came to patronise Kate Hamilton's brothel in Prince's Street, off Leicester Square, where she used her visits (though she was never regularly employed there) to meet well-connected young army officers and other gentlemen-about-town. She made the acquaintance of the proprietor of a successful livery stables in Bruton Mews, adjacent to Berkeley Square, who employed her to advertise his services by riding one of his handsomest horses on Rotten Row in Hyde Park or along 'Ladies' Mile' on the north side of the Serpentine. She was soon attracting crowds of admirers in the park, and was even painted by Sir Edwin Landseer as *The Pretty Horsebreaker*. She made the acquaintance first of William Frederick Windham (known from his days at Eton as 'Mad' Windham on account of his madcap behaviour), the dissolute and irresponsible son of General Windham of Felbrigg Hall in Norfolk, and later, in 1862, of Spencer Compton Cavendish, Lord Hartington, eldest son and heir to the 7th Duke of Devonshire.

With Hartington she had a protracted and torrid affair (insofar as it was possible to be torrid with one so lumpish), driving him from the side of the beautiful Louise ('Lottie'), Duchess of Manchester, until family pressure forced him to take panicky refuge in the USA, while Skittles emigrated in the opposite direction to the spa town of Ems in the Rhineland. Here she found herself pursued by another lover, Aubrey de Vere Beauclerk, a lurid young nobleman from Northern Ireland who was already married. He insisted on leaving his long-suffering young wife and fleeing with Skittles to New York, where she found herself in the middle of the American Civil War with two discarded lovers, both temperamentally totally opposed to each other. Beauclerk eventually returned to his wife with his tail between his legs, while Hartington came back to patch things up with his family and with the glamorous Lottie.

Catherine spent the rest of the 'Gay Sixties' in Paris. At the time the city, elaborately improved by the imperial minister Haussmann, attracted the attention of much of fashionable Europe, its dazzling and gilded surroundings providing the setting for a social life profligate to the point of degeneracy. Since she had little French, Catherine gravitated towards the English colony there, one of whose fashionable *cocottes* (known disrespectfully to Parisians as '*les horizontales*'), Cora Pearl, once tried to shock by having herself served to her dinner guests out of a silver platter wearing nothing but a string of pearls and a few sprigs of parsley, and then doing a few high kicks on top of the table. Another of the *demi-mondaines*, known as La Barucci, renowned for her habitual lateness and reproached for it by the Duc de Grammont-Caderousse when she appeared before him in a daringly low-cut gown, turned her back on him, flipped up her voluminous skirts and presented him with her white-clad buttocks. It was in Paris that Catherine accepted the protection of Achille Fould, Napoleon's bearded and elderly minister of finance. He installed her in a sumptuous apartment in the Avenue des Champs Elysées and allowed her to make her daily excursions to the Bois de Boulogne, where she outshone on horseback many other fashionable *équestriennes*. She even made the acquaintance of the Emperor himself, when she was introduced to him at dinner. He said he had never heard of the game of skittles, but sportingly agreed to a competition in an adjacent room, where footmen set up nine champagne bottles to be used for the purpose: he bowled at them and knocked over two to sycophantic applause, while Catherine, who had not lost her touch, knocked over the remaining seven with a single shot.

Fould, shrewd and kindly, lavished much time and money on Catherine, improving her halting French and taking her to concerts and galleries, while asking for little in return. He introduced her to the fashionable balls at the British Embassy, where she met Lord Hubert de Burgh (later Earl of Clanricard) and met also a young man, very junior in the embassy and slightly younger than herself, called Wilfrid Blunt. He was a writer of sentimental poetry and fell madly in love with her, inveigling her to spend three days and nights of passion with him in the Rue Jacob, where she – unusually for one so level-headed – also fell in love with him. Both agreed, however, that a marriage between them was impracticable, and, though they remained thereafter in each other's thoughts, they met only briefly and occasionally thereafter. Blunt was posted to Lisbon, to Frankfurt and finally to Buenos Aires (he eventually returned to England and married Lady Anne King-Noel, granddaughter of Lord Byron), while Catherine remained in Paris. But she was growing bored with her life there, and was spending an increasing amount of time in England, where every season she indulged her passion for fox-hunting, chiefly in Leicestershire with the Quorn or the Billesdon ('South Quorn') hunts. After the death of Fould in 1867 and the fall of Paris in 1871 during the Franco-Prussian War, she never lived in France again.

She had previously met Edward, Prince of Wales, while she was still in Paris, and now took up with him once more. Like him, Catherine had the common touch, sharing also his enthusiasm for fox-hunting. Finally she became his lover. She also got to know Squire Tailby, Sir Arthur Hazelrigg and Harry, the young Marquis of Hastings, together with the whole group of other great Leicestershire hunting figures. At this time she incurred the lasting enmity of Lady Stamford, the wife of the Master of the Quorn, who never rode to hounds again after a quarrel with her husband in which she presented him with the choice of herself or Catherine in the hunt (unfortunately he chose wrongly).

Catherine also spent a good deal of time in London, taking a house in Chesterfield Street. Here for the first time she was introduced to W. E. Gladstone, the Leader of the House of Commons (known to other members of Catherine's profession as 'Old Glad-eye' because of his reputed fondness for trawling the city streets to save fallen women and then taking them home with him for a cup of cocoa.[1] Gladstone talked to Catherine in a courtly fashion and brought her a pound of tea as a present. Oddly, they found they had a lot in common. Their background circumstances were quite different, but both were born in Liverpool and remained fond of it; thereafter Catherine always had a letter from him on her birthday. In 1872 she moved to South Street, which was closer to the Park and to Piccadilly.

By the end of the 1860s, Gladstone was Prime Minister, and 'Bertie', the son and heir of Queen Victoria, whose style of life he hated, often entertained Catherine at Marlborough House. Gladstone thoroughly disapproved, writing to the Foreign Secretary: 'To speak in general terms, the Queen is invisible and the Prince of Wales is not respected.' The 1870s came and Catherine, sadly, was beginning to feel the onset of middle age. She was outshone by the youthful Empress Elizabeth, wife of the Austrian Franz Josef, who spent a good deal of time in England and often appeared on the hunting field. Nevertheless, Catherine took up the new craze of roller-skating enthusiastically in 1876, though she was not as good at it as she would have wished. Soon she began to suffer from incipient arthritis in the joints, and so found walking increasingly difficult. Bertie, meanwhile, had taken up with Lillie Langtry, and was as devoted to her as his inconstant soul would permit. Catherine shortly after met her last amour, the Hon. Gerald Le Marchant de Saumerez, who attached himself to her when he was scarcely out of Eton, and was as young and unsophisticated as the youthful Blunt had been, but in his case never as much interested in her as he was in his own career. A keen soldier, he served in the Ashanti wars with the Lancers, and distinguished himself in the Boer War with the Rifles. Though over the age of military service at the time of the First World War, he dyed his hair black and saw active service in France as a gravedigger on the Western Front.

By the beginning of the new century, Catherine Walters was an old lady. In 1901 the Queen died, and in 1910 Edward VII passed on in his turn. All her friends were dying around her: Hartington, now 8th Duke of Devonshire, in 1908, and his wife Lottie shortly after. Most of Catherine's Parisian friends and rivals had now also died. About this time she began to be known as Mrs Baillie, though whether she had actually married Alec Baillie (brother of Col. Jim Baillie in the Fernie country at Illston Grange), as Edward had asked him to do, or whether this was a title of convenience is not precisely known. Like many others, she was deeply shocked at the outbreak of the Great War. She knew the Kaiser and thought him such a charming young man when she met him. She had received several letters from him, which she later sold, giving the money to help the wounded soldiers. During the war, she continued to live in South Street, and from time to time met her old flame, Wilfrid Blunt, whose own wife was now dead. She also kept in touch with Gerald de Saumerez, but at the age of eighty she was in a wheelchair, half-blind and very frail. She died in 1920. On her death certificate she was described as a 'Spinster of no occupation'.

THE CASE OF RUTH ELLIS: A CRIME OF PASSION

Ruth Ellis, in 1955, was the last woman to be hanged in Britain. Her execution, for murder, which was hotly debated at the time not only for its lack of mercy but also for its conspicuous lack of justice, was passed through the courts and hurried on by the political authorities for fear of encouraging the wider debate on the whole question of the appropriateness of the death penalty. As the law stood at the time, her condemnation was correct; but the circumstances of her conviction were so tragic that in the minds of the public they reflected more on the state of the criminal law than they did on the guilt of the accused.

On the evening of Easter Sunday 1955, Ruth Ellis, a glamorous nightclub hostess, waylaid her lover in a London street, shot him as he was about to get into his car, and then, as he lay at her feet, emptied all the remaining five chambers of her revolver into his body, inflicting multiple injuries and killing him almost immediately. Her victim was the public-school-educated David Blakeley, man-about-town and rather unsuccessful driver of racing cars, indulged by his wealthy parents and continuing as a racing driver even though he never won a race. He had been her lover for eighteen months in a squalid and tempestuous affair. After her arrest, the solicitor she chose was John Bickford, middle-aged and undistinguished, who recommended for her defence the well-known criminal lawyer Melford Stephenson QC, and, as his junior, the man who later became Lord Rawlinson and Attorney-General. The leader for the prosecution was the talented and sometimes unscrupulous Christmas Humphreys QC, who had scored a string of successes in a large number of well-publicised criminal cases. When her counsel met Ruth Ellis before the trial, they found her shabby and unkempt. In prison she lacked the bleach that kept her hair a stunning platinum blonde, so that instead it had become pale brown and patchy. Worse still she seemed depressed and defeatist. She had done wrong, she felt, and wanted to be hanged so that she could 'rejoin David'. She had committed murder, the ultimate crime, and believed she *should* hang – it was a matter of 'an eye for an eye', she said. With difficulty she was prevailed upon to plead not guilty, not because there seemed to be much chance of an acquittal, but chiefly so that her whole story could be brought out in court.

She came up at the Old Bailey towards the end of June, before Mr Justice Havers, not known as a 'hanging judge', and with a jury of ten men and two women. The defence proposed to concentrate on the way the victim had treated her, as extenuation of her behaviour. Humphreys' approach was simpler. He simply asked Ruth Ellis if she had shot David Blakeney, and when she said 'Yes' he asked her if she meant to kill him. Again she said 'Yes'. At this point the judge stopped the trial, sent out the jury and interviewed both counsel *in camera*, reminding them that the penalty the law prescribed for murder was death, and that the earlier conduct of the victim was irrelevant to the case. He therefore ruled that evidence of provocation was not admissible. The defence team were effectively at a loss, Rawlinson being forced to admit that he could not ask the questions he had planned without inviting the jury to ignore the judge's ruling. The trial was over in one and a half days, and the jury took just fourteen minutes to find the prisoner guilty. Not having heard of the provocation the accused had suffered, they made no recommendation for mercy. The judge put on his black cap, and pronounced sentence of death. In the light of the law at the time, this was perfectly proper.

Today, the defence of provocation could, and would, be brought in court. Ruth Ellis might well have escaped conviction. Even if the jury had produced a guilty verdict it would have recommended mercy, and the judge would have taken this into account in the light of today's much more flexible sentences. But at that time there was no such latitude either in the conduct of the case or in the sentence imposed.

Behind the hard and brittle surface of Ruth Ellis as a club 'hostess' lay a tragic personal story. She came from a needy South London family, her father an itinerant musician forced by the decline of the music halls to take poorly paid menial work. The family settled in Brixton in the early 1930s. Her mother was a staunch Roman Catholic forced by her circumstances into periodic fits of depression. Ruth had three sisters and two brothers. During protracted spells of unemployment, her father took out his frustration on his children, knocking them about and abusing at least two of the girls, Ruth and her elder sister Muriel. The elder girl claimed that he began abusing her sexually at the age of ten, when he forced her to sleep with him and submit to his attentions. Muriel eventually became pregnant at the age of fourteen, and gave birth to his baby. Although her mother knew that Muriel had not been associating with other males, she refused to believe that it was her husband who was the father of her daughter's child. After this episode he left Muriel alone, but transferred his attentions to Ruth, who was forced in the same way to sleep with her father.

At the outbreak of the war, Ruth was a teenager and beginning to grow up. She enjoyed going out dancing with Allied troops in London. By the time the war ended she was seventeen and going steady with a Canadian serviceman, and in due course bore him an illegitimate son, André. When he returned to Canada after the war he promised to return to fetch her, but he never did, and later she learned that he was a married man with three children. She and Muriel went to work for £2 a week in the local Oxo factory, but this soon palled for Ruth, and she moved on to do waitressing in Lyons' teashops in the West End. She was already a smart and personable young woman with startlingly peroxided blonde hair. Ruth was soon invited to pose for what were euphemistically called 'glamour photos', and went to work as a hostess in a sex club, serving drinks, chatting with the clients, and, at £20 a week (nearly ten times what she had been earning before, and the height of luxury), steadily beginning the slow slide into what effectively was prostitution. In the club she met and fell for George Ellis, a successful dentist. The two were married, but he soon showed himself too fond of drink and when he came home was often violent with her. Ellis tried to counter his addiction by taking treatment at a local centre for alcoholism, but Ruth thought his periods of absence meant he was having affairs with other women, and like her mother began to suffer from depressions. Hence she was prescribed the antidepressants that she took for the rest of her life. Soon afterwards she decided to leave him.

In August 1953 she resumed her career as a hostess in the Cavell's Little Club in London's clubland. It was here she first met and fell for David Blakeley who showed himself chiefly interested in women, drink and racing cars. He moved into her flat 'above the shop' and entered into a deeply passionate affair with her. He was good-looking but with a weak, selfish character and something of a cry-baby. The two would quarrel violently, separate, and then in floods of tears be reconciled, with Blakeley buying her gifts and promising not to quarrel again. Bystanders soon came to the view that Blakeley really thought little of Ruth and was merely using her for the sexual satisfaction she gave him.

In February 1955 she met at the club Desmond Cussens, the other man in her life. He became increasingly smitten with her. In June, while Blakeley was away racing at Le Mans, the two became lovers. Cussens looked after her: he paid her son's school fees, and when Ruth was forced to move he paid for her new flat. When Blakeley found out he was furious and quarrels thereafter became more frequent and more vicious. Ruth became pregnant again in March, but during a particularly violent quarrel, Blakeley punched her in the stomach, the baby died and she miscarried. Showing no remorse he walked out on her, this time going to lodge with Carol and Antony Findlater in Hampstead. She was a former lover of Blakeley's, he Blakeley's mechanic at the garage. Blakeley eventually sent Ruth a card, the two were reconciled and he promised to come back to her to spend Easter. However, he did not show up, and Cussens offered his help in pursuing him. On Easter Sunday, she went round to the house in Hampstead, knocked repeatedly on the door, and when she got no response began to bang on his car parked outside, doing some minor damage to the paintwork. Findlater appeared, told her to leave, and then the police arrived and moved Ruth away. Later that evening, about 7.30 p.m., Cussens drove her round there again, and this time she waylaid Blakeley as he left the house, shot him and killed him.

At her trial, Cussens was not even questioned about Blakeney's treatment of the accused, nor was any attention paid to where Ruth Ellis got the gun. The psychiatrist called to give evidence on her mental state was unhelpful and woolly in his testimony, and alienated the sympathies of the judge. Ellis seemed to go out of her way to incriminate herself, and appeared almost relieved when sentence was passed on her. Afterwards, in Holloway, John Bickford her solicitor could not persuade her to appeal, and a visit from George Rogers, an MP and a pioneer in advocating the abolition of the death penalty, had difficulty in getting her to change her mind. For her son's sake she eventually consented to appeal, but Bickford so fumbled her case that in a fit of irritation she sacked him, choosing in his place the youthful Victor Mishcon, at this time embarking on his distinguished legal career. He tried to arrange an appeal, and, when this failed, to apply for a reprieve.

The Home Secretary at the time was Major Gwilym Lloyd George, mediocre son of the former great Prime Minister. He was timid and hesitant, afraid to act too decisively for fear of precipitating a full-scale debate on the future of the death penalty. It was his view that if Ruth Ellis were reprieved it would be difficult ever again to hang a woman, or perhaps anybody. At first she refused to give her full co-operation to Victor Mishcon, not seeming to care whether she got a reprieve or not. In particular, she would not say where she had obtained the gun. Only later she broke down and confessed, as Mishcon suspected, that it had been given to her by Desmond Cussens, and that, even if he had not actually incited the murder, he was her accomplice not only during, but before, the crime. The two had sat together for the whole of the afternoon in question, commiserating with each other and drinking Pernod, until eventually he drove her to Hampstead later that evening, when the murder took place. She took the view that the murder was her responsibility alone; she was going to hang for it, and she did not wish that Cussens should have to go to prison, too. Nevertheless, Mishcon decided to ask for a stay of execution until Cussens could be examined and the extent of his complicity revealed. Time, however, was getting short. Unusually, Ruth Ellis' words in her interview with her solicitor in Holloway were disputed – on the grounds that a female warder present during the interview had made a statement to the police that did not fully tally with Mishcon's own notes on it. When the police decided to act they did so half-heartedly, looking for Cussens for a couple of days to question him, and then giving up. So Mishcon did not apply to the Home Secretary until literally the day before the execution was scheduled. Unfortunately, when he did, Lloyd George was at the races and could not be contacted. Home Office civil servants asserted that even if he had been contacted it would have made no difference to his decision: when very late the application was referred to him, he simply refused to grant a reprieve.

So Ruth Ellis was hanged, and the whole sorry story reached its seemingly inevitable conclusion. The administrative bungling behind it did not become public knowledge until much later; when it did, it reinforced the indignation many felt that she should have suffered death in such questionable circumstances. Certainly, at the time, the public expressed its deep shock and horror at the scandal of her execution, and the case helped to move the nation in the direction of the final abolition of the death penalty.

CHRISTINE KEELER:
THE PROFUMO CASE

The affair of John Profumo, Minister of War in the Macmillan government in the early 1960s, with the showgirl Christine Keeler, brought the disgrace of the Conservative government and helped in its defeat in the general election of 1964 after thirteen years in power. While illicit liaisons between public figures and women of easy virtue were not unheard of, the effect of the affair was to discredit the Conservatives for many years, losing them office and pursuing them with rumours of political 'sleaze' for the rest of the century. Christine Keeler herself, the occasion of the whole scandal, was mercilessly pilloried in the press in articles usually adorned with photographs of her unclad or partially unclad; but whether she was the black-hearted siren she was alleged to be today seems questionable.

The Sixties were a curiously ambivalent decade: staid and conventional on the one hand, and casual and permissive on the other. For those of the older generation with memories of the war, times were better than they had ever been; on the other hand, the younger generation were much more brash and uninhibited than their elders, shamelessly experimenting with soft drugs, strip joints and trial marriages, and going along with the shameless suggestion in the new satirical magazine, *Private Eye*, that the nation had 'never had it so *often*'.[1] With the popular press gloating pruriently over its details, the affair was meat and drink to satirical TV broadcasts and continued to scandalise the mass of the public for years.

John Profumo became Minister of War in the Macmillan cabinet in July 1960. Something of a 'toff', Profumo was balding, educated, and extremely rich – the very epitome of Conservative respectability, his main claim to distinction being that he was married to the British film star Valerie Hobson. It was this very respectability that made his disgrace so shocking. In July 1961, Profumo and his wife were among about twenty other rich and influential people, including Ayub Khan, the new President of Pakistan, whom Lord Astor invited to a weekend party at Cliveden, his estate in Berkshire. At the same time, and unknown to them, another weekend party had been arranged by Dr Stephen Ward, a fashionable West End osteopath who had been offered by Lord 'Bill' Astor a house on his estate called 'Spring Cottage' on the Thames where, at a nominal rent, he spent most weekends. In addition to his flourishing practice, Ward was a talented artist earning good fees producing pencil sketches of leading figures for various magazines. He was also a name-dropper and something of a socialite who cultivated the acquaintance of a wide group of trendy friends, entertaining them almost weekly at his fashionable address at Cliveden, where he enlivened the evenings after dinner with sex games, wife-swapping and other fashionable sixtyish pursuits. To this end, Ward had built up a clientele of nightclub hostesses and go-go dancers as young female 'escorts', including Mandy Rice-Davies and Christine Keeler, to provide his guests with the sort of services they required.

Christine Keeler was a twenty-year-old who had left home at sixteen after a self-induced abortion and had found work in London as a topless dancer in the West End, where she mingled with the customers between acts, peddling them overpriced drinks at their tables and occasionally supplementing her slender earnings by selling sexual services to them. She was young, dark-haired and attractive, and quite undeniably good-looking, but much less than the manipulative whore the papers made her out to be. Indeed, beneath her sophisticated veneer, Christine was still at heart a teenager, having nightly to fortify herself with stiff glasses of whisky before taking her top off and dancing bare-breasted at the club. She was also genuinely shocked the first time Ward's cut-glass guests unaccountably embarked on a group striptease, the ladies first gaily taking their own clothes off and then starting to disrobe the gentlemen. Her relations with Ward himself were close without being intimate; as Christine put it, he never 'took advantage' of her. In London, the pair of them shared his flat in Wimpole Mews; they may have had sex, but he was always a gentleman and always treated her with consideration. To her he was something of a father figure, her own father having walked out on the family while she was still very young. In later testimony, she agreed that she gave Ward money, but said it was for rent – and that in any case he always gave her back far more than she ever gave him.

At his weekend party, Ward had the permission of Lord Astor to add a little distinction to the occasion after dinner by using the swimming pool in the grounds of the estate. Unfortunately, Christine had no swimming costume with her, and the one she borrowed was not a good fit, so she was encouraged by Ward to enter the bath without one. While she was in the water, Profumo and Lord Astor came upon her during their after-dinner stroll in the grounds, and having swum round aimlessly for some minutes in the safety of the bath, she eventually tried to scramble from the water to put on her costume. Unfortunately, Ward got to it first and threw it into the bushes, and Christine was forced to resort to a quite inadequate towel to preserve her modesty. Profumo gave chase, and in the ensuing horseplay she lost the protection of her towel and was left completely nude. It was at this juncture that Mrs Profumo and the rest of the party arrived at the pool. Unexpectedly, the two sets of guests got on quite well, and instead of reproaching the minister for his behaviour agreed to renew their contacts by meeting again at the pool the following evening.

The following evening, one of the guests was Eugene Ivanov, a young man about town serving as naval attaché in the Soviet Embassy, fluent in English, and one of Ward's carefully cultivated circle. Ivanov also happened to be a serving member of the KGB. In the course of the evening both Profumo and Ivanov asked for, and got, Christine's telephone number. However it was Ivanov who drove her home on that occasion. He cracked a bottle of vodka with her in Ward's flat, and ended the evening by having sex with her on the hearthrug. In the course of the next few days, Christine became mistress to both of them. It did not take Ivanov long to realise that he was holding a trump card with his new acquaintance, but Profumo remained oblivious of the security implications of his new conquest and behaved quite indiscreetly, taking Christine with him on visits quite publicly in his ministerial car and often alternating with Ivanov in meeting her at Ward's flat at Wimpole Mews – though the two never actually met there. Later he realised he could not go on making such regular visits to the flat, and suggested instead that she come to him in his house in Regent's Park while his wife was away; he even suggested that he should get Christine a flat. She, however, was unwilling to abandon Ward's protection. Her liaison with a minister of the Crown much exercised MI5, which warned Ward of a possible security risk and advised him not to associate with Ivanov. Ward was delighted to have become so readily the centre of attention, and tried to play both ends against the middle, telling MI5 what it knew already – that Ivanov was a Soviet agent – but suggesting that with a little effort he might be persuaded to defect and work for Britain. At the same time he (Ward) jokingly asked Christine to find out in the course of her pillow talk with Profumo the location of US missile bases in Britain, information which he rightly judged would be of prime importance to the Soviet Union's espionage service. There is, however, no evidence that Christine ever asked for, or was ever given, any classified security information: to this day, she continues to insist that she would never do anything to betray her country. Nevertheless, tongues were already beginning to wag, and rumours of the affair soon surfaced in the gossip columns of the newspapers. When the matter of Profumo's indiscretion began to be mentioned in the corridors of Westminster, he thought it safer to discontinue the association, so he wrote Christine a farewell letter, and after one final meeting (when they had sex on the back seat of his car) finished his affair with her. Christine subsequently claimed that she became pregnant as the result of this meeting and tried to preserve Profumo's reputation in any scandal by procuring an abortion.

Thereafter Christine resumed her modelling career, appearing in a number of commercial advertisements, and making various professional appearances in West Indian clubs in London. One of her new lovers was one 'Lucky' Gordon, a demanding and quick-tempered individual who held Christine prisoner at knife-point on more than one occasion and repeatedly raped her. Escaping back to Ward's flat she bought herself a handgun for protection, and accepted the protection of Johnny Edgecombe, another West Indian who had intervened to protect her in a fight with Gordon. He had sided with her in a quarrel and had been severely slashed in the face for his pains. He had had taken possession of her gun and was now seeking to claim proprietary rights over her. Again she fled back to Ward, but Edgecombe came after her, and when she refused to admit him to the flat in Wimpole Mews, tried to shoot the lock off the door and took a shot at his cowering victim whom he had glimpsed in an upstairs window. The police came and arrested him, and threatened to charge him with attempted murder. It was clear that the whole affair was about to blow. If Christine appeared in the witness box and was questioned in public about her contacts the whole sorry story of her involvement with Profumo might come to light. Ivanov therefore took a flight back to

Moscow, and Ward decided to smuggle the frightened girl out of the country. Tracked down in Spain by reporters from the *Daily Express* she sold the 'full and frank' story of the entire affair to the papers for £800. But Lord Beaverbrook refused to publish it, on the grounds that if he did the paper might be sued for libel. So the white establishment closed ranks against the threat. Hence when Edgecombe came to trial at the Old Bailey, Christine did not appear in the box. Instead MI5 intervened to persuade the police to drop the attempted murder charge, thus protecting Profumo from any enquiry into his behaviour, and as a result Edgecombe was sentenced to seven years on the lesser charge of possessing an illegal firearm.

But by now the cat was really among the pigeons. The newspapers insinuated all they dared about Profumo's involvement with Christine, while in Parliament the inter-party conspiracy of silence was broken by veteran Labour MP George Wigg, who demanded assurances from the government that the rumours about Profumo were false and that there had been no breach of security in the minister's personal conduct. Profumo was not in the chamber when the question was asked, but he later came to the dispatch box and sought to brazen it out by denying any impropriety in his relationship with Christine. She, still in Spain, was again approached by the newspapers and sold them the story – this time for £2,000 – that the rumours were entirely false and that she was innocent of any wrongdoing. She then returned to a public hullabaloo in London.

For a time it looked as if Profumo would get away with his denial, but the security forces, puzzled by the ambiguities of Stephen Ward's behaviour and perhaps looking for a scapegoat, embarked on a detailed enquiry into the doctor's affairs. For a long time he stuck to his story that the rumours about Profumo were unfounded; but finally, harassed both by the police and by MI5, he confessed, in letters both to the Home Secretary and to George Wigg, that he knew all about the minister's affair with Christine and that his denials had been intended to shield him. Profumo, on holiday in Venice, realised the game was up, made a clean breast of it and resigned. His cabinet colleagues were furious with him – not so much for being involved in a sex scandal, but more for being caught out lying about it afterwards.

The police, meantime, interviewed 140 possible witnesses, and formulated charges under the Sexual Offences Act that Ward had been living on 'immoral earnings', even bringing pressure to bear on one unfortunate to testify that Ward had been her pimp. Mandy Rice-Davies spent a fortnight in Holloway on a trumped-up charge of possession of a forged driving licence in order to get her on to the witness stand, and Christine herself was afterwards sentenced to eighteen months for alleged perjury in 'Lucky' Gordon's case. Nevertheless, she was able once more to sell her account of the scandal to the papers, this time for £23,000. She used the money to get a new home for her mother, now an invalid, who was distraught with the whole business. Ward sought to defend himself, but found himself in his hour of need deserted by all his former friends. They all denied coming to his cottage at Cliveden, or, if they had come, denied that anything out of the way had happened there. Bill Astor denied that he had ever had sex with Mandy Rice-Davies, providing her with her chance of producing her historic retort: 'Well, he would, wouldn't he?' Ward was unable to bear the humiliation of his trial, or, worse still, the sense of betrayal he felt at his friends' desertion, and on the night before the jury reached its verdict killed himself with an overdose of Nembutal. Before he died he left a letter addressed to the Home Secretary making a full statement of the circumstances of the affair. That letter has never been made public. A later enquiry aiming at improving the nation's security and conducted by Lord Justice Denning concerned itself chiefly with protecting leading politicians from the scandal, and for the most part occupied itself with the easier task of blackening Ward's and Christine Keeler's characters.

Profumo's career was ruined, though he managed to salvage his marriage; it took forty years for him to hold his head up again in public. Macmillan was defeated by Harold Wilson at the election of September 1964, and thirteen years of Conservative government came to a discreditable end. Christine Keeler found it impossible to find employment afterwards on account of prejudice against her, and, with her mother now dead, was forced to live in straitened circumstances on social security benefit. Stephen Ward became the 'fall guy' who paid with his life for the entire scandal.

Mature judgement suggests that Christine Keeler was not by any means a wicked woman, but rather a lonely and unhappy youngster who found herself out of her depth in the 'swinging sixties'; that there was no real danger to Britain's security from Ivanov's role in the KGB, but rather that, in the absurdly exaggerated postures struck during the Cold War, government security felt itself obliged to make a master spy out of a society playboy. Finally, members of the 'establishment' did their best to stand together to hush things up from the threats of Ivanov, Ward and Christine Keeler, no matter what the cost to their lives or reputations.

PART 9

MONSTERS

LADY MACBETH: MONSTER OR MYTH?

Macbeth, ruler of Moray in the area around the present Inverness, was a real and not a fictional Scottish king of the eleventh century. A general of the army of his predecessor King Duncan, he replaced him in 1040 and ruled wisely and well for fourteen years before facing a rebellion in 1054 from Duncan's son Malcolm and being defeated and killed by him at Dunsinnan in 1057. His reputation as a strong and generous ruler has been superseded by the image created of him in Shakespeare's play that bears his name, a play featuring a king called Duncan, another called Macbeth, a prince called Malcolm, another called Donalbain (Donald Bàn – 'the Fair' or 'the White'), an earl called Siward of Northumbria and a Scottish nobleman called Macduff of Fife. How accurate historically was Shakespeare's portrait of the events of Macbeth's reign?

Shakespeare drew his material from Raphael Holinshed's *Chronicles* of 1577, and he in turn drew his story from two main sources, John of Fordun's *Scotichronicon*, from around 1380, and Andrew of Wyntoun's verses *Orygynale Cronykil*, from about 1420. The former was probably the better historian; the latter more steeped in the poetic tradition of folk tales. Both stories were included in the writings of Hector Boece, Principal of King's College, Aberdeen, in the early sixteenth century, whose work was translated into English later still by John Bellenden. It was this work that was developed by Holinshed and embroidered by Shakespeare. What is interesting is the material that is *not* included by any of these writers: the three witches, the character of Banquo, and, most important, Lady Macbeth.

There are some close correspondences of the play to the story told by the chroniclers: Macbeth did in fact quarrel with Macduff and drove him to flee to England; he did build a great house on Dunsinane Hill near Perth (but not a castle, and he did not hide there in anticipation of Siward's attack); he was safe until 'Birnham Wood be come to Dunsinane' (it is quite possible that Siward concealed his numbers from the waiting king by hiding them in greenery lopped from 'Brynnane'); he would only be killed by a 'man not of a woman born' (the nameless knight who slew him, says Fordun 'wes nevyr borne').

But some of the fairytale elements of the story stem from Fordun's account, and this was written more than three hundred years after the events it describes and may well have contained substantial elements of folk lore. What seems fairly certain is that Macbeth was beset by the 'temptations' of ambition and *not* beguiled by witches; that Duncan was *not* assassinated by Macbeth as he slept, but killed in battle; and that Macbeth's wife was *not* the scheming ogress of the play who incited him in his crimes – indeed, she was not called 'Lady Macbeth' at all. Macbeth's wife's name was in fact Gruoch, and she was the widow of his cousin Gillecomgain, who had ruled Moray during the years of Macbeth's minority, and so was much older than her young spouse. The pair were married in 1033, shortly after Macbeth inherited his title, and though they never had any children there is no evidence that she exercised any influence, baleful or otherwise, over him.

So how are we to explain this extraordinary tale of wickedness and cruelty that Macbeth and his wife had wished upon them?

Partly the legend stems from a tale of horror similar to the one of which Shakespeare accuses Macbeth. In 995 Macbeth's great-grandfather Kenneth II, who had eliminated a number of dynastic rivals to his throne in earlier years to consolidate his position as King of Moray, was treacherously done to death as he slept by a rival and great-nephew, Giric, in a castle belonging to a ruthless and scheming noblewoman Finella, the castle's owner. This deed was condemned by all the chroniclers, one of whom was Fordun himself. The murder at Finella's castle was later either accidentally or deliberately confused with criticisms aimed at Macbeth and his wife Gruoch.

But why was there this wish to blacken the names of two innocent people? Possibly the main reason for the calumny was the fact that Macbeth and his whole line were men of Moray, and that the line of Moray had been, and remained, the main obstacle to the Normanising, Anglicising house of Malcolm III (Ceann-mór, or 'Big-head'), who succeeded to Macbeth's elected successor (and Gillecomgain's son) Lulach in 1058. English interference in Scottish affairs, either through Strathclyde or through Northumbria, had been usual ever since the reign of Edgar in England in the mid-tenth century, and it would have been surprising if Macbeth's memory had not come to be associated in the minds of the new ruling aristocracy with the fear and the hatred associated with the last of the Celtic rearguard.

It is perhaps more surprising that Shakespeare did not write a play about Donalbain instead. He ruled after Malcolm Ceann-Mór, in the 1090s, and his fate was closer to the tragedy of the real Macbeth. He was no lover of his elder brother Malcolm's English ways, and he too tried to return to the idea of Celtic kingship. He died, old and blinded, in 1099, having been twice King of Scots and twice deposed by his own nephews. Like Macbeth and Lulach, he was buried on the Isle of Iona 'of the Kings'. But who his wife was, and whether she deserved the reputation that was attributed to the fictional Lady Macbeth, the chroniclers do not relate.

LADY ROCHFORD:
FALSE WITNESS

The chief claim to fame of Lady Rochford was the evidence she gave against her husband and against her sister-in-law, Queen Anne Boleyn. This evidence was vital in securing their condemnation, but it was almost entirely without foundation. Historians and Lady Rochford's apologists have struggled to explain her motives, and hover between theories of jealousy and insanity. Her subsequent involvement in Queen Catherine Howard's peccadilloes was to lead to her downfall and execution, in which the Queen appears as the tragic heroine and Lady Rochford as the Svengali.

Lady Rochford was born Jane Parker in Norfolk in about the year 1505. She was the daughter of Lord Morley and Alice St John. Morley was related to Henry VIII through the Beaufort line, but although of noble birth he was not rich, and spent his time as a scholar rather than an owner of vast estates. Even so, since the family was well connected, Morley was able to send his daughter to court, probably in her early teens, where she joined the household of Henry VIII's first wife, Catherine of Aragon. Little is known of her life at court, but she was present at the Field of the Cloth of Gold (1520) which was Henry's sumptuous and extravagant state visit to France. It may be that this experience gave her an insatiable taste for court life which was to prove her undoing.

Since there is no extant portrait of her it is difficult to know what Jane looked like, but in 1522 she represented one of the seven female virtues at a masque given at court, and all the seven participants were said to be in the bloom of youth and beauty. Two of Jane's future sisters-in-law, the Boleyn girls, took part in the masque, and Jane must have been well acquainted with the Boleyn family, and in particular George Boleyn, Viscount Rochford, brother of the two girls, whom Jane married in the winter of 1524/25. George's father, Sir Thomas Boleyn, demanded a £300 dowry which Lord Morley could not afford, and King Henry kindly subsidised it from the Privy Purse.

The quality of the marriage is vital in determining Jane's motives in later denouncing her husband. George was described by a contemporary as handsome and lecherous, a not unusual combination for young Tudor courtiers. He is said to have deflowered virgins, forced himself upon widows, and raped at will. Jane's apologists insist that this was a happy marriage, but most observers suggested it was not. At the very least he was unfaithful, at worst homosexual, but this latter charge was unsubstantiated, and may refer to some of the unnatural practices he is said to have indulged in with female partners. That Jane was unhappy at some of her husband's antics seems likely, but in themselves, given contemporary mores, they do not seem sufficient to explain her later willingness to denounce him in court.

Similarly there is a great deal of uncertainty about Jane's attitude towards her sister-in-law, Anne Boleyn. Anne was proclaimed Queen in 1533, even though Henry's first wife Catherine of Aragon was still living. And although Jane was supposed to be serving Catherine not Anne, she, like most of the court, had seen the way the wind was blowing and had transferred her allegiance to Anne long before Anne was formally recognised as Queen. Once Anne became queen she might have expected Henry to be more circumspect in his dalliances, but he kept his roving eye and in 1534 Anne and Jane collaborated to remove one of Henry's latest conquests from the court. Henry was so annoyed at Jane's part in the affair that she, too, was banned from the court for several months. But even the hot and cold running water at the Rochford home of Beaulieu Palace was not enough to compensate Jane for the loss of the pleasures of court, and no doubt she was glad when Henry's anger subsided and she was able to return to Anne's side. Yet Anne's and Jane's friendship had soured. Perhaps Jane thought that her exclusion from court was Anne's fault, or perhaps that George was closer to his sister than he was to her. In July 1535 Jane took part in a demonstration in favour of Lady Mary (Catherine of Aragon's daughter) and ended up briefly in the Tower for her impertinence.

Anne's days were by now numbered. She had angered a number of influential men, the most important of whom was Thomas Cromwell, the King's chief minister. She had opposed Henry's reconciliation with the Holy Roman Emperor, Catherine of Aragon's nephew, because he would never recognise Anne as Queen. But Cromwell believed that an agreement with the Emperor was essential to England's security; he therefore determined to get rid of Anne. This he did by using the close intimacy of court relationships to concoct a fictitious series of charges of adultery against Anne. As only one of the men accused, Mark Smeaton, was a commoner, he was the only one likely to have been tortured and thus was the only one to confess to the charges. Adultery was bad enough, but if Anne was to be thoroughly discredited something more was needed to destroy all public sympathy for her. Jane was questioned closely about the relationship between Anne and Anne's brother, Lord Rochford. There is no doubt that they were close, but there is also no doubt that the accusation of incest that emerged was preposterous. Jane repeated her evidence against both Queen and husband, Lord Rochford, at their trial on 15 May 1536, the records of which were destroyed on Henry's orders soon after the trial ended, so precise details are lacking. But enough emerged from those present at the trial to show that Jane's evidence was a vital part of the Crown case. Ordinary instances of sibling affection were distorted by her in court into something much more sinister. Various explanations have been offered for Jane's extraordinary behaviour: she was jealous of Anne's closeness to her brother, or she was punishing Rochford for his various infidelities. Jane may have felt that Anne was doomed anyway since several men had already been arrested, and that her evidence would make little difference. But the notion that she denounced her husband to make him plead guilty and thus give him a better chance of the King's mercy seems over-fanciful.

After her husband's execution, Jane fell upon hard times. Lord Rochford's property had been confiscated and Jane had to beg Cromwell for help. He managed to secure for her an annual pension of £100, enough whereby a lady could live comfortably but not extravagantly. But Jane was determined to return to court, and she did so within a few months, becoming a lady-in-waiting to Jane Seymour, Henry VIII's third wife. Queen Jane died soon after giving birth to Prince Edward (later Edward VI). So Lady Rochford had to find a new patron, and soon became an important member of the entourage of the next queen, Anne of Cleves. But for various reasons Henry's marriage to Anne turned out to be a disaster, and in July 1540 Henry instituted proceedings to dissolve the marriage; these proceedings were aided by Lady Rochford's testimony that the marriage had never been consummated.

So it is not surprising that Lady Rochford soon became an important member of the household of Henry VIII's fifth wife, Catherine Howard. She was a very inexperienced slip of a girl, still in her mid-teens, married to a king more than three times her age and more than three times her size. Lady Rochford was now a matron in her mid-thirties, much experienced in court life, and in a position to influence the new young untutored Queen for the good. Instead she indulged her. When, in 1541, the Queen began a liaison with Thomas Culpeper, Jane, with a few other ladies of the court, facilitated Catherine's secret meetings with Culpeper, and even, on one occasion, found pretexts for keeping the King away when he came to claim his conjugal rights. Whether secret meetings led to anything more than just intimate conversation, as Catherine was later to claim, is uncertain. But such meetings were difficult to keep secret and the brother of a disgruntled maid-servant saw revelation as a route to self-advancement. The Howards' Catholic sympathies made them anathema to the religious reformers and Archbishop Cranmer took upon himself the pleasurable duty of laying the sordid facts before a distraught Henry. Both the Queen and Lady Jane were placed under arrest.

While the Queen was closely guarded at Syon House, Lady Jane was taken to the Tower where she was subjected to searching questioning. As a viscountess, she was too noble to be tortured, but she might have feared it, and took refuge in feigning madness. After several months of deliberation the King decided not to proceed against them by a court trial but to have them both declared guilty by Act of Parliament. Such an Act of Attainder would make it unnecessary to produce evidence or witnesses, and would prevent any gratuitous references to the King's age and alleged impotence being aired in open court.

> ... be it enacted that the said queen Katherine and Jane, Lady Rochford, for their said abominable and detestable treasons ... shall be by the authority of this present parliament, be convicted and attainted of high treason ...
>
> (Act of Attainder, 1542)

Henry disposed of Jane's madness by having Parliament enact that those convicted of treason or misprision of treason should not escape the death penalty merely on account of madness. On 13 February 1542, Queen Catherine, in a virtual state of collapse, was beheaded on Tower Green. Lady Jane followed shortly afterwards; she had shed her madness, confessed her sins, and made a godly end. She was buried in the Tower near to the resting places of those she had served and betrayed.

Lady Jane Rochford's addiction to court life led her to serve five of Henry's queens. Her anxiety to remain in favour led her to abandon Anne Boleyn when her cause appeared lost, and to indulge Catherine Howard when she should have guided her. Her unfaithful husband made court life preferable to married life, and seems to have encouraged her vindictive streak. She may have had personality defects, but it is very unlikely that these bordered on madness. She was a more typical Tudor courtier than is often acknowledged; others courted favour, denounced those out of favour, and survived the hothouse atmosphere of Henry's court. Perhaps Jane was just unlucky.

ULRIKE MEINHOF AND THE RED ARMY FACTION

Ulrike Meinhof, together with Andreas Baader, were the pair who were the leaders of the notorious Baader-Meinhof Gang, also known as the Red Army Faction (or Rote Armee Fraktion), which terrorised Germany and to a lesser extent the remainder of Europe in the 1970s. They threatened direct action, involving robberies, assassinations, bombings, kidnappings and sometimes indiscriminate street violence against complete strangers, as a means of achieving their largely left-wing objectives. It was only with the greatest difficulty that they were first contained and later dealt with by Konrad Adenauer's West German government. With loose affiliations to the unilateralist movement and to the German Communist Party, the Baader-Meinhof Gang sprang from a student protest movement, but later, under the leadership of its two main protagonists, developed into a revolutionary grouping of such unexpected seriousness that it threatened the stability of the entire West German state, and was contained and finally suppressed only with considerable difficulty.

Ulrike Marie Meinhof was born in 1934 in Oldenburg, the family moving to Jena when her father, art historian Dr Weiner Meinhof, became director of that city's museum. Her father died of cancer during the war, and in 1946 the family moved back to Oldenburg when Jena fell into the Soviet occupation zone after the war. She took her secondary school exams in Weilburg in 1955 and went on to college at Marburg, where, in common with many adolescents at the time, she became involved with student political activities. In 1957 she moved on to the University of Münster, where her political activities became more time-consuming.

She joined the Socialist German Student Union, protested against the Federal Government's rearming of the *Bundeswehr*, became a spokeswoman of the Anti-Atomic Death Committee (*Anti-Atomtod-Ausschuss*) and an activist in the General Committee of Students (*Allgemeiner Studierendenausschuss*) where she wrote articles for a number of radical student newspapers. She married, and had produced twin children, Bettina and Regina, before her divorce from her husband, Klaus Rainer Röhl, in 1967. By this time her writings show her to have become a rabid and fearless revolutionary.[1] She had joined the banned German Communist Party (KPD) in 1959, and was by 1962 editor-in-chief of the magazine *Konkret*, extolling the virtues of direct revolutionary action.

In the late 1960s, in the course of her writing on the subject of firebombing as a means of political protest, she made the acquaintance of Andreas Baader and Gudrun Ensslin, perpetrators of a series of arson attacks in Frankfurt in protest against the Vietnam War. She left her job at *Konkret*, and joined them in their campaigns (she later vandalised the magazine offices where she had formerly worked), embarking on a new life as an urban guerrilla. The terrorist group began its activities in 1968 by firebombing department stores. Baader and Ensslin were arrested and convicted, but were released pending an appeal, and fled. In May 1970, Meinhof participated in the 'break-out' of Baader, though his assisted escape was not from prison, but from a research institute he was visiting at the time, an occasion on which an elderly librarian was mortally shot with a pistol, and two security staff wounded. The federal government offered a 10,000 DM reward for their apprehension. The group fled to Jordan and set themselves up in a training camp run by the Popular Front for the Liberation of Palestine, where they crawled in the sand, climbed through thickets of barbed wire and learned how to use small arms. These – apart from the last – were useless as accomplishments for urban guerrillas, and in any case their promiscuous behaviour soon shocked their El Fatah hosts, who were glad to see the back of them when they eventually left.

When the group returned to Germany later in 1970 they devised their 'RAF' name, their manifesto and their logo – a machine-gun. Meinhof did the thinking, writing many pamphlets glorifying direct action,[2] and Baader and his fellow agitators, known to their contemporaries in Munich as *shickeria* (or 'trendies'), stole Porsches and BMWs, and burned up the town in them. This eventually translated into a wave of bombings and murders in which thirty-five individuals, including prominent businessmen, bankers and judges, were killed. The group bombed a US Officers' Club in Frankfurt in 1972, kidnapped and brutally killed Hans Martin Schleyer[3] in 1977, and hijacked a Lufthansa aircraft in 1977 after take-off in Majorca, a plane in which they flew to Mogadishu in Somalia, after refuelling in Rome, before the plane was eventually stormed on the runway by a German special forces team. By then, a number of their leaders had been arrested and were under lock and key, and were brought to trial in 1975 in front of an elderly federal judge, Eberhard Foth, who leaned over backwards in order to be fair to them. The accused were granted unheard-of privileges during their detention in Stammheim prison: they were allowed to meet and to fraternise, and as a result of their continued plotting, their messages to other gang members were smuggled out of prison and further action planned. The trial lasted 192 days. Meantime, their keepers were astonished and appalled by their unruly behaviour, their recklessness and their defiance.[4] They were, however, finally found guilty of murder and attempted murder, and were sentenced to life imprisonment. A number of them refused to attend court to hear their sentences. By this time, Meinhof was already dead. She committed suicide in May 1976 and was found hanged by a rope fashioned from a prison towel in her cell. She was buried in Berlin-Mariendorf six days after her death.[5] The results of the official enquiry into her death were not published until 2001, and were never accepted by the RAF; they chose to believe that she had been secretly murdered by the prison authorities.

Meinhof's suicide brought to an end years of popular insurrection – a period of chaotic challenges on her part, and of uncertainty and dithering on the part of the federal government in Bonn, a government that did not itself last long thereafter, brought to an end by the reunification of Germany in 1990. Perhaps she was the only one of the whole group who gave any thought to what they intended to do – not that this made her popular among her followers[6]; all the others seem to have been mindless layabouts who were in it for the fun it gave them. But even she was not fighting a real enemy. She turned all her hatred on a mild German democratic system that was more indulgent than it was oppressive – what she was really fighting was the ghost of an oppressive Nazism that had perished in ignominy a generation earlier. Her life was not untypical of a postwar generation that, in the shameful shadow of a defeated Nazi autocracy, and blinded by a fanatical loyalty to juvenile ideas, could not grapple with the complexity of changed circumstances, so that she led her young followers along a path that ultimately led only to their disillusion and self-destruction.

ROSEMARY WEST: 'SHE MUST HAVE KNOWN'

Rosemary West featured in one of the most sordid and degrading crimes of the later twentieth century, when she was convicted in 1995 of being involved in the torture and murder of at least ten young women in Gloucester. Her husband, Frederick Walter Stephen West, who committed suicide in prison while awaiting trial, was accused of twelve instances of rape and murder (the first two before he had met Rosemary), crimes in most of which Rosemary was said to be his willing accomplice, though he himself avoided being sentenced by committing suicide in his cell in Winson Green Prison, Birmingham, by hanging, prior to the delivery of any verdict on him for his crimes. Rosemary was convicted in his place in November 1995, her judge, Mr Justice Mantell, observing when he sentenced her: 'If attention is paid to what I think, you will never be released.' She was imprisoned for life, a sentence for at least twenty-five years, later confirmed by the then Home Secretary, Jack Straw, as a 'full life sentence', at HMP Bronzefield, Ashford, Middlesex. She is still in prison in spite of efforts to review her sentence, though questions have been subsequently raised about the appropriateness and justice of the verdict.

Rosemary Pauline Letts was born in 1953 in Barnstaple after a difficult pregnancy on the part of her mother. She was a difficult child who grew up into a moody teenager and performed badly at school. She had something of a weight problem in her youth, although this did not prevent her from showing sexual precociousness and an interest in older men. Her mother and father separated when she was a teenager after alleged instances of violence on the part of her father; but in spite of this she left her mother and went to live with her father, just before meeting Fred West at the age of fifteen. Rosemary's father disapproved of West, threatened him, and also threatened to call in social services for their help, but in vain, and by 1970 Rosemary was living with him as well as caring for West's daughter Anne-Marie by a previous marriage. She also found herself pregnant by him.

Fred West, though bland and harmless-looking, was in fact the real monster. Moving from his parents' rural home in Herefordshire, he committed a number of minor offences before he moved to Gloucester, took a job in an abattoir, and continued his life of petty crime. Later, his criminal proclivities became more marked. He married Catherine (Rena) Costello, a prostitute who gave him two children, Charmaine and Anne-Marie, though one was the daughter of a client rather than his own. Later his wife left him. When she returned in 1966, she found him living with Anna McFall, who was heavily pregnant with his child. Fred murdered Anna and buried her in a field near Much Marcle. Shortly afterwards, Rena left him a second time. At this point he met Rosemary West, whom he introduced to a life of prostitution. The couple at first were living together in a caravan in Bishop's Cleeve, and later moved into a house in Midland Road, Gloucester. There she gave birth to her first child, Heather Anne, in October 1970[1] while still supposedly looking after Fred's children Charmaine and Anne-Marie. Charmaine died in 1971 about the time Fred was serving a prison sentence for unpaid fines; after he came out he dismembered her and buried her body under the floor. When Rena returned to seek out her children in August 1971 he killed her too, stripped and dismembered her body and buried it in a field near his childhood home.

It was at this point that the couple moved into the property he later used for the disposal of the bodies of his many victims, at 25 Cromwell Street, Gloucester. He harvested his scattered corpses from the graves he had dug for them, and began to rebury them under the cellar floor, until this was packed full of bodies and he had perforce to start on the garden. He began by attacking Caroline Owens, who was seventeen and employed as their children's nanny. She was assaulted and raped, an attack in which she later testified both Fred and his wife played a part. But she escaped with her life, and the court, not having experienced this type of behaviour from him before, chose to let the couple off with a fine. Subsequent victims were not allowed to escape. In rapid succession after the spring of 1973, Fred killed, stripped and dismembered first Lynda Gough, then Carol Anne Cooper, and then Lucy Partington, whom he abducted at a bus stop and detained for about a week before murdering her. In 1974 he murdered Therese Siegenthaler and Shirley Hubbard. In 1975 he murdered Juanita Mott, in 1978 Shirley Robinson and in 1979 Alison Chambers. His last victim was his own sixteen-year-old daughter Heather Anne, in 1987, whom he murdered and buried in the garden behind the house, where she remained for seven years before being discovered. It was at this point that the Wests' criminal activities came to the attention of the police. They were investigating incidents in 1992 when West was alleged to have raped his thirteen-year-old daughter, filmed the assault, and later to have gone on to rape her twice more. This she divulged to her brothers and sisters, who talked about it at school, and so it became known to the authorities. In August, Fred West was charged with three counts of rape and one of buggery against this daughter, but nearly a year elapsed before the police uncovered the first of many bodies. In the meantime, the rape case against Fred West and the charges of child cruelty against Rosemary collapsed when the two main Crown witnesses, members of the Wests' own family, refused to testify. Between February and April 1994, after extensive excavations at 25 Cromwell Street and elsewhere, West was arrested and charged with multiple murders. Rosemary was charged merely with sex offences. West confessed, retracted his confession, and then confessed a second time, this time only to the murder of his daughter Heather Anne, and denying that Rosemary was involved. She was not arrested until April 1994, and then only for sex offences, but she was subsequently charged also with a number of murders. The two came to trial in Gloucester in June 1994, Fred charged with eleven murders and Rosemary with ten. It was while he was in police custody that Fred West hanged himself in prison in January 1995.

Rosemary West went on trial alone in October 1995. In the heat of public indignation over the grotesque details that were coming to light, there was considerable local and national interest in, and much press reporting of, the details of the crimes, and there was pressure, too, on the police authorities to press for the prosecution of the remaining miscreant.[2] Other features of the case were also of critical importance.

The case came before Mr Justice Mantell at Winchester Crown Court, well away from the location of the crimes under consideration. The judge was an avuncular figure with a twinkle in his eye, firm but always very ready to explain court proceedings to the jury and anxious that they should understand; but it is difficult to excuse him from a latent bias in his attitude towards the case. When counsel asked him for a ruling, this was almost invariably given against the defence team. For example, when the defence made an application that 'similar fact' evidence should be excluded on the grounds that it was 'disputed evidence' rather than 'similar fact', the judge rebuffed his assertion that evidence from the dead and from the living were fundamentally not 'similar evidence' by allowing both types of evidence to be introduced, and again ruled against his objections on the grounds that the treatment of the dead girls was remarkably similar and similarities could properly be deduced from it relating to each others' deaths. Likewise, the judge dismissed the defence submission that the five cases the police had 'cherry-picked' to base their case on were different from the other seven, and selected because they were 'easier'; the judge's view was that the police were merely saving court time and were acting quite properly. The defence took the view that certain of the bones were coloured differently, suggesting the bodies had been buried before, and that bits of the bodies – the small toe-bones, the finger-bones, certain vertebrae, some patellas (knee-caps) and, in one case, a shoulder-blade – were missing, confirming this treatment and reinforcing the accused's statement she knew nothing about it. Counsel also petitioned for three of the ten cases to be tried separately on the grounds that these victims had perhaps been subject to some sort of sexual attack, thus distinguishing them from the others and giving the accused a sort of motive (though not for murder); but the judge, considering the defence submission over the weekend, rejected even this, ruling against a separate trial for the three, and saying that he would not allow damaging inferences to be made from these three for the others, since his rulings would be enough to prevent such misleading inferences being drawn. In fact, all these submissions pointed to a common feature of the multiple-murder charge: the premises at Cromwell Road were so restricted, and the murder proceedings so protracted and bloody, that even if she had not been a willing accomplice of her husband's actions, the couple were *in it together*, and Rosemary West *must have known* of the events that were afoot, so that in effect she was as guilty as her husband.

This dangerous assumption was not dispelled by the conduct of the case. Rosemary West's dress and demeanour in the dock deepened rather than weakened the prejudices against her. She said nothing to the warders escorting her; she spoke little, except in her monosyllabic answers; she looked 'more like a supermarket manageress' than a murderer, and seemed indifferent to the proceedings in the court and generally quite untroubled when very pointed comments were made about her by counsel. But at every turn, the prosecution was at pains to stress the 'pattern' of the killings, and the 'striking similarity' between the forensic evidence relating to the murders. Counsel insisted that there were sexual motives behind the stripping of the victims, and that the bodies had not merely been undressed in order to facilitate their dismemberment; it was 'plainly unthinkable that Rosemary West was not aware of, or involved in, the crimes'. The relations between the pair were 'of such closeness that she *must have known* about those who were brought to Cromwell Street and buried there'. This was the burden of the frequently repeated refrain in the Crown's case against her.

The parade of witnesses that followed was used by the prosecution to stress the closeness between Fred West and Rosemary, and by the defence to suggest the fear in which she held her husband. Some witnesses were clear, others confused; a few, as the defence pointed out, very damning, having already sold their stories to the newspapers and now in line for substantial rewards if the prosecution succeeded. The defence was not happy with the testimony of Caroline Owens, not only because she too had sold her story to the newspapers, but chiefly because the evidence she gave related to her maltreatment by and escape from the Wests, and fell into that category of 'similar evidence' that defence had been trying to disbar from the hearing on the grounds that it did not relate to the murder charges under consideration. Her declaration about Mrs West – 'She seemed evil to me' – weighed heavily with the jurors, but scarcely counted in the matter of her guilt of murder. Other evidence, too, concerning Rosemary West's dubious moral character, was admitted for consideration, all pretty distasteful, but none, in the view of the defence, 'probative of murder'. The testimony of one witness, 'Miss A', was of such precise detail as to be quite chilling to the court in the matter of sexual assault by both the Wests, but once again was weakened by the revelation that she stood to gain £30,000 in the case of a conviction, and by the twin facts that she had herself received treatment in a clinic for gonorrhoea, and treatment for a mental disorder involving notions of stalking and hallucinations in which she 'saw people with other people's heads on their shoulders'. Other witnesses gave testimony that was broadly along the same lines, but which the defence found deeply disappointing. Witnesses had given ample proof of Rosemary West's depraved character, but nothing more. Defence counsel said: 'You have heard evidence of sexual bondage, ropes and gags and so on. But what does that say? The Crown has built a careful but speculative case. The stack of cards on which it rests is that all the victims were sexually abused, and that Rosemary West was a necessary ingredient in that mix ... But even if you accept that she was perverted, that is proof of that, and nothing more ... Because there can be no evidence as to how these girls met their deaths, the Crown have filled that void with prejudice and speculation.'

The last witness called by the defence was Rosemary West herself. This strategy enabled defence counsel to elicit the information he considered relevant, but entailed a good deal of risk, since it enabled the prosecution to cross-examine her and might in fact succeed in confusing her in her testimony. In fact she bore up well as defence counsel questioned her, showing convincingly that she lived in terror of her husband, and genuinely regretted the death of her daughter Heather Anne. She sobbed as she averred that she did not know that Fred was a murderer, however improbable that sounded. When he opened his cross-examination, prosecuting counsel was not slow to point out by his questions the common-sense belief that *'she must have known'*. She replied 'No, sir' to everything to do with the murders: she had never witnessed any attacks, she had never heard any noises or screams, she had never seen a body, she had never seen bloodstains either in the house or on her husband's clothing, and so on. The court clearly did not believe her. Counsel was then allowed to go on to question her about her sexual behaviour, though its relevance was questionable. She was not a convincing witness: she had a faulty memory at one point, but remembered with crystal clarity at the next; she was sharp and obstreperous at one moment, but meek and persuasive at the next; above all, she totally rejected any suggestion that her conduct was morally reprehensible. Taped interviews of her husband's testimony to the police were played to the court; she kept her eyes downcast, and their contents shed very little light (mixture of truth and falsehood as they were, Fred perhaps had intended that they *should* cast little light) on the whole muddled story.[3] A final witness, a Mrs Janet Leach, gave evidence of a 'plot' between Fred West and his wife, by which, if she were released, he would take the blame for everything: she was to say nothing, while he was to lay a smokescreen by saying 'a lot of nonsense' with a view to escaping culpability, and she was to stay 'mum'. The witness worked herself up into a terrible state during her testimony, even forcing an interruption of the trial until she recovered her composure; but the defence was merciless in pursuing her, and eventually forced her to admit that she had reached a verbal agreement with a newspaper whereby she accepted £100,000 for her full revelations when the case was over, an admission that effectively discredited her in the eyes of the jury.

After the concluding speeches of the two barristers, the judge gave his summing-up. He could see that members of the jury were torn between an acquittal, on the grounds that there was not enough direct evidence to warrant a life sentence for murder, and a conviction on the grounds that she was a wicked woman who *must have known* about the monstrous behaviour of her husband. He spent four days on a speech that he said he intended to clarify their predicament, but which in fact drove the nails firmly into the defendant's coffin. Warning them not to draw unwarrantable inferences from the evidence, he virtually encouraged them to do this by defining *murder* so widely[4] that they were invited to do exactly that. He spent a good deal of time on the charge relating to sixteen-year-old Charmaine, reminding them that the defence had failed to challenge evidence that she had died while Frederick was in prison (which was the obvious thing to do if they thought Rosemary's assertion that her husband committed the crime was true). He even glossed over the mercenary role of the newspapers in influencing the content of evidence by saying that such reporting was 'a fact of life; it happens'.

The judge rose from his lengthy summing-up on 20 November, and the jury retired to consider its verdict. Two days later they filed back in to enquire (a) whether the absence of direct evidence, other than the presence of remains, is an obstacle to a guilty verdict, and (b) whether they could rely on the 'similar evidence' offered by witnesses in the case, in relation to the presence of remains. They were reassured by the judge on both counts. When the defence counsel asked the judge to recall them again to tell them that it was 'too great a leap' to infer guilt on one matter by reference to guilt on another quite different matter, he refused. The jury took twenty-three more minutes to reach their final verdict of guilty on all charges.

Four months later, Rosemary's counsel lodged an appeal against the verdict based on seven grounds. These were carefully considered by the three appeal judges in the Court of Appeal in London, and in a judgement which broadly endorsed the use of *similar fact*, said the jury had been right to reject Rosemary West's defence: the view that individual crimes of murder had been committed at these premises concurrently with grave sexual abuses of other girls committed concurrently by husband and wife together, without the wife being party to the killings was inconceivable, and was quite correctly rejected by the jury. The judgement in each case was therefore upheld.

In spite of the verdict and the apparent finality of the rejection of the appeal, there remain many questions about the justice of Rosemary West's sentence. The whole matter of 'similar evidence', especially in the case of evidence of one crime in relation to a quite different crime, seems fraught with problems and likely to lead to injustice. And there is the further question of whether – even if she was the accomplice of her husband in these crimes – this constitutes 'guilt' in the accepted sense of the word. There is ample clinical evidence of a state of mind, known to the psychiatrists as *folie à deux*, when a powerful personality so fascinates and overwhelms the character of another that the obsessed person becomes the willing tool of the dominant one, and carries out his instructions to the letter, no matter how obscene they may be. This syndrome is specially effective in cases where there is elaborate secrecy, and/or in cases where crimes of grisly violence are involved, and where the dominant figure is able to supplant the will of the dominated character with his own will. In such cases there is reason to say that the inferior member of the criminal partnership is not so much *guilty* as *sick*.

PART 10

POLITICAL LEADERS

MADAME ROLAND AND THE FRENCH REVOLUTION

Madame Roland, French writer-philosopher and radical revolutionary, was one of those leading figures who dominated the Revolution in its early idealistic days, believed in it and fought for it, and in the end died for it on the guillotine. She was by no means unique as a revolutionary figure, but in a male-dominated age she was set apart by her gender as a serious thinker and politician, and helped to set the scene on which the great drama of the Revolution was played. Her salon in Paris, where many of the issues at stake were discussed and debated, became the headquarters of the so-called Girondin Party, from which she persuaded her husband, Jean Marie Roland, to attack Danton and after him Robespierre in the National Convention, where he sat as a member and a former minister. These attacks were events that contributed to the split between the Girondins and the Jacobins, the two main parties at the time. When the Jacobins reached the pinnacle of their power in the Reign of Terror, she was arrested, imprisoned and finally executed in November 1793. Her husband never recovered from the shock and committed suicide shortly afterwards.

Jeanne Manon Roland de la Platière (*née* Phillipon) was born in 1754 of a well-to-do bourgeois family in Paris. Her father was an engraver. She married Jean Marie Roland de la Platière in 1780. Unusually for a girl of her class, she was thoroughly educated, first in a convent school, and later privately, and went on to become a woman of letters, much influenced by the writings of Plutarch and Rousseau. She established a salon in Paris in 1791 where the political and philosophical issues of the day were debated,[1] attracting the attention of many of the would-be politicians who flocked to the capital to resolve the problems confronting the country following the meeting of the Estates General in 1789. Reputed for her advanced revolutionary opinions, she was at first slow to discard her royalist sympathies, and, partly because of her origins and outlook, never had much truck with the *enragé* extremists of the Jacobin 'Mountain', whom she regarded as uncultured and fanatical. Her husband served for a time in 1792 as Minister of the Interior before the fall of the monarchy, and it was she who wrote the letter of protest to the King concerning his failure to take effective action in government, which brought about the minister's dismissal. They both considered themselves to be supporters and members of the Girondin Party, which, since it originated in the south-west in the area of the Gironde, was sometimes suspected of anti-Parisian attitudes (though there was very little justification for this). With the King's flight to Varennes in 1791 and the final fall of the monarchy at the end of 1792, she adopted more strongly anti-royalist attitudes, and advocated even the end of the monarchy, though eventually she came to realise that perhaps the revolution had got out of control and had gone too far.

In the preceding years, Mme Roland's respect for Louis XVI had steadily soured. But she disapproved more strongly of the aristocrats, on whom she was much more inclined to put the blame for the country's predicament. She looked on the continuing *jacqueries* as the peasants' way of voicing their displeasure with the way the noblemen had kept them in misery and subjection. Commenting on the burning of *chateaux*, she wrote rather smugly: 'The aristocrats make a great noise about it, but really it is not such a bad thing. I see no cause for public lamentations.' She saw the ills that their social role had fostered, causing great hardship, and noted at the same time that bad harvests and ineffective distribution of corn supplies (often exacerbated by the dealers in their own interests) in 1790 and 1791 intensified the problems resulting from the attack on the Bastille in July 1789. Large numbers of unemployed farm workers and domestic staff (laid off after the beginning of the emigration of aristocrats) brought masses of disaffected people into the capital, and their repeated acts of disorder threatened life and property in the city. But, though she felt so threatened that from time to time she withdrew from the city, at least it had the effect of making Paris the central theatre of the Revolution.[2]

Her opinion of Louis took a sharp turn for the worse after his attempted flight to Varennes with his wife and family in June 1791. The King's ministers were dismissed, and even the leaders of the National Guard fell under popular suspicion for carrying out the court's instructions. Mirabeau was losing ground and was heavily overworked; almost nobody seemed prepared to respect the King's constitutional rights. Mme Roland withdrew from the capital to her local village to escape the continual violence in Paris. This did not stop her reminding her friends that 'public opinion has made the revolution, and public opinion would save it – if only the people had arms!' Moderate opinion was dwindling and before the end of the summer voices were being raised in favour of a republic. Brissot's *Patriote*, supported by Mme Roland, was one of about a dozen publications denouncing Louis and calling for a republican form of government. But the deputies hesitated. Writing to Robespierre in late September, she despaired of the passivity of the Assembly. Their inaction, she said, proved that 'the least aberration from the orbit of equality and liberty tends to degrade human nature'. However, the constitution of 1791 at least made provision for the election of a new assembly, and these elections were carried out in the late summer and autumn of 1792, though without the full process by which some 40,000 electors should have given their votes. But the new Convention was radically different from its predecessor, not only in its design but in the sort of people represented in it. Mme Roland believed that the 'country has grown two centuries older in two years', so rapidly was their experience of democratic government advancing. It was headed by figures such as Vergniaud, Gensonné, Guadet and Buzot, but one of the powers behind the scenes was Mme Roland herself, who had returned to the capital convinced that she could show the Girondins the way to conduct the Revolution.

For some time, the Paris *sections* had been trying to recover the control they had lost over the National Guard. Louis XVI, with all the deviousness of a stubborn man out of his depth, was seeking to block any efforts by the populace and the deputies to recover this control, and vetoed the assembly's attempts to reinforce the armed forces with bodies of *fédérés* from the provinces. It was this situation which led Mme Roland to send a letter (or rather a lecture) dictated from the Ministry of the Interior in June, not so much by the minister as by the minister's wife. In it she said the King was making too free with his veto, and unless he mended his ways there would be further insurrections in Paris. ('The revolution is complete in men's minds: unless provision is made against evils which can still be avoided, it will be accomplished at the price of bloodshed, and will be cemented in blood.') This blunt and uncalled-for warning merely resulted in her husband being dismissed from office within the week, and further efforts to recover the initiative by the court.

By July 1792 the *fédérés* were starting to arrive. Some, like those from Brest, were not keen to fight the Parisians' battles for them in the capital, but others, like those from Marseilles,[3] and their fire-eating leader Charles-Jean-Marie Barbaroux, delegate from the city, quite clearly intended to carry out the wishes of the *Conventionels* to dethrone the King and create a republic. Mme Roland had been granted her wish, but she was nor sure whether she liked it.

On 10 August, the Parisians, egged on by columns of the *fédérés*, attacked the Tuileries, where the King and the royal family had been housed since their return to Paris from Versailles in 1789. He fled to the assembly, which eventually decided to lodge him at the Temple in conditions amounting to imprisonment. The Jacobins, in what was in fact a coup d'état, seized executive power and set up the Committee of Public Safety, under Danton's leadership, aided by Desmoulins, Robespierre and Marat, and ruled until he was replaced by Robespierre in July 1793. They were no longer ministers of the Crown, but employees of the Assembly. Mme Roland at first continued to exercise some sway with them, but the public crowds began to think that the remaining Girondins in the government were not to be trusted, and that the elegant dinners they gave at the Ministry of the Interior (to which M. Roland had been recalled) were used by Mme Roland and her clique to vent their hostility towards the Paris mob and the Commune. As a result they came to be suspicious of her.[4] Within six months, M. Roland had been dismissed from office again and his wife was threatened with prison.

At the beginning of June 1793, François Hanriot, the hard-faced ex-clerk of the *octroi* who had been newly appointed as commandant of the National Guard, arrested Mme Roland and purged the Convention by arresting key Girondins. Members of the party considered abandoning Paris and setting up their own government in the provinces, but nothing came of it and the Girondin elements in the administration gradually faded away. Mme Roland was still sufficiently feared to be denied a hearing before the Revolutionary Tribunal, or to speak in her own defence. She was imprisoned in the Sainte-Pélagie and the Conciergerie for five months until early November 1793, then dragged from her cell to a radiant martyrdom before the statue of Liberty. Reputedly, her last words before her head was struck off were: 'Oh, Liberty! What crimes are committed in your name!'

MARGARET THATCHER:
BRITAIN'S FIRST WOMAN PRIME MINISTER

Margaret Thatcher was the first woman Prime Minister of Great Britain and leader of the Conservative Party in the later years of the twentieth century. She was admired by many as the leader who rescued Britain from the dead hand of state socialism and who championed the market economy, all of which led to a revival of Britain's prosperity in the 1980s. But to those on the left-wing of politics it was axiomatic that she was a disaster for the country; they could not believe that any contrary opinion is even arguable.

Margaret Hilda Roberts was born at Grantham in Lincolnshire on 13 October 1925, daughter of Alfred Roberts, a local grocer, and Beatrice Roberts (*née* Stephenson). She was brought up as a Methodist, and after education at the local grammar school she went up to Somerville College, Oxford, to read chemistry and after graduation became a research chemist. But she soon abandoned this career to read for the law and became a barrister in 1954. In the intervening years she had entered politics, met and married Denis Thatcher, a successful businessman, in 1951, and had given birth to twins, Mark and Carol, in 1953. Unlike most women of that era she did not allow marriage or motherhood to interfere with her political ambitions and was soon putting herself forward for selection as a Conservative candidate in parliamentary elections. From the first, she encountered traditional Tory prejudice against women in politics, and it was some time before she could even get chosen as a candidate. At first she was only nominated for safe Labour seats such as Dartford in Kent, but in 1959 she was selected for Finchley in North London for the general election of that year. After a vigorous and effective campaign, she won the seat that she was to retain until 1992.

She soon made her mark in the House of Commons, and in 1961 was appointed junior pensions minister in Harold Macmillan's government. Edward Heath included her in his shadow cabinet during the long years of opposition (1964–70), and upon the Conservative success in the general election of 1970 made her his Education Secretary. Paradoxically the move to comprehensive education gathered pace during her secretaryship; she saw to it that local authorities were no longer compelled to abolish grammar schools as they had been under Labour, but most authorities were too far advanced with their comprehensive plans to put them into reverse. Her abolition of free school milk for primary school children provoked much anger and derision, and labelled her 'Margaret Thatcher, milk snatcher'; at that time child obesity was still comparatively rare. Heath's political miscalculations in 1974 led to his defeat in the general election of that year, and much disgruntlement among the Conservative rank and file; Margaret was never to forget how the miners held Heath to ransom and eventually brought down his government. As the party hierarchy jostled to challenge Heath for the party leadership, Margaret Thatcher's first inclination was to support Keith Joseph, but in the end allowed her own name to go forward, came higher than Heath in the first ballot, and following his withdrawal, beat William Whitelaw to become party leader in the second.

She was fortunate during the next four years to have plenty to oppose as leader of the opposition. Inflation, a spiralling national debt, and a stranglehold on government policy by powerful trade unions all gave Margaret Thatcher plentiful ammunition for her effective and withering attacks upon the successive Labour governments of Harold Wilson and James Callaghan. Both learned to fear her onslaught during Prime Minister's Questions. In May 1979, following 'a winter of discontent' of strikes and uncollected garbage, Callaghan was forced to face a general election, which the Conservatives won with a majority of just over forty seats. Margaret Thatcher became Prime Minister, a post she was to hold for eleven and a half years. Her promise, on appointment, to substitute harmony for discord[1] was not fulfilled as she would have liked, but for most of her premiership the Labour Party was consigned to the political wilderness. This was in part due to her political courage and her determination to see policies through without compromise. She took a firm stand on Northern Ireland even though ten IRA prisoners starved themselves to death in 1981 in an attempt to force the government to cave in on the issue of the rights of political prisoners. She set her face firmly against any compromise with the IRA that would undermine British sovereignty in Northern Ireland. She responded to the Argentinian invasion of the British Falkland Islands, another challenge to British sovereignty, by raising a huge task force to ensure their reconquest. Despite later criticism, she was supported at the time by all the main political parties.

Not surprisingly, she won a landslide general election victory in 1983, when the Labour Party appeared to be lurching to the left under Michael Foot. She showed undoubted courage at the Conservative Party Conference in the autumn of 1984 when the IRA bombed the Brighton hotel in which many of the Conservative delegates were staying, killing five of them. She defiantly insisted on continuing the conference rather than abandon it, which she said would have been tantamount to giving in to terrorism. She effectively organised government resistance to the miners' strike in 1984–85 as part of her policy to clip the wings of the trade unions and overall to modernise industry. The miners' strike of 1974 was vivid in her memory, and she was determined to defeat the miners despite some temporary unpopularity. After her success against the miners, she was able to use new legislation effectively to cut down the unions to size, stripping them of their cherished illusion that it was really they who ran the country. There were no more tea and sandwiches at Number 10 Downing Street for trade union leaders. The new weakness of the trade unions allowed her to deprive the state of whole areas of responsibility where previously it had been very busy on citizens' behalf. It scrapped, or sold off (i.e. privatised), vast networks of economic activity such as the gas and electricity industries, coalmining, the water industry, the railways – called significantly by Tory statesmen such as the geriatric Harold Macmillan 'the family silver'. She was even suspected by opponents of wishing to privatise the Post Office and the National Health Service.

Her firm stance against the imperialist character and policies of the Soviet Union earned her some grudging Russian respect, the soubriquet (which she was rather proud of) 'the Iron Lady', and the firm friendship of President Reagan of the USA. British sovereignty, which she had been so keen to protect in the Falklands and against the European Union, must, she felt, be protected against the Soviet threat in alliance with a pliant USA that was prepared, on the whole, to protect British interests.

Margaret Thatcher's style was deliberately confrontational at home as well as abroad. She rejected the notion of consensus pursued by Harold Macmillan, Edward Heath and other 'one-nation' Tories (despite her 'harmony' speech in May 1979) and tried to redefine the meaning of conservatism in individual moral terms. She made it clear that to her conservatism 'meant governing a society rather than managing an economy'. She always remained something of an outsider. Her social background was similar to Heath's, yet she was never accepted as completely as he was. Her plain, unsophisticated ways were ridiculed in private, and she remained the target of that snobbish elitism that was one of the less attractive features of Conservatism. One critic observed that 'she is still basically a Finchley lady'. Francis Pym revealed his essentially dismissive attitude towards her when he said: 'We've got a corporal at the top and not an officer.' These superior 'one-nation' Tories seemed to think that their polish would eventually rub off onto Margaret Thatcher and 'civilise' her, thinking that her directness showed the insecurity of a woman who had not yet gained the easy self-confidence of being 'at the top'.

Her critics were astonished when she continued to insist on what she believed to be the Tory 'basics'. As Nicholas Ridley, one of her admirers, put it in 1979: 'Her basic beliefs were clear enough: sound money, reform of the trade unions, targeting welfare to where it was needed, low taxation, rebuilding Britain's position in the world ... The 1979 election was to be the start of a long period of rigorous reform.' The battle within the party soon came to be described as one between the 'Wets' and the 'Dries'. It centred on monetarism[2] and featured in her budgets from the start. The 'Wets' were 'one-nation' Tories, some of whom, like Heseltine, wanted to use the powers of the state to pursue a more effective economic policy.[3] The 'Dries', on the other hand, like Biffen and later Howe and Lawson, became monetarists by different routes and soon counted themselves among her supporters. Old Etonian Ian Gilmour had published a book, *Inside Right*, in which he stressed the importance of creating what he called a 'sense of community'. But Margaret Thatcher was more individualistic and more radical than that. She even went so far at one point as to say: 'There is no such thing as society.'

When Thatcher's monetarist policies brought soaring inflation in the early 1980s, and unemployment topped three million, the Wets thought that their hour had struck, but Margaret stuck relentlessly to her guns and said: 'There is nothing else to try. There is no alternative.' This phrase, sometimes abbreviated in the press as TINA, and other similar phrases such as 'The lady's not for turning' were characteristic of her simplicity, frankness and conviction: 'Deep in their instincts people know that I am saying and doing right. And I know it is, because that was the way I was brought up. I regard myself as a very normal, ordinary person, with all the right instinctive antennae.' Sustained by this inner conviction, Margaret Thatcher went on to weed out those whose dryness she doubted, replacing them with her own creations, and simultaneously extending the limits of prime ministerial power. She carefully controlled Cabinet agendas, limiting discussion of controversial issues. She used her Press Office, and her loyal henchman, Sir Bernard Ingham, to watch over ministers and to leak information on them in order to damage them if they had outlived their usefulness. Those who succumbed – St John-Stevas, Gilmour, Prior, Pym – lost any influence they had once had; others, like Heath, glowered from the backbenches and kept aloof from any kind of public comment on her. By 1985 her supremacy was almost unchallenged.

Above all, she wanted to give the country leadership, and a leadership it could understand. She hated the muddle and drift of the 1960s and 1970s – the endless stop-go, the crippling strikes, the country's ailing industrial performance, continuing national decline – and wished to regenerate prosperity and success.

Throughout her period of office, Margaret Thatcher had two great advantages: grassroots support and a parliamentary party close to her both in her views and in her social background. Grassroots support showed itself at party conferences, where she was in her element – unlike most cabinet ministers, who loathed them. Margaret saw conferences as an annual opportunity not to decide what to do, but to re-bond with right-thinking folk. To her mind, these ordinary people represented precisely that sort of public opinion with which the Tory grandees were out of touch. The obsequious attention of television cameras, with the best 'sound-bites' reported on the evening TV news, all confirmed her easy and familiar ascendancy. She showed this at her very best with her handling of the Brighton bombing in 1984.

But Thatcherism was never an 'ideology'. To her the word ideology meant slavish adherence to some abstract blueprint created in advance. She rejected such a notion vigorously. Yet she gave many observers the impression of being ideological herself. This was because her policies conveyed a similar feeling of movement, direction and purpose. Thatcherites aimed to do 'the right thing', and shared fairly definite ideas as to what the 'right thing' was. She sometimes made references to what she called 'Victorian values', giving the impression that she was perhaps a nineteenth-century Gladstonian Liberal. But it would have been more accurate to say that she went back further than that, perhaps to Adam Smith.[4] Her view of Britain was drawn in three concentric circles; starting with the individual, it moved to the family to foster the individual's development, and arrived only last at the state, where the individual and the family could flourish and develop. It was in this sense that she meant that there was no such thing as society – rejecting the corporatist view that society exists in its own right as a vast welfare agency and assimilates the role of the individual to its own pattern. It was not for nothing that she was brought up as a Methodist; her view was profoundly religious, moral and individualistic.

It was also uncompromisingly single-minded. The Conservative general election victory in 1987 only slightly dented the large Conservative majority and seemed to confirm her mandate for further necessary reform. She had long been determined to get rid of the Greater London Council, in her view a hotbed of socialism, and succeeded in doing so in March 1986. Her success here emboldened her to tackle another long-standing issue of local government, namely its financing. Many Conservatives, and even some members of other parties, were highly critical of a system by which local finance[5] was levied on only a minority of the electorate (i.e. householders). Margaret Thatcher was convinced that if almost all voters paid for local finance they would have a greater sense of responsibility in exercising their vote. She therefore proposed to replace 'rates' with the Community Charge whereby local authorities determined a fixed sum per head to be paid by all adult voters with very few exceptions. It was to be introduced in Scotland in 1989 and in England in the following year. It met with almost universal opposition; critics emotionally dubbed it the Poll Tax[6] and called it regressive since it did not vary according to income. Her aim was to make the individual pay for his new freedom by shouldering his share of the Community Charge, but it foundered on the reluctance of those who demanded their share of political power but were happy that others should foot the bill. Riots in Edinburgh in 1989 were followed in 1990 by similar disturbances in England and Wales. The popularity of the Thatcher government slumped, coinciding with Thatcher's increasing difficulties in Cabinet.

These partly arose out of Margaret's unwillingness to compromise or change direction. Michael Heseltine was already waiting for an opportunity to challenge the Prime Minister, and in November 1990 Sir Geoffrey Howe, Margaret's Deputy and leader of the House of Commons, resigned from the Cabinet over Margaret's unwillingness to seek closer ties with Europe. She had already fought a vigorous battle to limit Britain's contribution to the coffers of the European Community but had very recently, and with considerable misgivings, agreed to join the European Exchange Rate Mechanism.[7] Her insistence on national sovereignty – in a curious way the counterpart to individual sovereignty – led her to resist further subordination to supranational Europe, and to reject going so far as a common currency. Howe's resignation showed the Cabinet division over Europe, but it also revealed wider divisions. Her didactic leadership style had offended not only the 'Wets' but also many colleagues who were broadly in sympathy with her views. When Michael Heseltine challenged Margaret for the leadership of the Conservative Party, she won, but not by the two thirds majority she needed to confirm her authority. In order to secure that majority Margaret was prepared to go to a second ballot, but was dissuaded, most reluctantly, from doing so by some of her Cabinet colleagues. She withdrew from the ballot on 22 November and resigned from the premiership on 28 November. Her fall was as dramatic as it was unexpected.

Margaret Thatcher stayed on as an MP until the general election of April 1992. She was appointed to the peerage as Baroness Thatcher of Kesteven two months later. Unlike Heath, she did not show silent hostility to her successor, John Major, and did what she could to ease the transition. She became an elder stateswoman. She was much in demand for highly paid after-dinner speeches, especially after she left the House of Commons, but tended not to make comment on controversial political matters. When Labour came to power in 1997 she had several private conversations with Tony Blair who, while bitterly opposing her policies, admired her political skills and formidable intellect. She also met Gordon Brown, Blair's successor, in 2007, but by that time her vigour had been affected by what seemed to be several small strokes and her increasing forgetfulness was an indication of incipient dementia. Nevertheless, she continued to make occasional public appearances throughout 2008.

Her political legacy was considerable. She had so far redefined public attitudes towards the state that even when Blair led Labour's return to power in 1997 he dared not reverse the innovations she had introduced, but instead redefined Socialism just as she had redefined Conservatism. As the result of her prime ministership, the whole of British politics had been shunted decisively from corporatism to individualism.

BENAZIR BHUTTO: FIRST WOMAN LEADER OF A MUSLIM NATION

Benazir Bhutto was a political leader who led the Pakistan People's Party, and was the first and only woman elected to lead a Muslim state. She served as Prime Minister twice, from 1988 to 1990, and again from 1993 to 1996, on both occasions being dismissed on charges of corruption. She proclaimed a 'people's revolution', but was assassinated in 2007 before she could start to bring it about. The matter of her probity, and even of her sincerity, remains still very much an open question.

Benazir Bhutto was born in Karachi in June 1953, daughter to Zulfikar Ali Bhutto, former Prime Minister of Pakistan, and his wife the Begum Nusrat Ispahani, another woman politician and a Pakistani of Kurdish descent. She went to two convent schools, passed her O-levels at the age of fifteen, then went on to Karachi Grammar School, where she completed her A-levels. She went on to university at Harvard University in the United States, where she took a degree *cum laude* in comparative government. After this she went on to Oxford, where she took a degree after a course in Philosophy, Politics and Economics at Lady Margaret Hall, after which she took a further course in International Law and Diplomacy at St Catherine's College. In 1976 she was also President of the Oxford Union, the university's prestigious debating society. In 1987 she married Asif Ali Zardari in Karachi, later giving him three children, two daughters, Bakhtawar and Asifa and a son Bilalwal.

From the beginning, her experience of Pakistani politics was a very troubled one. She returned to Pakistan from abroad in 1977 shortly after the military coup led by General

Mohammed Zia ul-Haq against her father, Prime Minister Zulfikar Ali Bhutto, with promises to hold a general election within three months. No election took place. Bhutto was accused of the murder of dissident politician Ahmed Raza Kasuri, and in spite of clemency appeals from all over the world was hanged in April 1979. Benazir and her mother were held in detention either under house arrest or in a variety of prisons until January 1984, when she was allowed to go into exile abroad. In the meantime, she had been clandestinely organising a new coalition, the Movement for the Restoration of Democracy (MRD) out of her own party, the Pakistan People's Party and a number of other opposition groupings, with which to oust Zia's regime. In exile, she explained her case in faultless English and with an appealing, girlish manner. Martial law was lifted in Pakistan at the end of 1985, and she returned home the following April. She was elected Prime Minister after the death of President Zia in mysterious circumstances.[1] After the first open election in a decade in November 1988, her party, the PPP, won the largest bloc of seats in the National Assembly, and she was sworn in as prime minister of a coalition government in December, becoming at the age of thirty-five the youngest person – and the first woman – to head a Muslim state in modern times. In 1989 she was awarded the Prize for Freedom by the Liberal International. In her first term, she achieved an uneasy compromise with the junta representing the Pakistani Army, improved relations with India, and brought Pakistan back into the Commonwealth. Her defenders hailed these achievements as initiatives for nationalist reform and modernisation. But in 1990 she was dismissed from office by presidential decree, and was accused of corruption, though these charges never reached the courts. Her replacement was Zia's former protégé Nawaz Sharif, who came to power after elections in October 1990.

In new elections in October 1993, Benazir Bhutto's PPP was victorious, and once again she became prime minister and set about redeeming her election pledges. She had promised to improve the lives of women by repealing controversial laws (the so-called Hudood and Zina ordinances) discriminating against women. But in fact little was achieved.[2] She even came out forcefully in opposition to abortion, accusing the West of seeking to impose its own social standards on developing countries. By 1995, disappointment began to spoil her reputation, and in September an army plot was uncovered to remove her from office. By 1996, much of the active criticism focused on her husband, Asif Ali Zardari, whom she had appointed Minister of Investments.[3] One of her main achievements was in recognising the Taliban as the dominant grouping in Afghanistan, and one likely to extend Pakistani influence in that country. She was not alone in regarding the Taliban in its early stages as a force for stability in that country, but together with a number of western countries came later to regret her support. However, at the end of 1996, she was dismissed from office on corruption charges against herself and her husband, disqualified from politics, and sent into exile in Dubai. Defeated in the elections of 1997, she was replaced by Nawaz Sharif and in 1999 by Pervez Musharraf. Her appeal against her conviction was successful in 2001, but she still could not return to Pakistan because of the continuance of suspicions of corruption and she remained in exile until October 2007, when she returned to take part in the election campaigns for the 2008 elections.

By this time, the situation in Pakistan was extremely troubled. Much of the opposition came from President Pervez Musharraf, who had amended the constitution in 2002 to prevent any prime minister (i.e. Benazir Bhutto) from holding office more than twice, and now declared a state of emergency in the country in the light of numerous terrorist attacks on politicians and on civilian crowds by unnamed 'terrorists', producing scores of fatalities by bombs and gunfire. For her part, she retaliated by supporting the Supreme Court's recent ruling that Musharraf could not legally be installed as President following the elections of October 2007 until he retired from his appointment as general in the Pakistani Army. She took care not to blame Musharraf for the civilian disturbances, but the four individuals she named were all close associates of his. Under considerable pressure, Musharraf eventually relaxed his state of emergency, but violence still continued and hundreds more died.[4] Eventually she herself was killed after an election rally in a terrorist attack using revolvers and bombs in Rawalpindi in late December 2007.[5]

The international reaction to the assassination was one of strong condemnation. The UN Security Council unanimously denounced it, the European Commission President and the Arab League secretary likewise; the US President and the UK Prime Minister condemned it; even from the Vatican came the statement that 'the Holy Father expresses sentiments of deep sympathy to the members of her family and the entire Pakistani nation'. The Pakistani government even asked Scotland Yard detectives to investigate the assassination, in the event fruitlessly; though at the same time they refused to assent to any post-mortem examination of Mrs Bhutto's body. In the end, the world was left with the feeling of regret, mixed with some bewilderment at the intransigence of the Pakistani authorities.

Even today, a final verdict on Mrs Bhutto's career has not been agreed. She still commands respect for her clarity of judgement and her political wisdom, and admiration for her charm and determination; but the accusations of political manipulation and corruption have not been entirely dispelled. She has been accused, perhaps somewhat unfairly, of misjudgement over her attitudes to the Taliban; she has been accused of divulging nuclear secrets to the North Korean administration; she has been said to have been at least ambivalent if not precisely dishonest in her professions to be a champion of women's rights, and of her country's reform and modernisation; and, looming over all, accusations of corruption continue to be made about her and especially about her husband, who still figures largely in Pakistani politics. Her final book, *Reconciliation: Islam, Democracy and the West* (2008), echoes the high ideals and disinterested motives she always proclaimed for herself, but the actual progress she made towards such a final reconciliation remains very small, and often much bemired in the sordid day-to-day details of her country's administration.

AUNG SAN SUU KYI:
THE LOST POLITICAL LEADER OF BURMA

Burma, a country that achieved independence in 1948, proved itself thereafter to be prone to threats from popular-supported communists and local rebels such as the Karen tribesmen. At first General Aung San was its leader. He was a powerful figure who founded the modern Burmese Army and used it to oust the British by collaborating with the invading Japanese in 1942; later he became the architect of his country's independence from British colonial control in 1947. He was assassinated in 1947 and was succeeded as head of the Burmese government by U Nu, who in 1958 felt obliged to call on the help of the military to keep order in the country, allowing them to install a military dictatorship there. Aung San Suu Kyi was the daughter of this Aung San. She is often referred to as Mrs Suu Kyi, or Dr Suu Kyi (the second part of the name taken from her mother's name and the first part from her grandmother's – she has no 'surname' in the European sense), and she was born during these troubled times in June 1945.

Suu Kyi was barely two years old when her father was murdered by his political opponents in 1947. She grew up with her mother and two brothers, one of whom was drowned in an ornamental lake at home in Rangoon while he was still only a boy, the other later emigrating to America and becoming a US citizen. After her brother's death, the family moved to a house close to Inya Lake, where she met people of diverse backgrounds, religious views and political opinions. Though educated chiefly at Roman Catholic schools, Suu Kyi remained a Theravada Buddhist. Her mother was a leading Burmese political figure who served as Ambassador to India and Nepal during Suu Kyi's teenage years. She took a degree at New Delhi University in 1964, and went on to take a further degree at Oxford in 1969. With a marked talent for languages, Suu Kyi lived in New York for about three years, working for the United Nations on budgetary affairs. In 1972 she met and married Dr Michael Aris, a scholar on Tibetan culture living abroad in Bhutan. In 1973 she gave birth to a son, Alexander, and in 1977 to another, Kim. She took her PhD in 1985 in the School of Oriental and African Studies at London University, where she became an Honorary Fellow in 1990, and went on for the next two years to embark on a course of advanced study at Shimla in India. Returning to Burma at the end of the 1980s chiefly to take care of her ailing mother, she effectively left behind her husband, who fell ill, and, though he appealed to the junta to allow him to visit his family in Burma, died of prostate cancer in 1999. For her part, though she was asked to go to help care for him, she was not able to go to his side, fearing that if she left to see him she would be refused re-entry, since she mistrusted the junta's assurance that she could return to Burma when she wished.

By this time Suu Kyi was a major force in Burmese politics. Entering politics in 1988, she became General Secretary of the National League for Democracy (NLD) and took part in the general election called in 1990. Her opponents resisted her plans, and the junta strengthened their powers with the introduction of the State Law and Order Restoration Council (SLORC) partly as a means of getting her out of the way. But the election results were decisive: the NLD succeeded in gaining over 80 per cent of the votes cast, and won 394 out of the 492 seats in the Burmese parliament. However, SLORC nullified the election results, and, instead of calling Suu Kyi to office, placed her under arrest at her home, denying her access to her party supporters, to foreign visitors and even to her absent husband, and allowing only limited visits by her doctor to supervise her indifferent health.[1] For more than fourteen of the following twenty years, she was shut away, cut off from the world, and even in the brief periods when she was restored to liberty it was made clear that if she left the country for any reason she would not be allowed to return. On one of the occasions she was released, in 2002, proclaiming a 'new dawn for the country', she was attacked in the northern village of Depayin by government-supported protesters, compelled to flee for her life, and was later re-arrested and imprisoned for three months at Insein Prison in Rangoon. Sentenced to house arrest on three or four different occasions after 1990, she has been detained for longer than even Burmese law allows.[2] All efforts to secure her release have so far failed.

From the beginning, international opinion rallied almost universally to her cause. The United States and the United Nations repeatedly tried to intervene on her behalf, and other countries, either separately, like South Africa or Japan, or jointly, like the Association of South-East Asian Nations (ASEAN, of which Burma was a member), sought to bring pressure on the Burmese government to treat her more leniently. Suu Kyi was awarded the Sakharov Prize for Freedom of Thought in 1990, and went on to win the Nobel Peace Prize in 1991, which cited her 'non-violent struggle for democracy, human rights and ethnic conciliation' in its award.[3] As well as neighbouring countries acting independently, as Indonesia, Thailand and the Philippines did on a number of occasions, the UN attempted to broker dialogue between its representatives and the Burmese junta.[4] Razali Ismael, UN special envoy, tried to establish dialogue but resigned when he was repeatedly denied entry to Burma at the end of the 1990s; Ibrahim Gambari, under-secretary of the UN Department of Political Affairs, met both with Burmese officials and with Suu Kyi herself in 2006 but with little result; the UN Working Group for Arbitrary Detention requested her release in 2007, a request that was ignored; Gambari's second visit to Burma in 2007 produced no tangible results; UN Secretary-General Ban Ki-Moon was rebuffed in 2009 when he renewed UN efforts to help Suu Kyi.

Visiting and exiled politicians from Burma met twice, in 1995 and again in 2002, at Bommersvik in Sweden to press for reforms in their home country. They demanded in the first instance the release of Suu Kyi and other imprisoned leaders, and in the second the reform of the Burmese government along the lines laid down by the 1990 elections (now ignored for twelve years), asserting that 'the military's refusal to honour the election results in no way diminishes the validity of these results'. But once again their protests were ignored.

Meantime, her cause was repeatedly taken up by the USA. Following the so-called 'trespass incident'[5] of 2009, US Senator James Webb visited Burma and pleaded for Suu Kyi's release, junta leader Than Shwe eventually agreeing to return her to house arrest. She had already been decorated with the Congressional Medal of Honor by President G. W. Bush in 2008. In 2009, the new President, Barack Obama, taking up the cudgels on her behalf, now pleaded with the Burmese leadership for the release of all political prisoners, including Aung San Suu Kyi, and for the removal of the 1975 Security Law under which she had been detained for so long. The junta replied that though the 1974 Constitution had been revoked the 1975 Security Law passed under it still remained in operation and could not be revoked. In effect this meant Suu Kyi would not be able to play any part in the elections promised for 2010 – the first elections for twenty years. President Obama could get no further than extracting from the junta the possibility of her release in time for her to help to organise the NLD in this election, but the junta, in spite of continuing international protests, refused to be drawn on the question of whether she herself would be allowed to run as candidate. Aung San Suu Kyi thus remains excluded from the political process in Burma, and the prospects for the democratisation of the country seem to be as distant as ever.

SHIRLEY WILLIAMS:
WAS SHE AS RADICAL AS SHE CLAIMED?

Shirley Williams was one of the leading British political figures of the later twentieth century, playing a major role in a number of the key developments of the British political left from 1960 onwards. Originally a Labour MP and a minister for Harold Wilson, she was one of the 'Gang of Four' who broke away to form the Social Democratic Party (SDP) in 1981, later to be merged with the old Liberals to make the Liberal Democratic Party in 1988. Elevated to the peerage in 1993 as Baroness Williams of Crosby, she subsequently served as Leader of the Liberal Democrats in the House of Lords from 2001 to 2004. She also received a number of distinguished academic appointments throughout her career both in the United States and in Britain. Though in her autobiography Climbing the Bookshelves *(2009) she modestly confesses to having little in the way of leadership qualities, she nevertheless has never quite been forgiven by the militant left for pulling the rug from under them after the fall of the Callaghan administration in 1979.*

Born Shirley Vivian Teresa Brittain Catlin in 1930, she was the daughter of the political scientist and philosopher Sir George Catlin and the radical pacifist Vera Brittain, said by her daughter to be 'conscientious but rather remote', author of the poignant *Testament of Youth* (1933), which brought her to acclaim as the biographer of the 'lost generation' of the First World War. Shirley had a very privileged childhood, noting, though never quite understanding, why she had plenty of toys and clothes, while others less fortunate went to school on alternate days because they had only one pair of shoes between them. She attended Talbot Heath School in Bournemouth, and then, during the Second World War, was evacuated to the USA with a number of other fortunate children whose parents could afford to send them. In the New World, she was chiefly in the Middle West in Minnesota, where she saw American attitudes change from truculent isolationism to commitment to the war after Pearl Harbor. In her youthful teenage mind she was able to contrast the more informal and relaxed methods of US education with the tightly-buttoned attitude she came back to in England in 1945. On her return to Britain she went to St Paul's Girls' School in Hammersmith, which she preferred to a boarding school, and from there to Somerville College, Oxford, where she took an open scholarship. She graduated in 1951 in Philosophy, Politics and Economics (with some freely acknowledged help from her father in philosophy, a subject which she admits to being rather shaky in), and subsequently converting her BA into an MA. She also was a keen member of the University's dramatic society OUDS[1], and became the first woman to chair the University's Labour Club. Later she was a Fulbright Scholar and studied economics at Columbia University in New York – this was at the height of the tide of McCarthyism, when popular feeling against the spread of communism was flooding the United States. When she returned to Britain she began her career as a journalist in 1952, working briefly for the *Daily Mirror*.

She threw in her lot with the political left, and took her first steps towards a career in politics. She moved in circles in which personal acquaintance with the political figures of the day, such as Hugh Gaitskell and members from the other side like Sir Edward Boyle and William Clark (Anthony Eden's Press Secretary at the time of the Suez crisis), was very much taken for granted.[2] Her travels in Africa prepared her for the world stage when she got to know Kwame Nkrumah, the brilliantly successful leader of the newly independent Ghana. She had unsuccessfully contested a by-election in Harwich in 1954, and afterwards was defeated again in the general election of 1959 when she failed to be elected for Southampton Test. But she did in 1959 witness the valiant, though unsuccessful, efforts of Hugh Gaitskell to modernise the Labour party by jettisoning Clause Four[3] at the Labour Party Conference of that year. In the following year she became General Secretary of the Fabian Society, a gradualist socialist movement with deeper roots in the Labour movement than more modern Marxist ideas.

Shirley Williams, as she now was after her marriage in 1955 to Bernard Williams, Fellow in Philosophy at New College, Oxford, finally succeeded in entering Parliament after being elected Labour MP for Hitchin in Hertfordshire in the 1964 general election. The first things that struck her about Parliament was its 'clubbishness', its unsocial hours and its complete lack of provision for the admittedly small number of female MPs at that time. She met with little sympathy in her protests, and eventually learned to live with its manifest disadvantages. She rose swiftly to junior ministerial rank: between 1971 and 1973 she served as Shadow Home Secretary; from 1974 to 1976 she took the newly created office of Secretary of State for Prices and Consumer Protection under the Wilson government, and when he was succeeded in 1976 by James Callaghan took two cabinet positions simultaneously, as Secretary of State for Education and Paymaster General. She came to have considerable admiration for Callaghan, but saw him in great difficulties struggling with the value of the newly devalued pound and trying to maintain a prices-and-incomes policy, at first voluntary and then statutory, in the face of sustained pressures from the labour left and the militant trade unions pressing for big pay increases. There followed the disastrous 'winter of discontent' in 1978/79, followed by the defeat of Labour at the 1979 election.

In that election, she lost her seat – the only Cabinet minister to do so – to Bowen Wells, the Conservative candidate for the Hertford and Stevenage constituency, newly created under boundary changes that had taken place in 1974, changes that were partly responsible for her defeat.[4] This defeat she found very wounding. It was by a mere 1,295 votes, and even her rivals Mervyn Rees and Norman St John-Stevas paid tribute to her achievements in office. She was especially exercised by the recent role of the trade unions and the militant left of the labour movement since the 1960s and 1970s. She felt that power had been allowed to slip from the hands of the more responsible elements into the hands of extremists, many of whom were intent on pursuing their own pay claims irrespective of the national interest; and that the result of this, as long as it continued, was bound to be a general turning away from the historic Labour Party at the polls. She believed that Callaghan had been overwhelmed by their strident and destructive self-interest, and that until the militant left had been brought into line the party would never come back to power. This extremism was not the result of any organised strategy, but the anarchic consequence of an unrepresentative handful of populist shop stewards of whom not only the rank-and-file of the party but even the official union leadership lived in dread. Supported by an extremist group known as the Revolutionary Socialist Party and another called the Militant Tendency, they practised the technique known to the old leadership as 'entryism' i.e. joining the party as a means of subverting it for their own purposes. She felt that the time had come to deal with this destructive group; to recover the initiative in the interests of continuing reform.

She was one of a small group of distinguished Labourites, including Bill Rodgers, Roy Jenkins and David Owen, known as the 'Gang of Four', who splintered away from the Labour Party in 1981 to form what they called the Social Democratic Party (SDP). Within weeks they were joined by thirteen other Labour MPs (and even one Conservative, Christopher Brocklebank-Fowler). The new party decided to challenge the old Labour Party as soon as possible, and in November 1981 Shirley Williams overturned a Tory majority of nearly 20,000 in the Crosby (Liverpool) constituency by winning back her place[5] in Parliament with a majority of over 5,000 votes. Her victory was closely followed by that of Roy Jenkins at Glasgow Hillhead in March 1982. But the SDP never fulfilled its early promise, even though the unreformed Labour Party still continued its suicidal tactics.[6] In the general election of 1983, in spite of her becoming President of the SDP, she was defeated at the polls and lost her seat at Crosby; in 1987 she was again defeated in the general election, this time at Cambridge. By now she had come round to supporting a merger with the Liberal Party, and this merger took place in 1988. In her private life, her marriage to Sir Bernard Williams was dissolved in 1974, and in 1987 she married again, this time to Harvard professor and presidential historian Richard Neustadt, who died in 2003.

After the crumbling of her parliamentary career, Shirley Williams moved into other important areas of public life. In 1988 she went to live in the United States where she became a full professor at Harvard's Kennedy School of Government, a post she occupied until 2001, when she became Public Service Professor Emerita of Electoral Politics. She remained active in public service not only in the USA and Britain, but also internationally. She was instrumental in drafting constitutions in Russia, the Ukraine, and in South Africa. She was also a board member and an active director of Harvard's Institute of Politics (IOP), and a member of the EU's *Comité des Sages*. In 1993 she was elevated to the House of Lords as Baroness Williams of Crosby, and subsequently served as Leader of the Liberal Democrats in the House of Lords from 2001 to 2004. She worked also for a number of other public bodies in both the UK and the USA, including the Ditchley Foundation, the Institute of Public Policy Research, the Council on Foreign Relations, the Century Foundation, and the US think tank Nuclear Threat Initiative (NTI). A lifelong supporter of comprehensive education, she remains deeply committed to education, and has served as the Chair of Judges of UK teaching awards.

It is difficult to make a judgement on her achievements in a career so varied and multifarious. She wrote half a dozen books in politics, chiefly focusing on her aspirations for people and relating to the Labour Party, the Liberals and the SDP, and also worked from time to time in journalism, chiefly for the *Daily Mirror* and repairing a gap she perceived in her own outlook by doing a stint with the *Financial Times*. She was an active participant in the public media, appearing in a number of TV question-time programmes – it is said she appeared on the BBC *Question Time* programme more often than any other politician. She has from time to time bewailed her lack of leadership ability, but as far as consistency, application to detail, and political 'door-stepping' at election times go, she still leaves little to be desired. Even her opponents have admitted she has always seen things clearly, consistently, and moderately, and has never been diverted from her path by considerations of career or personal profit. There are few who seek to condemn her for dogmatism, even if they do not accept her views. For every one who condemns her political moderation and the foundation of class privilege in which her attitudes are rooted, there are several more who praise her for exactly those same qualities. Without her, the story of political development in the Labour Party, the SDP, the Liberal Democrats, and even 'New' Labour, would not have been the same.

PART 11

EARLIER FAMOUS QUEENS AND RULERS

THE QUEEN OF SHEBA:
CLASSICAL ICON OF GRACE AND BEAUTY

The tradition of the Queen of Sheba pervades more than five thousand years of history. She is remembered, and her story related, by Jewish, Christian, Muslim, Arab and Persian chroniclers. The writers of the Old Testament used her to embellish the reputation of King Solomon, whose name even today is equated with wisdom and learning. To the Muslims she was an Arabian princess, beautiful and deeply revered. Arab traders and storytellers enshrined her memory in their own stories, blending her exoticism with the legends of their own traffic in rare and precious spices. Even the Ethiopians claimed her as the ancestress of their own historic ruling dynasty.

But in historical fact, no one knows where Sheba actually was; nor is there any contemporary record, even among the more settled and peaceful areas of the north, of any early kingdom ruled by a woman. All the evidence in such early writings is imprecise; different names are used to identify her, and most writers are content to say that she came from some unspecified place in 'the South'.

She figures in the First Book of Kings, where her appearance is used by the Old Testament chroniclers to enhance the reputation of the powerful King Solomon. The same story is repeated in the Second Book of Chronicles. The Queen, having heard of Solomon's great wisdom,[1] travels to Jerusalem 'with a very great train' of camels bearing precious stones, costly spices and 'very much gold'; when she arrives, she tells him she has come 'to prove him with hard questions', presumably some sort of cryptic riddles, to test his wit and his learning. Evidently Solomon performed very well in his interrogation, for she says to him: 'It was a true report that I heard in mine own land of thy acts and of thy wisdom ... The half was not told me: thy wisdom and prosperity exceedeth the fame which I heard. Happy are thy men and thy servants which stand continually before thee and hear thy wisdom.' Before she departs, she gives the King 'an hundred and twenty talents of gold, spices of very great store, and precious stones; never again was such an abundance of spices as these given to King Solomon.' The scriptural account tells us how the King used these gifts to beautify his temple and his palace with pillars, ornaments and with musical instruments.

More cryptically, we are told that the King 'gave unto the Queen of Sheba all her desires, whatever she asked' in addition to all his gifts of royal bounty. Some have interpreted these desires as being of a sexual nature. Some even say that the Queen had a son by Solomon. Such embellishments are fanciful; indeed the whole story sounds like an elaborate fairytale. Solomon, the first builder of the temple in Jerusalem, dedicated his whole reign to the consolidation of the power bestowed on him by his father David; and it is true that he extended the trade links he had with his neighbours until he 'outdid all the kings of the earth in wealth and wisdom, and all the world courted him'. But it is doubtful whether Israel at this time was anything more than a small kingdom with essentially a parochial outlook, or that the powers surrounding it would have paid much attention to it or to its rulers. Solomon, it is true, had trading links with neighbouring countries in the Near East, and even with Arabia, far to the south, but it is also doubtful whether there was much of a spice trade between Israel and its neighbours at this time: four or five hundred years would elapse before such a trade was even begun. Nevertheless the story made the Israelites think themselves of some importance in the tenth century BC.

The Jewish historian Josephus (AD 37 – *c*.100) accepts the story and says that the Queen of Sheba was 'the marvellous queen of Egypt and Ethiopia'; the early Christians, too, like Matthew and Luke, incorporate the story into their Gospels, but are less precise about her origins, telling us only that 'she came from the ends of the earth'.

In Arabia, too, the story of the Queen of Sheba makes its appearance, and also, hundreds of years later, in the Holy Koran. In the Koran, the story goes that King Solomon was told of the Queen by a small bird, the hoopoe, and writes a letter to her, given to the hoopoe for delivery, and commanding her to come to visit him. Her journey is said to have lasted seven years. When she arrives, she goes to the royal palace, but, mistaking Solomon's glass floor for a pool of water, lifts her skirts to step in, and lets the King see her legs. These legs are said to have been hairy, evoking his criticism that 'hairy legs are fine for a man, but disgusting for a woman'. All the same, the visit was a success, and finally the Queen is said to have 'praised and worshipped the One God'.

The Queen appears also in Ethiopian tradition, though there is a discrepancy of dates here, where she is said to have been the mother of that country's first Emperor, Menelik I (204–179 BC), the direct antecedent of that country's last Emperor, Haile Selassie (1930–74), who vainly sought Saudi help by claiming kinship with the ruling Saudi Arabian dynasty on the strength of the story.

The Queen is dubbed with a variety of different names. The Arabs called her Bilquis, or Belkis; Josephus calls her Nikaulis; the Ethiopians give her the name of Makeda. In the Koran, as in the Bible, she is given no name at all. The place of her provenance is equally hazy. There is general agreement that her home lay towards the south, although exactly where nobody knows. Arabia is frequently suggested as her home, though Egypt and, more often, Ethiopia are put forward in the later stories. Perhaps the most likely place is Saba, a former tribal kingdom in modern-day Yemen, just inland from the southern tip of the Arabian Peninsula. Such a place, however, is extremely unlikely to have been ruled by a woman. Furthermore, the journey from here to Jerusalem would have been long and extremely difficult, even today, involving a trek across several hundred miles of scorching, trackless desert inhabited by fierce and warring Bedouin tribes, living in tents and inspired by fierce personal loyalties unintelligible to outsiders. Such tribes are quite unlike the civilisation that is supposed to have produced the Queen of Sheba, and though there are some architectural remains of ancient civilisations to be found in the Arabian desert, none is near here, nor goes as far back as the tenth century BC.

LIVIA:
WOMAN BEHIND THE THRONE

The first Roman emperor Augustus wielded enormous power. He had eliminated political opposition, he had reduced the Roman Senate to a bunch of fawning sycophants, and he had extended and consolidated Rome's imperial frontiers. By his side for fifty-two years was his wife Livia. She was believed by many contemporaries and subsequent historians to have been the power behind the throne, who gave Augustus determination when he dithered, and who dissuaded him from his commitment to restore the republic. Her ambition was said to have known no bounds and she engineered her son Tiberius' accession to the imperial throne, not hesitating to stoop to murder in doing so. She is said finally to have hastened Augustus out of this world by using poisoned figs. Was she really the woman of whom Robert Graves paints such an appalling picture in his I, Claudius?

Livia was born into a noble Roman family in 59 or 58 BC. Her father was Marcus Livius Drusus Claudianus and his support for Julius Caesar's assassins put his family in jeopardy, especially when, at the age of fifteen, Livia was married to Tiberius Claudius Nero. He was a political opponent of the young Octavian, later (the title of Augustus not granted by the Senate until 27 BC) to be known as Augustus. Livia's son Tiberius was born in Rome in 42 BC, but increasing political tension caused the family to flee from Rome in 40 BC. They returned in 38 BC and Livia's father, having decided that Augustus really did intend to restore the liberties of Rome and to step down from office when the situation was stable enough, now offered Augustus his support. Even so, he probably had little influence on his daughter's sudden determination to divorce her husband and to marry Augustus. There were a few major obstacles in the way. Livia was five months pregnant, Augustus was married (his second marriage) with a wife close to term, and the divorces would have to be approved by the Senate. Livia's motives in this matter are disputed. Certainly, Augustus was the rising political star of Rome. Marriage to the head of state would give her much greater importance than continued marriage to a mere nobleman, and there were the future prospects of Tiberius and (the unborn) Drusus to consider. The timing of the divorces was very unfortunate and it might have been better for both of them to have delayed. But on Augustus' part at least, the marriage was one of passion, Livia was in her youth considered to be a very beautiful woman, and Augustus was a desirable young man, even though physically a little delicate. The events leading to their marriage caused much scandal-mongering in Rome, not fully allayed by the suggestion that the union had been blessed by the Gods.

It certainly was not blessed with children. Both Livia and Augustus had had children by previous marriages, and Augustus had had several children by other women. The suggestion that the marriage was not consummated can hardly be true if it was a marriage of passion, and Livia was rumoured to have had at least one miscarriage or stillbirth since her marriage to Augustus. But the absence of heirs was to give Augustus a major headache throughout his long period in power. Through his daughter Julia he had a number of grandchildren, and their successive demises gave rise not only to the suspicion that their deaths were unnatural, but also to the accusation that Livia, in order to advance Tiberius' claim to the succession, had had a hand in each of the deaths. This is certainly the theme of *I, Claudius*.

It was undoubtedly unfortunate that Augustus' efforts to name an heir to his title of *princeps* (which gave him virtually absolute power) were dogged by disaster. At first he favoured his nephew Marcellus, whom he married to his daughter Julia. This certainly caused resentment among some of Augustus' closest circle, including Agrippa, his long-standing friend and military comrade. But Agrippa had no need to be unduly concerned because in 23 BC, at the tender age of nineteen, Marcellus fell sick, and despite the close attention of Livia's and Augustus' doctors, soon died. Agrippa was named as successor by Augustus during a bout of illness similar to that which had carried off Marcellus. Agrippa was married off to Tiberius' widowed daughter Julia, and the marriage was fruitful enough to produce three sons, Gaius, Lucius, and Postumus, all of whom would take precedence over Tiberius as Augustus' direct descendants. Agrippa was of strong physique, Augustus was rather weakly, yet eleven years after Marcellus' death Agrippa died suddenly at home on his estate when he was only fifty. It is difficult to see how Livia could have profited from his death, or even how she could have been involved in it.

But in the meantime, as Augustus' grandsons were still minors, Tiberius was expected to act as Augustus' presumed successor until Agrippa's sons reached manhood. It was not a role that Tiberius relished, especially as he was expected to become Augustus' son-in-law by marrying Julia, whose husbands so far had been so short-lived. Tiberius soon tired of his new responsibilities and went off in a sulk to live on the island of Rhodes, leaving Livia to take care of his interests in Rome. She decided to leave him there as long as possible so that he would be so bored in Rhodes that he would be desperate to return. In AD 2 Lucius died in mysterious circumstances in Marseilles on his way to Spain, and Gaius never recovered fully from a wound he received in Armenia. Despite the best treatments sent especially from Rome, and which no doubt had Livia's personal attention, he died in Lycia on his journey home in AD 4. Augustus now had little choice but to adopt Tiberius and Postumus (aged fifteen) as joint heirs. But within three years Postumus had been disgraced and banished for depravity, yet he was to claim that he was innocent and that the evidence against him had been fabricated.

So in the last few years of Augustus' life, Livia's son Tiberius was Augustus' sole heir, and as Augustus was growing steadily frailer Livia was undertaking more and more of his administrative duties. In AD 14 Augustus fell ill. He had long suffered from stomach disorders, but this time the attack was much worse. He restricted his diet to fresh figs and ordinary bread, but to no avail, and within a few days he was dead. He had, of course, reached the ripe old age of seventy-eight – not bad for a man of weak physique in Roman times. Nevertheless, there was soon a rumour that he had been poisoned, and that Livia had been responsible for it in order to prevent Augustus from recalling Postumus from exile. There was plenty of rumour but little substance, and little likelihood that a rehabilitated Postumus would have been in a position to pose an effective challenge to Tiberius. Nor was there any evidence that Livia had had a hand in any of the other mysterious deaths which had eased Tiberius' path to power.

In fact, Livia had been a dutiful and supportive wife. It is most likely that she influenced her husband's decisions, and she was most instrumental on several occasions in persuading him not to restore the Republic because the time was not yet ripe for it. She played a major role in promoting charities, receiving foreign embassies and in instigating the construction of major public buildings. Both she and Augustus prided themselves on promoting traditional Roman values. Augustus always gave the impression that Livia was at home attending to domestic duties and that she spun and wove the cloth from which his garments were made. She certainly practised frugal economy in her household, and preferred food that was plain and wholesome to that which was rich, luxurious and expensive. Yet she had a fondness for costly jewellery and precious stones, which she was careful not to display on public occasions.

After Augustus died, Livia pushed for his deification and became a priestess of his new cult. As the widow of a god and mother of the new Emperor Tiberius, she occupied a unique status in Roman society. There were even plans to give her a *lictor* to precede her at public ceremonies, but it is uncertain whether the plans were fulfilled. She did allow statues of her to be portrayed in the guise of various goddesses, particularly Ceres, the goddess of fruitfulness and harvest. When she died in AD 29 at the ripe old age of eighty-seven, the Senate hastened to pay her the ultimate honour – a triumphal arch – previously only awarded to successful generals. Tiberius accepted this great compliment to his mother, said he would pay for it himself, and then conveniently failed to do so. It was her grandson the Emperor Claudius who in AD 42 accorded her the highest honour by having her deified as 'diva Augusta', the goddess Augusta. Livia would certainly have approved of that.

Of the two Livias, the unscrupulous murderess and the dutiful and devoted wife, the evidence inclines towards the latter. There is no specific evidence that she was involved in the murder of anyone. That she was ambitious, interfered in affairs of state, and craved public adulation seems undeniable, but the unproved accusations against her are most likely nothing more than the imaginative creations of those who opposed the Empire and wanted to restore the Republic. And these make the more interesting reading.

BOUDICA:
THE WARRIOR QUEEN

Not so long ago every school child had heard of Boadicea. Wronged by the Romans she gathered together her armed warriors. They covered their faces in woad, and armed the wheels of their chariots with scythes. They sacked the Roman settlements of Colchester, St Albans and London and burnt them to the ground. Finally, against the overwhelming odds of the Roman legions led by Suetonius, Boadicea charged into the thick of the battle, her red hair flying in the wind, and inspiring her men with her leadership. But it was to no avail, and rather than suffer the humiliation of a Roman captive, she took her own life. How accurate is all this?

In the first place her name was not Boadicea. This seems to have arisen out of an inaccurate transcription of the Roman historian Tacitus' Boudicca. There are only two letters that have been wrongly copied, u to a, and c to e, and that would have been easy to do. But it is likely that even Tacitus' spelling is incorrect. Boudica is from the Celtic word for 'victory', and it is the most probable spelling of the lady's name, bearing in mind that the Celts left no written records at that time from which to verify it.

Boudica was the widow of Prasutagus, chief of the Iceni whose main territory lay in Suffolk and Cambridgeshire. Tacitus, writing fifty years later, but having first-hand information from his father-in-law Agricola who was present during the rebellion, calls Prasutagus 'King'. Whether the Celtic chieftains of Britain were kings in any modern sense is uncertain, but Prasutagus had certainly been wealthy enough, and Catus Decianus, the Roman in charge of the local finances, decided to ignore Prasutagus' will, leaving only half his wealth to the Emperor, and to confiscate the deceased ruler's entire estate. Whether entitled to succeed her husband or not, Boudica was bound to protest against the disinheriting of herself and her two daughters. The Romans responded by having her flogged, and her daughters raped in her presence. The flogging may well have been symbolic to represent Rome's domination and the subservience of the Iceni. The raping of the young women was a traditional way in which the Romans asserted their superiority over a conquered people; they had practised it ever since the legendary rape of the Sabines some five centuries earlier. Conquest and humiliation were thus the twin driving forces of the Iceni rebellion, and the absence of Suetonius in his efforts to destroy the Druid stronghold in Anglesey made the moment opportune. General dissatisfaction with Roman rule led neighbouring tribes to throw in their lot with the Iceni. Boudica's part in originating and fomenting the uprising is not clear, but it seems she was given overall command of the uprising, whether substantive or merely titular.

So it is not certain whether Boudica was personally involved in any of the British atrocities which ensued. At Camulodunum (Colchester) sufficient alarm had been caused by British ravaging of the surrounding countryside for the city to send for help from London. A mere 200 troops were sent, all of whom perished in the subsequent slaughter. Catus, whose excesses had prompted the rebellion, had time to flee into Gaul, but Colchester was left to its fate. The British poured into the city. The inhabitants were massacred, irrespective of age or sex, women were subjected to rape before being hacked to pieces, and the buildings burnt in a great conflagration. The attackers were not content to massacre the living; they desecrated the Roman cemetery and they destroyed statues and monuments – anything symbolic of Roman rule.

Suetonius, summoned in haste, arrived in Londinium (London) with his cavalry, only to find that the city, not yet Britain's capital, had no defensive walls and was incapable of effective defence. Suetonius sent for the Second Legion based at Gloucester, but its acting commander refused to take risks and failed to move. To wait for the arrival of his own infantry would have been suicidal with the British closing in, flushed with their triumph at Colchester. Unmoved by the tears of the inhabitants, he galloped out with as many of London's citizens as could keep up with him. The enraged fury of the British then fell upon London. As with Colchester it was burnt to the ground. Its attackers seemed to have indulged in an orgy of beheadings. Destruction and fire encompassed its buildings and death its inhabitants. And then the British moved on to Verulamium (St Albans). But its Romano-British inhabitants had been forewarned. They fled. Their city was totally consumed by fire, but here casualties were light compared to Colchester and London. Yet, in their haste to destroy all traces of Roman civilisation in their destruction of the three cities, it did not seem to have occurred to Boudica and her commanders that a better strategy would have been to have left the cities alone, and to have destroyed Suetonius while he was at his most vulnerable. Without infantry, Suetonius could have been overwhelmed, but the British seemed so confident in their huge numbers that they expected to destroy whatever Roman legions were thrown at them.

This British overconfidence was largely responsible for the disaster that followed. The two main accounts of what ensued are those of Tacitus, and Cassius Dio writing a hundred years later. Both are obviously hostile, and although Tacitus had information from his father-in-law, neither account is objective nor necessarily accurate. Their failure, however, to mention swords on the chariot wheels is borne out by archaeological evidence, and the universal application of woad turns out to be a few tattoos. The description of Boudica sounds more like a stylised portrait of a warrior chief than an actual portrait of Boudica, although she may well have had wild red hair and sturdy limbs.

The British preoccupation with pillaging and destroying the cities gave Suetonius the breathing space to gather his infantry and with 10,000 men he was prepared to give battle. His troops were professionals, highly trained and well-equipped. Their seven-foot javelins, and their shields, which could be locked together to make an impenetrable wall, gave them a great advantage in defence, and their two-foot swords were invaluable in attack. Moreover, the Roman infantry wore light body armour as far as the waist, whereas the British wore no protection. The British swords were longer than the Roman ones, but since many of the British were hurriedly assembled farmers, they were not trained in their use. The British had superior numbers (although perhaps somewhat fewer than the Roman sources suggest); yet their forces were inflated by large numbers of women and children who assembled in wagons to watch the battle, and the men lacked the training and discipline of the Romans. Their main strategy was the wild charge augmented by much shouting and yelling. Their courage was uplifted by a stirring appeal to patriotism by Boudica before the battle commenced, and there is no reason to doubt that this took place; it was customary for Roman generals to inspire their troops in this way, and the British followed their example.

Suetonius' main concern was to prevent his troops being encircled, so he chose a position in front of dense woods which gave him protection from the rear. The British assembled their wagons on a ridge – for a better view – and effectively blocked any line of retreat. The British attack foundered against the Roman shields and Suetonius' counter-attack used infantry in the centre and cavalry on the flanks. The British were cut down by javelins and corralled into an ever-diminishing circle by their own wagons. In the slaughter that followed, men, women, children and horses were put to the sword mercilessly, and Tacitus estimated the British killed at 80,000 compared with a Roman loss of 400. If Boudica actually led her troops into battle she miraculously survived the Roman attack because she, presumably with her daughters, committed suicide by poison later. It seems more likely that her commanders led the fighting and that she watched, and perhaps gave orders, from one of the wagons.

The precise location of this battle is not known. Since Suetonius had been trying to gather reinforcements from the west it seems likely that the battle was away from Iceni territory in the West Midlands, possibly somewhere near Towcester. If so, Boudica would not have had a royal burial on alien soil. Suetonius' policy of vigorous repression would not have allowed any honour being paid to the rebel queen, even after her death. But his policy was ameliorated in the reign of Nero and there is a possibility that Boudica's remains were taken back to Iceni territory some years later and given a grand funeral. But if so, the site of the burial remains unknown.

So the classic depiction of Boadicea is little more than legend repeated. It is not certain what Boudica looked like, whether she was *de facto* or titular head of the Iceni, and whether that carried the title of Queen. Neither legend nor the Roman historians suggest that she was personally responsible for the atrocities in the Romano-British cities. Yet if she was queen regnant she must have not only known of the fate of these cities, but also have been responsible for the policy of razing them rather than destroying Suetonius. There were no wheel-scythes and no woad, and no certainty about the manner of her death or the place of her burial. Yet she is more substantive than King Arthur or Robin Hood, and her stand against tyranny makes her one of the grandest of historical heroines.

THE TWO QUEEN MATILDAS

In the middle of the twelfth century England enjoyed the doubtful luxury of two Queen Matildas. One was the daughter of Henry I, her title of Queen arising from her father's effort to secure her succession to the English throne. The other was Matilda the queen consort, wife of Stephen who had usurped the throne of England in 1135 to the exclusion of the other Matilda. As Henry's daughter was the widow of the Holy Roman Emperor and was known in Germany as the Empress Maud it will be easier to distinguish her from Stephen's consort by calling her Maud, despite the fact that as Queen of England she was never known by that name. Historians have painted a vivid contrast between the two. Matilda led a blameless life, was a loyal consort and great female warrior and was universally loved and respected. Maud was praiseworthy in her youth and in old age, but when she was fighting to secure the throne she was tyrannical, overbearing and was universally detested.

Both queens were closely related. Maud was the daughter of Henry I who had married another Matilda, daughter of Malcolm III of Scotland. Maud was born in 1102. Matilda was the daughter of Eustace III, Count of Boulogne, who had married Mary, another daughter of Malcolm III; so they were first cousins. Maud was also cousin to her rival Stephen, both being grandchildren of William the Conqueror. Maud had not expected that her destiny lay in England. In 1114 she had married the Holy Roman Emperor, Henry V, a man twenty years older than Maud, and believed her future to be closely tied to the affairs of Germany. But in 1120 a severe gale and a drunken helmsman decreed otherwise. The *White Ship* began to sink, Prince William went back to rescue the women onboard and was drowned in the attempt. His death deprived Henry I of a male heir, and although at first Henry toyed with the idea of adopting his nephew Stephen as his successor, Maud was able to return to England in 1125 on the death of her husband. She had had no children and there was therefore no reason why she should remain in Germany. On Christmas Day 1125 Henry I extracted from his leading clerics and nobility an oath to recognise and accept Maud as his successor. There was no English precedent for this, and there was always a danger that the oath might be repudiated. Maud's pleasure at the prospect of becoming Queen of England was tempered when Henry insisted on her marriage to Geoffrey of Anjou. From a first husband so much her senior Maud now acquired a teenage husband very much her junior. The marriage had to wait eight years before their first surviving male child was born in 1133 (Henry, later Henry II).

Throughout these early years Maud had been a submissive daughter and wife. As a child she had been in no position to defy her father over her marriage to the Emperor, and she had had no choice but to obey her new husband as all dutiful twelfth-century wives should. He sent away her English servants, and insisted on German as the language of his court. While her brother William lived, she expected nothing more than life as a German princess. After his drowning and the death of her German husband, life's prospects improved, but her father's determination to add Anjou to his French possessions meant that Maud again became a political marriage pawn. She must have found it doubly humiliating – both the arranged marriage and the juvenile husband, but there is no record of her resorting to haughty defiance, either of her father or her new husband. The contrast between the submissive Maud of these years and the arrogant Maud of the 1140s has been much commented on but rarely explained.

Matilda had a happier early life. She certainly married young, and to her cousin Stephen. Her parents thought him eminent enough to be a suitable match for their daughter, and he was only a mere nine years older than she. Since contemporary chroniclers unite in describing him as the handsomest man in Europe it is not surprising that she did not find his nine years' seniority a handicap to a happy marriage. Stephen was fairly unique among contemporary monarchs in having no illegitimate issue after marriage; his one bastard son Gervais of Blois was born several years before. Matilda had three sons and two daughters by him, and it seems that she and Stephen were devoted to each other. Certainly there was no indication in the early years of their marriage of the woman of decisive action and independent judgement that she was later to become.

Both queens could be cited as exemplars of the dutiful and obedient consorts which queens were expected to be at this time. But then in 1135 Henry I died. His nobility had sworn to accept Maud as their ruler, but they had done so under duress and with the greatest reluctance. The English had never had a queen regnant, and they were generally averse to the idea. They were also averse to the prospect of being ruled by Maud's husband Geoffrey, a foreigner whose interests were French rather than English. So when Stephen rushed across the Channel and had himself proclaimed King of England before Maud and her husband could make their move, there was little that Maud could do. Not until 1139 did the deteriorating situation in England enable her to challenge Stephen. Ill-advised, she landed in Sussex where Stephen's greatest strength lay, and only escaped from Arundel to Bristol because Stephen was chivalrously reluctant to take her prisoner. Maud's husband Geoffrey was far more interested in capturing Normandy for himself than England for his wife, so Maud, with the aid of her half-brother Robert, had to do much of the decision-making. She had already shown initiative and courage by escaping from one close encounter by wrapping herself in a shroud and being carried through enemy lines on a bier. When Stephen was defeated and captured at the battle of Lincoln in 1141, she showed that she was decisive by imprisoning Stephen in chains and moving quickly to London for her coronation.

But it never took place. The chroniclers describe her as haughty and imperious. In fact she was concerned not to undo the centralising feudalism of her father, and it was in this that she faced an almost impossible choice. To maintain her father's work she would encounter the bitter opposition of the nobility, which wanted its privileges back, and the citizens of London, who wanted their freedom back. To give in would give way to anarchy. She refused to restore the ancient liberties of Londoners; they refused to grant her a large subsidy. She refused pleas on behalf of Stephen and Stephen's nephews; she cancelled all the grants and privileges that Stephen had made, both lay and clerical. To do otherwise would make her the subservient tool of a reckless nobility, but she could get little support because so few wanted to preserve and consolidate her father's work, and to most the idea of being ruled by a woman was anathema. So it was easier for the chroniclers to blame her for recalcitrance than it was for them to blame the nobility and townsfolk for their obstinacy. They do comment on her Angevin bad temper, something she was to pass on to her son Henry; she is said to have boxed the ears of the King of Scotland in one of her rages.

Meanwhile, Matilda swung into action on behalf of her husband. While she appealed, unsuccessfully, to Maud to mitigate the rigours of her husband's imprisonment, she raised a large army in Kent and supplemented them with Flemish mercenaries. She succeeded in capturing Maud's half-brother Robert and, using him as a bargaining tool, was able to negotiate Stephen's release. Her appeal to Londoners for help was much more successful than Maud's, but then Matilda was queen consort, not queen regnant, and she was acting on behalf of Stephen. So successful was she that she and Stephen were able to trap Maud at Oxford in December 1142 and only Maud's courage in descending from a high window by rope and escaping across the frozen and snow-covered Thames in a white sheet saved her.

The civil war lasted another eleven years but neither side was able to get the upper hand. While Matilda left the fighting largely to her husband, Stephen entrusted her with negotiations with David of Scotland and with the betrothal of their son Eustace to the sister of the King of France. Maud spent several years trying unsuccessfully to win over the English barons to her cause, and even less successfully in imploring her husband Geoffrey for help. On the death of both Geoffrey and her half-brother Robert, Maud quitted England in 1147, effectively transferring her claim to the throne of England to her fourteen-year-old son Henry. It seemed to leave Stephen and Matilda triumphant, but Matilda's death in 1152 devastated Stephen and was a major factor in bringing him to the negotiating table. His eldest son Eustace died a year later. Stephen's surviving son William did not want the English throne, so Stephen secured peace by recognising Henry as his heir in the Treaty of Wallingford in 1153. In losing his wife and eldest son, Stephen, it is said, lost the will both to carry on the fight and the will to live; observers noted how appallingly he had aged. He died in 1154, and was buried alongside Eustace and Matilda in Faversham, an abbey that he and the Queen had recently founded as a thanksgiving for peace.

Maud, however, survived the war, and for the next thirteen years took on the role of Queen mother. Despite her alleged temper, her behaviour was exemplary. She gave her son advice which he frequently asked for, but she did not thrust it on him. She advised strongly against the appointment of Thomas Becket as Archbishop of Canterbury, advice which Henry II chose to ignore. As the quarrel between Becket and Henry developed, Maud was an active, if unsuccessful arbitrator, and she tried to persuade the Pope to restrain Becket while she in turn tried to calm down her hot-headed son. She died three years before Becket's murder, was buried in Rouen, and was remembered at the time not so much for her failure in war and her hot temper, but for her gentleness and her charitable works.

There is much similarity between these two women. In the normal course of events both would have led the lives of twelfth-century consorts, submissive and supportive of their husbands. Events decreed otherwise. Maud had the tougher assignment. She needed to persuade men to accept a woman ruler, and in that she was four centuries too early. Matilda gathered more support, not because she was necessarily a better person than Maud, but simply because she was fighting for her husband, not the throne. Maud resumed the womanly role in 1154, and undoubtedly Matilda would have done so had she lived. From both we get a glimpse of what twelfth-century women might have achieved if released from the conventions of the time.

QUEEN ISABELLA: REGICIDE

Isabella, French wife of Edward II, King of England, has for long enjoyed a bad reputation among historians. She was known as notoriously rapacious and extravagant. She was unfaithful to her husband and took a lover. With her lover, Roger Mortimer, she engineered the overthrow and deposition of her husband. And worst of all, she and Mortimer planned and effected the grisly death of Edward. His screams emanated from Berkeley Castle, Gloucestershire, on the night of 21 September 1327, and it was soon alleged that he had been done to death by having a horn thrust into his rectum and a red hot poker inserted via the horn into the ex-king's lower abdomen. Those who saw the body could see no visible signs of violence, but it was commonly said that the countenance was 'distorted and horrible to look upon'. It was given out that Edward had died during the night of a 'sudden disorder'. That Isabella could have been responsible for so appalling a murder horrified both contemporaries and posterity, and it is not surprising that Thomas Gray's description of Isabella as 'the she-wolf of France' was adopted later by nineteenth-century historians. But have they been fair to Isabella?

Isabella was born probably in 1295, daughter of Philip IV (The Fair) of France and Queen Jeanne of Navarre. Three years later, with Edward I tied down in Scotland and Philip IV sick of war, a marriage alliance was arranged between Isabella and Prince Edward of England, her senior by twelve years. When King Edward started to blow hot and cold on the arrangement, Philip offered to restore Gascony to England immediately and the official betrothal took place in 1303. Edward had acquired Gascony, and Philip envisaged his grandson on the throne of England, a prospect which promised peace rather than war. During the four-year engagement, Prince Edward failed to send his bride-to-be any courtly message or presents. He already preferred a handsome face to a pretty one. But he had promised his father on his deathbed to honour the engagement, and six months after his father died in the summer of 1307, Edward II proceeded to Paris for his wedding. Since Isabella was only twelve years old it is unlikely that the marriage was immediately consummated, or that Isabella, later famed for her beauty, had captivated her new husband. Indeed he seemed indifferent to her, and on his return from France with his new bride he threw himself into the arms of his favourite, Piers Gaveston, hugged and kissed him, and called him brother.

The English nobility might have tolerated Gaveston had not Edward showered him with lands and influence, and by elevating *him* excluded *them* from power. Isabella remarkably was on good terms with Gaveston, partly out of duty to her husband and partly because she was as yet not fully aware of the nature of Edward's relationship with Gaveston. But the nobility, incensed by Gaveston's arrogance and contempt for the rule of law, resorted to rebellion. Gaveston was captured by his enemies and beheaded, and the sullen Edward promised to mend his ways. For a few years he seemed to be keeping his promise, and Isabella bore him four children. Throughout these years Isabella had behaved as the dutiful wife, bearing her husband's children and tolerating his odd predilections. She did take an interest in state affairs and influenced her husband's decisions in foreign policy, and sometimes secured the appointment of her own favourites to vacant bishoprics. She collected jewels and manors to feed her taste for ostentation and display. Unlike the English, she had frequent baths, as the several bills for the repair of her bathtubs testify. She shared her husband's devotion to Thomas Becket and they made several visits to his shrine in Canterbury. But her husband was not particularly solicitous of her safety and on three occasions – 1312, 1319 and 1322 – she had to make hasty flights south to escape capture by the Scots, on each occasion without direct assistance from Edward.

By 1321, Hugh Despenser had risen rapidly through the court to become the King's favourite. He was young and handsome, and since homosexuality was then regarded as both a crime and a mortal sin Edward would have done well to keep his liaison with Despenser on a more discreet footing. But Edward flaunted it, and alienated Isabella both by his indifference towards her and by the public shame it brought upon her. Edward had learnt nothing from the Gaveston tragedy, and proceeded to shower the young Despenser and his father with estates and power. For six years they used their authority to crush all opposition, and even went so far as to have the King's cousin, the Earl of Lancaster, executed. Isabella now despaired of a normal relationship with her husband. She was particularly alienated by the confiscation of her estates in 1324 on the pretext of an impending French invasion, especially since this was done without compensation. That her children were also taken from her certainly suggests that the Despensers regarded her, sister of the King of France, as a potential traitor. She therefore argued strongly for peace with France and inveigled Edward into sending her there to negotiate a treaty with her brother King Charles the Fair, and then refused to return.

Roger Mortimer, 1st Earl of March, had long been an enemy of the Despensers, and Isabella had sided with her husband against him. But now in France she saw Mortimer as an English exile and an ally against the Despensers, and she became besotted with him. Led by Mortimer and urged on by Isabella, the English exiles, 2,000 in number, planned to invade England, crush the Despensers, secure revenge for the wrongs suffered at their hands, and restore English liberties. That their invasion was a resounding success was due in no small measure to the failure of England, and especially London, to rally to Edward's support. The Despensers fled, were captured, and were put to death with the full atrocities and venom of medieval law. Edward was captured, and in the great hall of Kenilworth Castle a parliamentary deputation declared him deposed in favour of his son Prince Edward. Isabella refused to join her husband in the lifelong captivity that was planned for him; she saw her future as lying with Mortimer. Although the Church made tentative efforts to urge Isabella back to her husband, she felt justified in refusing reconciliation with a man who had never loved her, and regarded her part in his deposition as a necessary contribution to the overthrow of tyranny. It was also a great opportunity for her to enrich herself at the expense of Mortimer's enemies, and the confiscation of their estates made her a great landowner.

It was one thing to plan her husband's overthrow; it was very much another to plan his murder. Certainly there was no immediate need for it. Although there was some plotting among the defeated party, there was no serious attempt to rescue Edward, but he did manage to escape briefly on one occasion, and there was enough plotting among his friends to alarm Roger Mortimer who, with Isabella, now ruled the country in the name of her son Edward III. The Earl of Lancaster, despite having lost his elder brother to the Despensers' executioner, felt some pity for Edward and treated him appropriately and with kindness at Kenilworth. While the ex-king lived, Mortimer could not feel absolutely secure, but it seems likely that, in order not to trouble her conscience, he did not keep Isabella fully informed of his plans for the ex-king. So he ordered Edward to be removed from Kenilworth and entrusted this task to Sir John Maltravers whose hatred of the Despensers had not been assuaged by their deaths. Sir John forced the former king to travel mostly by night, as if to prevent knowledge of his final destination, and after several months brought Edward to Berkeley Castle.

Lord Berkeley, who owned the castle, treated the captive courteously, but was taken ill while visiting his manor of Bradley, and was unable to return to the castle as promptly as he intended. According to the 'poker' story, Mortimer entrusted the care of Edward, during Lord Berkeley's absence, to Thomas Gurney and William Ogle. Apparently following instructions, they attempted at first to suffocate Edward with cushions, but when that failed they pinioned him and despatched him with horn and poker. They could not have pinioned him very effectively because no bruising from his bonds was visible on the body which was exposed next day to the many who poured into the castle as witnesses; and if there was no bruising from the bonds Edward could not have writhed much during the proceedings. No one accused Isabella of being present at the murder; she was told of her husband's death three days later. It is highly unlikely that she had been privy to the exact details of how he was to be murdered, nor was she given these details after the event. She did, however, refuse to bury him in London – it would have seemed inappropriate to her for so wicked and immoral a reprobate to be buried in St Paul's – but his presumed corpse was buried in Gloucester three months later. Isabella showed much grief as was the common practice, and much money was spent on making it a grand occasion. But Isabella's enemies thought that she was a good actress and that the funeral in no way diminished her responsibility for Edward's death.

At first, Edward's death was reported without detail, both in England and abroad where Edward's few followers would surely have tried to make propaganda out of so appalling an act of cruelty. The first account of the 'poker' appeared several years later in a northern chronicle, and although it soon gained popular acceptance, it was still not being repeated in newer chronicles as late as the 1340s. Only after this does the 'poker' gain universal acceptance, and with it the involvement of Isabella in planning and carrying out the murder.

For centuries afterwards chroniclers and historians have accepted the brutality of Edward's death as fact, and have dismissed or ignored anything that might throw doubt on it. The delay in the surfacing of the horrible details of Edward's murder and the northern source of the story throw some doubt on its veracity. The rule of Mortimer and Isabella had rapidly become unpopular, especially in the north, and since Mortimer and Isabella were believed to have sanctioned the murder, an embellished and fabricated account of it could help to undermine them. The murder story itself looks suspicious. That the murderers could not hold Edward down sufficiently to suffocate him, yet could render him immobile while they inserted horn and poker into his rectum seems a little dubious. And as for those screams (the 'wailful noise') which so many heard that night, but had not remembered for several years, would the murderers have wanted them heard? They would surely have preferred a windowless or at least secluded room for the deed, such as the one to the left of the castle keep in which legend has it that the murder took place. Only if the murder was committed in the spacious courtyard would the screams be likely to be heard at a distance from the castle, and then probably not as far as the village.

Edward, according to the story, died that night, and was despatched in a few brief but excruciating hours. Some modern medical opinion suggests that the poker would cause considerable damage in the lower abdomen, but that he was unlikely to have died immediately. He was more likely to have died a few days later of peritonitis or organ failure or both, unless Gurney and Ogle were periodically reheating the poker throughout the night. Perhaps the shock might have killed him earlier, but Edward, at forty-three, was physically strong and had fought valiantly against the cushions. He had also, it appears, been impervious to attempts to starve him to death (wouldn't Mortimer have wanted a *quick* result?) and to overpower him with the stench of rotting animal carcasses. Gurney and Ogle would not have found it easy to murder Edward unless they had the assistance of accomplices, and accomplices talk.

There is therefore considerable doubt about the reliability of the 'poker' story and therefore of Isabella's alleged part in it, and it seems that if Edward was murdered in 1327 it was more likely by cushion or pillow than heated steel. This doubt about

Edward's death is reinforced by the Fieschi letter. Manuele de Fieschi was a Genoese priest in the service of Pope John XXII. Early in 1337 he sent Edward III a letter. In it he makes reference to a previous communication (no longer in existence) containing information he says he got directly from Edward II. He then proceeds to give details of Edward's secret meanderings before arriving at Berkeley; he describes Edward's escape, the killing of a gatekeeper to effect the escape, and the convenient use of the gatekeeper's body for the funeral at Gloucester. He gives details of Edward's itinerary after his escape and how he finally found refuge in Lombardy as a recluse. That this is a genuine letter has never been challenged by historians who have, however, in the main disputed the accuracy of its contents as they are so much at variance with the stories of the murder. Yet the letter contains details known only to a few, and which are not found in any of the chronicles until several years after the letter was written. Since the few were by now dead, he could have got his information only from men of lower rank – but he would have had no idea who they were or how to get them secretly to Italy even if he did – or from Edward himself. His claim that he obtained his information directly from the exiled Edward ought not therefore to be dismissed out of hand.

But if Edward had escaped and was still alive, why did he not return to England to reclaim his throne? Of course he could not do so until after Mortimer had been overthrown in 1330. Nor, even after Mortimer's overthrow, could he be certain of Isabella's reaction; she had refused to take her husband back when he was alive – would she now want him on his return from the dead? And would Edward III be willing to give way to a father long believed dead, and would the people of England who had failed to support him when he was alive rally to his support if he came back from the dead? They would probably think of him as another impostor. And Edward might well, in the circumstances, have turned to religion. He had alienated his wife and son, he had lost Hugh Despenser, he had committed mortal sin, and kingship had brought him more sorrow than joy, and as demonstrated at his abdication, he was shattered in mind and spirit if not in body. Yet he had once escaped from his captors, in June 1327, and was it not possible that he could have escaped again? Those responsible for his incarceration might well have been unwilling to admit his escape to the vengeful Mortimer, and the corpse buried in Gloucester Cathedral might indeed have been the murdered gatekeeper. The only person to have examined the body closely after death was the woman embalmer, and Isabella, without Mortimer's knowledge, had a private interview with her soon after the funeral. Since this was not to buy her off – there is no record of any extra payment to her – it is a strong possibility that Isabella wanted such information about Edward's death as the woman could provide. She would hardly cross-question the woman secretly if she knew everything already.

Edward III would have had ten years to wonder about the manner of his father's death, and the extent of his mother's involvement in it. But in 1337 the Fieschi correspondence suddenly presented him with evidence that his father was still alive. He would not now undermine his own position by making such information public or even telling his mother, but it is significant that, having for so long vigorously pursued his father's murderers, he now employed Sir John Maltravers on diplomatic missions abroad. It is unlikely that Edward III ever believed the rumours concerning Isabella and his father's murder. After Edward III had overthrown Mortimer in 1330, Isabella at first feared her son's retribution, not for his father's death but because of her liaison with Mortimer. But he continued to treat her with filial duty, respect, and lavish provision. The Fieschi correspondence cleared Isabella of the worst of the crimes attributed to her, a crime of which her son at least did not believe her guilty. In subsequent years Edward listened to his mother's advice and sometimes took it. Isabella admitted some pangs of conscience over her treatment of her husband in her correspondence, and spent much of her time doing good works. But she did not modify her lavish lifestyle; living mainly in her favourite Castle Rising, she expected and received lavish gifts from the Norfolk locals, her household bordered on the extravagant, she loved property and money, and she ran true to form in trying to delay handing over the properties due to her daughter-in-law Philippa. But in her final year she joined a lay branch of the Franciscans and greatly increased her charitable works. Death came in 1358, and she was buried in the Grey Friars' Church at Newgate, to which she had been a very generous benefactor in her lifetime. Edward III gave her a 'sumptuous funeral' as a devoted son should do.

So 'she-wolf' originates from the exaggerations of Isabella's enemies. She was accused of regicide and adultery. She was probably innocent of the first and had some justification for the second. Though greedy for riches, she was generous to servants and friends. Though vindictive against the Despensers, she did try to mitigate the severity of the judgement on the elder Despenser and she did speak up unavailingly for Lancaster. She also tried to help Gaveston's widow. And although on occasions she seemed too ambitious, too ruthless and too hardened to be a romantic courtly woman like her daughter-in-law Philippa, she was no more than typical of her age. Perhaps if Edward II had been more like Edward I or Edward III, Isabella would have come down in history as an exemplary queen consort.

DIANE DE POITIERS: THE BLACK WIDOW

Many kings have had mistresses, but few of the mistresses are ever remembered. Diane de Poitiers is one of the few exceptions. She advised two French kings, was mistress to one of them and just possibly the other, and she was considered by some historians to have had a hand in policies that led to the French Religious Wars. Most mistresses are ephemeral, but Diane was the constant companion of Henry II of France for at least twenty years, despite the fact that she was almost twenty years older than he was. What was the secret of her success?

Diane de Poitiers was born on 3 September 1499, the daughter of Jean de Poitiers, Seigneur de St Vallier, and his wife Jeanne de Batarney. His was an ancient and noble line, and so it was with little difficulty that, as a child, Diane was found a place at the court of Anne of Beaujeu, regent of France. At the age of fifteen she married Louis de Brézé, grand seneschal of Normandy, a nobleman at the court of Francis I. He was forty-one years older than Diane, hunch-backed and notoriously ugly. Throughout the marriage, Diane was a dutiful and loyal wife, and it was fruitful enough to produce two daughters. From her husband, Diane learned much about the conduct of public affairs, and about the factions which surrounded the Crown. In 1524 she faced a crisis when her father became involved in the Constable de Bourbon's conspiracy and was sentenced to death. Legend has it that Diane saved her father's life by a personal appeal to King Francis and the reprieve arrived when her father's head was already on the block. But suggestions that this involved the sacrifice of her honour are unsubstantiated, and it is believed that Diane led a blameless life throughout the whole of her marriage. Despite, or perhaps because of, her purity she became lady-in-waiting to two successive queens of France, and exercised great influence over the King's children. In 1526, when Francis' two sons were taken to Spain as hostages,[1] it was Diane who bade them farewell with a kiss, and on their return four years later Diane was entrusted with the position of companion and teacher of courtly etiquette to young Prince Henry. Her influence over Henry showed when, in 1531, Henry publicly saluted Diane at a tournament before he so honoured Francis' new queen Eleanor. His infatuation with Diane was obvious to all. Even so, Diane and her husband approved young Henry's marriage to Catherine de Medici in 1533, despite the opposition of many at court who thought the Medicis inferior. Soon afterwards, de Brézé died, leaving Diane a widow, and she took care henceforth to wear clothes which were predominantly black, occasionally relieved with a little white or grey. Henry succeeded his brother young Francis as Dauphin in 1536, and Diane became his mistress soon after. Henry and Catherine were still childless and Diane placed her country's interests before her own by encouraging Henry to occupy the marital bed as frequently as possible. Even so, it was not until 1543, ten years after her marriage, that Catherine had the first of her ten children. In 1547 Francis I died, Henry became king as Henry II, and Diane became queen in all but name.

Diane's great influence over Henry was twofold. In the first place, contemporaries agreed in acclaiming her great beauty, even though this is not fully borne out by her surviving portraits. But she undoubtedly took great pains over her personal appearance. In an age when personal cleanliness was regarded as a fad rather than a necessity, she horrified contemporaries by washing, even on the coldest mornings, in water straight from the well. She was careful in the use of make-up; most ladies laid it on like plaster. She dressed tastefully within the colours to which she had restricted herself, and she succeeded in retaining much of her beauty until she was well on in her fifties. Henry did not appear to be concerned about the very large age difference, although he did from time to time have brief liaisons with other women.

But Henry was as much attracted by Diane's intellect as her beauty. After her husband died Diane took over her husband's duties, and emoluments, of grand seneschal of

Normandy, taking for herself the title of seneschale.[2] She showed legal skill by challenging in the courts to keep the royal lands that went with the post. During the reign of Francis I, she made an enemy of the King's mistress, Madame d'Étampes, who regarded Diane as a sorceress, yet Francis consulted Diane and retained her within his inner circle. Henry II was uncomfortable with women and found them difficult to talk to, but Diane would talk to him freely about affairs of state, religion, war and manly sports so that he was able to regard her as a companion and adviser as well as a sexual partner. He had such regard and trust for her high intelligence that he allowed her to write many of his official letters and to sign them with a joint name: HenriDiane. She was even a signatory to the first marriage contract between Henry's son Francis and Mary Queen of Scots. Such was Diane's power that the Queen, Catherine de Medici, was pushed into the background, and even the Pope found it tactful to send Diane a gift when he was honouring the Queen. Catherine and Diane did join forces when threatened with a new favourite. Most lasted very briefly; neither queen nor mistress would tolerate an interloper. When Lady Fleming, of Mary Queen of Scots' entourage in France, boasted, rather too loudly, that she was pregnant by the King, she was sent back in disgrace to Scotland.

Diane's position as mistress did not carry with it the stigma such a position would have had centuries later. She was able to negotiate fine marriages for her two daughters: one married the Duke of Bouillon, the other married the Duke of Guise's son. Such alliances often determine the political groupings and Diane found herself supporting the Guises and the extreme Catholic position towards the end of Henry's reign (1547–1559). She secured the appointment of her own nominee as Keeper of the Seals, and through him exercised powers that were normally reserved for the Chancellor. Thus her influence over policies was very considerable. She gave approval to the anti-Protestant measures that Henry introduced, but there is no evidence that she encouraged the burnings that accompanied them. Even so, she made a practice of demanding the confiscated property of heretics and thus built up a considerable fortune in land and other assets. But her interests were more artistic than religious. She loved the artistic manifestations of the Renaissance, although she was less interested in its intellectual accomplishments. She used the best architects and artists in the building of her chateau at Anet (on the Eure, west of Paris and north of Dreux), she patronised sculptors and musicians, and constructed beautiful gardens in the contemporary style. She helped bring up and educate the Queen's children and also Mary Queen of Scots when she joined the French court in 1548. Mary was afterwards to recall that the days spent at Anet with Diane were the happiest days of her life.

Diane was not without personal ambition. She became Duchesse de Valentinois in 1548 and Duchesse d'Étampes in 1553. Not content with Anet, she admired and coveted the lovely royal Chateau de Chenonceau and persuaded Henry to sell it to her at a cut price. He also gave her the Crown jewels to look after, which Catherine bitterly resented. The lands inherited from her husband and those given her by the King made Diane a very rich woman, but her power and much of her wealth depended upon the King's favour. In July 1559, Henry II was mortally wounded at a tournament by the Duke of Montgomery's lance. The lance had splintered as it struck: a splinter entered the

King's eye, the shaft entered his body. As he lay dying and calling for Diane, Catherine enjoyed her moment of triumph. She not only refused to allow Diane to visit the dying king, which would have been a serious breach of etiquette had it been allowed, but she also barred her from attending the funeral. She encouraged her daughter-in-law Mary Queen of Scots, the new Queen of France, to demand the return of the Crown jewels, and she did so the day after Henry's death. A bitterer blow was Catherine's insistence on the return of Chenonceau to the Crown in exchange for the Chateau of Chaumont. Diane lived there briefly before returning to spend her remaining days at Anet, where she died aged sixty-six in April 1566.

To contemporaries, Diane was a woman of enormous power, whose influence over the policies at home and abroad of Henry II was incalculable. More recent historians have been inclined to challenge this view and to say that her personal influence has been exaggerated. That she was a very formidable character is beyond dispute, especially in keeping at bay the notorious Catherine de Medici. She must bear some of the responsibility for the harsh measures against the Huguenots, and insofar as France failed to achieve success abroad, Diane must take her share of the blame. It would therefore be mistaken to underestimate her success in determining policy and in bending a besotted king to her will.

CATHERINE DE MEDICI: QUEEN EXTRAORDINARY

Catherine de Medici was successively Queen and Queen dowager of France. Her influence during the reigns of her sons Charles IX (1560–74) and Henry III (1574–89) was such as to make her almost a queen regnant, and she guided France through eight religious civil wars. Historians have long argued about her responsibility for the massacre of French Huguenots (Calvinist Protestants) which took place on St Bartholomew's Day, 24 August 1572. It resulted in the deaths of thousands of Huguenots, and in much damage to Queen Catherine's reputation.

Caterina Maria Romula di Lorenzo de' Medici was born in Florence, the power centre of the Medicis, on 13 April 1519; she simplified her name to Catherine de Medici after her marriage to a French prince in 1533. She was the daughter of Lorenzo II, the Medici Duke of Urbino, and her mother was Madeleine de la Tour d'Auvergne, Countess of Boulogne, so Catherine was already half French before her marriage. Her great uncle, Cardinal Giovanni de Medici, became Pope Leo X in 1513, and after a brief interlude in 1521–23 he was succeeded by another Medici Pope, her uncle, Clement VII. Despite her close link to the all-powerful papacy, Catherine had a very traumatic childhood. Both her parents died when she was in infancy and she was brought up at first by an aunt, and, when she died, by a cousin. When the Medicis were overthrown in Florence in 1527, Catherine was moved by the enemies of the Medici from one convent to another as a virtual prisoner. The Pope felt obliged to ask the help of the Holy Roman Emperor, Charles V, in restoring the Medici rule in Florence, and Charles laid siege to the city in 1529. This placed Catherine in grave danger. Citizens clamoured for her to be killed, and on one occasion soldiers forced her to ride through the streets on a donkey, jeered on by a hostile crowd. When Florence was taken by the Emperor's troops in 1530, the Pope sent for Catherine to live in Rome where he could give her greater protection and use her as a diplomatic bargaining counter.

Catherine did not grow up to be a great beauty, but she was renowned for her elegant hands. She was small and thin and had protruding eyes, but this did not matter unduly in an age when marriages were arranged. Many suitors of high rank sought her hand, lured by the prospect of a huge dowry and papal support, among them the impecunious James V of Scotland. But the Pope wished to secure the alliance of France against the all-powerful Habsburgs who ruled both the Empire and Spain. When, therefore, Francis I of France proposed that Catherine should marry his second son, Henry, Duke of Orleans, the Pope hastened to accept the offer. Betrothal was followed by a two-year-long engagement on account of the youth of the young couple. The marriage eventually took place on 28 October 1533 in Marseilles. Consummation is said to have been achieved in the presence of King Francis, although the Pope had a little more decorum and did not enter the bedroom until the next morning to give the young couple his blessing. The Pope died in the following year and the new Pope (Paul III) who was not a Medici, refused to pay Catherine's dowry, much to King Francis' chagrin. The papal alliance with France was now under threat, Catherine seemed to be infertile, but the hint of divorce was soon smothered by the realisation that the time was inopportune for divorce talk.[1] The death of Henry's older brother Francis in 1536 made Henry heir to the throne and Catherine became Dauphine. She was now under intense pressure to provide an heir for Henry. In 1538 Henry took as his mistress Diane de Poitiers, a renowned beauty twice his age. In must have been galling for Catherine to see the favours he gave her, including the beautiful Chateau of Chenonceau which straddles the river Cher, and to know that Diane repeatedly urged Henry to perform his marital duty with Catherine in order to produce the longed-for heir. It is said that in desperation Catherine resorted to the use of mule's urine and cow dung. Perhaps these had some effect for at last in 1544 Catherine gave birth to Francis (named after his grandfather), and thereafter she bore her husband nine more children, six of whom survived infancy.

With the death of Francis I in 1547, Prince Henry became King Henry II of France with Catherine as queen consort. She was crowned in 1549. Henry had no intention of sharing any power with her. He spent as much time as he could with Diane de Poitiers, and if he ever discussed state affairs with a woman he discussed them with her. But he did allow Catherine to be regent occasionally when he was absent abroad, although the powers he entrusted to her were very limited. In April 1559, France and Spain made peace by the Treaty of Cateau-Cambrésis and the peace was to be cemented by marriage between Philip II of Spain[2] and Elizabeth, Catherine's eldest daughter. A great tournament was held to celebrate the marriage during the course of which the French King was mortally injured by the Duke of Montgomery's lance which struck the King full in the face and splintered into several fragments. Catherine's son Francis, who in 1558 had married the young Mary Queen of Scots, now became King Francis II at the age of fifteen.

Mary Queen of Scots was the daughter of Mary of Guise, and the Guises had, during Henry II's reign, become the most powerful noble family in France. The new queen's uncles, the Guises, now effectively took control of the government, and since Francis was, though only fifteen, considered to be of age, Catherine as queen dowager had no claim to be part of it. She therefore found it expedient to work with the Guises, but she gained some personal satisfaction by making Diane de Poitiers hand over the French Crown jewels to the new Queen Mary and to give back Chenonceau to the Crown; Catherine immediately began ambitious plans to make Chenonceau a residence fit for herself. The Guises adopted a policy of religious persecution in view of the growing Protestant movement which threatened to undermine France's traditional Catholicism. Both Francis I and Henry II had adopted shifting religious policies, which were more political rather than religious in intent. Thus when France wanted to court the Habsburgs and the papacy, burnings of Huguenots became commonplace; when relations with the Habsburgs cooled persecution largely ceased. King Henry is known on one occasion to have expressed the opinion that if the Huguenots kept their religion private they should have freedom to practise it.

But they did not keep their religion private. By 1560 the Huguenots had become not only a considerable religious force but also a major political one. Once Huguenotism spread among the highest nobility, the survival of Catholicism in France seemed to be under threat. Admiral Coligny and Prince Louis of Condé, the most notable Huguenots, were ambitious to drive the Guises from power and to end all discrimination against their religion. The Guises, therefore, became the vanguard of the Counter-Reformation in France, determined to maintain the Catholic faith, wipe out Protestantism, and strengthen their grip on power. Catherine belonged to neither faction, nor at first did she have one of her own. She was therefore compelled to resort to expediency; her aim was to preserve the monarchy intact for her sons, so she had no choice but to play off one faction against the other. Her own inclination, at least until the late 1560s, was to grant some religious toleration to the Huguenots. But while she had strong political acumen she did not understand the reasons for, or the strength of, the religious divide. Intensity of religious fervour, so common to both factions, escaped her. She valued much more the predictions of her astrologers than the absolution of her confessors.[3]

Catherine spoke up for a measure of religious toleration to an Assembly of Notables in August 1560, but she did not think it inconsistent to have the Huguenot leader Condé arrested for raising an army for which he was sentenced to death. Nor did she see any incongruity in arranging that Condé's brother, Antoine de Bourbon, should give up his claim to a future regency in return for his brother's release. Catherine had already realised that her son King Francis was very ill, and made political capital out of it. Indeed, Francis did die of an ear infection in December 1560, and Catherine was able to claim the regency for herself on behalf of his successor Charles IX, her nine-year-old son.

Her main aim now was to prevent civil war. Both factions were raising armies and preparing for conflict despite a concessionary edict allowing Huguenots a measure of religious toleration for which Catherine and her Chancellor, Michel de l'Hôpital, were mainly responsible. But when the Duke of Guise's troops massacred a large number of Huguenots worshipping in a barn at Vassy in 1562, Coligny ignored the Duke's subsequent expression of regret and called his followers to arms. Civil war followed. Catherine's concern was to prevent the conflict giving an excuse for foreign intervention, which would weaken France. She was alarmed at the negotiations for Mary Stuart to marry the Spanish prince Don Carlos and persuaded her daughter Elizabeth, Queen of Spain, to place every obstacle in its way. At the same time she tried to bring the opposing sides together. The murder of the Duke of Guise in 1563 strengthened Catherine's position as regent and she was able to broker a temporary peace. But Condé now demanded a voice in the government and, fearing that the Huguenots were becoming too strong, Catherine had Charles IX declared of age when he was barely thirteen. She also conducted negotiations with Spain – a warning to the Huguenot leader not to press her too far. Nevertheless, Charles IX's refusal to grant full toleration to the Huguenots led to a renewal of civil war in 1567, which, after a brief respite the following year, ended in 1570 with the Huguenots gaining limited rights of public worship.

Peace was very necessary as Philip of Spain seemed poised to overwhelm the incipient Protestant rebellion in the Netherlands, and the Spanish-Scottish marriage alliance discussions had been revived after Elizabeth of Spain's death even though the Queen of Scotland was a prisoner of Elizabeth I of England. France seemed in danger of being surrounded by hostile Habsburg enemies, internal unity was essential, so Catherine invited Coligny to court in 1571. It was a mistake. Coligny's charm, reputation and charisma won over the impressionable young king and Catherine became concerned. She was afraid that Coligny's plan to use French troops to help the Protestant William of Orange of the Netherlands in his revolt against Philip of Spain would damage French interests and advance the Huguenot cause. Too many broken truces had brought her to the conclusion that the Huguenot leaders could not be trusted. She was annoyed that Coligny opposed the elevation of her favourite son, Francis of Anjou, to the throne of Poland, and she could not help being but a little jealous that Charles IX listened to Coligny in preference to her.

Political assassination was a favourite sixteenth-century weapon. The Duke of Guise had been murdered in 1563 and Condé in 1569. The murder of Coligny had probably been discussed by the Guises as far back as 1565 and they were certainly on the alert for a suitable opportunity. The court delivered one in 1572. Catherine had been anxious to marry her youngest daughter Marguerite to the Protestant Henry of Navarre, who would have the strongest claim to the French throne if Catherine's sons should prove childless. Margaret was not at all keen, but the marriage nevertheless took place on 18 August 1572 in the presence of large numbers of Huguenot leaders who had travelled from all over France for the ceremony and subsequent festivities. Two days later, a rather slipshod marksman attempted to murder Coligny but succeeded only in wounding him with a shot from an arquebus. There is little doubt that Catherine was privy to the murder attempt, and that the Guises were probably also involved. Charles' immediate reaction was an order to hunt down those responsible, but Catherine was alarmed that if an investigation took place her part in the assassination attempt would become public. In any case the attempt on Coligny would be certain to provoke a Huguenot reaction and Huguenot fury would be unmanageable if her involvement were known.

So Catherine, accompanied by her younger son Anjou, and several others of the extreme Catholic faction, hastened to see Charles to persuade him that Coligny was plotting against the Crown and that only his removal and that of other Huguenot leaders would save it. Charles eventually agreed:

> By God's death since you insist that the admiral must be killed, I consent; but with him every Huguenot in France must perish, that not one may remain to reproach me with his death, and what you do, see that it be done quickly.

Whether Charles really meant every Huguenot, or merely every Huguenot leader has been a matter of much controversy. It seems probable, however, that Catherine did not intend a general religious massacre, but simply wanted a limited political one. Haste was, as Charles implied, essential. On St Bartholomew's Day, 24 August 1572, the massacre began. At dawn assassins broke into Coligny's house, attacked him with their swords and disembowelled him, and while he was still alive they threw him naked from a window. Alarm bells were rung throughout Paris and the Catholic populace set about massacring every Huguenot they could lay their hands on. Similar scenes were enacted throughout France, especially in towns where the Huguenots were numerous, such as Rouen. Nearly 2,000 died in Paris and about 10,000 in the rest of France. Catholic Europe was delighted; the Pope issued a commemorative medal, Philip II of Spain danced a jig around his bedroom, but Protestant Europe was appalled and horrified, and Elizabeth of England kept the French ambassador waiting for three days before she would grant him an interview.

The accusation that Catherine had planned the destruction of the Huguenots runs contrary to the evidence. Her aim to preserve the balance of power is shown by her encouragement of the marriage negotiations between her son Henry of Anjou and Elizabeth of England that had been taking place as late as January 1572. And she had forced her daughter Marguerite to marry the Protestant Henry of Navarre rather than the Catholic Henry of Guise, to whom she had given her heart. Yet she had seen Coligny's schemes as an attempt to embroil France in a dangerous adventure in the Netherlands which would bring the wrath of the Habsburgs upon France without the certainty of an English alliance. So she had resorted to political assassination, not mass murder.

One consequence of the massacre was the renewal of civil war as the Huguenots sought to avenge their terrible suffering. Another was the rise of a moderate faction, sick of bloodshed and anxious for religious compromise, known as the *Politiques*. These moderate Catholics joined with the Huguenots in opposing the ambitions of the Guises, and Catherine virtually identified herself with them. Charles IX died in 1574 and was succeeded by his brother Henry of Anjou, as Henry III. A regency was not needed, since Henry was twenty-two when he came to the throne, but he lacked the energy and enthusiasm for affairs of state and left the government largely in the hands of Catherine and her civil servants. Since Henry was generally considered incapable of fathering children, his younger brother Francis, Duke of Alençon, was next in line to the throne. He incurred Catherine's wrath by giving too much support to the Huguenot cause, instead of treading the narrow path of the *Politiques*, and while Catherine wanted Spain to encounter continued difficulties in the Netherlands, Alençon undertook military intervention there and put himself forward as a major suitor for the hand of Elizabeth of England. His death in 1584 meant that the Protestant Henry of Navarre[4] was now heir presumptive to the French throne, and the Catholic League, headed by the Guises, was determined to change the succession and exclude Navarre. Catherine devoted her time to rallying support against the Guises, but the Catholic League was too strong, and by 1588 most of northern France was under its control. Catherine urged Henry to leave Paris for his own safety. In the autumn of 1588, Catherine became ill with a chest complaint and Henry took the opportunity to thank his mother for all she had done for him, and dismissed all the ministers she had appointed. He then summoned the Duke of Guise to a meeting and had Guise murdered, an act which horrified Catherine. She died two weeks later, on 5 January 1589, probably from a recurrence of the chest complaint.

There is some element of truth in the Protestant contemporaries who damned Catherine as a scheming Machiavellian. Her aim was always to preserve France intact for her sons, and to make good marriages for her daughters regardless of moral and ethical considerations. And if her sons were too weakly to have heirs she preserved the Valois line by marrying her daughter Marguerite to the Protestant Henry of Navarre, and thus preserved the French throne for her grandchildren through the female line. It was said that she was ruthless, but she made great efforts to come to an understanding with the Huguenots, and with the Protestant Elizabeth of England, and found her political home with the *Politiques* after the St Bartholomew's Day Massacre. She was said to have been cruel, and she did witness the execution of Huguenots at Amboise in 1560, but she did not instigate it. She did resort to physical violence against her daughter Marguerite for having a secret affair, and she is known to have berated Alençon for his lack of political judgement and Marguerite for her scandalous affairs. But it is most unlikely that she murdered the Queen of Navarre with poisoned gloves in 1559. Yet she was undoubtedly courageous, both in her appearances on the battlefield and in her tours of Huguenot areas of southern France.

There was a gentler side to her character. She brought up Mary Queen of Scots with her own children and Mary afterwards described those years with Catherine as the happiest of her life. After the death of her husband she avoided ostentatious dress but she did like sumptuous architecture displayed with her development of Chenonceau and the new palaces of Hotel de la Reine and The Tuileries. These she filled with great works of art ranging from paintings, tapestries, and china to exquisite furniture and musical instruments. And she promoted musical performances, especially those which combined drama and dance, precursors of the ballet. Perhaps, as she juggled with all the great political questions of the day, there was a Renaissance queen struggling to get out. In better times she could have been a patron of the arts and a model queen.

Her son-in-law, the Protestant Henry of Navarre, wrote her a fitting epitaph:

What could a woman do, left by the death of her husband with five little children on her hands, and two families of France who were thinking of grasping the crown – our own (the Bourbons) and the Guises? Was she not compelled to play strange parts to deceive first one and then the other, in order to guard, as she did, her sons, who successively reigned through the wise conduct of that shrewd woman? I am surprised that she never did worse.

ELIZABETH OF YORK: WISE PRINCESS

Elizabeth of York, wife of the first Tudor monarch, Henry VII, is often portrayed as a queen of little importance and of virtually no influence. She is depicted as a dynastic pawn, much under the influence of her ambitious mother, Elizabeth Woodville, the dowager queen. Her husband, King Henry, used her to produce his children, but otherwise treated her coldly, and on her early death wasted no time in looking for another wife. Does this picture require any modification?

Elizabeth was born on 11 February 1466. She was the eldest daughter of Edward IV, the Yorkist king, and his wife Elizabeth Woodville, and from the first it was clear that Elizabeth would be a valuable prize in the European royal marriage market. Although at the age of three she was affianced to one of the Neville family, this was merely to strengthen support for the Yorkists in the ongoing Wars of the Roses. But Edward IV triumphed over his enemies at the battle of Barnet in 1471, the Yorkist victory was complete, and successful negotiations were concluded with France for Elizabeth to marry the Dauphin. Since Edward IV was now secure on the English throne, the French had much to gain and little to lose by a dynastic alliance with England. For seven years the engagement apparently remained in force until, at the end of 1482, the Dauphin was affianced to the infant daughter of Mary of Burgundy, and Elizabeth, now sixteen years of age, was left in the cold. By sixteen most princesses had married, and Elizabeth needed to be found another suitor. It was not that Elizabeth was necessarily unattractive. No contemporary portraits of her exist, and eyewitness descriptions of her later in life comment on the fact that she was stout and big-breasted. But physical attraction was not a major marketing point for princesses; of much greater importance was their social standing and their wealth, and how diplomatically important they would be in the international kaleidoscope of shifting alliances.

But Elizabeth's father did not have time to arrange another betrothal for her; he died suddenly in April 1483. Within weeks Edward IV's brother Richard had seized control of Edward's young son Edward (now Edward V), and in alarm Elizabeth Woodville took her daughters and younger son into sanctuary at Westminster. In June, Richard proclaimed himself King Richard III and had Parliament declare Edward IV's daughters and sons to be bastards.[1] For the next few months Elizabeth and her children remained in sanctuary, and constituted a possible focus of opposition to Richard's usurpation. Towards the end of 1483, the new Lancastrian claimant to the throne, Henry Tudor, swore an oath to consolidate his claim by marrying young Elizabeth, and her mother appears to have been involved in a secret agreement to that effect with Henry's mother, Margaret Beaufort. Rumours of an agreement and definite news of the oath thoroughly alarmed Richard. Since Henry Tudor seemed to have little chance of immediate success, Richard decided to make Elizabeth's mother a better and more immediate offer. He promised her and her children personal safety, financial security and dowries for the girls. His offer was accepted and Henry Tudor was mortified.

Only a year earlier Richard had declared Elizabeth and her sisters to be bastards, but now there was no further talk of bastardy as Richard planned to marry off Elizabeth to his son, the Prince of Wales, but the young prince died at Middleham Castle before anything came of it.[2] Then Richard's wife Anne became ill, and after lingering more than a month died, with the usual suspicion of poisoning promoted by Richard's enemies. He now wanted a new wife to provide him with an heir, and for a while he is said to have toyed with the idea of marrying his niece Elizabeth, but was persuaded against it by horrified advisers even though the Pope would probably have granted a dispensation. Richard now publicly proclaimed that such a repulsive idea had never entered his head.

By the summer of 1485, Richard had become sufficiently unpopular in the south of England[3] for Henry Tudor to make an invasion attempt, and it achieved rather surprising success at the Battle of Bosworth; some of Richard's trusted friends proved less than trustworthy during the battle. It is not clear precisely where Elizabeth was during the crisis; she was at Sheriff Hutton for a short while with her cousin the Earl of Warwick, but the victorious Henry moved her to London, placing her in the care of her mother Elizabeth Woodville. Henry had every intention of uniting the two royal houses of Lancaster and York by marrying Elizabeth; her views about the marriage were not sought. But she was well aware of her own importance. After coming out of sanctuary, she had appeared at Richard's court dressed in similar clothes to his queen, and marriage to Henry would satisfy her newfound taste for court life. Moreover, Henry was in the prime of manhood, and not the consumptive wreck of a man he was to become in his final years. From his point of view marriage to Elizabeth was vital to consolidate his claim to the throne. Furthermore, he could not allow her to marry a foreign prince, thus giving her spouse the right to interfere in English politics while Henry's tenure of the throne remained insecure, nor could he allow her to marry an English nobleman and thus become the potential focus for the disaffected. Elizabeth thus really had no choice, and she could not really hope for a better offer. Any scruples about the fate of so many of her close relatives at and after Bosworth would have to be set aside, and at this time she did not even know what had happened to her two younger brothers, the princes in the Tower.

Henry was careful to delay the marriage until *after* Parliament had granted him the crown and had petitioned him to marry Elizabeth. The marriage took place on 18 January 1486; Elizabeth was twenty years of age, Henry was twenty-eight. Henry had taken the trouble to secure a papal dispensation for the marriage, even though he and Elizabeth were only distantly related. The dispensation arrived two months after the wedding. In just over eight months Elizabeth gave birth to her first child, Prince Arthur, and her coronation, which Henry had delayed as long as possible for political reasons, took place in September 1487. Only after the coronation did Henry make any separate financial provision for her, assigning property to her from her mother and later from her grandmother.

It is uncertain whether his mulcting of Elizabeth Woodville's property was simply a reassigning of resources within the royal family or a specific snub because of Elizabeth Woodville's uncertain loyalties. Lambert Simnel's rebellion in 1487 led Henry to suspect that the Queen's mother had given some kind of encouragement to Simnel's supporters (if only that she had given them an accurate description of the Earl of Warwick, who Simnel claimed to be). And it was not only Elizabeth's mother whom Henry treated harshly. The real Warwick was still closely confined in the Tower, her half-brother, the Earl of Dorset was arrested, and others had suffered confiscations and fines. How Elizabeth reacted to all the decimations and despoliations is not known, but as Henry's queen she would have to bite her tongue and keep her silence. In fact, Henry quite quickly learned to trust his wife and to value her judgement. When Perkin Warbeck's rebellion was finally crushed in 1497, Lady Catherine Gordon, Warbeck's wife, was entrusted to the Queen. She joined the royal court, and was treated by Elizabeth 'with great kindness'. Elizabeth could, on occasions, show that she was not entirely in her husband's shadow; when a Welsh tenant of the King's uncle Jasper complained of injustice it was Elizabeth who sent Jasper a sharp reprimand. Elizabeth would have taken a keen interest, and probably some part, in the negotiations that led to the marriages of her eldest son Arthur to Catherine of Aragon in 1501 and her daughter Margaret to James IV of Scotland in 1502. Henry tended to rely on Elizabeth to court former Yorkist supporters, and she received very large numbers of gifts from those seeking her goodwill.

Elizabeth is often regarded as playing an inferior role to that of her mother-in-law, Margaret Beaufort. And certainly it was Margaret who fostered literature and drama at Henry's court, supported by Elizabeth. But Elizabeth had interests of her own; she encouraged composers and musicians, and it was her design which was used for the new royal building at Greenwich. Margaret played a major role in the bringing up of the royal children, but it was Elizabeth who comforted the inconsolable King on the sudden death of Prince Arthur in April 1502. And if Elizabeth's marriage was born out of political expediency it could not have been loveless, partly because she bore the King seven children of whom three survived infancy, but even more so because there are no infidelities recorded or rumoured on either side; this constancy is almost unique in royal annals.

Elizabeth gave birth to her last child at the beginning of February 1503, and died of the complications of childbirth nine days later. Henry spent £2,800 on her funeral, an enormous sum in those days, especially for a man so notorious for his parsimony, and if Henry, after a relatively brief period of grief, began looking for a new wife he was doing no more than other monarchs had done in similar sad circumstances – a royal marriage is always a saleable commodity either for cash or diplomatic advantage. Elizabeth's passing was universally mourned, and by many who knew her she was much loved. All agree that she was good and gracious, and if she was not powerful she was certainly influential, and without her Henry VII's reign would have been demonstrably the poorer.

QUEEN ELIZABETH TUDOR AND HER FRIENDS

A great deal has been written on the subject of palace intrigue and the influence of courtiers in the reign of Elizabeth I, especially of men such as the Earls of Leicester and Essex with whom the royal name was closely linked, but less has been written on the subject of the many devoted women friends who served the Queen so loyally in the course of her long reign, from Lady Byron who nursed her as a baby and worried over her infant teething troubles to the last moment when, regretting the passing of her close friend Catherine Carey, Countess of Nottingham, she lay her head on her arm and slipped away alone in her seventieth year in March 1603. How important are these women in explaining the character of Elizabeth's reign?

There were a number of men who thought to attract the attentions of the Queen, such as Christopher Hatton, the captain of the bodyguard, and Walter Raleigh, the adventurer and soldier, who clearly fancied their chances with her, but the two most important would-be suitors in Elizabeth's life were Robert Dudley, Earl of Leicester and brother of Guildford Dudley, husband of Lady Jane Grey, and Robert Devereux, Earl of Essex, an adventurer and the great-nephew of Anne Boleyn and so a cousin of the Queen. Dudley passed from favour because of the lingering suspicion that he had been involved in the death of his wife Amy Robsart, though he spent the next twenty years pursuing his suit for Elizabeth. Devereux, seeking wealth and glory in exploits in the Lowlands, Spain and the New World, and, quarrelling with the Cecils (whom he saw as deliberately standing in the way of his greatness), finally got himself sent to Ireland in the late 1590s, where he fared ignominiously, returned unbidden to England to face public disgrace and, after a feeble attempt at a rebellion, underwent public execution in 1601. Elizabeth knew how to be loyal to men who served her well, as she showed by her devotion to both Cecils, father and son, throughout her reign, but was able to recognise that many of those who crowded round her were merely sycophants devoted to their own advancement.

Her earlier, rather unsubtle, encounters with ambitious men, such as Thomas Seymour, did little to improve her unfavourable impressions. Thomas was brother of Edward Seymour, Duke of Somerset, and gave diplomatic, military and naval service to Henry VIII in the later part of his reign. On Edward VI's accession he was created Lord Admiral and Baron. He married the royal widow, Catherine Parr, and, after her death in childbirth, even made overtures for marriage to the teenage Elizabeth. He was a man three times older than Elizabeth, and she found his attentions absolutely repellent, saying of him: 'He is a man of much wit, but very little judgement.' It may be a mistake to put down her later unmarried state to memories such as these (more likely she thought that she was born to rule, but that she could not be a good wife and a good queen at the same time), but they certainly served as a salutary reminder of the merits of spinsterhood.

Some of the women the Queen knew were too close to her own family and too close to the focus of dynastic politics. She knew Jane, Catherine and Mary Grey, daughters of the Brandons and granddaughters of her aunt Mary, but did not take to any of them as friends: Jane's religious fervour bordered on fanaticism, while Elizabeth was completely sincere when she said she 'did not wish to open windows into men's souls'; Catherine was inclined to be silly and arrogant, while Mary was an odd little woman without pretensions to either beauty or intelligence. She never actually met Mary Stuart, descended from her other aunt Margaret, who married her first cousin Henry Stuart, Lord Darnley, and produced the strange uncouth son who one day would succeed Elizabeth to the English throne; if they had it is hard to see how there could have been much friendship between the one so impulsive and indiscreet, and the other with such judicious self-possession, whose abiding care was for the well-being of the nation she ruled. Elizabeth's friends were taken from those who were not her relatives.

Her favourite women, she knew, were not so dedicated to their own careers. One of them was Katharine Ashley, daughter of Sir Philip Champernowne of Modbury in Devon. She was introduced to the court by Thomas Cromwell, who appointed her governess to the three-year-old Elizabeth in 1536. Later she married John Ashley – a Boleyn connection – in 1545. Kate, as the young Elizabeth called her, was a good teacher who gave her firm educational foundations. Kate was a friend of Roger Ascham, and, though she spent some time in the Tower after Somerset arrested her, never wavered in her devotion to Elizabeth. She was sent packing by Elizabeth's sister Mary during her short reign because of her Protestant affiliations, but returned to the Queen's side for some years before her death in 1565. She was an attractive woman with dark eyes and a lively countenance, and a powerful force on Elizabeth in her formative years.

Another was Blanche Parry, offspring of a Welsh border family (like the Vaughans and the Cecils) who had followed the Tudors into England and set themselves up as influential people who shared their good fortune. Blanche was a Renaissance woman, born in Herefordshire in 1508, who was made a lady-in-waiting while Elizabeth was still a little girl. Her second husband was Sir William Herbert, a natural son of the Earl of Pembroke, and as chief Lady of the Household she ruled the Princess' household with a firm but kindly hand. She shared with the Queen a love of beautiful clothes and jewels, and a consuming interest in books. When Kate Ashley died, Blanche succeeded her as chief gentlewoman. She became a person through whom the Queen could be approached, but without any corruption or intrigue. As well as being a royal go-between, Blanche shared with Elizabeth an interest in astrology, which passed at the time for scientific research, as exemplified by the career of Dr John Dee, the sixteenth-century scientist; but the later suggestion that her influence was damaging because it embroiled the Queen in necromancy ignores the enormous contribution made to science by Dee as a mathematician, geographer and navigator.

In 1587, Blanche, whose eyesight had been failing for some time, eventually went blind, and handed over her duties to Mary Radcliffe, a cousin of the Earl of Sussex, on whose impartial advice the Queen relied almost as much as she did on the Cecils. Mary was as dependable as he was, and gave many years' loyal service to the Queen, taking over the stewardship of the royal jewels, and sharing her interests in beautiful things – such as the carpets and rugs and other rich gifts bestowed by Ivan the Terrible on Elizabeth when Sir Jerome Horsey returned from his mission to Moscow in 1573. Mary was sometimes called the Queen's 'merry guardian' because of her social graces and her kind heart – it was she who even attempted (at Essex's request) a reconciliation between Essex and Elizabeth in the 1590s, though not so much because she felt sorry for him as because she thought that a meeting might thaw the Queen's frosty feelings for her former favourite. Mary outlived the Queen, and like her royal mistress died unmarried. She wound up her care of the royal jewels by making an inventory of them after Elizabeth's death, but so disliked the level to which the court sank after James I's accession that she retired from it altogether.

Among Elizabeth's other female friends and confidantes were the wife, sister and daughters of Henry Carey. One of the Queen's first actions was to grant him the manor of Hunsdon in Hertfordshire, previously owned by her great-grandmother, the Countess of Richmond, and to make him a Baron. Lady Hunsdon was a close friend of Elizabeth, as was his sister Catherine, the wife of Sir Francis Knollys. His daughters, Philadelphia and Catherine Carey, were chosen as Gentlewomen of the Privy Chamber and remained so until the Queen's death in 1603. Catherine (or 'Cate' as the Queen called her) was a gay, light-hearted woman and a bit of a tomboy in her youth. Later she married Charles Howard who became Lord Admiral, and Lord Howard of Effingham, at the time of the Spanish Armada. She later became Countess of Nottingham when her husband acquired the title of Earl, and it was her death, only a few days before Elizabeth's own, that was said to have hastened the Queen's end. Philadelphia was also in the Queen's inner circle, both before and after her marriage to Thomas, Lord Scrope. She sat with the Queen as she lay dying, and interpreted her signs, when she was beyond speech, that Archbishop Whitgift should continue his prayers.

Another staunch friend who shared this last vigil was Anne, Lady Warwick. She was Leicester's sister-in-law, being the wife of his brother Ambrose. Anne was the daughter of the Earl of Bedford and much younger than Ambrose. When the couple were married in 1565 the Queen laid on lavish entertainment at the Palace of Whitehall; she took care not to allow her feelings towards Leicester to colour her attachment to his kinsfolk, any more than she bore resentment for quarrels that had taken place over her mother while she was still an infant. Anne spent forty years in close attendance on the Queen; she shared her love of sport and when the plague visited London she supervised the move to Windsor, where she and Elizabeth spent much time in hunting and hawking. When Ambrose died in 1589 she lived with her sister Margaret, Countess of Cumberland, and together brought up Anne Clifford, Margaret's daughter. Both were patrons of Edmund Spenser, who celebrated his attachment to them in his poetry. After the Queen's death they both retired from court, both of them finding the company of James I uncouth and vexatious.

Lady Warwick's sisters, Mary and Catherine Dudley, were also among Elizabeth's friends. Mary was the wife of Henry Sidney, a Gentleman of the Bedchamber and a close friend of Edward VI. She was a sweet and agreeable lady, and resisted all the efforts of her kinsman Leicester to use his family connections to further his suit for the Queen. Mary remained staunchly loyal to Elizabeth even in 1562 when the Queen caught smallpox. She remained with her and nursed her, even though she caught the disease herself and carried the disfigurement with her to the grave. Catherine, Mary's sister, also spent many years as a Lady of the Bedchamber and an intimate friend of the Queen. Their intimacy continued even when Catherine married Henry Hastings, heir to the Earl of Huntingdon, who was descended through the Countess of Salisbury from the Duke of Clarence.[1] But the Queen harboured no such defensive reservations as her father, and found Catherine loyal enough to be exempted from any suspicion – and in any case, the Huntingdons were childless.

Apart from Englishwomen, the Queen counted also among her close friends a number of foreign ladies, the most notable of whom was Helena von Snakenborg, a young Swedish girl of only fifteen when she came to England in 1564, but who turned out to be one of her most devoted friends.[2] The auburn Helena, whose hair-colouring the Queen admired (it reminded her of her own), stayed behind when her royal mistress went home to Sweden. She had formed an amorous attachment to William Parr, Marquess of Northampton, who was a member of the Queen's Privy Council and (after a brief flirtation with the Lady Jane Grey episode in 1553) a kind of uncle to the young Elizabeth. Northampton seems to have been equally avuncular to the youthful Helena, though it was not until 1571 that he actually married her. But six months later he was dead. All the same her new rank (the Queen called her 'my good Lady Marquess') kept her securely lodged in England, and she became a Lady of the Bedchamber, and often deputised for her mistress at dinners and christenings, of which there were a great many, the Queen being fond of children and of good food, and soon received lands and riches on her own account. In 1577, Helena married again, this time to Sir Thomas Gorges, who was one of the Grooms of the Privy Chamber, and later served as Ambassador to Sweden with his new wife. The Gorges bought Longford estate in Wiltshire, and later built Longford Castle there. Both of them outlived the Queen and attended her funeral;

indeed, Helena lived to a ripe old age and did not join her husband in Winchester Cathedral until 1635.

What influence did these friends and allies have on the reign of Queen Elizabeth? More than perhaps a man, Elizabeth was often a lonely woman in her elevated social position, and, surrounded by fawning flatterers and self-seeking courtiers, yearned for some human company she could trust. Her father and mother and all Henry's other wives were dead, her half-brother died when he was still in his teens, and her half-sister Mary, her reign marred by religious extremism and marital unhappiness, was dead too; she really had very few close relations left. So the circle of friends the Queen gathered about her provides a strong clue to the sort of people she felt she had need for. They were nearly all clever, versatile, witty, well-read, artistic, and high-spirited; above all, they were *disinterested*, and did not pursue their own private agendas. The Queen was herself highly strung, and needed an atmosphere in which she could relax from the worries and fatigues (and even dangers) of her endless work and sink back into the domestic comfort of a normal household. These women provided such a background, and she could trust them not to intrigue against her or provoke her with disloyalty. History has her striding manfully among her soldiers at Tilbury, urging them to renewed efforts of martial gallantry; but the picture of her at rest at Windsor, following her hawks, or in the evenings at St James's Palace, sewing or playing on her virginals, also forms an important part of her royal portrait.

PART 12

LATER FAMOUS QUEENS AND RULERS

QUEEN CHRISTINA THE UNPREDICTABLE

The reign of Queen Christina of Sweden merits no more than a paragraph or so in most history books of the seventeenth century, which usually dismiss her as a loose cannon and, perhaps worse, a lightweight one as well. David Ogg says, in a book which ran into its eighth edition in 1960,[1] that she 'had all the vanity, caprice and imperiousness of Queen Elizabeth, but, unlike the English queen, she had no sense of responsibility, no patriotism and no common sense'. In fact, she was a much more interesting and complex figure than would appear from Ogg's rather sweeping dismissal.

She was born in December 1626, daughter to the Swedish warrior king Gustavus Adolphus, who fell in battle at Lützen in the Thirty Years' War in Europe in 1632. From her early childhood, she showed remarkable ability and promise. Perhaps because she was an only child, he wanted the very best for her from the beginning. In some ways she was an odd girl. She was uninhibited and outspoken, given to bouts of intrigue and prevarication and to moods of imperiousness and ruthlessness; she was careless in dress, masculine in manner – but without any hint of lesbianism.[2] Yet at the same time she had a great capacity for sustained hard work, and a strong intellectual curiosity which she combined with a deep love of art, music and the theatre. In later years she built up one of the finest art collections in northern Europe. She ruled Sweden for ten years from 1644, when she attained her majority, to 1654, when she abdicated the throne. At that point she abandoned Lutheranism, the religion of the country, in favour of Roman Catholicism and after a stay in the Lowlands finally settled in Rome, where she spent the rest of her life.

Before he died, her father gave strict instructions for her upbringing to his trusted Chancellor, Axel Oxenstjerna, regarding the Princess' education. She proved herself a stranger from female ways and mannerisms, and evinced a complete indifference to the company of women. She was a good swordswoman, an excellent shot and a fine rider. She was impervious to discomfort and hardship. She was not deliberately unfeminine; it was just that her education was not designed to bring her up as a beautiful lady, any more than was the education of other females in that epoch. She was put into the charge of three separate men: her governor, her sub-governor and her preceptor (a man called John Matthiae, who had been chaplain to Gustavus Adolphus, and whom she liked best of all). The *Riksdag* (the Swedish parliament) also had views on her education and submitted that she should receive instruction in foreign manners and customs, but that her lessons should focus particularly on those of Sweden, especially in matters of the national Lutheran faith. In fact, as was not unusual at that time, her studies centred on the classics, in Latin, where she became acquainted with a wide selection of Roman authors like Livy, Caesar, Cicero and Terence, speaking their language as well as writing it, and in Greek, where she read some of the works of Thucydides, Polybius and Plutarch. She also learned Spanish, Italian, Flemish, German (the language of her mother, Maria Eleanora of Brandenburg) and French (taught her by Matthiae). Beyond languages, she also learned arithmetic, geography and astronomy. She also made a study of politics and was devoted to heroes such as Caesar, Alexander and Cyrus the Great of Persia – but she paid little attention to the workings of the Swedish constitution, preferring its classical forerunners. Above all, it was thought extremely important to give her a solid grounding in religious instruction. But she soon proved unhappy with the teachings of Lutheranism, and grew especially restive under the long and gloomy sermons to which she was obliged to listen. As early as the age of nine, she grew to have a strong distaste for Lutheranism and a personal preference for the teachings of the Catholic Church. In philosophy she grew to prefer Epicurus and the Stoics, and Epicurus' Roman follower Lucretius, but never saw any contradiction between their pagan, materialistic teachings and those of the Roman faith.

Through her interest in music, art, the theatre and education, she also undertook the creation of a 'Court of Learning', and invited the French philosopher and scholar René Descartes to come to Stockholm, where he lived for two years, before suddenly becoming ill and dying in 1650. Her plans were thus frustrated and no Academy was ever set up in Sweden.

Christina also began early collecting works of art. In the course of the Thirty Years' War, many paintings, sculptures and other *objets d'art* were plundered in southern Germany, many of them stored in the Hradschin Palace in that part of Vienna at the time occupied by the Swedes. These were reserved for her by Königsmarck, the commander-in-chief, and were packed up and dispatched to her in Stockholm. She thus acquired nearly 500 pictures, including works by a wide variety of Italian artists such as Leonardo, Raphael, Michelangelo, Titian and Bellini, and other famous figures, too, like Dürer and Breughel. Moreover, there were books, ceramics, statues, jewels, silver, furniture and manuscripts.[3] Later she also acquired other works of art by purchase, as from the Buckingham collection. Christina's whole collection was catalogued shortly before her death in 1689. They were later dispersed among a large number of other collectors, among which may be listed the Scottish National Gallery; the National Gallery in London; Castle Howard, Yorkshire; and the Bowes Museum at Barnard Castle, in County Durham. The Queen's interest in, and commitment for, the arts goes some way to redressing the often unfavourable light in which her achievements were viewed.

Of course, Christina was interested, too, in diplomacy and politics. Coming to the throne at the age of six, she watched the old Chancellor, Axel Oxenstjerna, at work as head of government and regent for her until she came of age in 1644; even after that date, when she became full queen after her coronation, she continued with him as her chief advisor. She had her doubts, however, about the wisdom of continuing the war in the light of the heavy drain it imposed on the country's slender resources, and it was against her Chancellor's advice that she insisted on the signing of the Treaty of Westphalia ending the war in 1648. Her decision to make peace did not meet with universal approval; many put it down to her supposed defects of character. She was often presented as flippant, superficially knowledgeable, vain and a ruthless egotist; in fact she sometimes showed that this was a mistaken judgement. She had a shrewd idea of the underlying weakness of the Swedish economy, and a Machiavellian grasp of the realities of politics, with a sure eye to her own advantage. She shouldered responsibility and took decisions with astonishing assurance, and soon showed herself to be in every way her father's daughter. She was, however, in her freedom of language and her swift decisions, less strait-laced than was expected of her. Her lack of proper Lutheran solemnity gained for her a name for frivolity and godlessness, but this she almost certainly did not deserve. In two particular respects she was looked at askance: her doubtful allegiance to the Lutheran faith and her Romish tendencies; and in her scarcely concealed wish to abdicate from the Swedish throne.

It used to be thought that Christina's decision to convert to the Catholic faith led to her decision to abdicate from the throne; it now seems more likely that her decision to abdicate made possible the conversion to Catholicism that she desired. When her minority ended in 1644 she was already promised to her first cousin, Charles Gustavus.[4] As children, the two had been brought up together by Charles' mother, and had developed a boy-and-girl affection for one another; but when they met up again in 1646 she made it clear she did not love him enough to wish to marry him; indeed she seemed to suggest she would not get married at all, though she offered to make him her heir. She informed the Swedish Diet of her intentions in January 1649, and in August 1651 laid it officially before her Council. Members seemed to be apprehensive that Charles Gustavus, being six years older than Christina, might be ill-disposed towards waiting until her death for the throne, and might attempt a coup, especially since in the same month she sent a mission to Pope Innocent X indicating her intention to convert.

All these developments encouraged the growth of an opposition party to the Queen. During the Middle Ages, Sweden had been an elective rather than a hereditary monarchy; it was only with the accession of the Vasa dynasty in 1523 that possession of the crown was confirmed in the Vasa family. Even at that time aristocratic elements had objected to their exclusion from power and at the clear preference of successive Vasa sovereigns for government through 'low-born' secretaries instead of through them. They contended that the offer of the hereditary crown made by the Diet of Västerås in 1544 was a kind of *contract* (contracts at that time being a fashionable sixteenth-century philosophical concept) that held good only for as long as their government remained good. Now Christina was stepping into her father's shoes by replacing Oxenstjerna with a new 'rule of secretaries', once again excluding them.

At the same time, she could also see that the Swedish government's recent policies of alienating Crown lands in exchange for sums of money, which had so facilitated (and some would have said modernised) the conduct of the recent war, was an unwise one, since it was bound to end in the impoverishment of the Crown through the dispersal of its estates.[5] This was why, at the Coronation Diet of 1650 she was able to achieve the adoption of Charles Gustavus as her heir by putting to the three lower orders of the Estates (the clergy, the burgesses and the peasants) the urgent need to curtail noble privileges, which brought them over to support the Crown's position, and compelled noble acceptance of Charles Gustavus as heir. When she had prepared the way for Charles Gustavus' succession by securing the Diet's acceptance of her proposals, she calmly threw over her alliance with the lower orders, but achieved it by such means as retained their affection and loyalties. This adroit manoeuvring enabled her to abdicate without serious opposition in 1654.[6] Not until after the disasters of Charles X's reign would the aristocracy be in a position to dictate terms to an elected king.

Christina had now secured for herself the title she desired – the unchallengeable title of 'Queen' – and the financial maintenance for herself that she thought was fitting.[7] Now calling herself Maria Christina Alexandra, she left Sweden in 1654 disguised as a man, and eventually reached Rome, where she lived in a palazzo filled with art and books, which later became a centre of culture as a salon. She became a firm ally of the papacy in its counter-reformationary efforts to recover its old supremacy over Europe, but she was nevertheless aligned with the progressive wing of the Church, and turned her face firmly against draconian methods of reconversion. However, she was prepared for all other kinds of shady dealings – with Mazarin and even with Cromwell – to ensure her money supplies, and was ruthless in her exercise of royal rights. She even ordered the summary execution of her royal steward Monaldesco in her presence in 1656 when he betrayed her plan to become Queen of Naples to the Spanish Viceroy. In another failed scheme she tried to obtain the throne of Poland with the support of her friend and confidant Cardinal Decio Azzolino. It was this Azzolino who became her sole heir in 1669 when she died. She was buried in St Peter's Basilica – an unusual honour for a woman.

HENRIETTA MARIA: DYNASTIC FEMME FATALE OF THE STUARTS

Queen Henrietta Maria was the French princess who became the wife of King Charles I of England. Her uncompromising Catholic faith was widely believed to have been a major factor in determining Charles I's resolve to defy Parliament, and thus his fate. Her influence was held responsible for undermining the politically necessary Protestant allegiance of her sons, in turn respectively Charles II and James II, thus ensuring that they were the last kings of the Stuart dynasty. How great an impact did she have on the political history of England?

On 25 November 1609 Queen Marie of France gave birth to another daughter. The newborn princess was named Henrietta, after her father King Henry IV, and Maria, after her mother Marie de Medici, but she was not actually christened until 1614. In the meantime, her father had been stabbed to death by a mad monk in 1610, and her mother, as regent for Henrietta's brother Louis XIII, became in effect ruler of France. So Marie had little time to spare for the upbringing of her children, and anyway royal children were usually offloaded onto some trusted servant for their care and supervision. Madame de Montglat, who took charge of her, was to be a powerful influence over Henrietta long after Henrietta had left her care. She seldom saw her mother, who was busy arranging foreign alliances, and it must have been quite clear to her what her destiny was to be. Her sister Elisabeth was betrothed to a Spanish prince (later King Philip IV) and her brother, King Louis, to the Spanish Infanta. Some dynastic alliance would doubtless be in store for her.

In 1617 the queen mother lost her power and was estranged from her son Louis XIII. There was a reconciliation two years later, but the young Henrietta found it prudent to avoid taking sides between mother and brother. As early as 1620, an English marriage for Henrietta had been mooted at the French court. But James I wanted help for his daughter and son-in-law in the Palatinate and thought that he was more likely to get it from an alliance with Spain.[1] But Spain had no real intention of either marrying the Infanta to a heretic, or providing military support for another one, and contented itself with keeping the negotiations as prolonged as possible. Charles and his adviser Buckingham returned from Spain empty-handed, and, furious at Spain's prevarication, urged war with Spain. For this to be realistic England needed an alliance with France.

France proved far more amenable than Spain. Cardinal Richelieu, France's chief minister, welcomed an English alliance in view of the uncertainties of the Thirty Years' War and increasing Protestant unrest at home. He certainly did not want a hostile England to the north in alliance with a hostile Spain to the south. Even so he felt obliged to push for religious concessions from England. It was eventually agreed that, as the wife of the future king of England, Henrietta could have her own Catholic chapels, an army of Catholic servants and retainers (she brought 200 eventually) and the services of twenty-seven priests and a bishop. By a secret clause, James I promised not to enforce the recusancy laws against Roman Catholics; he could not repeal them without the consent of Parliament, and he knew that such consent would be impossible to achieve. But he promised freedom of conscience to Roman Catholics provided that they did not flaunt their religion.

Surprisingly, despite Prince Charles being a heretic, and she his second choice, Henrietta seemed keen on the match. Her enthusiasm was kindled in part by the English emissaries' over-rosy picture of England, and the impression she received from them of Charles being tall, dark and handsome. In fact he was only about 5 feet 4 inches tall. Nevertheless, Henrietta was very small, and only reached as high as Charles' shoulder, but she was generally agreed to be 'of good shape' if rather thin, a good dancer and highly intelligent. She was consoled too by the Pope's willingness to accept the marriage, even if his dispensation was partly motivated by political considerations. He told her that she must act as protectress of her co-religionists in England, a duty she was never to forget. Her preparation for her new role included intense religious brainwashing, intended to make her impervious to her new heretical surroundings, but oddly enough no one was deputed to teach her any English, a language of which she understood hardly a word.

The marriage treaty was signed in December 1624. There was little popular support for it in England, although the Londoners enjoyed the free beer and wine that accompanied its signing. It was intended that a proxy wedding should take place at the church door of Notre Dame in Paris, with the Duke of Buckingham standing in for Charles. But the death of James I in March delayed the ceremony until May, and Henrietta had to make do with one of her French relations instead of Buckingham. Many English guests attended, but nearly all ostentatiously walked away from the cathedral before the nuptial mass. A few weeks later Henrietta arrived in England, a country which she found greatly fell short of her expectations – it was cold, miserable, and relatively poor. The marriage fell short of English expectations too: Louis XIII had no intention of going to war on behalf of Frederick and Elizabeth, and Buckingham had angered Louis by making the usual nuisance of himself with the ladies, especially with Louis' wife, Anne of Austria.

The marriage got off to a bad start. Henrietta found the physical side of the marriage unpleasant and avoided it whenever she could. There were disagreements about Henrietta's entourage and Charles' determination to impose some English Protestant ladies-in-waiting on her. Buckingham assumed the role of peacemaker, but in reality he was concerned lest Henrietta begin to supplant him as Charles' chief adviser, and his efforts to conciliate proved unhelpful, and Henrietta took an instant dislike to him. Henrietta's refusal in 1626 to be jointly crowned with her husband by Protestant bishops meant that she was queen consort rather than a crowned queen. Continued marital friction exasperated Charles, who decided that Henrietta's vast French entourage was encouraging her contumacy. He therefore suddenly ordered it to leave the country. A compromise peace was eventually patched up, and Henrietta became more compliant. When Charles went to war on behalf of the Huguenots of La Rochelle she deliberately avoided taking sides, and when Buckingham was murdered in 1628 Henrietta rushed to Charles' side to console him in his agony of grief. The death of Buckingham proved a turning point. From then on Charles needed a new confidante to replace him, and his wife, who had resented Buckingham's intimacy with Charles, fitted the bill. She was now fairly fluent in English and able to engage her husband in intellectual conversation. She was also now a proper wife to Charles because a miscarriage in 1629 was followed by the birth of Prince Charles (later Charles II), Mary in 1631, James (later James II) in 1633, Anne in 1637, Catherine in 1639, Henry in 1640 and Henrietta in 1643. Of these only Charles and James lived to reach the age of thirty.

It was essential that young Prince Charles should be brought up as a Protestant and Henrietta was unable to prevent him being christened by the Dean of the Chapel Royal, William Laud. Although she knew that full toleration for Catholics would be politically impossible she did urge the King to avoid enforcing the anti-Catholic legislation as far as possible. She carefully refrained from proselytising, except among her Protestant ladies-in-waiting, but she did delight in the large numbers of the English who came to her

Catholic services. Her frequent contacts with Rome placed her under Puritan suspicion, but she had no intention of being used to bring England back into the Catholic fold, nor was she in a position to do so. And she certainly had no intention of meddling in foreign affairs apart from using diplomatic means to try to help secure peace with France in 1629; here she was not taking the initiative but simply trying to bring about the peace that both sides wanted.

She was to some extent dragged into the international arena when her mother Marie finally broke with her son Louis XIII in 1631 and went into exile. Marie blamed Richelieu for the breach, and so, in support of her mother, did Henrietta. She thus shared her husband Charles' distrust of the Cardinal. But the 1630s were on the whole Henrietta's happiest years. She enjoyed, produced and acted in many of the lavish masques that were put on for the court's entertainment. She loved theatre, music and dancing. On one occasion, she challenged a courtier to a boat race on the Thames which she won, together with a handsome wager. Her obvious enjoyment of life did not go down well with the Puritans who were growing in numbers and influence. William Prynne, so soon to be famous for losing his ears, denounced women actors as 'whores', and anti-Catholic agitation, sometimes leading to riots, was on the increase. There were certainly riots in Scotland when Charles attempted in 1637 to impose the English prayer book there. Henrietta expressed anxiety to Charles about the danger of a Scottish rebellion, which was of more concern to her than what precise form of heresy the Scots chose to subscribe to. By 1640 Scottish contumacy had led Charles to summon an English parliament after a gap of eleven years. It demanded redress of grievances before making any contribution to the royal revenue and it was promptly dissolved. Henrietta tried to raise money from English Catholics for Charles' Scottish expedition, but it raised barely a third of the amount promised and a new parliament proved as intransigent as the previous one. Puritan influence led to growing hostility towards Catholics, not specifically against Henrietta, but certainly against her mother Marie de Medici who had arrived in England with a vast retinue in 1638, and was proving an enormous drain on the royal exchequer.

The Long Parliament had major political issues to raise with the King, but it courted the support of the populace by raising the religious question. It made frequent attacks upon the growth of Catholicism at court, hinted that Henrietta was trying to convert her husband and that Archbishop Laud was Catholicising the Church of England with a view to restoring it to Rome. Some of Henrietta's adherents were summoned before the House and subjected to intimidating questioning. Henrietta made unsuccessful efforts to save Wentworth, the Earl of Strafford, both with the King and with some of the parliamentary leaders. But the dangerous riots in London alarmed Charles and forced his hand, and Strafford was executed in May 1641. So hostile had Parliament and the London mobs become that Henrietta began to fear for her own safety. In November 1641 Parliament forced her to give up her son Charles into its custody to remove him from Catholic influences. She responded by intensifying efforts to procure financial help from the Pope and from France, but Richelieu was an old enemy and the Pope would not stir unless Charles converted or promised to convert. Parliament was now unjustifiably and openly accusing her of treason in promoting the Irish rebellion, so it is not surprising that she was now urging her husband to be firm. It was widely believed that she was behind Charles' abortive attempt to arrest the five members of Parliament in January 1642; whether in fact she was proved far less important than the widespread belief that she was.

Soon afterwards, Henrietta left England for Holland whose crown prince had recently married her daughter Mary. But she got no help there; she even had great difficulty in pawning her jewels. After the outbreak of hostilities between King and Parliament, Henrietta returned to England with such funds as she had collected and landed in Yorkshire. After a brief stay in York she moved south with a Royalist army to join the King in Oxford. Henrietta believed that Charles' best chance of success lay in raising an Irish army, especially as the Scots were now openly supporting the Parliamentarians. At Oxford there was for a few months a pale imitation of the old glittering Whitehall court of the 1630s. But Henrietta was now pregnant for the final time, and it seemed safer for her leave for France.

Throughout the remainder of her husband's reign, Henrietta took on the role of his chief adviser, and furnished him with a stream of letters urging him to stand firm. Their relationship in the early years of the reign had made such a role impossible and in the 1630s unnecessary. But in the 1640s Charles was overwhelmed by conflicting advice, and Henrietta felt it essential to strengthen his resolve at such a time of crisis. From her point of view, no compromise was possible with those who would destroy the power of the monarchy. From her base in the Louvre, and supported by her sister-in-law Anne of Austria, Henrietta used all her newly forged diplomatic skills to secure help for Charles from any who would listen. But Cardinal Mazarin, who had succeeded Cardinal Richelieu in 1642, was delighted to see England removed from the international chess board by civil war, and gave her nothing but fair words. Most other countries were more concerned with the Thirty Years' War, which was closer to home, and the Pope wanted too much in religious concessions for his support. Henrietta's efforts to raise foreign armies to assist Charles were revealed in intercepted letters seized by Parliament, and helped to strengthen the popularity of Parliament's cause in England. The news of the execution of her husband in January 1649 reached Henrietta over a week later and sent her into prolonged paroxysms of grief.

Although she retired at intervals to a convent in the years that followed, her main concern was to support her son, Prince Charles now Charles II, in his efforts to secure the English throne. But her son-in-law William II of Orange in whom she had placed great hopes died suddenly in November 1650, Charles' hopes in both Ireland and Scotland came to nothing, and his English venture ended in disaster at the battle of Worcester. All Henrietta could do was to push for foreign support, but the Frondes paralysed France, and the rise of Cromwell and England's growing naval power made continental powers think twice about embarking on a risky English business. Henrietta was anxious about Charles' increasing dependence on the advice of Sir Edward Hyde and made the mistake of making an enemy of him. There was a brief period of hope when England found itself at war with both Holland and France, and Henrietta tried to persuade her youngest son Henry to convert as this would encourage Catholic powers to support the Stuart cause. But Henry resisted the intense pressure put upon him, and anyway England's peace treaties with both Holland and France included recognition of Cromwell's government and expulsion of the Stuarts. Henrietta and her daughter were allowed to stay in France but her son James was forced to leave the French army in 1656. Henrietta's influence with Charles had largely disappeared by 1655. He had been enraged by her attempts to convert Prince Henry and by her quarrel with Hyde, whose advice Charles heavily relied upon.

Since she had little political influence, Henrietta turned even more in the late 1650s to religion, and she spent much of her time at the nunnery in Chaillot and at the chateau of Colombes, which a grant from the French clergy and finance from her sister-in-law Anne of Austria enabled her to buy. By 1658, her son Charles was living in Brussels, virtually penniless. Cromwell's death in September 1658 seemed to her to be divine retribution, but politically less important than her concern over Mazarin's current intention for Louis XIV to marry a Savoy princess rather than her own daughter, Henrietta Anne. Peace between France and Spain in 1659 provided for the marriage of Louis to the current Spanish Infanta, and Henrietta's hopes were dashed.

Henrietta was surprised and ecstatic over the news from England in 1660. The restoration of the English monarchy for which she had so long worked and prayed came with surprising suddenness and virtually no bloodshed. She bombarded Charles with letters of advice, which he politely acknowledged but whose contents he deliberately ignored; Hyde was his chief counsellor. Henrietta's return to England was delayed while negotiations were concluded for Henrietta Anne (whom Charles nicknamed Minette) to marry Louis XIV's brother, Philip of Orleans. But the scandalous marriage between her second son James and Anne, daughter of Edward Hyde, infuriated her and she was anxious to get to England to sort them out. She arrived in October 1660, but gave way to Charles' urgings to reconcile herself to James' unfortunate marriage.[2] Pepys, who saw her at court, famously described her as 'a very little plainly dressed old woman' (she was only fifty-two). After a brief visit to France for her daughter Henrietta Anne's wedding, she returned to take up residence in Somerset House where her refurbishment attracted Pepys' approval but where her Catholic chapel caused public resentment.

By 1665 the tuberculosis which had been held at bay in her earlier years returned to plague her. She looked ill and thin, the English climate did not suit her, and she returned to France for good. She divided her time between Chaillot and Colombes, living the life almost of a religious recluse. When war began between France and England in 1666 Henrietta used her family influence to try to mediate, and Louis XIV made some use of her in the peace negotiations of 1667. The war interrupted her income from England and caused her a great deal of inconvenience as her letters of complaint to Charles showed. By 1669 she was increasingly ill, suffering from bouts of fever and worsening insomnia. On 10 September 1669 she died in her sleep, probably as an immediate result of excess of opiates prescribed for her insomnia. Her nephew Louis XIV financed her state funeral at St Denis, and her passing was hardly noticed in England.

James I had shown his religious ambivalence by marrying his daughter Elizabeth to a Protestant prince and his son Charles to a Catholic princess, but in doing so he laid up a store of trouble for the future. Henrietta Maria was never a major influence on her husband's policies. But she unwittingly became the hated symbol of Catholicism and despotism, and as such an important factor in bringing about the English Civil Wars. She was at her most influential during the 1640s when her main concern was not to direct specific policies but to give strength to her husband's resolve. Her son Charles was never close to his mother, and, while a French pension tied them in an unnatural alliance until 1652, Charles relied on more expert advisers. Yet the deathbed conversion of Charles II in 1685 and James II's Catholicism can both be traced to Henrietta Maria's example and influence. A Protestant queen might have saved the Stuarts; a Catholic queen was their death knell.

BESS OF HARDWICK: NOBLEWOMAN AND QUEEN-MAKER

Elizabeth Hardwick, Countess of Shrewsbury, widely known as 'Bess', was almost a legend in sixteenth-century England. Born a Derbyshire yeoman's daughter in 1520, she was fiercely successful in the highly competitive and largely men's world of Tudor England, accomplished and extremely wealthy, and perhaps the nearest thing in British history to a female kingmaker, or in her case queen-maker. Acquiring four progressively richer husbands – Robert Barlow, Sir William Cavendish, Sir William St Loe and then George Talbot, Earl of Shrewsbury – each of them dying and obligingly leaving her all his money – she was involved in the cause of Mary Stuart (Queen of Scots), actually helping her current husband on royal instructions to hold the captive queen under house arrest. Finally she hoped to put her own granddaughter Arabella Stuart on the English throne. These actions gave Bess a good deal of prominence; but they also got her into a lot of trouble.

Bess came of a rather impoverished family in north Derbyshire, and in her childhood knew what it was to go hungry. Although her father, Robert Leche, was one of the rural squirearchy, he did not live long after she was born, and left her only a small dowry in his will. She was put out to service at the tender age of twelve in the household of Sir John Douche at Codnor Castle near Ripley, and was only a little older when in 1534 she married for the first time. Her husband was Robert Barlow, a young man also in service, and even younger than she was herself. He was, however, a sickly youth and did not live long enough to consummate the marriage. His death gave the usual widow's jointure to Bess, amounting to a third of Robert's small income, but it did give her also title to a bit of land.

Bess' second husband, Sir William Cavendish, however, was over twenty years her senior. He has served Henry VIII well as one of the commissioners arranging the dissolution of the monasteries, and, like many of these officials, had come into ownership of much of the wealth the church possessed and a substantial area of monastic land. When Bess married him, she persuaded him to move from Suffolk to her native Derbyshire, where, in 1549, he bought estates in Nottinghamshire and Derbyshire, including the manor of Chatsworth. Here he embarked on building her a new home in the boggy valley of the Derwent, fringed to the east by inhospitable moorland and a few miles west of Chesterfield. Before building could start, Bess and her husband undertook the enclosure of the nearby village of Edensor (pronounced Ensor) and depopulated it, moving the whole of it comfortably out of sight about a mile away (not the last time in their lives they did this). Though the Tudor Chatsworth did not survive – apart from its imposing Hunting Tower, dating from the 1580s, on the precipitous scarp east of the house – they took the first steps towards building one of the finest country houses in northern England. Bess gained from her husband valuable experience in accounting and estate management, and these stood her in good stead in later life.

The marriage between Bess and Sir William Cavendish was by all accounts a fruitful one. In the ten years of their marriage they produced eight children of whom six survived childhood, their second son William becoming Baron Cavendish in 1605 and Earl of Devonshire in 1618.[1] However, their marriage was often tempestuous, but, as was quite usual in those days, the couple stayed together, and gradually accommodated themselves to each other's personalities. Sir William, however, became ill, and died heavily indebted in London in 1557, leaving his widow with extensive estates of land but not much in the way of disposable income. It was not long, however, before the attractive widow achieved importance in London by being appointed lady-in-waiting to the new monarch Elizabeth I, and soon was able to find herself a new husband.

In 1559 she married for the third time to another Sir William, this time Sir William St Loe, a wealthy widower who generously settled all her debts at their espousal. However, her experience at court was not all plain sailing. She was inclined to gossip. In 1561, Bess spent seven months in the Tower[2] when Elizabeth learned that she had been privy to the affairs of Lady Catherine Grey,[3] whose grandmother was the younger sister of Henry VIII – a fact which brought her close to the childless Elizabeth's throne. This Lady Catherine had secretly married the Earl of Hertford, and was by now pregnant by him. Bess declined to break this unwelcome news to the Queen, and Elizabeth, who always set a high store by loyalty, made an example of her by imprisoning her. But Bess did have a stroke of better luck when her husband died quite suddenly in 1565. As the result of a family quarrel arising from an alleged murder plot, Sir William before his death had broken off relations with his younger brother and heir, Edward, and as a result left his wife all his money and lands, including what he called his 'honest sweet Chatsworth'. This had the effect of swelling her fortunes further.

After an appropriate period of mourning, Bess returned to court to take up her old position there, and shortly afterwards married her fourth husband, George Talbot, 6th Earl of Shrewsbury. Their two families were further linked by the marriage of Mary Cavendish, Bess' twelve-year-old daughter, to Gordon Talbot, George's son, and that of Henry Cavendish, her eighteen-year-old son, to Grace Talbot, who was only eight.

The combined holdings of the Cavendish and Talbot families stretched right across the Midlands, and included Sheffield Castle, Wingfield Manor, Worksop Manor, Welbeck Abbey, Rufford Abbey, Buxton Hall and Tutbury Castle. Bess knew she was back in the royal favour when in 1569 she learned that her husband and she were to be the guardians of Mary Queen of Scots, who had fled Scotland after a skirmish at Langside and thrown herself on the mercy of her cousin Elizabeth. The trio of prisoner and two jailers were thrown into each other's company for sixteen years (1569–1585), first at Tutbury Castle in Staffordshire, and later at their other properties, Sheffield Manor, Wingfield Manor, Buxton Lodge, and even at their beloved Chatsworth. All this time Bess, an extremely jealous woman, could see for herself that Mary Stuart was very attractive; she hated the fact that Mary was forced to spend so much time with her husband, so in self-defence she took up Mary's acquaintance herself and became close to her, the pair of women spending their time in tapestry, embroidery and even simply in conversation.

Though the two women were close, there is no real evidence that Bess plotted to put Mary Queen of Scots on the English throne. Elizabeth may have thought so, but Cecil,[4] who doubtless monitored Mary's correspondence thoroughly for evidence of such a plot, never seems to have found any. Shrewsbury himself kept a close eye on Mary, and foiled more than one attempt to rescue her, as well as weeding out conspirators and spies from her numerous entourage. As time went on, both the Shrewsburys were left with a sense of grievance at their never-ending custodianship. The miserly Elizabeth had only ever paid the Earl £2,000 a year for housing Mary and her numerous household and dealing with her endless demands for comforts and necessities – and she reduced even this meagre allowance by a quarter in 1579. Bess, for her part, had, without royal consent, on one occasion moved her husband from Wingfield to Buxton to take the waters when he fell ill, and Elizabeth flew into a tantrum and threatened them both with the Tower. Only Bess' blunt assertion that she valued her husband's health more highly than her duty to the Queen seems – oddly – to have satisfied Elizabeth. Both Bess and her husband asked repeatedly to be relieved of what had become for them an expensive and irksome chore, but Elizabeth did not in fact excuse them until 1585.

Bess, meanwhile, was always anxious to establish her family's fortunes as securely as she could, and if possible bring them closer to the throne, and so had in 1574 invited Countess Lennox to Rufford Abbey with her son, Charles Stuart. He was the youngest brother of Mary's former husband Lord Darnley, who had met his death so mysteriously at Kirk o'Field in 1567. The Countess fell ill for a week at Rufford and Bess nursed her back to health. During that time Bess' daughter, Elizabeth Cavendish, was left to entertain the young man, and the two fell in love. Bess lost no time in engineering a match between her daughter and the young earl, as a result of which Elizabeth in due course gave birth in 1575 to a girl, Arabella Stuart, who through her father was a direct descendant of Henry VII, and so was second-in-line to the English throne after Mary's son James.[5]

Queen Mary Stuart was furious at the shabby way she felt she had been treated by her erstwhile friend, and relations between the two women rapidly cooled. She wrote to Cecil, passing on malicious gossip that Bess had revealed to her in confidence about the

Queen herself – how, for example, the elderly Elizabeth had flirted outrageously (and even slept) with the Duke of Anjou, the French prince who was currently wooing her – himself no oil painting – and with his servant Jean de Simier; how the loyal courtier Sir Christopher Hatton had been so embarrassed by Elizabeth's shameless fawning on the Frenchman that he had felt he had to quit the court, and how finally the ladies at court found it hard to keep straight faces at the ridiculous flattery that it was the custom to heap upon the Queen, when in fact she was so old and decrepit. Mercifully, Cecil did not show her Mary's letter (otherwise the fat would have been in the fire!) but she was aware that Bess, in her anxiety to promote the family's fortunes, and Arabella's chances of preferment, had embarked on the elaborate pretence of distracting the royal attention from her own affairs by suggesting that her own husband was still engaged in his adulterous relationship with Mary. There was even the suggestion that Mary had had a child by him! Elizabeth guessed that something was amiss, and sent for Bess and two of her sons. She forced them to kneel abjectly before her and confess that all these rumours were no more than malicious gossip. Shrewsbury naturally denied all of it, but when Bess shortly afterwards went on to accuse him of carrying on an affair with an attractive serving maid at court called Eleanor Britton, the two finally quarrelled with each other and decided to live apart. Bess angled for a reconciliation, but Shrewsbury had clearly had enough of her, and called her a 'sharp, bitter shrew'. So he went to live at Handsworth Manor, Sheffield; she returned to Chatsworth. It was not until 1585 that Shrewsbury was allowed to give up the guardianship of Mary Queen of Scots to Sir Ralph Sadler, when he confessed he was glad to have been delivered from those 'two demons', his wife and his prisoner.

In the last twenty years of her life Bess went on to extend her properties further. She bought Hardwick Old Hall at Doe Lea, near Bolsover, using some of her Chatsworth furniture to equip it. She went on later to replace the Old Hall entirely with a new one (though the Old Hall still stands next door). The new Hardwick Hall was a serious rival for Chatsworth; people commented on its fine, large, shapely windows with the phrase: 'Hardwick Hall, more glass than wall'.

The Earl of Shrewsbury died in 1590. With her own and her deceased husband's estates she was, next to Elizabeth herself, the richest woman in England. She had an income of over £10,000 a year, a sum equivalent to more than a million today. She owned iron foundries in Staffordshire, iron works and glass works near Wingfield, coal pits at Bolsover, Hardstoft and Tibshelf, whose products were carted as far as Clowne and Sheffield to be sold, and she had extensive estates in Staffordshire, Nottinghamshire and Yorkshire as well as in her native Derbyshire. Her lands were so extensive that she employed the services of seventeen estate managers to run them.

With the death of Queen Elizabeth in 1603, Bess' granddaughter, Arabella Stuart, came very close in line to the English throne. In 1604 there was a plot – the so-called Main Plot – to remove James and to put Arabella Stuart, his first cousin, on the throne. A number of influential Englishmen joined the conspiracy, including, it was believed, Sir Walter Raleigh, who had seen his colonial policies reversed and had been deprived of several of his offices as the result of the Stuart succession. The plot secured the support of the Spanish government, who saw it as a way of restoring the Catholic faith. Happily for James, the intentions of the plotters and a list of their names was given to the King by Henry Brooke, Lord Cobham, one of their number, who had been disgusted by the brazen way the new King had distributed his favours to his supporters, but now drew back from open rebellion and confessed the scheme to the King. James was able to arrest the plotters, several of whom, including Brooke himself, were executed, but three were reprieved to show how merciful the new King was. Raleigh, however, never recovered from his disgrace; he remained cooped up in the Tower until 1616, when he was allowed to head another expedition to Guiana, but was arrested and executed on his return. Arabella Stuart, the focus of the Main Plot, had been for some time under her grandmother's tutelage at Hardwick, where Bess was grooming her for her new role as queen, and at the same time angling for a suitable marriage for her, preferably to an Englishman, but even a foreigner would do if he were sufficiently distinguished. Bess was quite clear, however, that she had no wish to support the plot if it meant restoring Catholicism in England; but in any case the plot failed and Arabella was not directly implicated in it. She was able to return to James' court, still single.[6] So Bess' role as queen-maker was ultimately denied her. Bess of Hardwick died in 1608, and was buried in All Saints Church (now the cathedral) of Derby.

ANNE OF DENMARK: THE UNDERRATED QUEEN

The wife of James VI and I of Scotland and England has received short shrift from historians. She has been variously described as a 'dumb blonde' (Maurice Ashley) and 'frivolous to the last', and she was undoubtedly extravagant and fond of expensive jewellery. Her unsavoury associates would sometimes be a political embarrassment, and her conversion to Catholicism was a contributory factor to the Gunpowder Plot. Yet she was a great deal more intelligent than is usually supposed, and her political importance was not entirely negative.

Anna was born on 12 December 1574, the daughter of Frederick II, King of Denmark, and his wife Sophia. Of their seven children, Anna was the second daughter, and her eldest brother Christian was to become King of Denmark in 1588. At first Anna was brought up by her grandparents, the Duke and Duchess of Mecklenburg, but later returned to Denmark to her mother's household. From an early age she was bilingual in Danish and German, and later she learned French in order to speak the language of the Scottish court. She needed to learn English when she moved to England in 1603. Anna remained Anna until she became queen consort when she became popularly known as Anne, but she continued to sign herself as Anna throughout her life. It was during her childhood that Anne became familiar with and grew to love music, dancing and the theatre. And these were the sort of pursuits generally frowned upon by many Presbyterians in the sombre court that she was later to join in Scotland.

In keeping with contemporary custom among royals, there were plans to marry off the Danish princesses long before they reached puberty. A Scottish marriage was mooted for one of them in the early 1580s. But sovereignty over Orkney and Shetland was a problem between Scotland and Denmark, and Elizabeth I of England cast a jaundiced eye over any attempt by James VI of Scotland to get married at all. If he must marry, Elizabeth preferred him to marry the Huguenot Catherine of Navarre. The Scots, however, saw trading advantages to be gained by an alliance with Denmark, but the execution in England of Mary, James' mother, caused further diplomatic delays, and by the time a Scottish delegation arrived in Denmark in 1588, Elizabeth, the older princess, had already become engaged to the Duke of Brunswick. James had to swallow his mortification that he would not be marrying the King of Denmark's oldest daughter and would have to make do with the younger Anne instead.

The proxy marriage took place on 20 August 1589 and it required sixteen ships to accommodate Anne's splendid trousseau for the voyage to Scotland. Anne set sail two weeks later. Two exploding cannons marred her departure and tremendous storms marred the voyage. Her fleet took shelter in Norway and it was in Upslo (now Oslo) that the impatient James, who had hastened to Norway to find her, met his wife for the first time on 19 November. His expectations were surely satisfied, for Anna was nearly fifteen, and by all accounts a very attractive young lady. Hers were probably less satisfied: James was described in later life as stumpy-legged, his head was too big for his body, and his tongue too big for his mouth, so that it was often hanging out: court artists were somewhat kinder to him. But whatever scruples Anne had, she must have stifled them. With the return to Scotland delayed, the young couple had been invited to spend their honeymoon in Denmark, and it was soon reported that they were indulging in 'familiaritie (sic) and kisses', to the consternation of some of the strait-laced Scots. James was certainly not exhibiting the homosexual tendencies that were attributed to him in later life; at least marital relations appeared normal as Anne was to suffer a miscarriage a few months later.

After delaying in Denmark to attend Anne's sister's wedding, Anne and James left for Scotland and arrived on 1 May 1589 without mishap, even among the welcoming cannons. Anne's coronation took place two weeks later. At first Anne took little part in politics, and even allowed James to choose most of the Scottish ladies of her household. In 1591 Scotland and James were absorbed by the witchcraft trials, at which it was alleged, among other things, that witches opposed to the Danish marriage had stirred up the storms that prevented Anne's first journey to Scotland. Anne seemed to have shown little interest in these proceedings; she lacked the outdated superstitions and prejudices of her husband. But by 1592 she had become more politically active; she quarrelled with the Scottish chancellor, John Maitland, and she persisted in close friendship with the Earl of Bothwell, whose political unreliability seemed to be a family trait. On occasion, she defied James, and marital quarrels ensued, especially when James' desperate shortage of money led him to pawn the jewels he had given her.

Anne was further angered when James insisted that the heir to the throne (Prince Henry, born in 1594) should be brought up in the household of the Earl of Mar, as he himself had been. Those opposed to the Earl of Mar rallied to the Queen's support. Among those was William Gowrie, Earl of Ruthven, who became involved in 1600 in a rather mysterious plot to assassinate James, or at least to coerce him. Anne's close connection with the Ruthven family, and her unwillingness to dismiss the Earl's sister, Lady Beatrix, from her household was an embarrassment to her husband, especially as Anne continued a clandestine correspondence with Beatrix after the Ruthven family had been exiled. Even more embarrassing was Anne's religious conversion. When she arrived in Scotland a number of the Scottish ladies of her court were Roman Catholics, and they worshipped in private. Anne was permitted to continue in the Lutheran faith, but was expected to attend public services in the Calvinist form. She tended to avoid the lengthy sermons which accompanied them, and her private Lutheran services began to show increasing Catholic tendencies. Under the influence of Henrietta Stewart, Countess of Huntly, Anne spent increasing amounts of time at her favourite residence in Dunfermline, surrounded herself with Catholic friends, and began to adopt Catholic religious practices. This was less distasteful to James than might be expected because he was already engaged in a struggle with the more extreme Calvinists in the Scottish Church to retain bishops, and he was prepared to use Anne's Catholicism as a bargaining tool with the Pope, with English Catholics, and with those in Scotland whose strict Calvinism showed bigoted religious intolerance.

In their final years in Scotland, James allowed Anne, with her own chosen advisers, to tackle the royal debts, a task in which she showed administrative skill, if not complete success. Then in March 1603 came news of Queen Elizabeth's death, and James' accession to the throne of England. James hastened south, but Anne was pregnant, and delayed her departure until June, having in the meantime won a battle with the Earl of Mar for custody of Henry, the heir to the throne. English Catholics had sought out James in Scotland before Queen Elizabeth's death to try to secure a promise from him to relax England's anti-Catholic laws. It suited James to give them some hope, so that his accession to the English throne was greeted with universal enthusiasm. English Roman Catholics believed that surely a king with a Catholic wife would honour his half-given promises. But the English government was alarmed at the open and growing manifestations of Catholicism, and believed that they posed a threat to the security of the state. It insisted on renewed enforcement of the anti-Catholic laws to the letter, and James' popularity with the Catholics plummeted. The government sought to frighten James into acquiescence in 1605 by fostering the Catholic plot to blow up the English Houses of Parliament as the opening move in a Catholic takeover of the English government. The plot had virtually no chance of success, but it was sufficient to alarm James, and all talk of concessions to the Catholics ceased. Anne found it convenient not to flaunt her religion, although she still continued to practise it.

Within three years of becoming Queen of England, Anne had experienced her last pregnancy. Her several miscarriages, and the deaths of several children before they reached adulthood, had profoundly affected both parents, and after the death of daughters Sophia in 1606 and Mary in 1607 Anne and James refused to attend funerals. From this time marital relations seem to have ceased, and although James and Anne remained in a reasonably cordial relationship, his obsession with male favourites had begun by 1609. Domestic sorrow seemed to make Anne more determined to insist on her royal prerogatives and status. She was described by the Venetian ambassador in 1607 as being 'full of kindness for those who support her ... but terrible, proud and unendurable to those she dislikes'. She greatly disliked Robert Carr, Earl of Somerset, who had become the King's favourite. She disliked even more Sir Thomas Overbury, Carr's great friend, who, she believed, had behaved insolently towards her. She supported those who sought to replace Carr with the young George Villiers, although she did have the prescience to observe that Villiers was full of his own importance and would become a law unto himself.[1] Getting rid of Carr was probably a useful service to her country, but the choice of his replacement turned out to be questionable.

Anne had two main interests other than politics. One was her encouragement of the arts. The masque, with its drama, singing and dancing was the principal entertainment at court, and Anne promoted several of these, including four by Ben Jonson. These masques incurred the wrath of the Puritans for their supposed frivolity, and Anne's performing in some of them compounded their sinfulness. She had her own company of actors who presented plays at court, and helped to foster the widespread belief that the court was preoccupied with self-indulgence. Nor did her love of music meet with Puritan approval; Puritans tended to think of music as the work of Satan, and Anne was a performer on viol, lute and virginals. She lavished money on masques and music, but also on the art collection which she began, and which was to form the basis of Charles I's great art collection. She chose with great care and discernment, but her considerable use of royal revenue for buying great works of art incurred much contemporary criticism.

Her other interest was in helping to arrange suitable marriages for the royal children. Not unnaturally she tended to want Catholic marriages for them. Various Catholic countries showed an interest and sent negotiators to London. No sooner were Anne and James installed in England than Anne was scheming for a marriage between Henry (aged ten) and the Spanish Infanta. Nothing came of it, and Anne turned her attention to pairing off Princess Elizabeth with the Duke of Savoy, but James showed one of his occasional fits of firmness by refusing to allow it. The sudden death of Prince Henry in November 1612[2] devastated the parents, but negotiations had already begun for an engagement between Elizabeth and the Protestant Elector Palatine. Anne was noted to have 'no great grace nor favour to this match', but she did not sulk for long and attended the wedding in February 1613.[3] She now turned her attention to finding a suitable bride for Prince Charles, at first favouring a Spanish match. But Anne's brother, Christian IV of Denmark, preferred a French match for his nephew, not wanting to risk an increase of Habsburg influence in Germany. By the time of Anne's final illness in 1619, no firm decision had been made, and Charles, now almost twenty, was still unmarried.

Anne's life in England had been plagued by ill-health. She endured gynaecological problems from 1606, and chest illnesses weakened her. In 1613 she made her first trip to Bath in search of a cure. By 1615 she was suffering from dropsy. She was so ill by September 1618 that she was unable to leave Hampton Court, and on 2 March 1619 she died there overcome by dropsy and tuberculosis. James gave her a funeral for which no expense was spared, and Anne was buried in Westminster Abbey.

Anne was not merely a meek consort. She had more backbone than her husband James, more artistic interests, and in some ways more political sagacity, particularly when it came to choosing advisers. James may have been dubbed 'the wisest fool in Christendom', but Anne was wise without being foolish. She usually gave James good advice which he did not always heed, although until her final years, when James became obsessed with royal favourites, he had tended to rely on her a lot. She was not always so skilful in choosing her own friends as advising James on the choice of his. Her change of religion caused problems and helped to motivate the foolish Gunpowder Plotters, as well as inclining Prince Charles towards a Catholic marriage. But she was not a catalyst for the Civil War; the main responsibility for that lay with others.

CATHERINE OF BRAGANZA AND THE MARRIAGE TREATY OF 1661

Catherina Henrietta, daughter of John IV, Duke of Braganza, and sister of the imbecilic King Alfonso VI of Portugal, was married in May 1662 to Charles II of England in accordance with the provisions of the Anglo-Portuguese marriage treaty signed in Whitehall the previous June. This treaty was intended to produce a renewed friendship between England and Portugal and held the promise of the substantial dowry of two million cruzados *for the English king, extensive privileges for English merchants trading with Portugal and its colonial empire, and the future gain of Bombay in India and Tangier in North Africa for England, in return for the promise of English ships and troops for the defence of Portugal. This treaty proved to be of little real value to the Portuguese but of substantial importance both for the English king's finances and for the future of the English colonial empire in India.*

England and Portugal had been allies since the fourteenth century. The services of the English contingent at the battle of Aljubarrota in 1385 had been more than repaid by the contribution of Portuguese galleys a few years later to the English fleet in their struggle against a superior Castilian navy. But by the sixteenth century, England was a bigotedly Protestant country and Portugal devotedly Roman Catholic – witness the fact that the Jesuit movement was powerful and popular in Portugal while it was banned in England during the Reformation on penalty of death. All the same, both remained, for different reasons, deeply hostile towards Spain. So, though their differences continued, the alliance continued in the sixteenth century and was also was renewed in 1642 by the Stuart monarchy, and even by the Puritan government of Cromwell in 1654 and also in 1661.

News of a marriage alliance was received with more enthusiasm in Portugal than it was in England. The Portuguese were not keen to lose Tangier, which they had held against Moorish attack since 1471, but welcomed the possibility of English support against Spain, and hoped also that it would give them some respite in their long struggle against Dutch depredations in the colonies. The English were marginally relieved to know that the agreement would ease their sovereign's financial difficulties, but had hoped he would marry some handsome German princess[1] instead; likewise, while there was little or no opposition in Parliament, the acquisition of Tangier or Bombay does not seem to have been greeted with much enthusiasm. Charles' own enthusiasm dwindled, too, when the Portuguese found difficulty in raising the necessary finance for the dowry at the time of the handing over of Tangier. They offered little more than half of the first instalment, and much of that only in promissory notes on future trading cargoes and in bills of exchange; indeed by 1668 only £160,000 had reached the English Exchequer, and the rest was not settled until 1680. All the same the King went to meet her on her arrival at Portsmouth in May 1662, and there the marriage went ahead. However, they slept separately that night, and he confided to his journal:

> I went into my wife's chamber who I found in bed ... it was happy for the honour of the nation that I was not put to the consummation of the marriage last night for I was so sleepy having slept but two hours on my journey, that I am afraid that matters would have gone very sleepily ...

At the same time he expressed modest satisfaction with his new bride:

> Her face is not so exact as to be called a beauty, and nothing in her face that in the least degree can shock one; on the contrary she has as much agreeableness in her looks as ever I saw, and if I have any skill in physiognomy she must be as good a woman as ever was born, her conversation is very good for she has wit enough and a most agreeable voice ... in a word I think myself very happy, for I am confident our two humours will agree very well together.

She was a well-educated, intelligent young woman, nicely spoken and not without humour. Her portrait, too, shows her to have been dark-eyed, full-lipped and with fine white shoulders and long black hair in falling ringlets, wearing a fine silk off-the-shoulder gown and looking a little pensive and cautious, though not bad-tempered. She was a rather lonely twenty-four-year-old, marooned in a foreign country with almost none of her compatriots.

So she felt very insecure in England at the beginning, and a witness of her state entry into London commented that she looked like a prisoner at a Roman triumph. And she had to endure also many trials and tribulations at her faithless husband's hands. He forced her to receive the infamous Lady Castlemaine almost immediately, and later there were

Barbara Villiers, Duchess of Cleveland, Louise de Kérouaille, Duchess of Portsmouth, and a string of at least five others. He sent Catherine's ladies-in-waiting back to Portugal – they were old-fashioned in their dress and very plain – and picked others more agreeable to his royal eye. All the same, Catherine loved him from the very first as she felt she should, and seems to have felt for him quite a passionate devotion (in spite of the fact that the marriage was fruitless – all three of her children were stillborn). Pepys saw her riding with Charles in St James' Park in 1664, and commented: 'she looked well in a white laced waistcoat and a crimson short pettycoat, and her hair long, and dressed *à la négligence*'. The King was all eyes for her, said Pepys, ignoring, for once, Lady Castlemaine.

In time, the young Queen schooled herself to tolerate her consort's succession of mistresses, and to endure, without becoming in the least contaminated by it, the licentious atmosphere of the court and the ribald reputation of 'Chuck the Lad', as his vulgar admirers called him – but the process was a long and rather painful one for a simple, but loyal, spouse.

Nevertheless, Charles repeatedly rejected any suggestion – as from the pro-Spanish Lord Bristol – that he should divorce her; he rebuffed his chief minister Lord Shaftesbury, too, when he suggested that he should 'put her by' on grounds of her sterility. At the time of the 'Popish Plot',[2] when anti-Catholic sentiment reached unparalleled heights, he flatly declined to reject his Queen by reason of her religion. It was she who played a part in his later, and clandestine, conversion to Catholicism. Charles may have treated her shabbily throughout their married life, but she repaid him in true Christian fashion by doing her best to save his soul by bringing him back to the true faith. And, despite her frequently unpleasant experiences in England, she eventually came to like the country. She also proved a good friend to England when, after the death of her husband, she returned to Portugal in 1692, following the Glorious Revolution, when she became regent for her young brother Pedro II. Her influence over her own government was exerted in favour of alliance with England in the early stages of the War of Spanish Succession,[3] and continued until her death in 1705.

QUEEN CAROLINE:
THE POWER BEHIND THE THRONE

Queen Caroline of Ansbach was the wife of George II, King of England. She was widely believed by contemporaries to have greatly influenced his decision-making, and to have been largely responsible for raising Sir Robert Walpole to be Prime Minister, and for maintaining him in power when George's inclination was to get rid of him. Modern historians have differed from this view, and argue that Caroline's importance has been greatly exaggerated. Which view does the evidence support?

Wilhelmina Caroline was born in Ansbach, south Germany on 1 March 1683. Her father was Johann Friedrich, Margrave of Brandenburg-Ansbach, and her mother was his second wife Eleanore. Her mother was widowed in 1686 and in 1692 the family moved to Saxony when Eleanore married its Elector. On her mother's death in 1696 Caroline moved to Brandenburg whose Elector was her guardian. Eleanore became very close to Sophia the Electress, and was a vital part of the glittering court which Sophia found it necessary to have, especially once Brandenburg became the kingdom of Prussia in 1701, with Sophia as its first queen. Here Caroline received very little education, but she came into frequent contact with artists, musicians and intellectuals, one of whom was Leibniz the philosopher and historian. He was to remain a close friend until his death in 1716.

Caroline grew up to be widely acclaimed for her beauty and her intellect, and she came under pressure to marry the Archduke Charles, later Emperor Charles VI. But she did not take kindly to Jesuit instruction and refused to abandon her Lutheranism to promote the match. In the meantime she had been seen and much admired at the Prussian court by George Augustus, the Electoral Prince of Hanover, who refused to consider any other choice of bride. No sooner had the Habsburg match fallen through in 1705 than he married her in September of that year. Their first child Frederick Louis was born in 1707. George's devotion was soon tested when his bride fell ill with smallpox and then pneumonia, and he attended her personally throughout her illnesses. After 1707 Caroline had seven more children of whom the last was Louisa in 1724.

At the time of her marriage, Caroline would have been aware of her husband's destiny. Queen Anne had lost her last surviving child in 1700, and an Act of Parliament had settled the succession on James I's granddaughter Sophia. She was Hanover's dowager Electress, and the grandmother of Caroline's husband George. Sophia took a special interest in Caroline and began grooming her for her eventual role as Queen of England. Caroline started corresponding with a few of the most important ladies of England's aristocracy, in French, as her English was not yet good enough. She made progress in English, eventually being able to speak it but not fluently, and she could never write accurately in any language. Her letters in English were taken care of by Mrs Howard, Caroline's great friend. Her first political venture was to try to persuade her husband to visit England in the dying days of Queen Anne's reign to build up support for the Protestant succession. But Elector George would not give his son permission and the proposal came to nothing.

By 1714 Sophia had reached the advanced age of eighty-four and a rush for shelter during a heavy shower proved too much for her; she collapsed and died in Caroline's arms. Caroline's father-in-law, the Elector, was now heir to the English throne, and succeeded to the kingdom as George I on the death of Queen Anne a few weeks later. Both Georges, father and son, left for England in September and Caroline followed a month later, but was forced to leave young Frederick in Hanover. This was to maintain the fiction that George was not abandoning Hanover for better pastures in England. And in a sense it was not abandonment because George I spent much of his reign in Hanover leaving Prince George as regent.

George I's frequent absences and his intense dislike of social life left Caroline and Prince George to fill the gap. They patronised opera and the theatre, they took walks in the royal parks, they regularly and publicly attended church as if to emphasise their Protestantism and rejection of the Stuart Catholic faith. They gave their patronage and support to the composer George Frederick Handel who had written works for Caroline in Hanover, and could now in England be properly financed. In 1717 there occurred a rift between father and son. Prince George resented his father's neglect to consult him on important matters of state, and joined with the opposition in publicly opposing the Peerage Bill which would have limited the Crown's power to create new peers, and in effect inhibit a new king from changing his ministers on his accession. King George was furious with Caroline for her strong support of her husband, but nevertheless tried to use Caroline to broker a peace with the prince. Caroline entered into negotiations with Sir Robert Walpole, a former minister who was now prepared to back the King on Walpole's own terms. These negotiations sowed the seed of Caroline's admiration for and friendship with Walpole.

In the early years of George I's reign Caroline played an important role in Church patronage in which her father-in-law had little interest. She secured the appointment of her own nominee as Archbishop of Canterbury and was influential in the choice of other bishops. Her involvement in patronage diminished somewhat after the family rift in 1717, but revived again after her husband's accession in 1727 as George II. Of the thirteen bishops appointed between 1727 and 1737, Caroline was directly involved in the selection of eight of them; she was well aware, not only of their religious role, but also of their membership of the House of Lords and their political importance. In the days when royal favour was vital to political success the change of sovereign alarmed Walpole, who had in effect been England's Prime Minister for six years.[1] He had at one time been allied with Prince George in opposition but had made his peace with George I. George II distrusted him, believing that Walpole had secured a royal family reconciliation in 1720 largely for his own political ends. But on his accession George II found that there was no politician who could effectively manage the House of Commons better than Walpole and the only possible rival, Sir Spencer Compton was notoriously inadequate and incompetent. Even so, it was Caroline who reconciled the reluctant George to keeping Walpole in office, and it was her unflinching support for Walpole that persuaded George to retain him during the political crises of the reign.

Throughout the crisis over the Excise Bill in 1733[2] Caroline urged the King to stand by Walpole. A result of this was the deflection of the anti-Hanoverian agitation from George to her, as in the rhyme ostensibly addressed to the King, but which concludes: 'We know 'tis Queen Caroline, not you, that reign.'

The crisis of 1733 brought Walpole's political enemies, old and new, out of the woodwork; his political position was no longer so secure, and the opposition was more vociferous. Young Prince Frederick was nineteen in 1736, and beginning to feel that he should be given more responsibility. In that year, when George was away in Hanover, he quarrelled with his mother over her conduct of the regency and began colluding with the opposition. He did not attack his father directly but used Caroline as a foil through which to criticise the King's government and its policies. To her, Frederick's conduct threatened the stability of the government and possibly even the Hanoverian succession itself. She thought Frederick showed her scant respect, and his brusqueness and rudeness served to exacerbate his political naivety. She was so enraged that she vilified her son in public, on one occasion wishing that 'the ground would open up and sink the monster to the lowest hole in hell'.

Caroline died on 20 November 1737 as a result of a rupture that surgeons had been unable to deal with successfully. She told George, as she lay dying, that he must marry again. Frederick did not come to her bedside. Walpole was grief-stricken, not only for the loss of such a dear friend, but also for fear of the effect of her death on his own political position, and indeed Walpole's pre-eminence became increasingly shaky during his remaining five years of office. Caroline had not only strengthened the dynasty, but through collaboration with Walpole she had also helped to strengthen the stability of Parliament. In the absence of effective political parties, patronage was the oil which made Parliament work and Walpole used Caroline not only for ecclesiastical patronage, but also to help strengthen his grip on lay lords and MPs. Also, in collaboration with Walpole, she had persuaded George II to keep out of the War of Polish Succession; he had felt quite strongly that it was in Hanover's interest to join the war, but she insisted that a continental war would seriously damage England's trade and prosperity. So her influence was not confined to domestic politics. Her passion for landscaping and gardening was eagerly followed by many of the aristocracy and limited the time they could spend making mischief in politics. Her patronage of some contemporary artists and composers often lacked discrimination, apart from her love of Handel, but her preservation and expansion of the royal portfolio of Old Masters was to lay the foundations of the great royal art collection of her son Frederick and her grandson George III. Caroline's influence was many-faceted, and men of influence often consulted her before consulting the King on matters artistic, religious and political. George II had great trust in her political wisdom, and felt her death as not only a personal loss, but also a political one. On the whole the judgement of Caroline's contemporaries who knew her carries more weight than the assessment by twentieth-century historians who dismiss her.

PRINCESS MATHILDE: EMPRESS MANQUÉE OF THE SECOND EMPIRE

According to Caroline Murat, niece of Princess Mathilde, her aunt would have made a far better Empress of the French during the reign of Napoleon III than ever did Eugénie de Montijo, the Spanish noblewoman the Emperor married in 1853.[1] Whether this estimate of Princess Mathilde's importance is a valid one, or whether no more than family approval of her worth by her near relatives, there is no real way of knowing.

Princess Mathilde[2] was born in May 1820 in Trieste, daughter of Jerome, former King of Westphalia and the youngest brother of Napoleon Bonaparte. Louis Napoleon, who later achieved eminence for the role he played in French affairs, was the son of another brother Louis, French King of Holland, and thus her first cousin. Jerome, badly strapped for cash, lived in straitened circumstances, adopting the title of Prince de Montfort; his wife was Catherine, daughter of Frederick of Würtemburg, who spent much of her royal fortune on him. Mathilde was brought up in Rome, within a stone's throw of Madame Mère, Napoleon's mother, in the Piazza Venetia. Every Sunday she met Hortense, daughter of the Empress Josephine and wife of the very trying Louis Bonaparte, and sometimes his surviving son Louis Napoleon, a young man twelve years older than herself. She was never allowed to forget that she was Napoleon's niece; her home was virtually a museum dedicated to his memory. In 1831 the family moved to Florence. Matilde's mother died in 1835, and her aunt Hortense invited her to Arenenberg, Louis' chateau on the shores of Lake Constance. Here, at the age of fifteen, she began a long association with Louis Napoleon, then a young man of twenty-seven.

The two were not exactly in love, but he was drawn to her, and she, a very self-possessed young lady, flirted with him and won his parents round to the idea of a match. It was about a year later that she left Arenenberg. Louis gave her a ring set with a turquoise forget-me-not and a locket containing a lock of his hair; then, in 1840, he went off to Boulogne to stage a comic-opera *coup*[3] against Louis Philippe, was arrested and exiled to America for his pains. Jerome told her in no uncertain terms to break off her engagement; she, ever the obedient daughter, did so, and in 1840 married Anatole Demidoff, an incredibly rich young Russian with estates in the Urals containing immense deposits of iron ore, platinum and silver (though he himself was only descended from a blacksmith). Jerome utilised his son-in-law's wealth to solve his own financial problems – graver after his wife's death – and Mathilde saw it as a chance to escape provincial exile and to establish herself in Paris. The young couple, however, did not get on,[4] and in 1846 Mathilde appealed to Tsar Nicholas I to agree to arrange a divorce for her. Her separation was a generous one: she kept all her jewels and was allotted an annuity of 200,000 francs. She made the acquaintance of Alfred-Émilien, Comte de Nieuwerkerke, and moved into a small *hôtel* he found for her in the rue de Courcelles. But her new acquaintance was scarcely more prepossessing than her former husband; he was indolent, frivolous, unreliable and shallow. But she fell in love with him and he helped her to establish a successful salon, and she soon brought the world of the arts to the door of No. 10, Rue de Courcelles.

In 1848 Louis Napoleon returned to France after the revolution that overthrew Louis Philippe. Mathilde pawned her jewellery in an effort to help him in his campaign to win the presidency of the Second Republic; she even contemplated leaving Nieuwerkerke and trying to win Louis' affections once again. But she thought better of it. Louis Napoleon became President in 1850; he staged another coup in 1851[5] against the Second Republic and set himself up as Emperor Napoleon III by a plebiscite almost a year later in November 1852.

In 1853 the Emperor married a Spanish noblewoman, Eugénie de Montijo, and Mathilde had to content herself with her second-rate husband and her splendid new salon, a little further along the Rue de Courcelles at No. 24, given to her by the new Emperor, in which for nearly twenty years she ruled the literary and artistic life of Paris. Here you might meet Baron Haussmann, formidable Préfet de la Seine who created the Second Empire Paris, Alfred de Musset, the elder Alexander Dumas, Saint-Saëns, Gounod, Théophile Gautier, Flaubert, and many others. Her alter ego, Charles-Augustin de Sainte-Beuve, a magisterial figure in French intellectual life, gave her great help in creating a calendar of national artists of all kinds; he introduced her also to members of the intelligentsia closer to the centres of real power – Renan, the Goncourts, Ferdinand de Lesseps, Pasteur and senators and generals of all kinds. Mathilde herself was no intellectual, but she was a warm, possessive woman of great charm and éclat who remained for almost two decades one of the central figures of the Empire.

She broke with Napoleon III only over the Franco-Prussian War, when she advised him strongly against the challenge[6] and begged her ailing cousin not to take command and not to go to the front. She felt sure the war could have been avoided, and confided to Caroline Murat: 'If I had been Empress we should not have lost Alsace and Lorraine.' Her views were frank and unorthodox, her assessment of the role of Empress Eugénie bitterly critical – she thought Eugénie did more than anybody to encourage the conflict.[7] In the end she broke with her cousin in a scene of remarkable violence, and abandoned him to his fate.

She fled to Brussels in the dark days of the Siege of Paris and the Commune, returning only in 1872 to set up a new salon in the Rue de Berry. She remained 'Notre Dame des Arts' under the Third Republic and did not die until 1904.

QUEEN VICTORIA: QUEEN OF GREAT BRITAIN AND EMPRESS OF INDIA

At present, Victoria is most remarked for being Britain's longest-serving monarch. Just eighteen at her accession to the throne, she reigned for sixty-four years until her death in 1901, during which time enormous changes took place in British society, and in Britain's world position. In the middle part of her reign she excited some criticism because of her behaviour after the death of her beloved Albert, when she was regarded as being stiffly distant and unapproachable, as well as humourless ('We are not amused' – an observation she always stoutly denied ever having made); but the very length of her reign, and the fact that she was the head of perhaps the most extended and influential ruling family in the world at the time, meant that she also enjoyed considerable respect, both in Britain and internationally. She survived the often vociferous sentiment of republicanism in the early years of her reign, and laid the lasting foundations of the pro-royalist sentiment that flourished in the twentieth century. What is less well known is that she was possessed of a sharp line in repartee, and a considerable though completely untutored gift of mimicry. She also sometimes surprised her hearers by her loud explosions of boisterous laughter. She remained a passionate and sensitive woman, with finely honed artistic sensitivity, and capable of great loyalty and devotion to those to whom she was attached; and, although these feelings may have been somewhat blunted in her later years, she nevertheless remained a deeply affectionate parent and grandparent to the end of her days.

Alexandrina Victoria, born in 1819, was the product of an essentially loveless marriage between Prince Edward, Duke of Kent (1767–1820), and Victoire of Saxe-Coburg-Saalfeld (1786–1861), the highly ambitious widowed dowager princess of Leinigen, a German minor royal house. Edward was the third surviving son of George III after the Prince of Wales (later Prince Regent and then George IV on the death of his father in 1820) and William, Duke of Clarence (later William IV). Her birth was the result of the unseemly race to the throne after the death of the Prince Regent's wife, Princess Charlotte in childbirth in 1817 when Clarence, Kent and even Cumberland (the youngest son of poor mad old George), put aside their cards, their dice and their assorted German mistresses in their efforts to produce an heir. 'Drina' was, quite naturally, the apple of her father's eye. He said of her to his admiring courtiers: 'Look upon her well, for she will be Queen of England!' It was, however, perhaps fortunate that the two were never really close. Kent was a sadistic man with a vicious temper and few scruples; but he died when Drina was still only a babe-in-arms, and left her isolated and lonely. She had no contact with other children of her age; she scarcely knew her half-brother and sister, Karl and Anne, the earlier children of her mother. Uncle Leopold, her mother's brother, stayed in London for some time to help look after her mother, and became an object of her childish affection; but in 1831 he became King of Belgium and moved out of her life.

For the first eighteen years of her life, therefore, she was left exposed to the scheming ambition of her mother, and to Charles Conroy, a would-be Irish gentleman and adventurer, to whom the duchess became attached after her husband's death. Both regarded Drina as their meal-ticket to a life of political influence and indolent luxury. On the way to it, the young princess was bullied, snubbed and humiliated at every turn; she even slept in her mother's bedroom until she was eighteen as a means of insulating her from outside influences. Apart from her mother and the grasping Conroy, the only other people she came into contact with were her governess, Louise (later Baroness) Lehzen, and her tutor, the Reverend George Davys, both of whom educated her solidly, if not brilliantly well. After his succession in 1830, William IV's health as king was not good, and clearly the Duchess entertained hopes of becoming her regent if William died before Drina became eighteen.[1] King William, who was aware of the momentous nature of the young princess' calling, and hoped to advise and influence her in appropriate ways, was even more disturbed by the Duchess' possessiveness towards Drina, than he was enraged at her studied rudeness to his own wife, Queen Adelaide. But any advice or guidance from her caring uncle, the Duchess resolutely refused to countenance. When the princess was seventeen he quarrelled openly and publicly with her mother in 1836, telling her 'I trust my life will be spared nine months longer. I should then have the satisfaction of leaving the royal authority to the personal exercise of that young lady, and not in the hands of the person now near me.'

All this could not but help frighten and overawe the young Victoria. She grew up a solemn, solitary young woman well able to keep her own counsel, and disinclined to give her full affection to anyone. She is said to have been completely kept in the dark about her own future prospects, and only to have learned of her destiny through her personal reading. Likewise she is said to have promised, to Lehzen, that she would 'try to be good'. She certainly made a favourable impression on Lord Melbourne when he first encountered her, still in her dressing-gown, on the morning after her uncle's death, as she did on the rest of her ministers when she appeared at her first ministerial meeting in 1837. She was young, intelligent, dignified and apparently well aware of what was expected of her as monarch even then. She looked up to and admired her Whig Prime Minister, Lord Melbourne, whose avuncular manner appealed to her young and feminine side; the fatherless Victoria always looked to strong men to mentor her. But she loved her newfound independence. She moved her mother out of her bedroom, insisted on dining alone, and resolutely refused to appoint Conroy as her secretary as her mother suggested. She left Kensington Palace and moved the short distance to Buckingham Palace as her new home, dispatching her mother to far-off apartments, though keeping Lehzen in the room next to hers. Her new freedom sometimes led to unwise partisanship in politics in the first few years of her reign, as during the 'Bedchamber Crisis' in 1839, when she refused the incoming Peel's Conservative nominations to the number of her ladies-in-waiting,[2] so in effect preventing him from setting up a successor ministry to Melbourne.

Later she learnt the error of her ways and strove to behave less impetuously. But she was not long without male guidance. Even before the fall of Melbourne and a new administration headed by Sir Robert Peel, she renewed her acquaintance with her cousin, Prince Albert of Saxe-Coburg-Gotha (1819–1861),[3] whom she had met once before for a few days when he visited England. The two were attracted to each other; she proposed to him[4], and the pair were married in February 1840. There was no doubt that Albert, though actually three months her junior, was the dominant partner in the marriage; Victoria was happy to submit to his wishes, even in the choice of her clothes. He arranged for Lehzen to be pensioned off, and even effected a reconciliation between Victoria and her mother, though she never felt warmly towards the Duchess again.

The reign did not begin in auspicious circumstances. The monarchy, after the dissolute behaviour of many members of the royal family to that time, had left the new Queen unpopular and despised. There were three assassination attempts on her in the first four years, the first in June 1840, and the other two within weeks of each other in 1842. Victoria did her best to restore the fortunes of royalty, believing that the royal family should set the nation an example. Her stern views helped to change the moral climate of the country, though at the same time they contributed to the opinion that the Queen herself was prudish and repressed. Such was far from being the case.

The marriage was a conspicuously successful one, the Queen's youthful passion (she confided to her diary that 'he does look so beautiful in just his shirt only') steadily deepening into genuine love. Albert was always the true centre of her life. Together they produced five daughters and four sons, all of whom survived infancy – an unusual feat for that age – and were married into the royal families of Europe. It was said that in the later years of her reign the majority of European royalty addressed the Queen of England as 'Grandmama'. Albert saw the act of procreation as more of a duty than a pleasure, but the Queen usually enjoyed lovemaking, and treasured memories of it into her old age.[5]

She also took the view that Albert deserved everything of the very best. Apart from their official residences in London and Windsor, Victoria had Osborne House built for them on the Isle of Wight, and, while this was still under construction, bought also Balmoral Castle in Scotland in 1852. The two became their main royal residences.

He also took an enormous part of her life.[6] It began with the pair discussing issues of policy, and deciding which course of action was for the best; in the end, though it was quite unconstitutional and frowned upon by her ministers, the two sat side by side as they went through the Queen's 'boxes', adding thoughtful little notes to the documents they were working on, and Albert carefully blotting Victoria's signature when she made it. The clerk to the Privy Council, Charles Greville, observed in 1845: 'the Prince is so identified with the Queen that they are one person ... it is obvious that while she has the title, he is really discharging the functions of the sovereign. To all intents and purposes he is the King.'

Albert took a great interest in the social conditions of the country. His genuine concern for the working conditions of women and children gave the reform movement momentum and political acceptability, and was reflected in the increasing body of reform building up during his lifetime. He also had artistic and intellectual interests, and in education and public health; and all these also made considerable headway. His interest in technology led to the decision to hold the Great Exhibition in 1851, effectively the first World Fair. He masterminded the whole project and selected the Crystal Palace as its setting, designed by Joseph Paxton and built in Hyde Park to house its world-famous exhibits. The exhibition made a resounding profit, which the Prince planned to spend on establishing the Victoria and Albert Museum in Kensington. Curiously, this did little to give him popularity or respect: he continued generally to be regarded as a meddling interloper, and a foreigner to boot.

Undoubtedly, the provision of social and parliamentary reforms did achieve something in the way of lowering revolutionary pressures in mid-century Britain. When Europe was riven by successive revolutions in 1848, the British monarchy remained intact and the Chartists' demands for radical changes fizzled out in a massive but essentially pointless demonstration on Kennington Common.

Nevertheless, the Queen's, and Albert's, impact on matters of foreign policy was frequently resented as much by politicians as by the common people. Here, where Victoria and Albert were undoubtedly better acquainted with the crowned heads of European states than were the ministers, their tolerance towards, say, the Habsburgs led to their leniency towards Austrian and Italian policies, which ministers much resented;

the royal couple also called for greater tolerance during the years of the Indian Mutiny, and later urged neutrality in the American Civil War, which Lord Palmerston, Foreign Secretary at the time regarded as an invasion of his own sphere of authority. Albert in particular detested Palmerston, whose militant chauvinism appalled him as much as it delighted popular opinion. Albert and Victoria clashed frequently with Palmerston. In 1850, Victoria sent him a memorandum[7] to remind him of his obligations to her as one of her ministers – but it was his firm belief that he knew his job better than she did, and he continued to behave as before. Indeed, in 1861, his intemperate language nearly led to war with the United States; only Albert's toning down of the furious dispatch to Washington over the incident in which the British mail ship Trent was boarded in mid-Atlantic by a US warship and two Confederate agents removed under arrest, prevented war with the USA.[8]

In December 1861, twenty-one years after their marriage, Prince Albert contracted typhoid fever. The disease was misdiagnosed and the Prince died. Victoria was devastated at his loss. She never forgave her eldest son, Edward ('Bertie'), Prince of Wales, for his loss.[9] She was tortured by grief: she was said to have even contemplated suicide, and she spent the rest of her life dressed in mourning for her 'dear one'. She passed more than ten years in mournful seclusion at the houses on the Isle of Wight and in Scotland, where they had spent so many happy hours together. She built memorials to Albert at Buckingham Palace and on the site of the Great Exhibition in Kensington. Her retreat from public life (she was often called the 'Widow of Windsor') damaged her popularity and furthered the republican movement. She was only persuaded to return to her duties by two men – the next important figures in her life.

The first was Benjamin Disraeli, who came from a Jewish[10] background, who served her twice as Prime Minister during the 1860s and 1870s, and who flattered her[11] and flirted with her outrageously on the occasions he did business with her at the Palace. His elaborate courtesy was, however, largely feigned; indeed, he is reputed to have said: 'When it comes to flattering royalty, you have to lay it on with a trowel.' He was the only minister ever invited to sit down in her presence.[12] He eventually persuaded her to resume the monarchical duties she had so neglected since Albert's death. He went on to inspire her by detailing his grandiose (and largely unfulfilled) plans for the extension of the Empire she so loved and admired. He bought up a half-interest in the Suez Canal for her in 1876, and encouraged her in her hostility to the 'horrid Russians'[13] before the war crisis in the Balkans in 1877. Eventually, she gave him a peerage, making him Earl of Beaconsfield (where he had his home).

The other man was John Brown[14] (1836–83), who had been Albert's faithful ghillie and favourite at Balmoral, and who now became her most trusted manservant. He came to occupy a centrally important position both in her life and her affections; indeed, it was even rumoured that the two were secretly married to each other. Certainly she permitted him freedoms never allowed even to members of her family. He dispensed with the normal court conventions, and even – perhaps inadvertently – referred to her sometimes as 'Woman' instead of 'Ma'am'. Victoria liked him because he was honest and direct, and was not afraid of showing his true feelings. He wept readily at misfortune, and more than once she observed in her diary that 'good Brown was quite overwhelmed'. He was a fierce disciplinarian with the rest of the servant household. He liked his whisky, though he was never drunk. He often disapproved of the insincere conventions of polite courtesy, and exchanged sharp words more than once with visiting grandees and even members of the family – he held a particularly scathing opinion of the future Edward VII. All the same, there is no evidence that his relationship with the Queen was in any sense improper, or that relations between the two were unduly familiar. It seems likely that the suggestion that Victoria was 'Mrs Brown' was no more than malicious gossip. But he frequently stepped in to defend her, and on more than one occasion averted a threat to the Queen's life; his advice was generally sound and sensible, as when he joined with Disraeli in beseeching Victoria to re-engage herself with the nation's life. When he died in 1883 she was distraught, and, as in Albert's case, so afflicted with grief that she was confined to her room and temporarily lost the use of her legs.

Her last little 'passion' was expended on her Indian servant, Abdul Karim, with whom she became very close after he was presented to her as a servant at the time of the Golden Jubilee in 1887. She soon became quite infatuated with him. Abdul Karim was twenty-four years old, slim and clever, and from the start he turned the Queen's head. He treated her with grave oriental courtesy; he was seldom out of her sight; he waited upon her; he cooked Indian curries for her to savour; he even began to teach her a few words of Hindustani.[15] However, as outsiders began to note, he was always on the lookout for favours for himself and for his numerous family, and as a result was unpopular with his contemporaries. It was not long before he objected to waiting at table, claiming that he was a *munshi* (a clerk, and not a menial – this was technically true since he had worked in Agra Jail as a clerk at ten rupees a month). The Queen accepted this, promoted him, and delegated clerical work to him.[16] He created ill-feeling by securing Victoria's approval for his obtaining grants of land near Agra, and even asking permission for his father to attend a durbar in 1890.[17] The slights inflicted on him by ministers and courtiers had the effect of increasing Victoria's sympathy for Karim: she forbade the use of the term 'black men' for people of Indian extraction at court; she more than once tried to urge mercy for offenders condemned for offences in the sub-continent in the last decade of her reign; she urged India's rulers not to interfere too readily with the seclusion of widows, nor educate the men there to be able to read what she thought was 'objectionable European literature'; she even recommended greater tolerance for Islamic teachings in India, believing that non-Christians could have 'the spirit of Christ in them' as much as her own co-religionists.[18] Karim got his picture into the French press in 1895; the Queen, at the time of her visit to Germany in the same year, introduced him into the household of the Empress Frederick, saying that the munshi ranked as a gentleman in her entourage and, though a vegetarian, would 'not be too troublesome'. Her whole attitude at this time casts doubt on the frequently held opinion that Victoria's attitudes were those of a blinkered and hidebound reactionary in her later years.

There is no doubt that, at the time of the Diamond Jubilee, the Queen's opinions were more tolerant than those of her court and ministers. They had begun by this time to treat her as a harmless old bat who had to be humoured rather than accommodated. Their excuse was that her partiality for the Muslim side was encouraging to the one side in the Hindu-Muslim riots in India in 1897–98, and this was creating difficulties for the India Office, a view that perhaps had some truth in it. In the end, the Queen allowed herself to be muffled, though her sympathies for Karim continued unabated. After her death in 1901, a bonfire of the munshi's papers was made by Edward VII at Frogmore House, one of his homes, in 1902, and a later similar bonfire was burned after Karim's death at Karim Lodge, Agra, in 1909. If anything, this destruction of the evidence seemed to magnify rather than terminate Abdul Karim's political importance in the period before the death of the old Queen.

Victoria died at Osborne House in 1901 after a reign during which she came to count among her people a greater number of subjects in her kingdom and her empire than any earlier ruler. Many saw her Golden and Diamond Jubilees of 1887 and 1897 as the highpoints of her reign, and the peak of Britain's world position. Through her daughter Victoria, who married the future Frederick III of Prussia, she was the grandmother of the future Kaiser Wilhelm II. Through her daughter Alice, her granddaughter, also called Alice, married Tsar Nicholas II of Russia. Her second son, Prince Alfred, was elected King of Greece, though he did not take up his throne. Her daughter Marie married King Ferdinand of Romania. Her funeral was the occasion of a grand and solemn meeting of most of the royal houses in Europe in a time that was still a placid and prosperous one. Many believed that the world would never see her like again.

LILIUOKALANI: QUEEN OF HAWAII

Liliuokalani, Queen of Hawaii, was born in 1838, and was the first and the last Queen of Hawaii. The end of her reign witnessed the extinction of the Hawaiian monarchy in the US annexation of the Hawaiian Islands in 1900. To the end of her days she believed that she and her people had been sold out to the USA by American business interests and Hawaiian collaborators working on behalf of the United States, and by American ambition and prejudice against what they thought was a backward native government.

Liliuokalani was born in Honolulu in 1838, a Hawaiian princess and a member of the country's ruling royal family. Her father, Kapaahea, was a high chief and her mother, Keohokalole, was at one time one of the fifteen senior advisors to King Kamehameha III, who had reigned from 1824 to 1854. His predecessors and namesakes, Kamehameha I (the Great) and II, had united the tribes of the Hawaiian Islands under their royal rule, and for a time successfully resisted the encroachments of the white man.

The islands, discovered by Thomas Cook in 1778, and at first called the Sandwich Islands, had become of interest to Europeans, attractive both to Christian missionaries, who flocked to convert the heathen, and to traders, who valued them as the source of sugar, one of the main staples of the West Indian trade at the time. It was, in particular, valuable to American mariners as a base for the expanding whale-hunting trade, as also for other merchants as a halfway point in the growing China trade. By the end of the 1840s Honolulu was a very cosmopolitan town, with shops opened to sell American shirting, machine-made shoes, New England rum and a whole host of other cheap US manufactures. As early as 1842 Secretary of State Seward assured the islanders that the USA would not permit Hawaii to be annexed by any other foreign power, but this did not protect the islanders from the United States themselves, and before the end of the 1840s a treaty of annexation between the then King and the Washington government was put forward, and failed only because it would have made Hawaii a State of the Union instead of merely a Protectorate. For a time, the American Civil War distracted US attention from overseas issues, but in 1875 these were renewed with the signing of a reciprocity treaty agreeing exclusive trading rights between the two states, and this was confirmed in 1887 with another which ceded Pearl Harbor on the island of Oahu as a US naval base. After this American capital poured in, and by 1890, 99 per cent of Hawaiian exports valued at $20 million went to the United States.

This was the kind of atmosphere in which Lydia Kamakaeha Kaolamali (later known as Liliuokalani) grew up. At the age of four she went to a missionary school where she learned to speak English, and in 1862 at the age of twenty-four she married a non-Hawaiian, a government official called John Dominis whose relations with her brought her little happiness. A photograph of her at the time shows her dressed in sombre Victorian costume with enormous crinoline skirts. She was also a talented musician, and is best remembered for her composition of the song '*Aloha Oe*' ('Farewell to Thee')[1] which became the country's national anthem. In 1874 her brother David Kalakua became king, and after the death of their brother Leleiohoku she became heiress apparent, changing her name to Liliuokalani, and acting as regent during his absences. She performed her duties conscientiously. She set up schools and represented her country during a world tour in 1887,[2] during which time the King submitted to the pressure exerted on him by a cabal of US financiers and sugar-plantation owners, and not only accepted a new constitution which drastically curtailed the power of the monarchy, but at the same time conferred unprecedented trading rights on the Americans and also ceded Pearl Harbor to them.

When she eventually acceded to the throne in 1890 she was fifty-two, a strong, resolute and graceful woman, speaking excellent English and dignified in her manner. But she was far from happy. She resented the McKinley Tariff Bill of 1890, which imposed a punitive tariff on imported sugar in favour of US sugar producers, and she chafed at the restrictions on her traditional powers by the new American-imposed constitution. He felt that this constitution would not have been so bad had it genuinely represented native interests, but she felt that it was designed for the purpose of consolidating the powers of the *haole*, the clique of foreign businessmen and traders, nearly all American, who acted as a pressure group on the Hawaiian government. This *haole* began to moot the idea of total annexation of the islands by the USA, an idea which she as queen felt obliged to resist.

At the beginning of 1893 she determined to overthrow her brother's constitution, on the grounds that it did not represent Hawaii's best interests, and aimed to restore power to the monarchy. She appeared at Government House resplendent in a diamond-studded tiara and a feather cloak to announce her constitution, but was frustrated by the actions of two of her cabinet ministers whom the Americans had persuaded to change their minds. In spite of a large demonstration of natives demanding support for their Queen, the coup proved to be a damp squib and failed. The self-styled 'democratic reform' movement, shrewdly backed by the Americans was, on the other hand, operated swiftly and was well-organised. It was backed by the money and power of American interests, and was headed by Sanford Dole, son of a missionary and a veteran of Hawaiian politics. He portrayed the Queen as a scheming reactionary, and urged the US Government to give armed support for what he represented as a 'democratic coup'. The use of the magic word 'democratic' by the United States was enough to swing world support for Dole's side, and American troops were sent to Honolulu, forcing the Queen to abdicate.

It was, however, not to the local junta that the Queen capitulated, but to the United States itself. Shrewdly she put her faith in the justice of US policy, and, in a letter to the President, Grover Cleveland, expressing 'the certainty which I feel that your government will right whatever wrongs may have been inflicted on us'. When the President discovered that the bulk of Hawaiian citizens were against the coup, he declined to condone the annexation and demanded the Queen's reinstatement. But the Provisional Government ignored both her and him, and in 1894 declared the independence of the Republic of Hawaii. Liliuokalani was involved in another failed uprising in 1895, and was placed under house arrest in the former royal palace and compelled to recognise Dole as the new President of Hawaii, at the same time giving up her throne. When the US government finally annexed the islands in 1898, Hawaii became a United States territory and Dole became its territorial governor.

Liliuokalani was heartbroken, and spent the next twenty years of her life searching in vain for international aid in recovering her lost kingdom. The cause of an independent Hawaiian monarchy had failed, and she suffered a stroke and died in 1917.

PART 13

INFAMOUS QUEENS AND RULERS

QUEEN AELFTHRYTH:
THE WICKED STEPMOTHER

The wicked stepmother figures largely in a number of fairy stories, but Aelfthryth (Elfrida) was a real-life stepmother who was accused by contemporaries of committing one of history's most appalling crimes.

Aelfthryth was born about the year 945, the daughter of the Earl of Devon who had vast lands and influence in the West Country. Her mother was of royal Wessex blood, so Aelfthryth was obviously a marriageable young lady who could help to cement a political alliance. King Edgar certainly thought so; an alliance with a West Country earldom would be of great value to him, since his main strength lay in Mercia, (the Midlands) and when he heard that Aelfthryth had the additional recommendation of being a great beauty he decided to marry her. He was a widower and Aelfthryth had also been married before. Contemporary legend asserts that Aelfthryth's first husband Aethelwald had been sent by Edgar to see if she would make a suitable second bride for the King, but Aethelwald was so entranced by her beauty that he married her himself. How convenient therefore that Aethelwald was soon after killed in a supposed hunting accident, and Edgar was able to marry the heartbroken widow in 964 or 965.

Aelfthryth gave Edgar two sons, one of whom died in infancy, the other, Ethelred, born in 968, survived. But Edgar already had a son Edward by his first wife Aethelflaed, and although the laws of primogeniture were not fully established it was generally accepted that Edward was Edgar's heir. By 973 Edgar had declared himself as King of all the English, so he ordered a second coronation to consolidate his claim. Aelfthryth was crowned queen at this ceremony, the first authentic evidence of an English consort's coronation. Edgar did not live long to enjoy his united kingdom but died in 975 at the early age of thirty-two. Needless to say he had left no specific provision for the succession.

Aelfthryth saw Edgar's unexpected death as an opportunity to advance the cause of her young son Ethelred. She claimed, without any real supporting evidence, that Edward was illegitimate and that Ethelred was the only surviving legitimate son of Edgar, and she gathered around her a considerable band of supporters. But she had to reckon with Archbishop Dunstan who led the stronger faction. He had been responsible for major reforms in the Church, particularly the introduction of clerical celibacy, and he had greatly encouraged the Church's acquisition of much land from those hoping for salvation or doing expiation. Dunstan had enemies within the Church and among the nobility, but he held all the cards, in particular custody of young Edward, who was no more than fourteen or fifteen years of age. So Dunstan secured the recognition and coronation of Edward, while Aelfthryth continued her intrigues with the support of the powerful Earl of Mercia. Even so, for three years there was no effective challenge to Edward's and Dunstan's rule.

Aelfthryth's efforts to undermine to King Edward's authority did not prevent Edward from forming a strong attachment to his stepbrother Ethelred and an apparent willingness to forgive and forget. In March 978 Edward was in Dorset hunting when it occurred to him that as his stepmother and stepbrother were nearby at Corfe Castle he might as well pay them a courtesy visit . Edward let most of his attendants continue the chase and arrived at Corfe without adequate escort. Aelfthryth and her son Ethelred, who was only nine at this time, appeared at the outer gate of the castle to welcome him, and invited him in. But Edward did not wish to be parted long from the hunting party, refused with thanks to dismount, and merely asked to drink a toast to them both while he was still in the saddle. Wine was brought, and as Edward raised the cup to his lips one of Aelfthryth's servants, who had been quarrelling with Edward's retainers, stabbed him in the back. Servants do not normally stab kings unless they have been suborned to do so. Edward was not killed outright but spurred his horse to flight. He was rapidly losing blood, and fell from the saddle in a faint. One foot was caught in the stirrup and Edward was dragged some considerable distance over very rough ground until loss of blood and injuries from his being dragged through the woods killed him. His servants followed the blood trail and soon found his disfigured corpse which they burnt, and buried the ashes a few miles away at Wareham. The *Anglo-Saxon Chronicle* commented, with some hyperbole: 'No worse deed than this had been committed among the English peoples since they first came to the land of Britain.'

Ethelred was now expected to become the new king, but this did not prevent him from weeping copious tears at the loss of his beloved half-brother, nor Aelfthryth from giving him a severe beating for such a demonstration of weakness. Dunstan tried to persuade one of Edgar's illegitimate daughters to take the throne but she preferred to remain in the relative safety of her nunnery at Wilton. Dunstan therefore was obliged to crown Ethelred, the son of an alleged murderess, on Easter Day 979, but not before he is said to have uttered a profound curse over him during the ceremony. Aelfthryth now exercised great power through her son, and Dunstan's influence never recovered. But there were some who could never forgive what Aelfthryth had done, and even her supporters became increasingly jealous of her excessive influence. As Ethelred grew up her followers diminished and her importance declined. In 984 Ethelred was declared of age at sixteen and his mother ceased to witness his charters. She withdrew from the court and from public affairs, but she did play a major role in helping bring up Ethelred's children by Aelgifu of Northampton.

In her later years she became deeply religious, endowing churches and supporting the abbey at Wherwell. Her enemies attributed her newfound piety to remorse and fear of Hell's torments. Her final years are shrouded in mystery, but it appears that she retired to her favourite abbey at Wherwell near Winchester where she probably became a nun. Her death occurred somewhere between 999 and 1001, by which time the Viking incursions into England had been renewed with a vengeance, and she would have had time to reflect on what might have appeared to her as the direct result of Dunstan's curse. There is no doubt that Aelfthryth had schemed for the replacement of Edward with Ethelred, but how deep was her complicity in his murder it is difficult to determine. It was one thing to scheme to deprive Edward of his throne, quite another to scheme to deprive him of his life. Edward's willingness to visit Corfe without his full entourage strongly suggests that he felt he had no reason to suspect foul play. At worst his death was an opportunist murder for which she must take much of the responsibility, at best it resulted from a scuffle between unruly servants. So the wicked stepmother she must remain until and unless some new contemporary source comes to light which can exculpate her.

QUEEN EMMA:
THE UNFEELING PARENT

Queen Emma, wife of Ethelred II and subsequently of Cnut, was notorious for her alleged inconstancy, her involvement in the death of her son Alfred, and her possible treachery towards her first son Edward the Confessor. Her preference for her son by Cnut over her sons by Ethelred caused adverse comment at the time by the chroniclers, and her attempts to enhance Norman influence in England eventually aroused the wrath of patriotic Anglo-Saxons, notably Earl Godwin.

Emma was born about the year 985, the daughter of Richard I, Duke of Normandy, and his Danish second wife Gunnora. Emma's half-Danish ancestry had given her the name Aelgifu, but sometime after her arrival in England she preferred and used her Norman name Emma. It was usual for chroniclers to talk up marriage-worthy princesses, and they dubbed Emma the 'Flower of Normandy', and it seems that she probably was tall, blonde and beautiful. Ethelred II of England, not content with a life and death struggle against the Danes, had taken it upon himself to quarrel with Normandy. The Pope, in alarm for the safety of Christendom under the Viking threat, acted as mediator, and the seventeen-year-old Emma was offered in marriage to Ethelred as part of the settlement. Ethelred was twenty years older than Emma, had been married before, and had a mistress. A few months after the marriage, Ethelred ordered the annihilation of his Danish subjects, and the massacre of St Brice's Day in November 1002 must have horrified a queen who was half-Danish herself. Ethelred treated his new young wife badly, ignoring her and making no attempt to conceal his various illicit liaisons.

Emma responded with numerous bitter complaints to her brother whose reaction was to arrest all the native English who happened to be in Normandy and murder some of them. Despairing of her brother's help it is alleged that Emma intrigued secretly with Sweyn, King of Denmark, who was anxious to invade England and avenge the St Brice's Day massacre. Whatever the truth of that accusation it is true that Sweyn's invasion of England which followed the massacre was greatly assisted by the surrender of Exeter, a town held by one of the Norman nobleman who had come to England with Emma.

During the years which followed Emma bore Ethelred's children, and Sweyn's repeated invasions were bought off by Ethelred with increasing amounts of gold. By 1012 Ethelred's position, 'abandoned, deserted and betrayed' had become untenable, and Sweyn had become master of the kingdom. Ethelred hastily quitted London and fled to the Isle of Wight from which he sent his children and Emma to the court of her brother at Rouen. Ethelred had doubts about his own reception in Normandy after so many quarrels with his brother-in-law, but Richard chivalrously agreed to give Ethelred asylum. But only six weeks after he had been accorded the title of King of England, Sweyn died, and the witan that had welcomed Sweyn now invited Ethelred to return, provided he promised to govern better. For three years Ethelred fought intermittent war against Cnut, Sweyn's son, and when Ethelred died in 1016 after a short illness, the witan chose not one of Ethelred's legitimate children by Emma , Edward or Alfred, but one of his illegitimate sons, Edmund Ironside, as the new king. Edmund was of age and a renowned soldier, and Emma's two sons were mere minors and were being brought up in Normandy. Nevertheless, Emma must have felt that Ethelred's notorious inconstancy had been sanctified by the witan's choice.

Edmund had only varying success against the Danes and in the autumn of 1016 he felt obliged to sign a treaty with Cnut partitioning the kingdom between them, but at the end of November Edmund died and Cnut was acknowledged, unchallenged, as King of England. Emma's position was difficult. Her husband's enemy was now king, and he began his reign by proscribing and killing Anglo-Saxon leaders who had fought against him, and the witan now excluded from the throne all the descendants of Ethelred, legitimate or illegitimate. Emma and her sons had taken refuge with her brother once again. He made noises on behalf of his nephews Edward and Alfred, demanding that Cnut surrender England to them. Cnut did not want a hostile Normandy close to England's shores no matter how limited Normandy's resources or how futile Richard's demands. Emma's choices appeared to be exile at her brother's court or a nunnery, neither of which seemed very attractive. She must have been surprised to learn that Cnut and Richard had settled their differences and that she was to marry Cnut as part of the settlement and thus be restored as Queen of England. How enthusiastic she was for this arrangement is not recorded, but it is said that Cnut wooed her and she consented. What choice she had in the matter is not clear. The English had never greatly liked Emma with her Viking blood and her Norman sympathies. They therefore condemned the marriage as 'unnatural', although the remarriage of widows was common enough in an age when war and pestilence were endemic. Even so, Emma was marrying the man who caused her husband's ruin and probably hastened his death. It did not seem to worry Richard that Cnut had been married before, although this marriage had never had the sanction of the Church. His first wife, Aelgifu of Northampton, bore his sons, was put in charge of northern England, and later became Cnut's regent of Norway on behalf of her son Sweyn. To Emma it must have seemed that Aelgifu was at least Cnut's mistress, and that, like Ethelred before him, he was an unfaithful husband. A legend dating from the end of the eleventh century suggests that Emma herself was later accused of infidelity, with a bishop no less, and had to prove her innocence by ordeal by fire, but there is no contemporary evidence for this story.

What Emma cannot be excused for by English chroniclers is her neglect of her sons by Ethelred whom she left to be brought up at the Norman court. But, considering the ferocity with which Cnut pursued the relations of Edmund Ironside and Ethelred, there is no certainty that Edward and Alfred would have been welcome or even safe at Cnut's court. But she did not give them any financial help, and the two boys were dependent on the rather meagre charity of their Norman relations. And as soon as Emma began bearing Cnut's children she seems to have lost interest in those of her first marriage, and was fully in sympathy with Cnut's aim to create a great Danish empire out of England, Denmark, Norway and Sweden, of which Cnut's children would be the inheritors. But he died comparatively young in 1035 with his ambitions not yet fully achieved.

Cnut had intended his dominions to be divided between his three sons, Harthacnut, his legitimate son by Emma, and his illegitimate sons by Aelgifu, Sweyn and Harold (nick-named Harefoot). There were strong contemporary rumours that the illegitimate sons were not sons of Cnut at all, but of a priest and a cobbler respectively. However, civil war was avoided as Emma, strongly supported by Earl Godwin held southern England for Harthacnut who was far too busy in Scandinavia to set foot in England, and, since possession of London was disputed with Harold, they held their court at Winchester. Even there, while the peace between the parties was being negotiated, Emma was not safe, for Harold fell upon Winchester and took possession of Cnut's treasury and valuables, much to Emma's chagrin. Emma's preference for her son by Cnut, but not his illegitimate ones, was soon evident when an invasion from Normandy by Edward (later the Confessor) was thwarted by the large army she and Godwin raised, and Edward escaped with difficulty back to Normandy, vowing never to return to England again. He certainly had good reason to be angry with his mother.

But the second invasion from Normandy had a much more sinister ending and helped to destroy Emma's reputation. In 1036 Edward and Alfred received a letter purporting to be from their mother, full of maternal affection, reproaching them with their indifference, and urging one of them to come to England to assert their joint rights against the tyrant Harold. This letter seemed so out of character with Emma's attitude towards her sons during Cnut's reign that it is surprising that both brothers were not suspicious. If she had written the letter she was dissembling and if she had not the letter was a forgery, possibly by Earl Godwin. The aim of the letter was to bring the brothers to England so that their threat to Harthacnut from Normandy could be neutralised. Even if Emma wrote the letter it seems most unlikely that she could have planned what was to follow. Not surprisingly, Edward refused but Alfred accepted the invitation. Yet instead of arriving in England without armed forces as requested in the letter he landed in Kent with at least 600 men. He marched without opposition into Surrey, avoiding Harold Harefoot's stronghold of London, and was met at Guildford by Earl Godwin. Godwin swore fealty to Alfred and promised to escort him to Winchester to meet his mother. But Godwin had now secretly switched sides and become a supporter of Harold. That evening he billeted Alfred and his forces in scattered lodgings throughout the town, and made sure they were plied with plenty of drink. That night as they were sleeping off their drunken stupor Harold's forces set upon them, rounded them up, and next morning all but one in ten of them were barbarously put to death. Alfred was sent to London, and from there, naked on a horse, with his feet tied beneath the horse's belly, Alfred was taken to Ely. A hostile Danish court condemned him as a disturber of the peace, and ordered his eyes to be gouged out. This was done so barbarously that he died of his injuries a few days later. It was Godwin's treachery that led to this disaster, but Emma's collusion in inviting Alfred to England in the first place cannot be disproved.

Shortly after the death of Alfred, Emma, abandoned by Godwin, who feared the growth of Norman influence in England, and threatened by Harold, found it convenient to escape to the continent, especially as Harold's own mother Aelgifu seemed to have taken charge of the government. Emma did not, however, choose to join her relations and her son in Normandy, but went instead to the court of Baldwin, Count of Flanders . She was no doubt rightly concerned about her reception should she venture to Normandy. Her exile was to last for the rest of Harold Harefoot's reign, during which Emma repeatedly urged Harthacnut to abandon his ambitions in Scandinavia and stake his claim to England. Eventually Harthacnut gathered a large force and sailed for Flanders to consult Emma. While there, a deputation of Saxons and Danes from England informed him of Harold's sudden death (1040) and offered him the English crown. So Emma's legitimate son by Cnut had gained the throne without having to fight for it, and Emma felt it safe to return to England. Before she did so, she was presented with *Encomium Emmae*, probably written by a Flemish monk, a panegyric of Emma's life and achievements that glorified her strengths, ignored her weaknesses, and even omitted the fact that she had once been married to Ethelred.

Harthacnut turned out to be a veritable Jekyll and Hyde. He massacred indiscriminately and taxed excessively. Yet he showed his horror at the death of his half-brother Alfred by having Harold Harefoot's corpse dug up, dismembered and thrown into the Thames. He tried to bring Godwin to trial for his part in the murder and Godwin was forced to clear himself by the compurgation (collective oath-swearing) of a large number of his supporters and a very expensive gift to the King. He also welcomed his other half-brother, Edward, to England and made him his heir. Godwin, now a supporter of Harthacnut again (he really did not have much choice) found it expedient to join forces with Emma, and they effectively ruled the country between them. Godwin, with treachery and murder in his background, needed Emma much more than she needed him. Harthacnut gave them no problem after the early months of his reign, since his main interests were excessive eating and excessive drinking, but within two years he was dead, after collapsing suddenly at a wedding feast.

Edward (soon to be known as 'the Confessor') was already in England, recognised as Harthacnut's heir, and had no difficulty in securing the overwhelming support of the witan. He was much put out when, before his coronation, Emma refused to help him when he was short of funds. He was even more put out when he suspected his mother of supporting the claim of King Magnus of Norway to the English throne and offering him free use of her treasury. So in the autumn of 1043, accompanied by Earls Godwin, Siward and Leofric, Edward hastened to Emma's stronghold at Winchester, seizing her treasure, cattle, corn and forage. Chroniclers are puzzled by Edward's harsh treatment of his mother, but he never forgave her for her part in Alfred's murder or her intrigues with King Magnus, and he was possibly indoctrinated by his Norman relations who had little reason to love Emma. Nevertheless, he held back from sterner measures and Emma was allowed to keep her lands. She remained at Winchester, shorn of power and influence, but in comfortable circumstances, and died there in 1052. Fittingly, she was buried there, next to Cnut.

Emma gets a buffeting from the chroniclers. Saxon chroniclers disliked both her Norman background and her Viking sympathies, and they regarded her second marriage as a betrayal. Norman chroniclers dislike her support for Sweyn and her alleged involvement in the entrapment of Alfred; they condemn her complete lack of any maternal instincts towards her children by Ethelred. She certainly found expediency the safest policy and she loved wealth and power. Whether she was quite such an unloving parent is debatable, but certainly Edward's early treatment of her would suggest so. In her defence she might argue that difficult times justify difficult decisions. She tolerated two marriages to inconstant husbands. She saw England's future as more secure in the Viking orbit than tossed between Saxon factions; she saw it as more secure in the hands of Harthacnut than the impetuous Alfred or the reclusive Edward. But she was not infallible and sometimes she got it wrong.

JUDITH: THE BETRAYER

Judith of Lens was William the Conqueror's niece, daughter of Adelaide, William's sister, and her second husband Lambert, Count of Lens. She was born in 1054. It was natural that William should seek a worthy and profitable marriage for so close a relative. But Judith's behaviour, which was generally believed to have brought about her husband's downfall, was widely condemned both by contemporary chroniclers, and by subsequent historians.

After the rebellion of the north in 1069, William I dealt with the rebels in the usual Norman manner – their lands were laid waste and they were either executed or their bodies were maimed with loss of limb or foot. There was one notable exception to this savagery. Waltheof, Earl of Huntingdon was the most popular and influential of the Anglo-Saxon leaders, more so because of his great father Earl Siward of Northumbria than because of any qualities he himself possessed. But, after the Harrying of the North, William was concerned to win over rather than alienate any more of his new Anglo-Saxon subjects, and he accepted Waltheof's abject surrender, deciding to tie him effectively to the Norman cause by marrying him into his family. Thus Waltheof and Judith were married in 1070.

The marriage was relatively uneventful. Judith bore her husband three children during the years 1070–75. Waltheof's behaviour had been so exemplary that William promoted him to the earldom of Northumberland in 1072. And Waltheof followed the Norman practice of protecting his wife from a possible impecunious widowhood by transferring substantial estates from his earldom of Huntingdon into her possession. Then, in 1075, Waltheof and his wife were invited to a wedding in Norwich. Ostensibly this was to celebrate the marriage of Roger Fitz-Osborn, Earl of Hereford to Emma, daughter of the Earl of Norfolk. But this marriage had been forbidden by William, according to most authorities, and the wedding took place in defiance of William, and with the secondary purpose of fomenting rebellion among the new Norman barons and as many Welsh, Anglo-Saxons and others as could be recruited. Their prime target was Waltheof, and under the heady influence of the wine and with the atmosphere of enthusiasm around him he agreed to take part. But next morning 'when he had consulted with his pillow, and awaked his wits to perceive the danger whereunto he was drawn, he determined not to move in it.' Not only did he consult his pillow but he also consulted his wife Judith, giving her every detail of what was afoot. Nevertheless, he had sworn an oath of secrecy to the earls, promising not to divulge any of what had been discussed. So although he was privy to the discussions which had taken place at Norwich Castle, he was so alarmed by what was planned that he left Norwich on the day after the wedding and rushed to London, there to inform Archbishop Lanfranc of what he knew, despite his oath to the earls. Unknown to Waltheof, Judith had already betrayed him to William. Lanfranc was quick to alert William, who was in Normandy, and the rebellion was effectively nipped in the bud.

Although Waltheof had taken no part in the brief rebellion that followed the meeting in Norwich Castle, he was speedily rounded up with the other leaders and placed under arrest. It seems that, in her betrayal, Judith had revealed all she knew to her uncle, including information that Waltheof had withheld from Lanfranc. And she added for good measure the damning accusation that the Danish fleet, which was hovering off the Norfolk coast, had been invited there by Waltheof. It is arguable that her behaviour was motivated by Norman patriotism, but the more likely motive was that she had taken a fancy to one of the Norman barons, and wished her husband out of the way so that she could be free to remarry.

William had the Earl of Hereford sentenced to perpetual imprisonment, which was the usual Norman punishment for treason, but he agonised for several months over what to do with Waltheof. The Anglo-Saxon punishment for treason was death, and Waltheof was Saxon, not Norman. To put him to death, however, would rouse enormous Anglo-

Saxon resentment, and might even provoke another rebellion. William took advice from the leading Norman nobility, and Judith was prominent among those arguing that Waltheof was more of a danger to William alive than dead. He could be a focus for any Anglo-Saxon rebellion, and, after all, he had rebelled in 1069, and again in 1075, and therefore would be likely to do so again. So Waltheof was beheaded at Winchester in the early morning of 31 May 1076, so early in order to avoid any public demonstration in his favour. He was almost instantly regarded by the English nation as a saint.

Judith now expected to marry her Norman nobleman, but William forbade it. Rumours of Judith's motives must have reached him, and he would not allow Judith to profit from her treachery to her husband. He did, however, claim her as a ward, the legal nicety whereby widows were placed at the disposal of their lord. William now offered Judith another husband, Simon of St Luz, a French soldier of great repute who happened to be both lame and deformed. Judith did not use delicacy to turn him down, but rejected him with harsh and insolent words that could not help but hurt Simon's feelings. William was furious at her behaviour, expelled her from court, deprived her of the estates Waltheof had given her, and transferred these estates to Simon, who no longer had need of her as a wife. Judith, without property, was now reduced to poverty. Even her Norman relations shunned her when she fled to France, and on her return to England she spent her remaining years seeking shelter in remote places where her identity and thus her perfidy were unknown.

Judith's conduct was almost universally condemned by chroniclers, both Saxon and Norman. Typically they describe it as 'infamous'. It was in the interests of Norman chroniclers to highlight Waltheof's treachery and to condemn Judith's tactless rejection of Simon of St Luz. It was in the interest of Saxon chroniclers to highlight Waltheof's innocence and to condemn Judith's disloyalty towards him. In their efforts to reduce Waltheof's culpability in the 1075 rebellion (but one at least asserts that Waltheof was as guilty as the two earls) and to produce justification for William's harsh treatment of his niece, they may have found it convenient to exaggerate and blacken her part in these events. But as yet she has not found a champion.

LUCREZIA BORGIA: RENAISSANCE WOMAN

The Borgia family is renowned in history for its indulgence in every sin previously known to mankind, and in a number of others in which they were innovators. At the centre of this family were Rodrigo Borgia who in 1492 became Pope Alexander VI, his son Cesare Borgia whom he created a cardinal, and his daughter Lucrezia. Pope Alexander's twin goals were the advancement of his family – he was devoted, possibly over-devoted, to his children – and the advancement of the papacy by turning it into a territorial monarchy in the Romagna (Central Italy). Alexander pursued his aims relentlessly and without scruple; his most sycophantic apologist thinks him certainly guilty of only one of his many alleged poisonings; his son Cardinal Cesare Borgia was less restrained, and Lucrezia was widely regarded as an expert in the art of poisoning.

Italy, at the end of the fifteenth century, was a territory of many states, some so small as to be little more than towns with attached farmland. Others, like the Kingdom of Naples, were much more extensive. Naples was ruled by a branch of the Spanish House of Aragon, thus its interests were pro-Spanish, and the Borgias, whose origins were Spanish, were inclined to support them. Petty rivalries weakened the Italian states, which were only too ready to call in the foreigner and make Italy a battleground for the major powers. States like Venice played off one foreigner against the other – a game which Alexander VI was quick to learn. During his reign the French invaded Italy twice, in 1494 and in 1499. The first invasion had only fleeting success, but the second led to the French becoming established in both north and south Italy and it took several years to drive them out. Alexander feigned pro-French sympathies when France prospered in Italy; he feared a General Council and deposition or at minimum a loss of territory. But when France was on the defensive Alexander usually espoused the Spanish cause.

Thus the Italy of Lucrezia's childhood was in political turmoil. She was born on 18 April 1480. As the daughter of a cardinal, later Pope, she enjoyed a very privileged upbringing. There was nothing unusual in the fathering of children by men high in the church. Alexander's predecessor, Innocent VIII, had at least two, and possibly as many as sixteen children, Alexander had at least seven. It seems that in the fifteenth century a casuistic interpretation of the canon law on celibacy forbade clerical marriage, but had no categorical objection to clerical sex. Lucrezia's mother was Vannozza Cattanei who retained Alexander's affection for longer than most of his other women, but who was respectably married to successive husbands for nearly all her adult life. She kept a separate household, and from the age of three Lucrezia was brought up not by her but by one of Alexander's nieces. She wanted for nothing while her father was still a cardinal. And when he became Pope her prospects immeasurably improved.

The children of cardinals were sought after in marriage because of their fathers' possible influence in the secular and spiritual affairs of the papacy. Lucrezia had already been promised in two successive pre-nuptial agreements at the age of eleven. But when her father became Alexander VI in August 1492 she became even more marriageable, the pre-nuptial agreements were quietly set aside, and a suitor, more valuable to the papacy than his predecessors was looked for. Since the French were at any moment expected to invade Italy, and since the Borgias' Spanish origin would make them natural allies of Naples, Alexander was concerned about the French threat to Rome, and anxious not to antagonise the French. There was no better way for Alexander to show his good intentions to France than by showing favour to the Sforzas, the ruling House of Milan, who were France's supporters in the forthcoming French invasion. A junior scion of the

House of Sforza, Giovanni Sforza Count of Pesaro, was considered suitable. He was the right age – twenty-eight, Lucrezia was thirteen – he was sound in mind and limb, but his pockets were empty, and he expected that the papal treasury would help to fill them.

The wedding took place in the Vatican on 12 June 1493. No expense was spared. The guests included representatives of almost every noble family in Italy, with ambassadors from most European states. The wedding was not consummated immediately in view of Lucrezia's youth, but it must have been a frightening experience for her to be taken from her family and transported to the nearby palace at Portico, and eventually to Pesaro, where she knew nobody. It is unlikely, in view of Giovanni's coolness towards her, that she ever learned to love her husband, but she certainly found compensation in the receptions, balls, processions and plays which dominated daily life at Portico, together with the many church services which were *de rigueur* for the daughter of a Pope.

Lucrezia was, by all contemporary accounts, fair and beautiful, despite her receding chin. But Giovanni's main concern was not his wife, but the threat from the impending French invasion. The Pope had now switched sides and was supporting Alfonso of Naples, fearing the likely consequences of a French domination of Italy, and Giovanni felt himself in an impossible position. As an officer in the Milanese army he should have been friendly towards France, but as the Pope's son-in-law he should have sided with Naples. In the event he chose the worst of both worlds by accepting the post of an officer in the Neapolitan army, resigning his Milanese commission, but keeping Milan informed about the size and deployment of the Neapolitan forces. He was now terrified that his father-in-law would find out what he had been doing. When Milan made a separate treaty with the French the gulf between the Borgias and the Sforzas widened. At the Pope's insistence Giovanni returned to Rome, but he constantly had to watch his back. Lucrezia was privy to a Borgia plan to murder her husband, but at least she warned him of what was afoot. Giovanni wisely fled back to Pesaro leaving Lucrezia in Rome. Since she would not obey her husband's demand that she join him, and since he refused the Pope's request to return to Rome, Alexander abandoned the murder plan and turned instead to the idea of annulling his daughter's marriage.

Lucrezia was eventually to give her consent to the annulment, possibly with some reluctance, but since her father refused to allow her to leave Rome she suddenly moved into the convent of San Sisto. It is doubtful if she intended to become a nun; it is more likely that she wanted time and space in which to reflect on her position and her future. Her father ordered her to leave the convent and sent troops to drag her out when she refused to do so. But the prioress talked them out of carrying out their orders and Lucrezia remained in the convent for the time being. While she was there news reached her that the body of her younger brother Juan, Duke of Gandia, had been fished out of the Tiber; his throat had been cut. Since Juan was his father's favourite it was soon rumoured that he had been the victim of his brother Cesare's jealousy. Lucrezia was beside herself with grief. She consoled her grief by falling in love with Pedro Caldes, one of the Pope's emissaries to the convent. The Pope, meanwhile, stopped the preliminary investigations into Juan's murder and sent his son Cesare, the chief suspect, on a diplomatic mission to Naples. By now Lucrezia was pregnant. It was soon being put about that Lucrezia was pregnant, not by her lover or husband, but by her father. For this there was much rumour, largely originating from Giovanni Sforza who strongly resented the papal assertion that he was impotent. But there was little evidence to support either allegation.

Throughout the summer of 1497 the Pope had persisted and Giovanni Sforza resisted. When the Pope suggested that the childless marriage had never been consummated, Giovanni denied it and asserted that the childless marriage was Lucrezia's fault since his previous marriage had been fruitful. He could no longer use this argument once Lucrezia's pregnancy became obvious. It is said that Lucrezia appeared before a church court when six months pregnant and swore that she was a virgin. Fortunately the voluminous women's fashions of that era acted as a screen. When the Pope tried to refer to the pre-nuptial agreements as binding enough to invalidate the marriage, Giovanni referred to the legal and ecclesiastical opinions of 1493 which expressly denied any binding commitment. He was in a very difficult position. Since the French had now decided to push their claim to Milan instead of using the Milanese alliance, the Sforzas became enemies of France, while the Pope preferred to cultivate France's friendship, at least while France posed a new and immediate threat. But Giovanni clung to his papal marriage connection, both for its prestige and for the protection it might give him. He did not endear himself to the Pope by telling the Duke of Milan of his suspicions about incest, an accusation that he may have invented out of hatred for the Borgias and his disloyal wife. It was not until November 1497 that Giovanni finally consented to the annulment, and by then negotiations were already under way for Lucrezia's next marriage.

Not that Lucrezia's wishes were consulted in the diplomatic flurry. Her infatuation with Pedro Caldes had become an obsession, and the Borgias had not freed Lucrezia from the Sforzas so that she could be wasted on so inferior a person. It was even rumoured that Cesare and Lucrezia were unnaturally close, and that Cesare was intensely jealous of all Lucrezia's husbands and lovers. In March 1498 Caldes was assassinated in the Pope's presence, desperately clutching at the Pope's robe in the hope that Alexander would save him. Caldes' corpse, tied hand and foot, was a day or two later fished out of the Tiber. Lucrezia had only a few weeks before giving birth to either Caldes' or her father's child. Even so, new suitors swarmed in abundance, despite the unspeakable rumours of incest and Lucrezia's perhaps undeserved reputation as 'the greatest whore in all Rome'. Since the new King of France Louis XII wanted papal support for an annulment of his marriage and Cesare was trying to secure a Neapolitan marriage for himself, Alexander had greater freedom of manoeuvre. A marriage into the Neapolitan house of Aragon would further Cesare's ambitions in southern Italy, and Alfonso of Aragon, bastard son of Alfonso II became the favoured suitor. He was the brother of Lucrezia's sister-in-law Sancha, and was reported by her to be a fine young man (he was eighteen), handsome, physically strong, and mentally agile. With Lucrezia's unsavoury reputation growing ever stronger, a good marriage would be a safe refuge. The wedding took place in July 1498 and Alfonso was granted the lands and title of the Duke of Bisceglie. The wedding was a much less ostentatious affair than Lucrezia's first one, but it was marred by a riot between Cesare's and Sancha's servants which so frightened Alexander's servants that they fled.

At first all went well, and the young couple seemed happy enough. But Cesare had had enough of being a cardinal, and was allowed to renounce his vows in August 1498. He now set out on a diplomatic mission to France to persuade Louis XII of Papal goodwill, and eventually in May 1499 he married into the French royal family. His interests were now decidedly pro-French whereas Lucrezia was actively supporting the aims of her Aragonese in-laws. Cesare and the Pope were now so strongly supporting the French cause that Alfonso became alarmed for his own safety. He was well aware of what had happened to Giovanni Borgia. In August 1499 he fled from Rome, leaving behind a pregnant and indignant Lucrezia. In order to dissuade Lucrezia from following him, Alexander appointed her Governor of Spoleto, a town ninety miles north of Rome, and in the opposite direction to Naples. Here Lucrezia showed great maturity for one so young. She received ambassadors, dispensed justice, accepted petitions and organised the running of the municipality so effectively that she was much respected and admired by the townsfolk. She also sent abject letters to the Pope begging to be reunited with her husband.

Meanwhile, the French had invaded Italy again and seized Milan. Alexander feigned his disapproval of the French action effectively enough for Alfonso to think it safe to return to Rome. Lucrezia joined him. She gave birth to a boy, Rodrigo, named after his grandfather, at the beginning of November 1499, and soon after Cesare returned to Rome. The success of the French with whom he was now closely allied gave him confidence. He had been unscrupulous before in dealing with his enemies; now he became bold. Almost every night the Tiber received new victims. Some were stabbed, some were strangled, some garrotted and some presumably poisoned. On 15 July 1500 the Duke Alfonso of Bisceglie was set upon by ruffians outside St Peter's and was severely wounded. He was brought bleeding and unconscious into the Vatican. Few had any doubts about who was responsible for the outrage and Duke Alfonso's life was obviously still in grave danger. Lucrezia and Sancha took it upon themselves to nurse him back to health. They were particularly concerned to prepare his food with their own hands to eliminate the danger of poisoning, and within a month he had much improved, although still weak. On 18 August, fearing that a visitor might be intending to kill the duke, the two women rushed into an adjoining room to seek the Pope's protection for the sick man. During their brief absence Alfonso was strangled. Lucrezia was too fond of her husband to be a party to the killing, and she must have bitterly regretted her confidence in her father's ability or willingness to protect him. The two women were not allowed to be present at Alfonso's funeral, but Lucrezia's grief was genuine enough. It was at this time that rumours of Lucrezia's skill with poisons began to circulate. She was considered to be an expert in delayed-action poisons and mysterious potions such as *cantarella* and *aqua totana* were talked of. Yet at this time it was Lucrezia's Spanish friends, not her enemies, who were ending up in the Tiber, and there is no specific evidence to link her to any suspected death by poison. Of course most mysterious deaths at that time were assumed to be by poison unless proved otherwise.

She had not been a widow a month before new suitors came flocking. She refused several, but realised the need for personal security and less dependence on the Borgias.

The city of Ferrara in the valley of the Po was ruled by the Este family. It was close enough to the Romagna to be alarmed by Cesare's recent successes there in collaboration with the French. Even the Duke of Este thought it prudent to have the Pope on his side in case Cesare was to develop ambitions to the north of the Romagna. The negotiations were protracted, not because of any unwillingness on Lucrezia's part – she seemed keen on the match – but because Duke Ercoli of Este felt that his ancient and historic family would be demeaning itself by allying with the Borgias, and because he was too mean to grant his new daughter-in-law an appropriate allowance. He was won over by an enormous sum in ducats, but even so rejected as part payment any ducats that were underweight or defaced. During the long negotiations the Borgias entertained the delegates from Ferrara with enthusiasm. They attended a party at which fifty prostitutes were present, and they watched an unedifying episode in which four stallions were let loose upon two mares. Lucrezia probably attended both events; she was not delicate in her tastes. The wedding between Alfonso of Este and Lucrezia was finalised at Ferrara in February 1502 amid surprising magnificence considering how parsimonious Duke Ercole was.

From the outset Lucrezia was at loggerheads with her new in-laws. Nearly all her Spanish servants were sent away, and the Duke continued to keep her short of money. In turn she kept the Ferrarese at arm's length. Her relationship with her husband was normal enough, but this did not prevent her from entering into liaisons that gave rise to scandal. Ercole Strozzi was widely read in the literature of the Renaissance and a poet in his own right. Lucrezia was well-informed and well read. Soon Strozzi had become a favourite, with free access to her private apartments. When she became ill (poison was suspected) in the summer of 1502, a visit by Cesare alarmed the Duke, now thoroughly concerned about Cesare's activities in the Romagna. Thus the advantages of the Borgia alliance had faded away and Lucrezia's position became increasingly difficult. It was ominously felt in Ferrara that it would not be convenient for Lucrezia to die 'for the time being'.

In the autumn of 1502 Lucrezia met Pietro Bembo. He was a gifted young man who moved in humanist circles in Ferrara, where he was much admired for the depth of his learning and the wit of his conversation. He and Lucrezia fell in love. When he was very ill in 1503 she defied respectability by visiting him in his sickroom. His illness was not caused by poison, although this was the season of poisonings. Two cardinals who had fallen foul of the Pope were said to have succumbed to it, Cardinal Michiel of Venice and Cardinal Orsini. Then both the Pope and Cesare became ill, allegedly from a poison they had intended for another cardinal, but more likely from an ordinary fever. Whatever the cause, the Pope died on 18 August 1503. With his death died the influence and power of the Borgias. By the summer of 1504 Cesare had lost most of his conquests, was forced to surrender, and sent to a Spanish prison. The Este family might have been prepared to get rid of Lucrezia were it not for the huge dowry which would have to be paid back. At the end of the year Duke Ercole died, Alfonso succeeded him, and Lucrezia was now Duchess of Ferrara.

Lucrezia did not share her husband's interests. She loved literature, poetry and music; he loved artillery, majolica and other women. So the Duchess led a mainly separate life, apart from providing him with three children who survived infancy, although he did put the government of Ferrara into her hands when he went on his many foreign visits, and she handled the responsibility with considerable diplomacy and skill. She lost an old friend in one of Italy's most famous murders when in June 1508 Strozzi was struck down with twenty-two dagger wounds. While it was rumoured at the time that Lucrezia might have been responsible out of jealousy of Strozzi's wife Barbara, it is more likely that Barbara's enemies were responsible, anxious to reduce her to abject poverty. But Lucrezia had been using Strozzi to facilitate her clandestine correspondence with her attractive brother-in-law Gonzaga, Marquis of Mantua, and this throws some suspicion onto her Este relatives. Even so, when in 1509 Gonzaga was captured by the Venetians, Lucrezia contrived to send him gifts and messages without her husband's knowledge.

The next few years saw unprecedented political turmoil in Italy. The political ambitions of France, the papacy, Venice and Spain resulted in a shifting kaleidoscope of alliances and war. Alfonso's confidence that Ferrara could follow an independent policy led to his excommunication and invasion by papal forces. Eventually Ferrara was rescued by the French, although it lost territory. During these conflicts Lucrezia considered flight and exile for her own safety but was persuaded to stay on and face whatever the future had in store; it probably helped that she was much admired by the French general in Ferrara, Gaston de Foix. In 1510 she had founded her own convent where she could find spiritual consolation and inner peace; She may have been unaware that the Marquis of Mantua (now an enemy of Alfonso but certainly not of Lucrezia) had asked the Pope that he should be given custody of Lucrezia in the event of the fall of Ferrara. The political situation temporarily improved in 1513 with the death of Julius II, an old enemy of the Borgias, and the election of Pope Leo X, a friend of the Este family.

In the final years of her short life, Lucrezia was largely untouched by what was happening in Italy. She still corresponded with her former lovers Bembo and Gonzaga, but she mainly spent her time dealing with civil disputes, in which she was said to be a very capable judge, and in religious devotion. In 1518 she joined the order of St Francis and took to wearing a hair shirt under her robes. Although she avoided too much contact with her husband by frequent visits to her convent, to churches and other religious foundations, she nevertheless endured frequent pregnancies. In 1519 she was pregnant and ill. She gave birth on 15 June and died from fever some nine days later.

Lucrezia's reputation for wickedness has been much exaggerated. Her promiscuity was not out of the ordinary in the Italy of her day, although the rumours of incest did set her apart from most other women of her era. Even so her father's use of her as a political pawn was not for her to challenge, and she meekly accepted his choice of her husbands. She was, indeed, loyal to her husbands as a wife of those days should be, although lacking in devotion, except possibly to her second husband the Duke de Bisceglie. She did not connive at his murder, and was inconsolably distraught when it occurred. She was devoted to her children and worked hard for their advancement, even for the feckless Rodrigo of Bisceglie. She had little reason to join in the reign of terror of 1500–03, and those that died were mainly as pro-Spanish as she was. That poison was used at the court of Alexander there is no doubt, but Lucrezia's reputation as a poisoner is based on unsupported rumour rather than hard evidence. She was an able administrator, a competent linguist, a humanist and a woman of piety, and very much in conformity with the spirit of the age.

WAS MARY TUDOR A VILLAINESS?

Mary Tudor, the child of Henry VIII and his first queen, Catherine of Aragon, was born at Greenwich Palace in 1516. Her whole life was unhappy. She endured a miserable and stifling childhood, aware as only a child can be of the lack of love between her mother and father; she faced undeserved bastardy after her mother's separation and divorce; she was included in her father's will as successor to her younger brother, Edward, but debarred again by him during his reign; she came to the throne only after efforts to substitute for her the young Lady Jane Grey (the 'Nine Days' Queen') in July 1553; her reign was brief and sad, complicated by her unfortunate marriage to Philip II of Spain and marred by an orgy of Protestant burnings sparked off by her refusal to compromise her Catholic principles; she died in 1558, an unhappy woman at the early age of forty-two, of a wasting disease complicated by influenza, having lost England's last foothold on the continent of Europe through the capture of Calais by the French. Known to history as 'Bloody Mary', she is said to have uttered her own famous epitaph: 'When I am dead, you will find Philip and Calais engraved on my heart.'

Mary was the only surviving child of the royal marriage between Henry VIII and Catherine of Aragon. The King's eldest son, Henry, born in 1511, had died after no more than seven weeks. His sixth and last-born child died only hours old in November 1518. By the middle of the 1520s, when the Queen turned forty, it became evident that the marriage would bring the King no more children. It was unthinkable that he should be succeeded by a girl; a son was essential to carry on the royal line. Henry began to think that the match was frowned on by the Almighty, even though the Pope had consented to it.[1] He thought that the fault lay with him: he had committed a mortal sin by marrying his brother's widow, and this was God's way of punishing him.[2] Catherine, on the other hand, would admit of no flaw in the marriage, and bitterly resented her husband's efforts to get rid of her.

Such was the loveless household in which the young princess grew up. At the age of nine she was given the title of Princess of Wales and dispatched to Ludlow Castle, close to the Welsh border. A well-educated child, a talented musician and a capable linguist speaking Spanish fluently to her mother, Mary staunchly refused to accept that her mother's marriage was not legitimate, and she regarded her father's second marriage to Anne Boleyn in 1533, and all his subsequent liaisons before her mother's death in 1536, as bigamous. She had an unstable if not a violent relationship with Anne, her stepmother, and she disliked her young half-sister Elizabeth. But her religious convictions were as solid as Elizabeth's were flexible, and she remained stubbornly Catholic throughout her father's reign, refusing to accept, or even recognise, the Protestant Reformation. This was a dangerous course of action, for Henry was a choleric man, and to defy him might easily bring down on her imprisonment, if not worse. Henry relented sufficiently to include her in the succession, after Edward, in his will; but Edward's Protestant advisers – and the young King himself – mistrusted her, and feared that on the throne she might reverse all the reforming legislation they had brought in, and so kept her at arm's length and struck her from the succession a second time, complying with his adviser Northumberland's[3] plans to promote Lady Jane Grey as his successor. But Edward was a sickly child, and died when he was only fifteen in 1553, after a year or more suffering from consumption, mastoiditis, and from the congenital syphilis his father had given him.

But Mary was probably closer to the true feelings of the nation than the Reformers were, because although Lady Jane was proclaimed Queen, very few supported her. The nobility were affronted by Northumberland's naked pursuit of power, and the nation showed its loyalty to Princess Mary as readily as it did to the teachings of Catholicism instead of the newfangled notions of the Protestants. Northumberland's army was swiftly dispersed, and he was arrested and executed for treason. Jane and her young husband were imprisoned in the Tower. Mary, advised to show no weakness towards Northumberland himself, was inclined to be merciful towards the young couple, neither of whom seemed very anxious to supplant her; but Jane's fate was hazarded when her father Henry Grey, Duke of Suffolk, became involved in Sir Thomas Wyatt's rebellion against Mary, and finally sealed when Jane refused point-blank to recant her Protestantism. She, too, was beheaded in February 1554.

At the outset of her reign, Mary's policies were studiously moderate. She had seen her own childhood ruined and her own close relatives mutually antagonised by the quarrels resulting from her father's marital shenanigans, and had noted with regret the tranquillity of the whole nation disturbed by the reformers' arbitrary modifications of its traditional faith. She therefore tried to rock the boat no further, but to keep her own changes to the absolute minimum. She countermanded efforts to squeeze more money out of the Church, abandoned a number of recent Puritan changes in the style and content of worship, and winked at the disobedience of more traditional counties that had failed to implement earlier Edwardian decrees. For herself, Mary restored as much of the 'old order' as she thought possible. She reinstated some of the expelled Catholic bishops, and consented to the removal of the more zealous of religious reformers; but she dare not formally restore either the monasteries or papal supremacy in England, since she knew this would excite controversy. She did, however, pass a law invalidating her father's divorce from her mother, thus legitimising herself and, incidentally, bastardising Elizabeth.

But gradually pressure for more decisive leadership began to build up. The threat of dynastic conflict, and the need to obtain a secure succession to the throne, pushed her towards decisions that otherwise she would have wished to avoid. She had, of course, to marry, and if possible produce an heir.[4] Parliament and her ministers were keen to have her wed an Englishman, and quite a queue of noblemen grew up who shared this objective; but Mary lived in the shadow of the Wars of the Roses, and had a real fear of renewing dynastic strife between the great aristocratic families. Hence she preferred a foreign match. Her choice fell on Philip II of Spain, a dark-haired, good-looking man and a co-religionist over ten years her junior who kindled a spark of love within her and who seemed at first to be interested in her too.[5] But the Spanish match was the Queen's first mistake: her choice was extremely unpopular. Many believed that Philip would use the match to recreate papal supremacy in England, foist his own policies on his new subjects, and in effect make the country a mere appendage of Spain. Popular dissatisfaction with her choice led to the rising headed by Sir Thomas Wyatt in Kent in January 1554, which threatened the very instability that Mary so feared.[6] The rising, however, was badly organised and worse led. Minor risings in Devon and in the Midlands were easily crushed, and, though Wyatt had some success at Rochester and at the Thames crossing at Kingston, he barely reached Temple Bar before his forces dwindled away and he was easily defeated. He and the rest of the ringleaders were apprehended, tried and executed.

The Spanish match proved to be the first of a series of disasters for Mary. After her wedding in July 1554, Philip was granted the title of King, and became the only English King Consort in history. With the abdication of his father Emperor Charles V in 1556 while he was in Spain, he succeeded to that throne as well as England's. Philip was much more interested in the affairs of his own country than in England, and he returned to England only once after that date, when he spent a few months there between March and June 1557. Nonetheless, he made Spain's mark very clearly on English politics, radically influencing Mary's decisions. In 1554, Reginald Pole, Papal Legate and later Archbishop of Canterbury, restored England to the Holy See. While such a decision was widely welcomed in England by many, in its wake came the much less popular decision that heretics must be burned at the stake, a fate that befell nearly three hundred victims between 1555 and 1558.[7] There is not much doubt that little of this was welcome to the Queen, but once the wheels of retribution were turning, there seemed to be little she was able do to stop them.

Philip also continued to use England as his cat's paw in his foreign affairs. He enlisted the support of the English in his long-running feud with the French, which had witnessed campaigns in Italy, south-west France and in the east around Metz. Now the struggle was extended to the Spanish Netherlands, whence a Spanish army entered France in 1557 and laid siege to St Quentin. The capture of the city was, however, costly, and Philip, who had dreamed of a triumphal entry into Paris, had to content himself with a more limited victory. The Duke of Guise, formidable champion of the French cause, then counter-attacked in the Low Countries and recovered many of the places previously lost to the Spaniards. Finally he fell upon Calais, the last English stronghold on the continent, whose garrison Mary had allowed to fall below strength. The outlying forts were taken, the arrival of reinforcements prevented partly on account of the weather, and the citadel bombarded and finally seized in January 1558. Under the Treaty of Cateau-Cambrésis in April 1559, France retained many of her gains, including Calais. This loss sealed Philip's fate in the eyes of the English; already unpopular, his name was now execrated.

Meantime, Mary's reputation in England had fallen almost as low as Philip's own.[8] More principled and more conscientious than nearly all the Tudors, she felt her rejection by the nation deeply, believing it to be unmerited. She always strove to be just and merciful, to weigh the consequences of her actions carefully, and to refrain from policies that she thought vindictive, divisive or hasty. But the nation found it difficult to square the moderation she claimed for herself with the unbending ruthlessness with which her government acted. A woman in what was still preponderantly a man's world, she found herself cajoled, persuaded and finally outmanoeuvred by men whose minds were as clear as, but whose consciences were more easily appeased than, her own. They saw, which she did not, that the commitment to restore the Roman faith was expected to, and necessarily *did* lead to, the burnings of heretics, a policy with which she concurred, believing she could somehow mitigate its consequences. Only too late did she see the cruel brutality to which her Catholicism, and the Holy Inquisition in its wake, had led her. Her half-sister Elizabeth was subtler and less principled than she was in her handling, during her own reign, of religious matters, but even she was forced into 'opening windows into men's souls' (which she said she never wished to do) and punishing religious opponents, sometimes severely. Mary's principled conscientiousness was finally her undoing. She died deeply unhappy with the fruits of her policies, and indeed deeply unhappy with herself.

TZ'U HSI:
EMPRESS DOWAGER OF CHINA

The belief persisted in China until the death of the Empress Dowager in 1908 that Chinese civilisation was inherently superior to the rest of the world, and that any right-minded person was perfectly aware of this.[1] But it was an attitude of mind that was rapidly losing ground at the beginning of the twentieth century in face of the decay of Chinese power, the development of republicanism and the further loss of respect resulting from the suppression of imperial efforts at reform in 1898. Opening the gates of the Forbidden City did little to help, since imperial autocracy could only be overthrown if there was something effective to replace it. The dowager Tz'u Hsi[2] spent her lifetime trying to deny the need for change, and the old China passed away as the result.

The Empress Dowager was a very powerful woman. Born in 1835, she joined the Emperor's court in 1851 as an imperial concubine, quickly established herself at court and claimed the motherhood of the young Prince who came to the throne as the Emperor T'ung Chih in 1861. Her dominant personality soon asserted itself; she plotted the removal of officials who stood in her way, and on the early death of T'ung Chih in 1875, engineered a new regency for the youthful K'ang Yu-wei who replaced him. He ruled until 1908, and she remained the power behind the throne throughout that time.

Chinese government in the nineteenth century was a tightly organised and extremely reactionary bureaucracy, administered by a circle of scholar-officials called mandarins. They were very deeply set in their ways, and were unalterably opposed to the introduction of necessary reforms. Meantime, the mass of the population was desperately poor and oppressed by high taxes and high rents for their landholdings. Their discontent had already led to the Taiping Rebellion, which took fourteen years to crush and produced as many as 20 million deaths. But the most obvious evidence of Chinese decline was found in the inroads of the despised foreigners into Chinese territory. From the 1840s onwards, first the English, then the French, Germans, Russians and Americans carved out areas of influence for themselves. The British fought two so-called 'Opium Wars' against China, and on the second occasion destroyed the Summer Palace at Yuan Ming Juan, close to Peking. European powers came to control a string of strongpoints along the eastern seaboard from Hong Kong up to Port Arthur.[3] In 1894 the newly modernised Japan launched its career of aggression against China in a series of devastating victories.[4] By the peace treaty of 1895 Formosa was annexed by Japan, and Korea was given its independence and soon became a Japanese sphere of influence. Even Tz'u Hsi was forced to admit that China's enemies were 'slicing up the country as if it were a ripe melon'. All this generated a bitter hatred among the Chinese people of foreign interference, and a determination among a handful of the Chinese ruling class to introduce reforms to deal with it. This resulted in the sudden flood of changes introduced by the young emperor K'ang Yu-wei in 1898, and known as the Hundred Days of Reform.

But Tz'u Hsi was having none of it. While not fully identifying herself with the conservative faction, she nevertheless scotched many of the reforms before they came into action, and went on to cancel the rest, resumed the role of regent and even imprisoned the young Emperor for his role in them. But the low point in China's fortunes came two years later, with two successive harvest failures and a major flooding of the Yellow River. These disasters produced an explosive situation that was exploited by a secret nationalist society known as the 'Boxers'. This group began a series of murderous attacks on Christian missionaries and their Chinese converts, and in Peking foreign legations found themselves besieged by them. For several sweltering weeks the legations held out until finally they were relieved by an Allied Expeditionary Force that seized Peking and forced the Empress Dowager to flee westwards. She was forced to sign a humiliating peace treaty agreeing to pay £67 million in reparations. The Manchus had reached the nadir of their fortunes.

How far were Chinese troubles to be put down to the inflexibility of Tz'u Hsi? To the modern observer – and even to alert contemporary Chinese observers like Sun Yat-sen – she seemed obdurate and short-sighted to a degree, and with no more than a slight acquaintance with the realities of the international world. She simply refused to have any dealings with those she called 'barbarians' and lived in the same unchallenged Confucian universe in which all of the mandarins had been trained. She dismissed all suggestions that she was foolish and short-sighted, and denied all the rumours existing at the time, for example that she had neglected defence spending in favour of luxurious consumption, that she operated an arcane network of corruption and illegal tribute by inferiors[5] to sustain her authority, that she made high appointments in the administration through nepotism, or that she had salted away over eight million in Chinese money in foreign bank accounts to provide herself with a retirement fund. All these rumours, she said, were gross fabrications put about by her detractors. In practice she showed considerable administrative ability. Nearly all her decrees were drafted by her in person and show skill and judgement. She was served by capable officials, chosen by her and well-rewarded for their successes – some of them, like Tso T'sung-t'ang, ruler of the north-west provinces, and Li Hung-chang, diplomat and foreign relations expert, were the nineteenth-century equivalent of the twentieth-century warlords. Her influence was felt in ordinary life; for example she objected to railway locomotives on account of their dirt and noise, and preferred to see the railway tracks used for horse-drawn traffic. Generally her government was popular among the Chinese ruling classes, though they passed over the gaieties, the theatricals and the corrupt inner rule that characterised the later part of her government.

Though unpopular in the southern parts of China, where people such as Sun Yat-sen despaired of reform ever succeeding, Tz'u Hsi remained popular in northern China among the ordinary people. They gave her names like 'Motherly and Auspicious' and 'Old Buddha', and buried her with great pomp and ceremony when she died at the age of seventy-eight in 1908. Even so, her high reputation failed to prevent the overthrow of the dynasty in 1911. During her lifetime, too, she remained popular among the many foreign visitors who met her, many of whom commented on her fascinating personality, her caring nature, her love of dogs and flowers, her fondness for European cigarettes and her encouragement of Chinese theatre and opera. In the end, as the *Times* reporter who described her funeral said: 'The weaknesses of her character and the errors of her career are forgotten, and only her greatness remembered.'

PART 14

RADICALS AND PIONEERS

MARY ASTELL:
THE FIRST ENGLISH FEMINIST

Seventeenth-century women were expected to be content with their lot of childbearing, domesticity, and meek servility towards their husbands. Mary Astell did not conform to this stereotype. Her views on the equality of women were not only surprising in themselves, but remarkable for having gained the interest and support of some of the mightiest in the land.

Mary Astell was born in Newcastle upon Tyne on 12 November 1666. Her parents, Peter and Mary Astell, were comfortably off, since Peter was in charge of a local coal company just when demand for sea coal was beginning to increase. Mary was brought up as an Anglican in a royalist household, but her father died when she was twelve and the family fell upon hard times. They therefore found it necessary to give up their separate establishment and move in with Mary's aunt. Mary received no formal education, but did get some instruction from her uncle, a bibulous clergyman who overstepped even the Restoration's lax attitude towards clerical inebriation and was suspended from the priesthood.

After the death of her mother and aunt in 1688 Mary moved to London where her residence in Chelsea brought her close to the literary circle of women among the more notable of whom was Lady Mary Wortley Montague. They assisted her in her literary ambitions which were also furthered by the Archbishop of Canterbury, William Sancroft, who helped her to find a publisher. In her *Some Reflections on Marriage* (1700) Mary's views on the subordination of women are made crystal clear: 'If all men are born free, how is it that all Women are born Slaves?' She did not tackle the question historically, but rather philosophically, arguing that both men and women were blessed with the power to reason, therefore women as well as men should be allowed to develop their full potential. Yet, unlike Aphra Behn, she did not condemn or ridicule the institution of marriage, describing it as the only honourable way of continuing mankind, but she had little time for the subservient wife whose life was ordered according to her husband's needs. She preferred those who read pious books and did good works, and she had much sympathy for the unmarried maids and widows who were often poorly provided for, if at all.

But her most groundbreaking ideas were on women's education as propounded in *A Serious Proposal to the Ladies for the Advancement of their True and Greatest Interest* (1694) and *A Serious Proposal, Part II* (1697). Here she proposed the establishment of special institutions for the education of women. If women were to have equal chances with men for going to heaven they must be educated. Therefore they were to be accorded instruction both secular and religious, and all in a secluded nun-like institution where they would be protected in general from the sins of the world and in particular from the influences and demands of men. These ideas were well received among literary circles, but there was no finance to back them, and they were regarded as too Catholic for a Protestant society. But she was a devout Anglican, and her *Letters Concerning the Love of God* (1695) were much praised for their elegance and their rhetorical style, although her ideas on women's education were subjected to ridicule by Jonathan Swift.

Most of her work covers a fifteen-year span between 1694 and 1709, but she remained a powerful and influential figure after her literary work dried up. In May 1731, Mary died. She had a few months earlier been subjected to the horror of the surgeon's knife to remove her cancerous right breast. Towards the end she had a coffin installed in her room, refused to see any of her friends, and lived out her final days communing with God. She is of great interest, not so much for what she said, but for when she said it. She was well in advance of her time, and a worthy predecessor of the great feminists of the nineteenth century.

MARY WOLLSTONECRAFT AND THE RIGHTS OF WOMEN

Mary Wollstonecraft was a seminal figure of the women's rights movement, and the inspiration of most of the twentieth-century rights champions who followed her and claimed her as the prophet of the feminist movement. In her background, attitudes and experiences she resembled more the thinkers of the French philosophers of the eighteenth-century Enlightenment than the nineteenth-century radicals, but nevertheless, in spite of the hectic and unpredictable personal adventures of her lifetime and her many vicissitudes,[1] many of the philosophic theories of both made their first appearance in her writings.

Born in 1759 in London to a father who was first a handkerchief weaver in Spitalfields, but who had speculated most of his money away and then failed in business, Mary and her family first lived on a series of farms in the vicinity of London, finally moving to Yorkshire near Beverley in 1765. She became the close and often passionate friend of Jane Arden, whose intellectual pleasures in books and philosophy she shared, and later of Fanny Blood, of Hoxton, North London, who Mary believed 'opened her mind' to new influences. She became a 'lady's companion' to Sarah Dawson, a widow living in Bath, but found her a finicky and demanding mistress, and in 1780 returned home to care for her dying mother. After her mother's death she did not return to Bath, but made her home with the Blood family, further cementing the emotional bonds that bound her to Fanny. Aiming to prolong the 'female utopia' that linked them, the two young women set up a school together in Newington Green, near Islington, in London. Shortly afterwards, Fanny Blood married Hugh Skeys, who took her to Europe to improve her precarious health. Mary left the school in 1785 to help to nurse her, but it was in vain and shortly afterwards Fanny died in pregnancy, a tremendous shock to Mary (and the subject of her first novel in 1788).

Mary took up a position in 1786 as governess to a wealthy Anglo-Irish family at Mitchelstown Castle in County Cork. Again she found it difficult to get along with the mistress, Lady Kingsborough (objecting, rather oddly for someone so bohemian, to their profligate lifestyle), and decided after only one year to give up this career and to try her hand as an author – a very bold decision for the times. She moved to London, and, helped by the liberal publisher Joseph Johnson,[2] found a place to live and took up work to support herself. She taught herself French and German, and became a translator, writing also reviews for Johnson's periodical *Analytical Review*. She also attended Johnson's famous dinners, where she met such luminaries as Thomas Paine and William Godwin. Johnson's progressive circle welcomed the French Revolution, and when Edmund Burke in 1790 published his *Reflections on the Revolution in France*, responded with her *Vindication of the Rights of Men*, a work describing her ideal society in which ability and hard work should be rewarded quite irrespective of social class, and the game laws, slavery and the press gang should be abolished. She followed this in 1792 with her *Vindication of the Rights of Women*, in which she argued that by limiting women's participation in society their efforts were being wasted; girls should be eligible for a full education and should be encouraged to enter the professions and take up useful employment as well as being trained for marriage and for motherhood.

In London, meantime, Mary pursued a relationship with the artist Henry Fuseli, with whose brilliant personality she was entirely besotted. She even went so far as to propose a household *à trois* to Fuseli's wife, but she was disgusted, even though the basis of the arrangement was to be platonic, and broke off relations between her family and Mary.

In late 1792, as anti-radical sentiment in Britain was building up, Mary Wollstonecraft left for France to share in the exciting developments there. She arrived about a month before the revolutionaries sent Louis XVI to the guillotine. She encountered other British expatriates in Paris and breathed in the heady atmosphere of Jacobin revolutionary thinking. She also fell madly in love with an American timber-merchant and adventurer, Gilbert Imlay, with whom she conducted an impassioned affair; but he was less enthusiastic about marriage than she was, and when she gave birth to their first child, Fanny, in May 1794, he refused to legalise their extra-marital arrangement. Meantime, the political situation had worsened with the British declaration of war on the infant French republic, placing all British citizens in France in danger.[3] As a result, Mary went to live in Le Havre. Imlay had registered Mary as his wife at the end of 1793, even though they were not married, and she continued to refer to herself as 'Mrs Imlay' for some years afterwards, mainly to give legitimacy to little Fanny. But her 'husband' was drifting away from Mary, and his frequent and extended absences finally convinced her he was seeking to escape her domesticated clutches.

Seeking to locate Imlay, Mary returned to London in 1795, but he rejected her and she attempted suicide by taking laudanum. In a last desperate attempt to win him back, she undertook some delicate negotiations in Scandinavia on his behalf to recoup some of his heavy financial losses in timber-dealing, visiting Norway, Sweden and Denmark, accompanied only by a maid and her tiny daughter. On her return she was still rejected by him, and for a second time tried to kill herself, this time by standing in the rain to soak her clothes and then jumping into the Thames. She was, however, rescued by a passer-by. Reconciling herself to the loss of her loved one, it took her some time to recover, but eventually she became involved with Joseph Johnson's circle again and resumed her authorship. William Godwin read some of her work, and was drawn to her. Slowly their relationship deepened, and for a second time she found herself pregnant. This time things went better with the man of her choice, and the couple were married in March 1797. In August she was delivered of her second child, Mary Godwin.[4] At first, all seemed well, but she became infected during the birth process by the non-delivery of her placenta, which broke apart, a not unusual occurrence at that time, and she died of septicaemia in September 1797. She was buried in Old St Pancras churchyard, and a memorial was constructed to her there, though both her remains and those of William Godwin were later moved to Bournemouth.

The impact of Mary Wollstonecraft as a writer and as a thinker can scarcely be overestimated. Though until the twentieth century her life was read about because of her strange behaviour and her bizarre sexual exploits, where she was often regarded as a 'freakish' exception showing how women should *not* behave, gradually attention began to centre on her ideas and on her writing instead of merely on her adventures. Gradually she began to be recognised not as an early exponent of twentieth-century feminism, but more as a rather untypical creature of her time, formulating ideas which reflected the eighteenth-century context of sensibility, economics and political theory in which they were conceived.

In her *Vindication of the Rights of Men* (1790), she launched into Burke's defence of monarchy, constitutionalism and aristocracy with her own statement of republicanism and radical democracy. He had lamented: 'I had thought that ten thousand swords must have leaped from their scabbards to avenge even a look that threatened her [Marie Antoinette] with insult – but the age of chivalry is gone!' Yet Mary attacked him for his association of beauty with weakness and femininity, and for his employment of gendered language. To her, his conservative defence of the existing order set up two wholly unacceptable ideals – one an unequal society based on privilege and one founded on the passivity of women. Arguing that unreflecting conservatism would allow the continuance of slavery because this, too, was traditional, she showed that the rationalism of her utopian views was preferable, though radical, because it was based on 'true' feeling and not on 'false'.

In her *Vindication of the Rights of Woman* (1792), she extended her consideration of natural rights from men to women. She demanded that women should have a proper education, and claimed that women do essential work in educating the young, and ought to be 'companions' to their husbands and not merely ornamental. In particular, she fumed at the sexual prejudices of writers such as Jean-Jacques Rousseau[5] who would compel women to be mere 'spaniels' or 'toys' for men rather than individuals in their own right. Mary roundly asserted that many women were 'silly' or 'superficial', not because of any inherent intellectual limitations, but merely because of the deficient education that had been inflicted on them.[6] She did not suggest that men and women were *equal*, except in the sight of God, but she argued that the male attitudes which would elevate women's social position as a mere adornment for society, or as sentimental heroines, were in fact destroying the very thing they were idealising. In her twelfth chapter, on 'National Education', she outlines a co-educational form of education that will counteract these mistaken tendencies, and produce women who are intellectually more mature and better fitted to be equal partners of educated men.[7]

Her fictional works give an added dimension to her philosophical theories, fleshing them out in a coherent way. In *Mary* (1788), she shows how a woman is forced into a loveless marriage, and later fulfils her need for love and affection with two passionate friendships, one with a male and one with a female. In *Maria, or the Wrongs of Woman* (1798), she tells how a woman was locked in an insane asylum by her husband, and finds solace in friendships with a fellow inmate and one of her keepers. Female friendships are central to both books, but the fact that at least one of them cuts across classes as well as sexes is the first hint indication hinting at the future feminist theory that women in different class situations share the same type of interests simply because they are women. In her *Letters Written in Sweden, Norway and Denmark* (1796), the publication that brought her close to William Godwin,[8] Mary explores the relationship between the self and society, as well as giving a sociological and geographical picture of Scandinavian society. Here she departs from Rousseau's critique of society, but rather celebrates domestic harmony within it, and accepts rather than dismisses industrial progress. Her views on marriage, partnership and education remain, however, substantially the same.

It is only in the past fifty years that Mary Wollstonecraft's standing as a scholar and moral luminary has come to be recognised, and she came to be accepted as a pioneer of present-day feminism. Her reputation and standing came to suffer in the conservative climate of the nineteenth century simply because she was so unorthodox in her views and unpredictable in her behaviour; but by the end of the twentieth century her true importance had come to be appreciated.

MADAME DE STAËL AND THE IDEA OF LIBERALISM

Madame de Staël is sometimes accused by her detractors of never having had an original idea in her head, instead merely reflecting the current views of others of her generation; and her writing is criticised as florid and sentimental. She was nevertheless setting out important new

ideas at the time of the French Revolution, at the very bedside of the birth of modern history,
and these writings have subsequently moulded much of the political thinking that has gone into
the liberal and constitutional theory of the contemporary age. This qualifies her as a serious
contender for the title of literary and constitutional pioneer.

Mme de Staël was born in Paris in 1766 as Anne Louise Germaine Necker, daughter
of the prominent Swiss politician and financier Jacques Necker, famous as the reformer
who put forward a deceptive analysis of Louis XVI's budgetary predicament[1] and later
made suggestions for reform that the King was neither willing nor able to implement.
Her mother, before her marriage the object of an early amorous pursuit by the historian
Edward Gibbon, was a gifted socialite and mistress of one of the most popular salons of
pre-revolutionary France. Mlle Necker, unlike her mother, who was decorous and strictly
reserved, was in her youth something of a show-off, a flirt, and was always passionately
desirous of prominence and attention. She was conscious of being less attractive
physically than her mother, but she developed early quite remarkable literary skills and
wrote a good deal of fiction on the lines of the sentimental romanticism fashionable at
that time. She spent many of her early years at Coppet, her father's estate on the shores
of Lake Geneva, but returned to Paris in 1785. In 1786 she married Erik Magnus
Staël von Holstein, first an attaché at the Swedish Embassy, and later minister. He was
seventeen years older than her, but it was a genuine match; they produced three children
and there was never any scandal attached to either name.

Mme de Staël experienced some of the turmoil and excitement that preceded the
Revolution in 1789. She had already published a novel, anonymously, and now wrote
a somewhat uncritical series of letters, the Lettres sur J. J. Rousseau, which were more
remarkable for their enthusiasm than for their critical discernment. She did not see the
lapses of judgement or logic evident from a close study of his Contrat Social, nor the
abuses it would be used to justify in the darker days of the Revolution. She was, however,
gratified by the meeting of the Estates General in 1789, and even more delighted
with the recalling, shortly after, of her father from exile in Brussels to form his second
ministry for Louis XVI, though this turned out to be only short-lived. Her first son was
born just as her father finally left France in disgrace.

The troubled days preceding the Terror saw her siding with the more moderate
elements in Paris, but, only days before the September massacres started in 1792 (though
not herself in any immediate danger), she fled to Switzerland, where she gathered about
her a number of friends and fellow refugees, and launched a new salon, which over the
next twenty-five years made her famous among contemporaries. She also visited England,
where she placed herself at the centre of a colony of liberal émigrés finding safety from the
Paris mob in Mickleham in Surrey. However, in 1794 her mother died, and, with the fall
of Robespierre, she came back to Paris with her husband, now accredited as Ambassador
to the French Republic by the Swedish government. Her moderate sympathies accorded
well with the largely middle-class personnel of the Directory, many of whose chief
characters happened to be frequenters of her salon. Her preference was for moderate and
democratic government, and she became a close colleague of the constitutional expert
Benjamin Constant, whom she first met at Coppet in 1794. She had as little time for the

royalists as she did for the radicals, and hated and despised Bonaparte – a mistrust he heartily reciprocated. By this time, she had had two more children, Albert and a daughter Albertine (afterwards Duchess of Broglie), and in 1797 was separated from her husband. Then, in 1799, her husband was recalled, and died in 1802.

Dismayed at the violence shown in the crushing of the coup of 13 Vendémiaire 1795 (the famous 'Whiff of Grapeshot'), Mme de Staël criticised the royalist insurgents for unwittingly providing Bonaparte the opportunity of bringing armed force to bear on the situation in Paris. Shortly after this the Constitution of 1795 came into operation. All five of the Directors being regicides, they seized the chance of enacting, or re-enacting, the legislation against the royalists, which Mme de Staël (being essentially a moderate) deplored.[2] This made her unpopular with the Directors, and she was briefly exiled once more, before returning in time for the re-election of the second third of the Conventionels in 1797. As she predicted, all but eleven of the 216 members who retired under the constitution were defeated, so that the royalists increased their grip over Paris. Mme de Staël lamented: 'Louis XVIII reigns!' But the royalists were a quarrelsome lot, and both she and Benjamin Constant urged the government not to be panicked into repressive action. She founded her Constitutional Club to counteract the influence of the royalist Clichy Club, and suggested that the rigid separation of powers between the executive and the legislative should not be allowed to impede the efforts of the Directors to promote constitutional harmony by dealing effectively with royalist agitation. But the large number of factions, moderate and royalist, few of which made any effort to understand the position of the others, prevented a harmonious solution. This confused political infighting gave Bonaparte his chance to intervene militarily again, and on 18 Fructidor (4 September) 1797 to overpower the Directors and emasculate the Convention by banishing upwards of fifty Conventionels. By this time, the 1795 Constitution was little more than a dead letter, and the way prepared for the further coup which replaced it with the Consulate in 1799.

Thus Mme de Staël's efforts to walk the constitutional tightrope were ultimately unsuccessful – indeed, Talleyrand blamed her for not supporting the royalists strongly enough to prevent the emergence of the Bonapartists. Her view was that moderation was always preferable to extremism. In her writings and in her actions she consistently tried to formulate the theory and effect the practice of what she saw as constitutional freedom.

Her attitude remained unchanged during the whole Napoleonic period, for much of which she found herself hounded by the imperial police and forced into exile.[3] She spent much of her time in Switzerland, but when this passed into French control after 1799, she spent much time in Germany (in Mainz, Frankfurt and Berlin) and in Austria, at Vienna. It was from here that she moved into Galicia, and thence into Russia, Finland and Sweden. She always wished her work to be published in France, but Napoleonic censorship made this impossible. She wound up in England, where it is said she should have gone first of all if she had been really serious in her resistance to Bonaparte. The result was that her major work, *Considérations sur la Révolution Française*, was not published until after the Bourbon restoration in 1814. She then returned to Paris, but was faced with a difficult problem when the effort was made to restore Napoleon during the Hundred Days: she had to choose between the Royalists and the Bonapartists. She resolved her problem by fleeing to Coppet once more, though in the end she did return to France, where she found that in practice Louis XVIII was not as bad as she feared, proving as he did a welcome brake on the enthusiasm of the Ultra-Royalists.

During the period of the Allied occupation of Paris (which did not end until after Mme de Staël's death in 1817), she came into close and frequent contact with the Duke of Wellington, the Supreme Allied Commander, who had his HQ at Cambrai. They wrote to each other frequently. Impressed by the friendly and orderly conduct of British occupation troops in the capital,[4] she seemed almost to wish that Wellington could rule France, since she so strongly disapproved of the conduct of the Ultras and of the reactionary leanings of the Chambre Introuvable in 1816. Wellington, while responding chivalrously to her letters, tried his best to 'keep her light' by avoiding political subjects[5]; she flattered him grossly, but seems to have had a genuine regard for him and a respect for his integrity.[6] Wellington was quite firm in refusing to get embroiled in the detail of French politics. He recommended that she reconcile herself with the House of Bourbon (though he admitted that 'some of those who have been recalled' i.e. Artois, the future Charles X, were 'not as capable of ruling as one could have wished'). Mme de Staël had a stroke early in 1817, and Wellington became a regular visitor to her sickroom, showing a kindness and concern that were quite exceptional. She died on 14 July 1817, on the twenty-eighth anniversary of the storming of the Bastille, and only a year before the ending of the Allied occupation after the Congress of Aix-la-Chapelle in September 1818.

Her rejection of political extremism remained with her to the end of her days, as did her firm attachment to moderate and constitutional forms of government. Louis XVIII, who was somewhat like her in his conduct if not in his principles, protected her from the Ministry of Police, under Décazes, and enabled her to continue to extol the benefits of constitutional liberalism. It was a pity for the future of the royal dynasty that the other Bourbons did not pay more attention to either their restored king or their political writer.

HARRIET MARTINEAU: ECONOMIST, SOCIOLOGIST, HUMANITARIAN

Harriet Martineau was one of the leading intellectual figures of the nineteenth century, a bluestocking whose interests spanned so wide a field of subjects that she is perhaps best referred to as a 'philosopher'. She has also been called by contemporaries and by present-day commentators the first female sociologist in Britain. Her main areas of concern included literary criticism, as well as economics, sociology, abolitionism, social reform and feminism. Her own verdict on her work and career was modest, but not entirely unrealistic.[1]

Harriet Martineau was born in June 1802 in Norwich, Norfolk, her father a manufacturer of Huguenot parentage with strong Unitarian views. Her brother James was a clergyman of some mark in the tradition of English Dissent. She grew up in a home that was serious-minded, industrious and intellectual, but she herself proved to be the weakling of the family, being without a sense of taste or smell, as well as deaf from an early age, and obliged to use an ear trumpet. From the age of sixteen she was obliged to make a prolonged visit to her aunt Mrs Kentish's home in Bristol, where she was in agreeable company and became happier. She did, however, fall under the influence of another powerful figure, the Revd Dr Lant Carpenter, another Unitarian minister, whose stiff and respectable attitudes, she felt, helped to influence her character. About the age of twenty her deafness worsened. She began to write, at first articles for *The Monthly Repository*, a Unitarian periodical, and then her own works, publishing in 1823 her *Devotional Exercises and Addresses*.

In 1826 her elder brother died, followed by her father, leaving the family financially in a difficult situation. Her difficulties were compounded by the death of her fiancé at much the same time, and by the bankruptcy of the finance house in which all the family's monies were invested. Harriet found herself obliged to work for her living, and, being barred from teaching on account of her deafness, decided to become a professional writer. She wrote a number of successful stories, winning three prizes for them from the Unitarian Association, but still could not make enough to live on, and was obliged to take in needlework to supplement her income. At this time, popular interest in the new science of political economy was developing, and she decided to illustrate the subject by way of stories, and this she was engaged to do by the editor of *The Monthly Repository*, to which she had previously contributed. The success of these stories, much to everyone's surprise, was immediate and enormous. She went on in 1834 to complement these stories with four others on *Illustrations of Taxation*, supporting the new Whig Poor Law reforms of 1834. These stories were controversial, and excited the criticism of Tory paternalists and Radicals alike, the first objecting to the reforms as being too 'Malthusian', because they deprecated charity and provision for the poor, the second as too harsh in their consequences for those needing support. Only the Whigs supported her, and she came to be fêted in Whig high society as a result. But her writings certainly made her a lot of new friends. Her literary acquaintances came to include Thomas Malthus, John Stuart Mill, George Eliot (Mary Ann Evans), Edward Bulwer-Lytton, Elizabeth Barrett Browning and Thomas Carlyle. Florence Nightingale and Charlotte Brontë also became her friends.

In 1834, Harriet paid an extended visit to the United States, and gave her open support to the Abolitionist party, which was at that time small and rather unpopular. On her return, her publication of *Theory and Practice of Society* (1837) made it quite clear where she stood, and played its part in introducing the whole slavery question to the English public. Shortly afterwards she wrote *The Hour and the Man* (1840), a book in which she explained her admiration for the Haitian hero and leader Toussaint l'Ouverture.

On his return from his historic trip on the *Beagle*, even Charles Darwin got to know her, when his brother Erasmus, in London, spent some time in his carriage 'driving out Miss Martineau'.[2] During this time she continued to write, producing not only several in her handbooks series, but also providing a *Guide to Service* and another *Maid of All Work* on domestic work (leading to the widespread, though inaccurate, belief that she had once been in service herself). She also wrote her most successful work, a three-volume novel entitled *Deerbrook* (1839).

In 1839, too, her health broke down again, this time because of an ovarian cyst. In the late 1830s she had moved to Newcastle, and it was here that she took medical advice and as part of the remedy moved down the river to Tynemouth, where she lived for the next six years. She provided herself with a telescope, and looking through this at happenings in the locality was almost as good as getting about again. In 1844 she underwent a course of mesmerism, which for a time made her feel better, and the following year she moved to Ambleside in the Lake District where she built herself a new house, 'The Knoll', where she lived for much of the rest of her life. In 1846 she made a tour of the Near East, and, as she passed through each of the sites associated with the historic religions, she gave a good deal of thought to religious matters, at each step her ideas becoming more abstract and philosophical, as well as more agnostic. The book these thoughts generated, *Eastern Life, Present and Past*, caused her some unpopularity on account of its anti-religious tone, and was rejected by her publisher because of its 'infidel tendency', though it did find another publisher later. About this time, back in the Lake District, she wrote *Household Education*, a book postulating that freedom and rationality, rather than command and obedience, were the true forces driving education, and *The History of the Thirty Years' Peace, 1816–1846*, which summarised her ideas on the period from the point of view of a 'philosophical radical' and showed a current awareness of most of the political trends during these three decades. She followed this with *Letters on the Laws of Man's Nature and Development* (1851), which brought together her ideas in a mixture of morality, mesmerism, clairvoyance and philosophical atheism, regarded by many of her contemporaries as scandalous and irreligious. She went on writing tirelessly into the 1850s, contributing to *The Daily News* and the *Westminster Review*, as well as writing further books, such as her *Letters from Ireland*, composed as a result of a tour of that country in 1852.

In 1855 Harriet found herself suffering from a heart condition, and for a time persuaded herself that she was dying. She hastily embarked on her autobiography, though in fact her life was prolonged for a further twenty years and she did not die until June 1876. When Charles Darwin's epoch-making book *The Origin of Species* appeared in 1859 and Erasmus sent a copy to his old flame Harriet, she waxed lyrical,[3] taking the book as confirmation of her own religious stance (which in fact it was not), and rather regretting its author's occasional references to 'the Creator'.

But the remainder of her life was not spent in sterile religious disputation; she found time, too, to further her studies in economics and the social sciences. She never succeeded in finally distinguishing between the two – perhaps because at that time, in the infancy of both disciplines, there was little enough to define either of them. Economics had not yet acquired its statistical or mathematical dimensions, though she had succeeded in mastering the logical principles of laissez-faire capitalism. As for sociology, even the name was yet scarcely invented; indeed, it was not until 1839 that the first outlines of it were found in Auguste Comte's book *Philosophie Positive*. Harriet, on the other hand, had already published her impressions of America in her 1837 book *Society in America* and went on in the following year to set out her ideas in *How to Observe Morals and Manners*, a book pretty well on target in its basic premise that the life of any society was governed by general social laws, including the principle of progress, the emergence of science as the product of intellectual endeavour, and the dynamics of population vis-à-vis the environment. As a result of these theories, Harriet is sometimes referred to by contemporaries as the 'first woman sociologist'. At least it could be argued that her introduction of Comte to the English-speaking world was a point in favour of her recognition as a kindred spirit in the whole discipline of sociology.

Feminism, too, was a study that in her lifetime was as yet undeveloped, and she made no reference in any of her writings to any precise formulation of the subject as a coherent discipline. But her views were discovered later to relate closely to the feminist viewpoint in respect of women's rights, female suffrage, women's place in education and generally in the recognition of women's opinions on matters to do with society as a whole. Modern issues like the rights of women in matters to do with birth control, abortion, contraception, rape or domestic violence had not yet been spelled out and were not matters generally discussed in print in Victorian times, but the fact that she became recognised as a pioneer in the subject of feminism shows that she would have had views on such things, and that she was an originator rather than a follower, and did not entirely deserve the accusation of lack of originality that is sometimes levelled at her (and that she levelled at herself).

Her death in 1876 removed from the scene a major figure whose life was important in developing new ideas, and set back intellectual progress in a number of subjects, chiefly women's subjects, for forty or fifty years until the early part of the twentieth century. She was not a great economist like Ricardo, a great historian like Maitland, a great reformer like Shaftesbury, a great revolutionary like Bakunin or a great scientist like Darwin, but she was important as a significant populariser of new ideas, and had the gift of bringing them together and establishing links between them hitherto unobserved.

ISABELLA BEETON: VICTORIAN HOUSEHOLD MANAGER

Historical evidence on the subject of the world-famous home management specialist Mrs Beeton is curiously thin. This dearth of evidence about her (there seems to be only one photograph of her in her adult years, and this has been doctored) is due to a curious secretiveness created by

*members of her husband's family, in particular her fourth son, Mayson Moss Beeton. He seems
to have had a vested interest in creating an archive of material about her and then refusing
to allow anyone else access to it.[1] At one time, Lytton Strachey, author of the famous work*
Eminent Victorians, *had considered including her in his book, but perhaps it is just as well
that he did not, since he confessed he visualised her as 'a small tub-like lady, rather severe
of aspect and strongly resembling Queen Victoria', when in fact she was nothing like that
– indeed, born in 1836, she was almost too young to be called Victorian at all. Furthermore, her
appearance did not fit the pattern. She was slim rather than tubby, serene rather than severe,
and middle-class rather than regal.[2] But in some respects the Beeton story may be a Victorian
one, not least because of the deep and lasting feud that sprang up between the two sides of the
family, the Beetons on the father's side and the Maysons and the Dorlings on the mother's. The
story of her life was never comprehensively put together until 2005, when Kathryn Hughes
published her biography as* The Short Life and Long Times of Mrs Beeton. *This article
draws much of its information from that biography.*

The early history of the family has a Regency rather than a Victorian flavour. It has
its roots in an England that was rural and pre-industrial. Mrs Beeton's grandfather,
John Mayson, spent forty years in Cumberland serving as a curate in the late eighteenth
century because he lacked the social cachet of the Oxbridge degree that would have given
him preferment in the Church. Her father, Benjamin – biblically named as the third and
youngest child of the curate – took the opportunity of an industrialising Lancashire to go
into textiles, and in 1831 moved to the City of London as a 'Manchester warehouseman'
dealing wholesale in linen cloth. He married the daughter of a couple in domestic service
who had their roots near Chichester, one of whose father was head-hunted by the Duke
of Richmond as a groom at Goodwood and so moved in fashionable horsey circles,
while the other's father, also with rural roots but in Hampshire, set up a livery stable near
Marylebone. Isabella, born in 1836, was the daughter of this marriage. Her father died
suddenly in 1841 and the five-year-old Isabella was sent back to live with her grandfather
in Cumberland. Shortly afterwards her mother married again, to Henry Dorling, a young
printer, himself now a widower who had been a friend of the family. The Dorlings lived
at Epsom, a quiet town for most of the year, but blossoming annually for the races on
Derby Day. Henry and his father William – also in the printing business – made money
by printing race cards for the course (said to be 'Correct' or 'Genuine' i.e. accurate). In
1839 Henry was appointed Clerk of the Course, and soon became famous and quite rich
by investing in the Grandstand, specially built for the races in 1830. The couple built
themselves Ormond House nearby to house both the family and the printing business,
but, though roomy, it was not big enough to accommodate the whole Mayson-Dorling
brood, which came by the 1840s to number seventeen children – including four from
the marriage of Isabella's mother, four from that of her stepfather, and five from the new
match.[3] Indeed, Isabella, at twelve the steadiest and the eldest of the children, was now
expected to act as unpaid nursery-maid to the whole brood, and was given the run of the
Grandstand, which doubled its function both as racing grandstand and nursery.

Isabella's education was patchy. She went for a time to a little boarding school in
Islington, and then for rather more than two years to what passed as a 'finishing school'

in Heidelburg, under a Frau Heidel, where she learned a little about dance, music and domestic economy, but spent her time chiefly on arithmetic, French and German. This was relatively unusual for a girl of her class and background. She returned at the age of eighteen in 1854 to play the part of the 'daughter at home' in the interval between childhood and marriage.

Isabella Mayson and Samuel Beeton had bumped into each other many times before they started courting. They lived in close proximity in the City of London, Isabella for a time in Milk Street, and Samuel nearby, where his father kept the Dolphin public house at the junction of Milk Street with Cheapside. The Beeton family hailed from Stowmarket, and before becoming a publican, Sam's father, another Sam, had been a tailor who had later gone in for local politics as a Common Councillor for the Pattenmakers Guild.[4] The family was busy, locally important and socially active, even if not entirely respectable. The younger Sam went in for the paper trade in and around Fleet Street and the Strand, supplying stationery and newsprint for local firms, and even doing a bit of publishing on the side in unofficial partnership with printers' apprentices such as Frederick Greenwood, a typesetter, and Charles Clarke, who was a book-binder. As young men about town, the three of them saw what passed for the nightlife of the City, mixing with the riff-raff and the many prostitutes who frequented the streets. Clarke and Beeton's little firm scored an early hit with the English publication of Harriet Beecher Stowe's *Uncle Tom's Cabin*, pirated from the USA, selling in large numbers from a 1*s* railway edition to a luxury version, with illustrations, which was priced at 7*s* 6*d*.[5] Their luck, however, ran out with their publication of Mrs Stowe's sequel to *Uncle Tom's Cabin*, called *The Key to Uncle Tom's Cabin* (which turned out to be a rather tedious collection of the author's sources for the first book), and though the firm of Clarke and Beeton limped on for a few years it never made much money thereafter. It did, however, bring Beeton's name into public circulation.

Sam and Isabella knew each other for about two years before they became officially engaged in 1855. Theirs was a tempestuous engagement, chiefly because Isabella's family (and especially the Dorlings, who always thought – and said – that the young lady was marrying beneath her) found Sam pushy and not entirely honest. He certainly went to great lengths to avoid meeting them. Even Isabella, sweet on him as she was, could not help wondering what he thought he was doing making all these transparent excuses for avoiding them. Yet, in spite of his dislike and mistrust, Henry Dorling put on a good show for the wedding at Epsom in July 1856, though he could not help getting a bit of free publicity by arranging the wedding breakfast afterwards in the Grandstand at the course.

The newlyweds, after their honeymoon, took up residence in rented accommodation at Woodridings near Pinner, at that time a village about thirteen miles north-west of London. There is no evidence that the couple were not devoted to each other, but life was not the rural idyll that Isabella might have expected. Within a few months she found herself working as a journalist – and an unpaid one – for her husband; within a year she was compiling material for a *Book of Household Management*, and by 1860 she was editor of one women's magazine, *The Englishwoman's Domestic Magazine*, and was also helping in the launch of another. But before then, in May 1857, Isabella gave birth to her first son, named Samuel Orchart Beeton after his father. Both parents were deliriously happy, but both so busy with magazine business that there was a long delay before they could even find time to register the birth. However, the child was a sickly one, and within three months he died. Diarrhoea, croup and even cholera were suggested as the infant's cause of death, but the most likely explanation is congenital (i.e. prenatal) syphilis, the fruit of Sam's 'gay time' at the Dolphin.[6] It seems likely that Sam's increasingly unpredictable behaviour in his later years could be put down to incipient insanity caused by syphilis – but whether he was aware that he had the disease and had given it to Isabella is doubtful.

In spite of the shock of the death and the strain it placed on the household, Isabella was soon back at her literary work. After August 1857 she had embarked on her magnum opus, a book, originally titled *Beeton's Book of Household Management, edited by Mrs Isabella Beeton*, but which became better known under its later title of *Mrs Beeton's Book of Household Management*. It was this book, not finished until 1861, which made her name a byword for accuracy and thoroughness. Its crisp style, easy avoidance of any circumlocution and its didactic tone contrived to make her sound like an experienced matron of fifty with a lifetime of domestic know-how instead of the newly-married young girl of twenty-one that she really was.

The year 1861, however, did not see a happy ending to the family's troubles. Sam was always getting himself into scrapes of one kind or another, usually as the result of his slapdash book-keeping. Because he saw there was money in it, he took up with *haute couture*, and started a new magazine *Queen*,[7] with a respectful nod to the much-revered (but now, after the death of her beloved Albert, black-draped) Victoria, and aiming at women who took a pride in their appearance. He gave the editorship to Isabella, who made several trips to Paris in pursuit of publishable ideas. He broke rather acrimoniously with Charles Clarke, but continuing financial embarrassments led him to give up the house in Pinner and move back to London, where they now lived 'over the shop' in the Strand. He had to sell *Queen* to Edward Cox, and he promptly appointed one of his own friends – a woman – to the editorship. For her part, Isabella had produced another son – also called Samuel Orchart – in 1859, but he also was sickly, and died when he was little more than three, his family blaming the smoky air of London for his death.[8] It was here, over the publisher's offices in the Strand, that she gave birth to her third child, also a son. To break the jinx, he was christened Orchart, and he lived until 1947. Shortly afterwards, the family moved out of the City into Greenhithe, at that time a village on the Kent side of the Thames. Here, in 1865, she was delivered of her fourth son, Mason Moss Beeton.[9] Unfortunately she did not survive the ordeal. She contracted puerperal fever, possibly by reason of the transferral of bacteria from another birth by means of the unwashed hands of the doctor in attendance, and she died in great agony several days afterwards. Sam, of course, got the blame for overburdening his wife with work, and the Dorlings thereafter built up the legend of his being a cruel, dreadful man who married a clever, ladylike girl and reduced her to a drudge.

Thereafter, in due course, Sam took up with a Greenhithe couple, Charles and Myra Browne, who gave him both financial and editorial help in his continuing publishing work. It seems likely that she too gave him a child. Sam dabbled in variety of schemes ranging from high fashion through academic textbooks to pornography connected to flagellation and to the wearing of tight corsets. But most of his schemes failed and he was reduced to selling out many of his rights to Frederick Warne, including his rights to his much-prized book on *Household Management*. His finances, never his strong point, suffered further damage when he was caught up in the collapse of the discount house of Overend and Gurney in 1866, which brought ruin to thousands of businesses. He was still embroiled in the courts when, on the verge of bankruptcy, he finally sold his business completely to Ward, Lock and Tyler in 1867 for the paltry sum of £1,900 – though in compensation he did get a position in the company and a rising share of its profits. But it did not seem to do Sam any good. His frenzied style of life steadily degenerated into dementia and he died in 1877.

Mrs Beeton's Book of Household Management, which was the most lasting of her memorials, provides evidence of the Victorian love of system, neatness and order even in domestic affairs. It aimed to remedy the 'family discontent' caused by household mismanagement and it provided a valuable *vade mecum* for the middle-class housewife. Isabella provides an exhaustive index at the beginning rather than at the end, and in the best traditions of legal textbooks she numbers her paragraphs from 1 to 2751. She divides the book into sections: there are sections dealing with the 'arrangement of the kitchen' and, more widely, with the duties of the housekeeper and the duties and the recommended pay of the other domestic servants. There are even tips for the 'mistress' on the giving and returning of 'calls', the correct way to address a bishop, the writing of 'letters of introduction', on seating for dinner and on proper etiquette at table. There are sections on the rearing of children, the treatment of their illnesses from convulsions to worms, and the nursing of invalids.[10] The sections on the duties of housemaids, and particularly of the 'maid-of-all-work' (2340 to 2356), suggests that such people should have the patience of Job, the strength of an ox and that ideally, first to rise and last to retire, they should never need any sleep. But in the main the book is filled with recipes, of which there are literally hundreds. Grouped under headings like sheep, hogs, calf, birds and game, it deals also with vegetables, sauces, pickles, gravies, soups, and puddings, pastries and cakes. They were all very systematically treated, with the list of their ingredients given at the beginning instead of in their usual place at the end.

But in fact there is no evidence that Isabella Beeton was in the least interested in cooking, or indeed ever went anywhere near the kitchen either before or after writing the book. Considering the number of late meals she left for Sam congealing on the hot plate when he got back from work, and considering the witness of contemporaries who attested to the 'shocking meals' she served up to her evening guests, it seems perhaps a pity she did not pay more attention to her own published advice.

In reality her whole book was nothing more than a scissors-and-paste job from start to finish. Like many cookery specialists, before and after, she stole her recipes mainly from the collections of others. Some of the people she borrowed from were foreigners like Carême and Soyer[11]; others were people employed in grand British households of the aristocratic variety, like the Yorks or the Bedfords or even Queen Victoria herself.

If they were still alive, or famous enough to be recognisable, she usually acknowledged her sources and limited her borrowings to a few phrases; if they were dead, or obscurely foreign, she copied them out paragraph by paragraph or even page by page. Her favourite device was to quote a short passage with due acknowledgment and then follow it with more extensive extracts unacknowledged. Many of her recipes were sent in by loyal readers of her magazine. She could not even claim to have tried her recipes out. If she had done that she would never have left the kitchen during the time it took for the book to be prepared. Even the declaration she makes in the first sentence of her preface, that had she known beforehand the labour that this book would have cost her, she would never have embarked on the project, was not inserted because it was true (although it may well have been) but because it was the conventional preliminary admission to make, and other cook-book writers did the same.

Yet it is not the entire truth that she was a simple plagiarist. As well as the strong affection and the sense of wifely duty that made her complete the work imposed on her by her husband, there was an encyclopedist instinct driving her to make lists and tables and rules to provide a framework for the Victorian household, and there was also the scientific desire to do away with the baffling vagueness of existing cookery books by setting things in order and defining exactly how much is meant by a cupful, a spoonful or a drop.[12] As a magazine contributor, too, she knew how to appeal to the snobbish inclinations of the lower middle-class 'lady' who wished to outdo her continental competitors in their babas, madeleines and flans. Though she was not a great cook or housekeeper, she gives us plenty of evidence that she would like to have been.

ANNIE BESANT

Annie Besant is best remembered for her role in the Match Girls' Strike of 1888 and for her advocacy of contraception. But in her very long life she pursued a wide variety of philanthropic interests, published books, wrote for the press and was a major campaigner for women's rights and Indian independence. It could be argued that she was as eclectic in her choice of good causes as she was in her choice of men.

Annie was born in London in 1847, the daughter of William Wood and Emily (*née* Morris). The family originated in Ireland, and was respectably middle-class, but her father died when she was five and her mother tried unsuccessfully to support the family by taking charge of a boys' boarding house at Harrow. It was such a hard struggle that Emily eventually entrusted the upbringing of her daughter to a family friend. She received a good education, and was imbued with strong senses of moral responsibility and of female capability, and she was able to embark upon European travel, where she learned to admire the mystic and ceremonial aspects of Catholicism. These were to have a profound influence on her later spiritual development.

The main career for Victorian women was marriage and in 1867 Annie married the Reverend Frank Besant, soon to be vicar of Sibsey in Lincolnshire; by him she had two children. But she found marriage a strait-jacket. She had begun to earn money from her writing and Frank appropriated it, since a woman's property belonged by the law of the time to the husband. He was not very sympathetic to her interests, as women were expected to be meek and submissive, not stubborn and independent. His Tory views conflicted with her own which were becoming increasingly left-wing. Eventually she committed the ultimate crime of an Anglican clergyman's wife by refusing to attend communion. She left him, and taking her daughter with her, took up residence in London. Since divorce was virtually an impossibility for a clergyman, Annie remained married to, but separated from, her husband for the rest of his life.

Once in London Annie began part-time studies, but caused alarm among her teachers by the novelty and extremism of her political and religious views. Her attacks on organised religion brought her to the attention of the National Secular Society and Annie began writing for their newspaper, the *National Reformer*. This brought her into close contact with Charles Bradlaugh, its leader, and they lived together for a number of years, though not as sexual partners. Annie became one of the speakers for the Society and soon demonstrated a gift for oratory. As a result she was in demand up and down the country, and used the rapidly developing railway network to great effect. In 1877 she and Bradlaugh republished a book written by the American Charles Knowlton, *The Fruits of Philosophy*. He had argued the case for birth control and showed explicitly in his book how to achieve it. This caused pious Victorian hands to be raised in horror. It was one thing to be sexually liberated in private but very much another thing to flaunt such liberation in public. Anything with the faintest hint of sexual explicitness was generally regarded as pornographic, sinful, and criminal. So Charles and Annie were arrested, tried, found guilty, and released on appeal. The appeal succeeded, but only on a technicality. The trial generated much public interest and much newspaper correspondence. It brought the issue of birth control before the public in a way that its previous advocates had never been able to do, and after the trial the ban on distributing information about contraception came to an end. Charles and Annie saw their acquittal as a vindication, but Annie lost custody of her children to her husband who claimed that her advocacy of birth control made her an unfit mother.

Charles' political ambitions were achieved by his election to Parliament for Northampton in 1881, although his refusal to take the religious oath of allegiance led to a series of expulsions from the House of Commons and by-elections until he was finally allowed to take his seat in 1887. In the meantime, Annie had developed new political interests. She wrote in her newspaper columns in favour of Irish Home Rule and gave her support to Michael Davitt and his Irish Land League.[1] She took up the cause of unskilled working-class labourers, both rural and urban, and urged them to become unionised. Bradlaugh was not impressed. He had no enthusiasm for working-class militancy, less for women's rights, and even less for socialism with which Annie was now flirting. As her friendship with Bradlaugh cooled, her friendship with George Bernard Shaw,[2] one of the Fabian Society's founders, prospered. He persuaded Annie to join the Fabian Society. She in turn invited him to live with her, which he declined. She transferred her affections to Edward Aveling, a young socialist teacher who had boarded with her. He soon moved out to live with Karl Marx's daughter so Annie came under the influence of William Morris, the artist, who had established the Socialist League. Through him she became a Marxist, but instead of joining the Socialist League she joined the Social Democratic Federation in 1888, even though its revolutionary views were in contrast to those of the Fabian Society of which she still remained a member.

In the autumn of 1887 rising unemployment had led to increasing unrest and workers' protests. Annie agreed to speak at one of the protests arranged for Trafalgar Square on 13 November. The meeting led to violence, soldiers were called in to assist the police, and one of the protesters died. There were many injuries and many arrests. Annie provocatively invited the police to arrest her as well, but the police declined; they did not wish to incur any further adverse publicity for an event already described in the popular press as Bloody Sunday. She responded by organising financial and legal aid for those who were jailed.

She soon found a new cause to champion. She had fallen in love with Herbert Burrows, a young socialist who been in contact with Bryant and May's match girls and who was appalled at their working conditions. They received pitiful wages, eight shillings a week for a woman, four shillings for a girl, and fines were imposed for minor misdemeanours. Industrial disease was rampant since the phosphorus they used to make the match heads was poisonous to the lungs and caused rotting of facial bones with facial disfigurement.[3] Burrows and Annie published an article, 'White Slavery in London', describing their working conditions and calling for a boycott of Bryant and May matches. Matches were big business since virtually all forms of lighting (candles, oil, gas) required initial lighting by match. Bryant and May were very big and powerful and very horrified. The firm threatened legal action against Herbert and Annie and required all their employees to sign a document to attest that they were well treated. One girl refused to sign and was dismissed by the firm. To everyone's surprise, including Annie's, 700 match girls immediately downed tools and came out on strike. Annie not only gave them moral support, she organised them to hold meetings all over London, including the West End, where onlookers were appalled by their unhealthy appearance, their jaw disease and their inadequate clothing. The strike was eventually settled by arbitration which conceded to the match girls nearly all their demands: better pay, recognition of their union and the ending of fines.

Her success with the match girls emboldened her for participation with the dockers' strike of 1889. Although Ben Tillett was its prime mover, in this he received invaluable help from Annie in drawing up the rules of the Dockers' Union, and she organised and addressed meetings, and did her best to whip up public support for the dockers. They struck for a basic wage of 6*d* per hour (the dockers' tanner), came very near to defeat, but public sympathy and support throughout the world saw them through and they, too, gained most of their demands.

Annie was now very much a public figure. Apart from her active support of the match girls and the dockers she had cashed in on her notoriety to secure election to the London School Board in 1888. She was very much in demand for newspaper articles and in 1889 she was asked for a review of H. P. Blavatsky's book *The Secret Doctrine*, in which he expounded the theory of theosophy.[4] To this Annie was greatly attracted and its mysticism in a way conformed with the mysticism she claimed to have found in the Roman Catholic Church in her youth. By 1890 theosophy became her religion and her close links with British socialist groups had ended. She developed a deep friendship with Blavatsky, and when he died in 1891 she became one of theosophy's most important exponents. After some internal turmoil the Theosophical Society's main base was in India, which Annie first visited in 1893. The Society owed a great deal at first to Buddhism, but Annie steered the Society towards Hinduism and helped to establish the Central Hindu College for the training of young boys. This was to become the founder college of the Banaras Hindu University, established in 1917. Annie had, in 1907, been elected International President of the Theosophical Society and this greatly assisted her in her fundraising for the college and university. Annie had for some time shown interest in freemasonry, and when she discovered that there was a branch, The International Order of Co-Freemasonry, she and several friends had hastened to join in 1902. Within a few years Annie had founded several lodges in Britain and abroad and had become the Most Puissant Grand Commander of them – all this while she was so very active in furthering the Theosophical Society's work in India.

It was difficult to work in India and not be aware of the underlying political tensions. Shortly before the outbreak of the First World War, she joined the Indian National Congress. At first its concern was to provide educated Indians with some share in local government, but the outbreak of war was the nationalist opportunity. Annie edited *New India*, a newspaper demanding Indian home rule. In 1916 she helped to create the Home Rule League, an echo of Michael Davitt. The government's reaction was repression, and in June 1917 Annie was arrested and sent into confinement on a hill station. Nationwide protests followed demanding her release, strongly supported by both Congress and the Muslim League. The government of India backed down. It promised some moves towards Indian self-government and released Annie in September. Three months later Congress made her its president for a year, and Annie was the one of the only three Britons ever to have held the office.

One of those who had written demanding Annie's release was Mahatma Gandhi. He was one of the new leadership, and although he advocated non-violence Annie was concerned about Congress' lurch towards socialism. Her own socialism had become tempered over time. But Annie, arrayed in her own version of Indian costume, continued to work for Indian independence. She toured both India and Britain, effectively making the case for it. Age inevitably slowed her down, and she died at Adyar in India in 1933. She had, during her later years, formed a close bond with Jiddu Krishnamurti, who had been adopted as a young boy by the Theosophical Society in Adyar, and who had led his own Order of the Star of the East with their encouragement and support. When he broke his ties with the Society in 1929 Annie bought him land for his maintenance, and after her death he, with others including Aldous Huxley, built a school, the Besant Hill School, in her memory.

Annie Besant had a very long and very active life, and she was not averse to pursuing vastly different causes at the same time. She was one of the few Victorian women who refused to accept the place allocated to them by society, and outraged her contemporaries by breaking its implicit rules. In Britain she challenged convention; in India she challenged government. She had a considerable measure of success in both.

EMILY HOBHOUSE AND THE SOUTH AFRICAN WAR

Emily Hobhouse was the champion of the rights of ordinary folk threatened with internment in British concentration camps[1] at the time of the Second Boer War (1899–1902) in South Africa. In the face of prolonged and violent provocation, and the disapproval of many of her countrymen for her 'unpatriotic' actions in defending the national enemy, she eventually secured, almost single-handedly, the capitulation of the British government to her demands for fair and humane treatment of mostly innocent civilians.

Emily Hobhouse was one of the most highly controversial characters of her generation and was involved with a number of issues that put her, and kept her, in the public eye for most of her lifetime. She was born in 1860, fifth of six surviving children, in the Rectory of St Ive (pronounced 'Eve'), daughter of Archdeacon Reginald Hobhouse and his wife Caroline (*née* Trelawny, of the ancient Cornish family of Trelawny, the name that formed the subject of the Cornish national anthem 'And shall Trelawny die?'). The Archdeacon grew more cantankerous as he aged, and by the time of his death was quite hypochondriac. After his wife's death, and the departure of Emily's siblings, he kept his daughter at home to care for him until she was thirty-four, lonely, though in conditions of relative comfort.[2] Emily had been only very sketchily educated at a finishing school in London, but was highly intelligent and resentful that others, like Elizabeth Garrett, got on, while she was stuck at home. All this had predictable effects on her character: she was strong-willed, authoritarian and often acerbic; she gave a wigging to at least four British prime ministers, administered rebukes to hapless clerks and junior officers that still manage to curl the toes, and had endless and repeated trouble with domestic servants, who, if they were not dismissed, walked out of her service in high dudgeon. Her friends admired her directness and her unvarnished candour; her enemies branded her as overbearing, calculating and manipulative. Her biographer, John Hall, says of her that she was 'part Joan of Arc, part Florence Nightingale and part Vanessa Redgrave'.

Her father's death in 1895 set Emily free to enter the world and the means to endeavour to improve it.[3] To her startled brothers and sisters she declared her intention to carry out good works abroad, and set off for Minnesota, where, in a remote settlement known as Virginia City, not far from Duluth in the far corner of Lake Superior, she expected to find Cornish miners in need of her ministrations. In fact, if they were engaged in mining at all, it was only in the open-cast variety. She found the climate of the place insupportable: a mixture of forest and marshland, it was suffocatingly hot in summer, bitterly cold in winter. Nevertheless, she worked hard, often in the teeth of local corruption, and earned the respect of many of the locals. Unfortunately, she got herself taken in by one of them, John Carr Jackson. He proved a swindler who relieved her of the greater part of her fortune and then abandoned her, making off to Mexico under a charge of the embezzlement of municipal funds, but nonetheless continuing to pester her for money for a good time afterwards. She made a trip to the Caribbean and strenuous efforts to rescue the relationship, but in the end, back in England, she terminated her engagement, and sought a new outlet for her humanitarian aspirations in the South African war in 1899.

Here a conflict between the stolid Boers and go-getting English imperialists who dreamed of creating an 'all-red line' from the Cape to Cairo, resulted in open war over Boer repression of predominantly British mining immigrants, known to the Boers as *Uitlanders*. They had flocked to the country in search of the gold and diamonds to be found there, and were then heavily taxed there and denied civil rights. The imperialist champions were Cecil Rhodes, soon to become Prime Minister of Cape Colony, Joseph Chamberlain, British Colonial Secretary, and Alfred Milner, a diplomat who displayed a polished legalistic suavity, now British High Commissioner for South Africa. To Emily Hobhouse they represented all that she despised about career politicians; she had no time for any of them.

She became a member of the South African Conciliation Committee, founded only three weeks after the declaration of war in October 1899, and was immediately branded as a 'pro-Boer' and therefore a traitor, even before she set sail for South Africa. By the time she landed at Table Bay at the end of 1900, the British and Empire soldiers had effectively broken the back of the enemy army[4] and were now intent on subduing the two newly occupied Boer republics. She met Milner at Government House – he was almost as wary of meeting her as she was of him (he was distrustful of women, mainly because he was afraid of them) – and extracted from him almost every concession she could expect over the management of the concentration camps.[5]

There was no doubt that the camps were atrociously managed by the military authorities: there was an acute shortage of doctors and nurses; supplies of food, medicine and fuel were desperately short (the shortage of soap was the worst, making it difficult for the inmates to keep clean – the excuse that the Boers were a 'filthy lot', anyway, cut little ice with Emily), and as a result epidemics of cholera, typhoid and diphtheria were endemic, and fatalities were currently running at about 500 per month. Furthermore, the bell-tents employed by the camp authorities to house inmates were inadequate and quite unsuitable for people accustomed to living on the open veld. Emily dwelt obsessively on items like combs, needles and thread, stuffing for mattresses and, above all, soap – none of these items had occurred to the military mind. Scissors and thimbles were like gold, and were handed round from tent to tent. She virtually bankrupted herself paying out of her own purse for food and medical supplies, clothes and blankets to meet the needs of the inmates of the camps. She made no distinction between the 'hands-uppers', who favoured a policy of surrender, and the 'bitter-enders' who wanted to continue with the struggle to the end. And they all worshipped her.[6] The British officers in charge treated her with a mixture of blank incomprehension and bureaucratic obstruction. Soldiers were good at doing what they had been trained for, but much worse at carrying out humanitarian work. There were, however, a few who afforded her such gallant courtesy as to reduce her to tears. As well as British officials, Emily got to know a number of Cape Dutch, and some prominent Boer families as well such as the Steyns, the Fichardts, the de Villiers family and a number of others. Meantime, the camp inmates went on dying and producing babies as if nothing were amiss.[7] But by the time Emily sailed for home, the death toll in the camps had risen to over 1,000 per week.

Emily returned home aboard the *Saxon*, the same ship as brought Milner back to a hero's welcome and to ennoblement as Baron Milner of St James's and Cape Town.[8] He was sworn into the Privy Council and awarded the freedom of the city of London. Meantime, Emily produced a 40-page report on conditions in the camps, and a shorter pamphlet that she had had printed and distributed to the members of both Houses of Parliament. She had a two-hour interview with Sir Henry Campbell-Bannerman, the Leader of the Opposition, which visibly moved him and evoked his comment about British policies that has been so often quoted in the history books as 'methods of barbarism'. The radical Lloyd George (whom she did not much care for) was now her ally. She had come to his rescue once before in July 1900, when a public meeting they had been attempting to address in Liskeard had produced such uproar that he had to be smuggled out the back way in disguise as a policeman. Together and separately, they now held meetings all over the country. Emily found herself greeted with standing ovations or with boos and hisses, according to the sympathies of the audience. She addressed, or tried to address, over sixty meetings in the summer of 1901. At one of them, in Darlington, the pandemonium was so loud and sustained that she stood before her audience for an hour and a half waiting to speak, and eventually left without opening her mouth. The government imposed a ban on her ever returning to South Africa to continue her work, but nevertheless finally bowed to the storm, and decided to send an official commission to inspect the camps, but chose as its leader not Miss Hobhouse, but Mrs Millicent Garrett Fawcett.[9] She, too, came from Cornwall, but in other respects was quite different from Emily. She was an unrepentant believer in what she called 'the laws of economics' and rejected any attempt to protect women workers in mines or mills, or the efforts of what she called 'drawing-room philanthropists' to champion Bryant and May's match girls dying from phosphorus poisoning; above all, like Kipling, she was a great believer in Britain's imperialist mission to govern the lesser races (which she believed included the Irish). All the same, her final report, running to 300 pages and packed with damning statistics, broadly backed up Emily's devastating conclusions, and roundly condemned the camp authorities for their failure to implement elementary rules of sanitation, to check the spread of disease, to provide medical attention for the internees, or to feed them properly. In illustration of this, by the summer of 1901 camp mortality topped 2,500 per month, and in October reached 3,250.

All this confirmed Emily's private decision to defy the government's ban and to visit South Africa again. At the beginning of October she sailed for Cape Town aboard the *Avondale Castle*, but when she arrived the military authorities refused her entry and would not let her leave the ship. They offered instead passage home, first on the liner *Carisbrooke*, then, when she refused to transfer, on the troopship *Roslin Castle*. She used every device known to womanhood in wheedling them to let her remain in South Africa, but ultimately was manhandled and overpowered and forcibly removed from her cabin and placed aboard the waiting vessel.[10] Her journey home was one long litany of complaint, about the smells, the reek of tobacco smoke, the pitching of the ship, the vibration of the propeller and the discomfort aboard what was, after all, the smallest and the oldest troopship in service.

Emily arrived back in England at the end of November 1901, determined to make public her protest at the way she had been treated. The difference was that, the first time, the fuss had been about the concentration camps; now it was about Emily herself. Half the papers bewailed her fate; the other half continued their complaints about her conduct.[11] The controversy subsided only with the signature of the Treaty of Vereeniging, ending the war, at the end of May 1902.[12] The war cost the British taxpayer £250 million, and the peace treaty at its conclusion provided the only example of an indemnity paid by the victor to the loser. The death toll in the concentration camps finally topped 28,000, nearly all of them women and children.

About this time, Emily also wrote *The Brunt of the War*, accepted for publication by the London publisher Methuen. The book provides a detailed critique of the conduct of the Boer War, and is still an indispensable source on the camps. She visited South Africa a third time in the summer of 1903, this time without any of the dire consequences she had endured two years before, and this time saw the sorry straits to which the war had reduced the Boer homesteads on the veld. Nearly half a million horses, mules and cattle had been slaughtered, and food was desperately short. Enjoying the meagre hospitality offered her by the people she knew on the veld, she was often hungry and forced to raid her private hoard of *biltong* during the night, made up with bread she had filched into clandestine sandwiches. The sight of the devastation brought vividly to her mind the Valley of the Dry Bones in the Old Testament. In Bloemfontein she renewed old acquaintances with Martinus Steyn, President of the old Orange Free State but now an invalid, and his wife Isabella, long Emily's friend. She also made a friend of Louis Botha, one of the Boers' war heroes. She also got to know Jan Smuts, and remained his close confidante and pen-friend to the end of her life.[13] She rather shocked her Boer hosts by mingling with the native population and enquiring how the war had affected them.[14] Her experiences left her rather sceptical over the role of the organised churches during the war, and her churchgoing habits declined, though she stopped short of the outright agnosticism of her brother Leonard.

She did not return to England until the end of 1903, and played little part in the 'Chinese Slavery' question[15] that soon afflicted both South Africa and Britain at the time of the 1906 general election, though there was no doubt where Emily's sympathies lay. She inherited substantially at the death of her uncle Arthur, Lord Hobhouse, in December 1904, and visited South Africa for a third time in an extended visit from February 1905 to October 1908, during which time she built herself a house for her retirement (though she never used it) and acquired an enormous St Bernard dog that created a sensation in a country quite unused to such large hairy animals. The death of this dog, and Emily's retirement from her self-imposed assignment of creating 'spinning schools' for Boer woman (about sixteen in the Transvaal and a further twelve in the old Free State), were what lay behind her return to Britain at the end of 1908.

But Emily found it difficult to live without a cause to support. She dabbled with the suffragette movement, but failed to get excited over its main issue of 'Votes for Women', and in any case did not get on well with its leaders (hardly surprising, really, considering that they did not get on very well with each other). Some of her later causes were still centred on South Africa, which she visited yet again in 1913, observing the creation of a 120-foot sandstone obelisk, an impressive monument near Bloemfontein to those who had given up their lives in the war, at whose unveiling she spoke movingly in December. She also met, and struck up a friendship with, Mahatma Gandhi, who clearly trusted her, and whose cause she also embraced in trying to secure a better standing for Indian immigrants into South Africa.[16] She played a part in bringing him into touch both with Smuts, and with Prime Minister General Botha, whose guest she was at the time, and arranging the beginnings of the scaling down of the discriminatory legislation directed against the 100,000 Indian population in the country. Gandhi was immensely grateful to her – she had played, he said, 'no mean part in the settlement'. For much of the time, however, Emily's life was plagued by indifferent health, and her role was much less consistent than in her younger years.

But it was her extraordinary role in attempting a single-handed effort to halt the First World War with Germany that stands out as the final great endeavour of her life. Emily returned from her sojourn in South Africa in early 1914 to find a rapidly escalating international crisis between the major powers. She never believed the belligerent things that were said about 'the Germans, the poor dears', as she put it; and the outbreak of war in that hot summer left her with the unshakeable belief that it was all a mistake, and that a little common sense would sort out differences whose importance was being grossly overinflated. She found herself the unexpected ally of Mrs Fawcett in the Women's International League, condemning the stupidity of the generals in allowing themselves to be carried away by war fever, bewailing the carnage inflicted in its battles, and urging sensible negotiation to end it. Emily's nephew Stephen Hobhouse, younger son of 'Cousin Henry' Hobhouse, reinforced the government's already unflattering view of her as 'that bloody woman' by espousing the pacifist cause together with his wife, Rosa, and declaring himself a conscientious objector (for which he served a three-month sentence in Northampton Gaol). Emily, recuperating briefly in Rome at the start of 1916, hatched her one-woman peace strategy here, moved to Switzerland, and journeyed quite openly from there into Germany, where she was received by a somewhat sceptical German Foreign Minister Gottlieb von Jagow, who had her conducted on visits to Belgium, where she found the civilian population unbrutalised and the nuns there unraped, and to a prisoner-of-war camp near Berlin housing British soldiers captured in action and kept in conditions far better than those in the camps she had seen in South Africa.[17] All this confirmed Emily in the opinion she had already formed that the whole war was a mistake, and she returned home after nearly a month at the end of June to point out to the British government the error of its ways.

To say that the British government was surprised by this unilateral peace initiative would be an understatement. Some of its members demanded that she be shot immediately as a spy, or at least an enemy agent; others that she should be imprisoned for a very long time on whatever charge they could summon up; all were unanimous that her actions were plainly a breach of the Defence of the Realm Act, and that excursions of this sort into enemy territory had to be prevented in future by changes in the law. In the end, nothing happened to her at all, and the whole affair was swept discreetly under the carpet. Even those who agreed with her views said they thought 'she was sweet, but a little mad'.

After the Armistice she organised the mass feeding of children throughout Europe with fresh milk and cooked meals, and protested vigorously, and almost alone, against the ridiculous – but nonetheless pitiless – provision in the Treaty of Versailles that Germany should surrender 140,000 milking cows to the victorious Allies.

Emily Hobhouse's death in 1926 passed almost unnoticed, with very little comment in British newspapers. Her body was carried to Golders Green crematorium where she was unobtrusively cremated; then the casket of her ashes was sent to South Africa. She was buried under the same obelisk that commemorated the fallen Boers, after one of the finest funeral orations ever heard (from Jan Christiaan Smuts, part in Afrikaans, part in English). Today her name, famous in South Africa, is quite unknown in Britain.

FANNY LEE CHANEY: CIVIL RIGHTS CAMPAIGNER

Born in black poverty in 1921, Fanny Lee Chaney had an almost accidental introduction to prominence in the US civil rights movement, but found herself caught up in it and regarded as one of the leaders of it from 1964 until her death at the age of eighty-four in 2004. Like Rosa Parks, the pioneer of the bus boycott in Alabama, whose life and exploits she never wished to imitate, she found herself looked up to and revered for most of her later life; and when she died she had a sense of real fulfilment, and was widely admired by her fellow pioneers in the movement.

Fanny Lee Chaney was born to a working-class black family in Neshoba County, Mississippi, in September 1921. After she married she became a mother of five lively and intelligent youngsters who went on to enter useful employment in the locality. She herself was a baker. But she had no ambition to enrol in the rapidly developing civil rights movement until the middle 1960s, but this proved to be the direction in which events irresistibly pushed her.

In the early morning of 21 June 1964, she prepared breakfast for three young civil rights protesters, Andrew Goodman, Michael Schwerner and her own 21-year-old son James, who were off to take part in a protest against the burning of a black church in their neighbourhood. Though not part of it, they found themselves caught up in what later became known as the 'Freedom Summer' demonstrations in Mississippi. James' younger brother Ben was keen to accompany them in their protest, but Fanny, worried that, as someone so young, he might get into trouble, insisted that James leave without him; so he did.

James never came back. His dead body, together with those of his two white American colleagues, was found in an earth dam close by nearly two months later, so badly mutilated that it looked as though he had been in an aircraft disaster. The murders were part of a concerted onslaught on African Americans and civil rights campaigners by racist extremists. That summer literally thousands of US student volunteers travelled to Mississippi in a campaign to help African Americans to register their vote, as the federal government now permitted them to do. Within weeks there were numerous attacks on black campaigners, bombings of seven buildings associated with the campaign, four deaths by shooting and numerous beatings of civil rights campaigners. Because Goodman and Schwerner were white northerners, their murders aroused national and international attention to the problem. It emerged that the trio had been arrested for speeding, beaten with chains in jail, and subsequently handed over by the local sheriff to the Ku Klux Klan (KKK), of which he was a member. The hooded mob kicked them about for a while and then shot each of them in turn before dumping their bodies into the structure of the dam.[1] This was not Fanny Chaney's first experience of racial terror. Some years earlier, her grandfather had been killed by white extremists when he refused to sell his land to a white man. His body was never found. Mrs Chaney said they recovered only his glasses, his shoes and his watch.

It was her son's senseless murder that persuaded Fanny Chaney to join the civil rights movement. She sued five restaurants for racial discrimination against black customers. In return they got her fired from her job as a baker. KKK members planted burning crosses on her lawn (the usual form of greeting favoured by the Klan), and a firebomb was directed at her house.[2] She felt so threatened that she left Mississippi and went to work in New York, where for over thirty years she worked as a cleaner in an old folks' home. When she retired she went to live nearby in New Jersey.

But the question of race relations remained a central issue in US politics throughout the period of the Kennedy and Johnson administrations. At first the state authorities refused to investigate the charges against KKK individuals, pretending there was nothing wrong.[3] The result was that later in 1967 the federal government intervened and brought charges of violation of civil rights against nineteen offenders (according to the US Constitution a charge of murder could only be brought by the state, and this the state appeared unwilling to do). Local juries, however, proved very tolerant of such offences; all but seven of the accused were acquitted, the maximum penalty inflicted on those found guilty was seven years, and the suspected ringleader, Edgar Killen, a Baptist minister as well as local KKK leader, was completely acquitted (on the grounds that no one could possibly believe a minister was responsible for such crimes).

There the problem was left until 1980, when, in his presidential campaign, Ronald Reagan, the Republican candidate for the presidency, referred to it in his campaign speech at Neshoba County Fair. However, he made no reference either to local extremists campaigning against black rights, or to the deplorable record of the state courts in their leniency towards civil rights offenders; he confined himself to a few choice platitudes, and reaffirmed his devotion to the old doctrine of 'states' rights'. Reagan's Democratic opponents in Mississippi noted his ambivalent stand against such right-wing behaviour, and declared their opposition to policies which seemed to them to be tolerant of the reinstatement of the attitudes of the 1960s.

Revival of the old prejudices, however, was avoided, and in 2005 Killen was brought back to court to answer charges of murders committed nearly forty years earlier. By this time the old man was eighty-two and confined to a wheelchair. Local opinion held that the old ghosts of discrimination had finally been laid when he was found guilty and was condemned to a sentence of sixty years for his former crimes.[4]

Fanny Lee Chaney was less than ecstatic over this outcome. She was just as old as Killen, and thought he had got off very lightly. She commented: 'It took a mighty long time. There were many other killers, but most of them are dead by now.' She herself died in May 2007, aged eighty-four, and was survived by her younger son and her three daughters.

MARIA BOULDING: SCHOLAR AND PIONEER OF THE CHURCH

One of the great Catholic scholars and thinkers of the twentieth century, Dame Maria Boulding, OSB,[1] was an author, a scholar and a creative thinker in the Roman Catholic cause, translating, among other early works, St Augustine's Confessions, *his* Commentaries on the Psalms, *and the later devotional works of other scholars. She even worked on the translation of the* New Missal *on behalf of the Roman Missal Editorial Commission for use in the Roman Church. Her call to proclaim the Word as a John the Baptist, and to receive the Word as a Mary, elucidated in* Wisdom, *was by a fortunate chance the very book that was being read in the days before her death in November 2009, and this provides the modern reader with a summary of all that was best in her spirit, showing her, as the* Book of Wisdom *in the Apocrypha says, 'holy, unique, subtle, active, incisive, unsullied, lucid' (Wisdom 7.22).*

Born in London in 1929, the daughter of Reginald Boulding, a radar specialist, and his wife Josephine, Mary – to give her her baptismal name – lost her mother while still a schoolgirl and was left to take care of four younger siblings. At the young age of sixteen she felt the call to the contemplative life, and was accepted as a novice by Stanbrook Abbey, Worcester, shortly after her eighteenth birthday. Though she gained a state scholarship and was offered admission to Oxford, she turned the offer down and entered Stanbrook in 1947. She took solemn vows in 1952 when she was still only twenty-two years old.

Maria eventually took to the monastic discipline of silence, scripture and community demands, and found fulfilment in abbey life that was to last her for the next sixty-two years. At first there was a kind of malaise – the sort that often follows the irrevocability of life commitment to the discipline – but she put this down to a lack of intellectual stimulation, and remedied it by taking on a study of theology as an external student of London University while she was still carrying out the routine of monastic life. She welcomed the new focus brought about by the Second Vatican Council on the Scriptures and blossomed into an enthusiastic member of the Benedictine community. She held the appointment of novice mistress from 1965 to 1974, welcoming the chance to use her scholarly gifts to transmit her enthusiasm of monastic life to the novices, but in the end this was not enough and she came to feel an obligation towards communicating the word of God to a wider number of others. Blessed with a beautiful speaking voice, she took tuition from Alec Guinness on the technique of public speaking; she also embarked upon what proved to be a life-long enthusiasm for authorship

She began with participating in a collaborative enterprise with other members of the Benedictine Congregation's Theological Commission to articulate a theology of monastic life, published as *Consider Your Call* in 1978, and then went on to a series of individual publications from 1979 to 1987 which popularised the discipline and combined a theologically sound and informed approach to the liturgy and to personal prayer with a personal devotion to God reminiscent of the Cistercian fathers. All the books are still in great demand: *Marked for Life: Prayer in the Easter Christ* (1979), *The Coming of God* (1982) and *The Gateway to Hope* (1987). One of the aids to prayer that Sister Boulding valued was what she called 'enclosure', and this required seclusion and prevented her playing a personal role in publicising her works (though she did break her own rules to carry out a speaking tour in 1980 – the fifteenth centenary of St Benedict's birth – of the Far East, including Australia and the Christian community in Japan).

But increasingly she was called to deeper solitude, and for nearly twenty years undertook to live as a hermit in 1985, with no other company than her cat and her dog. She deeply valued being entirely alone, and valued, too, the opportunity this gave her for uninterrupted work. During this seclusion she participated in an Augustinian plan to translate the works of St Augustine for modern study, and this she did by translating his *Confessions*, which appeared between 2000 and 2004 in six volumes, a work still in great demand.

She returned to Stanbrook Abbey in 2004 to play once again her role in monastic life. In spite of her advanced years – she was now seventy-five – she threw herself into the immense task of packing up the abbey library of 40,000 books in preparation for the congregation's move to Yorkshire. No sooner was this completed than she was appointed to the Roman Missal Editorial Commission, a task that involved frequent meetings with her fellow commissioners in Britain, the United States, and not least in Rome. In spite of years of loneliness in her eremitical life, she got on well with the people, mainly men, she met, all of whom seemed to value and profit from her presence. Here she blossomed. She translated the Easter Vigil's *Exsultet*, a work described as a masterpiece, and finally in 2008 was appointed by the Vatican to a committee entrusted with the revision of the prayers of the Divine Office, a task marking the crowning of her life's work for the Church. Throughout she showed strong authority, fierce integrity and an incisive style. She had no time for small talk. She looked forbidding, until a radiant smile transformed her whole appearance. Two of her earlier works reinforced the impression she created of great power and authority: *Are Contemplative Nuns Wasting Their Time?* (1973) and *A Touch of God* (1982). This latter book contains an autobiographical chapter entitled 'A Tapestry from the Wrong Side' in which she contends that what we may see as 'messes' in life may look quite different to God, who is on the other side – the right side – and sees human life from another perspective.

Three days before she died in 2009, Maria Boulding completed her last book, *Journey to Easter*, a series of meditations on her thoughts about the Resurrection through pain and suffering, a book as yet unpublished. But her own death in the Abbey was a peaceful one.

PART 15

SOCIAL REFORMERS

SELINA HASTINGS, COUNTESS OF HUNTINGDON, AND THE RELIGIOUS REVIVAL OF THE EIGHTEENTH CENTURY

Leicestershire's part in the evangelical revival of the eighteenth century began in the north-west part of the county at Donington Park, at present the home of the celebrated motor-racing circuit, and close to East Midlands airport. Donington Hall still stands, but is now the headquarters of East Midlands Airways. In the eighteenth century it was the home of Selena Hastings, countess of Huntingdon.

Lady Selina Shirley was born at Staunton Harold Hall near Ashby-de-la-Zouch, Leicestershire in 1707, and at the age of twenty-one was married to the 9th Earl of Huntingdon. He died before he was fifty, but she outlived him by forty-five years and did not die until she was eighty-four. Until the end of her life, Lady Huntingdon could not mention his name without tears of bitter regret at their long separation. Shortly after his death Selina moved to Ashby-de-la-Zouch, where she lived for the rest of her life.

She always said that her religious impulse came from the childhood experience of witnessing the funeral, when she was eight, of a child of about her own age, and that this experience put into her own mind an awareness of her own mortality. She joined the funeral procession, and prayed on the spot that when her own time came she would face death without any fear. In later years she was stricken by a sudden, sharp illness that brought her childhood experience to mind, and she recalled the words of Lady Margaret Hastings, her sister-in-law, a devout woman and a committed Christian, and shortly after 'yielded herself to the gospel call, renounced every hope and for the first time knew the joy of believing'.

She already had some knowledge of the evangelical revival that was sweeping Britain in the 1730s. In Wales the revival made considerable progress under leaders such as Griffith Jones, Daniel Rowland and Howell Harris; in England, too, where George Whitfield, one of their converts, was preaching in Bristol and the South West. In the 1740s he came north into Leicestershire, and, like his contemporaries John and Charles Wesley, spread the word in mass meetings among ordinary working people. By the 1740s, the 'Great Awakening' was well under way. As yet the evangelical movement had made no sign of wishing to break from the Anglican Church, though the somewhat cool and conventional style of the typical Anglican clergy in it was much challenged by its supporters' populist and enthusiastic leanings. Preachers like the Wesleys[1] and Whitfield were a new phenomenon. Their habit of preaching to common workers in the open air and without the normal formalities led eventually to suspicion of their motives, and pulpits were increasingly closed to such itinerant clergymen. The prejudice against them was common also among the country gentry who looked down on agricultural workers and miners, and regarded them with fear and suspicion. So their true gospel preaching soon became the object of their ridicule, mockery and contempt. Uneducated though they might have been, the poor knew when they were being snubbed and ignored; they reacted bitterly to their rejection. They would rather listen to the evangelicals in the open air than set foot in a church, and they soon said so, denouncing their own clergy as rich, snobbish and out-of-touch.

The Countess of Huntingdon did not share the prejudices of the upper classes. She sympathised with the motives of the evangelicals and wanted to provide the opportunity of spiritual redemption for lower-class people as well as for her fellow gentry. She saw the preachers at work in Leicestershire, and developed close ties with the Charles and John Wesley[2] and with Whitfield.[3] In 1747 she made Whitfield one of her chaplains, and invited some of her titled friends to attend her chapel to hear him preach. Soon she came to expend much of her wealth on the construction of chapels in various parts of England and Wales, such as Brighton, Bath and Tonbridge. There were several in London. Indeed, before long she was called the 'patroness of the revival'. In 1768 she founded Trevecca College in South Wales for training evangelical clergy, and her friend George Whitfield preached at its dedication service. Her chapels were soon widely spread throughout England and Wales, and used by working-class people. In 1769 she was compelled by law to register her chapels as 'non-conformist meeting-houses', though she had never had any intention of being a non-conformist, and her chapels became known as the 'Countess of Huntingdon Connexion' – a title they bear to this day.[4]

People such as Whitfield, the Wesleys and the Countess of Huntingdon herself are sometimes said to have helped to save Britain from the same sort of bloody revolution as afflicted France in the later years of the eighteenth century. Evangelicalism certainly inculcated a passive acceptance of proletarian servitude – a 'quiet resignation' in the hope of eventual eternal salvation – and did not make contemporary political reform a big issue in its teachings. Indeed, it was exactly this sort of stoical acceptance of their degraded and miserable fate that led Karl Marx to denounce religion as the 'opiate of the people', cynically offering them a rich life in the future while their exploiters enjoyed a rich life in the present. The evangelicals would have been deeply affronted by his suggestion of this moral betrayal. It was not that the evangelicals were opposed to reforms – indeed, many of them were in the forefront of the movements towards factory legislation and the emancipation of the slaves – but, quite simply, to them the salvation of the body took second place to the salvation of the soul, which was, and remained, the prime target of their preaching. Nonetheless, the glad bearing of the cross inflicted on the lower orders by life did in fact produce a quiescence that broadly suited the lives of their exploiters.

The Countess died at her London home in 1791. In her funeral sermon she was declared to have been 'the greatest woman in the cause of the Gospel that had ever lived in the world'. Augustus Toplady[5] said she was 'the most precious saint of God that I knew', and Philip Doddridge[6] declared: 'I never saw so much of the image of God in any woman upon earth.' In the parish church at Ashby-de-la-Zouch there is a window bequeathed by members of Lady Huntingdon's Chapel in Spa Fields, London, 'in memory of one of the most distinguished persons associated with the Church', together with a brass plaque in her memory.

FRANCES BUSS:
EDUCATIONAL PIONEER

Headmistress of North London Collegiate School for Ladies, Frances Buss was one of the nineteenth-century pioneers of girls' schools in Britain, and together with Dorothea Beale, founder of Cheltenham Ladies' College, established the first successful schools in the country specifically catering for girls, so successfully plugging a notable gap in the market at the time. Previously education had virtually been denied to young females, apart from tutoring at home by governesses or tutors, and even then was usually confined to music, sewing, French and a few social arts thought necessary for prospective brides.

Born in August 1827 in London, Frances Mary Buss was the daughter of Robert William Buss, an etcher and a painter, and one of the original illustrators of Charles Dickens' *Pickwick Papers*, and Frances (*née* Fleetwood). She was one of six of their children who survived into adulthood. Her father was not very successful commercially, so the family lived within straitened means. As a result she did not get much formal education; but her grandparents eventually sent her to a private school in Aldersgate, from where she was later sent to a similar establishment in Kentish Town. Because of her father's continuing lack of success, and in order to augment the family's income, her mother herself set up a school in 1845 in Clarence Road, Kentish Town, and Frances found herself teaching there from the age of fourteen, and by sixteen was virtually left in charge of it. The ideas behind the new school were based on those of Johann Heinrich Pestalozzi,[1] so the school was progressive by any standards, and extremely so in comparison with other schools at the time that confined themselves only to basic literacy and numeracy skills, administered parrot-fashion in a dreary routine.

In her early twenties, Frances attended evening lectures at the newly-opened Queen's College in Harley Street, where she was taught by a number of nineteenth-century luminaries such as F. D. Maurice and Charles Kingsley, and where she gained certificates in French, German and Geography.

The school that she helped found and in which she worked was renamed the North London Collegiate School, and moved into larger premises in Camden Street in 1850, with Miss Buss as its first Principal, a job she continued almost until her death. In 1864

Miss Buss gave evidence to the Schools Enquiry Commission, and in its final report her school was singled out for exceptional commendation, as was she herself for putting the education of girls on a proper educational footing and offering a much wider variety of subjects to pupils than was usual at the time. In the later 1860s, further financial resources were provided both by the Brewers' Company and the Clothworkers' Company (two surviving ancient guilds), as the result of which the school was moved from Camden Town to Harrow-on-the-Hill and rehoused in more modern premises, still under Miss Buss's headship, and a further school was provided for girls in Camden.

In her later life, Miss Buss became famous, together with Miss Dorothea Beale of Cheltenham, Headmistress of Cheltenham Ladies College, as chief leaders in the reformed educational movement. They played a major role in the establishment and later success of the Girls' Public Day School Trust (originally the Girls' Public Day School Company), encouraging the bringing of girls' schools up to university entrance standard by the improvement of examinations, and working for the establishment of women's colleges affiliated to universities, and of teacher-training colleges for women. Some of these in the twentieth century became members of nearby universities, such as Homerton teacher-training college which became part of Cambridge University. Both ladies remained unmarried until their deaths, giving rise to the sardonic little rhyme:

> Miss Buss and Miss Beale Cupid's darts do not feel;
> How different from us, Miss Beale and Miss Buss.

Frances Buss was also a notable member of the Women's Suffrage Society, and a member of the London Suffrage Committee, as well as a regular participant in the Kensington Society, a discussion group for women. She also continued as headmistress of her school until the year of her death, 1894.

JOSEPHINE BUTLER AND THE CONTAGIOUS DISEASES ACTS

Josephine Butler was one of the pioneers of feminism and a tireless worker against what she regarded as the shortcomings of some of the health legislation of the mid-nineteenth century. In particular she spoke out against later instalments of what perhaps misleadingly were called the Contagious Diseases Acts. These acts had been introduced during the 1860s (in 1864, 1866 and 1869) as a form of regulation of the prostitution industry, about which the Victorians had very deeply held but prejudicial opinions.

The nineteenth century saw a great upsurge in health and sanitary legislation, especially in the form of public health measures. This process, though distinctly paternalist in tone rather than *laissez-faire*, began with the first Whig legislation of the 1830s, and continued in a steady stream for most of the rest of the century, during which time Britain moved from being a country entirely lacking in health laws to one that was systematically regulated. The 'sanitary idea', first put forward by a number of concerned medical men such as Dr John Snow (1813–1858) and Dr John Simon (1816–1904), as the result of their experiences in practice, was taken up by dedicated reformers such as the radical Edwin Chadwick (1800–1890), and transformed into a concerted offensive against the epidemic diseases and the long-standing environmental hazards of the industrial revolution. The main laws passed, amid a plethora of smaller measures, were the Public Health Acts of 1848 and 1875, but these acts did no more than touch obliquely on the problems posed by prostitution.

The Contagious Diseases Acts were no more than a minor branch of such health measures. The state regulation of prostitution aimed to prevent the spread of venereal diseases, especially in the British Army and the Royal Navy, and was modelled on similar legislation introduced during the early years of the Second Empire of Napoleon III. The law gave magistrates the power to order a genital examination of prostitutes for symptoms of VD (a process dubbed by opponents of the act, of which Josephine Butler was one, as 'surgical rape'), and to detain infected women compulsorily for three months to be cured. Refusal to consent to such an examination was to result in a term of imprisonment. An unsupported accusation of prostitution by a police officer was sufficient to order an examination, and the women accused often lost their jobs as a result whether they were prostitutes or not. The first acts applied only to seaports and garrison towns, but the 1869 Act, in its draft, proposed to extend the scope of the measure to the entire United Kingdom. This proposal led to strident opposition from Christians, feminists and from supporters of civil liberty, and to the establishment of the Ladies' National Association for the Repeal of the Contagious Diseases Act, a group whose very name should have been weighty enough to strike fear into the mind of the most assiduous radical. Josephine Butler was one of the prime movers of this association.

Josephine Elizabeth Grey was born in 1828 in Dulwich, at that time a village near London, and was the seventh child of John Grey, cousin of Charles Grey, 2nd Earl and the Prime Minister who worked to ensure the passing of the great Parliament Act of 1832, and his wife Hannah (*née* Annett). In 1833, John Grey was appointed estate manager of the Dilston Estate near Corbridge, Northumberland, and the family moved there.

In 1852 Josephine married George Butler, scholar and cleric, and later Dean of Winchester, and their union eventually produced four children, the youngest of which was a girl, Evangeline Mary. The Butlers had strong radical sympathies, and went on to support the North during the American Civil War (1860–65). The daughter died in 1863, and this led to Josephine undergoing some kind of moral change, the result of which was that she embarked on a course of ministering to those who in their lives had suffered great loss or pain. In 1866, when George had been appointed Principal of Liverpool College, the family moved there and Josephine began visiting Liverpool's

Brownlow Hill workhouse. Then her interests turned to working with prostitutes, first through taking them into her own home, and later by establishing a refuge for them. She was also interested in the education of women and in their educational opportunities, and in 1867 became the President of the North of England Council for the Higher Education of Women. She later petitioned Cambridge University on the subject of educational examinations for women, the result of which was the establishment of two affiliated colleges for women in the University: Girton in 1860 and Newnham in 1871. Her feminist philanthropy grew out of Christian beliefs but accepted the Victorian conceptions of gender role, which meant that she only marginally challenged the dominant assumptions of a separate sphere for women.[1] This was the context in which she developed her ideas on the Contagious Diseases Acts.

Her ideas on the moral and social aspects of the problem of prostitution were in fact the opposite of most of her generation. Victorian opinion generally – particularly male opinion – was *against* prostitutes (however much men may have availed themselves of the services they provided), so that generally they felt that if prostitutes got themselves infected by sexually transmitted diseases, this was their own fault and they had asked for it by their conduct; the same was to be said of men, who knew the risks they were taking when they used them. Josephine, and her Christian and feminist supporters in the Ladies' National Association, took the opposite view. They were *for* prostitutes, not because they approved of their style of life, but in the sense that they believed that these women were more to be pitied than blamed. They thought that to force humiliating medical inspection upon them as if they were cattle (the idea of legislation against transmitted diseases had originated from regulations relating to livestock), and to compel them to accept what amounted to imprisonment while they were compulsorily cured of their infection, were plain violations of their natural rights, and grossly discriminatory in that they did not apply to the men who were the real source of the infection. She was deeply suspicious of the real motives that led policemen to arrest them and bring them in, and took the view that if these women preferred not to be treated they had every right to claim exemption from it. She believed in the civil and moral rights of the women who were at the receiving end of what she called the 'diabolical triple power' of the police, magistrates and doctors. These men were using the law as a means of maintaining the oppression and surveillance of women, and were creating a double standard of morality for male and female.[2] While accepting that certain aspects of the legislation, such as the penalising of brothel-keepers and predominantly male pimps, were desirable, the main purpose of the act, they believed, was morally profoundly wrong.

Josephine performed strongly on public platforms, and in one meeting reduced one speaker, Hugh Price Hughes, Superintendent of the West London Mission, to tears, driving him from the stage. She often silenced her opponents by her sheer eloquence. Despite verbal vilification and even physical assault from her adversaries, she was finally successful in persuading Parliament to bring about the repeal of the Contagious Diseases Act in 1886.

It was in this spirit that she was drawn into the later 'social purity' campaigns associated with W. T. Stead, editor in the 1880s of the *Pall Mall Gazette*, and a pioneer against child prostitution and white slavery.[3] He had founded the so-called National Vigilance Association in 1885, which had as its main object the stamping out of such practices. He also published a series of sensational articles in his magazine under the title 'The Maiden Tribute of Modern Babylon', exposing the extent of child prostitution in London in the heyday of Victorian England, as the result of which the legal age of consent in Britain was raised from thirteen to sixteen.

Josephine was also active in spreading her campaign against the Contagious Diseases Act on the continent, and travelled widely in France and Switzerland with this aim in view, though in these countries, too, there was considerable reluctance to heed her advice. However, she was successful in setting up an International Abolitionist Federation to expose and eradicate prostitution and traffic in women and children, activities that she carried as far as British India in her continuing work for 'moral purity'.

After the death of her husband in 1890, however, she largely withdrew from public life, concentrating on writing her own *Recollections* of his life in 1892, and her own *Reminiscences of a Great Crusade* in 1896. She died in 1906.

OCTAVIA HILL: PIONEER OF HOUSING AND OPEN SPACES

The nineteenth century is full of eminent worthies who devoted themselves to improving the conditions of people who were poor and not so fortunately placed in society or so educated as themselves, and on whose behalf they dedicated themselves to act. One of these social pioneers, focusing her efforts on the housing of the poor, and the provision of open spaces for them to enjoy, was Octavia Hill (1838–1912). Why did she devote herself to this cause, and what were the influences that worked upon her in her philanthropic career?

Octavia Hill became a pioneer of housing management, a friend of the social philosopher John Ruskin, an adviser of politicians and ecclesiastical commissioners, and finished her career in helping to preserve the countryside for her fellow countrymen. The most important influence on her life came from her grandfather, Dr Thomas Southwood Smith, a close friend and colleague of Charles Dickens, who, in the year of Octavia's birth, was publishing his novel *Nicholas Nickleby* in monthly instalments in the popular press. Dickens learned a lot from the doctor, and Southwood Smith gained in the author an influential ally in his lifelong fight for better popular sanitation.

Southwood Smith enjoyed an importance in his own generation similar to that of Sir Alexander Fleming in the twentieth century. He began his career in the Church, first as a Baptist minister and later as a Unitarian, but increasingly devoted himself to the care of the bodies of his patients rather than the salvation of their souls. He built up a flourishing practice in the East End of London, and was appointed as a physician to the London Fever Hospital, the Eastern Dispensary and to the Jews' Hospital in Whitechapel. He wrote a number of seminal articles on the laws relating to epidemic diseases and the sanitary laws, and was largely responsible for the *Report on the Sanitary Conditions among the Labouring Classes in London* in 1838. Describing the conditions still existing in Bethnal Green and Whitechapel, his report made a deep impression on public opinion and shocked Dickens, too, who was made more aware of what conditions really were like. Southwood Smith followed this up with a report to the Children's Employment Commission in 1842, and then a second such report in 1843, both of which revealed conditions of slave labour among the juvenile workers of the conurbation. The scenes portrayed in Dickens' *Christmas Carol*, *The Chimes*, and in *Bleak House* provide telling testimony of the influence these publications had on the author. Southwood Smith went on in 1851 to make a submission to the Metropolitan Sanitary Association advocating improved working-class tenements, a plea taken up by other pioneers like Chadwick, Kay-Shuttleworth and Lord Shaftesbury in the years following.

Octavia was only a girl of thirteen in 1851, but through the meetings at her home and through her mother, who became at this time secretary to the newly founded Ladies' Co-operative Guild, she became aware of the importance of the work in hand, and for a number of her teenage years worked with juvenile toymakers, buying their materials, keeping their accounts, and even seeing that they ate properly and spread a clean cloth when they stopped working to have their meals. She went on in the later 1850s to be secretary of the London Working Women's College. But it was in 1864 that she began her main work. She used money provided by Ruskin (to the tune of £3,000) to purchase properties in Paradise Place, recondition them and provide homes for working-class families, starting savings clubs, teaching the women to sew and even providing jobs for the menfolk who had fallen out of work. She freely admitted she got her ideas from *Household Words*,[1] which achieved great influence at this time, from Dickens' other work and from readings arranged by her mother of Shakespeare, Browning and, of course, Ruskin. Before the end of the 1860s, she had persuaded Ruskin to buy other properties, all of which she reconditioned and brought into good use. Her work was recognised in the 1860s, and was supplemented by the establishment of the Peabody Trust, which devoted £150,000 and then a further £350,000 to the provision of working-class housing, and became crucial to the slum clearance programme of the Metropolitan Board of Works in the 1870s.

Octavia Hill's emphasis was always on individual responsibility and moral reformation, things which she believed could be achieved without state interference or control. She selected her tenants carefully, set her face against the accumulation of arrears and always insisted on the eviction of 'undesirables' among those she housed; indeed she always resisted Poor Law arrangements made by the state, either under the so-called Speenhamland system or under the new Poor Law of 1834; she even resisted efforts to legislate over wage levels. This meant that her achievements were always parochial and small-scale, and could do little more than trim the fringes of the social problem instead of tackling it head-on. Nonetheless, though limited, the changes she made were lasting and profound. She finished by achieving a good deal in a number of well-run blocks of property in various parts of London – a different sort of achievement from the Torrens Artisans' and Labourers' Dwellings Act of 1868.

Octavia Hill was also interested in preserving open spaces so as to benefit the health of city-dwellers. She failed to prevent Swiss Cottage Fields, where she herself had played as a child, from being built over, but there were many more areas, like Parliament Hill, Hilly Fields, and others, large and small, where she was successful. She worked with the Commons Preservation Society to protect open land from urban sprawl, and went on to prepare maps of footpaths and commons, and to establish where there were rights of way. For her, public access mattered as much as preservation. With Sir Robert Hunter and Canon Rawnsley, she tried vainly to prevent Thirlmere from being turned into a reservoir for Manchester. The Kyrle Society, which she helped to set up in 1875, encouraged the poor to enjoy open-air recreation, and from this there came the National Trust[2] 'to preserve places of historical interest and natural beauty' for stretches of coastline and fine buildings in 1895.

She died in 1912 and was buried in Crockham Hill churchyard, within sight of the countryside of Kent, and looking out on Ide Hill, Toys Hill and Mariner's Hill, which were among her own favourites and those of Charles Dickens. She was one of the social pioneers whose work made a lasting difference to the world we have inherited.

CATHERINE BOOTH:
MOTHER OF THE SALVATION ARMY

Although apparently deficient in doctrinal ideas, the Salvation Army was in its attitudes closest to the Methodist faith, in that both its original founders, William Booth and his wife Catherine, were of the Methodist persuasion. It was she who was the main mover towards the creation of the Salvation Army, encouraging her husband with the work and going on to devote her whole life to its cause in the years after their marriage. Even after she died she continued to contribute to it by bequeathing her house in Clacton to the Army for charitable purposes.

She was born Catherine Mumford in Ashbourne, Derbyshire, in 1829, the daughter of John Mumford, a coach-builder and his wife Sarah (*née* Milward). The family later moved to Boston, Lincolnshire, and then to Brixton, London. From an early age, Catherine was a serious and studious girl of deeply religious parentage. She is said to have read her Bible through eight times by the time she reached her teens. At the age of fourteen she was seriously ill and confined largely to bed, but she kept herself alert and busy, and developed her interest in matters of faith, as well as taking up an interest in the social problems resulting from alcohol. With this dissenting background and a progressive outlook, she joined the Brixton Methodist Church, and became a member of the Band of Hope and of the national Temperance Society. It was through her church that, at a prayer meeting, she met her future husband William Booth, a Methodist minister who came to preach in Brixton in 1852. It was she who persuaded him to continue with the street evangelism for which he became famous.

He was another serious-minded individual, a Nottingham man of humble parentage who was converted at the age of fifteen to an active practice of Christianity in 1844, when he joined the Methodist New Connexion. He undertook missionary activity in the East End of London, later described in his book *In Darkest England* (1890), and helped to galvanise public opinion by revealing the shocking social and moral conditions in which many of the lower orders languished. After a three-year courtship, the pair were married in 1855 at the Stockwell Green Congregational Church in London. Their wedding was simple and without ostentation, as they wanted to use their time and money for his ministry. Even during the period of their honeymoon, William was asked to speak at meetings, which he generally did.

Catherine gradually became more active in the work of her husband's church at Brighouse, and, though of a nervous disposition, found she enjoyed working with children and young people, and even found the courage to address them in meetings. At this time it was almost unheard of for women to speak in public, unless they were upper-class and well-educated, and there were many people who condemned such 'forwardness' on her part. But she had a simple belief in the rights of women to participate in the moral causes that she held dear, and when the opportunity was provided for her to make her public 'testimony' at Gateshead, she did not waste her chance. It was a great turning point both for her and her husband, and the start of what was to prove a lifelong ministry. She also began to visit people in their homes, especially those who were the victims of heavy drinking, urging them to make a new start and do something with their lives, as she herself had done.

The couple began the work of the Christian Mission in 1865 in the East End, William speaking to the poor, hungry and ragged, and Catherine undertaking the raising of funds by speaking to the more favoured people of the middle and working classes. It was not only those who had cash in their pockets who extended the hand of friendship to others less fortunate; fundraisers generally could find support from the honest working class as well, even if it meant taking up a collection in public houses. Those who made donations might generally reject charity as something distasteful, but in the case of the Army they were prepared to make an exception. For both Booths, this was a partnership that operated very successfully, and it helped to chip away at some of the typical prejudices that she and others had entertained of the 'drinking classes'.

In 1878, the name of their mission was changed to the Salvation Army, William becoming known as the 'General' in what was modelled as a spiritual replica of the armed forces, and Catherine becoming known as the 'Mother of the Army'. She went on to have eight children, Bramwell, Ballington, Kate, Emma, Herbert, Marie, Evangeline and Lucy, two of whom, Bramwell and Eva, became in their turn Generals in the Army. Catherine herself always maintained her interest in it also. It was she who designed the Army's flag, and the uniforms and bonnets for the female members.

There was, of course, a core of beliefs which the Army subscribed to, but these, while undoubtedly important, did not dominate the life of the organisation. The Army distributed free soup, food and warm clothing rather than sermons, and made available clean beds for the homeless without stopping to ask whether or not those in need of help were subscribing worshippers. Want, hunger and squalor were as much the enemy as Satan. Its soldiers were always glad when the recipients of their largesse turned to Jesus, but it was by no means an indispensable condition; to them the relief of social degradation was, in its effects, almost as valuable an achievement as preaching the word of God. And those who dug their hands into their pockets to help the Army felt they were helping a worthwhile social cause, whether they accepted the tenets of Methodism or not.

Catherine Booth died at the age of sixty-one in Clacton-on-Sea at Crossley House, which was transformed into a home for people with learning difficulties, and became a summer holiday home for those connected with the Army. The Booth family had rented it as a small seaside house in sight of the sea at Clacton, and it was here that she died in October 1890 in the arms of her husband and with her family around her. She was buried in Abney Park Cemetery, London, where her husband joined her in the family grave in 1912.

HARRIET BEECHER STOWE AND THE AMERICAN CIVIL WAR

Harriet Beecher Stowe was an American abolitionist and the author of the seminal novel Uncle Tom's Cabin *(1862) in which she gave a moving depiction of the plight of black slaves at the time of the American Civil War. It touched the hearts of millions of Americans and of as many English, both as a novel and later as a play, and played a vital role in focusing opinion on both sides of the Atlantic on the slavery question. It provoked widespread anger in the South by reason of its sentimentality and its gross bias, and a righteous conviction in the North in what many came to regard as the underlying cause of the war. The lists of facts and figures which were often supplied as an accompaniment to this text[1] were supposed to provide evidence for the views advanced, but were much less effective in concentrating the minds of readers than the story itself. Abraham Lincoln, on meeting the author, is reputed to have observed: 'So you're the little woman who started this war!'*

Born Harriet Beecher in Litchfield, Connecticut, in June 1811, she was the youngest daughter of the religious leader Lyman Beecher and his wife Roxana (*née* Foote), likewise a deeply religious woman who died while Harriet was still only very young. Her elder sister Catharine was an author and a teacher, and her two brothers, Henry Ward Beecher and Charles Beecher, were clergymen. Harriet was brought up in the family with puritanical strictness, and enrolled in her sister's Connecticut Female Seminary at Hartford in 1824, where she received a traditionally 'male' education. At the age of twenty-one she moved to Cincinnati, Ohio, to join her father, who had become president of Lane Theological Seminary, and in 1836 married Calvin Ellis Stowe, professor at the seminary and an ardent critic of slavery. The two took an interest in the issues arising from slavery, and supported the conspiracy known as the 'Underground Railway' whereby fugitive slaves were given hiding and refuge while arrangements were made to spirit them away in the direction of Canada, where under British law slavery had been illegal since 1833. The couple eventually moved to Brunswick, Maine, where Calvin taught theology at Bowdoin College. When in 1850 Congress passed the Fugitive Slave Law forbidding assistance to runaway slaves, both were moved to make public protest. Harriet felt obliged to present her objections on paper, and in 1851 went on to write the first instalment of *Uncle Tom's Cabin* for the anti-slavery journal *National Era*, published in Washington.

Before this they had both taken a lively interest in that other great problem of a rapidly growing society: intemperance. Almost from the beginning of the nineteenth century the dissenting churches had fostered temperance movements, and by 1825 had enrolled more than a million members in church-sponsored societies, publishing pamphlets, sending out speakers and employing professional organisers to further the work. The movement culminated in the formation in 1840 of the Washington Temperance Society. This society was the most successful of all, organising what it called 'Cold Water Parades' and popularising publications such as Timothy Shay Arthur's *Ten Nights in a Bar-Room* (a book that rivalled *Uncle Tom's Cabin* in its popularity). Calvin and Harriet were enthusiastic supporters of temperance, working towards improved education as one way of tackling drunkenness, and towards strengthening legislation controlling the sale of liquor. By 1860, laws had been brought in to achieve this latter aim in thirteen states, though it was not until the twentieth century that Prohibitionism achieved (and then only temporarily) its objectives.

But it was the anti-slavery movement that mainly occupied their attention. Harriet's book, *Uncle Tom's Cabin*, was one of the milestones of the anti-slavery campaign. The campaign had begun in earnest in the early 1830s when William Lloyd Garrison, the New England firebrand, had produced the first number of his abolitionist paper, *The Liberator*.[2] He formed the New England Anti-Slavery Society in Boston, an example swiftly followed in New York City, Providence, Philadelphia and Ohio. In 1850 Harriet threw her weight behind the movement. The abolitionists' arguments were set out with a coherence and force that shook the nation. In the first place, slavery was wrong on *moral grounds*; slave breeding, the refusal of slave-owners to recognise the validity of slave marriages, their willingness to break up slave families and to sell their members separately all went against the most fundamental precepts of society. It was irreligious and *contrary to scripture*, offensive to the teachings of all churches and rendering meaningless the efforts of missionaries of all kinds to convert the unbeliever. It was also *undemocratic*, unconstitutional and illiberal, and, based solely on the profit motive, and contrary to the whole 1776 spirit of American independence, standing in the way of social and humanitarian reform. Finally it was *inefficient*, wasteful and economically unsound, since it offered no incentive to the worker except that of avoiding the whip, and no way towards improving economic performance other than the swelling of the bosses' profits. *Uncle Tom's Cabin*, however, played more on people's feelings than on their intellects, and showed by the simplest and most direct route, that of storytelling, the real truth of the issues. Its sales in the USA were 500,000 copies in the first five years, and in Britain almost as many again, especially after the book was favourably reviewed by George Eliot (Mary Anne Evans). Its episodes dealt with the sufferings inflicted on slave workers by their owners: the brutality of the separation of wives from husbands, of mothers from children; the whippings and brandings; the filthy living conditions and the scant and unpalatable food – what the author herself declared to be 'a collection and arrangement of real incidents grouped together with reference to a general result'. The book was translated into twenty-three languages, and was followed in 1856 by another on a similar subject called *Dred: A Tale of the Great Dismal Swamp*.

Harriet lost some popularity in England later with her *Lady Byron Vindicated* (1870), even though the charges of incest against Lord Bryon with his half-sister proved in fact to be quite accurate. Her other successful books were those which dealt with life in New England, like *The Minister's Wooing* (1859) and *Old Town Folks* (1869). Harriet Beecher Stowe died in July 1896 at the age of eighty-five and was buried at Hartford, Connecticut.

MATILDA ASHURST BIGGS:
A WOMAN OF COURAGE, VISION & TALENT

There were many local women who played major parts in British history in the social and political movements of their time, even though they did not figure on any national stage during their lifetimes. Often of middle-class origin, their husbands local worthies in industry, trade or town government, they held opinions about, or took an active role in, affairs that sometimes reflected national movements through their local connections. Such a woman was Matilda Ashurst Biggs, wife of Joseph Biggs who was connected with one of the largest hosiery businesses in Leicester, and sister-in-law of its two proprietors John and William who went on to become involved in local politics, both of them eventually becoming radical Members of Parliament. Matilda was a member of a very vigorous Unitarian[1] church in the town, taking part in their secular as well as their religious activities. She was a principal player in the local and national women's rights movement and in its connections with the campaign for female suffrage, the education of girls, societies to help the plight of mistreated domestic servants, the care for prostitutes, and she also took part in the long and bitter struggle over the Contagious Diseases Act of 1866. She was involved also in a variety of local radical movements such as the Anti-Corn Law League, Chartism (where she was an associate of leading figures such as Henry Vincent and William Lovett); she played a part, too, in the anti-slavery movement both before and after the Abolition Bill in 1833. Finally, she took an interest in European as well as world affairs, supporting in particular the movement for Italian freedom and independence, and being a personal friend of the mid-century figure Giuseppe Mazzini. There were, in short, more pies than she had fingers to put in them.

Matilda was born at Muswell Hill, Middlesex, in 1817, second daughter of William Henry and Elizabeth Ann Ashurst (*née* Brown). She had three sisters, Eliza, Caroline and Emilie, and a brother William. She married Joseph Biggs, younger brother of John and William Biggs, owners of one of the largest hosiery businesses in Leicester, where she came to live in 1837. Matilda and Joseph were two very like-minded people: both came from a Unitarian background and both had family traditions of independent thinking and political radicalism.[2] Matilda's family was an intimate friend of Giuseppe Mazzini, in whose footsteps they followed in wishing to see the establishment of an independent and united Italian republic. His many letters to her have survived and provide an invaluable source of information about Matilda and her involvement in current political problems. Both her sisters and her daughters shared her enthusiasms. The Biggs brothers, too, supported the growing demands for women's rights, campaigned actively for the protection of women,[3] strove to improve standards of public health in the 1840s,[4] and, with Matilda's sister Eliza, campaigned against the Contagious Diseases Act.[5]

Matilda's work in creating and afterwards managing refuges for reformed prostitutes, supported chiefly by public subscription, dates back to the 1840s, and by the 1850s literally hundreds of such homes had been set up across the country. The 'homes' were a mixture of conservative evangelism, imposing a harsh workhouse-like regime on their inmates, and the more humane approach approved of by the Unitarians. This group did not write off the inmates as irredeemably wicked, but hoped through their tolerance and understanding, and the better conditions they offered, to give the 'fallen women' a better life and offer them a better chance of reforming themselves. In the matter of results, the record of these homes was patchy, but this did not discourage the organisers and there were a number of significant successes; this encouraged them to continue with their efforts.

As for female suffrage, all the Biggs' efforts did not persuade the Chartists to include this in their demands, and after the failure of Chartism in 1848 Matilda still continued to hope it might be achieved. Her pamphlets called for universal male and female suffrage – a very radical demand at the time – and justified it on the grounds that both paid tax, and so had equal rights to citizenship. She eventually wrote to the Northern

Reform Society, which appeared to be working towards the same goal, only to be fobbed off with the statement that they were concentrating on the male franchise only, believing this to be the best way forward.[6] In 1866, just before her death, she wrote a letter to John Stuart Mill in the House of Commons, and collected signatures for a massive petition on behalf of the Women's Suffrage Committee. He brought the matter to the notice of the House of Commons in 1867, on the occasion of the first parliamentary debate on women's suffrage. By this time, Matilda was herself dead, but her sister Caroline became a member, and eventually joint secretary, of a larger committee known as the London National Society for Women's Suffrage, whose results, unfortunately, were so meagre that they did not even secure the smallest mention in the House.

Matilda was also a lifelong opponent of slavery. She and her sister Eliza attended the World Anti-Slavery Convention in 1840, organised by the British Foreign Anti-Slavery Society in London, where they met a number of American women who shared the same objective. Hidden from public view by a discreet curtain, they had to endure the humiliation of a debate on their attendance in which they could not participate.[7] The Convention also emphasised the growing importance of the rather oddly named Ladies' Negro Friendly Society, originating in Birmingham in 1825, and later of importance throughout the East as well as the West Midlands.

There were other causes, too, where Matilda Biggs took an active interest. John Biggs' youngest daughter, Annie, had been affianced to one James Hollings before her unfortunate death from typhus in the 1840s. Afterwards he went on to marry her elder sister Sarah,[8] and brought education and his other interests into the Biggs' lives. He trained as a barrister, but does not seem to have practised very long. He went into teaching, and became Headmaster of the Proprietary School in what is now the Museum in New Walk and was later moved to London Road. It was not a very successful school and was often down to a mere handful of pupils, but Hollings went on to other things. He became President of the Leicester Mechanics' Institute in a building presently used as part of the municipal lending library, and later, on two occasions in the 1850s and 1860s, became President of the Leicester Philosophical Society, and even Mayor in 1859. He also was Editor of the *Leicestershire Mercury* for a number of years, and was able to use this paper as a means of promoting the political ambitions of his two brother-in-laws. The Biggs brothers' sympathies for such radical causes gave Matilda a firm foundation on which to base her radical activities throughout the middle years of the century.

But it was not only national problems which excited her sympathies. Her extensive correspondence with Mazzini shows her belief in his cause for the unification of Italy as a democratic republic, though she seems to have had some reservations, and to have preferred the actions of people such as Felix Orsini. The pressure group she joined (Society for the Friends of Italy, which had about 800 members of whom about 75 were women) favoured more direct methods, but the incident in January 1858, where Orsini threw three bombs at Napoleon III and his wife as they were driving to the opera – leaving them uninjured but killing eight innocent bystanders and wounding 150 others – alienated her feelings and led to a breach between them.[9]

Mazzini's later letters in 1864 show his increasing concern for Matilda's health. It was only after the proper drainage of Abbey Meadows that the town became a healthier place to live, and before that the family moved to Tonbridge in Kent after 1850. But, in spite of the move, she seems to have contracted tuberculosis in the 1860s.[10] She survived the winter of 1865, but she died in October 1866. After her death her husband and his daughters moved back into London, to Notting Hill.

Matilda left a feminist legacy for her daughters to follow. Daughter Caroline continued in the fight for women's suffrage; she joined the National Society for Women's Suffrage and contributed articles for the *Women's Suffrage Journal*, as well as publishing other written contributions to the campaign (she never joined the Pankhurst movement, however, since she died in 1889, but she did have a memorial established for her at Girton College, Cambridge, in 1903). Daughter Maude transferred her mother's enthusiasm for the Italian cause to Poland, where she worked for the deliverance of that country from Russian domination. She saw her hopes come to fruition at the end of the First World War with the establishment of a large and independent Polish republic. When she died in 1933 she left part of her estate to the Society for the Employment of Women, and another part to the Elizabeth Garrett Anderson Hospital in London.

HELEN SUZMAN AND THE STRUGGLE AGAINST APARTHEID

After thirty-six years in the South African parliament, where she was the single liberal voice against the state's avowed policy of apartheid, Helen Suzman was twice nominated for the Nobel Peace Prize, and was appointed an honorary Dame by the British Queen. She received thousands of letters from oppressed and dispossessed blacks in South Africa who were without property and employment, and were disfranchised in the South African political system. Denounced by a former Nationalist Prime Minister, P. W. Botha, as a 'vicious little cat', she steadily aroused the grudging admiration even of her opponents for her doggedness and determination. Usually she was the sole spokesman in the South African parliament to speak out against Apartheid legislation, and to highlight the frequent instances of institutionalised racial repression to which it gave rise. For more than five years she was the only woman among the 165 MPs, and obliged to endure the contempt of her male colleagues, who looked upon white supremacy as their birthright, and who regarded 'liberalism' as a dirty word.

Helen Suzman was born Helen Gavronsky in Germiston, a mining township outside Johannesburg, in 1917, daughter of a Jewish immigrant who had come to settle in the Transvaal from Lithuania, with, as she used to say, 'a bundle on his back'. She received her education at Parktown Convent in Johannesburg, and went on to read commerce and economics at Witwatersrand University in the middle 1930s. At the age of twenty, she got married to a much older man, Dr Moses Suzman before she graduated, but after the birth of her first child she returned to complete her studies and later took a first-class honours degree. After the Second World War, she taught economic history at Witwatersrand University for eight years before going into politics, and then was elected as a United Party representative for the Houghton constituency of Johannesburg in 1953. At that time, Dr D. F. Malan's Nationalist government had completed five years in office, and the Nationalists were enforcing the first apartheid legislation. Though elected as a member of the old United Party of General Smuts, she was one of those who broke away to form the Progressive Party in 1959, specifically to resist apartheid. The new party was all but wiped out at the polls in the general election of 1961. She was their only survivor, and continued as the sole parliamentarian unequivocally opposed to apartheid through the elections of 1966 and 1970, for thirteen years until 1974. She found herself constantly spied upon and harassed by the police, and her telephone was regularly tapped by their agents.[1] Her party never altered its fundamental stance against apartheid, though with the passage of time it merged with Harry Schwarz's Reform Party to become the Progressive Reform Party (the official Opposition), and later, joined by notable liberal colleagues such as Colin Eglin, became the Progressive Federal Party. Altogether she spent a total of thirty-six years in parliament.

During these years, Suzman's voice was frequently the only dissenting voice heard on the opposition benches. She took on the trio of Nationalist prime ministers, Hendrik Verwoerd, John Vorster and P. W. Botha[2] fearlessly, and condemned them for laws they brought in legalising detention without trial, and other savage punishments, such as the use of torture and the holding of detainees *incommunicado* and often in solitary confinement under the Terrorism Act and the Internal Security Act, both designed to reinforce state powers. She proved herself witty and fearless in debate, and a mistress of the pungent rejoinder. Frequently she had to stand alone amid furious anger and repeated verbal abuse, all the worse because she was an English-speaking Jewish woman in a parliament dominated by fully persuaded Afrikaner Calvinists. She was once accused by a hostile minister of asking questions that 'embarrassed South Africa', to which she sharply retorted: 'It is not my questions that embarrass South Africa; it is your answers.'

From the beginning, Suzman had taken a special interest in the conditions prevailing in South Africa's prisons. She visited Nelson Mandela on Robben Island in the early 1960s, and visited him several times thereafter, while he was serving eighteen of his twenty-seven years in prison after being imprisoned for life following a show trial for high treason. Her niece, Janet Suzman,[3] later said that her aunt was deeply fond of Mandela, but not afraid of challenging him: she said her aunt was one of the few people after his release who could ring up Mandela and say: 'Look here, what's going on?' Helen Suzman made it her duty also to visit squatter camps such as the one at Crossroads, and to bring conditions there to the notice of parliament. She pointed out, too, the steadily deteriorating standards of the South African judiciary, in particular in cases where whites beat blacks to death in the most brutal fashion, and got away with it scot-free in court, or else received scandalously light sentences. In 1989 she introduced the first censure motion ever – unsuccessful, as it turned out, since the motion was heavily defeated – in the South African parliament on a federal judge, J. J. Strydom, who had given no more than a short suspended sentence and a moderate fine to a white farmer who had beaten a black labourer to death. Generally speaking, white public opinion was massively in favour of keeping the blacks 'in their place'.

All the same, South Africa was on the brink of change. P. W. Botha gave up the leadership of his party in 1989 after suffering a stroke, though he still retained the state presidency (the office of prime minister had been abolished in constitutional changes in 1983), and his successor, F. W. de Clerk, was already half-persuaded of the need for a non-racist South Africa, with negotiations with members of the African Congress to settle the future shape of the state. The year 1989 also witnessed Helen Suzman, now seventy years of age, deciding to retire from politics, sensing that much of what she stood for was just about to come into being.

But she did not lose her critical edge. After Nelson Mandela came to power, she went on speaking out against what she saw as the failings of the country's post-apartheid ANC administrations, and in particular against the limited vision of a whole generation of black politicians and their failure to live up to the original high ideals of Mandela, allowing inequality and social exclusion, poverty, unemployment and particularly AIDS to continue to ravage the very people she had spent her whole life trying to champion. She was deeply disillusioned by what she called the 'flaccidness' of President Thabo Mbeki's policies both at home and in his external policies (for example, in the case of Zimbabwe), and utterly appalled by the corruption and crime that followed under his ambitious successor Jacob Zuma. Her opponents might say that all this was the predictable consequence of entrusting political power to the natives, but she remained convinced that the moral conscience of a nation must be kept alive, even when almost extinct, that hers was the only true way forward, and that Africa could and must survive the early growing pains of a genuine democracy. Her husband died in 1994; she herself died at the age of ninety-one on New Year's Day 2009.

MAYA ANGELOU:
GREAT AMERICAN SPIRIT

Maya Angelou, known at least in the United States as a philosopher, civil rights worker, poet and autobiographer, has been called 'America's most visible black female writer' and has become in her advancing years a public figure of considerable importance as well as a close acquaintance of national leaders like Hillary Clinton. Her works centre on themes as diverse as identity, family, racism, morality and sociology, and a number are used throughout the USA as set texts in schools and universities. Winner of numerous literary prizes and awards, some of her work is so controversial as to be challenged or even banned in US libraries.

Marguerite Ann Johnson was born in April 1928 in St Louis, Missouri, the daughter of Bailey Johnson, a black doorman, and Vivian Johnson, a surgical nurse and a real estate agent. She was given the nickname 'Maya' by her elder brother, who supposedly shortened it from 'my-a-sister'. In her childhood, after the break-up of her parents' marriage, she had many unhappy experiences with her grandmother in Arkansas, and then again, when she was returned to her mother in Missouri. Back in her own home she was beaten, abused and repeatedly raped by her mother's then boyfriend, as a result of which he was seized and battered to death by her uncles. This episode had a traumatic affect on the growing girl: there was a period of about five years when she retired into her shell and refused even to speak. At that time a family friend introduced her to the world of books, and she began to read voraciously – a number of American authors like Edgar Allen Poe, as well as many of the works of Shakespeare and Dickens. She studied at George Washington High School in the 1940s, and went on later to study dance and drama at the California Labour School, earning money working as a bus conductress for a time before becoming a professional dancer and singer. At the behest of the Purple Onion in San Francisco, where for a time she was employed as a dancer, she adopted the surname 'Angelou' from the Greek sailor she married at the age of twenty-one in 1949 – he was called Tosh Angelos – and went on to divorce and remarry several times in the course of her career.[1] Her dancing career was brief but quite spectacular. She toured Europe in 1954–55 with *Porgy and Bess*, studied modern dance with Martha Graham and appeared with Alvin Ailey in television variety shows (as Al and Rita, from her baptismal name Marguerite); she also experimented with West African tribal dancing, and even with ballet. At the end of the 1950s she reverted to writing and to politics as her main interest.

She found dancing very strenuous, and began to turn elsewhere.[2] In 1959 she joined the Harlem Writers' Guild, where she met one of the figures who was to be important to her in her later life, the African American author James Baldwin. She also heard Martin Luther King speak, and was moved to join the civil rights movement. She organised several benefits for King and he chose her as the northern co-ordinator of the Southern Christian Leadership Conference in 1960. She went abroad for a time as the common-law wife of the South African freedom fighter Vusumzi Make. When this association ended she moved to Egypt where she became associate editor of the *Arab Observer*, moving again to Ghana in 1962 to become feature editor for *The African Review* and an instructor in the University of Ghana's School of Music and Drama. In Ghana she also became a close friend of Malcolm X. She returned to the USA in 1964 to help him build a new civil rights association there. However, Malcolm X was assassinated in 1964, as was Dr King in 1968. She found these events unendurable and retreated into private life for a number of years, dealing with her grief chiefly by increasing her output of writing.

In 1973 she married Paul du Feu, British-born carpenter and remodeller, and moved with him to California. Over the following years she wrote articles, short stories and poetry[3] for a number of magazines; she also played Kunta Kinte's grandmother in the play *Roots*, and wrote a screenplay *Georgia, Georgia*, which was the first original script by a black woman to be produced. She later divorced de Feu and returned to the southern states in 1981, and accepted the lifetime Reynolds Professorship of American Studies at Wake Forest University at Winston-Salem, North Carolina. In 1993 she performed her poem *On the Pulse of the Morning* at the inauguration of President Bill Clinton, the first since Robert Frost recited at John F. Kennedy's inauguration in 1961. In the 1990s she began to take part in the US lecture circuit, appearing nearly a hundred times and charging upwards of $40,000 per appearance. She cultivated a rather dated southern formality in her manner, always addressing everyone she spoke to by their surname and insisting on being herself called Dr Angelou. A professional dealer in hope, she used her own poetry as the vehicle for popularising passionate and compassionate exhortation to improve the world.[4] She became a close friend of Oprah Winfrey, whom she first encountered in the 1970s, and appeared in a weekly show, *Oprah and Friends*, after 2006. In 1998, to celebrate her seventieth birthday, she went on a cruise as a present from Oprah Winfrey. In 2008, on her eightieth, she took part in a number of 'pricey soirées' including an appearance at Donald Trump's Mar-a-Lago Club at Palm Beach, Florida, where she was serenaded by some of the brightest stars in the US entertainment firmament.

Always on the edge of politics by the nature of her civil concerns, she entered into the mainstream of US presidential politics in 2008 when she threw her weight behind Hillary Clinton's efforts to rally support among the members of the black community. She appeared to think that the time was not yet ripe for a black President, but when Barack Obama finished twenty-nine points ahead of Hillary Clinton and took 80 per cent of the black vote in the North Carolina primaries she threw her support behind him, declaring: 'we are growing up beyond the idiocies of racism'. She still, however, maintained cordial relations with the defeated Hillary Clinton, and enthusiastically supported her nomination as Secretary of State in Obama's cabinet after his election in November 2008. By 2009 she had completed her purchase of a solid town house in Harlem, New York, though she did not settle there, but continued to travel widely.

Her literary and philosophical impact on the US remains extremely important today. Critics agree that her influence on American literature, especially in the genre of autobiography, has been epoch-making. Whereas before, black female writers in the US were marginalised to the point of invisibility, she set new standards of achievement not only for black women, but for her sex in general. Though she herself characterised her writings as autobiographical, her use of fiction-writing techniques in dialogue, plot and language resulted in the frequent placement of her work on the fiction shelves. Devices such as the abandonment of strict chronology, her use of poetic vocabulary so that her prose and her verse are very similar, her 'short-story techniques' in their content and style, and the use of what has been called the 'slave narrative tradition' of speaking in the first-person singular, but meaning 'we' – these are employed to get closer to the 'human truth' of her life. Racial and cultural identity, kinship concerns and motherhood are constantly referred to in her writing, her concerns leading through subtle resistance all the way to outright and active protest in the civil rights movement.

In recent years she has been showered with honours, from the Presidential Medal of Arts in 2000 to the Lincoln Medal in 2008. She has been awarded upwards of thirty honorary degrees by a wide variety of educational institutions. She remains sanguine in her old age about the prospects for continuing black advancement, suspending judgment on Obama's presidency beyond his first 'hundred days', and believing real improvement is going to be slow, taking years instead of days.

NOTES

Helen of Troy

1. This gave two new words to the English language: *spartan,* which means austere, hardy and rigorous, and *laconic,* which means pithy, brief, and terse.
2. It seems strange that the place should be known as 'Ilium' as well as 'Troy'. Its earliest name, relative to its two main districts, as used by the Hittites, was Wilusa and Taruwisa. With the passage of time, the 'w' came to be dropped by the Ionian Greeks (of whom Homer was one), so that (W)ilusa became Ilusa, and then Ilios, and Taru(w)isa became Taruisa and then Troia. Hence we get Homer's story of Ilios, the *Iliad,* and the wars of *Troia,* or Troy.
3. Probably not of a *thousand* ships, since each contained fifty oarsmen and thirty fully-armed warriors, and this would have paralysed the entire Mycenaean economy; but certainly several *hundred.*
4. Herodotus' version of the story denies that Helen was ever *in* Troy; if she had been, the Trojans would have preferred giving her up to condemning themselves to a costly war to keep her. Herodotus thinks she sat out the entire war in Egypt, and possibly sent an *eidolon* (a body double) to Troy.
5. Here Homer's story coincides again with Herodotus' history, which says she was in Egypt all along.

NOTES TO PART 1

Beatrice and Dante Alighieri

1. He also wrote *Canzonieri*, a collection of sonnets and short poems; *The Banquet*, a commentary on another of the poet's works; *On Monarchy*, expounding his theory of divinely inspired world government by a universal pope; and *On the Common Tongue*, in which he discusses the origin of language.

Aphra Behn

1. The English had settled along the Surinam river under the patronage of Lord Willoughby, governor of Barbados in the 1650s. But after changing hands several times it was finally ceded to the Dutch in 1667.

2. The Exclusion Crisis, in which the Whig opposition under Lord Shaftesbury tried to exclude the Catholic James, Duke of York, from the throne, had just ended with the Whigs routed.

Jane Austen

1. It was said that 'streams of water flowed; everything Mediaeval and Gothic became a fad; wild tales of mystery and horror were mightily cried up'.
2. Jane said of one critic of *Mansfield Park* that 'she liked it, but thought it was a mere novel'. Another criticised Austen for her 'want of taste' and said that 'she does not understand wit', while a third said of *Pride and Prejudice* that it was 'downright nonsense'.
3. As in the main plotline of *Sense and Sensibility*.
4. In *Pride and Prejudice* Elizabeth's mother was the daughter of a lawyer, and he, unless he happened to be a barrister, counted as a tradesman. Her other uncle was in trade. The prejudice against trade, however, did not prevent impoverished gentry from marrying into money by taking wealthy tradespersons' daughters as wives.
5. Like Mr John Knightley in *Emma*, the younger brother of the owner of Donwell Abbey.
6. In *Mansfield Park*, Edmund Bertram, younger son of Sir Thomas Bertram, has to see his father sell the right to the next presentation to the more profitable of his two livings to pay his elder son's debts, and so has to content himself with the second, much poorer, living.
7. The highest mentioned was the portion of Miss Gray in *Sense and Sensibility*, who had £50,000. The five Misses Bennet, in *Pride and Prejudice*, on the other hand, had only £1,000 each.
8. When Maria Ward, with only £7,000, married Sir Thomes Bartram in *Mansfield Park* the 'whole of Huntingdon exclaimed on the greatness of the match' because her uncle, the lawyer, knew she was 'at least £3,000 short of any equitable claim to it'. In other words, Sir Thomas' contribution amounted to at least £10,000.
9. Willoughby, in *Sense and Sensibility*, rejects Marianne Dashwood because her dowry is only £3,000, and sets his cap at Miss Gray, with £50,000. On the other hand, Anne Elliot, in *Persuasion*, regrets being persuaded to reject Capt. Wentworth the first time they meet because he had only his profession to depend on for his living.
10. Frank Churchill and Jane Fairfax, in *Persuasion*, were secretly engaged for about eight months because Frank's guardian refused her consent and Frank was financially dependent on her.

Elizabeth Barrett Browning

1. She exercised a great influence on his writing as he did on hers, though it is doubtful whether the influence was always beneficial. Her concern with public and social issues diminished and her obsession with spiritual matters correspondingly increased. Her father disinherited her, as he did all his children who married,

though one of the scholars who wrote about her (William S. Paterson in *Sonnets from the Portuguese* – 'Portuguese' was Browning's pet name for her) may not have been entirely serious in his judgement on her when he said: 'the Mrs. Browning of popular imagination was a sweet innocent young woman who suffered endless cruelties at the hands of a tyrannical papa but who nonetheless had the good fortune to fall in love with a dashing and handsome poet named Robert Browning, finally escaping the dungeon of Wimpole Street, eloping to Italy and living happy ever after.'

2. He never married but it is said that the local population are sprinkled with his descendants.

3. See, for example, Angela Leighton, *Elizabeth Barrett Browning* (Indiana University Press, 1986).

Helen Bradley

1. Ina Taylor, *Helen Bradley's Lancashire* (2002). The book is lavishly illustrated with many of Bradley's paintings and the wry commentaries with which she accompanied them.

2. The symbol of the fly comes from the artist's baptismal name, Nellie, and the children's skipping rhyme: *'Nellie Bly caught a fly / Tied it to a string / Let it out to fly about / But couldn't get it in.'*

3. This was at Saddleworth, where she told the great man she had difficulty painting figures. 'Paint only those you know well,' he is said to have told her. 'Go home and paint your mother.' This was kind but rather surprising advice, considering that she was already well into her sixties.

Coco Chanel

1. She said he broke her heart twice, first by marrying her, and then again when he was killed in a car crash in 1919.

2. First known as 'Eau Chanel', it was one of the first 'artificial' fragrances, not designed to smell like roses or jasmine, but as a 'compound fragrance' which, if it smelled of anything, smelled of pure fashion.

3. She is said by Cecil Beaton to have retorted to someone who complained of her associating with the enemy: 'Really, a woman of my age cannot be expected to look at his passport if she has the chance of a lover.'

4. She always claimed she wanted to free women from their corsets, and when fitting the curvy dancer Émilienne d'Alençon with a dress she grumbled, 'Why are you so fat?'

Enid Blyton

1. 'Golliwog' was another abusive term used to describe Negroes, though the appearance of golliwog dolls on Huntley's marmalade jars had originally no such overtones.

NOTES TO PART 2

Greta Garbo

1. This was her first attempt at romantic comedy, in which she parodied her own aloof image, and famously laughed. The cinema posters made a meal of it – 'Garbo *laughs!*' they said.

2. She always denied making such a request. What she had said, she maintained, was 'I want to be *left* alone.' In the film *Grand Hotel* in 1932, indeed, Grusinskaya (played by Garbo) says 'I want to be left alone.'

3. Two other women, Mercedes de Acosta in the 1930s and Louise Brooks in the 1940s, claimed in their writings to have had a lesbian relationship with Garbo.

Joyce Grenfell

1. Nancy Astor did not get on with Winston Churchill, and is once said to have told him: 'If I were your wife, sir, I would poison your coffee.' Whereupon he is said to have retorted: 'And if I were your husband, madam, I should drink it' – one of the few occasions when she did not come off the best.

2. Unsuccessful because, although he was articled to Sir Edmund Lutyens, the most famous architect of his generation, and was a kind and thoroughly nice person, was not the sharpest knife in the box. He later tried to work in Canada and the USA, but generally was forced to depend on his family for money. All the same, Nora seemed to love him, and he was suitable as a match. For the Phipps family tree went back to the Norman Conquest, while his mother, Jessie Butler Duncan, Joyce's paternal grandmother, had lived at No. 1, Fifth Avenue, New York, and was the daughter of an enormously rich banker and railroad tycoon.

3. Christian Science was a faith developed by the American Mary Baker Eddy and was fashionable in the first half of the twentieth century. Christian Scientists believe that God is responsible for all the good in creation, but that all evil and sickness is due to human error or illusion. Jesus is the Son of God and Saviour, and God is not an avenger but a spiritual embodiment of goodness. For Christian Scientists, all creation existed in spiritual ideas, and life should express itself through active love and charity. The Church had no ordained clergy, but there were Christian Science 'practitioners', trained in spiritual healing, who took the place of doctors.

4. ENSA stood for Entertainment National Service Association, which put on concert parties and other entertainments for servicemen, not, as was sometimes maliciously suggested, 'Every Night Something Awful'.

5. Like Marcus Aurelius, she did not regard God as someone 'up there' to be prayed to. Indeed, she did not believe in prayer. She said: 'I don't converse with God. I try to understand the ever-presence of Good. Good is already there, in everyone. If you recognise the good in anyone, you are recognising God.'

Marilyn Monroe

1. Where she put on a breathy, little-girl's voice to sing 'Diamonds Are a Girl's Best Friend'.
2. She won the Italian equivalent of an Academy Award, plus the French Crystal Star Award, and was nominated for a BAFTA award.
3. She was married three times, to James Dougherty, to the baseball player Joe DiMaggio, and to the playwright Arthur Miller. The second attachment seems to have been the strongest.
4. She took drugs to liven her up, to calm her down, to stay awake, and to go to sleep. She took methamphetamines by the handful when she had minor illnesses, and Secoral, Demerol and Nembutal, often mixed with chloral hydrate in a potentially lethal cocktail.
5. The Kennedys were of course one of America's leading Catholic families, and anything like a divorce would have been quite impossible for them.
6. It seems unlikely that Kennedy betrayed any state secrets to his new protégée, but enough was said for the matter to be brought to the attention of both the FBI and the CIA, who undertook a watching brief over Marilyn's home in Fifth Helena Drive, Brentwood, and began to tap her telephone.
7. She was face down, and not wearing the clean brassiere she usually put on at night in an effort to preserve the profile of her bust. There were no obvious puncture marks on the body to suggest a fatal injection, though there was slight bruising on the arms and lower back. The position and the attitude of the corpse looked as though the scene had been deliberately staged.
8. In particular, the autopsy found evidence that the subject had undergone 'multiple abortions', some of them relatively recent.

Gracie Fields

1. She had lost her British nationality as the result of her marriage, so that the announcement of the Honour in the *London Gazette* in February 1979 indicated that it was substantive rather than honorary. This, however, proved to be a distinction without a difference.

Margot Fonteyn

1. It was said that the ballet was like the royal court of the sovereign Louis XIV, one of the earliest patrons of this form of dance: the courtiers were the corps de ballet, the individual dancers were the ladies-in-waiting, the solo dancers the dukes, duchesses and other noblemen, and at the centre of the stage the queen of the ballet, the role filled by Fonteyn herself.
2. She retired in 1963 but retained her influence over the Royal Ballet for as long as she lived. She died in 2001 at the age of 102.
3. When he saw Nureyev perform, chain-smoking Fred Ashton exclaimed: 'Fuck me! He's better than Nijinski!'

4. He said they danced with 'one body, one soul' and that Margot was all he had, 'only her'.

5. Fonteyn performed in a ballet the very day she learned of his shooting, and afterwards devoted a good deal of her income and savings to providing care for her crippled husband. Fred Ashton joked that now he was immobile she might at last be able to get him to sit all the way through one of her performances.

NOTES TO PART 3

Laura Ormiston Chant

1. Some of the features of these acts were intended to be beneficial insofar as they were intended to close brothels and punish anyone profiting from prostitution. Yet they created great resentment from those who objected to the idea they contained of compulsory medical examinations for women believed to be prostitutes, on the grounds that it would be a violation of their rights and would treat them like cattle. In fact, legalised state brothels, on the model of those existing for servicemen in French seaports, with rigorous medical testing, might have brought benefits to the health of their clients – and even to the prostitutes themselves.

2. One was called, rather belligerently, *Why We Attacked the Empire*. This redoubled the hostility of Rudyard Kipling, who hated her anyway for the bigotry of her views.

3. Churchill had spent some time polishing a speech he intended to give to the recently established Entertainments Protection Society, which he had joined, denouncing Mrs Chant's work. But he found he was the only member of the public present at the meeting, so he gave up and went to the theatre instead.

Mary Whitehouse

1. Lord Reith was Director-General of the BBC from 1927–38. As his newsreaders were, until 1936, broadcasting on radio alone, the requirement for formal dress seems a little excessive, but it helped to give the BBC its great reputation as a highly respectable institution.

NOTES TO PART 4

Margaret Ann Bulkley

1. The Spanish historian, Las Casas, who was present, reported in 1817 on the visit of 'a medical gentleman' in the company of 'one of the captains of our station', and was struck by his slim build and youthful appearance, saying 'I mistook the captain's medical friend for his son or nephew'.

2. It casts an unexpected light on the total absence, or, if they occurred, the perfunctory character, of medical examinations in the British Army at that time, that a woman, without detection, could pass herself off as a man throughout the whole length of her professional career.

Marie Curie

1. Becquerel was himself a university teacher of chemistry, and a leading figure in the fields of electricity, magnetism and optics.

NOTES TO PART 5

Roxelana

1. Her first name was probably Anastasia, though Polish sources refer to her as Aleksandra Lisowska. In the European languages she was known as Roxelana (or Roxelane, or Rosselana, or Rossa); in Turkish as Hürrem, from the Persian Khurram, the 'laughing one', or the Arabic as Karima, the 'noble one'. 'Roxelana' might not have been a proper name, but a nickname referring to her Ruthenian origins, so it could be derived from 'Ruslana' meaning 'the Ruthenian one'. Again, it might also be a reference to the colour of her hair.
2. The Turkish Army was composed of two chief wings: the cavalry, which was drawn from the holders of the land as part of their conditions of tenure, which was not necessarily hereditary, and the infantry, which was drawn from the subject – and therefore mainly Christian – population, at the rate of roughly one per family. They were tall, strong, well-trained, and known as 'Janissaries', a term derived from the corruption of two Turkish words meaning 'new' and 'army'.
3. Sultans never married: they had such a choice of women and were so powerful that there was no need of dynastic matches. This tradition was reinforced by the legend of one of Suleiman's ancestors whose wife was captured by his enemies and forced to wait on her new masters naked at table. Thereafter, sultans never married again; their children were produced by their concubines. Indeed, all sultans were the sons of slaves.
4. There was even the suggestion that Ibrahim himself was Selim's father, because it was doubtful 'whether the true blood of the Ottoman race flowed in the veins of these twenty-five degenerates' (i.e. the rulers who followed Suleiman, according to Lord Eversley, who based his view on the opinion of the Italian Luigi Bassano, a contemporary who served as a page at the court of Suleiman). Certainly, the like of Suleiman was never seen in Turkish history thereafter.

Nell Gwynn

1. She disappointed Pepys, too, when he saw the play. He commented in his diary: 'I am most infinitely displeased with her being put to playing the Emperor's daughter, which is a great and serious part, and which she does most basely.'
2. 'Gay' here had its old sense of 'lively, playful, merry', not of 'homosexual'.
3. Nell is said to have played a dirty trick on Moll when, knowing she was about to go to bed with the King, she laced her drink with a powerful laxative.
4. See the entry for Catherine of Braganza on page xxx.
5. This did not mean they lost much affection of each other. Nell was very unkind about her, and called her 'Weeping Willow' on account of her mastery of the weapon

of tears. For equally unkind reasons (though such an affliction is not obvious from her portrait) she also called her 'Squintabella'.
6. In fact, in 1960, the property remained the only one on the south side of Pall Mall not owned by the Crown.
7. Charles is said to have uttered on his deathbed: 'Let not poor Nelly starve'.

Abigail Masham

1. See the entry for Sarah Churchill on page 74.
2. In those days, changes of government usually *preceded* general elections, which were held to confirm the new government in power. Government use of money and patronage almost invariably ensured the right result.
3. The Act of Settlement (1701) provided that Anne's successor, since her last child the Duke of Gloucester had died in 1700, was to be the Dowager Electress of Hanover.

Sarah Churchill

1. The Popish Plot began in 1679 with anti-Catholic hysteria whipped up by Titus Oates. His false accusations led to the execution of eighty innocent victims. Politically, the plot brought about attempts by the Whig-dominated Parliament to exclude the Catholic James from the succession.
2. George was not very bright and Charles II remarked of him: 'I've tried him drunk and I've tried him sober, but I can't make any sense of him either way.'
3. Bedchamber women were menials who emptied slops and slept on the floor. Ladies of the Bedchamber were the aristocrats of the court; they were expected to be present, but not to serve in any way that might be considered indelicate.
4. He was Prime Minister from 1754 to 1757, but not a very effective one.
5. Marlborough House was one of Sarah's few extravagances. She had built it with money borrowed from Anne's Privy Purse. The house was designed by Sir Christopher Wren.

Mme de Maintenon

1. Though her father, Constant d'Aubigné, was a Huguenot and a general of Henri IV, her mother, a fervent Catholic, was obliged through poverty to entrust her daughter's education to her sister-in-law, Mme de Villette, and she brought her up as a Protestant. Nonetheless, by 1650 she had reverted to Catholicism and remained faithful to it until her death.
2. Though she approved of the revocation of the Edict of Nantes in 1688, removing the right of French Protestants, granted in 1598 by Henri IV, to worship in their own way, she disapproved of the King's policy of using the billeting of his soldiery on recusant families (the so-called *Dragonnades)* to ensure their conversion.
3. She was wrong on this – and later admitted it when she said: 'There is nothing so clever as behaving oneself irreproachably.' It certainly proved to be the way to Louis XIV's heart.

4. Mme de Maintenon had a great reputation for devotion. In 1692 Pope Innocent XII granted her the right of visitation over all the convents in France.
5. It was said at court that she liked to escape from Versailles from time to time. The palace was large and draughty and the King was a fresh-air fiend who used to fling the windows open; when she got to St Cyr she could crawl into a warm bed and stay there as long as she liked.
6. This was inscribed with a simple couplet composed by Racine, which said:

> Elle est notre guide fidèle,
> Notre félicité vient d'elle.

7. Nothing less than a *lettre de cachet* from the King, relegating her to a life sentence in a distant convent.
8. Quietism led to an advocacy of poetic mysticism and pure love instead of deeds. It tended, too, towards non-attendance at church, since listening to sermons distracted believers' pure concentration on God. All this smacked of heresy, just as did their view that sin is permissible so long as one really loved God, which implied looser standards than were normally acceptable. In the end, Mme de Maintenon abjured Quietism when Louis XIV put his foot down and sent Mme Guyon to the Bastille for eight years.

Mme de Pompadour

1. The King's son, Louis the Dauphin, had died in 1711, and his son, Louis, Duke of Burgundy, in the following year, leaving the future Louis XV a mere child.
2. The Compagnie des Indes, under the direction of the Scotsman John Law, collapsed in the financial scandal of 1720, a 'bubble' resulting from the relentless self-promotion of the company, in which many investors were ruined. It was refloated more modestly later that year, but it forced the French government deeply into debt and was responsible for the devaluation of the currency.
3. At court, she promoted her father, too. In 1747, he received recognition for his 'services to the king' in the Works Department (the *Bâtiments*) and became Seigneur de Vandières, a small property he owned near Château Thierry. Later, his son Abel became known at court derisively as 'Monsieur d'Avant-hier' (Lord Day-Before-Yesterday).
4. Voltaire, who could grovel almost as well as he could sneer, wrote a sickening little verse to her, in which he rhymed 'Pompadour' with 'amour'.
5. Frederick had a healthy male contempt for women in politics. He called Pompadour 'Petticoat III' ('Petticoat I' was Maria Theresa, his Austrian foe, and 'Petticoat II', was Catherine II, the Great, of Russia, always threatening him with her troops on his eastern flank).
6. The *vingtième* was a 5 per cent tax equivalent to the English Land Tax (also at a shilling in the pound), but it was new and more sweeping. It was later doubled, and then actually tripled.

7. A *lit de justice* was a constitutional device whereby the King summoned his magistrates to his presence and commanded them to acknowledge their fealty and enregister an edict which they had previously refused to accept. This they were obliged to do on pain of banishment, but they usually found a way to repudiate it again afterwards.

8. A *billet de confession* showed that a dying person had confessed to a priest who accepted the Papal Bull *Unigenitus*, which signified acceptance of papal authority by rejecting the doctrines of the Jansenists, the opponents of the Bull. The Marquise was right in suspecting that these *billets* were an intrusion into private affairs, but wrong in suspecting the *Parlement* and the clergy of being allies – in fact many of the *parlementaires* were Jansenists.

9. From time to time, churchmen contributed voluntarily to government revenues by making a 'free gift' to the French Exchequer; though this was often quite substantial it was much less than they should have paid if they had been properly assessed. Historically, however, no one had as yet dared to challenge the churchmen's resistance to the claim that they should be liable for taxes like any other person.

10. All of them virgins, out of deference to the King, and because this lessened the risk to him of venereal disease.

11. She always suffered from her nerves, since she lived on the edge and drove herself hard to amuse the King and maintain her position; blinding migraines were the frequent result. Latterly she suffered from digestive problems and recurrent fevers, and finally died of bronchial pneumonia in April 1764, at the age of forty-two, not long after the Treaty of Paris ended the Seven Years' War.

Jeanne Bécu

1. The necklace was not finished before Louis XV died. Eventually, in 1785, the court jewellers wanted Marie Antoinette to buy it. Her unwillingness to do so led to a sordid attempt to entrap the Queen into its purchase. The 'Diamond Necklace Affair' helped to discredit the monarchy in the years leading up to the French Revolution. See 'How Diamonds were Not a Girl's Best Friend' in Ed Rayner and Ron Stapley, *Scandals in History*, (2008).

2. The *tricoteuses* were the women who sat around the guillotine, some knitting, some collecting the bloody tresses of the victims, and seldom showing any sympathy for the condemned.

Peggy Eaton

1. The mob trampled mud into the carpets, broke the crockery and the glasses, tore and smashed the furniture, and Jackson himself had to flee for his life through an open window. The crowd was only enticed from the house by putting open barrels of punch on the lawn.

2. Congressman Richard Call, for example, hearing that Peggy was a woman of easy virtue, tried it on with her when he got her alone, only to find that she snatched up a pair of fire-irons in her defence, and afterwards complained to Jackson of

the congressman's conduct. Jackson, ever the ladies' champion, sent for him and administered a blistering rebuke that he never forgot.

3. Thus he introduced into American life what is often called 'the Spoils System'. One of the criticisms made by Jacksonians against the previous President J. Q. Adams was that his civil service was corrupt; the new President remedied this by packing his government service from cabinet offices down to local postmasterships with hundreds of his own supporters. He justified this with the phrase 'To the victor, the spoils'. Of course, this did not improve the quality of the civil service; it merely extended the scope of the President's patronage.

4. The cotton estates of the South were rapidly becoming exhausted, and the tariffs imposed on imported manufactures by the federal government to protect northern industry made the people pay more for their imports. Southerners believed not only that the North was introducing tariffs chiefly in its own interests, but was also threatening slavery, the mainstay of the southern economy. Calhoun took the lead in producing the 'South Carolina Exposition', which protested against such policies and threatened 'nullification' of discriminatory laws, and eventually secession from the Union if the North continued with them. These 'states rights' beliefs were eventually the main cause of the American Civil War in 1860.

5. The Bank of the United States had been chartered for twenty years in 1816, and its renewal was due in 1836. Jackson opposed this, saying that its profits came out of the hard work of ordinary American citizens and went into the pockets of a few rich men (an assertion not without truth). He diverted government funds into smaller 'pet' banks and starved the federal bank out of business, a policy which may have been populist but which militated against the commercial interests of US business, as conservatives like Calhoun clearly saw.

6. This name was given to the little coterie of advisers who were the President's 'cronies' and discussed matters with him unofficially before matters came before the real cabinet. Many were ex-newspapermen; all were his personal acquaintances.

Lillie Langtry

1. A French actress of Dutch descent who had already achieved a formidable reputation in Paris.
2. Lord Mountbatten (Louis' son) always believed that Jeanne Marie was his half-sister.
3. In a letter of condolence, written to another widow, Lillie confided: 'I, too, have lost a husband, but alas! it was no great loss.'

Eva Braun

1. According to Albert Speer, she never slept with Hitler. She left the room 'as soon as dignitaries of the Reich appeared at the table'. She was 'obviously regarded as socially acceptable within strict limits. Sometimes I kept her company in a room next to Hitler's bedroom. She was so intimidated she did not dare leave the house for a walk without his permission.'

2. In the closing days of the war he attempted to escape from the Führerbunker to Sweden, his pockets full of cash and jewels, but was caught at it and hauled straight back. Out of hand, Hitler ordered him to be shot. Gretl was nine months pregnant at the time. After her sister's death, she subsequently named her daughter Eva.

Clara Petacci

1. Marcello was a doctor in the Italian Navy and was said to be making a mint from smuggling gold through his diplomatic bag, from his dealing in large sums of foreign currency and from his contacts with the Duce, which enabled him to place contracts and arrange profitable appointments. Mussolini was not interested in money, and certainly never helped Marcello to make any.
2. The main organs of this government were cut off from him in Salò and a number of other small north Italian towns; Mussolini's villa was in Gargnano, though he would dearly have liked to return to Rome.
3. They included Gottardi, Marinelli, Pareschi, his own kinsman Ciano and the 78-year-old Marshal de Bono. He would have liked to prosecute Grandi, Federzoni and Bottai, but they, together with a good many others, had taken to their heels and disappeared.
4. They were merely hoping that right-thinking Catholics would be distressed at his marital infidelity.
5. Buffarini-Guidi suggested he make for Switzerland; an old mistress, Francesca Lavagnini, invited him to join her in the Argentina; Clara suggested a fake car accident in which he could be 'killed'. He angrily rejected all of these.
6. Mussolini did not take long. Clara was still fumbling among the bedclothes, and when told to hurry up replied that she could not find her knickers. In the end she left without them.

NOTES TO PART 6

Anne Hathaway

1. He certainly died on 23 April, St George's Day, and tradition has it that it was on the date, too, that he was born, but this is not certain.
2. It does not excuse, however, his lack of generosity towards the twins, who received little or nothing.

Elizabeth Pepys

1. Regicides were the fifty-nine men who had signed Charles I's death warrant in January 1649. Ten of those still living in 1660 were executed by hanging, drawing and quartering.
2. The Dutch fleet sailed up the mouth of the Thames into the River Medway at Chatham, where they destroyed several ships and carried off the *Royal Charles*, the pride of the English fleet.

3. In 1678 the rogue Titus Oates was largely responsible for the Popish Plot which alleged treasonable activities by Roman Catholics or alleged Roman Catholics. At its height eighty men were tried and executed on Titus' false evidence. Samuel Pepys was under investigation and narrowly escaped trial himself in 1679. See Rayner and Stapley, *Scandals in History* (2008), pp. 93–99.

Mary Anne Disraeli

1. At a house party given by Lady Hardinge, she shocked her hostess by announcing at breakfast that she had slept the night before 'between the greatest soldier (Hardinge) and the greatest orator (Disraeli) of our times.' In fact she was referring to the location of her bedroom.
2. When the table talk turned to the subject of the great eighteenth-century Irish scholar and wit Jonathan Swift, she asked whether she might not invite him to one of her parties.
3. The very fact he was twelve years younger meant she was likely to predecease him, and then he would get nothing, since the London house was entailed to the relatives of her first husband.
4. His biographer Robert Blake says he rather overdid his passion for trees; he took pleasure in planting them, but Gladstone loved chopping them down.
5. This was some months after the Royal Titles Bill, which conferred the title of 'Empress of India' on Victoria, though in no sense (in spite of what is sometimes alleged) was it a 'payback' for this honour.
6. There is little evidence, however, that he ever deferred to her in political matters; these were his own particular province and he seldom if ever mentioned them to her.

Jane Carlyle

1. Carlyle was also a prolific writer on the general and political problems of his day, as well as on history: his editing of the letters and speeches of Oliver Cromwell was noteworthy, his *French Revolution* absolutely sensational (despite its first manuscript being supposedly used by John Stuart Mill's housemaid to light a fire) and his *Frederick the Great* ran to six vast volumes and was monumental although quite unreadable.

Lady Emily Tennyson

1. Her father, a gruff Lincolnshire man disapproved of Alfred's careless way of dressing, his raffish air and his lax religious views, and thought that he 'wasted himself in cigars'.
2. When he read in *The Times* of the Charge of the Light Brigade he sat down then and there to draft his poem on it. It so heightened his reputation that he was offered a Doctorate in Civil Law at Oxford and accepted it in 1855.
3. Emily wrote: 'He is a most striking figure, in his picturesque white poncho lined with red, his embroidered red shirt and coloured tie over it; his face is very noble, powerful and sweet, his forehead high and square.'

4. She wrote to her sister in 1890: 'Once or twice I have been very unwell, but of course I must keep things to myself as much as possible – I have a great many things to be thankful for!'

Alice Liddell

1. Its original title was *Alice's Adventures Under Ground*.
2. On his death, however, the book was bought by a consortium of US bibliophiles who presented it back to Britain, where it is now lodged in the British Library.
3. The note says 'LC learns from Mrs. Liddell that he is supposed to be using the children as a means of paying court to the governess – he is also supposed to be courting Ina' (the older sister by three years).
4. An article in the *Times Literary Supplement* (2003) says it was in fact written by Dodgson's great-nephew Jacques – though there is no handwriting evidence to support the claim.

Magda Goebbels

1. Friedländer later died in Buchenwald concentration camp.
2. (Paul) Josef Goebbels (1897–1945) joined the Nazis in 1924 and helped with his newspaper *Der Angriff* to build the party into a national force. He entered the Reichstag in 1928 and became *Gauleiter* of Berlin in 1929. In 1933, when the party came to power, he became Minister of Propaganda, controlling the national media, which he manipulated to ensure support for the regime.
3. He went to North Africa during Rommel's campaigns there, was captured and interned in a prisoner-of-war camp. His mother wrote him a farewell letter from Berlin early in 1945, in which she bemoaned the fate of her party and her country: 'Our glorious idea is in ruins.'
4. She refused, however, to intervene to save the life of her Jewish stepfather, Richard Friedländer, from the Holocaust, and he died in a concentration camp. She is on record as saying: 'The Führer wants it thus, and we must obey.'
5. See 'What Was the Fate of Adolf Hitler?' in Rayner and Stapley, *Who Was Mr Nobody?* (2007).

NOTES TO PART 7

Joan of Arc

1. George Bernard Shaw, in his *Prelude to Saint Joan*, makes something like the same point when he says: 'Joan must be judged a sane woman in spite of her voices because they never gave her any advice that might not have come from her mother wit.'
2. Joan seems to have suffered little progressive deterioration in her health over six years, which points away from the brain tumour theory, nor did her fifty-foot leap from the tower of Beaurevoir in an escape attempt during her imprisonment produce any haemorrhaging, as most likely it would in the case of a growing tumour.

3. It is quite wrong to infer from this some sort of condition relating to sex or gender e.g. that she was 'boyish'; in fact the condition is a recognised complication of tuberculosis.

Grace Darling

1. A cobble (or coble) boat is small, oared, flat-bottomed boat normally used on rivers and in estuaries.
2. The most lifelike was a watercolour by H. P. Parker, 1838, at present in the National Portrait Gallery.

Mary Seacole

1. A *creole* is the offspring of a first-generation mixed marriage, either of Amerindian or, more usually, of African blood. In fact, Mary's mother was a free mulatto with African blood, which makes Mary herself a *quadroon*. Her own children (if she had ever had any) would have been *octoroons*.
2. The Seacole family believed (and still believe) him to have been the second natural child of Admiral Nelson and Lady Hamilton, whose first child, Horatia, died when she was only two.
3. Nightingale also referred to the 'British Hotel' at Spring Hill as a 'bad house'. She may have meant only that it was a ramshackle wooden and sheet-iron hovel, but, more likely, she meant in the common parlance that it was a brothel.
4. Sarah ('Sally') Seacole, who helped her run the 'hotel' in the Crimea, was about fourteen years of age and was a young relative of the Seacoles. She called Mary 'Mammy', not unusual for youngster speaking to an older relative in Jamaica, but this was the cause of innocent confusion on the part of her hearers, but less innocent on Nightingale's part, who chose to believe that the girl was the illegitimate offspring of Col. Henry Bunbury, an officer in the 33rd. This regiment, however, had never been posted to the West Indies.
5. Nightingale was much too lady-like – or clever – to express any criticism in public, but privately she reacted venomously even to the mention of Mary's name. For her part, Mary was never even privately critical of Nightingale, though one of the other nurses at Scutari, Nurse Betsy Davis, spoke not only for herself when she said that Florence was 'an arrogant and cold-hearted petticoat out for power and glory at the expense of the sick'.
6. A returning war veteran asked in *The Times*: 'while the benevolent deeds of Florence Nightingale are being handed down to posterity with blessings and renown, are the humbler deeds of Mrs. Seacole to be entirely forgotten?'
7. She may have been Princess Alexandra's masseuse, for Alexandra, unpompous and jolly (and quite unlike Queen Victoria), suffered from deafness and from 'white leg', oedema of the legs caused by thrombosis, and needed massage to ease the condition. She and Mary got on famously.
8. She had converted to Catholicism in her middle fifties, shortly after the Crimean War.

Edith Cavell

1. Before her execution she saw the Anglican chaplain, the Revd Father Graham, and took Holy Communion. To him she expressed the opinion: 'Patriotism is not enough. I must have no hatred or bitterness towards anyone.' These words were later inscribed on the plinth of her statue in St Martin's Place, near Trafalgar Square.
2. The film, released in September 1939, featured Anna Neagle as Nurse Cavell, with a cast including a number of other distinguished actors such as George Sanders and May Robson. The film was in black-and-white, and was nominated (unsuccessfully) for an Oscar.

Eva Péron

1. Her birth certificate is dated 7 May 1922, and was later forged on her instructions to conceal her illegitimacy, at that time much frowned on in Argentina. Accurate details of her origins are provided by her baptismal certificate.
2. Juan Perón was born in 1895, entered the Argentine Military Academy when he was sixteen and joined the army in 1915. Posted to various provincial garrisons he was promoted to captain in 1926, and played a small role in the coup of 1930. In 1936 he became military attaché to Chile, and shortly before the outbreak of the war was sent to Europe, visiting Austria, Germany, Spain and Portugal. Much impressed by the theatrics of Benito Mussolini, he came to believe that the only real choice for the future was between communism and fascism.
3. This movement (the 'shirtless ones') had strong backing from the trade unions and represented the workers, the unemployed and the poor of the nation. As yet, Eva's own following was relatively small.
4. October 17 is still celebrated in Argentina as a public holiday – *Dia de la Lealtad* (Loyalty Day).
5. It built also entire communities, such as Evita City, which still exists today.
6. It was, however, displayed only briefly in her former office, on account of the ravages of her disease. The finished body, however, with its radical measures, was an embalmer's triumph, and survived a long time.
7. And even, too, by some Argentinians. One of her opponents said of her: 'She let down the poor, the shirtless ones by providing a glamorous façade for a fascist dictatorship, by salting away charity funds, and by distracting from her husband's protection of Nazi war criminals.'

Phyllis Thom

1. The programme, in thirty-one episodes, gave a semi-fictionalised account of the relations between a wide variety of classes and types of female prisoner-of-war during the Second World War and their insensitive and often brutal Japanese camp guards in Malaya. The programme was called 'Tenko', which was the answer required from the parade of prisoners at daily roll call by the camp guards.
2. He said that there would now be peace and the Japanese would be leaving Sumatra. He added that they could now be friends, an idea that was less than welcome to his victims.

Anne Frank

1. One of his employees was Hermann van Pels, a Jewish butcher who had fled Osnabrück with his family and now advised Otto Frank about spices used in the butchery business. His family shared the fate of the Franks in the 1940s.
2. These were Victor Kugler, Johannes Kleiman, Miep Gies and Bep Voskuijl, all employees, and Jan Gies (Miep's husband) and Johannes Viskuijl (Bep's father).
3. Miep Gies was actually present when Gestapo officers entered the office, moved the bookcase and discovered the hidden families. She managed to talk herself out of being arrested, and later went into the annexe and collected the documentation she knew to be Anne's diary and kept it hidden. She later gave it to Otto Frank. She originally came from Vienna in 1920, a sickly child, and was called Hermine Santruschutz (1909–2010). She took refuge in the Netherlands when trying to reach London, slowly recovering her health in Leiden. Later she applied for and got employment with Opetka. She was close to the Franks, since she was Viennese and they knew little Dutch. She subsequently met and married Jan Gies, a social worker for the Amsterdam City Council, and managed to secure the relevant paperwork about her 'Aryan birth' to satisfy the authorities and get married. She was one of the group of people who helped to secrete and supply the Frank family and their companions in 1942.
4. Victor Kugler and Johannes Kleiman were also arrested and detained. Kleiman was released in mid-September, but Kugler remained in detention at Amersfoort until the war ended in 1945.
5. Edith Frank was desperately ill and remained behind in Auschwitz where she later died of hunger.
6. A film, compulsorily screened in British cinemas, was made to put the conditions in the camp on record, but this did not prevent later Holocaust deniers from saying that the whole thing was a propaganda hoax.
7. They subjected the diary to detailed forensic examination as to its style and content and as to its constituent materials, paper, ink and binding. In 1986 they confirmed its authenticity.

Sophie Scholl

1. He did a gruelling spell of military service on the Eastern Front, and was among the fortunate minority who managed to get evacuated from Stalingrad in January 1943. After Sophie's death he married her elder sister Elisabeth.
2. Russian soldiers surrendered in vast numbers because of their inferior equipment and bad officering, and the Nazis had neither the manpower nor the food supplies to deal with them. Shooting was the easiest way to solve the problem.
3. In 2003, on the other hand, German viewers were invited by ZDF television to vote for the names of the top ten most important German figures in history, and Sophie and Hans Scholl took fourth place, above Bach, Goethe, Bismarck, Willy Brandt and Albert Einstein.

Princess Diana

1. Diana's maternal grandmother, another Lady Fermoy, was a long-term friend and lady-in-waiting to Queen Elizabeth, the Queen Mother.

2. In London, she liked to drive round Buckingham Palace, sizing it up as a future home; one of Charles' great recommendations, she thought, was that as Prince of Wales he *couldn't divorce her.*

3. If the Duke of Edinburgh, for example, wished to take lunch with the Queen, he would send his footman with a little note to her social secretary, and she would send a written message back, accepting or declining.

4. She was furious when she caught him wearing cuff-links that Camilla had given him – she never realised this was no more than a trick played by his manservant (with whom Diana had had a little spat), who did everything for the Prince. The notion that Charles could or would choose his own cuff-links was quite ridiculous.

5. Even the Queen's comment was a warm one: 'Thank God he hasn't got his father's ears!'

6. Disrespectfully, she called President Reagan a 'Horlicks', which is Sloane-speak for a hopeless, doddery old duffer without an idea in his head.

7. At about this time, too, there occurred the mysterious appearance of two (clearly nefariously obtained) audiotapes which made the rounds and were eventually published: the 'Camillagate' tape, in which Charles was heard making very indiscreet and intimate observations to Camilla Parker-Bowles, and the 'Squidgygate' tape, between Diana and her current amour James Gilbey. 'Squidgy' was the nickname Gilbey used for Diana.

8. She found Mugabe a 'frightening little man' who 'never stopped sweating' the whole time she was with him.

9. It is true that she wrote to him in extremely affectionate terms, and she may well have given Dodi the idea that she was seriously contemplating marriage to him. But she always wrote warm and loving letters (even to Prince Philip, whom she called 'Darling Pa') and certain of her close friends acknowledged that she always wrote 'very effusively'. To these friends, however, she admitted that she 'needed marriage like she needed a rash on her face'. It is difficult to avoid the conclusion that there was an element of duplicity in her character.

10. The pursuing paparazzi got the blame for the accident, and bitter public odium for taking pictures of the wrecked car and its occupants (pictures that were never published), but in fact they were the most deeply grief-stricken of all, not only at the loss of a woman they loved and admired, but of their entire livelihoods.

NOTES TO PART 8

Skittles

1. See 'Was W.E. Gladstone a Whited Sepulchre?' in Rayner and Stapley, *Scandals in History* (2008).

Christine Keeler

1. The Prime Minister, Harold Macmillan, using what was for him unfamiliar popular parlance, had boasted at the previous election that the nation 'had never had it so good'.

NOTES TO PART 9

Ulrike Meinhof

1. She wrote: 'Protest is when I say "This does not please me". Resistance is when I ensure that what does not please me no longer takes place.'
2. She declared rather portentously that her aim was 'to throw bombs into the people's minds'. She also wrote the pamphlet *The Concept of the Urban Guerrilla* to set out in detail their ideology.
3. He was an industrialist who had been abducted and held in an effort to get recently arrested RAF leaders 'sprung' from prison.
4. One of her warders, Horst Bubeck, said of Meinhof that the first time he met her in 1974, on remand from Ossendorf Prison in Cologne, she immobilised him by kicking him hard in the crotch; thereafter she referred to him as 'pig-dog', 'fascist rat' or 'arsehole'. Nevertheless, she always asserted her intellectual superiority. He was astonished at the number of privileges the group were allowed: they spent up to eight hours together daily, they had TV sets, record players, newspapers, cooking facilities and even a gym cell.
5. Her daughter Bettina discovered after her death that her brain had been removed and kept by the hospital in Magdeburg without permission, the hospital having performed a post-mortem at the request of a local psychiatrist who claimed her 'terrorism' might have been due to surgery on her head in 1962 to remove a brain tumour.
6. Baader in particular detested her for her earnestness – he called her 'a fat cow'.

Rosemary West

1. Rosemary produced eight children altogether: after Heather Anne, there was Mae (June 1972), Stephen Andrew (August 1973), Tara (December 1977), Louise (November 1978), Barry (June 1980), Rosemarie (April 1982) and Lucyanna (July 1983). Some of these children were fathered by a variety of clients, since Rosemary was encouraged by her husband to continue with her work as a prostitute. Her father, Andrew Letts, also visited the house and had sex with Fred's daughter Anne Marie.
2. The police had been aiming mainly to prosecute Fred, and had compiled masses of evidence with this aim in view, but there was relatively little time to get the case together against Rosemary.
3. The tapes concluded ghoulishly: 'Keep your promises to me. You know what they are. I have no present. All I have is my life. I give it to you. Come to me, I will be waiting.'

4. Rosemary West would be guilty of murder if: (a) she struck the fatal blows herself, or (b) if she jointly participated as an accomplice in the acts, or finally (c) *she intended the people named in the charges should either be killed or should suffer serious bodily harm.*

NOTES TO PART 10

Madame Roland

1. Robespierre himself attended on a number of occasions, though he was gauche and awkward in company and never had much to say for himself.
2. In rural France events did not move so fast. Mme Roland found to her dismay that the people of her village knew nothing of the Declaration of the Rights of Man and of the Citizen more than a year after its publication.
3. They brought with them Rouget de Lisle's famous 'battle hymn of the Marseillais', the *Marseillaise,* which still serves as France's national anthem: '*Allons, enfants de la patrie, le jour de gloire est arrivé...*'
4. There was a day in the autumn of 1793 when she made a speech at the bar of the House and was received with enthusiastic applause by members, but the public gallery was conspicuously silent. Marat observed shrewdly: 'Perhaps they know better than we do.'

Margaret Thatcher

1. 'Where there is discord, may we bring harmony. Where there is error, may we bring truth. Where there is doubt, may we bring faith. And where there is despair, may we bring hope.'
2. Monetarism: control of the economy by careful management of the money supply, as opposed to Keynesianism with its deficit spending as a cure for a failing economy.
3. Michael Heseltine resigned from the Cabinet in January 1987 when he disagreed with Margaret Thatcher over defence policy. He was now free to challenge her leadership of the party.
4. Adam Smith's *Wealth of Nations*, published in 1776, was widely regarded as the foundation stone of free trade capitalism.
5. It was largely financed by government grants. Ratepayers contributed only about 20 per cent of local government needs.
6. The Poll Tax of 1377 (not the first one by any means) was notorious for precipitating the Peasants' Revolt of 1381 led by Wat Tyler. It was assessed at four pence per head, a very large sum for an impoverished peasant.
7. Known as the ERM, it tied participating currencies to each other within narrow limits.

Benazir Bhutto

1. He was killed by a bomb placed on his plane, which exploded over Bahawalpur in August 1988, killing him and, in addition, his top generals and the US ambassador to Pakistan.

2. The Zina Ordinance was not repealed until 2006, ten years after she left office.

3. Pakistani investigators claimed to have uncovered a network of bank accounts linked to the family's lawyer and crediting profits to him as chief shareholder. He was said to be accepting substantial backhanders from a French company supplying the country with fighter jets, and to have an exclusive licence to import gold into Pakistan which brought him profits of more than $10 million. He was said to have bought several million-pound properties in various European countries, including Britain and France. He denied the charges, declared that the documents were forgeries, and his wife said the criticisms were politically motivated.

4. The worst toll was as a result of a suicide bomber's attack which killed 136 people and injured a further 450. There were also attacks on banks, petrol stations, railways and shops.

5. Al-Qaeda claimed responsibility for the attack, saying that Mrs Bhutto was 'America's most precious asset'.

Aung San Suu Kyi

1. Her 'severe weakness' was eventually traced to physical causes and in 2003 she underwent a hysterectomy.

2. Under the State Protection Act of 1975, later reinforced by similar laws directed against 'subversion', the government took the power to imprison people for up to five years without trial. Suu Kyi has been imprisoned for over fourteen.

3. When she used the prize money to establish a health and education trust for the Burmese people, and to help the London-based charity Prospect Burma to bolster higher education for Burmese students, state-run newspapers reacted by suggesting that Suu Kyi be prosecuted on tax evasion charges for spending the money outside the country.

4. In 1997 SLORC had been replaced by the State Peace and Development Council (SPDC), but this was much the same kind of body as before.

5. In May 2009 a US citizen, John Yettaw, swam across the lake uninvited to her island home on Inya Lake, supposedly to meet her, and stayed for two days because of 'exhaustion', thus violating the terms of her house arrest. After a farcical trial she was found guilty and sentenced to imprisonment in a military base outside the city. She spent her sixty-fourth birthday thus imprisoned, before international pressure brought her return once again to her home. Yettaw was deported.

Shirley Williams

1. She actually played Cordelia in *King Lear*, and later toured the USA with the production.

2. She met Herbert Morrison, newly succeeding Ernest Bevin as Foreign Minister, when she was still in the sixth form, and told him rather severely that he had no right to the Foreign Office because he did not know what the letters 'MRP' (*Mouvement Républicain Populaire*) stood for in French politics – Morrison gravely agreed she was quite right!

3. This clause in the 1918 Labour Party constitution committed Labour to a policy of widespread nationalisation, and had become increasingly an electoral obstacle to the party in its efforts to achieve power; unfortunately it was very popular with the Labour left and the trade unions, who succeeded in retaining it.

4. She also lost support by appearing to renege on a commitment to increase teachers' pay, even provoking the moderate Assistant Masters' Association (AMA) to threaten to strike.

5. Though she had lost her place on the Labour benches, she still remained a key member of the National Executive after 1979, until she left the party in 1981.

6. It was only under Tony Blair in the 1990s that the Party grasped the nettle and finally ditched Clause Four, easing the transformation to 'New Labour' in preparation for his victory in 1997.

NOTES TO PART 11

The Queen of Sheba

1. Several books were attributed to him as a wise man, including the Song of Solomon, the Wisdom of Solomon, the Proverbs and certain of the Psalms. He also constructed the first Temple of Solomon in Jerusalem. His wisdom is illustrated in the Book of Kings by the story of the two women, one of whom, when her baby dies, steals the other one's child and pretends it is hers. Solomon, unable to decide which is telling the truth, is said to have sent for a sword and ordered the child to be chopped in two, and half given to each claimant; the woman who could not bring herself to agree to the division being then awarded the baby as her own true child.

Diane de Poitiers

1. Francis I had been taken prisoner at the battle of Pavia in 1525 and had been unable to pay the stipulated ransom.

2. The office of seneschale made her the King's representative in the province.

Catherine de Medici

1. The Pope could hardly give Prince Henry of France a divorce when he was refusing one to King Henry VIII of England.

2. His last wife, Mary Tudor of England, had died in November 1558, so his period of mourning was very brief.

3. Catherine had received two warnings from her astrologers forecasting her husband's death in 1559, and she herself had dreamt of it the night before.

4. Navarre had converted to the Roman Catholic faith to save his life at the time of the St Bartholomew's Massacre, but had gone back to Protestantism shortly after on the grounds that his 'conversion' had been secured by force. He was to become a Catholic again in 1593.

Elizabeth of York

1. It was asserted that Edward IV had, before his marriage to Elizabeth Woodville, been engaged to another woman, thus making his marriage to Elizabeth bigamous according to contemporary church law.
2. This plan for an eleven-year-old boy to marry an eighteen-year-old girl seemed to raise few eyebrows at the time.
3. He was still much loved in the north.

Elizabeth I

1. Clarence was the elder brother of Richard III, and was supposed to have met his end by his mysterious drowning in a cask of malmsey wine. His Plantagenet blood would have been thought a threat to the Tudor dynasty, and would have been enough in Henry VIII's reign to have sent him to the Tower, if not to the scaffold.
2. Eric XIV, King of Sweden, was the son of Gustavus Vasa, who had wrenched his kingdom from the control of Christian II, King of Norway, Sweden and Denmark in 1523. Conditions similar to those in England in the Wars of the Roses led Eric into an effort to strengthen his new kingdom by securing a powerful foreign ally, and thus he became a suitor for Elizabeth's hand, sending his sister Princess Cecilia, who had recently married the Prince of Baden, to England in 1564, with Helena in her entourage.

NOTES TO PART 12

Queen Christina

1. David Ogg, *Europe in the Seventeenth Century* (8th edition, 1960).
2. She did have a close relationship with a lady-in-waiting, Countess Ebbe ('Belle') Sparre, with whom for many years she maintained a lively correspondence, continuing for years after the countess married and left court. It was said that they sometimes 'shared a bed', but this does not necessarily imply a sexual liaison between the two.
3. There was also, among her trophies, a live lion, which presented some problems to her packers.
4. Charles Gustavus was the son of Gustavus' elder sister, Catharine, who had married John Casimir, Count Palatine of Zweibrücken.
5. The benefits of liquidating landed assets, whose revenues were small and slow to materialise in wartime, in favour of lump cash sums which were available for immediate spending had already appealed to Gustavus Adolphus, but of course had

extended the grip that the wealthy purchasers (usually members of the aristocracy) had over the lives of their tenants and peasants.

6. Christina felt she could not give the nobility the chance of declaring the 'contract' of Västerås annulled because she had deserted her throne; only an abdication by consent could ensure the unconditional accession of her cousin.

7. It was finely ironic that the revenues she demanded should have come from the Crown lands she had insisted should be restored to, and guaranteed for, the royal family.

Henrietta Maria

1. The Protestant Frederick had unwisely accepted the throne of Bohemia and thus precipitated the Thirty Years' War (1618–1648). He had by now lost both Bohemia and the Palatinate, and he and Elizabeth were penniless exiles. James I was seeking financial and military support for them, and was banking on the rivalry between the Austrian and Spanish Habsburgs.

2. Apparently Anne was already pregnant when the marriage took place.

Bess of Hardwick

1. The 4th Earl became Duke in 1694 on the strength of his support for William III, invited to England by the 'Immortal Seven' Whig magnates to take the throne from James II in 1688.

2. The Tower of London was a royal stronghold built by the Normans in the eleventh century, but its apartments were increasingly used by Tudor monarchs as a place of detention for those who had offended them.

3. She was the younger sister of the unfortunate Lady Jane Grey, who had briefly been queen for just nine days in 1553 on the death of Edward VI, and who was later imprisoned and executed by Queen Mary Tudor.

4. Sir William Cecil, Baron Burghley, was Elizabeth's chief finance minister and head of her intelligence service.

5. When Mary Queen of Scots was executed in 1587, James became heir to the English throne, and in 1603 united the two countries as James VI of Scotland and I of England.

6. Arabella had the misfortune to be loved by the very man James would not allow her to marry, Seymour, Earl of Hertford, who himself had a claim to the throne through Lady Jane Grey. In 1610 they married secretly, were imprisoned by the King, escaped and fled. Hertford reached Ostend, but Arabella was arrested at sea and was sent back to the Tower, where she died in 1615.

Anne of Denmark

1. Villiers was made Duke of Buckingham and led the country under James' successor, Charles I. Villiers was responsible for organising the disastrous La Rochelle expedition of 1628 and was murdered at Portsmouth in that year. Villiers' incompetence was one of the many grievances of Charles I's early parliaments.

2. A tennis match appeared to be too much for him. He was only eighteen, but already considered to be the intellectual superior of his brother Charles, later Charles I.
3. Elizabeth's daughter Sophia was eventually to marry the Elector of Hanover, and their son George preserved the Protestant Succession as George I of England.

Catherine of Braganza

1. Charles refused this notion with the opinion: 'I hate Germans, and all the princesses of cold countries.'
2. See also 'How did Titus Oates Try to Save England from the Popish Plot?' in Rayner and Stapley, *Scandals in History* (2008).
3. She was close with the two Methuens, Sir John Methuen, who became envoy to Portugal in 1691, and his son Paul, both men career diplomats. Sir John returned as Ambassador in 1703 and joined her in her native country; he negotiated the two Methuen treaties, the first bringing Portugal into the Grand Alliance against Louis XIV, and the second lowering duties on English cloth entering Portugal and on Portuguese wines entering England, both treaties securing Catherine's support.

Queen Caroline

1. Sir Robert Walpole is usually considered to be England's first Prime Minister, a post he held from 1721–42. No first ministers before him equalled his firm hold on power, and his parliamentary management.
2. The Excise scheme was the proposal to use bonded warehouses for tobacco, and later wine, to curb smuggling. Parliamentary opposition to it was such that Walpole had to abandon it.

Princess Mathilde

1. In her *Memoirs* in 1910, Caroline Murat said: 'It is possible, indeed very probable, that had my aunt been Empress of the French the Franco-Prussian War would never have taken place, and many lesser errors of the Second Empire would have been avoided. She would have made an admirable Empress.'
2. Her full name would have sunk a battleship if it scored a direct hit: it was Laetitia Mathilde Frédérique Aloïssia Élisabeth. Laetitia was the name of her grandmother, Madama Mère, Napoleon's mother; Mathilde was the name of her mother's stepmother, Charlotte Augusta Matilda, daughter of George III of England, and Frédérique recalled the name of her maternal grandfather, King Frederick of Würtemburg.
3. This was his second attempt at a *coup;* he had performed even more disastrously at Strasbourg in 1836.
4. Demidoff was blatantly unfaithful; he was inclined to homosexuality; he suffered from venereal disease; he behaved boorishly and was inclined to violence against his wife (she said he used the whip on her).
5. On the anniversary of the battle of Austerlitz in early December; Napoleon had a fine sense of theatre. This was the coup of which Karl Marx wrote so excoriatingly in his *Eighteenth Brumaire of Louis Bonaparte.*

6. The Empress, on the other hand, urged him to take up the challenge.
7. She wrote to her nephew Joseph Primoli: 'My profound conviction is that she was the principal cause of our misfortune. She took eighteen years to destroy the Emperor, and she wore him out. This woman, who is reckoned virtuous because she had no lovers, has ruined the best of men, and our poor country with him. She undermined our society by her excessive luxury, by giving more importance to the outward appearance of things than she did to their essential qualities.'

Queen Victoria

1. Indeed, even after her daughter's eighteenth birthday, she proposed postponing her majority until she was twenty-one, suggesting that the Princess was still so naive and immature that a regency under her own control was the best way forward.
2. She did not like Sir Robert Peel at first; his stiff, formal manner repelled her – she said he had a smile 'like coffin handles'. Later, however, she came to respect his great ability and his personal integrity.
3. He was a solemn, rather studious young man, recommended by his uncle King Leopold of Belgium, who was, of course, Victoria's own uncle, as a future spouse. She seems to have given her affections to the younger man from the beginning, confiding in her diary: 'Albert is extremely handsome ... a beautiful figure, broad in the shoulders and a fine waist: my heart is quite gone on him.' She wanted to make him King Consort, but Melbourne warned her against it and recommended instead the title of 'Prince Consort', which Albert duly took. Melbourne also pared £20,000 from the Prince's personal allowance voted for him in Parliament, which Albert primly denounced as a 'truly unseemly vote'.
4. Since she was a reigning monarch, the law required that she had to take the first step towards marriage.
5. The act of childbearing, on the other hand, she did not find so pleasant. She called it 'the shadow side of marriage'. Victoria rather shocked the royal physician by asking him whether there was not some way of having sex without creating babies.
6. See also 'Prince Albert: Statesman or Foreign Meddler?' in Rayner and Stapley, *Debunking History* (2002).
7. The Queen's memorandum objected to the way he sent her Foreign Office dispatches too late for her to deal with properly, or ignored her suggestions, or even scratched out her amendments and sent dispatches willy-nilly. Palmerston accepted her reproof and apologised, but he was soon cheerfully at it again.
8. Victoria and Albert provided a tactful loophole through which the USA scrambled, suggesting that the whole affair was due to undue zealousness on the part of Capt. Wilkes, master of the warship, when he exceeded his orders and ordered the boarding. He therefore carried the can, and war was averted.
9. Albert had been obliged to travel to Cambridge to rebuke Bertie for an affair the undergraduate Prince was having with an actress. On this occasion they had walked together in the cold, and this was thought to have brought on Albert's illness.
10. He was only ethnically Jewish, his father having earlier converted to Christianity.

11. He referred with a sigh to the problems of authorship with the phrase: 'Ah, we authors, ma'am.' He was something of a writer himself, penning quite successful political novels. Here he was referring to the Queen's own literary efforts in writing her somewhat more modest *Journal of Our Life in the Highlands* (1861).

12. On the other hand, she never liked Gladstone, whom she found obstinate and patronising – she said that he addressed her as if she were a public meeting.

13. She wrote letters to him, on the subject of the Balkan crisis, and said 'if the Queen were a man, she would like to go and give those horrid Russians such a beating!'

14. See also 'Queen Victoria or Mrs Brown?' in Rayner and Stapley, *Debunking History* (2002).

15. She noted in her diary her interest in the language and the people, and showed a quite astonishing lack of xenophobia toward foreigners, as if banishing racial prejudice by royal example.

16. The two held 'instructive conversations' and Victoria even allowed him access to her 'boxes'. Some ministers, especially those in the India Office, suspected that he was selling state secrets to the Afghan Government at the time, with which British forces were engaged in a struggle for supremacy.

17. This request was sharply turned down by the Viceroy on the grounds that his father earned less than 3,000 rupees a year, the minimum 'qualification' for entry to a *durbar*.

18. She took serious objection to the view that Karim was of little account because he came from humble origins, commenting: 'to make out that the poor *Munshi* is so low is really *outrageous* in a country like England ... she has known archbishops who were sons respectively of a butcher and a grocer.' And later she commented acidly: 'How dare the India Office say her *munshi* was not a gentleman when the Gaekwar of Baroda was raised to a prince from a goatherd?'

Liliuokalani

1. The tune is melodious and plaintive, and she composed it as she watched two young lovers bidding farewell to each other. She said it symbolised the pain she felt when the country was taken away from the Hawaiians.

2. In Europe, she met Queen Victoria, and said she found her 'one of the best of women and greatest of monarchs'. Describing the meeting, she wrote: 'the Queen of England kissed me on the forehead ... and said "I want to introduce you to my children", and one by one they came forward and were introduced.'

NOTES TO PART 13

Mary Tudor

1. Catherine had first been promised to Henry's elder brother Arthur, and had become his wife in 1499. Unfortunately, Arthur died of consumption in 1502, and Henry, the ten-year-old Duke of Cornwall and the future Henry VIII, became

heir apparent. Henry VII was anxious to preserve strong links with the Spanish monarchy, and mercenary enough to wish to retain Catherine's substantial dowry in his own coffers; so he persuaded Pope Julius II to grant an annulment – on grounds of non-consummation of the marriage – for Prince Henry to marry her instead. This he did in 1509, when he was eighteen, a few weeks after he came to the throne.

2. Those of his advisors who agreed with him in such an interpretation made great play with Leviticus 20.21, which threatened childlessness to a man who married his brother's wife. But such advice overlooked the positive injunction in Deuteronomy 25.5 that a man *ought* to marry his brother's widow rather than send her away.

3. John Dudley, Earl of Warwick and Duke of Northumberland, who succeeded Edward Seymour, Duke of Somerset (Edward's uncle), as Lord Protector in 1549, took the precaution of ensuring the continuance of his own dominance by marrying his fifth son Guildford to Lady Jane Grey.

4. By the age of thirty-seven, Mary had come to regard herself as a spinster. She was unfortunately not overly attractive to the male species: like her half-brother she inherited congenital syphilis from her father, which gave her a weak constitution, bad eyesight, regular headaches, and a sort of rhinitis that meant that her breath always smelt bad.

5. He was not, however. His ardour for her soon cooled, and his sexual attentions soon became occasional and somewhat perfunctory.

6. Princess Elizabeth herself was implicated in the plot and spent some time confined in the Tower.

7. They included Thomas Cranmer, former Archbishop of Canterbury (a scholar and author of a new translation of the Bible and a new Protestant Prayer Book); Hugh Latimer, Bishop of Worcester; and Nicholas Ridley, Bishop of London, who were all burned outside Balliol College, Oxford, in 1555–56; and Rogers, Canon of St Pauls; and Bishops Hooper and Ferrar at Gloucester and Carmarthen. These executions were recorded and published by John Foxe in his *Book of Martyrs*.

8. There had been, indeed, efforts to depose her and her husband, such as that of Sir Henry Dudley at the end of 1555 and in the early months of 1556, and to replace them with Elizabeth, whom they proposed to marry off to Edward Courtenay, a distant relative descended from Edward IV. But news of it leaked out, and the conspirators were either arrested or forced to flee.

Tz'u Hsi

1. The Emperor Ch'ien Liung, writing to George III, acknowledged graciously, 'I am impressed and greatly pleased by your genuine respectfulness and friendliness', and Commissioner Lin Tse-hsu, writing to Queen Victoria about the opium traffic in 1839, recommended her 'to check your wicked and sift out the vicious people before they come to China ... to show further the sincerity of your politeness and submissiveness'.

2. In Pinyin spelling, now frequently used, her name is spelt 'Cixi'.

3. These European possessions were described as 'a modern hem sewn along the edge of an ancient garment'.

4. At about this time, Tzu Hsi had used millions in silver to restore the Summer Palace at a time when the Chinese navy needed the money to build modern new ships against the Japanese, and many of her critics blamed her for losing the war.

5. Until 1870 she sent out – and after 1870 allowed to continue without countermanding such missions – court eunuchs to visit appointees in the provinces, inviting them to make her gifts of money or valuables to show their appreciation of her patronage. Contributions were exacted from subordinates; these in turn exacted them from their subordinates until eventually the burden fell on those who had no subordinates at all (and were usually the poorest). These payments were a rough equivalent of modern 'protection money'.

NOTES TO PART 14

Mary Wollstonecraft

1. The historian J. H. Plumb takes a very dim view of her and calls her life 'squalid'. He says of her and her circle: 'The intellectual bohemians, Godwin, Shelley, Mary Wollstonecraft and their circle sinned for the sake of revolt rather than for enjoyment, then they justified themselves by the principles of liberal philosophy.'

2. He was a very far-sighted and progressive publisher and published works by Joseph Priestley, Richard Lovell Edgeworth and Erasmus Darwin.

3. Thomas Paine, author of *The Rights of Man*, for example, was arrested and held for some time; others were actually executed by the leaders of the Terror.

4. She became Mary Shelley after her marriage to the famous poet Percy Bysshe Shelley.

5. To many self-styled educational philosophers, and even to Rousseau, in his *Émile*, male writers seemed to deny women education except to allow them to be educated for the pleasure of men.

6. She rejected the stereotyped view of female value as superficial: 'Taught from their infancy that beauty is women's sceptre, the mind shapes itself to the body, and roaming round its gilt cage seeks only to adorn its prison.'

7. Nonetheless, her views are essentially bourgeois. She was no real friend of the poor; indeed, after the age of nine, she advocates that the poor should be separated from the rich, apart from the most gifted of them, and taught in another school.

8. At their first meeting in 1787, he had found her rather confrontational and abrasive, but now he said of her work: 'If ever there was a book calculated to make a man in love with its author this appears to be the book.'

Madame de Staël

1. His famous *Compte Rendu au Roi sur les Finances de la Nation* in 1781, by a feat of creative auditing, had announced a surplus of revenue over expenditure of 10

million livres, instead of the true figure of a deficit of 40 million livres – figures which were accepted by the uninformed public as genuine, although the ministers and the court knew they were false.

2. In her book, *The Passions*, published in 1796, she spoke out for moderation: 'Extremes are in the minds of men, not in nature. No one faction can exist without giving rise to an opposing one, and the struggle only results in the triumph of the intermediate belief.' (This was curiously Marxist in style.)

3. From the title of her book *Dix Années d'Exil*, not published until after the Bourbon Restoration, she dated her conflict with Napoleon from 1804, but she had clashed with him before, and had resisted him even before he assumed the imperial crown.

4. The army of occupation did not consist of 'mixed' units; each power kept to its separate zone and ran it without reference to the commander-in-chief. The Prussians were systematic but brutal, while the Cossacks and the Austrians carried out 'cold and methodical' looting of French property.

5. He wrote to her (in a charming mixture of French and English): '*Je déteste parler politique.*' And she responded warmly: '*Parler politique pour moi c'est vivre.*'

6. 'You can succeed only by conciliating, never by oppressing, and you have so much charm that you could join the glory of being France's liberator to that of being her conqueror.'

Harriet Martineau

1. In 1876 she said of herself: 'Her original power was nothing more than was due to earnestness and intellectual clearness within a certain range. With small imaginative and suggestive powers, and therefore nothing approaching to genius, she could clearly see what she could see, and gave a clear expression to what she had to say.' In short she could popularise, but could neither discover nor invent.

2. He shared her Unitarianism and her Whig politics, but the Darwin's father was unwilling to consider her as a daughter-in-law for Erasmus Darwin because 'her politics are so extreme'. Charles Darwin himself considered her 'very agreeable' but at the same time he said 'I am surprised to find how ugly she is!' Her impression of him she recorded in equally unflattering terms: 'he is simple, childlike, painstaking', but 'effective'.

3. She wrote: 'What a book it is! – overthrowing Revealed Religion on the one hand and Natural Religion on the other. The range and mass of knowledge take away one's breath!'

Isabella Beaton

1. She died very young in 1865, and yet recipe books in her name continued to appear after her death, as if her family were attempting some sort of immortality for her. By 1880, *Mrs Beeton's Shilling Cookery*, *Mrs Beeton's Everyday Cookery* and *Mrs Beeton's Cottage Cookery* were minting money for the publishers Ward, Lock, who had purchased Sam Beeton's copyrights. The latest two such books were products of the

twentieth century, and were called *Mrs Beeton's Caribbean Cookery* and *Microwaving with Mrs Beeton.*

2. The *Daily Express* critic said she looked as if she had just sent her cook from the room a minute before – in fact Mrs Beeton didn't have a cook.

3. It must have been extremely noisy at times. Indeed, when Henry complained to his wife about the racket, she is supposed to have said: 'That, Henry, is *my* children and *your* children fighting *our* children.'

4. Pattens were strap-on platforms that raised the wearer's footwear above the level of the stinking detritus that mired London's streets in the early nineteenth century.

5. They were able to do this because there was no copyright agreement between the USA and Britain until 1891. On the other hand, they took the prudent precaution against pirating of inserting into the book additional explanatory material of their own, drafted by Greenwood, which meant that they could sue other publishers who in turn stole their work, and then seize their printed material and sell it on as their own.

6. Syphilis starts with ulcerous swellings around the sexual organs, followed by fever, a rash, a sore throat and general debility, but then often subsides for years or even decades afterwards. During this remission the sufferer may imagine that the disease has spontaneously cleared up. But then it returns in the tertiary phase with hideous physical and mental symptoms that eventually prove fatal. Little was known about the disease in Victorian times, and the remedies on offer were as painful as they were useless. But the shame attached to the disease was very real – that is why sufferers kept it quiet.

7. The magazine still exists as half of the sophisticated weekly *Harpers & Queen.*

8. The death certificate gave the causes of his demise as 'suppressed scarlatina' and 'laryngitis', which match the bright rash and the wheezy snuffles that are characteristic of infant syphilis. The odd thing is that no one questioned Isabella's own health, in spite of the numerous miscarriages she suffered in her short married life.

9. It was he who in his later years took up the self-appointed task of preparing a biography of his mother as her memorial. He died in 1947.

10. Here she quoted freely from Florence Nightingale's *Notes on Nursing*, covering herself against a charge of plagiarism with a perfunctory 'Miss Nightingale says'.

11. Alexis Soyer was part chef, part showman. He invented the large-scale soup-kitchen and shipped it to the Crimea at his own expense to show the French and British troops out there how to make the best of their rations.

12. Mrs Beeton rightly pointed out that the size of a 'drop' depended partly on the size of neck of the vessel it came from and partly on the viscosity of the fluid. She went on to say that the College of Physicians asserted that the quantity of a 'drop' amounted to *one grain*, 60 drops making one *fluid drachm*. Their drop, she concludes, is one-sixtieth part of a fluid drachm, or a *minim.*

Annie Besant

1. An organisation to support the rights of Irish peasants and to fight against tenant evictions.
2. A young Irish playwright who opposed capitalism and advocated socialism through gradual democratic means. He had helped found the Fabian Society in 1884 to promote these ideas.
3. Since it mainly affected the jawbone, the disfigurement was popularly known as 'Phossy Jaw'.
4. A mystical doctrine asserting the spiritual nature of the universe and the divine nature of man.

Emily Hobhouse

1. These camps were where Boer civilian populations were 'concentrated' in one place, after the burning of their farms and homes, so as to prevent them offering shelter and aid to Boer 'commandos' who were fighting a scattered guerrilla war against British and Empire troops in the later stages of the Boer War. The name 'concentration camp' was later hijacked by the Nazis and used to describe punishment camps of a quite different character.
2. He had had an undistinguished career at Oxford, finishing with a 'fourth', but inherited over £10,000 from his father, as well as his clerical stipend of £362 per annum. The family was well-connected: her uncle Arthur was Lord Hobhouse, and her other two uncles a bishop and a Member of Parliament. She was also related more distantly to Leonard Courtney, MP for East Cornwall, to the Potter girls, one of whom became Mrs Beatrice Webb, and another who became the mother of Stafford Cripps.
3. Her share in her father's will alone amounted to £6,000 (well over a quarter of a million pounds in today's money), and was in addition to several smaller bequests from other relatives she received at about the same time.
4. Redvers-Buller, whose troops were besieged in the towns of Kimberley, Ladysmith and Mafeking after the Boer incursion into Natal, had been replaced by Lord Roberts (Kipling's 'Bobs'), with Kitchener as his second-in-command, fresh from his exploits in the Sudan; and they combined to defeat Cronje at Paardeberg and marched into Bloemfontein in March 1900. Thereafter the remnants of the Boers engaged in guerrilla actions, harassing the occupying forces and forcing them into making wide 'sweeps' to mop up their opponents.
5. All the same, his mistrust of the Boers still remained. He said of their government that it was 'the most disgusting system of espionage, subornation, bribery and humbug'.
6. She met an old couple of about ninety, both hungry and she almost naked. Emily had no food for them, but she slipped off her own petticoat to give the old woman something to wear.
7. 'You can't stop the course of nature,' Emily said. Indeed it is remarkable how many girl children in the camps were given the name of 'Emily' in the course of the next few years.

8. Emily snorted derisively that the landless Milner was the first peer 'to name himself after his lodgings'.
9. She was thirteen years older than Emily, tiny in stature but forceful in character, the first women to be awarded a doctorate by a British university for her work in women's higher education. She was the younger sister of Elizabeth Garrett Anderson, and the widow of a blind Cambridge professor and MP.
10. Her removal from the *Avondale Castle* involved 'the services of a stretcher, body straps, a file of Tommies, half a dozen women and an assortment of other people' while she 'kicked and scratched and yelled more than any coloured woman run in for drunkenness'.
11. Chamberlain, in the House of Commons, commented on Mrs Fawcett's 'Blue Book' in a debate in which he said: 'Every visitor to the camps, with the exception of Miss Hobhouse, has recognised the efforts of all concerned to do their best for the poor people in their charge.'
12. The prospects here did not look good, either, until Kitchener, in a whispered aside to Smuts, said: 'Look here, Smuts. I can only give it to you as my opinion, but my opinion is that in two years' time a Liberal government will come to power, and when it does it will grant you a constitution for South Africa.' Then the Boers jumped at the chance.
13. By then 'Dear Miss Hobhouse' had become 'Dear Missus' and 'Dear General Smuts' had evolved into 'My dear, dear Oom Jannie' ('Oom' was the Afrikaans word for 'Uncle', though in fact he was ten years younger than her).
14. She met the Zulu evangelist preacher Alexander Tschwangtwe, who called her the 'English Missis', but always insisted of using the back door, which he said was more suitable for *kaffirs*.
15. Chinese indentured labour had been introduced into the mines on account of the difficulties attendant on the recruitment of black labour, and Boer opinion generally was hostile to the introduction of yet another racial element into their social mix. Liberals like Lloyd George and Campbell-Bannerman in Britain seized the opportunity to attack 'Chinese slavery', which they said was backed by the Tories.
16. From this time, too, the first beginning of a split between her and the majority Boer opinion in South Africa can be discerned, with her questions about their treatment of the native majority. Humane to the end, she commented on the suppression of the native population in her accusation that 'South Africa's whites were withholding from others in your control the very liberties and rights you have valued and won for yourselves'.
17. One of the English prisoners in Ruhleben said, in a letter home: 'The lady was very nice to me. She said I looked very well and asked if she could do anything for me … She did not explain what she was doing in the middle of Germany.'

Fanny Lee Chaney

1. Their story was the subject of the 1978 feature film *Mississippi Burning*.
2. Fortunately for her, it missed – but it struck her neighbour's house and burnt it down.

3. Martin Luther King visited Neshoba County in 1967 and spoke to the crowds assembled there. He said he had no doubt that 'the murderers of Goodman, Chaney and Schwerner are within range of my voice'. A voice among the white men there replied: 'Damn right. We're right here behind you!'

4. All the same, he was convicted of manslaughter, not murder, on the grounds that 'there was insufficient evidence for a murder charge'.

Maria Boulding

1. Order of St Benedict. Benedict was a monk of the sixth century in Nursia who conceived a monastic rule of discipline in pursuit of which hundreds of Benedictine Abbeys were later founded throughout Europe.

NOTES TO PART 15

Selina Hastings

1. The Wesley brothers had already at Oxford University earned themselves the nickname 'Methodist' because of their organised style of life and worship, though the name 'Enthusiast' would have been equally appropriate.

2. John Wesley preached in the Midlands in 1741, and got to know the Countess at Donington Hall when he preached at nearby Melbourne and at Markfield, a village close to Leicester.

3. She did not, however, fully accept all their teachings. The Wesleys and George Whitfield himself were Arminians, but Selina inclined to a more radical Calvinist viewpoint.

4. After her death, the Connexion was directed by Lady Anne Erskine, and it still exists today as a small independent church.

5. Augustus Montague Toplady, Vicar of Broad Hembury in Devon, was one of the most notable of evangelical hymn-writers in the eighteenth century, and the author of 'Rock of Ages' in 1775.

6. Philip Doddridge studied at the Dissenting Academy at Kibworth (Leics.) and went on to help set up a new such academy at Market Harborough (Leics.), where he taught in the 1720s and 1730s. Anxious to prevent the splintering of the Non-conformist movement, he worked to keep them all within the Church of England.

Frances Buss

1. Born in Zurich, Pestalozzi (1746–1827) accepted the teachings of J. J. Rousseau as expressed in *Émile*, and set up a residential farm school for his waifs and strays at Neuhof in Switzerland in 1774. He was never very successful, because he was a better propagandist than an administrator, but his writings became very influential in the nineteenth century and his schools were widely copied.

Josephine Butler

1. She regarded men's and women's roles as complementary: men's role was as breadwinners and suited to outward-looking enterprise; women's natural strength lay in their moral pre-eminence, nurturing and protecting the weak and defending the home. She particularly rejected the double standard that permitted men greater sexual freedom, but condemned women who sought the same freedom.
2. They did not accept, or even understand, the commonsense view that medical inspection was in the interests of women and helped to treat their diseases, and was ultimately protective of their male clients as well.
3. He claimed to have *bought* a twelve-year-old girl for a few shillings as part of this grim traffic, and finished up in court for it as part of his campaign to end white slavery.

Octavia Hill

1. This was a weekly paper edited by Charles Dickens, which became one of the vehicles for transmitting information on household matters to people wishing to improve themselves. It was Octavia Hill's idea, and it included contributions from people like Dame Henrietta Barnett and Beatrice Webb.
2. She preferred the name 'Commons and Garden Trust', but Sir Robert Hunter pencilled in the margin of her letter 'National Trust' and this was how it came to be known.

Harriet Beecher Stowe

1. These facts were later consolidated into a publication called *The Key to Uncle Tom's Cabin* (1853) which was much more informative, and a good deal more boring, than the novel, containing a massive array of data on the institution of slavery.
2. 'I am in earnest,' he declared. 'I will not equivocate – I will not excuse – I will not retreat a single inch, and I WILL BE HEARD.'

Matilda Ashurst Biggs

1. Its chief doctrinal tenet was the assertion that there was only *one* God, not the usual trio of Father, Son and Holy Ghost; its political views were equally radical, and supported many reforming opinions at the time. Like the Quakers, the Unitarians were well-known for their evangelism, and their support of advanced political causes.
2. The *Biographical Dictionary of Modern British Radicals* claims that Matilda's father 'encouraged his daughters to be independent and they achieved some notoriety as unconventional cigar-smoking bohemians'.
3. William founded the Institution for Improving and Enforcing Laws for the Protection of Women, created a Home for Penitent Women in Blue Boar Lane in 1846 – a refuge for reformed prostitutes – and repeatedly pressed the leaders of the Chartist movement to include votes for women in their programme.

4. Leicester at the time was a fairly unhealthy place; much of it was low-lying in the valley of the Soar and flooded regularly, giving rise to the spread of 'Leicester fever', which probably was typhoid. There was also typhus about. John Biggs' younger sister Annie died of it in Stoneygate in the 1840s.

5. Some of the features of these acts (the most controversial of which was the Act of 1866) were beneficial, in that they were intended to close brothels and prosecute anyone profiting from them, but they created great resentment from those who objected to the idea they contained of compulsory medical examinations for women believed to be prostitutes, on the grounds that it would be a violation of their rights and would treat them like cattle. In fact, the act legalised state brothels, on the model of those existing for servicemen in France, which, rigorously managed, might have brought benefits to public health of their clients – and even of the prostitutes themselves. (See the entry on Josephine Butler on p. 315)

6. But with considerable bravado they went on: 'The Society will be glad of women's subscriptions, and trust they will use their best efforts to promote its extension.'

7. Leading British representatives asserted that the participation of women was 'subversive of the traditions of the country, and contrary to the word of God' and went on roundly to declare that 'it was unthinkable that these females should be admitted' – perhaps affirming their own unfitness for their declared purpose. This debate had at least one beneficial result: it lasted a whole day and was the first time that the restricted position of women had been given such a public airing.

8. He was very unfortunate here since his wife Sarah also died of typhus in 1862.

9. Matilda was keen also on Napoleon III as the embodiment of the French national spirit, and disapproved of Orsini's methods of reminding him of the promises he had made to aid the Italian cause – if, after all, he had killed the Emperor his promise to help Italy acquire Savoy and Nice would *never* have been fulfilled.

10. In a letter of July 1865 he said to Emilie: 'Yes, dear, Matilda is doomed: bronchi, larynx or trachea, she is in the last stages of consumption.'

Helen Suzman

1. She developed her own techniques for dealings with phone-tappers, one of which was to blow a whistle into the mouthpiece of her telephone in the course of the call.

2. She said of them that they were 'as nasty a trio as you would encounter in your worst nightmares', though she secretly confessed that Verwoerd was 'the only man who has ever scared me stiff'.

3. She was a successful stage, screen and TV actress who remembered her aunt in vivid detail.

Maya Angelou

1. She has always refused to clarify how many times she has been divorced – she says 'for fear of appearing frivolous'.

2. Her experiences are related in some detail in her three autobiographies: *I Know Why the Caged Bird Sings* (1969), *Gather Together in My Name* (1974) and *Singin' and Swingin' and Gettin' Merry Like Christmas* (1976. However, these books have been challenged for their content. Readers, especially parents, have criticised their irreverence towards religion, their violence and even their pornographic explicitness; some schools and libraries have even banned them for this reason.

3. There were several volumes of poetry, one of which, *Just Give Me a Cool Drink of Water 'Fore I Die*, was nominated for a Pulitzer Prize.

4. Her public face commanded great respect. As in the introduction to one of her later books she said: 'Try to be a rainbow in someone's cloud. Do not complain; never whine. Be certain that you do not die without doing something wonderful for humanity.'

SELECT BIBLIOGRAPHY

Algrant, Christine P., *Madame de Pompadour, Mistress of France*, 2003.

Armstrong, Richard, 'Grace Darling: Victorian Heroine', *History Today*, May 1965.

Ashton, Rosemary, *Thomas and Jane Carlyle: Portrait of a Marriage*, 2002.

Bellonci, Maria, *Lucrezia Borgia*, 2000.

Bennett, J. & G. Gardner, *The Cromwell Street Murders*, 2006.

Brown, Peter & Patte Barham, *Marilyn: the Last Take*, 1992.

Brown, Tina, *The Diana Chronicles*, 2007.

Butterfield, John & Isobel-Ann, 'Joan of Arc', *History Today*, September 1958.

Charles-Roux, Charles, *Chanel: Her Life, Her World, the Woman Behind the Legend*, 2009.

Douglas-Home, Jamie, *Stately Passions*, 2006.

Fraser, Antonia, *The Warrior Queens*, 1993.

Grant, Sally & David & Robert Yaxley, *Edith Cavell: Nurse and War-Heroine*, 1995.

Hall, John, *That Bloody Woman: The Turbulent Life of Emily Hobhouse*, 2008.

Hampton, Janie, *Joyce Grenfell*, 2002.

Hughes, Bettany, *Helen of Troy: Goddess, Princess, Whore*, 2006.

Hughes, Kathryn, *The Short Life and Long Times of Mrs Beeton*, 2005.

Jordan, Jane, *Josephine Butler*, 2001.

Kamm, Josephine, *How Different From Us: A Biography of Miss Buss and Miss Beale*, 1958.

Kemp, Sandra & Judith Squires (eds.), *Feminisms*, 1997.

Knecht, R. J., *Catherine de' Medici*, 1988.

Macdonald, Roger, *The Man in the Iron Mask*, 2005.

Masson, Georgina, *Queen Christina*, 1968.

Masters, Brian, *She Must Have Known: The Trial of Rosemary West*, 1996.

Mitford, Nancy, 'Mme de Maintenon as Educationalist', *History Today*, January 1965.

Manton, Jo, *Elizabeth Garrett Anderson*, 1958.

Oxford Dictionary of National Biography, 2004.

Oxford History of the Classical World, 1986.

Paris, Barry, *Garbo*, 1995.

Perry, Ruth, *The Celebrated Mary Astell: An Early English Feminist*, 1986.

Plowden, Alison, *Henrietta Maria*, 2002.

Robinson, Jane, *Mary Seacole*, 2005.

Sackville-West, Vita, *Aphra Behn: The Incomparable Astrea*, 1927.

Sackville-West, Vita, *Saint Joan of Arc*, 1955.

Schama, Simon, *Citizens: A Chronicle of the French Revolution*, 1989.

Spada, James, *Monroe: Her Life in Pictures*, 1982.

Stenton, F. M., *Anglo-Saxon England*, 1947.

Suzman, Helen, *In No Uncertain Terms: A South African Memoir*, 1993.

Taylor, Ina, *Helen Bradley's Lancashire*, 2002.

Todd, Janet, *Mary Wollstonecraft: A Revolutionary Life*, 1992.

Weir, Alison, *Henry VIII*, 2002.

Weir, Alison, *Isabella*, 2006.

Williams, Shirley, *Climbing the Bookshelves*, 2009.

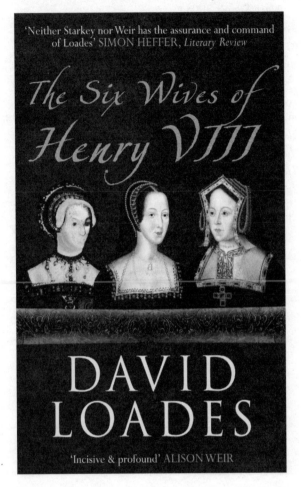

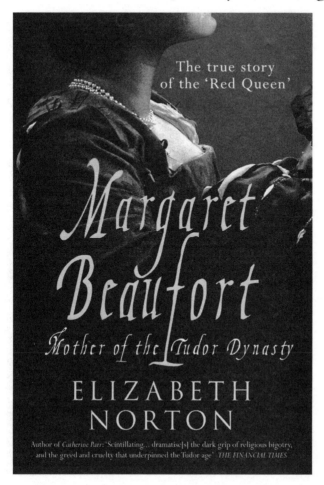

Available from June 2011 from Amberley Publishing

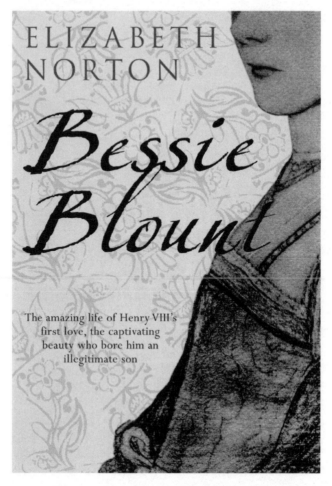

Beautiful, young, exuberant, the amazing life of Elizabeth Blount, Henry VIII's mistress and mother to his first son who came tantalizingly close to succeeding him as King Henry IX

Sidelined by historians until now, Bessie and the son she had by the king are one of the great 'what ifs' of English history. If Jane Seymour had not produced a male heir and Bessie's son had not died young aged 17, in all likelihood Henry Fitzroy could have followed his father as King Henry IX and Bessie propelled to the status of mother of the king.

£20 Hardback
30 illustrations (20 colour)
288 pages
978-1-84868-870-4

Available from June 2011 from all good bookshops or to order direct
Please call **01285-760-030**
www.amberleybooks.com

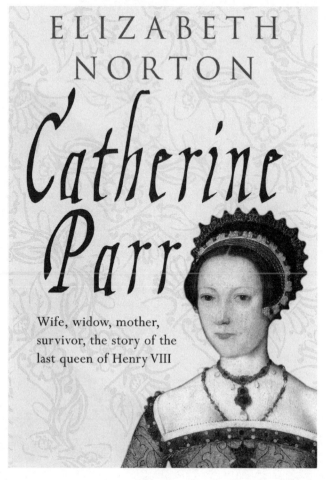

Also available from Amberley Publishing

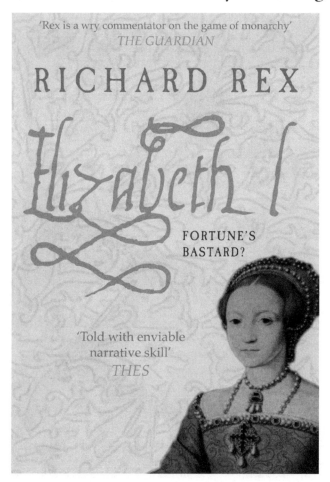

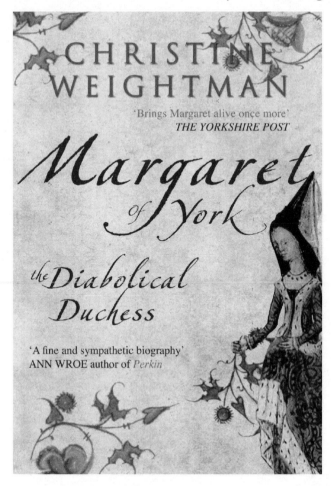

Also available from Amberley Publishing

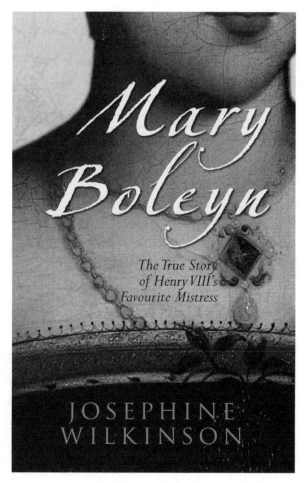

The scandalous true story of Mary Boleyn, infamous sister of Anne, and mistress of Henry VIII

Mary Boleyn, 'the infamous other Boleyn girl', began her court career as the mistress of the king of France. François I of France would later call her 'The Great Prostitute' and the slur stuck. The bête-noir of her family, Mary was married off to a minor courtier but it was not long before she caught the eye of Henry VIII and a new affair began.

Mary would emerge the sole survivor of a family torn apart by lust and ambition, and it is in Mary and her progeny that the Boleyn legacy rests.

£9.99 Paperback
22 illustrations (10 colour)
224 pages
978-1-84868-525-3

Available from all good bookshops or to order direct
Please call **01285-760-030**
www.amberleybooks.com

INDEX